THE NATION, 1865-1990

THE NATION
1865-1990

Selections from the Independent Magazine of Politics and Culture

Edited by KATRINA VANDEN HEUVEL

Introduction by E.L. DOCTOROW

Afterword by VICTOR NAVASKY

THUNDER'S
MOUTH
PRESS
NEW YORK

Introduction copyright © 1990 by E.L. Doctorow

All other contents copyright © 1990 by The Nation Company

All rights reserved.

Published by Thunder's Mouth Press

54 Greene Street, Suite 4S

New York, N.Y. 10013

Second printing, 1992.

Poem on page 499 from *Poems 1960-1967* by Denise Levertov.

Copyright © 1966 by Denise Levertov Goodman. Reprinted with

permission of New Directions Publishing Corporation.

Library of Congress Cataloging-in-Publication data:

The Nation, 1865-1990 : selections from the independent magazine

   of politics and culture / edited by Katrina vanden Heuvel ;

   introduction by E.L. Doctorow ; afterword by Victor Navasky.

      p. cm.

  ISBN 1-56025-001-1 : $21.95 (cloth)

  ISBN 1-56025-023-2 : $14.95 (pbk.)

  1. United States—Civilization—20th century. 2. United

States—Civilization—1865-1918. 3. United States—Politics

and government—20th century. 4. United States—Politics and

government—1865-1900. 5. Progressivism (United States

politics)

  I. vanden Heuvel, Katrina. II. Nation (New York, N.Y. : 1865)

        E169.1.N37412   1990

        973.9—dc20   90-10920

                           CIP

Text design by Loretta Li.

Composition by Stanton Publication Services, Inc.

Manufactured in the United States of America.

Contents

E.L. DOCTOROW, Introduction   *xi*

Editor's Note   *xv*

Original Prospectus for *The Nation* (1865)   *1*

The Danger of the Hour [editorial] (1865)   *2*

HENRY JAMES, Saratoga (1870)   *5*

E.L. GODKIN, The Moral of Tweed's Career (1878)   *12*

The Week [circus clowns and journalists] (1882)   *15*

E.L. GODKIN, The Execution of the Anarchists (1887)   *15*

W.P. GARRISON, The Pesky Anti-Imperialist (1902)   *19*

The Week [military spending] (1908)   *22*

The Week [the tango] (1914)   *22*

ARTHUR GARFIELD HAYS, American Liberalism [letter to the editor] (1919)   *23*

ROBERT C. BENCHLEY, The Making of a Red (1919)   *24*

WILLIAM MACDONALD, The Madness at Versailles (1919)   *27*

The Week [Lenin and Trotzky and baseball] (1919)   *32*

THEODORE DEBS, No Newspapers for Debs [letter to the editor] (1919)   *32*

Sowing the Wind to Reap the Whirlwind [editorial] (1920)   *33*

HERBERT J. SELIGMANN, The Conquest of Haiti (1920)   *36*

GILBERT SELDES, *Ulysses* [book review] (1922)   *41*

The Week [Tut-ankh-amen's tomb] (1923)   *46*

SINCLAIR LEWIS, Minnesota: The Norse State (1923)   *47*

WILLA CATHER, Nebraska: The End of the First Cycle (1923)   *49*

H.L. MENCKEN, H.L. Mencken (1923)   *53*

CHAIM WEIZMANN, Zionism—Alive and Triumphant (1924)   *56*

A Net Spread in Vain [correspondence between Oswald Garrison Villard and George Bernard Shaw] (1924)   *61*

W.E.B. DU BOIS, Georgia: Invisible Empire State (1925)   *62*

ADOLF HITLER, Class Justice in Germany [letter to the editor] (1925)   *66*

MARY HEATON VORSE, The War in Passaic (1926)   *67*

MARK VAN DOREN, First Glance [book review—T.S. Eliot's poetry] (1926)   *70*

LANGSTON HUGHES, The Negro Artist and the Racial Mountain (1926)   *72*

CRYSTAL EASTMAN, Mother-Worship (1927)   *76*

UPTON SINCLAIR, Poor Me and Pure Boston (1927)   *80*

Justice Underfoot [editorial] (1927)   *83*

SERGEI EISENSTEIN, Mass Movies (1927)   *89*

EZRA POUND, The Passport Nuisance (1927)   *92*

MOSHE MENUHIN, Yehudi Menuhin [letter to the editor] (1927)   *95*

CARLETON BEALS, With Sandino in Nicaragua (1928)   *96*

FREDA KIRCHWEY, Out of Bondage (1928)   *100*

HEYWOOD BROUN, It Seems to Heywood Broun (1929)   *102*

LIONEL TRILLING, Is Literature Possible? (1930)   *106*

ALBERT EINSTEIN, The 1932 Disarmament Conference (1931)   *110*

OSWALD GARRISON VILLARD, The Pot and the Kettle (1932)   *112*

JAMES THURBER, The 'Odyssey' of Disney (1934)   *114*

EMMA GOLDMAN, The Tragedy of the Political Exiles (1934)   *116*

MARGARET BOURKE-WHITE, Dust Changes America (1935)   *121*

MARY MCCARTHY and MARGARET MARSHALL, Our Critics, Right or Wrong (1935)   *124*

JAMES T. FARRELL, The Fall of Joe Louis (1936)   *129*

JOHN DOS PASSOS, Big Parade—1936 Model (1936)   *133*

BERTRAND RUSSELL, On Being Modern-Minded (1937)   *136*

NORMAN THOMAS, The Pacifist's Dilemma (1937)   *139*

THOMAS MANN, I Stand with the Spanish People (1937)   *144*

LOUIS FISCHER, Spain's Tragic Anniversary (1938)   *147*

GEORGE S. KAUFMAN, Einstein in Hollywood (1938)   *151*

I.F. STONE, Making Defense Safe for Alcoa (1941)   *153*

HENRY MILLER, Mother and Son [book review — *Thomas Wolfe's Letters to His Mother*] (1943)   *158*

I.F. STONE, For the Jews — Life or Death? (1944)   *160*

ARCHIBALD MACLEISH, The People Are Indivisible (1944)   *163*

One World or None [editorial] (1945)   *168*

HANNAH ARENDT, French Existentialism (1946)   *171*

JEAN-PAUL SARTRE, Americans and Their Myths (1947)   *176*

JAMES AGEE, Film [*The Treasure of the Sierra Madre*] (1948)   *178*

STEPHEN SPENDER, Writers in America (1949)   *182*

GUY ENDORE, Life on the Black List (1952)   *185*

NELSON ALGREN, American Christmas, 1952 (1952)   *187*

Bill of Rights Day [editorial] (1953)   *189*

EDGAR SNOW, Red China at Geneva (1954)   *192*

ARTHUR MILLER, A Modest Proposal (1954)   *197*

DAN WAKEFIELD, Justice in Sumner (1955)   *204*

JOSEPHINE HERBST, The Ruins of Memory (1956)   *208*

SARAH BOYLE, Spit in the Devil's Eye (1956)   *214*

HAROLD CLURMAN, Theatre [*Long Day's Journey into Night*] (1956)   *219*

DALTON TRUMBO, Blacklist=Black Marketing (1957)   *221*

KENNETH REXROTH, Jazz Poetry (1958)   *231*

RALPH NADER, The *Safe* Car You Can't Buy (1959)   *234*

It's Only Nikita, After All [editorial] (1959)   *239*

Are We Training Cuban Guerrillas? [editorial] (1960)   *241*

RICHARD CONDON, "Manchurian Candidate" in Dallas (1963)   *242*

HUNTER S. THOMPSON, The Motorcycle Gangs: Losers and Outsiders (1965)   *245*

MARTIN LUTHER KING, JR., The Last Steep Ascent (1966)   *254*

JAMES BALDWIN, A Report from Occupied Territory (1966)   *261*

Paradise Reagan-ed [editorial] (1966)   *269*

JACK NEWFIELD, One Cheer for the Hippies (1967)   *270*

As We See It [editorial—the 1968 Presidential election] (1968)   *274*

ERNEST GRUENING, On Vietnam (1969)   *277*

WILLIAM SHIRER, The Hubris of a President (1973)   *282*

BARBARA L. BAER and GLENNA MATTHEWS, The Women of the
    Boycott (1974)   *288*

TODD GITLIN, SDS Around the Campfire (1977)   *299*

ARTHUR SAMUELSON, The Dilemma of American Jewry (1978)   *308*

JAMES PETRAS, White Paper on the White Paper (1981)   *319*

E.P. THOMPSON, East, West—Is There a Third Way? (1983)   *325*

ANDREW KOPKIND, The Return of Cold War Liberalism (1983)   *332*

The Long Shadow [editorial] (1983)   *351*

KURT VONNEGUT, The Worst Addiction of Them All (1983/1984)   *353*

CALVIN TRILLIN, Uncivil Liberties (1986)   *356*

GORE VIDAL, Requiem for the American Empire (1986)   *358*

CARLOS FUENTES, Land of Jekyll and Hyde (1986)   *366*

The Revenge of Ahab [editorial] (1986)   *368*

MOLLY IVINS, Tough as Bob War and Other Stuff (1986)   *369*

KATHA POLLITT, The Strange Case of Baby M (1987)   *372*

STEPHEN F. COHEN, Sovieticus (1987)   *383*

CHRISTOPHER HITCHENS, Minority Report [the death penalty]
    (1987)   *386*

JOHN LEONARD, Delirious New York [book review—Tom Wolfe's *Bonfire
    of the Vanities* and *Dissent* special issue] (1987)   *388*

ALEXANDER COCKBURN, Beat the Devil [the legacy of My Lai]
    (1988)   *397*

For Jesse Jackson and His Campaign [editorial] (1988)   *403*

DANIEL SINGER, In the Heart of Le Pen Country (1988)   *410*

PENNY LERNOUX, Casting Out the 'People's Church' (1988)   *416*

ROBERT SHERRILL, White-Collar Thuggery [book review — Russell Mokhiber's *Corporate Crime and Violence*] (1988)   *422*

EDWARD W. SAID, Palestine Agenda (1988)   *432*

DARRELL YATES RIST, The Deadly Costs of an Obsession [with responses by Martin Bauml Duberman and ACT UP] (1989)   *436*

ARTHUR DANTO, Art [Andy Warhol] (1989)   *446*

PAUL KRASSNER, Abbie (1989)   *452*

MEREDITH TAX, March to a Crossroads on Abortion (1989)   *454*

ALICE WALKER, The Right to Life: What Can the White Man . . . Say to the Black Woman? (1989)   *460*

RICHARD J. BARNET, Bush's Splendid Little War (1990)   *463*

Poetry

D.H. LAWRENCE, Bare Almond Trees (1923)   *471*

ROBERT FROST, The Bear (1928)   *472*

EMILY DICKINSON, Four Poems (1929)   *473*

FEDERICO GARCIA LORCA, Song of the Little Death (1936)   *475*

LOUISE BOGAN, The Dream (1938)   *476*

W.B. YEATS, Long-Legged Fly (1939)   *477*

WALLACE STEVENS, On an Old Horn (1939)   *478*

W.H. AUDEN, Matthew Arnold (1939)   *479*

CARL SANDBURG, Memory (1940)   *480*

MARIANNE MOORE, The Mind is an Enchanting Thing (1943)   *481*

ROBERT LOWELL, The Death of the Sheriff (1946)   *483*

RANDALL JARRELL, A Game at Salzburg (1949)   *485*

WALLACE STEVENS, The Plain Sense of Things (1952)   *487*

LAWRENCE FERLINGHETTI, What Happened the Day a Poet Was Appointed Postmaster (1958)   *488*

WILLIAM CARLOS WILLIAMS, A Brueghel Nativity (1958)   *489*

SYLVIA PLATH, Two Views of a Cadaver Room (1960)   *492*

ANNE SEXTON, The Starry Night (1961)   *493*

LEROI JONES, After the Ball (1963) *494*

ROBERT DUNCAN, Up Rising (1965) *495*

ROBERT BLY, Johnson's Cabinet Watched by Ants (1966) *497*

DENISE LEVERTOV, What Were They Like? (Questions and Answers)
  (1966) *499*

W.S. MERWIN, Gift (1972) *500*

MARGARET ATWOOD, Marsh, Hawk (1973) *501*

ERNESTO CARDENAL, The Arrival (1975) *503*

JAMES WRIGHT, To a Blossoming Pear Tree (1975) *505*

MAY SWENSON, Teeth (1978) *507*

OCTAVIO PAZ, Nightfall (1979) *508*

PABLO NERUDA, Injustice (1981) *509*

JOSEPHINE JACOBSEN, Tears (1981) *511*

VICTOR NAVASKY, Afterword *513*

List of Illustrations

BEN SHAHN, Sacco and Vanzetti (1952) *88*

DAVID LEVINE, I.F. Stone (1982) *156*

ROBERT GROSSMAN, Cold War II (1983) *342*

EDWARD SOREL, "It's Only a Theory" (1987) *402*

FRITZ EICHENBERG, Woodcuts (1930–1980) *467*

Introduction

When, in the dark broadcloth days of 1865, E.L. Godkin undertook publication
of a new journal called *The Nation,* his first priority was to create a forum for
the discussion of what his publisher, Joseph A. Richards, called "the topics of the
day." This was right and proper, the suitably plainspoken objective of the good
journalist. Of course his magazine would try to conduct a discussion at a level
commensurate with the complex problems of a modern industrial society recently
at war with itself and its Constitution. It would attend to matters of culture as well
as government. But there was no high-flying claim of intellectual grandeur, no
visionary aesthetic, no philosophy, theology or other eternal prospect from which
his writers could look down. There would be no looking down. There would be
level engagement with "the topics of the day."

In the post-war exhaustion of 1865 we needed such ordinary witness. *The Nation* was claiming for itself the right of citizens in a democracy to carp, protest,
condemn, revile, applaud, celebrate, prophesy and otherwise give themselves to
the articulation of their circumstances. The subtext of the original prospectus
says: To conduct our discussion we may first have to put together a little money
to pay the printer; but we require no accreditation from anyone but ourselves – we
are self-appointed authorities in such topics of the day as history, like a managing
editor, assigns us.

And so it began. The editors never published anything less than what was ur-
gently on their minds. The generations of free-lances wrote of immediate matters,
the daily topics that turn yellow with the newsprint. Yet, here and now, in this
collection of pieces covering the hundred-and-twenty-five-year life of the magazine, it is apparent that whoever writes hard and heedlessly in the present, under
all its teeming deadlines, and is moved to define what is specifically intolerable,
or to decide what is suddenly momentous, or to praise what is especially beautiful, or to laugh at what is hugely ridiculous, may hope, even as time antiquates
his diction, to write for posterity.

I am not making a necessarily literary claim. Some topics of the day are endur-
ingly topical. They create writers. In an editorial from the September 31, 1865
issue, you will find E.L. Godkin writing of President Johnson's Reconstruction
policy that it may reconstruct "a society so closely resembling slave society as to
reproduce most of the phenomena which made slave society politically obnoxious . . . " And W.E.B. DuBois writing in the January 21, 1925 number that
"side by side with that warm human quality called 'Southern' stands the grim fact
that right here and beside you, laughing easily with you and shaking your hand
cordially, are men who hunt men: who hunt and kill in packs, at odds of a hundred

to one under cover of night." Later, James Baldwin, writing from Harlem in his "Report from Occupied Territory" of July 11, 1966, appends his demand "for the recognition of our common humanity. Without this recognition, our common humanity will be proved in unutterable ways . . . "

Thus the topic of the day turns out to be the torment of the generations. And the modest objective of a weekly magazine transforms in time into a kind of narrative depicting an awesome journey of the national spirit.

It was Chekhov who said to an aspiring writer that if he wanted to represent the moon, he should not describe it in the sky, but rather let us see its reflection in a broken bit of glass at our feet. This book gives us glimpses of our historical life as refracted in the eyes of witnesses. It is written not from an omniscient point of view but in a multiplicity of first persons. We can see history flashing up through its disasters with our alarmed writers running alongside. Albert Einstein writes of the importance of the 1932 Disarmament Conference. Thomas Mann explains why he stands with the Loyalists in the Spanish Civil War. Emma Goldman speaks with anger and pity of the tens of thousands of political exiles of dictatorships of the right and left "turned into modern Ahasueruses, forced to roam the earth, admitted nowhere." And a few years later, I.F. Stone is desperate to get the American government to provide sanctuary for European Jews who will otherwise die under Hitler. (He will fail.)

As with all narratives we find complexity, ambiguity, unexpected turns. Somewhere in time, perhaps in the 1930s, American history as conceived in *The Nation* widens to include the world. There are many reasons for this, not all of them having to do with the editors' deepening perception of monumental world crisis. There is also the desire of American intellectuals to spring us from the bonds of provincialism. A *Nation* literary critic asking in 1930 "Is Literature Possible?" affirms that though it has thus far in the twentieth century failed to match the European achievement, our literature need not continue to fail: "The salvation of American art certainly lies . . . in its becoming subversive and dangerous to the social order," declares Lionel Trilling, not yet the author of *The Liberal Imagination.*

Then, with the end of the war, Hannah Arendt is here to give us a provocative look at a new intellectual phenomenon—French Existentialism. And in 1947 Sartre himself comes over to have a look at us: "When we walk about New York," he says, "we see the most pathetic visages in the world, uncertain, searching, intent, full of astonished good faith." But the days of our national cultural inferiority complex are over. A brilliant refugee generation of European writers, composers, artists, scholars, and scientists, has settled here, and the old invidious distinctions are passé. In any event, with our country triumphant in the war, the saviour of self-destructing Europe, it is hard to remember what we were so sensitive about.

But then the awful political puritanism of the cold war is upon us – as if, having emerged from the Second World War with our combative spirit unassuaged, we must now turn it upon ourselves. The topics of the day are loyalty, blacklists, patriotism. In response Arthur Miller makes the "Modest Proposal" that every citizen submit himself to "patriotic arrest" for judgement and classification by a "Court of Clearance." If that citizen attended a meeting of any group or organization included on a government list of proscribed organizations he can be found to be an "Action Traitor;" if he engaged in any conversation not "Positively Conducive to the Defense of the Nation" he can be found a "Conceptual Traitor." On the other hand he will be cleared as "unclassified" if he is unable to speak or understand the English language, is chronically listless, committed to institutions for the insane or homes for the aged and infirm, or is an agent of the FBI.

A few themes now begin to emerge from our national novel: How very much of the political argument or analysis is actually the articulation of conscience, or ethical perception, for example; or the astonishing degree to which patriotism – if it is the love of justice for the nation, justice in its laws and structures – is slandered and reviled in periods of American tribal righteousness. We see our very own current global America coming into view now, the familiar names – Nixon, Reagan, the familiar places – Vietnam, Nicaragua. The texture of the book thickens and its narrative advance becomes less pronounced as the lines are written, drawn, in the diction of grim modernity – consumer rights, civil rights, human rights. We begin to wonder if the ideological deformation of our culture in the past forty-five years is not revealed as much by the numbers of writers who have excused themselves from the pages of *The Nation* as by the writings of those who have risen to the task as to a topic of the day.

For solace, counsel, and enlightenment, we turn of course to the poets, the transcendent among us who can remake the world in a line. And what a company they are, these poets of newsprint: Yeats and D.H. Lawrence, Dickinson and Frost, Garcia Lorca, Neruda, Auden, Bogan, W.C. Williams, Moore, Lowell, Plath and Wright – for starters.

Or we can turn back to our stylish entry by Henry James (Henry James? Yes, Henry James) as he describes the season at Saratoga in 1870; or to H.L. Mencken's confident tirade against J.P. Morgan, the Supreme Court and the Anti-Saloon League. Or resort to our resident wits: George S. Kaufman describing how Albert Einstein is invited by a Hollywood studio to make a movie of the Theory of Relativity; or James Thurber calling upon Walt Disney to do an animated version of *The Odyssey* now that he has made his mark with his epic *Three Little Pigs*.

But I see I have strained to breaking my metaphor of the weekly journal as historical novel. Put it aside. Think instead that you can dig through this anthology as you would a hope chest, finding and holding up to view its mementos, treasures, jewels — its laces and old valentines. You begin smiling and then you catch your breath. This is your family's life you have in your hands.

E.L. DOCTOROW
New York City
April 1990

Editor's Note

This is not a typical anthology, one made up of "the best of . . . " or one devoted to a particular theme or designed to serve as a historical record. I have selected articles and essays which are representative of *The Nation* spirit—its passion, commitment, idealism and skepticism; which are good examples of their authors' work; and which startle, provoke and entertain. If there is an undercurrent that runs through these selections, it is that most are in the "critical spirit" forecast by *The Nation*'s founders in the original prospectus of 1865, and emblematic of dissenting journalism. Also, I have chosen pieces that illustrate those issues on which the magazine's commitments have been steadfast: passionate support for civil rights and civil liberties, opposition to racism in all its guises, and unrelenting struggle against militarism, imperialism, corruption and abuse of power. It is remarkable how many of the controversies that engaged the moral and political concern of *The Nation* twenty-five, fifty or seventy-five years ago still do.

Mark Van Doren, *The Nation*'s literary editor in the 1920s, once wrote: "I have always believed that an anthology should be one-sided, that it should reflect only the prejudices of the editor. . . . It will then be interesting to certain readers at any rate; and if in the long run it prove all wrong, surely that will be the next best thing to having proved all right." Although others have given generously of their opinions, the prejudices are mine. Any one of us might have made somewhat different choices from the tremendous array of articles, essays, poems and drawings that make up nearly six thousand issues of *The Nation*. It was a task that filled me with trepidation for nearly a year.

Although this book does not provide a complete picture of the development of *The Nation* since 1865, it does, I believe, reflect the dominant concerns of the magazine in its first 125 years. The bias, admittedly, is towards the fairly recent past. A few articles have been edited for reasons of space; the poetry is untouched, and the material is arranged in chronological order. In all cases, the original text has been followed in word and style.

Sadly, space limitations compelled me to omit some of *The Nation*'s landmark pieces and important contributors. Here I would mention Fred Cook's groundbreaking special issues on the Hiss case, the FBI, the CIA and the "Shame of New York," as well as the many important pieces by Frank Donner on politics and civil liberties. The piles of photocopied second choices, third choices, things I would have liked to reprint if Thunder's Mouth Press had given me several hundred thousand words more, have become a traffic hazard in my small office.

I wish to thank Valentina Fratti, Morgan Neville, Christopher Johnson and Gideon Forman for their research assistance; and Richard Lingeman, Elsa Dixler, George Black, JoAnn Wypijewski and Micah Sifry for their valuable suggestions and ideas. Grace Schulman was a wonderful guide to *The Nation*'s remarkable poetry. Finally, I thank Victor Navasky for living up to the magazine's long tradition of anti-interventionism.

KATRINA VANDEN HEUVEL
New York City
April 1990

THE NATION, 1865-1990

Original Prospectus for *The Nation*   July 6, 1865

THE NATION

A WEEKLY JOURNAL OF POLITICS, LITERATURE, SCIENCE, AND ART WILL BE PUBLISHED JULY 6, 1865.

Terms: — Three Dollars per annum, in advance; Six Months, Two Dollars.

ITS MAIN OBJECTS WILL BE

First. — The discussion of the topics of the day, and, above all, of legal, economical, and constitutional questions, with greater accuracy and moderation than are now to be found in the daily press.

Second. — The maintenance and diffusion of true democratic principles in society and government, and the advocacy and illustration of whatever in legislations or in manners seems likely to promote a more equal distribution of the fruits of progress and civilization.

Third. — The earnest and persistent consideration of the condition of the laboring class at the South, as a matter of vital interest to the nation at large, with a view to the removal of all artificial distinctions between them and the rest of the population, and the securing to them, as far as education and justice can do it, of an equal chance in the race of life.

Fourth. — The enforcement and illustration of the doctrine that the whole community has the strongest interest, both moral, political, and material, in their elevation, and that there can be no real stability for the Republic so long as they are left in ignorance and degradation.

Fifth. — The fixing of public attention upon the political importance of popular education, and the dangers which a system like ours runs from the neglect of it in any portion of our territory.

Sixth. — The collection and diffusion of trustworthy information as to the condition and prospects of the Southern States, the openings they offer to capital, the supply and kind of labor which can be obtained in them, and the progress made by the colored population in acquiring the habits and desires of civilized life.

Seventh. — Sound and impartial criticism of books and works of art.

The Nation will not be the organ of any party, sect, or body. It will, on the contrary, make an earnest effort to bring to the discussion of political and social questions a really critical spirit, and to wage war upon the vices of violence, exaggeration, and misrepresentation by which so much of the political writing of the day is marred.

The criticism of books and works of art will form one of its most prominent features; and pains will be taken to have this task performed in every case by writers possessing special qualifications for it.

It is intended, in the interest of investors, as well as of the public generally, to have questions of trade and finance treated every week by a writer whose position and character will give his articles an exceptional value, and render them a safe and trustworthy guide.

A special correspondent, who has been selected for his work with some care, is about to start in a few days for a journey through the South. His letters will appear every week, and he is charged with the duty of simply reporting what he sees and hears, leaving the public as far as possible to draw its own inferences.

The following writers, among others, have been secured either as regular or occasional contributors: —

Henry W. Longfellow, James Russell Lowell, John G. Whittier, Samuel Eliot (Ex-President Trin. College, Hartford), Professor Torrey (Harvard), Dr. Francis Lieber, Professor Child (Harvard), Charles E. Norton, Judge Bond (Baltimore), Edmund Quincy, Professor W. D. Whitney (Yale), Professor D. C. Gilman (Yale), Judge Daly, Professor Dwight (Columbia College), Judge Wayland, Frederick Law Olmsted, Rev. Dr. McClintock, Rev. Dr. Jos. P. Thompson, Rev. Phillips Brooks, Rev. Dr. Bellows, C. J. Stillé, Henry T. Tuckerman, Bayard Taylor, C. A. Bristed, C. L. Brace, Richard Grant White, William Lloyd Garrison, Sydney George Fisher, Theodore Tilton, James Parton, Gail Hamilton, R. H. Stoddard.

JOSEPH H. RICHARDS, Publisher
130 Nassau Street, N.Y.

The Danger of the Hour
[*editorial*]

September 21, 1865

This editorial by E.L. Godkin, *The Nation*'s co-founder and first editor, is an endorsement of the early Reconstruction program. Within the space of two decades, however, *The Nation* had virtually reversed its position.

The whole question of the wisdom or folly of President Johnson's plan of reconstruction, as he is at present carrying it out, turns upon the amount of confidence which ought to be reposed in the good faith and good intentions of the Southern people. He is evidently of opinion, if we may judge by his action in the Sharkey-Slocum case in Mississippi, as well as by his language to the Southern delegations, that there is not and ought not to be any limit to this confidence. We are given to understand that before very long he means not only to permit the militia to be called out in all the Southern States, but to recall the Federal troops, except a few garrisons, and leave our Southern brethren entirely to their own devices.

Those who defend his course and his opinions do so by ridiculing the notion that there is any danger of a renewed attempt at insurrection in the South, but this is simply fighting a man of straw. There are very few people at the North who apprehend anything of the sort. The Chicago *Tribune* the other day showed, by an elaborate calculation, that the permission to call out the Southern militia would place 161,000 men under arms, most of them disbanded rebel soldiers, smarting under their defeats and still fired by the passions of the struggle, and gave its readers plainly to understand that it was fair to anticipate from these people a fresh effort to throw off the "Yankee yoke." We think this arming of the Southern militia to be unquestionably a very unwise and dangerous proceeding, but not because we expect it to lead to a fresh revolt.

There is nobody who has the least knowledge of the actual physical and moral condition of the South but must treat all such apprehensions as chimerical. There has probably never been a people, since the Gauls, so thoroughly beaten in war as the Southerners have been. The completeness of their overthrow has been in the exact ratio of the vigor and obstinacy of their resistance, and resistance more vigorous and more obstinate was probably never offered by any population of the same size. This generation is certainly completely at the mercy of its conqueror, and incapable of offering the least opposition to his mandates. Should it be able to bequeath its passions and hopes to the next one, there might be a possibility of the latter renewing the struggle, but the next generation is twenty years away, and we are not disposed to look forward so far.

What we fear from the President's policy is, not a renewal of the war, but the restoration of the state of things which led to the war. We, of course, do not anticipate a revival of slavery "pure and simple;" but it was not the fact of slavery in itself which led to the revolt, but the state of feeling and of manners which slavery bred—the hatred of democracy, the contempt for human rights, the horror of equality before the law, the proneness to violence which always results from inequality, the tone which all these things communicated to Southern manners, literature, education, religion, and society. What we fear now is the reconstruction at the South, not of "slave society," properly so called, but of a society so closely resembling slave society as to reproduce most of the phenomena which made slave society, politically, so obnoxious, and so dangerous, to the public peace and prosperity. The great lesson which we have learned from the war, if we have learned any lesson at all, is that homogeneousness, social as well as political, is the first condition of our national existence. This government, we now know as well as we know anything, cannot be carried on, if any portion of the population which lives under it is legally kept in degradation, or legally excluded from the enjoyment of any of the rights or privileges possessed by the rest of the community.

The great question to be answered, therefore, by those who propose handing the South over immediately to the control of the Southern whites, is not whether they can be trusted not to revolt again, or not to restore slavery again—we know them to be physically unable to do either of these things—but whether they can be trusted to establish among them that form of social organization which we know to be necessary to the peace and happiness of the nation, to the vindication of our own principles before the world, and to secure which we have spent millions of treasure and torrents of blood. Nobody will venture to answer this in the affirmative. Nobody has answered it in the affirmative. The partizans of the South content themselves with calling attention to the resignation with which they gave up slavery, after it had been destroyed by force, and the alacrity with which they laid down their arms, when further resistance meant slaughter or starvation. But can they be trusted to take measures for putting the negro fairly under the protection of the laws—that is, giving him, weak, helpless, and degraded as he has been, those guarantees for life, liberty, and the pursuit of happiness which the white race, strong, rich, powerful, and energetic as it knows itself to be, declares to be essential for *its* liberty and security? Can they be trusted with the sole management of one of the most difficult and delicate of political processes, the endowment of slaves with the feelings and aspirations of freemen, when they have up to the last moment fought against it sword in hand, and at this moment make no secret of the loathing and rage which it excites in them, of their confidence that it will fail, and of their hopes that it may fail?

He must be a very sanguine or very simple person who will say yes to all this, when we see that all through the South the men whom the people elect to take charge of the work of reconstruction which Mr. Johnson is committing, as we believe, most recklessly to their hands, are those who are notoriously most thoroughly impregnated with the old pro-slavery vices, the old pro-slavery passions, hates, and prejudices. The most popular man in South Carolina to-day is Wade Hampton, and there is not another in the South who hates freedom, and the North, and the Union more thoroughly. We might go through every one of the revolted States and cite cases of the same kind. The men who are animated by Northern ideas are either nobodies or persons in whom their neighbors have no confidence. The men whom President Johnson has put in office are often like the redoubtable Perry, persons who make speeches in Charleston which are not intended to be heard in Washington. This personage, as our readers may remember, avowed himself at Greenville a humiliated, outraged, unrepentant, Yankee-hating Southerner, who believed that "freedom would be a curse to the negro;" but on receiving his appointment as provisional governor, two days afterwards, he made his appearance at Washington, with eight friends, in the character of a "wandering sheep," and matched himself to bleat "Union sentiments" against any loyal wether in the capital.

What we fear is, that we are now about to witness a phenomenon for which many calm and shrewd observers have all along looked with fear and trembling: the free States once more overcome by that disposition to temporize, compromise, and put off the evil day, and hope for the best, to which whatever of shame, humiliation, and disaster there has been in the history of the last forty years may be directly traced. We are all more or less affected by the languor which was sure to follow the prodigious efforts of the war. The public mind is a little weary of contention and agitation; trade is rapidly reviving, and Southern orders are just as sweet and as soothing, Southern tongues just as glib and as smooth, as ever they were. The restoration of a Union of some kind or other seems within easy reach, and it is no more difficult for Southern orators and traders to persuade their Northern friends that all trouble is over and that the political millennium is at hand, than it was to persuade them ten years ago that the very existence of Northern society depended on Southern favor and encouragement. We are but witnessing to-day, in the impression produced on Northern opinion by Southern professions, a fresh display of that consummate political ability which, for half a century, laid a large, acute, intelligent, and industrious community prostrate at the feet of a few thousand slave-owners, the product of a society on which civilization had left only the faintest traces. And we run great risk at this moment of being dragged into compromises, the consequences of which our children will rue, as we have rued those of our fathers.

HENRY JAMES

Saratoga

August 3, 1870

Henry James was only twenty-two when he wrote "The Noble School of Fiction" for the magazine's first issue. James wrote, in all, over two hundred essays and book, art and theater reviews for *The Nation*.

Saratoga, August 3, 1870.
One has vague irresponsible local previsions of which it is generally hard to discern the origin. You find yourself thinking of an unknown, unseen place as thus rather than so. It assumes in your mind a certain shape, a certain color which frequently turns out to be singularly at variance with reality. For some reason or

other, I had idly dreamed of Saratoga as buried in a sort of elegant wilderness of verdurous gloom. I fancied a region of shady forest drives with a bright, broad-piazzaed hotel gleaming here and there against a background of mysterious groves and glades. I had made a cruelly small allowance for the stern vulgarities of life—for the shops and sidewalks and loafers, the complex machinery of a city of pleasure. The fault was so wholly my own that it is quite without bitterness that I proceed to affirm that the Saratoga of experience is sadly different from this. I confess, however, that it has always seemed to me that one's visions, on the whole, gain more than they lose by realization. There is an essential indignity in indefiniteness: you cannot imagine the especial poignant interest of details and ac-cidents. They give more to the imagination than they receive from it. I frankly ad-mit, therefore, that I find here a decidedly more satisfactory sort of place than the all-too primitive Elysium of my wanton fancy. It is indeed, as I say, immensely different. There is a vast number of brick—nay, of asphalte—sidewalks, a great many shops, and a magnificent array of loafers. But what indeed are you to do at Saratoga—the morning draught having been achieved—unless you loaf? "Que faire en un gîte à moins que l'on ne songe?" Loafers being assumed, of course shops and sidewalks follow. The main avenue of Saratoga is in fact bravely enti-tled Broadway. The untravelled reader may form a very accurate idea of it by recalling as distinctly as possible, not indeed the splendors of that famous thoroughfare, but the secondary charms of the Sixth Avenue. The place has what the French would call the "accent" of the Sixth Avenue. Its two main features are the two monster hotels which stand facing each other along a goodly portion of its course. One, I believe, is considered much better than the other—less prodi-gious and promiscuous and tumultuous, but in appearance there is little choice between them. Both are immense brick structures, directly on the crowded, noisy street, with vast covered piazzas running along the façade, supported by great iron posts. The piazza of the Union Hotel, I have been repeatedly informed, is the largest "in the world." There are a number of objects in Saratoga, by the way, which in their respective kinds are the finest in the world. One of these is Mr. John Morrissey's casino. I bowed my head submissively to this statement, but pri-vately I thought of the blue Mediterranean, and the little white promontory of Monaco, and the silver-gray verdure of olives, and the view across the outer sea toward the bosky cliffs of Italy. Congress Spring, too, it is well known, is the most delicious mineral spring in the known universe; this I am perfectly willing to maintain.

The piazzas of these great hotels may very well be the greatest of all piazzas. They are not picturesque, but they doubtless serve their purpose—that of afford-ing sitting-space in the open air to an immense number of persons. They are, of course, quite the best places to observe the Saratoga world. In the evening, when the "boarders" have all come forth and seated themselves in groups, or have begun to stroll in (not always, I regret to say, to the sad detriment of the dramatic interest, bisexual) couples, the vast heterogeneous scene affords a great deal of entertainment. Seeing it for the first time, the observer is likely to assure himself that he has neglected an important feature in the sum of American manners. The rough brick wall of the house, illumined by a line of flaring gas-lights, forms a harmonious background to the crude, impermanent, discordant tone of the assembly. In the larger of the two hotels, a series of long windows open into an immense parlor—the largest, I suppose, in the world—and the most scantily furnished, I imagine, in proportion to its size. A few dozen rocking-chairs, an equal number of small tables, tripods to the eternal ice-pitchers, serve chiefly to emphasize the vacuous grandeur of the spot. On the piazza, in the outer multitude, ladies largely prevail, both by numbers and (you are not slow to perceive) by distinction of appearance. The good old times of Saratoga, I believe, as of the world in general, are rapidly passing away. The time was when it was the chosen resort of none but "nice people." At the present day, I hear it constantly affirmed, "the company is dreadfully mixed." What society may have been at Saratoga when its elements were thus simple and severe, I can only vaguely, regretfully conjecture. I confine myself to the dense, democratic, vulgar Saratoga of the current year. You are struck, to begin with, at the hotels by the numerical superiority of the women; then, I think, by their personal superiority. It is incontestably the case that in appearance, in manner, in grace and completeness of aspect, American women vastly surpass their husbands and brothers. The case is reversed with most of the nations of Europe—with the English notably, and in some degree with the French and Germans. Attached to the main entrance of the Union Hotel, and adjoining the ascent from the street to the piazza, is a "stoop" of mighty area, which, at most hours of the day and morning, is a favored lounging-place of men. I am one of those who think that on the whole we are a decidedly good-looking people. "On the whole," perhaps, every people is good-looking. There is, however, a type of physiognomy among ourselves which seems so potently to imperil the modest validity of this dictum, that one finally utters it with a certain sense of triumph. The lean, sallow, angular Yankee of tradition is dignified mainly by a look of decision, a hint of unimpassioned volition, the air of "smartness." This in some degree redeems him, but it fails to make him handsome. But in the average American of the present time, the typical leanness and sallowness are less, and the individual keenness and smartness at once equally intense and more evenly balanced with this greater comeliness of form. Casting your eye over a group of your fellow-citizens in the portico of the Union Hotel, you will be inclined to admit that, taking the good with the bad, they are worthy sons of the great Republic. I find in them, I confess, an ample fund of grave entertainment. They suggest to my fancy the swarming vastness—the multifarious possibilities and activities—of our young civilization. They come from the uttermost ends of the continent—from

7

San Francisco, from New Orleans, from Duluth. As they sit with their white hats tilted forward, and their chairs tilted back, and their feet tilted up, and their cigars and toothpicks forming various angles with these various lines, I imagine them surrounded with a sort of clear achromatic halo of mystery. They are obviously persons of experience—of a somewhat narrow and monotonous experience certainly; an experience of which the diamonds and laces which their wives are exhibiting hard by are, perhaps, the most substantial and beautiful result; but, at any rate, they are men who have positively actually lived. For the time, they are lounging with the negro waiters, and the boot-blacks, and the news-venders; but it was not in lounging that they gained their hard wrinkles and the level impartial regard which they direct from beneath their hat-rims. They are not the mellow fruit of a society impelled by tradition and attended by culture; they are hard nuts, which have grown and ripened as they could. When they talk among themselves, I seem to hear the mutual cracking of opposed shells.

If these men are remarkable, the ladies are wonderful. Saratoga is famous, I believe, as the place of all places in America where women most adorn themselves, or as the place, at least, where the greatest amount of dressing may be seen by the greatest number of people. Your first impression is therefore of the— what shall I call it?—of the *muchness* of the feminine drapery. Every woman you meet, young or old, is attired with a certain amount of splendor and a large amount of good taste. You behold an interesting, indeed a quite momentous spectacle: the democratization of elegance. If I am to believe what I hear—in fact, I may say what I overhear—a large portion of these sumptuous persons are victims of imperfect education and members of a somewhat narrow social circle. She walks more or less of a queen, however, each unsanctified nobody. She has, in dress, an admirable instinct of elegance and even of what the French call "chic." This instinct occasionally amounts to a sort of passion; the result then is superb. You look at the coarse brick walls, the rusty iron posts of the piazza, at the shuffling negro waiters, the great tawdry steamboat cabin of a drawing-room—you see the tilted ill-dressed loungers on the steps—and you finally regret that a figure so exquisite should have so vulgar a setting. Your resentment, however, is speedily tempered by reflection. You feel the impertinence of your old reminiscences of Old-World novels, and of the dreary social order in which privacy was the presiding genius and women arrayed themselves for the appreciation of the few—the few still, even when numerous. The crowd, the tavern loungers, the surrounding ugliness and tumult and license, constitute the social medium of the young lady whom you so cunningly admire: she is dressed for publicity. The thought fills you with a kind of awe. The Old-World social order is far away indeed, and as for Old-World novels, you begin to doubt whether she is so amiably curious as to read even the silliest of them. To be so excessively dressed is obviously to give pledges to idleness. I have been forcibly struck with the apparent absence of any warmth and richness of detail in the lives of these wonderful ladies of the piazzas. We are freely accused of being an eminently wasteful people: I know of few things which so largely warrant the accusation as the fact that these consummate *élégantes* adorn themselves, socially speaking, to so little purpose. To dress for every one is, practically, to dress for no one. There are few prettier sights than a charmingly dressed woman, gracefully established in some shady spot, with a piece of needlework or embroidery, or a book. Nothing very serious is accomplished, probably, but an aesthetic principle is considered. The embroidery and the book are a tribute to culture, and I suppose they really figure somewhere out of the opening scenes of French comedies. But here at Saratoga, at any hour of morning or evening, you may see a hundred brave creatures steeped in a quite unutterable emptyhandedness. I have had constant observation of a lady who seems to me really to possess a genius for being nothing more than dressed. Her dresses are admirably rich and beautiful—my letter would greatly gain in value if I possessed the learning needful for describing them. I can only say that every evening for a fortnight, I believe, she has revealed herself as a fresh creation. But she especially, as I say, has struck me as a person dressed beyond her life. I resent on her behalf—or on behalf at least of her finery—the extreme severity of her circumstances. What is she, after all, but a regular boarder? She ought to sit on the terrace of a stately castle, with a great baronial park shutting out the undressed world, mildly coquetting with an ambassador or a duke. My imagination is shocked when I behold her seated in gorgeous relief against the dusty clapboards of the hotel, with her beautiful hands folded in her silken lap, her head drooping slightly beneath the weight of her *chignon*, her lips parted in a vague contemplative gaze at Mr. Helmbold's well-known advertisement on the opposite fence, her husband beside her reading the New York *Sun*.

I have indeed observed cases of a sort of splendid social isolation here, which are not without a certain amount of pathos—people who know no one—who have money and finery and possessions, only no friends. Such at least is my inference, from the lonely grandeur with which I see them invested. Women, of course, are the most helpless victims of this cruel situation, although it must be said that they befriend each other with a generosity for which we hardly give them credit. I have seen women, for instance, at various "hops," approach their lonely sisters and invite them to waltz, and I have seen the fair invited most graciously heedless of the potential irony of this particular form of charity. Gentlemen at Saratoga are at a premium far more, evidently, than at European watering-places. It is an old story that in this country we have no leisured class—the class from which the Saratogas of Europe recruit a large number of their male frequenters. A few months ago, I paid a visit to a famous English watering-place, where, among many substantial points of difference from our own, I chiefly remember the goodly number of well-dressed, well-looking, well-talking young men. While their sweethearts and sisters are waltzing together, our own young men are rolling up greenbacks in counting-houses and stores. I was recently reminded in another way, one evening, of the unlikeness of Saratoga to Cheltenham. Behind the biggest of the big hotels is a large planted yard, which has come to be talked of as a "park." This I regret, inasmuch as, as a yard, it is possibly the biggest in the world; while as a park I am afraid it is decidedly less than the smallest. At one end, however, stands a great ball-room, approached by a range of wooden steps. It was late in the evening: the room, in spite of the intense heat, was blazing with light, and the orchestra thundering a mighty waltz. A group of loungers, including myself, were hanging about to watch the ingress of the festally minded. In the basement of the edifice, sunk beneath the ground, a noisy auctioneer, in his shirt and trousers, black in the face with heat and vociferation, was selling "pools" of the races to a dense group of frowsy betting-men. At the foot of the steps was stationed a man in a linen coat and straw hat, without waistcoat or cravat, to take the tickets of the ball-goers. As the latter failed to arrive in sufficient numbers, a musican came forth to the top of the steps and blew a loud summons on a horn. After this they began to straggle along. On this occasion, certainly, the company promised to be decidedly "mixed." The women, as usual, were a great deal dressed, though without any constant adhesion to the technicalities of full-dress. The men adhered to it neither in the letter nor the spirit. The possessor of a pair of satin-shod feet, twinkling beneath an uplifted volume of gauze and lace and flowers, tripped up the steps with her gloved hand on the sleeve of a railway "duster." Now and then two ladies arrived alone: generally a group of them approached under convoy of a single man. Children were freely scattered among their elders, and frequently a small boy would deliver his ticket and enter the glittering portal, beautifully unembarrassed. Of the children of Saratoga there would be wondrous things to relate. I believe that, in spite of their valuable aid, the festival of which I speak was rated rather a "fizzle." I see it advertised that they are soon to have, for their own peculiar benefit, a "Masquerade and Promenade Concert, beginning at 9 P.M." I observe that they usually open the "hops," and that it is only after their elders have borrowed confidence from the sight of their unfaltering paces that they venture to perform. You meet them far into the evening roaming over the piazzas and corridors of the hotels—the little girls especially—lean, pale, and formidable. Occasionally childhood confesses itself, even when motherhood stands out, and you see at eleven o'clock at night some poor little bedizened precocity collapsed in slumbers in a lonely wayside chair. The part played by children in society here is only an additional instance of the wholesale equalization of the various social atoms which is the distinctive feature of collective Saratoga. A man in a "duster" at a ball is as good as a man in irreproachable sable; a young woman dancing with another young woman is as good as a young woman dancing with a young man; a child of ten is as good as a woman of thirty; a double negative in conversation is rather better than a single.

An important feature in many watering-places is the facility for leaving it a little behind you and tasting of the unmitigated country. You may wander to some shady hillside and sentimentalize upon the vanity of high civilization. But at Saratoga civilization holds you fast. The most important feature of the place, perhaps, is the impossibility of realizing any such pastoral dream. The surrounding country is a charming wilderness, but the roads are so abominably bad that walking and driving are alike unprofitable. Of course, however, if you are bent upon a walk, you will take it. There is a striking contrast between the concentrated prodigality of life in the immediate precinct of the hotels and the generous wooded wildness and roughness into which half an hour's stroll may lead you. Only a mile behind you are thousands of loungers and idlers, fashioned from head to foot by the experience of cities and keenly knowing in their secrets; while here, about you and before you, blooms untamed the hardy innocence of field and forest. The heavy roads are little more than sandy wheel-tracks; by the tangled wayside the blackberries wither unpicked. The country undulates with a beautiful unsoftened freedom. There are no white villages gleaming in the distance, no spires of churches, no salient details. It is all green, lonely, and vacant. If you wish to seize an "effect," you must stop beneath a cluster of pines and listen to the murmur of the softly-troubled air, or follow upward the gradual bending of their trunks to where the afternoon light touches and enchants them. Here and there on a slope by the roadside stands a rough unpainted farm-house, looking as if its dreary blackness were the result of its standing dark and lonely amid so many months, and such a wide expanse, of winter snow. The principal feature of the grassy unfurnished yard is the great wood-pile, telling grimly of the long reversion of the summer. For the time, however, it looks down contentedly enough over a goodly appanage of grain-fields and orchards, and I can fancy that it may be good to be a boy there. But to be a man, it must be quite what the lean, brown, serious farmers physiognomically hint it to be. You have, however, at the present season, for your additional beguilement, on the eastern horizon, the vision of the long bold chain of the Green Mountains, clad in that single coat of simple candid blue which is the favorite garment of our American hills. As a visitor, too, you have for an afternoon's excursion your choice between a couple of lakes. Saratoga Lake, the larger and more distant of the two, is the goal of the regular afternoon drive. Above the shore is a well-appointed tavern—"Moon's" it is called by the voice of fame—where you may sit upon a broad piazza and partake of fried potatoes and "drinks;" the latter, if you happen to have come from poor dislicensed Boston, a peculiarly gratifying privilege. You enjoy the felicity sighed for by that wanton Italian princess of the anecdote, when, one summer evening, to the sound of music, she wished that to eat an ice were a sin. The other lake is small, and its shores are unadorned by any edifice but a boat-house, where you may hire a skiff and pull yourself out into the minnow-tickled, wood-circled oval. Here, floating in its darkened half, while you watch on the opposite shore the tree-stems, white and sharp in the declining sunlight, and their foliage whitening and whispering in the breeze, and you feel that this little solitude is part of a greater and more portentous solitude, you may resolve certain passages of Ruskin, in which he dwells upon the needfulness of some human association, however remote, to make natural scenery fully impressive. You may recall that magnificent passage in which he relates having tried with such fatal effect, in a battle-haunted valley of the Jura, to fancy himself in a nameless solitude of our own continent. You feel around you, with irresistible force, the serene inexperience of undedicated nature — the absence of serious associations, the nearness, indeed, of the vulgar and trivial associations of the least picturesque of great watering-places — you feel this, and you wonder what it is you so deeply and calmly enjoy. You conclude, possibly, that it is a great advantage to be able at once to enjoy Ruskin and to enjoy what Ruskin dispraises. And hereupon you return to your hotel and read the New York papers on the plan of the French campaign and the Twenty-third Street murder.

E.L. GODKIN

The Moral of Tweed's Career   *April 18, 1878*

As editor, between 1865 and 1881, E.L. Godkin waged war on municipal corruption. What he had to say about the downfall of Boss Tweed's career offers lessons to citizens of New York even at a later date.

The death of Tweed, the late Boss of this city, has drawn forth the usual number of funeral discourses, both from the press and the pulpit, and by most of them he has been made to serve as a warning of extraordinary solemnity against dishonest practices and sensual indulgence. We cannot help thinking that this is great waste of a fine and conspicuous example. The only preacher, within our observation, who has turned it to proper account is the New York *Times*, in pointing out that what Tweed's career most effectively illustrated was not the inexpediency of individual wickedness, but the badness of the social conditions in which such wickedness could be so successful. There is no city in the civilized world which does not contain plenty of men capable of doing all that Tweed did and more, if they got a chance. London, Paris, Vienna, Berlin, Boston, and Philadelphia, all have them in abundance; men, we venture to say, with full as much ability and audacity, with as huge a greed for money and as capacious stomachs. In every one of these cities there are scores of "mute inglorious" Tweeds, waiting for an opportunity to play his part. If we never hear of them the reason will be, not that *he* was a man of matchless powers of mischief, but that the community they live in will not give them a chance of imitating him. He was undoubtedly an eminent man in his field, but he was not an eminently bad man. With similar culture and manure dozens like him could be raised in a year in any great capital, and by going to any State prison much more valuable illustrations of the consequences of knavery might be produced for the use of the Sunday-school teacher.

To say that he was produced by certain social conditions is, however, not strictly accurate. He was produced by certain political conditions which grew into existence almost without the knowledge of the American public, and to which their eyes were only fairly opened by his rise and fall. American political theories and traditions had made absolutely no provision and provided no place for the community which raised him. According to these theories and traditions, when a number of capitalists, owning or controlling vast amounts of property, collect for the transaction of business at the mouth of a great river and draw around them hundreds of thousands of poor, ignorant, or shiftless persons to work for them in their warehouses and factories and docks, these hundreds of thousands become animated by an eager desire for efficient, orderly, and economical municipal government, and unite with the property-owners for its creation and maintenance; they become, in short, the personage known in American jurisprudence as "the people," inheriting the supposed attributes of the sovereign of the Old World— that is, a perspicacious, vigilant, upright master, keeping a watchful eye over the public interests, and careful in the selection of public servants. In fact, however, the growth of American cities has followed no such lines. The population by which they have been rapidly built up during the past twenty-five years has had many of the characteristics of a plebs, and rapidly began to ask for leaders which should put it in the way of living off the rich without violating the law. Tweed succeeded because he was the first to perceive the work which this class wished to have done, and the first to discover the way of doing it. Having once secured, through the ignorant, greedy vote, the control of the local taxation, he introduced Americans to another startling novelty—the wholesale corruptibility of legislatures composed of country farmers and lawyers of small means, by the use of sums which far exceeded with most of them the possible savings of a frugal and successful life. With the instruments in his hands, his work, as we all know, was perfectly easy. He met with no check from the very first until the exposure came. And let us remember that he fell without loss of reputation among the bulk of his supporters. The bulk of the poorer voters of this city to-day revere his memory, and look on him as the victim of rich men's malice; as, in short, a friend of the needy who applied the public funds, with as little waste as was possible under the

13

circumstances, to the purposes to which they ought to be applied—and that is to the making of work for the workingman. The odium heaped on him in the pulpits last Sunday does not exist in the lower stratum of New York society. We can appeal for the truth of this to any one who has during the past six years taken the trouble to test the opinion of this stratum on Tweed's life and fate.

The intelligent and wealthy classes, of course, do not like to believe these things, and men with political ambition, if they believe them, do not dare to utter them; but they are none the less true and important. They constitute "the great-city problem," which is perhaps now the most pressing one of American politics, but which politicians and primitive Americans (with the New England town governments still fresh in their minds, however) either refuse to see or shrink from dealing with. It is the problem, too, by which the seeds of that communistic spirit which is now assailing the nation's finances was sown and is being steadily fostered. The power lodged in the hands of the penniless muncipal voter over large masses of property furnishes either a constant lesson in spoliation or a temptation to spoliation, and is keeping alive or stimulating all over the Union the schemes for getting a living out of the Government by hook or by crook which are now showing themselves in the arena of national politics, and even becoming the foundation of a party. In this new field—new in America—Tweed was simply the earliest worker, but he was not a particularly skilful worker. He lost his head very early in the day, and thus precipitated his downfall. Had he gone more slowly and carried on his operations on a smaller scale, and been simpler in his habits and less ostentatious in his pleasures, he could have retained his power until now, and might have strengthened it and made his overthrow far more difficult. A villain of more brains would have had a modest dwelling and would have guzzled in secret. He found, however, the seizure of the government and the malversation of its funds so easy at the outset that he was thrown off his guard. His successors here and elsewhere will not imitate him in this, but that he will have successors there is no doubt. The resolute refusal of the community which he spoiled and corrupted to make any essential change in the system by which he rose, or even to acknowledge the desirableness of a change, is a kind of standing invitation to all the demagogues of the world to come here and try their hands on us again, and the taxing system of nearly every city in the Union offers them a ready instrument for the attempt.

The Week

[circus clowns and journalists]

Paragraphs of (unsigned) comment on current affairs called
"The Week" filled the first three or four pages of the magazine
from 1865 to 1936. Items often reflected the editor's view that
the function of a weekly was not to explain or report or celebrate the national virtues, but to take a consistently critical view
of "the idols of the tribe." Here the topic was the vices of the
press, one of Godkin's favorite targets.

A circus clown has been telling a St. Louis newspaper that the best days of the
circus are over. One of the reasons he gives for thinking so is that, for success
in the circus, training must begin early in life, and the societies for the prevention
of cruelty to children are so active that they prevent anything of the kind. There
may be something in this; but a more serious difficulty, we fancy, is that the part
taken in the performance by the clown is much less attractive than it formerly
was, owing to the fact that a great deal of the talent which once found its way
into this business now goes into journalism, the mental outfit of a really able
"funny man" being very much what that of a successful clown used to be. The
press makes a business of supplying daily just such jokes as the circus used to
provide, and ambitious humorists, who would formerly have worn stripes and
spangles in the ring, now entertain the public through a newspaper. The clown
proper has consequently run down, because the profession no longer attracts the
best humor, as any one may satisfy himself by going and listening to a modern
clown trying to make jokes. There is obviously no remedy for this decay, which
really gives a new illustration of the wonderful power of the press.

E.L. GODKIN

The Execution of the Anarchists   *November 10, 1887*

Certain pages in *The Nation* make strange reading. On May 3,
1886, Chicago police killed and wounded half a dozen demonstrating workers. The following day, when the police broke up
a protest meeting at Haymarket Square, someone threw a bomb
into the crowd; seven people were killed and over sixty injured.
Though the actual perpetrator of the bombing could not be
found, a Cook County judge held that those who incited the
deed were as guilty as those who committed it. Under this rul-

ing, the judge found eight anarchists guilty of murder and sentenced one to imprisonment and seven to death by hanging. No credible evidence was ever introduced linking the defendants to the bombing. Godkin wrote several pieces calling for the hanging of the Chicago Anarchists; the magazine, under his editorial control, also opposed trade unions and attacked socialists.

There is much to be said in favor of such slowness of judicial process as has marked the Anarchist cases, but there is one great objection to it, and that is the opportunity it affords to people to forget the atrocity of the crime, the sufferings and sorrows of its victims, and to lash themselves into sympathy with the doomed criminals. It is now a year and a half since the bomb-throwing in Chicago. During the following six months people's minds were occupied with the horrors of the resulting slaughter and maiming of the police, about forty of whom were killed or disabled in the discharge of their duty, and with the devilish malignity of the attack on them. At that time nobody—not even, we think, the firmest opponents of capital punishment—ventured to suggest that there was any place in this world for the bomb-throwers, or that the removal from it of such tigers was not a solemn duty to human society.

Since then, however, a good many people—some of them clergymen, some philanthropists, and some simply soft-headed people who sign all papers presented to them which do not impose pecuniary obligations—have had time to forget all about the police, and all about social security, and all about the Anarchists' teachings and aims, and are trying to get Governor Oglesby to commute the sentences of the men now awaiting execution. We have no fear that he will be weak enough to pay any attention to them. But there is great reason to fear that the agitation in their behalf may do much to weaken the deterring influence of their fate on their surviving brethren, seeing that several men of good standing and repute for common sense and patriotism are lending their countenance to it. There are some considerations which these persons have apparently overlooked in doing so; and we would therefore earnestly urge upon their attention, and the attention of all concerned, the following points:

(1.) That anybody who has any doubt of the complicity of the whole seven malefactors now awaiting sentence in the awful crime of May 4, 1886, either has not read the judgment of the Supreme Court of Illinois, on the appeal, in which the whole case, both facts and law, is elaborately reviewed; or if he has read it and has not been convinced by it, should so far question his power of weighing the pros and cons of a case of this nature as to feel it his duty to be silent about it, and to abstain from all attempts to influence the conduct of those whom the law obliges to act in it. Nothing but thorough acquaintance with the evidence produced on the trial, and thorough mastery of the reasoning applicable to questions of probability, warrants anybody in asking Gov. Oglesby for a pardon of the prisoners on the plea that they, or any of them, are innocent, or that some are less guilty than others. That is to say, that any one who tries to embarrass him or shake his nerves in the performance of such an awful duty as now devolves on him, without feeling well assured that he knows thoroughly what he is talking about, is guilty of a gross violation of social morality.

(2.) That those who ask for a pardon through dislike of capital punishment, should remember that the opposition to capital punishment in modern times has been everywhere based on the assumption that murder will be committed through private, individual hate, or for purposes of robbery, and that the substitutes suggested for this punishment have not had in view attacks on the whole social organization by sects of conspirators, claiming the right of slaughter and devastation as in open war; that therefore, holding the lives of Anarchists sacred, after they have massacred policemen, would be very like promising foreign invaders that resistance to them with weapons of any description would be strictly forbidden, and that the most they had to fear in case of failure was a short period of detention.

(3.) That should Gov. Oglesby even commute their sentences, the arguments in favor of commutation would, as the memory of the crime grew more faint, be every year used, and with increasing force, in favor of complete pardon; that, in fact, their right to a pardon would become a political issue in the State elections, and that demagogues would soon bring about their liberation, until probably, in five or six years from this time, we should witness the shocking spectacle of the joyous, unrepentant freedom and activity of a band of convicted assassins preaching with renewed vigor the gospel of arson and murder in the very streets which they had reddened with the blood of the officers of the law. No civilized community can afford to offer such a sight as this.

(4.) That although, as Judge McAllister of Chicago says, the hanging of these men may make "them martyrs in the opinion of thousands of people," this is the less of two evils. Society can stand their being considered martyrs by a great many thousands of people; but it cannot stand their finding ready imitators even among a few hundreds. Nobody is hurt by anybody's considering Spies or Lingg "a martyr," but it would hurt a great many to have even a dozen men conclude that there was no risk in following his example.

(5.) That it must not be forgotten that these criminals are all but one foreigners and new arrivals, who have left behind them in Europe thousands infected with their ideas and as averse from the dull routine of regular industry, who are watching the case of their forerunners in this country with intense interest, to see if armed attacks on the social organization can be made with more safety here than in Europe. To allow the murderers of the Chicago police to get off with what would certainly prove a short term of imprisonment, would confirm them in their belief that the absence here of the great display of police and soldiery with which they see the law made terrible in the Old World, really means weakness of the public force, and inability of society to defend itself against anybody who chooses to disregard its obligations or dispute its authority. It would, in fact, operate as an invitation to all the ferocious malcontents of France, Germany, and Russia to come here and work out their theories whenever they could raise their passage money, or found the pursuit of the hangman in Europe too hot for them.

There are signs that the discovery of bombs in the cell of Lingg, the Anarchist, in the Chicago Jail is doing something to bring the friends of "clemency," in that region at least, to their senses, and the petitioning for pardon or commutation has visibly declined. The probabilities are that Lingg meant to blow up himself and as many others as possible whenever he found that hope was at an end and the inevitable hour had come. In other words, his tigerish nature was not in the smallest degree softened by the long period of suffering and anxiety through which he had passed.

A great deal of the effort made to save the Anarchists from the gallows is due to the impression that they are being punished for their opinions, and that even if it be just, it is bad policy to punish men for their opinions, because, if these opinions are noxious, the persecution or martyrdom of the authors only helps to spread the poison. It has to be borne in mind that the State of Illinois has acted on this theory for several years. For fully ten years the city of Chicago has been a hotbed of Anarchy, in which the slaughter of well-to-do people and the destruction of their property was freely and openly advocated, without any interference from the authorities. The result was that the militant or homicidal Anarchists every day gained strength, and the dreamy, persuasive Anarchists were every day pushed more and more into the background.

The lesson of all this is, that the only opinions which a civilized community can treat with either respect or indifference are opinions which, even if embodied in action, would not menace its existence. Our traditional Anglo-Saxon respect for free speech is based on the assumption that public speech is always intended in free countries to persuade people into agreement with the speaker for purposes of legislation, and that the agreement aimed at is therefore a lawful one. The notion that we must tolerate speech the object of which is to induce people to break up the social organization and abolish property by force, is historically and politically absurd. The notion that we must not do whatever is necessary to prevent men's publicly recommending murder and arson, because they are sincere in thinking murder and arson good means to noble ends, is worse than absurd. It is, as we see, full of danger for everything we most value on earth.

It is a great pity that we cannot shut up the mouths of the Anarchists by love. But as we cannot shut them up by love, we must do it by fear, that is, by inflicting on them the penalties which they most dread; and the one most appropriate to their case when they kill people, is death. The frantic exertions they are making just now to escape the gallows, and the joy with which they would welcome a "life sentence," shows clearly that the gallows is the punishment the case calls for. For violent incitements to murder and pillage, imprisonment will doubtless suffice; but for actual murder and pillage there is nothing likely to prove so effective a deterrent as death. Those who oppose this view can only do so successfully by maintaining that society has no right to defend its own existence, and that murder and arson are evils only when the murderer's motives are low and selfish; that if he can show that he means well, and has at heart the elevation of the poor, he should be treated with the respect due to prophets and apostles. If the propagators of these grotesque fancies only knew the encouragement they were giving to the contempt for law which makes both the rich briber and the semi-barbarous lyncher the curse of American politics at present, we feel sure they would pause in their efforts to save the community the loss of the vagabonds and ruffians who are now awaiting execution at Chicago.

WENDELL PHILLIPS GARRISON

The Pesky Anti-Imperialist   *May 8, 1902*

> Imperialism was anathema to *The Nation*. The prospect of the annexation of a sovereign people without their consent, and the stories of atrocities committed by U.S. troops in quelling the Filipino insurrection, aroused the fierce indignation of many Americans and inflamed public opinion. People of the most diverse views rallied under the banner of anti-imperialism. This satirical editorial exemplifies the magazine's indictment of imperialism masquerading as patriotism.

It is most provoking, we know, for Anti-Imperialists to pretend that they are still alive. They have been killed so often. After 1899 we were to hear no more of them. In 1900 they were again pronounced dead, although, like the obstinate Irishman, they continued to protest that, if they were dead, they were not conscious of it. Last year the slain were slaughtered once more, and that time buried as well, with all due ceremony. Yet the impudent creatures have resumed activity during the past few months just as if their epitaphs had not been composed again and again.

And the worst of it is that they seem to have acquired a strange power over the public and over Government. What the lonely and ridiculous Anti-Imperialist was whispering in the closet, a year ago, thousands are now shouting from the house-tops. The impossible measures which the absurd fellow was demanding have been adopted by the President of the United States, and have even compelled the approval of Congress. When Gen. Funston, for example, began his blethering, it was the foolish Anti-Imperialists who said that the President ought to reprimand and silence him, and how the jeers arose! That was just like the silly old impracticables—attacking a popular hero. But presently the said hero had a gag forcibly inserted between his teeth by Executive order, just as if the Anti-Imperialists had been right about it from the beginning. It is not necessary to recall the triumphs of the mistaken beings in the whole matter of the Philippine investigation and of courts-martial for the implicated officers. Enough to say that, in the entire affair, the Administration and Congress have acted on the demand and as if by the advice of that handful of out-of-date and laughable persons, the Anti-Imperialists.

The phenomenon occasions much scratching of the Imperialist head. How to account for it? Imperialist editors and statesmen are puzzled. Their despised and helpless opponents are actually swaying the policy of the Government! It is absurd, of course, really quite preposterous, but there stands the fact. It is all very fine, and it's lots of fun, to make merry at the expense of wrong-headed people who get in the way of national progress, and hope to turn back the hands on the dial of evolution, but how if they succeed? Prodigiously unreasonable, it goes without saying, and truly disgusting to the well-ordered mind of the Imperialist; but what is the explanation?

Very simple, cocksure brothers of the Empire, we assure you. All you have to do is to remember that Anti-Imperialism is only another name for old-fashioned Americanism, and all will be clear to you. An American who has a settled body of convictions, as to which he is ready to speak out at a moment's notice, and which he is ready to apply promptly and sharply to every fresh set of circumstances that turns up; who with his inherited ideas has an inherited courage, an inherited love of equality and of justice; who has also a sense of humor which cannot be imposed upon by Uncle Sam masquerading in Louis Quatorze garments—why, he is a natural born Anti-Imperialist, and it is simply his Americanism that makes him think and act as he does.

We have had some beautiful illustrations of this truth in the weeks last past. What is the true American way of dealing with a rampant military banqueteer like Funston? Or with news from the Philippines that makes the blood curdle? It is to say on the spot what you think, is it not? Well, that is exactly what the Anti-Imperialists did. It was the other sort who looked at each other in wild surmise, wondered if they dared say anything at all, kept still until shame finally drove them into mumbling speech, and acted in all ways as if they were the terrified and hunted minority afraid to say their souls were their own. Is that Imperialism? We do not know. We only know that it is not Americanism, and that in this case, as so many times before, the citizens who first found their voices, who first spoke out their honest indignation and made their righteous demands, were the ones to move public opinion and to influence official action, while the palterers and the apologizers had to come shamefacedly after.

And it is, too, the "ancient humor," as well as the elder stanchness, of true Americanism that has been coming to its own in the recent successes of the Anti-Imperialist cause. What are our anxious and solemn Imperialists thinking of when they imagine that Uncle Sam has forgotten how to take a joke? They gather about the old gentleman with attentive flatteries, and keep serious faces when he nervously asks them how his ermine hangs, and if his crown is on straight. All the while he would much prefer to have them laugh at him openly and tell him not to be a durn fool. Mark Twain is showing us to-day how true is his descent in the right line of American humor by his continued satires on the airs and graces of our Imperialists. He speaks in the very voice, if not in the numbers, of Hosea Biglow, and with all his sarcasm at the expense of the high and mighty ones who think to arrange all matters of statesmanship and of national policy without consulting the inquisitive democrat of field and shop—

"Wal, it's a marcy we've gut folks to tell us
The rights an' the wrongs o' these matters, I vow."

This, in a word, is what makes the Anti-Imperialist so pesky—he is American to the core. He has fed on his country's tradition. With him, as with Gov. Andrew and with Lincoln, justice does not depend upon the color of a man's skin. He cannot distinguish between the flag and the principles which first set the flag flying. With John Quincy Adams he believes that the Declaration of Independence is the very Alcoran of American political doctrine. And he does not in the least mind being in a minority. He remembers that the history of success is the history of minorities. Sneers and jeers are alike indifferent to him, and when the Red Slayer thinks to have made an end of him, he turns and passes and comes again. He is content to bide his time, knowing that the road of popular persuasion is a long one, though sure in the end, and that republics cannot march to their goal with "the decisiveness and consistency of despotism." Withal, he knows how to shoot a dart of ridicule at Imperialist folly as it flies, and derives amusement as well as hope from Uncle Sam's humorous appreciation of his present plight. This might well be caricatured to-day, as we have heard it suggested, by a picture of your Uncle ruefully contemplating his Philippine extremities, enormously swollen by ulcers and boils, and saying with whimsical melancholy, "And they call this expansion!"

The Week

[military spending]

"More than a million dollars a day for military purposes"—this is not an estimate of the autocratic Russian government's expenditure to keep itself in power, nor of the bill paid by Germany to maintain a great fleet and keep up a standing army of 600,000 men. It is merely a conservative guess at what our peace-loving United States is to be asked to pay during the next fiscal year. Congressman Tawney has pointed out that the estimates already received call for the enormous amount of $406,011,216, at a moment when our balance sheet may show a deficit of one hundred millions in the year 1908–1909. This total includes, of course, pensions; but, as Mr. Tawney pointed out:

> This stupendous sum of $406,011,216 is asked for simply for the military side of the government, and is larger than appropriations for the entire expenses of the government for any fiscal year since the civil war down to 1890, and not appreciably less than appropriations for any fiscal year prior to 1897, for the Spanish-American war.

But, as the Washington *Times* points out, this is not all, for it does not include the twenty-one millions paid out for the maintenance of the War and Navy Departments, or the forty millions asked for new battleships. If Mr. Roosevelt's military mania were to be allowed full sway, we should expend $467,000,000 in 1908–1909 for war purposes, past, present, and future, or one and one-third millions for every day in the year. There never was a more stupid spectacle than that of this country's assuming all the burdens of that Old-World militarism which annually drives to our shores thousands of immigrants.

The Week

January 29, 1914

[the tango]

Why are Americans ceasing to read good literature? It is the fault, of course, of the tango. Beneficial as the new dance may be in certain respects, its most ardent advocates do not claim for it that it induces a longing for Shakespeare or even Alfred Noyes. But the tango does not stand alone in this respect. The automobile must bear part of the blame. We are the surer of the soundness of this contention when we recall that some years ago one of the greatest hindrances to the spread of good literature was the bicycle. What it was before that is less clear, although we imagine that the record would show that in the thirties good literature was neglected because of the influence of the railway, just as still earlier the invention of the steamboat caused people to lose interest in worth-while books. It is thus the unfortunate truth that in every age of the republic there has been something which has made us cease to care for good literature. Every generation has been devoted to books of the highest value, but every succeeding generation has ceased to care for them. Some day, perhaps, we shall have exhausted every other form of activity, and then our native love of good literature will no longer be denied.

American Liberalism
[letter to the editor]

January 11, 1919

Arthur Garfield Hays, a young lawyer in 1918 when he wrote this letter to the editor, later became director of the American Civil Liberties Union.

TO THE EDITOR OF THE NATION:

SIR: "It seems to me," said one of my guests at a dinner party, "that we are not getting all the news from Russia. We hear rumors now and then of the other side of the story. Perhaps our intervention was a mistake and our troops should retire. One also hears suggestions that it will be necessary to employ armed forces in Germany for years, in order to avoid the terror the Socialists may cause. No, I don't think the Socialists are all Bolshevists, nor am I inclined to believe that the Bolshevists are Anarchists.

"Have you noticed the talk of huge indemnities – punitive I think Wilson called them when he disapproved? Resentment arising from economic slavery does not make for an enduring peace. At any rate, the Socialists are not the Pan-Germans who caused the war.

"The Espionage Act? It seems to me that now that the war is over, it ought to be repealed. Why should Burleson and Creel carefully select the premises from which we must draw conclusions? Hearst? No, I don't think he's a traitor. You ask about the British Labor Party? Its principles are inspiring. Yes, it's socialistic, but what of that? – the world is changing."

My guest departed early. "He's a Socialist," said one. "He's an Anarchist," said another. "I am not so sure," said a third, "but from what he said I am sure you will all agree that he's a pacifist and a pro-German." And they all did.

New York December 24, 1919   ARTHUR GARFIELD HAYS

ROBERT C. BENCHLEY

The Making of a Red

> The playwright, humorist, critic and actor Robert Benchley
> wrote this satirical piece at the height of the Red Scare in 1919.
> Benchley captures the hostility to radicals, the antipathy to
> foreigners and the jealous protection of the status quo that were
> hallmarks of the time.

You couldn't have asked for anyone more regular than Peters. He was an eminently safe citizen. Although not rich himself, he never chafed under the realization that there were others who possessed great wealth. In fact, the thought gave
him rather a comfortable feeling. Furthermore, he was one of the charter
members of the War. Long before President Wilson saw the light, Peters was advocating the abolition of German from the public-school curriculum. There was,
therefore, absolutely nothing in his record which would in the slightest degree
alter the true blue of a patriotic litmus. And he considered himself a liberal when
he admitted that there might be something in this man Gompers, after all. That
is how safe he was.

But one night he made a slip. It was ever so tiny a slip, but in comparison with
it De Maupassant's famous piece of string was barren of consequences. Shortly
before the United States entered the war Peters made a speech at a meeting of the
Civic League in his home town. His subject was: "Inter-Urban Highways: Their
Development in the Past and Their Possibilities for the Future." So far 100 per
cent. American. But, in the course of his talk, he happened to mention the fact
that War, as an institution, has almost always had an injurious effect on public
improvements of all kinds. In fact (and note this well; the Government's sleuth
in the audience did) he said that, all other things being equal, if he were given
his choice of War or Peace in the abstract, he would choose Peace as a condition
under which to live. Then he went on to discuss the comparative values of mac-
adam and wood blocks for paving.

In the audience was a civilian representative of the Military Intelligence service. He had had a premonition that some sort of attempt was going to be made
at this meeting of the Civic League to discredit the war and America's imminent
participation therein. And he was not disappointed (no Military Intelligence
sleuth ever is), for in the remark of Peters, derogatory to War as an institution,
his sharp ear detected the accent of the Wilhelmstrasse.

Time went by. The United States entered the war, and Peters bought Liberty
Bonds. He didn't join the army, it is true, but, then, neither did James M. Beck,
and it is an open secret that Mr. Beck was for the war. Peters did what a few

slangy persons called "his bit," and not without a certain amount of pride. But he did not hear the slow, grinding noise from that district in which are located the mills of the gods. He did not even know that there was an investigation going on in Washington to determine the uses to which German propaganda money had been put. That is, he didn't know it until he opened his newspaper one morning and, with that uncanny precipitation with which a man's eye lights on his own name, discovered that he had been mentioned in the dispatches. At first he thought it might be an honor list of Liberty Bond holders, but a glance at the headline chilled that young hope in his breast. It read as follows:

PRO-GERMAN LIST BARED BY ARMY SLEUTH
Prominent Obstructionists Named at Senate Probe

And then came the list. Peters's eye ran instinctively down to the place where, in what seemed to him to be 24-point Gothic caps, was blazoned the name "Horace W. Peters, Pacifist Lecturer, Matriculated at Germantown (Pa.) Military School." Above his name was that of Emma Goldman, "Anarchist." Below came that of Fritz von Papen, "agent of the Imperial German Government in America," and Jeremiah O'Leary, "Irish and Pro-German Agitator."

Peters was stunned. He telegraphed to his Senator at Washington and demanded that the outrageous libel be retracted. He telegraphed to the Military Intelligence office and demanded to know who was the slanderer who had traduced him, and who in h–l this Captain Whatsisname was who had submitted the report. He telegraphed to Secretary Baker and he cabled to the President. And he was informed, by return stage-coach, that his telegrams had been received and would be brought to the attention of the addressees at the earliest possible moment.

Then he went out to look up some of his friends, to explain that there had been a terrible mistake somewhere. But he was coolly received. No one could afford to be seen talking with him after what had happened. His partner merely said: "Bad business, Horace. Bad business!" The elevator starter pointed him out to a subordinate, and Peters heard him explain: "That's Peters, Horace W. Peters. Did'je see his name in the papers this morning with them other German spies?" At the club little groups of his friends dissolved awkwardly when they saw him approaching, and, after distant nods, disappeared in an aimless manner. After all, you could hardly blame them.

The next morning the *Tribune* had a double-leaded editorial entitled "Oatmeal," in which it was stated that the disclosures in Washington were revealing the most insidious of all kinds of German propaganda – that disseminated by supposedly respectable American citizens. "It is not a tangible propaganda. It is an emotional propaganda. To the unwary it may resemble real-estate news, or perhaps a patriotic song, but it is the pap of Prussianism. As an example, we need go no further than Horace W. Peters. Mr. Peters's hobby was inter-urban highways. A very pretty hobby, Mr. Peters, but it won't do. It won't do." The *Times* ran an editorial saying, somewhere in the midst of a solid slab of type, that no doubt it would soon be found that Mr. Peters nourished Bolshevist sentiments, along with his team-mate, Emma Goldman. Emma Goldman! How Peters hated that woman! He had once written a letter to this very paper about her, advocating her electrocution.

He dashed out again in a search of some one to whom he could explain. But the editorials had done their work. The door-man at the club presented him with a letter from the house-committee, saying that, at a special meeting, it had been decided that he had placed himself in a position offensive to the loyal members of the club, and that it was with deep regret that they informed him, etc. As he stumbled out into the street, he heard someone whisper to an out-of-town friend, "There goes Emma Goldman's husband."

As the days went by things grew unbelievably worse. He was referred to in public meetings whenever an example of civic treachery was in order. A signed advertisement in the newspapers, protesting, on behalf of the lineal descendants of the Grand Duke Sergius, against the spread of Bolshevism in Northern New Jersey, mentioned a few prominent snakes in the grass, such as Trotzky, Victor Berger, Horace W. Peters, and Emma Goldman.

Then something snapped. Peters began to let his hair grow long, and neglected his linen. Each time he was snubbed on the street he uttered a queer guttural sound and made a mark in a little book he carried about with him. He bought a copy of "Colloquial Russian at a Glance," and began picking out inflammatory sentences from the *Novy Mir*. His wife packed up and went to stay with her sister when he advocated, one night at dinner, the communization of women. The last prop of respectability having been removed, the descent was easy. Emma Goldman, was it? Very well, then, Emma Goldman it should be! Bolshevist, was he? They had said it! "After all, who is to blame for this?" he mumbled to himself. "Capitalism! Militarism! Those Prussians in the Intelligence Department and the Department of Justice! The damnable bourgeoisie who sit back and read their *Times* and their *Tribune* and believe what they read there!" He had tried explanations. He had tried argument. There was only one thing left. He found it on page 112 of a little book of Emma Goldman's that he always carried around with him.

You may have read about Peters the other day. He was arrested, wearing a red shirt over his business cutaway and carrying enough TNT to shift the Palisades back into the Hackensack marshes. He was identified by an old letter in his pocket from Henry Cabot Lodge thanking him for a telegram of congratulation Peters had once sent him on the occasion of a certain speech in the Senate.

The next morning the *Times* said, editorially, that it hoped the authorities now saw that the only way to crush Bolshevism was by the unrelenting use of force.

WILLIAM MacDONALD

The Madness at Versailles *May 17, 1919*

> *The Nation* was the first journal of opinion to denounce the
> Treaty of Versailles. The editors noted proudly in 1920 that "if
> *The Nation* had done nothing else in this decade it would yet
> have justified itself by the position it then took and has main-
> tained ever since."

It was not to be hoped that there would be a generous peace. The wickednesses
of the German armies were too obvious, the bad faith of the German Imperial
Government had been too clearly demonstrated to admit of any settlement which
did not impose heavy penalties and exact specific and ample guarantees. The temper of the victorious Allies as a whole was too harsh, and that of the French in
particular too strained with nervous dread, to make possible a peace under which
Germany would have much power to recuperate rapidly. Moreover, official
reports and unofficial intimations from Paris, although dealing for the most part
with scattered details rather than with larger or connected topics, have been
sufficient to indicate that the Peace Conference was little disposed to make concessions, and increasingly inclined to be drastic. For a rigorous peace, in short,
the world was already somewhat prepared. But it was not prepared for a peace
of undisguised vengeance, for a peace which openly flouts some of the plainest
dictates of reason and humanity, repudiates every generous word that Mr. Wilson
has ever uttered regarding Germany, flies in the face of accepted principles of
law and economics, and makes the very name of democracy a reproach. In the
whole history of diplomacy there is no treaty more properly to be regarded as an
international crime than the amazing document which the German representatives
are now asked to sign.

Only as one keeps in mind the high professions with which the war was
conducted—professions of which Mr. Wilson, more than any one else, was the
polished and unctuous mouthpiece, and which the Allies by their applause impli-
edly accepted—is the enormity of what has happened to be fully comprehended.
The world was to be made safe for democracy. German militarism was to be
crushed, and the German Constitution itself was to be so changed as to emanci-
pate the German people from autocratic rule and make impossible the repetition
of such a war as this one had proved itself to be. The German people, who, it
was repeatedly affirmed, had had no part in bringing on the war, and who at the
worst were the helpless instruments of its prosecution, were to be freed from
tyranny and given a chance to take their place among the peoples who love liberty
and practice righteousness. Again and again, in the rhetorical documents in which

Mr. Wilson expounded to a waiting world the divine order of human society, he declared that America, at least, had no quarrel with the German people, that it begrudged them no greatness which their industry and intelligence might attain, and that a victorious peace, if it meant punitive damages or harsh restraint, would be worse than useless as a world settlement. And for the attainment of these ends and their sanctification a League of Nations was to be set up, with Germany itself, if it would cease to do evil and learn to do well, as one of its members.

How have these generous professions, honorable alike to those who made them and to those who trusted them, been carried out? The treaty affords only one answer. Germany and the German people are virtually to be destroyed. The burdens which the treaty imposes are heavier than any people can bear and progress. To begin with, German territory is to be diminished. Including Alsace-Lorraine, Silesia, Posen, the Saar Basin, and other areas, Germany is to lose 35,175 square miles, in addition to 8,572 square miles in Schleswig and East Prussia which will presumably have to be parted with in consequence of referendum votes on the question of allegiance for which the treaty provides. Even conceding that the whole of Alsace-Lorraine ought to be restored to France, and that the inhabitants of the designated portions of Schleswig and East Prussia should be allowed to determine their allegiance, the loss of territory still aggregates 29,575 square miles. In addition to deprivation of territory in Europe, Germany is to renounce in favor of the Allies and the other so-called associated Powers all its overseas possessions, including not only its colonies but its rights and property in China, Siam, Liberia, Morocco, Egypt, Turkey, and Bulgaria. The destruction of Germany's military and naval power is virtually complete; its army is reduced to 100,000 men, its navy is cut down to a handful of vessels, conscription is abolished, the further construction of wireless stations is forbidden, and most of its cables are appropriated by the victors. Within a zone of fifty kilometres east of the Rhine all fortifications are to be destroyed.

All this, drastic as it is, forms only the opening chapter. There are to be reparations, indemnities, and strangling economic punishments as well. What the aggregate amount of indemnities and reparations is to be has not, apparently, yet been determined, but, whatever it is, Germany is to go on paying it for thirty years, beginning with an initial payment within two years of a billion pounds sterling. At the same time it is required to devote its economic resources directly to the restoration of the invaded regions of Belgium and France; to deliver annually for ten years to those countries and to Italy great quantities of coal (one of its principal coal fields, the Saar Basin, having in the meantime been surrendered); and to grant to the Allied and associated Powers preferences and concessions in trade which will go far toward destroying German competition in any branch of industry. As if deliberately to add insult to penalty, the victors further propose to exact from Germany most-favored-nation treatment for their own vessels in the German fishing and coasting trade, and even in towage; while as a guarantee that the requirements of the treaty will be met, German territory west of the Rhine, together with the bridgeheads on that river, is to be occupied by Allied and associated troops for fifteen years, unless in the meantime the requirements of the treaty are fully complied with.

Nor is this all. The provisions for the disarmament of Germany, which might easily, had the victorious Powers so chosen, have been made a beneficent illustration of how a great state might live in peace and happiness without an army or a navy greater than the needs for a police, are wholly negatived, so far as moral value is concerned, by the failure of the treaty to provide for any measure whatever of disarmament on the part of the Allies and their associates. As the treaty stands, Germany is to be stripped of its means of defence as well as of offence, while its conquerors hover about it fully armed. If there were still need of proof that the League of Nations, as a device for insuring world peace, is only an alliance of three great Powers to enforce their will upon all the others, the treatment accorded to Germany at this point should furnish the demonstration. Further, what is to be said for a treaty which requires Germany to "hand over to the associated Governments, either jointly or severally, all persons" accused of "having committed acts in violation of the laws and customs of war," together with "all documents and information necessary to insure full knowledge of the incriminating acts, the discovery of the offenders, and the just appreciation of the responsibility," one of the alleged offenders being the former Kaiser, now outside of German territory; to concede in advance the validity of treaties yet to be made with Austria-Hungary, Bulgaria, and Turkey, including the decisions which may be made regarding their territory; to recognize in advance any new states that may be formed out of the territory of the three Powers mentioned, with such boundaries as may be agreed upon; to accept in advance the decisions of prize courts of the Allies regarding ships or goods; and to admit the jurisdiction of a League of Nations of which it is not a member, and which it cannot enter save with the unanimous consent of the Powers which are seeking its destruction?

Such are the terms to which the representatives of Germany are asked to set their hands without demur. Such is the treaty which is to end a war fought to overthrow autocracy and militarism and to enthrone democracy and peace. Such is the settlement to which the President of the United States has given his approval, and which the Senate of the United States will be asked to ratify. The heinousness of its offending, the calculating harshness of its demands and impositions, the gross repudiation of moral obligations and good faith which it involves, its gross injustice to the Allied peoples themselves and to their moral standing, become only the more apparent as its terms are studied. It is a peace of vengeance, not of justice. It will not restore Germany to the family of nations; it will destroy Germany as a Great Power. What will be the fate of Germany if the treaty prevails is, however, quite the least important aspect of the matter; the great and startling question now is what will be the fate of democracy, of political and economic liberty, of morals and ideals? How stands it with the peoples at this grave moment in the world's career?

It would be idle now to mince words. The meaning of the treaty is obvious. After nearly five years of strenuous effort and high expectancy, the hopes of the peoples have been destroyed. The progress of democracy as either a theory or a practice of social righteousness has been suddenly and forcibly checked. The great reforms which were to substitute the rule of peoples for the rule of Governments, abolish war as a means of aggression or of settling international disputes, break down alliances and balances of power, put secret diplomacy under the ban, do away with discriminating tariffs, establish the right of self-government for all peoples who desired it and were fit to exercise it, and bind the nations in a world league in which all would enjoy equal rights and equal opportunity, have been checked in their progress. In place of these helpful things of which patriots had dreamed, and which the peoples of the world for one brief moment imagined they were about to grasp, there has been enthroned at Versailles an arrogant and self-sufficient autocracy of five Great Powers, two of which are practically at the mercy of the other three; an autocracy owning no authority save its own will, deliberating in secret, parcelling out privileges and territory as best serves its own interests, turning a deaf ear to protests and closing its eyes to facts, observing no sounder principles than those of political compromise, and ordering all things by its own self-centred notions of how the peoples may best be controlled. It is this Versailles autocracy which, in crushing Germany as a world Power, has itself assumed the rôle of world dictator. That it is vindictive as well as powerful, that its resources are immense, and that it intends to have its way with the peoples and their aspirations, no one now need cherish any doubt whatever. Progress henceforth is to go by favor, and the favor will be that of the Big Three.

History, perhaps, will some time tell us how, among the men who have dominated the proceedings at Versailles, the responsibility for this state of things should be apportioned. None, surely, who have had a hand in the determinations of the Peace Conference can go unblamed, save as they may have been overborne by the weight of authority. Yet the verdict of history will not, we think, be incorrectly forecast if the larger blame for the check which liberty and democracy have received is laid to the charge of Woodrow Wilson. To Mr. Wilson, more than to any other man who has ever lived, it fell to voice the aspirations of the world's peoples and to receive their homage. The times and the opportunity were alike supremely great. The stream of revolt against privilege and privilege-begotten wealth, the demand for the abolition of autocracy and the substitution of a political and economic régime in which the people should rule in fact as well as in name, had risen to the point where all that was needed, apparently, was wise and inspiring direction to make it an instrument of the greatest gains for human welfare that the race had ever known. It was Mr. Wilson's achievement to give to this great yearning of the world's masses, not indeed constructive leadership, for he has builded nothing that will endure, but a winning exposition and a moral unction which caught the imagination of peoples everywhere, riveted their attention upon him as the one man living who sounded their motives and voiced their aspirations, and made him their idol as well as their guide and friend. The trust which the peoples gave him, the appeals which they fondly directed to him, and the high expectations with which they hung upon his words, were as pathetic in simplicity as they were imposing in weight and mass. He was the hope of democracy, and the fear of his enemies was the confidence of his friends.

How Mr. Wilson has repaid the confidence which the peoples gave him, all the world now knows. The one-time idol of democracy stands today discredited and condemned. His rhetorical phrases, torn and faded tinsel of a thought which men now doubt if he himself ever really believed, will never again fall with hypnotic charm upon the ears of eager multitudes. The camouflage of ethical precept and political philosophizing which for long blinded the eyes of all but the most observing has been stripped away, and the peoples of the world see revealed, not a friend faithful to the last, but an arrogant autocrat and a compromising politician. And with the loss of the robes which gave him sanctity goes also the loss of all liberal and ennobling support. There will still be many to applaud the treaty, and to join hands with Mr. Wilson in remorseless effort to push vengeance to completion, but they will not be the liberals who long acclaimed him as their leader nor the masses who once saw in him a second Providence. Those who stand with him now — strange transformation when one recalls the years of his ascendancy — are the staunch supporters of power and privilege, the controllers of great wealth and dictators of social favor, the voluble champions of the established order against every form of revolution, the preachers of hate and prejudice, and the timid and dependent whose souls are not their own. These are the ones who now do Mr. Wilson honor.

It is well that the line should at last be clearly drawn, for with the publication of the German treaty the real battle for liberty begins. All that has gone before — the overthrow of Czardom in Russia, the constitutional struggle in Germany, the establishment of a Soviet Government in Hungary, the revolt against tyranny or constraint in all quarters of the globe — are only the preliminaries of the great revolution to whose support the friends of freedom must now rally everywhere. Less and less, as that struggle widens, will the world have place for either liberals or conservatives: Versailles has forced men into two main camps, the radicals and the reactionaries. Heaven grant that the revolution may be peaceful, and that it may destroy only to rebuild! Whatever its course, it is the peoples who have been deluded and ignored who will play the leading part, for with the appalling example of Mr. Wilson and the Peace Conference before their eyes, the peoples will have small use for any leadership save their own. This is the scene which the moral collapse at Versailles opens to the world, this the promised land toward which the peoples of the world will now press with all their strength. With Germany crushed and autocracy enthroned, with the strong hand of power at the throat of liberty, the battle opens which is to make men free.

The Week
October 4, 1919

[Lenin and Trotzky and baseball]

The news from Russia, genially reported by *The Public Ledger* (Philadelphia), that Lenin and Trotzky are not only watching the World Series, but are willing to bet two to one on the Reds, is of the kind which may at last persuade our public to turn back from its unthinking drift towards internationalism before it is too late. It is all very well for Lenin and Trotzky to observe our political antics, for those are, after all, the concern and exercise of the few; but for them to trifle with our national sport is another matter. It is ours and they cannot have it. Foreigners, we all heard, while our army was acquainting itself with hand grenades, cannot throw. Notoriously they are mere women when it comes to perceiving the fine points or even following the bare plot of a baseball game. By what right then do Lenin and Trotzky, dreadful Dioscuri, begin to dabble in our particular affairs? Our Junkers are right: once these blinking Bolshevists are allowed a foothold they will never turn back. Like the cuckoo's brat in the nightingale's nest, when they get an inch they take a mile; like any capitalist, when they get a tip they make a bet. If only they did not show themselves so unpardonably colored by their own prepossessions we might still endure it. But between our Reds and their reds there is a difference. Whatever our Reds may do, the red rag of the Bolshevists shall never fly over our bleachers. Some things *are* sacred.

No Newpapers for Debs
October 18, 1919

[letter to the editor]

Eugene Debs was the Socialist Party's candidate for president five times between 1900 and 1920. In 1918, Debs was convicted and sentenced to ten years' imprisonment for violating the Espionage Act. *The Nation* ran editorials calling for Debs's release and advertisements asking readers to contribute to the "Debs cause." In the 1920 elections, Debs received nearly a million votes, although he was serving a term in the federal penitentiary in Atlanta. In 1921, at the age of sixty-six, Debs was released.

TO THE EDITOR OF THE NATION:

SIR: In behalf of Eugene Debs, as well as for myself, I wish to thank you for having had *The Nation* sent to his prison cell. Ever since his removal to Atlanta all papers and periodicals, including *The Nation*, are denied him; and he is not allowed even newspaper clippings, enclosed in letters. The other day I enclosed in a letter to him a small newspaper cut of the proposed building to be erected at Indianapolis by the Comrades, which is to be known as the "House of Debs," but before the letter was delivered the little picture was removed therefrom.

It is quite evidently the purpose of the Administration to cut him off completely from the outside world in the ardent hope of breaking his spirit. Of course he is permitted to read light fiction furnished by the prison library, but in these days when history is being written as never before, this is as nourishing and satisfying to the mentality of a student of events as skimmed milk is to the body of a famished child.

Several years ago Gene planted a little peach tree in his yard. It struggled for existence, but with careful nursing it survived. This year for the first time it bore a few peaches. Knowing the care Gene had bestowed upon this little tree, Mrs. Debs packed half a dozen of the peaches and sent them to him in care of the Warden. They were not delivered, although at the very time he had just been removed from his cell to the hospital.

Terre Haute, Ind., September 15, 1919   THEODORE DEBS

Sowing the Wind to Reap the Whirlwind
[editorial]   *January 17, 1920*

Oswald Garrison Villard became editor in 1918 and dedicated *The Nation* to the defense of civil liberties. Villard helped to found the American Civil Liberties Union in 1920.

The unprecedented outburst of terror and terrorism which at the moment is venting itself upon Socialists, Communists, "Reds," and agitators of all sorts in this country grows in volume and intensity from day to day. Every morning now brings news of more raids, more scores or hundreds of men and women arrested, more tons of papers seized, more offices and assembly rooms wrecked, more plans for deportation, more promises of purgings yet to come. Ellis Island is crowded to repletion with the victims of the dragnet; one transport loaded with undesirables is just arriving in Europe, and two or three others, it is rumored, are being prepared. Public meetings are broken up or prevented from being held; a Socialist Congressman-elect is ejected from Jersey City by a captain of police. Every radical thinker or reformer in the United States today who belongs to any organization which the Department of Justice has put under the ban, or who expresses sympathy with the men and women who have been pounced upon, puts his personal liberty in danger if his sympathies be known.

It is well, in times of general unreason and hysteria, to fix the mind on simple, fundamental things. If any of the persons, whether aliens or not, upon whom the Department of Justice has descended have violated the law, they should be indicted, tried, and punished for their offense. The Constitution of the United States defines the crime of treason and the conditions under which alone a charge of treason can be sustained; and the courts, in numerous decisions, have made clear the scope and application of the Constitutional provisions. Sedition and conspiracy are offenses known to the law, provable by rules which the law lays down, and punishable by penalties which the law defines with precision. The attempted or actual destruction of life or property, no matter what public motive the perpetrator may announce, belongs in the category of crimes or misdemeanors for which the laws of the United States and of every State provide sufficient and even drastic penalties. There is no "sacred right of revolution" to which the aggrieved citizen may appeal without at the same time imperilling his personal liberty or even his head; the only justification for revolution which courts or governments can recognize is the complete success of the revolt. No government can be expected to allow its foundations to be undermined by treason or sedition without defending itself, and it will defend itself by preventing attacks in advance as well as by meeting assaults in the open.

The case of the alien is as clear as that of the citizen. Barring treaty stipulations, the alien is a guest. The privileges which he enjoys are of the nature of hospitality, resting upon the comity of nations and an accustomed reciprocity of privilege and opportunity. And with the privileges go obligations—obligations to obey the law of the land, to respect the government and its institutions. If, as often happens, the alien is also enjoying the right of asylum, he is further under moral obligation not to plot against the government from whose jurisdiction he has fled; and he certainly violates grossly the spirit of hospitality if he plots attack upon the government which gives him shelter. What shall be done with him if he offends, or if for any reason his further presence is not desired, is for the Government to say. He certainly may be arrested and punished like any citizen if he breaks the law; he may as certainly be expelled or deported if the Government is willing to risk an international controversy.

If such commonplaces of American law covered the whole case of any or all of the thousands of men and women who are being swept into the clutches of the Department of Justice, about all that could be done would be to express regret that so many criminally-minded agitators had been living among us, and to hope that the Department would soon make an end of the unsavory job. Unfortunately for our good name as a nation, however, and for our standing with a Great Power with which we must some day make peace and with which we are already anxious to trade, they do not by any means cover the case. Far the larger number of the persons who have been arrested and confined, and over whose heads, if they be aliens, hangs the prospect of deportation to Russia or elsewhere, appear to have been seized merely upon suspicion. The particular charges against them and the evidence upon which the charges are based have not, so far as we have observed, been made public save in vague or sweeping terms quite insufficient as bases for an opinion. Membership in the Socialist or Communist parties is not a crime even for an alien, nor is a member of a political party answerable at law for the acts of the party, or of any member of it except himself. Few of the persons arrested appear to have been given a preliminary hearing in court, or allowed to furnish reasonable bail, or assured of an opportunity to meet their accusers and offer a defense, although hitherto aliens have always been regarded as entitled to these privileges along with citizens. It would even appear that in numerous cases the persons arrested have been denied the privilege of communicating with their friends or their families. The Government, on the other hand, has not hesitated to issue drum and trumpet statements which, whatever their purpose, have unquestionably had the effect of inflaming the public mind against aliens in general and Russians aliens in particular.

What must happen if this sort of thing goes on, every sober-minded citizen knows. Wholesale arrests and deportations such as we are now witnessing will not breed respect for government or crush out socialism or communism; they will only multiply a hundredfold the number of radicals, and increase many times the volume of discontent. The belief, startlingly confirmed only the other day by no less respectable a body than the Carnegie Foundation, that there is in this country one law for the rich and powerful and another for the poor and weak, will be strengthened; as will the conviction that free speech, free debate, and free publication of opinion, whether for the citizen or the alien, are rights to be enjoyed by such only as say what the Department of Justice and powerful business interests approve. If the rights which the Constitution guarantees to every citizen, and which by general consent have been conceded as privileges to the alien, are to be jeopardized wholesale the country over because some alien agitators have abused them, then assuredly will new and revolutionary doctrines grow apace. We shall not safeguard liberty by repressing it; we shall not raise American prestige abroad by sending overseas the disillusioned and the unassimilated. The only way to end dangerous discontent in the United States is to remove its causes. Unless that is done, those who today are sowing the wind will before long reap the whirlwind.

HERBERT J. SELIGMANN

The Conquest of Haiti   *July 10, 1920*

Between 1918 and 1932 *The Nation* carried more than fifty articles and editorials on conditions in Haiti. Evidence of torture and massacres uncovered by *The Nation*'s 1920 inquiry into the American occupation of Haiti led to a congressional investigation and helped bring the island independence in 1934.

To Belgium's Congo, to Germany's Belgium, to England's India and Egypt, the United States has added a perfect miniature in Haiti. Five years of violence in that Negro republic of the Caribbean, without sanction of international law or any law other than force, is now succeeded by an era in which the military authorities are attempting to hush up what has been done. The history of the American invasion of Haiti is only additional evidence that the United States is among those Powers in whose international dealings democracy and freedom are mere words, and human lives negligible in face of racial snobbery, political chicane, and money. The five years of American occupation, from 1915 to 1920, have served as a commentary upon the white civilization which still burns black men and women at the stake. For Haitian men, women, and children, to a number estimated at 3,000, innocent for the most part of any offense, have been shot down by American machine gun and rifle bullets; black men and women have been put to torture to make them give information; theft, arson, and murder have been committed almost with impunity upon the persons and property of Haitians by white men wearing the uniform of the United States. Black men have been driven to retreat to the hills from actual slavery imposed upon them by white Americans, and to resist the armed invader with fantastic arsenals of ancient horse pistols, Spanish cutlasses, Napoleonic sabres, French carbines, and even flintlocks. In this five years' massacre of Haitians less than twenty Americans have been killed or wounded in action.

Of all this Americans at home have been kept in the profoundest ignorance. The correspondent of the Associated Press in Cape Haitien informed me in April, 1920, that he had found it impossible in the preceding three years, owing to military censorship, to send a single cable dispatch concerning military operations in Haiti, to the United States. Newspapers have been suppressed in Port au Prince and their editors placed in jail on purely political grounds. Even United States citizens in Haiti told me of their fear that if they too frankly criticised "the Occupation," existence in Haiti would be made unpleasant for them. During my stay of something over a month in Haiti several engagements occurred between Haitian revolutionists and United States Marines. Early in April, Lieutenant Muth, of the Haitian gendarmery, was killed, his body mutilated, and a marine wounded. In that engagement, as in others which occurred within a few weeks of it, Haitian revolutionists or *cacos* suffered casualties of from five to twenty killed and wounded. No report of these clashes and casualties, so far as I know, has been published in any newspaper of the United States. The United States Government and the American military occupation which has placed Haiti under martial law do not want the people of the United States to know what has happened in Haiti.

For this desire for secrecy there are the best of reasons. Americans have conceived the application of the Monroe Doctrine to be protection extended by the United States to weaker States in the western hemisphere, against foreign aggression. Under cover of that doctrine the United States has practiced the very aggressions and tyrannies it was pretending to fight to safeguard weaker states against. In 1915, during a riot in the capital of Haiti, in which President Vilbrun Guillaume Sam was killed, the mob removed a man from the sanctuary he had claimed in the French legation. It is said the French threatened to intervene, also that the German Government had, before the European war, demanded control of Haitian affairs. In justifying its invasion of Haiti in 1915, the United States makes use of the pretext with which the Imperial German Government justified its invasion of Belgium in 1914. The invasion was one of defense against any Power which, taking control of Haiti, a weaker state, might use its territory as a base for naval action against the Panama Canal or the United States.

Instead of maintaining a force of marines at Port au Prince sufficient to safeguard foreign legations and consulates against violence, the United States proceeded to assume control of the island. The American hold was fortified by a convention empowering the United States to administer Haitian customs and finance for twenty years, or as much longer as the United States sees fit; and by a revised constitution of Haiti removing the prohibition against alien ownership of land, thus enabling Americans to purchase the most fertile areas in the country. Thenceforward Haiti has been regarded and has been treated as conquered territory. Military camps have been built throughout the island. The property of natives has been taken for military use. Haitians carrying a gun were for a time shot at sight. Many Haitians not carrying guns were also shot at sight. Machine guns have been turned into crowds of unarmed natives, and United States marines have, by accounts which several of them gave me in casual conversation, not troubled to investigate how many were killed or wounded. In some cases Haitians peaceably inclined have been afraid to come to American camps to give up their weapons for fear they would be shot for carrying them.

The Haitians in whose service United States marines are presumably restoring peace and order in Haiti are nicknamed "Gooks" and have been treated with every variety of contempt, insult, and brutality. I have heard officers wearing the United States uniform in the interior of Haiti talk of "bumping off" (i. e., killing) "Gooks" as if it were a variety of sport like duck hunting. I heard one marine boast of having stolen money from a peaceable Haitian family in the hills whom he was presumably on patrol to protect against "bandits." I have heard officers and men in the United States Marine Corps say they thought the island should be "cleaned out"; that all the natives should be shot; that shooting was too good for them; that they intended taking no prisoners; that many of those who had been taken prisoners had been "allowed to escape," that is, shot on the pretext that they had attempted flight. I have seen prisoners' faces and heads disfigured by beatings administered to them and have heard officers discussing those beatings; also a form of torture—"sept"—in which the victim's leg is compressed between two rifles and the pressure against the shin increased until agony forced him to speak. I know that men and women have been hung by the neck until strangulation impelled them to give information. I have in my possession a copy of a "bon habitant" (good citizen) pass which all Haitians in the interior have been required to carry and present to any marine who might ask to inspect it. Failure to carry the pass formerly involved being shot or arrested. Arrest for trivial offenses has involved detention in Cape Haitien and Port au Prince for as long as six months. In justice to the officers and men of the Marine Corps, it should be said that many of them detest what they have had to do in Haiti. One officer remarked to me that if he had to draw a cartoon of the occupation of Haiti he would represent a black man held down by a white soldier, while another white man went through the black man's pockets. Other officers and men have criticised the entire Haitian adventure as a travesty upon humanity and civilization and as a lasting disgrace to the United States Marine Corps. But the prevailing attitude of mind among the men sent to assist Haiti has been such determined contempt for men of dark skins that decency has been almost out of the question. The American disease of color prejudice has raged virulently.

The occupation points with pride to military roads. These roads were in large part built by Haitian slaves—I intend the word literally—under American taskmasters. An old Haitian law of corvée, or enforced road labor, rarely if ever invoked, authorizing three days' work in each year on roads about the citizen's domicile, was made the excuse for kidnapping thousands of Haitians from their homes—when they had homes—forcing them to live for months in camps, insufficiently fed, guarded by United States marines, rifle in hand. When Haitians attempted to escape this dastardly compulsion, they were shot. I heard ugly whispers in Haiti of the sudden accumulation of funds by American officers of the Haitian gendarmery who had the responsibility of providing food for these slave camps. Charlemagne Peralte, an important political leader under the Zamor Government, arrested for political activity, was forced to labor in prison garb on the streets of Cape Haitien, where he was well known. He escaped in September, 1918, flaming with hatred and became known throughout Haiti as Charlemagne, one of the most resourceful of revolutionary leaders in the Hinche district until he was killed in the autumn of 1919. It is no coincidence that his power was greatest and the revolt severest in the regions where the corvée slavery had been most in use.

Colonel John Russell, at present brigade commander in Haiti, who is struggling with an impossibly difficult situation, largely created by his predecessors, formally abolished the corvée late in 1919. That was not undoing the damage which had been done. Colonel Russell could not, even by issuing the most stringent orders against indiscriminate murder of Haitians by marines, wipe out what had occurred under a former commanding officer who had been sent to Haiti although it was in his record that he had been court-martialled for brutality to natives in the Philippines.

Another creation of the Americans in Haiti, although it is now improved in personnel and leadership, fanned the flames of hatred and violence which swept the island. I refer to the Gendarmerie d'Haiti. This is a military force of black men, officered with one or two exceptions by corporals and sergeants of the Marine Corps promoted to lieutenancies and captaincies over Haitians. Many of the white men were ignorant and brutal. Some of the Haitians enlisted in the gendarmerie were notorious bad men. Several of them have been shot for murder and extortion among their own people.

The armed peace which has resulted from the conquest of Haiti by the United States has opened a new field for American investors. Already the Banque Nationale d'Haiti, the bank of issue of all Haitian paper currency, is owned by an American bank. The National Railways of Haiti are owned by Americans. Sugar mills and lighting plants are in American control. Groups of Americans are purchasing or are endeavoring to purchase the most fertile land in the country. The representative of one company told me they owned 58,000 acres. In this scheme of American "protection" of Haitian welfare, the Haitian's place is illuminated by a remark which I heard one American entrepreneur make. He advocated that Chinese coolies be imported to supplant uninstructed Haitian labor.

After an indefensible invasion of a helpless country, after the professions of solicitude and good-will which accompanied the crime, what has the United

States to offer in extenuation? Military roads, which the Haitian people do not particularly want, a civil hospital in Port au Prince, and the Haitian Gendarmerie. The present Government of Haiti which dangles from wires pulled by American fingers, would not endure for twenty-four hours if United States armed forces were withdrawn; and the president, Sudre d'Artiguenave, would face death or exile. No beginning has been made in combatting with teachers the appalling illiteracy of the Haitian people. No attempt has been made to send civilian doctors or even military doctors to minister to the needs of diseased Haitians in the interior. These sins of commission and of omission are attributable less to the men confronted with the overwork and the difficulties, and often with the inferior food which their Government sends them, in Haiti, than to an Administration, and especially a State Department ready to countenance armed invasions without plan and to undertake, by a nation which has signally failed in administering its own color problem, the government of a black republic.

The jumble of jurisdictions imposed upon Americans in Haiti by the irresponsible gentlemen in Washington would paralyze even a genuine attempt at regeneration of Haitian government. The customs receipts and the disbursements of Haiti are administered by two Americans independent of the military command. Of the customs administration, suffice it to say that not one business man to whom I talked, and there were prominent Americans as well as Haitians among my informants, had a word to say in its favor. There is no appeal from the scrupulously inept customs rulings except to Washington. The fiction of a Haitian republic is maintained, although the American military command can suppress newspapers and virtually controls Haitian politics and elections. The Haitian Government, such as it is, either yields perforce to American pressure or finds itself in feeble and ineffectual opposition. The gendarmerie, theoretically under the Haitian Government's command, is officered by American marines, paid by both Haiti and the United States.

This militarist, imperialist burlesque on the professions with which the United States entered the war in behalf of weaker states leaves the Haitians little to do but to wonder what the United States intends. If they had power, they would drive the armed invader into the sea. They have not the power. They are disarmed and cynical, those who can think. If Haitian government was not conspicuously successful, lives of Americans and other foreigners were safe before the invasion. For the rest, in the absence of any plans for Haiti's regeneration except through "development" of the country by exploiters, the Haitian may derive what spiritual nourishment he can from the Wilsonian phrases with which United States thuggery disguises its deeds.

GILBERT SELDES

Ulysses
[book review]

> Literary and film critic Gilbert Seldes, author of an influential
> study of popular culture, *The Seven Lively Arts* (1924),
> reviewed James Joyce's *Ulysses* in 1922. The novel was banned
> in the United States for indecency until 1933.

Ulysses. **By James Joyce. Paris: Shakespeare and Company. 150 francs.**

"Welcome, O life! I go to encounter for the millionth time the reality of experience and to forge in the smithy of my soul the uncreated conscience of my
race. . . . Old father, old artificer, stand me now and ever in good stead." With
this invocation ended James Joyce's first novel, "A Portrait of the Artist as a
Young Man." It has stood for eight years as the pledge of Joyce's further achievement; today he has brought forth "Ulysses," a monstrous and magnificent travesty, which makes him possibly the most interesting and the most formidable
writer of our time.

James Joyce is forty years old and these two novels represent his major work;
there are in addition "Chamber Music," a book of exquisite lyrics; "Exiles," a
play; and "Dubliners," a collection of eighteen superb short stories. As some of
these antedate the "Portrait" it is fair to say that Joyce has devoted eighteen years
of his life to composing the two novels. Except that he is Irish, was educated at
a Jesuit school, studied medicine, scholastic philosophy, and mathematics on the
Continent, where he has lived for many years, nothing else in his biography need
be mentioned. Among the very great writers of novels only two can be named
with him for the long devotion to their work and for the triumphant conclusion—
Flaubert and Henry James. It is the novel as they created it which Joyce has
brought to its culmination; he has, it seems likely, indicated the turn the novel
will take into a new form. "Ulysses" is at the same time the culmination of many
other things: of an epoch in the life of Stephen Dedalus, the protagonist of the
"Portrait"; of an epoch in the artistic life of Joyce himself; and, if I am not mistaken, of a period in the intellectual life of our generation.

"A Portrait of the Artist" is the story of the interior life of Stephen Dedalus,
from his earliest memories to the time of his leaving home with the invocation
quoted above. It is easy to distinguish it from contemporary autobiographical
novels, for they resemble it only in what they have borrowed from it. It is a work
of the creative imagination more than of the memory; it is marked by a dignity
and a lyric beauty almost without equal in prose fiction; the concern is the soul

of a young man destined by circumstances to be a priest and by his nature to be a poet. He struggles against the forces which urge him to repair the family fortunes, to be loyal to the faith, to fight for Ireland. "He wanted to meet in the real world the unsubstantial image which his soul so constantly beheld." Against the sense of sin excited at the school was his ecstasy: "He closed his eyes, surrendering himself to her, body and mind, conscious of nothing in the world but the dark pressure of her softly parting lips. They pressed upon his brain as upon his lips as though they were the vehicle of a vague speech; and between them he felt an unknown and timid pressure, darker than the swoon of sin, softer than sound or odor." And his joy: "A girl stood before him in midstream; alone and still, gazing out to sea. . . . Her long slender bare legs were delicate as a crane's and pure save where an emerald trail of seaweed had fashioned itself as a sign upon the flesh. Her thighs, fuller and soft-hued as ivory, were bared almost to the hips where the white fringes of her drawers were like feathering of white down. . . . Her bosom was soft as a bird's, soft and slight, slight and soft as the breast of some dark-plumaged dove. But her long fair hair was girlish; and girlish, and touched with the wonder of mortal beauty, her face." There was also his clear proud mind.

"Ulysses" is, among other things, a day in the life of this same Stephen Dedalus, an average day after his return to Dublin from Paris. As an average day it marks the defeat of the poet; he has encountered and been overcome by the reality of experience; the ecstasy and lyric beauty are no more; instead of it we have a gigantic travesty. That is, as I see it, the spiritual plot of "Ulysses." And as Stephen, in addition to being a created character, is both "the artist" generically and specifically James Joyce, "Ulysses" naturally takes on the proportions of a burlesque epic of this same defeat. It is not surprising that, built on the framework of the "Odyssey," it burlesques the structure of the original as a satyr-play burlesqued the tragic cycle to which it was appended; nor that a travesty of the whole of English prose should form part of the method of its presentation. Whether a masterpiece can be written in caricature has ceased to be an academic question.

The narrative of "Ulysses" is simple. The portions corresponding to the story of Telemachus tell of a few hours spent by Stephen Dedalus on the morning of June 16, 1904: he visits the Nestorian head of the school where he teaches, goes to the modern cave of the winds in a newspaper office, tests the "ineluctable modality of the visible." It is in the newspaper office that he first sees one Leopold Bloom, né Virag, an advertising solicitor whose early day has already been recounted. Him we see in all the small details of his morning, preparing his wife's breakfast, going to a funeral, trying to get a reading notice for an advertiser, gazing a bit wistfully at the intellectual life of Dublin, under the name of Flower carrying on amorous correspondence with young girls, to the first climax of his day when he gets into a quarrel in a public house and is stoned as he drives off because he reminded a Cyclopean citizen there that Christ was a Jew. From this he goes to his second climax, an erotic one caused by observing a young girl on the rocks near Sandymount—an episode which officially corresponds to that of Nausicaa, but more interestingly to the scene in the "Portrait" I have quoted. Bloom sees Stephen a second time at a lying-in hospital where he goes to inquire the issue of an accouchement. Much later that evening Stephen and Bloom encounter each other in a brothel in the nighttown of Dublin. Bloom protects Stephen from an assault by a drunken soldier and takes him to his home where they talk until nearly daybreak. After Stephen leaves, Bloom goes to bed, and the catamenial night thoughts of his wife, thoughts of her first lovers and of her adulteries, complete the book. Bloom being Ulysses, his wife is Penelope. The authoritative version makes her also Gea, the earth-mother.

This is what is technically known as a slender plot for a book which is the length of five ordinary novels. But the narrative is only the thread in the labyrinth. Around and about it is the real material of the psychological story, presented largely in the form of interior monologues—the unspoken thoughts of the three principal characters and at times of some of the others, separately or, in one case, simultaneously. In a few words, at most a few pages, the essential setting is objectively presented; thereafter we are actually in the consciousness of a specified or suggested individual, and the stream of consciousness, the rendered thoughts and feelings of that individual, are actually the subject matter of the book. There is no "telling about" things by an outsider, nor even the looking over the hero's shoulder which Henry James so beautifully managed; there is virtually complete identification. The links in the chain of association are tempered by the nature and circumstances of the individual; there is no mistaking the meditations of Stephen for those of Bloom, those of either for the dark flood of Marion's consciousness. I quote a specimen moment from this specimen day: "Reading two pages apiece of seven books every night, eh? I was young. You bowed to yourself in the mirror, stepping forward to applause earnestly, striking face. Hurray for the Goddamned idiot! Hray! No one saw: tell no one. Books you were going to write with letters for titles. Have you read his F? O yes, but I prefer Q. Yes, but W is wonderful. O yes, W. Remember your epiphanies on green oval leaves, deeply deep, copies to be sent if you died to all the great libraries of the world, including Alexandria? Someone was to read them there after a few thousand years, a mahamanvantara. Pico della Mirandola like. Ay, very like a whale. When one reads these strange pages of one long gone one feels that one is at one with one who once. . . . "

The swift destructive parody in the last sentence is a foretaste of what arrives later in the book. In the episode at the *Freeman's Journal* Joyce has sown headlines through the narrative, the headlines themselves being a history by implication of the vulgarization of the press. In the public house a variety of bombastic styles sets off the flatness of the actual conversation; on the beach the greater part of the episode is conveyed through a merciless parody of the sentimental serial story: "Strength of character had never been Reggy Wylie's strong point and he who would woo and win Gerty MacDowell must be a man among men" and so on. Here the parody creates itself not in the mind of Bloom, but in that of the object in his mind, and renders the young-girlish sentimentality of Gerty with exceptional immediacy and directness. The burlesque of English prose, historically given, against which great complaint has been made, is actually only some sixty pages long; the parodies themselves I find brilliant, but their function is more important than their merit. They create with rapidity and as rapidly destroy the whole series of noble aspirations, hopes, and illusions of which the centuries have left their record in prose. And they lead naturally, therefore, to the scene in the brothel where hell opens.

This is the scene which, by common consent, is called a masterpiece. The method is a variation from that of the preceding; the apparent form is that of a play with spoken dialogue and italicized stage directions. The characters at the beginning are the inhabitants of nighttown; they and the soldiers and Bloom and Stephen have this real existence. But the play is populated by the phantasms and nightmares of their brains. Bloom's dead parents appear and converse with him; later his inflamed imagination projects him successively in all the roles he has played or dreamed of playing, from seducer of serving wenches to Lord Mayor of Dublin; he is accused of his actual or potential perversions; the furies descend upon him; he is changed into a woman, into a pig. Stephen's mother, at whose death-bed he refused to pray and who literally haunts his conscious thought, appears to him. In the Witches' Sabbath brute creation and inanimate things give voice; the End of the World appears and dances on an invisible tight-rope; and the Walpurgisnacht ends in a hanging of totally unnamable horror. It is here that Bloom recognizes Stephen as his spiritual kin.

The galvanic fury in which this episode is played is, one feels certain, not equalled in literature; it is a transcription of drunken delirium, with all the elements of thought and imagination broken, spasmodic, tortured out of shape, twitching with electric energy. The soft catlike languor of the whores, the foulness of the soldiers, the whole revel of drink and lust, are only reliefs to the implacable terrors in the subconscious minds of Stephen and Bloom. At the end of it Bloom accepts Stephen as the man his own son, and so himself, might have been; Stephen, more vaguely, seems to see in Bloom the man he himself may become. The orgy dies out in a cabman's shelter, in dreary listlessness, and after a description of their affinities and differences, given in the form of an examination paper, the two men part. The poet defeated by his self-scorn and introspection, the sensualist, with his endless curiosity, defeated by weakness, disappear;

and in the thoughts of Mrs. Bloom something coarse and healthy and coarsely beautiful and healthily foul asserts itself. Like the Wife of Bath, she can thank God that she has had her world, as in her time.

Although her last words are an affirmation that her body is a flower, although she morally rejects her brutal lovers in favor of Stephen and ends with a memory of her first surrender to Bloom, there is no moral triumph here. For Mrs. Bloom there can be no defeat similar to that of the others, since there has been no struggle. Their impotence is contrasted with her wanton fornication; she occurs, a mockery of the faithful Penelope, to mark their frustration. In their several ways Bloom and Stephen have been seekers, one for experience and the other for the reality of experience; and finding it they have been crushed and made sterile by it.

If it is true, as Mr. Yeats has said, that the poet creates the mask of his opposite, we have in "Ulysses" the dual mask—Bloom and Stephen—of James Joyce, and in it we have, if I am not mistaken, the mask of a generation, the broken poet turning to sympathy with the outward-going scientific mind. (Bloom is completely rendered by Joyce, with infinite humor and kindness and irony, to give point to this turning.) Conscious despair turns to unconscious futility; in the end, to be sure, Stephen leaves the house of Bloom, to be homeless the last few hours of the night. And this homelessness, beside which is the homelessness of Joyce himself, strikes us as a joyful tragedy in Stephen's freedom and solitude and exaltation. The one thing one does not find in "Ulysses" is dismal pessimism; there is no "down" on humanity. Lust and superstition, Mr. Santayana has told us, are canceled by the high breathlessness of beauty; in this book love and hate seem equally forgotten in an enormous absorption in things, by an enormous relish and savoring of palpable actuality. I think that Nietzsche would have cared for the tragic gaiety of "Ulysses."

I have not the space to discuss the aesthetic questions which the book brings up nor to indicate what its effect upon the novel may be. I have called Joyce formidable because it is already clear that the innovations in method and the developments in structure which he has used with a skill approaching perfection are going to have an incalculable effect upon the writers of the future; he is formidable because his imitators will make use of his freedom without imposing upon themselves the duties and disciplines he has suffered; I cannot see how any novelist will be able (nor why he should altogether want) entirely to escape his influence. The book has literally hundreds of points of interest not even suggested here. One must take for granted the ordinary equipment of the novelist; one must assume also that there are faults, idiosyncrasies, difficulties. More important still are the interests associated with "the uncreated conscience of my race"—the Catholic and Irish. I have written this analysis of "Ulysses" as one not too familiar with either—as an indication that the book can have absolute validity and interest, in the sense that all which is local and private in the "Divine Comedy" does not detract from its interest and validity. But these and other points have been made in the brilliant reviews which "Ulysses" has already evoked. One cannot leave it without noting again that in the change of Stephen Dedalus from his affinity with the old artificer to his kinship with Ulysses-Bloom, Joyce has created an image of contemporary life; nor without testifying that this epic of defeat, in which there is not a scamped page nor a moment of weakness, in which whole chapters are monuments to the power and the glory of the written word, is in itself a victory of the creative intelligence over the chaos of uncreated things and a triumph of devotion, to my mind one of the most significant and beautiful of our time.

The Week
[Tut-ankh-amen's tomb]

The opening of Tut-ankh-amen's tomb after 3,400 years seems to have afforded the one touch of nature that makes the whole world kin. All classes are reading the news of the discoveries with an avidity which shows not only that we are not altogether war-shocked into insensibility, but that we still have imaginations to be stirred. No such public interest attended the news that three men talked by wireless from New York to London the other evening and were heard in a public hall with absolute distinctness—one actually *coughed* across the Atlantic. A generation that sees a new scientific invention every week, and in its own homes triumphs over space, may perhaps be pardoned for being a bit blasé over things which a generation ago would have made the whole world gasp with astonishment. But the far, far distant past still stirs us; the thought of a king's grave rediscovered untouched after three millenniums—that sinks in. Fashion-makers tell us we are to have our jewelry and our garments made in the manner of Tut-ankh-amen's age. The past, not the future, is to strengthen its hold upon us. Hard on Shaw's Methuselah comes the news that we are to have a cave-man film to show us whence we sprang and how our remotest ancestors lived thousands upon thousands of years before Tut-ankh-amen. Multitudes who are envying the Pharaoh his gilded lion-couches, Lebanon cedar canopy, and alabaster vases will instead echo Oliver Herford's view of the descent of man from the trees:

> I'm glad we sprang; had we held on
> We might for aught that I can say
> Be horrid chimpanzees today.

46

THESE UNITED STATES

From 1922 to 1925, *The Nation* asked some of America's pre-eminent writers to contribute to the series "These United States." *Nation* editor Ernest Gruening, who commissioned the forty-nine articles – one for each state – wrote that he "presented no specific formula except a general purpose to bring out, in whatever way the author desired, the state's individuality." In addition to the selections published below by Sinclair Lewis, Willa Cather and W.E.B. DuBois, the series included Theodore Dreiser on Indiana, Edmund Wilson on New Jersey, H.L. Mencken on Maryland and James Cain on West Virginia. Gruening hoped *The Nation* would do a similar series every fifty years.

SINCLAIR LEWIS

Minnesota: The Norse State   May 30, 1923

Best known for his novels *Main Street* (1920) and *Babbitt* (1922), Sinclair Lewis made the revolt against small town life and businessmen a popular preoccupation.

. . . No fable is more bracing, or more absurd, than that all the sons and grandsons of the pioneers, in Minnesota or in California, in Arizona or Nebraska, are racy and breezy, unmannerly but intoxicatingly free. The grandchildren of the men who in 1862 fought the Minnesota Indians, who dogtrotted a hundred miles over swamp-blurred trails to bear the alarm to the nearest troops – some of them are still clearing the land, but some of them are complaining of the un-English quality of the Orange Pekoe in dainty painty city tea-rooms which stand where three generations ago the Red River fur-carts rested; their chauffeurs await them in Pierce Arrow limousines (special bodies by Kimball, silver fittings from Tiffany); they present Schnitzler and St. John Ervine at their Little Theaters; between rehearsals they chatter of meeting James Joyce in Paris; and always in high-pitched Mayfair laughter they ridicule the Scandinavians and Finns who are trying to shoulder into their sacred, ancient Yankee caste. A good many of their names are German.

Naturally, beneath this Junker class there is a useful, sophisticated, and growing company of doctors, teachers, newspapermen, liberal lawyers, musicians who have given up Munich and Milan for the interest of developing orchestras in the new land. There is a scientific body of farmers. The agricultural school of the huge University of Minnesota is sound and creative. And still more naturally, between Labor and Aristocracy there is an army of the peppy, poker-playing, sales-hustling He-men who are our most characteristic Americans. But even the

He-men are not so obvious as they seem. What their future is, no man knows—
and no woman dares believe. It is conceivable that, instead of being a menace,
in their naive boosting and their fear of the unusual, they may pass only too soon;
it is possible that their standardized bathrooms and Overlands will change to an
equally standardized and formula-bound culture—yearning Culture, arty Art. We
have been hurled from tobacco-chewing to tea-drinking with gasping speed; we
may as quickly dash from boosting to a beautiful and languorous death. If it is
necessary to be Fabian in politics, to keep the reformers (left wing or rigid right)
from making us perfect too rapidly, it is yet more necessary to be a little doubtful
about the ardent souls who would sell Culture; and if the Tired Business Man is
unlovely and a little dull, at least he is real, and we shall build only on reality.

The nimbler among our pioneering grandfathers appropriated to their private
uses some thousands of square miles in northern Minnesota, and cut off—or
cheerfully lost by forest fire—certain billions of feet of such lumber as will never
be seen again. When the lumber was gone, the land seemed worthless. It was
good for nothing but agriculture, which is an unromantic occupation, incapable
of making millionaires in one generation. The owners had few of them acquired
more than a million, and now they could scarcely give their holdings away. Suddenly, on parts of this scraggly land, iron was discovered, iron in preposterous
quantities, to be mined in the open pit, as easily as hauling out gravel. Here is
the chief supply of the Gary and South Chicago mills. The owners of the land do
not mine the ore. They have gracefully leased it—though we are but Westerners,
we have our subsidiary of the United States Steel Company. The landowners
themselves have only to go abroad and sit in beauty like a flower, and every time
a steam shovel dips into the ore, a quarter drops into the owner's pocket.

This article is intended to be a secret but flagrant boost. It is meant to increase
civic pride and the value of Minnesota real estate. Yet the writer wonders if he
will completely satisfy his chambers of commerce. There is a chance that they
would prefer a statement of the value of our dairy products, the number of our
admirable new school-buildings, the number of motor tourists visiting our lakes,
and an account of Senator Nelson's encouraging progress from poverty to mag-
nificence. But a skilled press agent knows that this would not be a boost; it would
be an admission of commerce-ruled barrenness. The interesting thing in Minnesota is the swift evolution of a complex social system and, since in two generations we have changed from wilderness to country clubs, the question is what the
next two generations will produce. It defies certain answer; it demands a scrupu-
lous speculation free equally from the bland certitudes of chambers of commerce
and the sardonic impatience of professional radicals. To a realistic philosopher,
the existence of an aristocracy is not (since it does exist) a thing to be bewailed,
but to be examined as a fact.

There is one merit not of Minnesota alone but of all the Middle West which must be considered. The rulers of our new land may to the eye seem altogether like the rulers of the East—of New England, New York, Pennsylvania. Both groups are chiefly reverent toward banking, sound Republicanism, the playing of golf and bridge, and the possession of large motors. But whereas the Easterner is content with these symbols and smugly desires nothing else, the Westerner, however golfocentric he may be, is not altogether satisfied; and raucously though he may snortle at his wife's "fool suffrage ideas" and "all this highbrow junk the lecture-hounds spring on you," yet secretly, wistfully he desires a beauty that he does not understand. . . .

WILLA SIBERT CATHER

Nebraska: The End of the First Cycle

September 5, 1923

Willa Cather's novels and stories—*My Antonia* and *Death Comes for the Archbishop* among others—shared a single theme: the superiority of the moral values of the past over the material interests of the present. Cather contributed this piece on Nebraska to the series "These United States."

. . . When the first courageous settlers came straggling out through the waste with their oxen and covered wagons, they found open range all the way from Lincoln to Denver; a continuous, undulating plateau, covered with long, red, shaggy grass. The prairie was green only where it had been burned off in the spring by the new settlers or by the Indians, and toward autumn even the new grass became a coppery brown. This sod, which had never been broken by the plow, was so tough and strong with the knotted grass roots of many years, that the home-seekers were able to peel it off the earth like peat, cut it up into sticks, and make of it warm, comfortable, durable houses. Some of these sod houses lingered on until the open range was gone and the grass was gone, and the whole face of the country had been changed.

Even as late as 1885 the central part of the State, and everything to the westward, was, in the main, raw prairie. The cultivated fields and broken land seemed mere scratches in the brown, running steppe that never stopped until it broke against the foothills of the Rockies. The dugouts and sod farm-houses were three or four miles apart, and the only means of communication was the heavy farm wagon, drawn by heavy work horses. The early population of Nebraska was largely transatlantic. The county in which I grew up, in the south-central part of the State, was typical. On Sunday we could drive to a Norwegian church and listen to a sermon in that language, or to a Danish or a Swedish church. We could go to the French Catholic settlement in the next county and hear a sermon in French, or into the Bohemian township and hear one in Czech, or we could go to church with the German Lutherans. There were, of course, American congregations also.

There is a Prague in Nebraska as well as in Bohemia. Many of our Czech immigrants were people of a very superior type. The political emigration resulting from the revolutionary disturbances of 1848 was distinctly different from the emigration resulting from economic causes, and brought to the United States brilliant young men both from Germany and Bohemia. In Nebraska our Czech settlements were large and very prosperous. I have walked about the streets of Wilber, the county seat of Saline County, for a whole day without hearing a word of English spoken. In Wilber, in the old days, behind the big, friendly brick saloon — it was not a "saloon," properly speaking, but a beer garden, where the farmers ate their lunch when they came to town — there was a pleasant little theater where the boys and girls were trained to give the masterpieces of Czech drama in the Czech language. "Americanization" has doubtless done away with all this. Our lawmakers have a rooted conviction that a boy can be a better American if he speaks only one language than if he speaks two. I could name a dozen Bohemian towns in Nebraska where one used to be able to go into a bakery and buy better pastry than is to be had anywhere except in the best pastry shops of Prague or Vienna. The American lard pie never corrupted the Czech.

Cultivated, restless young men from Europe made incongruous figures among the hard-handed breakers of the soil. Frederick Amiel's nephew lived for many years and finally died among the Nebraska farmers. Amiel's letters to his kinsman were published in the *Atlantic Monthly* of March, 1921, under the title "Amiel in Nebraska." Camille Saint-Saëns's cousin lived just over the line, in Kansas. Knut Hamsun, the Norwegian writer who was awarded the Nobel Prize for 1920, was a "hired hand" on a Dakota farm to the north of us. Colonies of European people, Slavonic, Germanic, Scandinavian, Latin, spread across our bronze prairies like the daubs of color on a painter's palette. They brought with them something that this neutral new world needed even more than the immigrants needed land.

Unfortunately, their American neighbors were seldom open-minded enough to understand the Europeans, or to profit by their older traditions. Our settlers from New England, cautious and convinced of their own superiority, kept themselves insulated as much as possible from foreign influences. The incomers from the South — from Missouri, Kentucky, the two Virginias — were provincial and utterly without curiosity. They were kind neighbors — lent a hand to help a Swede when he was sick or in trouble. But I am quite sure that Knut Hamsun might have worked a year for any one of our Southern farmers, and his employer would never have discovered that there was anything unusual about the Norwegian. A New England settler might have noticed that his chore-boy had a kind of intelligence, but he would have distrusted and stonily disregarded it. If the daughter of a shift-less West Virginia mountaineer married the nephew of a professor at the University of Upsala, the native family felt disgraced by such an alliance.

Nevertheless, the thrift and intelligence of its preponderant European population have been potent factors in bringing about the present prosperity of the State. The census of 1910 showed that there were then 228,648 foreign-born and native-born Germans living in Nebraska; 103,503 Scandinavians; 50,680 Czechs. The total foreign population of the State was then 900,571, while the entire population was 1,192,214. That is, in round numbers, there were about nine hundred thousand foreign Americans in the State, to three hundred thousand native stock. With such a majority of foreign stock, nine to three, it would be absurd to say that the influence of the European does not cross the boundary of his own acres, and has had nothing to do with shaping the social ideals of the commonwealth.

When I stop at one of the graveyards in my own county, and see on the head-stones the names of fine old men I used to know: *"Eric Ericson, born Bergen, Norway . . . died Nebraska," "Anton Pucelik, born Prague, Bohemia . . . died Nebraska,"* I have always the hope that something went into the ground with those pioneers that will one day come out again. Something that will come out not only in sturdy traits of character, but in elasticity of mind, in an honest attitude toward the realities of life, in certain qualities of feeling and imagination. Some years ago a professor at the University of Nebraska happened to tell me about a boy in one of his Greek classes who had a very unusual taste for the classics — intuitions and perceptions in literature. This puzzled him, he said, as the boy's parents had no interest in such things. I knew what the professor did not: that, though this boy had an American name, his grandfather was a Norwegian, a musi-cian of high attainment, a fellow-student and life-long friend of Edvard Grieg. It is in that great cosmopolitan country known as the Middle West that we may hope to see the hard molds of American provincialism broken up; that we may hope to find young talent which will challenge the pale proprieties, the insincere, conventional optimism of our art and thought. . . .

Of course, there is the other side of the medal, stamped with the ugly crest of materialism, which has set its seal upon all of our most productive common-wealths. Too much prosperity, too many moving-picture shows, too much gaudy fiction have colored the taste and manners of so many of these Nebraskans of the future. There, as elsewhere, one finds the frenzy to be showy; farmer boys who wish to be spenders before they are earners, girls who try to look like the heroines of the cinema screen; a coming generation which tries to cheat its aesthetic sense by buying things instead of making anything. There is even danger that that fine institution, the University of Nebraska, may become a gigantic trade school. The men who control its destiny, the regents and the lawmakers, wish their sons and daughters to study machines, mercantile processes, "the principles of business"; everything that has to do with the game of getting on in the world—and nothing else. The classics, the humanities, are having their dark hour. They are in eclipse. Studies that develop taste and enrich personality are not encouraged. But the "Classics" have a way of revenging themselves. One may venture to hope that the children, or the grandchildren, of a generation that goes to a university to select only the most utilitarian subjects in the course of study—among them, salesmanship and dressmaking—will revolt against all the heaped-up, machine-made materialism about them. They will go back to the old sources of culture and wisdom—not as a duty, but with burning desire.

In Nebraska, as in so many other States, we must face the fact that the splendid story of the pioneers is finished, and that no new story worthy to take its place has yet begun. The generation that subdued the wild land and broke up the virgin prairie is passing, but it is still there, a group of rugged figures in the background which inspire respect, compel admiration. With these old men and women the attainment of material prosperity was a moral victory, because it was wrung from hard conditions, was the result of a struggle that tested character. They can look out over those broad stretches of fertility and say: "We made this, with our backs and hands." The sons, the generation now in middle life, were reared amid hardships, and it is perhaps natural that they should be very much interested in material comfort, in buying whatever is expensive and ugly. Their fathers came into a wilderness and had to make everything, had to be as ingenious as shipwrecked sailors. The generation now in the driver's seat hates to make anything, wants to live and die in an automobile, scudding past those acres where the old men used to follow the long corn-rows up and down. They want to buy everything readymade: clothes, food, education, music, pleasure. Will the third generation—the full-blooded, joyous one just coming over the hill—will it be fooled? Will it believe that to live easily is to live happily?

The wave of generous idealism, of noble seriousness, which swept over the State of Nebraska in 1917 and 1918, demonstrated how fluid and flexible is any living, growing, expanding society. If such "conversions" do not last, they at least show of what men and women are capable. Surely the materialism and showy extravagance of this hour are a passing phase! They will mean no more in half a century from now than will the "hard times" of twenty-five years ago—which are already forgotten. The population is as clean and full of vigor as the soil; there are no old grudges, no heritages of disease or hate. The belief that snug success and easy money are the real aims of human life has settled down over our prairies, but it has not yet hardened into molds and crusts. The people are warm, mercurial, impressionable, restless, over-fond of novelty and change. These are not the qualities which make the dull chapters of history.

H.L. MENCKEN

H.L. Mencken *December 5, 1923*

The most vociferous social critic of his generation, H.L. Mencken made it his business to expose bourgeois complacency. His columns in *The American Mercury*, the magazine he edited from 1924 to 1934, recorded the fatuousness and vulgarity of American life. Mencken joined *The Nation* as contributing editor in May 1921. This account was one in a series of articles by critics about themselves.

Ask a professional critic to write about himself and you simply ask him to do what he does every day in the practice of his art and mystery. There is, indeed, no criticism that is not a confidence, and there is no confidence that is not self-revelation. When I denounce a book with mocking and contumely, and fall upon the poor author in the brutal, Asiatic manner of a drunken longshoreman, a Ku Kluxer, or a midshipman at Annapolis, I am only saying, in the trade cant, that the fellow disgusts me – that his ideas and his manners are somehow obnoxious to me, as those of a Methodist, a golf-player, or a clog-dancer are obnoxious to me – in brief, that I hold myself to be a great deal better than he is, and am eager to say so. And when, on the other hand, I praise a book in high, astounding terms, and speak of the author as if his life and sufferings were of capital importance to the world, then I am merely saying that I detect something in him, of prejudice, tradition, habit of mind, that is much like something within myself, and that my own life and sufferings are of the utmost importance to me.

That is all there ever is in criticism, once it gets beyond cataloguing. No matter how artfully the critic may try to be impersonal and scientific he is bound to give himself away. In fact, his very effort to be impersonal and scientific is a form of giving himself away, as the writings of my eminent colleague, Prof. Dr. Erskine, well demonstrate. I have never had the honor of being presented to Erskine, but I know quite as well as his grandmother that he is essentially a shy man – that the winds of doctrine alarm him and he has no stomach for rough adventure. Hence his plea for decorum and tradition, i. e., for what has passed the stage of experiment and danger, i. e., for safe harbors and refuges. He can no more get himself out of his criticism than he can get himself out of his skin. Nor can, at the other pole, the critical Bolsheviki of Greenbaum Village—all of them as foreign and as loathsome to Erskine, I daresay, as so many Nietzsches or Beethovens. When these bright young men print profound aesthetic treatises upon the art of Fatty Arbuckle, Gertrude Stein, and the "Parisian Widows" burlesque troupe, they say, of course, nothing that is pertinent to aesthetics, but they do say something extremely amusing about their own tastes, and hence about themselves. More, they say something even more amusing about the seminaries where they were bred to the humanities.

With criticism thus so transparent, so unescapably revelatory, I often marvel that the gentlemen who concern themselves with my own books, often very indignantly, do not penetrate more competently to my essence. Even for a critic I am excessively garrulous and confidential; nevertheless, it is rare for me to encounter a criticism that hits me where I live and have my being. A great deal of ink is wasted trying to discover and denounce my motive in being a critic at all. I am, by one theory, a German spy told off to flay, terrorize, and stampede the Anglo-Saxon. By another I am a secret radical, while professing to admire Coolidge, Judge Gary, and Genghis Khan. By a third, I am a fanatical American chauvinist, bent upon defaming and ruining the motherland. All these notions are nonsense; only the first has even the slightest plausibility. The plain truth is—and how could it be plainer?—that I practice criticism for precisely the same reason that every other critic practices it: because I am a vain fellow, and have a great many ideas on all sorts of subjects, and like to put them into words and harass the human race with them. If I could confine this flow of ideas to one subject I'd be a professor and get some respect. If I could reduce it, say, to one idea a year, I'd be a novelist, a dramatist, or a newspaper editorial writer. But being unable to staunch the flux, and having, as I say, a vast and exigent vanity, I am a critic of books, and through books of *Homo sapiens,* and through *Homo sapiens* of God.

So much for the motive. What, now, of the substance? What is the fundamental faith beneath all the spurting and coruscating of ideas that I have just mentioned? What do I primarily and immovably believe in, as a Puritan believes in hell? I believe in liberty. And when I say liberty, I mean the thing in its widest imaginable sense—liberty up to the extreme limits of the feasible and tolerable. I am against forbidding anybody to do anything, or say anything, or think anything so long as it is at all possible to imagine a habitable world in which he would be free to do, say, and think it. The burden of proof, as I see it, is always upon the policeman, which is to say, upon the lawmaker, the theologian, the right-thinker. He must prove his case doubly, triply, quadruply, and then he must start all over and prove it again. The eye through which I view him is watery and jaundiced. I do not pretend to be "just" to him—any more than a Christian pretends to be just to the devil. He is the enemy of everything I admire and respect in this world—of everything that makes it various and amusing and charming. He impedes every honest search for the truth. He stands against every sort of good-will and common decency. His ideal is that of an animal trainer, an archbishop, a major general in the army. I am against him until the last galoot's ashore.

This simple and childlike faith in the freedom and dignity of man—here, perhaps, stated with undue rhetoric—should be obvious, I should think, to every critic above the mental backwardness of a Federal judge. Nevertheless, very few of them, anatomizing my books, have ever showed any sign of detecting it. But all the same even the dullest of them has, in his fashion, sensed it; it colors unconsciously all the diatribes about myself that I have ever read. It is responsible for the fact that in England and Germany (and, to the extent that I have ever been heard of at all, in France and Italy) I am regarded as a highly typical American— in truth, as almost the archetype of the American. And it is responsible equally for the fact that here at home I am often denounced as the worst American unhung. The paradox is only apparent. The explanation of it lies in this: that to most Europeans the United States is still regarded naively as the land of liberty *par excellence,* whereas to most Americans the thing itself has long ceased to have any significance, and to large numbers of them, indeed, it has of late taken on an extreme obnoxiousness. I know of no civilized country, indeed, in which liberty is less esteemed than it is in the United States today; certainly there is none in which more persistent efforts are made to limit it and put it down. I am thus, to Americans, a bad American, but to Europeans, still unaware of the practical effects of the Wilson idealism and the Roosevelt saloon-bouncer ethic, I seem to be an eloquent spokesman of the true American tradition. It is a joke, but the joke is not on me.

Liberty, of course, is not for slaves: I do not advocate inflicting it on men against their conscience. On the contrary, I am strongly in favor of letting them crawl and grovel all they please—before the Supreme Court of the United States, Gompers, J. P. Morgan, Henry Cabot Lodge, the Anti-Saloon League, or whatever other fraud or combination of frauds they choose to venerate. I am thus unable to make the grade as a Liberal, for Liberalism always involves freeing human beings against their will—often, indeed, to their obvious damage, as in the cases of the majority of Negroes and women. But all human beings are not congenital slaves, even in America. Here and there one finds a man or a woman with a great natural passion for liberty—and a hard job getting it. It is, to me at least, a vast pleasure to go to the rescue of such a victim of the herd, to give him some aid and comfort in his struggle against the forces that seek to regiment and throttle him. It is a double pleasure to succor him when the sort of liberty he strives for is apparently unintelligible and valueless—for example, liberty to address conventions of the I.W.W., to read the books of such bad authors as D. H. Lawrence and Petronius Arbiter, to work twelve hours a day, to rush the can, to carry red flags in parades, to patronize osteopaths and Christian Science healers, to belong to the best clubs. Such nonsensical varieties of liberty are especially sweet to me. I have wrecked my health and dissipated a fortune defending them – never, so far as I know, successfully. Why, then, go on? Ask yourself why a grasshopper goes on jumping.

But what has liberty to do with the art of literary criticism, my principal business in this vale? Nothing – or everything. It seems to me that it is perfectly possible to write profound and valuable literary criticism without entering upon the question of freedom at all, either directly or indirectly. Aesthetic judgments may be isolated from all other kinds of judgments, and yet remain interesting and important. But this isolation must be performed by other hands: to me it is as sheer a psychological impossibility as believing that God condemned forty-two little children to death for poking fun at Elisha's bald head. When I encounter a new idea, whether aesthetic, political, theological, or epistemological. I ask myself, instantly and automatically, what would happen to its proponent if he should state its exact antithesis. If nothing would happen to him, then I am willing and eager to listen to him. But if he would lose anything valuable by a *volte face* – if stating his idea is profitable to him, if the act secures his roof, butters his parsnips, gets him a tip – then I hear him with one ear only. He is not a free man. Ergo, he is not a man. For liberty, when one ascends to the levels where ideas swish by and men pursue Truth to grab her by the tail, is the first thing and the last thing. So long as it prevails the show is thrilling and stupendous; the moment it fails the show is a dull and dirty farce.

CHAIM WEIZMANN

Zionism—Alive and Triumphant   *March 12, 1924*

In 1924, Chaim Weizmann, the president of the World Zionist Organization, traveled to the United States to generate support for his cause. Just a few years earlier, Weizmann had been involved in securing from the British government the Balfour Declaration, in favor of a Jewish national home in Palestine – then still under British control. Weizmann, who helped garner U.S. support for the formation of the state of Israel, became that country's first president.

Of all the concepts which are associated with the Jewish problem and the outstanding effort which is being made toward its solution, perhaps none has become involved in obscurer controversy than "political Zionism." So keen and even acrimonious have the debates become that the doctrine which this phrase inadequately represents has been torn out of its setting of history and reality, like a sentence wrenched out of its context, and has become a sort of *Ding an sich*, a self-inclosed system of ideas, or, better still, an incantation, capable of effecting a wonderful transformation in the relationship of Palestine to the Jewish people.

Yet political Zionism can no more be dissociated from practical affairs than law from natural process. For us there is only Zionism—and "cultural Zionism," "practical Zionism," "political Zionism" are only convenient figures of speech, arbitrary approaches or methods of discussion. To talk of political Zionism as something which the Zionist can either accept or deny is to talk of granting permission to two and two to make four. Political Zionism is not something outside of the process of building up a homeland in Palestine which may be added to that process or withheld from it. It is inherent in every step. Every affirmative act in the creation of a Jewish center in Palestine is political.

Political Zionism, in brief, is the creation of circumstances favorable to Jewish settlement in Palestine. The circumstance most favorable to Jewish settlement in Palestine is the existence of a Jewish settlement in Palestine. The larger the Jewish settlement the greater the ease with which it can be increased, the less the external opposition to its increase; the smaller the Jewish settlement in Palestine the more difficult its increase, the more obstinate the opposition.

One does not create political Zionism by affirming it, any more than one destroys it by denying it. Men who have never heard the phrase, and others who have combated it, have been political Zionists. Those first pioneers of nearly half a century ago, who went out to Palestine and founded the first modern colonies, who laid the foundations of the still small but flourishing Jewish settlement, were actually the founders of political Zionism. They built up positions, they furnished proof of the practicality of the scheme, they gave the most convincing demonstration of the will behind the demand; their work, whatever they intended, reached beyond the immediate achievement and beyond the Jewish people. The world respects the settlements in Palestine more than all the protestations of the Jews.

Those who believe, or who affect to believe, that some sort of system can be devised whereby Palestine can be "given" to the Jewish people are talking of a Zionism which is not political but metaphysical. A country is not a thing done up in a parcel and delivered on demand. England can no more "give" Palestine to the Jews than it can give them history or a culture. All that England can do—and is making serious efforts to do—is to create conditions whereby the Jews cannot "take" Palestine but can grow into it again, by a natural and organic process.

England could not even give Palestine to the Jews if that country were entirely uninhabited. It could permit Jewish immigration "as of right and not on sufferance"—which is precisely what it is doing now. The rest is in the hands of the Jewish people. That Jewish immigration into Palestine should be recognized as being "of right and not on sufferance" is the triumph of political Zionism. The preamble to that part of the British Mandate over Palestine which says: "Whereas recognition has been given to the historical connection of the Jewish people with Palestine and to the grounds for reconstituting their National Home in that country," is the triumph of political Zionism. This recognition is not British alone, but is common to all the nations which combined to give the Mandate, and to America, which indorsed the essential part of the Mandate in a special resolution.

But the idea that England should "give" Palestine to the Jews is particularly crude and Utopian when it is linked up with the suggestion of expropriation or removal of the Arabs. Fortunately no such suggestion has ever come from a responsible Zionist leader. For apart from its inherent impracticality and immorality, the idea again betrays a complete dissociation from the realities of the situation. England would not commit such an act even if the Jewish people were to demand it. And the Jewish people would not demand it because it realizes that, in laying the foundations of its old-new home, it must not tolerate even a suspicion of faith in those vicious imperialist principles which have been the source of half its woes.

If there is any significance at all in the rebuilding of a Jewish homeland, it must be made evident first in the attitude of the Jewish people toward the nations in the midst of which that homeland is being built. Friendliness with the Arabs is not simply a matter of convenience or expedience; it is a cardinal doctrine; it is an essential part of the Jewish outlook, an aspect of the spiritual dream which the Jewish homeland is to embody. If we reject the vicious shifts and tricks of what is inaccurately called *Realpolitik* it is not only because of its essential stupidity and ineffectiveness, but because our entire history has been a living protest against it. To solve one problem by the creation of two others is a method which is not unapproved in the world of practical men. Perhaps it pays in the case of fly-by-night nations, though even most of these live long enough to witness the undoing of their practical wisdom. In the case of the Jews, who are, as it were, a permanent institution, there is a reputation to be cherished and maintained. Nor is Jewish-Arab cooperation a new concept. The ideal already has an illustrious history. It is not so long ago — as history, and particularly Jewish history, goes — that Jews and Arabs worked hand in hand from Granada to Bagdad in founding and spreading one of the most brilliant civilizations: when the rest of Europe was still steeped in the dark slumber of the Middle Ages, Spain, Mesopotamia, and Northern Africa were brightly illumined by a great Arab Jewish culture. That culture has never disappeared; it survived, transmuted and disguised, in the Renaissance to which it contributed generously; its unacknowledged issue today forms part of our Western civilization.

For I would make it clear that the primal appeal of the Jewish homeland in Palestine is spiritual. Zionism cannot solve immediately, it can only relieve to some extent, the Jewish world problem. If Palestine were empty today, if it could absorb fifty thousand immigrants a year (and by the way these two conditions are not supplementary: an empty Palestine could not absorb Jews more rapidly than Palestine as it is), it would still fail to solve the problem of eight million of Jews subject to the moods and caprices of unfriendly surrounding nations. But even at that the refugee problem in its relation to Palestine has another aspect. Our plea to the Western world to open its gates to the persecuted Jews loses much of its cogency if that part of the problem which is in our own hands remains unsolved. When we are sending as many refugees into Palestine as that country can absorb, we have a double claim on the sympathy of the world.

One must not, of course, talk of "sending Jews into Palestine" as though this were purely an arithmetical problem. Jews "sent to Palestine" cannot stay there unless they can be absorbed healthily into the economic life of the country. Preparation must be made for every Jew who wishes to enter Palestine. In the last three years we have sent over thirty thousand Jews into the country. Tens of thousands more await the opportunity to enter it. They cannot be admitted pell-mell and at random, lest the emigration from Palestine finally counterbalance the immigration into it. And by preparation we mean of course the growth and development of the country's resources and the integration of newcomers with its economic life. Money is needed for this task; but we need equally a sense of organic construction. Restriction of immigration into Palestine has nothing to do with political conditions. Given the means we could double and treble the immigration, though we must understand that even unlimited means would not enable us to ship a hundred thousand Jews a year to Palestine. It takes time for a small country like Palestine to digest and assimilate fifteen or twenty thousand newcomers.

It would be false to see the ultimate possibilities of the Zionist experiment in terms of Palestine alone. The peculiar position of Palestine fits it to play a role of extraordinary importance in the Near East—a role which it has already entered on. The development of Palestine is the key to the development of a vast territory once the most fruitful in the world, today cut off from the centers of civilization and given over to neglect and decay. Unfortunately hunger is impatient, and the immense resources of the Mesopotamian hinterland are neglected because they cannot be developed in a day. Yet the first steps toward this development have already been taken. The linking up of Bagdad with Haifa is the tangible evidence. The carrying of mail in seven hours between these two points—separated hitherto by three and a half weeks of laborious traveling; the immediate prospects of a railway track which will carry freight back and forth in three days, these are both symbols and achievements. Their creation was made possible only with the awakening of Palestine by Jewish enterprise, and Jewish enterprise is perhaps destined to play an exceedingly important part in the economic reconstruction of the Near East.

Yet I must repeat that if the question of the Jewish refugee gives a new spur to the Zionist effort, it is not and never was the primal motive. There was something more affirmative behind the first stirrings of the movement—and that something became more coherent and self-conscious as the movement gathered momentum and power. Zionism envisages more than the negative relief of suffering, more than philanthropic effort, and Palestine to the Zionist was never merely a last desperate opportunity to escape the persecution of the world. Indeed, whatever fortuitous cooperation there has been between anti-Semitism and Zionism, it would be quite wrong to make the two interdependent. The Jew does not depend on anti-Semitism for his existence, and Zionism is the strongest expression of the Jewish will to live.

The hope and lure of Palestine, its special appeal to the Zionist, lay in the authentic Jewish life and culture which could again develop there, after an interruption of twenty centuries. The concept of Jewish culture—and even Jewish culture in Palestine—has too often been of a "literary" nature. It is true that Zionist effort has succeeded in reviving the Hebrew language so that throughout an entire public-school and high-school system Hebrew is the language of tuition, so that Jewish children again use Hebrew as their natural medium. It is equally true that within a few months the Hebrew University is to be opened. It is equally true that concomitant with the Zionist renaissance there has come an extraordinary resurgence of Hebrew poetry—certainly the finest we have produced since the time of the Spanish singers—and perhaps the finest since the days of the Hebrew prophets. But culture must not be dissociated from life, and when we talk of a renewed Jewish culture, an authentic Jewish culture, in Palestine, we are not talking only of schools and literary people.

A civilization is whole and complete. The Jewish village in the valley of Jizreel, the Jewish cooperative colony under the shadow of Mount Hermon, the Jewish merchants of Tel-Aviv and Jerusalem, the young men and women who are building roads and draining marshes—these are, after all, the material of the new Jewish culture. These people, working in a world of their own, from clean and unspoiled beginnings, are apt to produce that now forgotten value—the purely Jewish culture. In all other countries, in all other colonies, the Jew comes to add and to adapt. He is nowhere free to be himself; he must be that which an established civilization will permit him to be. With the best will in the world a nation welcoming the Jew cannot remove the tacit pressure and demand of its civilization and culture on the individuality of the Jew. But in Palestine the Jew can, for the first time since his dispersion, enter again into direct relation with his foundations. No one there stands between him and the first principles of life. He is back on the soil in every sense of the word: it would perhaps be better to say that he is back on the earth.

It is idle to speculate as to the forms which Jewish life in Palestine will take in two or three generations from now. To say that the Jew will give this or that to the world, as the result of a restoration of Palestinian Jewish life, is to indulge in vicarious generosity. We must say frankly that we cannot foresee the end of the experiment. We can only say that its beginnings are extraordinarily auspicious, that all circumstances combine to convince us of the value of the effort, that the vitality and richness of the Jewish people precludes the fear that the final product will be either commonplace or meaningless. Given a chance to be himself, the Jew will certainly not serve the world less than when forced to be everybody but himself. And that restoration to himself implies, too, the rehabilitation of his reputation in his own eyes and in the eyes of the world.

A Net Spread in Vain
[correspondence]

August 24, 1924

MY DEAR MR. SHAW:

I understand a number of friends are writing to you and urging you to come to the United States. May I say how gratified we of *The Nation* would be should you come to us?

Yours very sincerely,
OSWALD GARRISON VILLARD, *Editor*

MR. GEORGE BERNARD SHAW,
10 Adelphi Terrace,
W. C. 2, London, England.

DEAR MR. VILLARD:

This conspiracy has been going on for years; but in vain is the net spread in sight of the bird. I have no intention either of going to prison with Debs or taking my wife to Texas, where the Ku Klux Klan snatches white women out of hotel verandas and tars and feathers them. If I were dependent on martyrdom for a reputation, which happily I am not, I could go to Ireland. It is a less dangerous place; but then the voyage is shorter and much cheaper.

You are right in your impression that a number of persons are urging me to come to the United States. But why on earth do you call them my friends?

Peebles (traveling), 4-8-21

G. BERNARD SHAW

W.E. BURGHARDT Du BOIS

Georgia: Invisible Empire State

January 21, 1925

An historian, educator, and author of *The Souls of Black Folk* and other works, W.E.B. DuBois led an intellectual revolt against the accommodationist principles of Booker T. Washington, which crystallized in the founding of the Niagara Movement in 1905. When this group merged with the newly founded National Association for the Advancement of Colored People (NAACP) in 1909, DuBois became editor of the association's journal, *Crisis*; he remained editor until 1932. W.E.B. DuBois contributed this piece on Georgia to the series "These United States."

. . . Georgia is beautiful. Yet on its beauty rests something disturbing and strange. Physically this is a certain emptiness and monotony, a slumberous, vague dilapidation, a repetition, an unrestraint. Point by point one could pick a poignant beauty—one golden river, one rolling hill, one forest of oaks and pines, one Bull Street. But there is curious and meaningless repetition until the beauty palls or fails of understanding. And on this physical strangeness, unsatisfaction, drops a spiritual gloom. There lies a certain brooding on the land—there is something furtive, uncanny, at times almost a horror. Some folk it so grips that they never see the beauty—the hills to them are haunts of grim and terrible men; the world goes armed with loaded pistols on the hip; concealed, but ready—always ready. There is a certain secrecy about this world. Nobody seems wholly frank—neither white nor black; neither child, woman, nor man. Strangers ask each other pointed searching questions: "What is your name?" "Where are you going?" "What might be your business?" And they eye you speculatively. Once satisfied, the response is disconcertingly quick. They strip their souls naked before you; there is sudden friendship and lavish hospitality. And yet—yet behind all are the grim bars and barriers; subjects that must not be touched, opinions that must not be questioned. Side by side with that warm human quality called "Southern" stands the grim fact that right here and beside you, laughing easily with you and shaking your hand cordially, are men who hunt men: who hunt and kill in packs, at odds of a hundred to one under cover of night. They have lynched five hundred Negroes in forty years; they have killed unnumbered white men. There must be living and breathing in Georgia today at least ten thousand men who have taken human life, and ten times that number who have connived at it.

Of religion as it exists in present-day Georgia one may well despair. Georgia is already religious to overflowing. Everyone belongs—must belong—to some church, and really to "belong," one should be Presbyterian or Baptist or Methodist. Episcopalians are unusual, Unitarians gravely suspect, Catholics and Jews feared and hated. But all these are within the range of understanding and misunderstanding. The hottest of hell-fire is reserved for any so unspeakable as to hold themselves freethinkers, agnostics, or atheists. Georgia's religion is orthodox, "fundamental." It continues to wash its "miserable sinners" in "the blood of the Lamb," but the blood of the mob's victim lies silent at its very doors. But outside of the church religion has its uses! When the Ku Klux Klan sent out its official instructions to delegates to the State convention, the Grand Dragon said: "It is the earnest desire of Mr. McAdoo to elect his friend Mr. John S. Cohen as national committeeman. Mr. Cohen is a high-class Christian gentleman, a member of the North Presbyterian Church of Atlanta." No, there is little hope in Georgia religion despite a light here and there.

Nevertheless, there are brave men in Georgia, men and women whose souls are hurt even to death by this merciless and ruthless exploitation of race hatred. But what can they do? It is fairly easy to be a reformer in New York or Boston or Chicago. One can fight there for convictions, and while it costs to oppose power, yet it can be done. It even gains some applause and worth-while friends. But in Atlanta? The students of white Emory College recently invited a student of black Morehouse College to lead a Y. M. C. A. meeting. It was a little thing — almost insignificant. But in Georgia it was almost epoch-making. Ten years ago it would have meant riot. Today it called for rare courage. When the Southern Baptists met in Atlanta recently they did not segregate Negro visitors. Such a thing has seldom if ever happened before in Georgia. It is precisely the comparative insignificance of these little things that shows the huge horror of the bitter fight between Georgia and civilization.

Some little things a liberal public opinion in Georgia may start to do, although the politico-economic alliance stands like a rock wall in the path of real reform. A determined group called "inter-racial" asks for change. Most of them would mean by this the stopping of lynching and mobbing, decent wages, abolition of personal insult based on color. Most of them would not think of demanding the ballot for blacks or the abolition of Jim Crow cars or civil rights in parks, libraries, and theaters or the right of a man to invite his black friend to dinner. Some there are who in their souls would dare all this, but they may not whisper it aloud — it would spoil everything; it would end their crusade. Few of these reformers yet fully envisage the economic nexus, the real enemy encased in enormous profit. They think reform will come by right thinking, by religion, by higher culture, and do not realize that none of these will work its end effectively as long as it pays to exalt and maintain race prejudice.

Of the spiritual dilemmas that face men today I know of none more baffling than that which faces the conscientious, educated, forward-looking white man of Georgia. On the one hand is natural loyalty to what his fathers believed, to what his friends never question; then his own difficulty in knowing or understanding the black world and his inbred distrust of its ability and real wish; there is his natural faith in his own ability and the ability of his race; there is the subtle and continuous propaganda—gossip, newspapers, books, sermons, and "science"; there is his eager desire to see his section take a proud place in the civilized world. There is his job, his one party, his white primary—his social status so easily lost if he is once dubbed a "nigger lover." Facing all this is lynching, mob murder, ignorance, silly self-praise of people pitifully degenerate in so many cases, exploitation of the poor and weak, and insult, insult, insult heaped on the blacks.

Open revolt comes now and then. Once Tom Watson tried to unite labor. He organized the Populist Party in Georgia and invited the blacks to help. It was a critical situation that developed in the early nineties, when it was increasingly difficult to keep the Negro disfranchised illegally and not yet possible to disfranchise him legally. In the first campaign it was easy to beat the Populists by the fraud of "counting them out." Immediately thereafter the captains of industry mobilized. By newspaper, by word of mouth, by lodge communications it was conveyed to the white workers that not only would Negroes benefit from any attempt to better the present industrial situation, but they would gradually displace the white workers by underbidding them; that any benefits for white workers must come secretly and in such a way that Negroes could not share in the benefits. Thus immediately the emphasis was put on race discrimination. And this race difference grew and expanded until in most cases the whole knowledge and thought of the workers and voters went to keeping Negroes down, rather than to raising themselves.

Internal dissension in the labor ranks followed. The Negroes were then blamed for not voting solidly with white labor, for selling out to capital, for underbidding labor. The whole movement swung into intense Negro hatred; and the net result was that the white labor vote turned eventually into a movement finally and completely to disfranchise Negro labor. The mob shot down Watson's Negro leaders in their tracks and the only way in which he could survive politically was to out-Herod Herod in his diatribes against Negroes and in coining new variants of appeals to prejudice by attacks on Catholics and Jews. To his death he kept a dangerous political power and even reached the United States Senate, but with his labor party cut in two and forced into additional disfranchisement by the "white primary" he could not menace the "machine."

A second way toward emancipation may lie through dissension in the high seats of power. When in Cleveland's day Hoke Smith opposed "free silver" he was read out of Georgia Democracy and his path to the United States Senate was blocked. Immediately he espoused the cause of "labor" and made a frontal attack on capital and the great corporations of Georgia. The white labor vote flocked to him, and instead of the "white primary" being the ordinary parade a bitter internal political fight developed. Smith and his opponents quickly came to terms. In the midst of the campaign Smith dextrously switched his attack on monopoly to an attack on Negroes as the cause of monopoly, and since this old game had often been played he played it harder and more fiercely. He went so far that the State was aroused as never before. Race bitterness seethed, and white labor took the bit into its teeth. It demanded economic disfranchisement of the Negro to follow political. The Negro must be kept from buying land, his education must be curtailed, his occupations limited.

This was overshooting the mark and destroying the whole bi-racial labor situation upon which the Secret Empire of Georgia is based. Quick action was needed. The minds of the mob must be turned again and turned from political and economic thought to pure race hatred. Immediately the sex motif arose to leadership. All subconsciously, sex hovers about race in Georgia. Every Negro question at times becomes a matter of sex. Voting? They want social equality. Schools? They are after our daughters. Land? They'll rape our wives. Continually the secrecy, the veiled suggestion, the open warning pivot on sex; gossip rages and horrible stories are spread. So it was at the culmination of the Hoke Smith campaign. All restraint was suddenly swept away and submerged in wild stories of rape and murder. Atlanta papers rushed out extra editions each with a new horror afterward proved wholly fictitious or crassly exaggerated. On a Saturday night the white Atlanta laborers arose and murdered every Negro they could catch in the streets. For three days war and rapine raged—then the streets of the Empire City sank into awful silence. Hoke Smith became Governor and Senator, and the industrial and political systems were intact.

All these occasions of revolt against the present political and industrial situation have thus ignored the Negro as an active factor in the revolution. But he cannot be ignored. In truth there can be no successful economic change in Georgia without the black man's cooperation. First of all the Negroes are property holders. Sixty years after slavery and despite everything Georgia Negroes own two million acres of land, a space nearly as large as the late kingdom of Montenegro. Their taxable property saved from low wages and systematic cheating has struggled up from twelve million dollars in 1890 to over sixty millions today; and now and then even the remnant of their political power strikes a blow. In 1923 in Savannah a fight within the "white primary" between the corrupt gang and decency gave twelve hundred Negro voters the balance of power. Efforts were made to intimidate the Negroes. Skull and cross-bones signed by the Ku Klux Klan were posted on the doors of eight of the prominent Negro churches with the legend, "This is a white man's fight; keep away." Warning slips were put under the doors of colored citizens. In vain. The colored voters held their own political meetings, financed their own campaign, went into the election, and of their twelve hundred votes it was estimated that less than a hundred went for the gang; the reform mayor was elected.

I am in the hot, crowded, and dirty Jim Crow car, where I belong. A black woman with endless babies is faring forth from Georgia, "North." Two of the babies are sitting on parts of me. I am not comfortable. Then I look out of the window. The hills twist and pass. Slowly the climate changes — cold pines replace the yellow monarchs of the South. There is no cotton. From the door of hewn log cabins faces appear — dead white faces and drawn, thin forms. Here live the remnants of the poor whites.

I look out of the window, and somehow it seems to me that here in the Jim Crow car and there in the mountain cabin lies the future of Georgia — in the intelligence and union of these laborers, white and black, on this soil wet with their blood and tears. They hate and despise each other today. They lynch and murder body and soul. They are separated by the width of a world. And yet — and yet, stranger things have happened under the sun than understanding between those who are born blind.

Class Justice in Germany
[letter to the editor]   *September 2, 1925*

> In *The Nation* of June 3, 1925, Louis Fischer wrote about "Class Justice in Germany." One response was this letter to the editor from Adolf Hitler. Fischer's article had reported on the extreme political bias of the Weimar Republic's judiciary. The judges, mostly declared enemies of democracy and the republic, meted out savage punishment to defendants on the left but were extremely mild with those on the right. Fischer was wrong about the length of Hitler's incarceration. Hitler was arrested on November 11, 1923, two days after the Munich Beer Hall Putsch; he was tried in March of 1924 and sentenced on April 1 to five years of fortress arrest, with explicit provision for early reduction of sentence — and that is what he got. He was freed on December 20, 1924. As for his privileges while inside, they were not so "abridged" that he was kept from writing a good deal of *Mein Kampf.*

TO THE EDITOR OF THE NATION:

SIR: In your issue of June 3 Mr. Louis Fischer says that "Hitler spent six months in a palace prison and was then released."

I was in prison at Sandberg a.S. thirteen months in all. A special decree on April 1, 1924, deprived me of all previous privileges. All privileges theretofore granted the prisoner were either abridged or wiped out. Count Arco was still benefited by these alleviations.

Uffing, June 28, 1925   ADOLF HITLER

MARY HEATON VORSE

The War in Passaic   *March 17, 1926*

Labor journalist, political organizer and activist Mary Heaton Vorse served as the publicity director for the more than 11,000 striking textile workers in Passaic in 1926.

The annual report of the Botany and Garfield Worsted Mills of April 21, 1925, showed net earnings of $2,229,550, a net credit to surplus of $1,731,298, and distributable earnings of $5.91 a share on class A stock and $1.91 a share on common stock. —ORIGINAL NOTE

The strike of the textile workers in Passaic, New Jersey, is a strike of hunger. It is the direct result of a 10 per cent slash in wages already far below a level of decent living. The pay of the textile workers is the lowest in American industry. They get from $12 to $22 a week. Heads of families work for $20, $17.50, and $15. It seems incredible that wages as low as these should have been cut by companies whose mills are among the richest in the country. But that is what happened. That is what has sent ten thousand textile workers streaming out of the mills. That is why after weeks of strike the picket line numbers thousands. That is why processions of workers march from Passaic to Garfield and Clifton singing. Never has a strike of such small numbers shown such mass picketing and such parades. Half the picket line is composed of young people. Mothers with children by the hand, older women and high-school boys and girls stream along, their heads thrown back, singing "Solidarity forever, the union makes us strong" to the tune of "John Brown's Body." The singing picket line has hope in it. Passaic sprawling in its winter slush and snow watches its mill-workers make a full-hearted protest against the intolerable conditions in the mills, against the inhuman and unbearable wage cut.

During the first weeks of the strike the numbers of strikers rolled up like a snowball. The Botany Mill came out first. One mill after another joined the strikers until nearly all the mills were involved. One day they formed a parade of twelve thousand to march from Passaic into Clifton. What a parade! Processions of baby carriages, bands of youngsters, older women, an old grandma of eighty-one. The undimmed, enthusiastic mill children, the youngsters in their teens.

This peaceful parade was set upon by the police as they tried to cross a bridge marching from one town to another. Clubbings of such brutal nature occurred that the daily press was filled with pictures of prostrate strikers and policemen with riot clubs in air. This clubbing did not dim their spirit. The big parade gave them a sense of power and solidarity. They had been striking against the wage cut — only that. Now they voiced demands: a 10 per cent increase over the old wage scale, the return of money taken from them by wage cut, time and a half for over-time, a forty-hour week, decent sanitary working conditions, no discrimination against union workers, and recognition of the union. Then came a further tri-umph, the Forstmann-Huffmann Mills with their four thousand workers joined the walk-out.

The outside world began to notice the strike. Noted ministers, writers, representatives of labor organizations, supporters of civil liberties streamed into Passaic. The town of Garfield invited the strikers to a meeting and the city council indorsed the strikers' demands completely, the only dissenting voices being those of the mayor and the chief of police.

At the beginning of the sixth week the mayor of Passaic menaced the strikers with a force of three hundred mounted policemen. This proved to be only a buga-boo. The picket line, two thousand strong, was practically unmolested, while the aged horses upon which a few policemen were mounted brought laughter from the crowd. Again the strikers formed a parade in the afternoon and marched into Garfield. Throughout all these demonstrations perfect order was preserved.

Then the authorities decided to break the peace. With tear bombs, mounted patrolmen, and a company of sixty-five foot police they tried to disperse a crowd of 2,000 strikers. They failed. The workers jeered and laughed at them. But finally, with the help of five fire companies battering the crowd with powerful streams of water the guardians of order broke the ranks of the strikers, smashing them with clubs when they attempted to halt in their flight or to reform their ranks. The next day the police did better still. They charged a crowd of 3,000 strikers, bludgeoned many men, women, and children, and smashed with deliberate intent the persons and cameras of the news photographers and motion-picture men pres-ent. That was their last victory. The strikers, armed with gas masks, helmets, and their unbending courage, defied the police successfully — and paraded in peace. Photographers took pictures through the slits in armored cars or from the safe vantage of a swooping airplane. The authorities were, temporarily at least, con-founded. As a result of the disorders of the week Justice of the Peace Katz issued warrants for the arrest of Chief of Police Zober and two patrolmen charged with clubbing orderly and inoffensive men and women. To the date of writing warrants are still hovering over the heads of these guardians of the public peace; none of their fellow-officers can be induced to serve them. Meantime the fight goes on and the picket line, an army of thousands, defies the police and greets the few remaining workers when the mill gates open.

The present Passaic strike is only a phase of the long fight of the textile workers for organization and a living wage. These million people who weave our cloth have always lived on the fringe of destitution. Employed by some of the richest corporations in America, their poverty is a by-word. The conditions under which they live is a disgrace to this rich country. We are indicted, tried, and condemned by our textile workers. From time to time they remind us of this fact by a strike.

Fourteen years ago all of us who saw the strike in Lawrence were horrified at the conditions we found. Heads of families were working for $9, for $12. People lived in dwellings that were no better than rat-holes. It was then that Vida Scudder, professor in Wellesley College, stated that the women of this country would refuse to wear cloth manufactured under such conditions if they knew the price in human life being paid for it.

Now after fourteen years we see people whose real wages are but little higher than those of Lawrence days. We see them living in tenements so ill-ventilated, in rooms so dark with walls that sweat so much moisture that the tenements of New York seem pleasant, airy places in comparison. Even in 1912 the laws of Massachusetts prevented some of the scandalous conditions of Passaic. Children under sixteen were not allowed to work in the mills. Passaic children of fourteen are permitted to work an eight-hour day. Night work for women was not permitted in Massachusetts. In Passaic we have the spectacle of hundreds upon hundreds of women, the most overburdened of all the population, the mothers of large families, forced by their husbands' low wages to work in the mills. These women, who may have six, seven, and eight children, go to work at night. They work for ten hours a night, five nights a week. They have no dinner hour. At midnight a recess of fifteen minutes is accorded them. They return home in the morning to get the children off to school and to do the housework. Most of them have children under school age as well and these they must attend to during the day—rest or no rest.

It is this night-work in the mills that marks the difference between the bright-looking, eager girls and the dragged, hopeless, tired older faces which one sees, faces blurred by fatigue. The bearing of many children, the constant fight against poverty, the existence in over-crowded, unaired rooms, the long, grilling, inhuman hours of night-work make these women's lives a nightmare of fatigue.

A law was passed by the legislature of New Jersey forbidding night-work of women. A group of women mill workers appeared at Trenton and begged to have this law repealed. Of course they did. How can a family of nine people live on $20? Of course these women will clamor to be allowed to kill themselves with night-work rather than forego the pittance which they make.

The recent wage cut was written in terms of life and death. The textile workers live so near the margin of destitution that 10 per cent taken from them means undernourishment and disease and eventually death. The men and women in Passaic have met the conditions imposed on them with heroism and have tried for their children's sake to make good homes out of nothing. In the miserable dark rooms in which they live you will find bright hangings, touching bunches of gay paper flowers, often spotless cleanliness, always an attempt at beauty. Through their strike the textile workers have again questioned our civilization.

It would be impossible for any right-thinking man or woman to go into the homes of Passaic and talk to the women who work on the night shift without feeling that a personal responsibility had been laid upon him or her. When there is such want and suffering, when conditions of toil are so degrading, when the places that human beings live in are so indecent it becomes the concern of the public at large to make its power felt and to see that this state of things is altered.

MARK VAN DOREN

First Glance
[book review—T. S. Eliot's poetry]

June 9, 1926

No story about *The Nation*'s 1920s can be told without mention of the Van Doren dynasty—brothers Carl and Mark, and their wives Irita and Dorothy. From 1920 to 1922, Carl ran the book section. He was succeeded by Irita, who later became literary editor of the *New York Herald Tribune*. Mark succeeded Irita. And Dorothy, who later became a successful novelist, was associate editor from 1919 until 1936. First and always a poet, Mark edited the magazine's book section from 1924 to 1928. His "First Glance" column ran from 1925 to 1928.

Several readings of "Selected Poems: 1909–1925," by T. S. Eliot (London: Faber and Gwyer: 7/6), have convinced me that the thing most worth saying at present about Mr. Eliot is not that he is an expatriated American, or that he writes "difficult" poems, or that he is one of the most interesting and austere (if also the most deliberately arid) of contemporary literary critics, or that he is perhaps the most unanswerable of living pessimists in verse, or that he is a desiccating satirist, or that he is elegant and tired, or that he is the spokesman *par excellence* for those fairly numerous spirits who believe that our civilization has come to a dead end. This last is the most important of the secondary things which could be said and are being said about Mr. Eliot, and I must confess that in itself it greatly interests me—as whom would it not? For, leaving aside the question whether or not our culture is truly dying or dead, Mr. Eliot's suspicion that it is obviously explains his subject matter and his style. It explains his preoccupation with bald old age and withered wisdom, with the mock-meanings of human passion, with nerveless gestures, with toothless thoughts in long-deserted heads; it accounts, I suppose, for his indifference to most of the current poetic themes; and it furnishes the key, certainly, to an otherwise baffling technique. In particular, of course, it explains The Waste Land, which bulks pretty large in the present volume—a volume of only ninety pages, though it contains most of Mr. Eliot's published poetry. But all this is no sufficient reason for calling Mr. Eliot one of the finest of twentieth-century poets, as I am convinced he is. The possibility that literary historians five centuries hence may be able to sum up our generation by quoting the badly fractured end of The Waste Land—that splintered passage in which the poet seems to be saying that there is no language any more wherewith to say the thing, whatever it is, which might be said and is not worth saying—does not affect the fact that for us here and now Mr. Eliot is fine.

What impressed me most in this rereading of the poems was their familiarity. I discovered that I had, without ever trying to do so, come very near to knowing many of them by heart; or if not that, I experienced the pleasure—for me perhaps the keenest of all pleasures—of recognizing a classic where I had not known any classic was. It is an achievement, surely, for a poet who has produced on the whole so little, and who has fashioned that little so ingeniously that always on its first appearance it was harsh or shocking, to have arrived in fifteen years at a position where he may be acclaimed beautiful and perfect. It is well known that the quatrain of Mr. Eliot's Sweeney poems has found many fascinated imitators, and no sensitive reader can ever have been unaware of the workmanship which went into the invention of that stanza or into the free verse of certain longer pieces. But no one has paid adequate tribute to Mr. Eliot's skill and felicity in everything he does. The thing next in order is an analysis, if one is at all possible, of Mr. Eliot's manner—or manners. Meanwhile I rest hugely content with The Love Song of J. Alfred Prufrock, Preludes, Rhapsody on a Windy Night, Morning at the Window, The Hippopotamus, all of the Sweeney poems, and most of The Waste Land.

LANGSTON HUGHES

The Negro Artist and the Racial Mountain

June 23, 1926

In 1926, black writers and artists were enjoying the flowering
of the Harlem Renaissance. Just a year earlier, Langston
Hughes had published *The Weary Blues*, the volume of poems
that brought him to artistic prominence. And over the next
generation, Hughes published other works of poetry, including
Fine Clothes to the Jew and *Shakespeare in Harlem*, as well as
novels, short stories, essays and an autobiography. Hughes's
piece is a manifesto of sorts: African Americans had an identity, he wrote—a spirit, a perspective on life, a culture, an
idiom—which was articulated in their speech and music, and it
was the responsibility of black writers to craft their art from
that medium.

One of the most promising of the young Negro poets said to me once, "I want
to be a poet—not a Negro poet," meaning, I believe, "I want to write like a white
poet"; meaning subconsciously, "I would like to be a white poet"; meaning behind
that, "I would like to be white." And I was sorry the young man said that, for no
great poet has ever been afraid of being himself. And I doubted then that, with
his desire to run away spiritually from his race, this boy would ever be a great
poet. But this is the mountain standing in the way of any true Negro art in
America—this urge within the race toward whiteness, the desire to pour racial
individuality into the mold of American standardization, and to be as little Negro
and as much American as possible.

But let us look at the immediate background of this young poet. His family is
of what I suppose one would call the Negro middle class: people who are by no
means rich yet never uncomfortable nor hungry—smug, contented, respectable
folk, members of the Baptist church. The father goes to work every morning. He
is a chief steward at a large white club. The mother sometimes does fancy sewing
or supervises parties for the rich families of the town. The children go to a mixed
school. In the home they read white papers and magazines. And the mother often
says "Don't be like niggers" when the children are bad. A frequent phrase from
the father is, "Look how well a white man does things." And so the word white
comes to be unconsciously a symbol of all the virtues. It holds for the children
beauty, morality, and money. The whisper of "I want to be white" runs silently
through their minds. This young poet's home is, I believe, a fairly typical home
of the colored middle class. One sees immediately how difficult it would be for
an artist born in such a home to interest himself in interpreting the beauty of his

own people. He is never taught to see that beauty. He is taught rather not to see it, or if he does, to be ashamed of it when it is not according to Caucasian patterns.

For racial culture the home of a self-styled "high-class" Negro has nothing better to offer. Instead there will perhaps be more aping of things white than in a less cultured or less wealthy home. The father is perhaps a doctor, lawyer, landowner, or politician. The mother may be a social worker, or a teacher, or she may do nothing and have a maid. Father is often dark but he has usually married the lightest woman he could find. The family attend a fashionable church where few really colored faces are to be found. And they themselves draw a color line. In the North they go to white theaters and white movies. And in the South they have at least two cars and a house "like white folks." Nordic manners, Nordic faces, Nordic hair, Nordic art (if any), and an Episcopal heaven. A very high mountain indeed for the would-be racial artist to climb in order to discover himself and his people.

But then there are the low-down folks, the so-called common element, and they are the majority — may the Lord be praised! The people who have their nip of gin on Saturday nights and are not too important to themselves or the community, or too well fed, or too learned to watch the lazy world go round. They live on Seventh Street in Washington or State Street in Chicago and they do not particularly care whether they are like white folks or anybody else. Their joy runs, bang! into ecstasy. Their religion soars to a shout. Work maybe a little today, rest a little tomorrow. Play awhile. Sing awhile. O, let's dance! These common people are not afraid of spirituals, as for a long time their more intellectual brethren were, and jazz is their child. They furnish a wealth of colorful, distinctive material for any artist because they still hold their own individuality in the face of American standardizations. And perhaps these common people will give to the world its truly great Negro artist, the one who is not afraid to be himself. Whereas the better-class Negro would tell the artist what to do, the people at least let him alone when he does appear. And they are not ashamed of him — if they know he exists at all. And they accept what beauty is their own without question.

Certainly there is, for the American Negro artist who can escape the restrictions the more advanced among his own group would put upon him, a great field of unused material ready for his art. Without going outside his race, and even among the better classes with their "white" culture and conscious American manners, but still Negro enough to be different, there is sufficient matter to furnish a black artist with a lifetime of creative work. And when he chooses to touch on the relations between Negroes and whites in this country with their innumerable overtones and undertones, surely, and especially for literature and the drama, there is an inexaustible supply of themes at hand. To these the Negro artist can give his racial individuality, his heritage of rhythm and warmth, and his incongruous humor that so often, as in the Blues, becomes ironic laughter mixed with tears. But let us look again at the mountain.

A prominent Negro clubwoman in Philadelphia paid eleven dollars to hear Raquel Meller sing Andalusian popular songs. But she told me a few weeks before she would not think of going to hear "that woman," Clara Smith, a great black artist, sing Negro folksongs. And many an upper-class Negro church, even now, would not dream of employing a spiritual in its services. The drab melodies in white folks' hymnbooks are much to be preferred. "We want to worship the Lord correctly and quietly. We don't believe in 'shouting.' Let's be dull like the Nordics," they say, in effect.

The road for the serious black artist, then, who would produce a racial art is most certainly rocky and the mountain is high. Until recently he received almost no encouragement for his work from either white or colored people. The fine novels of Chestnutt go out of print with neither race noticing their passing. The quaint charm and humor of Dunbar's dialect verse brought to him, in his day, largely the same kind of encouragement one would give a sideshow freak (A colored man writing poetry! How odd!) or a clown (How amusing!).

The present vogue in things Negro, although it may do as much harm as good for the budding colored artist, has at least done this: it has brought him forcibly to the attention of his own people among whom for so long, unless the other race had noticed him beforehand, he was a prophet with little honor. I understand that Charles Gilpin acted for years in Negro theaters without any special acclaim from his own, but when Broadway gave him eight curtain calls, Negroes, too, began to beat a tin pan in his honor. I know a young colored writer, a manual worker by day, who had been writing well for the colored magazines for some years, but it was not until he recently broke into the white publications and his first book was accepted by a prominent New York publisher that the "best" Negroes in his city took the trouble to discover that he lived there. Then almost immediately they decided to give a grand dinner for him. But the society ladies were careful to whisper to his mother that perhaps she'd better not come. They were not sure she would have an evening gown.

The Negro artist works against an undertow of sharp criticism and misunderstanding from his own group and unintentional bribes from the whites. "O, be respectable, write about nice people, show how good we are," say the Negroes. "Be stereotyped, don't go too far, don't shatter our illusions about you, don't amuse us too seriously. We will pay you," say the whites. Both would have told Jean Toomer not to write "Cane." The colored people did not praise it. The white people did not buy it. Most of the colored people who did read "Cane" hate it. They are afraid of it. Although the critics gave it good reviews the public remained indifferent. Yet (excepting the work of DuBois) "Cane" contains the finest prose written by a Negro in America. And like the singing of Robeson, it is truly racial.

But in spite of the Nordicized Negro intelligentsia and the desires of some white editors we have an honest American Negro literature already with us. Now I await the rise of the Negro theater. Our folk music, having achieved world-wide fame, offers itself to the genius of the great individual American Negro composer who is to come. And within the next decade I expect to see the work of a growing school of colored artists who paint and model the beauty of dark faces and create with new technique the expressions of their own soul-world. And the Negro dancers who will dance like flame and the singers who will continue to carry our songs to all who listen—they will be with us in even greater numbers tomorrow.

Most of my own poems are racial in theme and treatment, derived from the life I know. In many of them I try to grasp and hold some of the meanings and rhythms of jazz. I am sincere as I know how to be in these poems and yet after every reading I answer questions like these from my own people: Do you think Negroes should always write about Negroes? I wish you wouldn't read some of your poems to white folks. How do you find anything interesting in a place like a cabaret? Why do you write about black people? You aren't black. What makes you do so many jazz poems?

But jazz to me is one of the inherent expressions of Negro life in America: the eternal tom-tom beating in the Negro soul—the tom-tom of revolt against weariness in a white world, a world of subway trains, and work, work, work; the tom-tom of joy and laughter, and pain swallowed in a smile. Yet the Philadelphia clubwoman is ashamed to say that her race created it and she does not like me to write about it. The old subconscious "white is best" runs through her mind. Years of study under white teachers, a lifetime of white books, pictures, and papers, and white manners, morals, and Puritan standards made her dislike the spirituals. And now she turns up her nose at jazz and all its manifestations—likewise almost everything else distinctly racial. She doesn't care for the Winold Reiss portraits of Negroes because they are "too Negro." She does not want a true picture of herself from anybody. She wants the artist to flatter her, to make the white world believe that all Negroes are as smug and as near white in soul as she wants to be. But, to my mind, it is the duty of the younger Negro artist, if he accepts any duties at all from outsiders, to change through the force of his art that old whispering "I want to be white," hidden in the aspirations of his people, to "Why should I want to be white? I am a Negro—and beautiful!"

So I am ashamed for the black poet who says, "I want to be a poet, not a Negro poet," as though his own racial world were not as interesting as any other world. I am ashamed, too, for the colored artist who runs from the painting of Negro faces to the painting of sunsets after the manner of the academicians because he fears the strange un-whiteness of his own features. An artist must be free to choose what he does, certainly, but he must also never be afraid to do what he might choose.

Let the blare of Negro jazz bands and the bellowing voice of Bessie Smith sing-ing Blues penetrate the closed ears of the colored near-intellectuals until they lis-ten and perhaps understand. Let Paul Robeson singing Water Boy, and Rudolph Fisher writing about the streets of Harlem, and Jean Toomer holding the heart of Georgia in his hands, and Aaron Douglas drawing strange black fantasies cause the smug Negro middle class to turn from their white, respectable, ordinary books and papers to catch a glimmer of their own beauty. We younger Negro art-ists who create now intend to express our individual dark-skinned selves without fear or shame. If white people are pleased we are glad. If they are not, it doesn't matter. We know we are beautiful. And ugly too. The tom-tom cries and the tom-tom laughs. If colored people are pleased we are glad. If they are not, their dis-pleasure doesn't matter either. We build our temples for tomorrow, strong as we know how, and we stand on top of the mountain, free within ourselves.

CRYSTAL EASTMAN

Mother-Worship   *March 16, 1927*

> In 1926, seventeen women were invited by *The Nation* to ex-plore the personal sources of their feminism. The series was the brainchild of the young managing editor, Freda Kirchwey. "Our object," the editors announced with the first installment of "These Modern Women" on December 1, 1926, "is to discover the origin of their modern point of view toward men, marriage, children, and jobs." Anonymity was offered as an encourage-ment to uninhibited self-disclosure and as a protection against the hurt feelings of relatives or the abuse of strangers. This piece by Crystal Eastman, a dedicated feminist, pacifist and so-cialist, is of interest for the light it sheds both on the era of the twenties and on the feminism of today. (How accurately the last paragraph of "Mother-Worship" reflects Eastman's sentiments, however, is unclear. Eastman's last paragraph was changed by *The Nation*, and in letters to friends and relatives, Eastman made remarks such as: "It was much better as I wrote it, more honest and sure. Far more interesting.")

The story of my background is the story of my mother. She was a Middle-Western girl, youngest, cleverest, and prettiest of six daughters — children of an Irish gun-smith and a "Pennsylvania Dutch" woman of good family and splendid character. The gunsmith was a master of his trade but a heavy drinker, always ugly and often dangerous. My mother got away from home as soon as she could. After a year in a nearby coeducational college she taught school for a while and then married. The man she chose (for she was the sort of girl who has many chances) was a penniless but handsome and idealistic Yankee divinity student whom she met during that one college year. When he had secured his first parish, they were married.

For about eight years, during which there were four different parishes and four children were born, my mother was a popular, active, and helpful minister's wife. Then my father, who had always struggled against ill-health, suffered a complete nervous breakdown. He was forced to give up his church and his chosen profession. My mother had to support the family.

She began by teaching English literature in a girls' school. Before long she was giving Sunday-evening talks at the school. Then she began to fill outside engagements and finally she became a sort of supply-preacher to nearby country churches. About the year 1890, though she had had no theological education, she was ordained as a Congregational minister and called to be the pastor of a fairly large church in a well-to-do farming community. After three or four successful years, she and my father (who by this time had lost a good bit of money trying to be a farmer and a grocer but had begun to regain his health) were called as associate pastors to a big liberal church in a city of 40,000. It was my mother's reputation as a preacher that brought them this opportunity and she proved equal to the larger field. In time my father's health improved so that he could carry his share of the work, but my mother was always the celebrated member of the family.

I have a vivid memory of my mother when I was six years old. We are standing, my brother and I, in front of a run-down farmhouse on the edge of the town which had become our home. We have just said goodby to our mother and now we are watching her trip off down the hill to the school where she goes every day to teach. She turns to smile at us—such a beaming smile, such a bright face, such a pretty young mother. When the charming, much-loved figure begins to grow small in the distance, my brother, who is younger and more temperamental than I, begins to cry. He screams as loud as he can, until he is red in the face. But he cannot make her come back. And I, knowing she will be worried if she hears him, try to drag him away. By the time I was ten my mother had become a preacher.

Life was never ordinary where my mother was. She was always trying something new. She had an eager, active mind, and tremendous energy. She was pre-eminently an initiator. From the time I was thirteen we spent our summers like most middle-class, small-town American families, in a cottage beside a lake. And our life there, I suppose, would have been much like the life in thousands of other such summer communities, except for the presence of my mother. For one thing, she organized a system of cooperative housekeeping with three other families on the hillside, and it lasted for years. A cook was hired jointly, but the burden of keeping house, planning meals, buying meat and groceries from the carts that came along three times a week, getting vegetables and fruit from the garden, collecting the money, keeping track of guests, and paying the bills, shifted every week. At first it was only the mothers who took their turn at housekeeping. But as the children grew older they were included in the scheme, boys as well as girls. Toward the end we had all the fun of eating in a big jolly group and only one or two weeks of housekeeping responsibility during the whole summer.

We used to have Sunday night music and singing for the whole hillside at our cottage, with the grown-ups in the big room, and the children lying outside on the porch couches or off on the grass. We had "church" Sunday mornings, too, in our big room; after all we were the minister's family. But it was a very short informal "church" followed by a long swim, and any one who wanted to could preach. We took turns at preaching as well as at keeping house, and we could choose the subjects of our own sermons.

Then one summer my mother started "symposiums." Once a week the mothers and older children and any fathers who happened to be around would gather on somebody's porch, listen to a paper, and then discuss it. I read a paper on "Woman" when I was fifteen, and I believe I was as wise in feminism then as I am now, if a little more solemn.

"The trouble with women," I said, "is that they have no impersonal interests. They must have work of their own, first because no one who has to depend on another person for his living is really grown up; and, second, because the only way to be happy is to have an absorbing interest in life which is not bound up with any particular person. Children can die or grow up, husbands can leave you. No woman who allows husband and children to absorb her whole time and interest is safe against disaster."

The proudest and happiest moment of my college days was when I met my mother in New York, as I did once a year, and went with her to a big banquet in connection with some ministers' convention she had come down to attend. She always spoke at the banquet, and she was always the best speaker. She was gay, sparkling, humorous, intimate, adorable. I would sit and love her with all my heart, and I could feel all the ministers loving her and rejoicing in her.

Almost always it is painful to sit in the audience while a near relative preaches, prays, or makes a speech. Husbands, wives, brothers, sisters, and children of the performers ought to be exempt from attending such public functions. My brothers and I always suffered when father preached, although, as preachers go, he was pretty good. At any rate he was beautiful to look at and had a large following of enthusiastic admirers. But when my mother preached we hated to miss it. There was never a moment of anxiety or concern; she had that secret of perfect platform ease which takes all strain out of the audience. Her voice was music; she spoke simply, without effort, almost without gestures, standing very still. And what she said seemed to come straight from her heart to yours. Her sermons grew out of her own moral and spiritual struggles. For she had a stormy, troubled soul, capable of black cruelty and then again of the deepest generosities. She was humble, honest, striving, always beginning again to try to be good.

With all her other interests she was thoroughly domestic. We children loved her cooking as much as we loved her preaching. And she was all kinds of devoted mother, the kind that tucks you in at night and reads you a story, and the kind that drags you to the dentist to have your teeth straightened. But I must leave her now and try to fill out the picture. My father, too, played a large part in my life. He was a generous man, the kind of man that was a suffragist from the day he first heard of a woman who wanted to vote. One evening, after mother had been teaching for some time and had begun to know her power as a public speaker, she came to him as he lay on his invalid's couch.

"John," she said, "I believe I could preach!"

"Mary!" he cried, jumping up in his excitement, "I *know* you could!"

This was in those early days when he had given up his own career as a minister, when he had cheerfully turned small farmer and had begun, on days when he was well enough, to peddle eggs and butter at the back doors of his former parishioners. From the moment he knew that my mother wanted to preach, he helped and encouraged her. Without his coaching and without his local prestige, it is doubtful if she could have been ordained. And my father stood by me in the same way, from the time when I wanted to cut off my hair and go barefoot to the time when I began to study law. When I insisted that the boys must make their beds if I had to make mine, he stood by me. When I said that if there was dishwashing to be done they should take their turn, he stood by me. And when I declared that there was no such thing in our family as boys' work and girls' work, and that I must be allowed to do my share of wood-chopping and outdoor chores, he took me seriously and let me try.

Once when I was twelve and very tall, a deputation of ladies from her church called on my mother and gently suggested that my skirts ought to be longer. My mother, who was not without consciousness of the neighbors' opinions, thought she must do something. But my father said, "No, let her wear them short. She likes to run, and she can't run so well in long skirts."

A few years later it was a question of bathing suits. In our summer community I was a ringleader in the rebellion against skirts and stockings for swimming. On one hot Sunday morning the other fathers waited on my father and asked him to use his influence with me. I don't know what he said to them but he never said a word to me. He was, I know, startled and embarrassed to see his only daughter in a man's bathing suit with bare brown legs for all the world to see. I think it shocked him to his dying day. But he himself had been a swimmer; he knew he would not want to swim in a skirt and stockings. Why then should I?

Beyond the immediate circle of my family there were other influences at work. My mother, among her other charms, had a genius for friendship. There were always clever, interesting, amusing women coming in and out of our house. I never thought of women as dull folk who sat and listened while the men talked. The little city where we lived was perhaps unusual. It was the home of six or seven distinguished persons, and not all of them were men.

In this environment I grew up confidently expecting to have a profession and earn my own living, and also confidently expecting to be married and have children. It was fifty-fifty with me. I was just as passionately determined to have children as I was to have a career. And my mother was the triumphant answer to all doubts as to the success of this double role. From my earliest memory she had more than half supported the family and yet she was supremely a mother.

I have lived my life according to the plan. I have had the "career" and the children and, except for an occasional hiatus due to illness or some other circumstance over which I had no control, I have earned my own living. I have even made a certain name for myself. If I have not fulfilled the promise of my youth, either as a homemaker or as a professional woman, I have never wavered in my feminist faith. My mother has always been a beacon to me, and if today I sometimes feel a sense of failure it may be partly because I have always lived in the glow of her example. In their early struggle for survival against narrow-minded and prejudiced parents some of my contemporaries seem to have won more of the iron needed in the struggle of life than I got from my almost perfect parents.

UPTON SINCLAIR

Poor Me and Pure Boston

June 29, 1927

Upton Sinclair wrote frequently for *The Nation*. Best known for his novel *The Jungle*, Sinclair was a prolific writer, a socialist, and founder of the End Poverty in California (EPIC) movement.

Everybody admires "Lindy" because he does not talk about himself. I wish I could follow the same charming practice in telling about Boston and its censorship, but unfortunately all I know about it is what it has done to me.

Behold me, therefore, an author who had been known most of his life as the prize prude of the radical movement; a man who can say that he has never told a smutty story in his life, and who was once described by his former marital partner, through the newspapers of the civilized world, as "an essential monogamist"—a very old-fogyish thing to be. I am the author of some thirty books, and a Boston police magistrate has decreed that the last one "manifestly tends to corrupt youth." Let me say at once that "Oil!" is no different in this respect from any of the others. Judged by the Boston method, they are all equally vicious. They are being read throughout the rest of America and in other civilized lands, and Boston alone thinks they are obscene.

It is rather a joke on an author—sitting at his typewriter at home, engaged in work upon a book denouncing what he considers the really obscene writers of his country and time—to have his labors interrupted by a telegram advising him that his own book has fallen under the ban. I am happy to be able to say that I was not calling for the police, but for the moral forces of society to make war upon true obscenity. I wrote that "every time you get a censor, you get a fool, and worse yet, a knave, pretending to be a guardian of morality while acting as a guardian of class greed." And now the Boston censor has arisen to provide me with the proofs!

How does it work here? An Episcopal clergyman stopped me on the street yesterday and told me he knew the man who made the complaint to the police about "Oil!" The clergyman gave me his name, and added: "I have suppressed two reports damaging to his moral character." It is, you see, the old story of "Honi soit qui mal y pense."

The next step, under Boston practice, is that two detectives are sent to a bookstore to buy the book about which a complaint has been made. In this case they chose a bookseller who has the hard luck to be only a few doors from the courthouse. They bought the book from Mr. John Gritz, a clerk, who happens to be only twenty years of age and the nearest approach to a cherub that you can find wearing trousers.

The book is then turned over to an inspector. He is a busy man, and his business isn't reading. Here is a book of something over a quarter of a million words; naturally, he says, "What the hell?", passes the book to a clerk in his office, and says, "Hey, Joe, here's a juicy one." I am telling this not as a fiction writer, but as one who has been hanging round the courthouse for the past week, listening to the men on the inside gossiping about what did actually happen.

Next, "Joe" takes the book home and marks the passages which he thinks corrupted his morals. The book is returned to the inspector and he reads these passages and says: "Holy smoke, here this guy has a girl say to a fellow that she knows how to keep from having babies." Boston is 70 per cent Roman Catholic, you understand, and the percentage prevails in the police department. So the inspector goes before a magistrate, and the magistrate takes the book home overnight, and reads the marked passages. If he is an especially fair-minded man, he may have an impulse to read the whole book; but the law does not require him to do so. The law provides for the condemnation of a book "containing" anything, and under the governing decision only the passages complained of are required as evidence. "You are not trying any book except this," said the trial judge in a charge which the Supreme Court of Massachusetts upheld, "and only such parts of this as the Government complained of. . . . It makes no difference what the object in writing this book was, or what its whole tone is." The test is whether it contains, anywhere, anything "manifestly tending to corrupt the morals of youth." You can see that this confines modern writers to the juvenile department, and makes it impossible for them to write for adults.

For my part, I am not going to be bound by this limitation. I believe that grown people have experiences and needs which have to be dealt with in fiction. I will not deliberately corrupt anyone, of course, but if young people read my books they will learn what is going on in the modern world; also they will learn what I consider to be the cause of this moral breakdown, the presence of parasitism and exploitation in our society – the fact that a class of idlers are permitted to have enormous wealth without doing anything to earn it.

In the case of "Oil!" there are 527 pages, and the police object to nine; that does not seem to indicate an abnormal interest in the sexual aspects of life. The first scene they object to begins on page 193, and anyone who buys the book looking for obscenity – a great many people are now doing so – will find it rather slow in starting. There are four or five pages about a "petting party," and that is very bad, according to the Boston police; but on the other hand there are twenty-six pages about how to lease a tract of ground for a drilling-site, and really that does not seem to be giving undue emphasis to the "petting party" aspects of the life of a young "oil prince."

Of course, when a born preacher like myself puts such a scene into a novel, it is for a purpose. I am showing my young "oil prince" groping his way out of the customary life of his class and into a better one. The next time he is invited to a "petting party," he does not go – because he is looking for a better kind of love. Curiously enough, I was rebuked by the reviewer of *The Nation* for these little preachments. "To inject a paragraph of moralizing into the piquant incident of Mrs. Thelma Norman's attempt to be seduced in Bunny's cabin is absurdly priggish." I had hoped that what displeased *The Nation* reviewer might help me out with the magistrate, and I took a copy of the review to court, but alas, I was not allowed to show it, or to say a word. It can never be introduced, under the law, nor can the "petting-party" scene be judged in the light of what comes after, what lessons are drawn from it, what repudiation it meets with from the author and the hero later on in the book. Speaking strictly, I may get such testimony in if the Superior Court sees fit to admit it, but the court is under no obligation to admit it, and if it declines to do so the Supreme Court will not call it an error: such is the governing decision, brought out by a trial of the novel "Three Weeks."

I wanted to be the defendant in this case, instead of the cherubic Mr. Gritz. But alas, the police department of Boston does not want me. Mr. George E. Roewer, the unwearying defender of unpopular causes in Boston, approached the authorities with the customary proposition for a test case with a minimum fine upon conviction, but it appears that the police consider the birth-control utterance of my flapper, Eunice Hoyt, especially bad, and I am to go to jail for a year if they can get me. What I am going to do I will not say until after I have done it, but I can assure you I am not going to spend a year on Deer Island.

It is obvious that under this law very little standard English literature can be sold. Consider Smollett or Fielding, "Tess of the D'Urbervilles" and "Ann Veronica." Or consider Shakespeare and the Bible. One of the newspapermen here tells me that the public is sick of Shakespeare and the Bible, because every publisher of a book, obscene or claimed to be obscene, always proposes these tests. Nevertheless, poor Boston will have to go on hearing about it, until it changes its laws so that these two books can be legally sold and so that modern writers may be free to produce great literature if they can. I have called a meeting at Byron Street House, headquarters of the Community Church of Boston, for the morning of June 16, and I am there going to read the very offending passage of Act III, Scene ii of "Hamlet," and offer this book to the police at bargain prices. Then I am going to read the quite horrible piece of obscenity in Genesis 19, 30–38, and see if the police will buy that.

POSTSCRIPT—JUNE 16. *I offered a copy of the Bible to the police this morning. They would not buy it. I sold it to a Boston rationalist of very high moral standards who is distressed by the thought of how such a passage will corrupt youth and promises to appear before a magistrate and demand a warrant for my arrest. I then offered the police what they thought was a copy of "Oil." I did not say it was "Oil." All I did was hold it up before the audience. The police bought it and notified me to appear in court tomorrow. Then they examined the volume and found they had bought the Bible bound in a cover of "Oil." They demanded their money back, and I was too polite to keep it. The only way to fight this law is to make a monkey of it.*

JUNE 21. *At last I have found a policeman willing to buy a copy of "Oil" and have sold him one.*

Justice Underfoot
[editorial]

August 17, 1927

The tragic injustice of the Sacco-Vanzetti case dragged through the twenties, poisoning the decade. Many people wrote about the trial for *The Nation*, including editor Oswald Garrison Villard in this impassioned 1927 editorial. Villard also helped form the Citizens National Committee for Sacco and Vanzetti, which in 1927 forced a review of the case by the Governor of Massachussetts — all, it turned out, in vain.

One of the most momentous decisions in the history of American jurisprudence has been rendered — and Sacco and Vanzetti are condemned to death. Around the earth the news has winged its way as fast as light and wherever the tidings have reached millions of workers now believe that justice does not exist in America, that two innocent men are going to their doom in order that a social system may be upheld, a tottering social order may triumph. As we write no one can foretell the consequences of Governor Fuller's astounding decision, but from remote quarters there already comes the news of protest meetings, of protest strikes, of the windows of the American Consulate in Buenos Aires smashed, of a sense of horror-struck outrage in one country after another. Talk about the solidarity of the human race! When has there been a more striking example of the solidarity of great masses of people than this? Ten years ago people were reading of thirty thousand, forty thousand, fifty thousand men done to death in a single day in the war that statesmen, with horrible sacrilege, had falsely dedicated to democracy and to civilization. Those useless massacres nowhere stirred the neutral world as has the fate of these two Italian workers, who have dared to say that they were anarchists, but innocent of the murder with which they are charged. Wherever the American flag flies in foreign lands today, it has to be guarded; it appears the symbol of a monstrous wrong. Men may yet die by the dozen because of Governor Fuller's decision. Rightly or wrongly, we repeat, uncountable multitudes today believe that in America justice is dead.

For ourselves, we are shaken to the core. We had not believed such a decision possible. We do not retract one word from our praise of the industry Governor Fuller has shown, his painstaking examination of the topography of the scene of the crime, of witnesses and jurors, judge and prisoners. We recognize again his honesty of purpose; we acquit him of any charge of political maneuvering; we admit the superficial ability of his opinion. Yet we cannot for one instant accept this verdict in the face of facts known to us for years as they have been known to multitudes of others. It seems to us that he has missed all the important points in the case and that his decision reveals his complete inability to rise above the point of view of his surroundings, his class, and the setting in which great wealth has placed him. Nor are we convinced by the facile report of the Governor's committee of three eminent and conventional gentlemen, two chosen from the highest Boston social circles, all of one type of mind and not one of them representing the vast groups that have felt from the first that they had a vital stake in the fate of these men. After a brief investigation, partaking of the nature of a star-chamber in hearing Judge Thayer and his attorney without attendance of the defense's counsel, they have upheld the court.

As for Governor Fuller's judgment of the case, it no more closes it than the hanging of John Brown ended the Harper's Ferry raid and condemned him to execration and oblivion. More than half the people of this country refused to consider John Brown a traitor or a murderer, though his guilt was unquestionable and was openly confessed, whereas the masses believe Sacco and Vanzetti legally innocent and entitled to have their innocence determined by law and not by prejudice. The people saw behind John Brown issues of far-reaching moment that soon thereafter tore this country apart and for four long years drenched it in blood. They knew at once that the questions at stake were not settled on that Charlestown scaffold and could not be; that the lives and liberties of millions were involved, and the issue was whether or not the South should be ruled by a despotic economic oligarchy, whether poor whites and blacks alike should be masters of their bodies as well as their souls. Rightly or wrongly, the case of Sacco and Vanzetti has become identified with efforts to reconstruct the social order, just as the Dreyfus case came to mean infinitely more important things for France and the world than the fate of one Jewish major.

Absurd and unjustified, this interpretation of the Sacco-Vanzetti case seems to all conservatives. But it is there, and not Massachusetts alone, but the whole of the United States will have it to reckon with. Governor Fuller's opinion will never upset this belief. For the fact, the great and unanswerable fact, stands out that here is an instance of a headlong collision of certain viewpoints which are and must be hopelessly antagonistic. The liberals and the workers who are championing the cause of these men may also have their blind eyes. The truth remains that the question of the guilt of these men has been subordinated to the clash of these two vital currents of human thought, and the world at large knows that Sacco and Vanzetti have been judged and will have been executed by the representatives of one of these viewpoints alone. And still another fact, a great and unanswerable fact, stands out that in its essence the guilt or innocence of these men has been passed upon by only one judge; that what is forbidden in New York and is impossible in other States of the Union has come to pass in Massachusetts: the *evidence* — not the technical legal procedure — has been ruled upon only by the trial judge, he who, if a tithe of the charges against him by reputable witnesses is true, ought to be impeached and disgraced — even the Lowell committee admits what it kindly calls his "indiscretion."

Is it any wonder that M. Herriot, who has repeatedly, as Prime Minister of France and as the present Minister of Education, given proof of his friendship for America, has cried out in protest, against not only this final act of barbarity but what has gone on before. "To the depths of my soul," he declares, "I am against this punishment that has lasted seven years. I am sorry to be unable to make my voice heard, but I belong to the Government and my words might pledge the whole cabinet. Personally, I never varied my opinion. Sacco and Vanzetti ought to be released. They have earned such a measure of clemency." This is what affects the European opinion more than Americans can possibly realize – that these men have been in jeopardy of their lives for seven long years. We are informed on high authority that a group of the foremost London jurists, after devoting an entire evening to a discussion of the Sacco and Vanzetti trial, was unanimously of the opinion that they ought to be freed now, *whether guilty or innocent,* since even the crime of murder does not merit the cruel and unusual punishment of keeping men in such torture for seven years. Governor Fuller smugly condemns the defense for the delay – would he be as quick to denounce Messrs. Sinclair and Doheny and Fall and Daugherty for dragging out their trials for five years? – but the hideous circumstance is there. It is impossible in any other civilized country for men to be tortured as have been these. The London *Times* itself features bitter criticism of verdict and procedure. Even the New York *Times* is compelled to write thus:

> Yet it remains true that thousands of good citizens, while submitting to this grievously delayed working of the machinery of justice, will feel that there is something shocking in an execution so long after trial. We speak not of the "perverted zeal of clamorous agitators," though that will now doubtless flame afresh. Far more serious is the hurt to humane feeling and the doubt which will persist in candid minds whether the ends of justice could not better have been attained in some other way.

A just and pious wish! But, the world over, it is a *demand* by an outraged humanity. Even if Governor Fuller felt that he must uphold the decision, could not justice have been tempered with mercy? Yield to foreign or American threats of course he could not. But the hands of millions have been outstretched to him for pardon or commutation of sentence. A great executive would justly have taken note of that, would have strengthened justice by recognizing an unparalleled demand for clemency; might even have weighed the cost to his country of making martyrs of these men; could have upheld the majesty of the law far, far better by exercising forbearance than by a brutal insistence upon an eye for an eye, a tooth for a tooth, a life for a life.

As for Governor Fuller's opinion, he sweeps away the testimony as to the bias of Judge Thayer by affirming that the judge had a right to be biased after the testimony was in, whereas the affidavits of reputable men and women affirm that that bias was evident from the earliest stages of the trial. We pass over aghast his tribute to the "clear-eyed" and "courageous" witnesses – some of whom are of doubtful reputation, contradicted themselves, and testified to the impossible. Nor would we stress today the old question of the identifications or the fact that the deadly bullet was never proved to have been from Sacco's revolver; nor dwell upon the Governor's describing in one hundred words the Bridgewater hold-up which had nothing to do with the question of a fair trial in the Braintree case. As for the latter, the Governor is quite satisfied that Judge Thayer was right in denying all the seven motions for a new trial. He is not willing that the men should be given the benefit of a doubt, nor will he appeal to the legislature to start the machinery for a new trial in a different atmosphere under a different judge. Would that have rocked the foundations of Massachusetts justice? It might have inflamed the Back Bay clubs, but it would have meant joy and satisfaction wherever newspapers appear.

And not merely to radicals. It is *not* the radicals alone who fought for Sacco and Vanzetti. Noble souls have given years of their lives and their money to this cause who are neither Reds nor foreign-born Americans; nor have they belonged to those holding the anarchist views of the condemned. If there are finer types of our citizenship, or men and women of older American lineage, we should like to have them pointed out to us. They, too, have read every word of the testimony; they have examined the new witnesses; they, too, have studied the motions for a new trial and perused Judge Thayer's denials of them; they have read the affidavits against the judge and they are as good lawyers as the Governor himself. They are as eager as he for the good repute of Massachusetts and its courts, yet they are unconvinced. To them an incredible tragedy is being finished before their eyes; a judicial murder is being committed. Does not the passionate belief of these unselfish supporters of the right merit consideration, if not assent?

As for Sacco and Vanzetti, sometimes we have asked ourselves whether it was not intended that they should die, and whether it is not best for the cause of human progress that they should perish. In his wonderful address to the court—made to Judge Thayer, who did not once dare to look at the prisoners as he condemned them to the chair—Vanzetti voiced this in amazing exaltation of spirit:

> If it had not been for these thing, I might have live out my life, talking at street corners to scorning men. I might have die, unmarked, unknown, a failure. Now we are not a failure. This is our career and our triumph. Never in our full life can we hope to do such work for tolerance, for joostice, for man's onderstanding of man, as now we do by an accident. Our words—our lives—our pains—nothing! The taking of our lives—lives of a good shoemaker and a poor fish-peddler—all! That last moment belong to us—that agony is our triumph!

This, we believe, will be the verdict of history. Certain it is that if the precedents of history hold true, monuments are likely to be erected to Sacco and Vanzetti and the names of their prosecutors will fade out of history.

There is one other word from these men that we wish we might record from their lips before they step over into eternity. That is an appeal to all their fellow-workers of the world to refuse to be goaded by their deaths into any violence whatever. If we have any influence at all with those working-men whose cause

BEN SHAHN: *Sacco and Vanzetti* (1952)

we have so often sought to champion, we would make it count now if never again. Any violent reprisals can only do the cause of progress infinite harm. The life of every one brought into this case must be sacred. He who strikes at one of them strikes a blow at liberty and progress and justice and hope for a better world comparable to this execution of innocence. Should there be lawless violence, then reaction everywhere will not only retaliate in kind, but will seize upon it as proof of the necessity of maintaining itself by any means whatsoever. That way lie only madness and destruction. It is the American way to accept such a defeat in peace, however bitter the spirit, and then, by time-honored methods, seek to make a recurrence impossible.

As for those Tories who in their clubs and the marts of trade will rejoice that, innocent or guilty, Sacco and Vanzetti are going to their graves, we would delve into the past once more. The orator is Wendell Phillips:

> Men walked Boston streets, when night fell on Bunker's Hill, and pitied Warren, saying, "Foolish man! Thrown away his life! Why didn't he measure his means better?" Now we see him standing colossal on that blood-stained sod, and severing that day the tie which bound Boston to Great Britain. That night George III ceased to rule in New England. History will date Virginia Emancipation from Harper's Ferry. True, the slave is still there. So, when the tempest uproots a pine on your hills, it looks green for months—a year or two. Still, it is timber, not a tree. John Brown has loosened the roots of the slave system; it only breathes—it does not live—hereafter.

Let those who would uphold the present system by force beware lest it look green for a while, yet still prove timber and not a tree. Let them beware lest August 10, 1927, be forever recorded as the day of a great American change.

SERGEI MIKHAILOVICH EISENSTEIN

Mass Movies   *November 9, 1927*

> Sergei Eisenstein, the great Soviet film director, wrote "Mass Movies" for *The Nation*'s special issue on the tenth anniversary of the Russian Revolution. (Other Soviet contributors included Lenin's widow Nadezhda Krupskaya and the writer Mikhail Zoshchenko.) Two years later Eisenstein's film *Potemkin* was released.

I am a civil engineer and mathematician by training. I approach the making of a motion picture in much the same way as I would the equipment of a poultry farm or the installation of a water system. My point of view is thoroughly utilitarian, rational, materialistic.

When the little "collective" which I direct hits on a subject we do not draft plans in an office. Nor do I go and sit under an oak tree waiting for poetic inspiration. Our slogan is "Down with intuitive creation." Instead we wallow in life. Having chosen the village as the theme of our latest production, "Generalnaya Linya" (General Peasant Policy), we dip into the archives of the Commissariat of Agriculture. Thousands of peasant complaints are perused. We attend village soviet meetings and listen to village gossips. The picture—it will be finished on January 1—shows the power of the soil over man and aims to teach the town-dweller understanding and affection for the peasant. We took the actors from night-lodging houses; we picked them up on the road. The "heroine" must plow and milk a cow.

Our films do not center around an individual or a triangle. We want to develop the public, not the actor. This is a reflection of the spirit of collectivism which is abroad in the land. Nor do we attempt to excite vicarious participation in the lives of the persons of the drama; that is an appeal to sentiment. The cinema can make a far bigger contribution and a far stronger impression by projecting matter and bodies rather than feelings. We photograph an echo and the rat-a-tat-tat of a machine-gun. The impression is physiological. Our psychological approach is on the one hand that of the great Russian scholar, Pavlov, with his principle of reflexology, and on the other, that of the Austrian Freud—the principle of psychoanalysis.

Take the scene in "Potemkin" where the Cossacks slowly, deliberately walk down the Odessa steps firing into the masses. By consciously combining the elements of legs, steps, blood, people, we produce an impression—of what kind? The spectator does not imagine himself at the Odessa wharf in 1905. But as the soldiers' boots press forward he physically recoils. He tries to get out of the range of the bullets. As the baby carriage of the crazed mother goes over the side of the mole he holds on to his cinema chair. He does not want to fall into the water.

Our mounting method is a further aid in achieving such effects. Some countries in which the picture industry is highly developed do not use mounting at all. A sled rushes down a snowy toboggan and you merely see it sliding and skidding to the bottom. We photograph the bumps, and the movie goer feels them, and hears them, too, from the orchestra pit just as he did the throbbing of the engines when the armored cruiser "Potemkin" moved into battle. For this reason, probably, the movement of things and of machines in our pictures is not a part quickly to be passed over but one of absorbing interest. Mounting—the interlacing of close-ups, of side-views, top-views, bottom-views—is the most important part of our work. A picture is either made or unmade by it. Such methods cannot be adapted to the theater. I started in the theater, with the Proletcult, but left it for motion pictures. The theater, I believe, is a dying institution. It is the handiwork of the petty artisan. The movie reflects heavy, highly organized industry.

The scenic effect is calculated; so also is the ideological effect. We never start a picture without knowing why. "Potemkin" was an episode of revolutionary heroism calculated to electrify the masses. "Generalnaya Linya" seeks to encourage the bond between the city and the village – the outstanding political task of Bolshevism. "October," which will be shown all over the Union on November 7, depicts the ten days in the autumn of 1917 that shook the world. It shows history being made by the man in the street, by the worker from the foundry, by the lousy soldier from the trench. It identifies the common citizen of today with that history.

Conditions make our work easy. Night after night from four to five thousand Leningrad workers volunteered to participate in the storming of the Winter Palace which forms part of "October." The government supplied the arms and uniforms, as well as the army. In addition to workers and soldiers, we needed a mob. But word was whispered about and the militia had to be summoned to keep away the tens of thousands.

In "Potemkin" the Black Sea fleet was put at our disposal. On November 7, 1917, the flagship Aurora of the Baltic squadron joined the Communists and proceeded up the Neva to bombard the Winter Palace. The state lent us the Aurora for the reenactment of this scene in "October." We likewise had the use of tanks and artillery.

As we stick to life for our subjects so we stick to life for our scenery. We never build streets, or cities, or villages. The natural ones are truer. The detail of permission is easily arranged. No private owner or entrepreneur can object to the photographing of his premises or demand payment for the privilege. These things cheapen production.

"Potemkin" was a poster. "Generalnaya Linya" and "October" are subtler. They are nearer life. We are learning. We feel that our method is the only correct one and that its potentialities are unlimited.

Our method and America's highly developed movie technique ought to be a powerful combination. For this reason we are interested in an invitation to work in the United States during the next year. If our activities here permit, and if we are granted freedom of action in the United States, we may soon be there.

EZRA POUND

The Passport Nuisance

November 30, 1927

> *The Nation* never published Ezra Pound's verse, but it did
> publish his articles on the witlessness of passport officials
> (1927) and the sins of American libraries and musical found-
> ations (1929).

"The American people does not think." Very well, no mass of 120,000,000 people ever has thought; it takes but the most rudimentary knowledge of crowd-
psychology, unanimism, etc., to know that thought does not occur in such
aggregates. Why expect our nation to surpass, all so easily and so undesigningly,
the records of the past and "great nations of antiquity"?

"The American people does not remember." Another age-old quality or defect
of the populace, the traditional populace. Americans under thirty do not remember pre-war Europe, for the natural reason that they mostly never saw it; and in
consequence they cannot be expected to become especially enraged over particular imbecilities that have developed in Europe since 1914 or 1918.

Elder American tourists have not all of them been in Europe before; and we
are, let us suppose, the most patient and nebulous race of beings that have ever
moved on this planet. The majority of tourists appear to believe that European
conditions were always as bad as they now are; their historic perspective does
not reach back to, let us say, the causes of Wilson's first election. We are, as a
nation, educated to look not to the past but the future; as the simple-minded fresh-
man is told to look up—while you slip a bit of ice down the front of his collar.

The post-war annual exodus to Europe is divisible roughly into three or four
parts: (1) The studious, I mean the young, actively acquisitive explorers; (2) the
cultural, I mean the patient old ladies who have been saving up for some time;
(3) the drunks (a post-war phenomenon—this—in any such quantity as to demand
special treatment), and (4) the shoppers. I suppose these are all particularly patient classes. The old ladies have learned patience; the young are still accustomed
to be being interfered with by college deans and other such formenifera; the
drunks are so relieved by the prevalence of certain facilities that they are ready
to put up with anything; the shoppers are notably idiots, and besides they usually
have attendants to take trouble for them. (So also have the envoys of the Standard
Oil and other legendary monsters with whom the bureaucracy distinctly does
not monkey.)

While Europe still "groaned under tyranny" I wandered about the face of this
continent, I went on foot into its by-ways for sixteen years with no "papers," that

is to say with no brass checks, no government's petty officials' permission, nothing in fact, but for one year (1911, I think it was) an unstamped membership card to the Touring Club de France, and a tin button of that fraternity which helped me to get into a small inn at Chalus when covered with twenty miles of mud.

This comfortable period is "over"; not permanently, if I can help it, but at any rate suspended; and this suspension has continued for six or eight years too long. To trace the remote causes of any ill odor is a thankless task, especially if the search reveal such national treasures and sources of civic pride as the late Bryan, the late Wilson, and the unfortunately still extant personnel of the United States Department of State. It is, alas, almost wholly forgotten that Bryan gave Wilson to America; and that Wilson subsequently introduced into international affairs an academic mind; a mind used not to dealing with adults, but to administering petty formalities to an adolescent scholastic body. And whatever ultimately be said by Mr. Wilson's apologists, and whatever final praise be given to his aims and aspirations, there remains at least one private conviction that during his rule the civic organization of America suffered very great damage; that the individual welfare of the citizen went by the board; that the powers of all classes of officials were extended beyond the limits of decency, and beyond limits compatible with the permanent safety of the commonwealth.

Yes, these are very large words. Let 'em stand. What, gentle reader, *are* bureaucrats? Hired janitors who think they own the whole building. The French, being more given to speculation than we, have recently produced several students of bureaucracy, several authors who have studied the *fonctionnaire* as one studies other poisonous insects, and even tried to explain and account for his actions, his inhibitions. The result is not encouraging. One can sympathize with a tyrant, led on by some megalomania or some dream of ultimate benefit to the race or some decoration of his own personal glory; one can sympathize with the crook who does it for excitement, or the poor devil who steals to feed himself or his family; but for the *rond-de-cuir* who sits in an office devising, in perfect safety, some inane means of annoying others, one can have no tolerance.

Mr. Wilson might have made a fairly successful Emperor of Byzantium; in the year 853 few of his habits would have greatly annoyed the populace of that city. But a President who exceeds his functions naturally encourages the small fry to follow suit. There had been, before Wilson's election, very few Democrats; the supply for normal appointees was short, and for the abnormal war demands, still shorter. The war produced, if not a new ruling class, at least a new zealous bossiness.

I had my first meeting with the new civic order during the armistice. I was living in London. I was told that I "could not go to France unless I had business." I naturally had business. I received a lot of other improbable information from the under-sub-vice-assistant. My wife could not possibly accompany me unless she were ill. I naturally produced doctors' certificates. I could not move about in France; I must go to one place and stay there. At this point I was rescued by an elderly intelligent official from another department who took two hours off and swore to several contradictory statements in a manner showing great familiarity with the mind-ersatz of officialdom.

I went to France. When I got to Toulouse I found, as I had suspected, that the under-sub-vice-assistant's information was false. The young chap at the *mairie* told me I could do as I liked, and that I was free to walk into the Pyrenees. A few miles from the Spanish border an officer on horseback rode up behind me and asked where was I going. I said "Mt. Segur." He said "All right, go there. I am looking for French deserters."

This was, you perceive, before the so-called Peace of Versailles, and before all Europe had gone crazy over formalities. I had no trouble till I got back to Paris and entered the American consulate. There the vice-assistant-second-sub categorically forbade me to return to my home in London. I said: "I live there," and suggested that he ask the assistant-first-vice or some one higher up concerning the regulations. He disappeared behind a partition, and returned with a request that I "get a letter" from my employer, evidently knowing no strata of life save one where *everyone* has an employer. It was next suggested that I find some sort of "reference" for myself. Every American I had known in Paris before the war had left. I knew no one save the Ambassador whom I had met two days before. I thought vaguely that he might have other things to do—at that particular time —than look after passports. However, I stepped into a taxi and drove round to the embassy. The embassy dealt with the consulate, and I proceeded about my lawful occasions.

That was 1919, and Europe was, confessedly, in a mess, and errors might be exceptions. But what in heaven's name has that temporary confusion to do with 1924, 1925, 1926, 1927? What has it to do with the unending boredom of waiting an hour, a half-hour, three hours, in countless bureaus, for countless useless visas, identities, folderols?

England is not richer than we are; England is not less exposed to the immigration of undesirable units. The British passport costs seven shillings, sixpence (less than two dollars); it is good for seven years. Visas to other countries have either been mutually abolished or their cost reduced to a trifle.

The American official and executive group does not desire the comfort and convenience of the American individual. And what is more, we have one of the clumsiest systems of communication between individuals, and unorganized groups of individuals, that exists in any allegedly representative government. Apart from our tendency to put up with anything, and our instilled duty to be humorous instead of taking action, the normal American has no idea whatsoever as to how he should or can deal with any executive infamy. That, I take it, is part of the price we pay for having our national capital tucked away in a corner. The English who do most things badly are at least able to get at their rulers. Someone takes little Whiff or old Jiblet out on a golf-links and wrings his figurative neck; someone knows so-and-so and the matter gets a few moments' attention. Anything causing inconvenience to ten or twenty thousand literate people can be got on the floor of the House of Commons in, I should say, forty-eight hours. In the United States this could only happen if the issue affected some very large organized business.

Our ideal public servant was given a one-column-wide, four-inch newspaper boost some months ago: "Aged 70 and a bachelor, has not taken a vacation for 20 years, has never indulged in sports or other games, but occasionally enjoyed a good cigar."

Yehudi Menuhin
[letter to the editor]

December 28, 1927

TO THE EDITOR OF THE NATION:

SIR: It may interest you to know that Yehudi Menuhin loves his weekly *Nation* next best to his violin. It is upon his request that I am now asking you to see to it that we do not miss any copies. *The Nation* is of a great help to us to give Yehudi a liberal education. We prefer to teach him privately at home. He has not reached his tenth birthday.

A few days ago, while on a hike with his best friend through the Golden Gate Park, prior to his appearance with the San Francisco Symphony Orchestra as soloist in the Tchaikovsky Concerto, I overheard their heated debate about Debs. His friend told him that the high-school teacher had called Debs "a downright law-breaker"; to which Yehudi answered that on the contrary Debs was "not only a lover of humanity but also a lover of human individuals. . . . "

San Francisco, December 18, 1926   MOSHE MENUHIN

CARLETON BEALS

With Sandino in Nicaragua   *February 22-April 18, 1928*

For six years, from 1927 to 1933, Augusto César Sandino led
the resistance to the U.S. Marines' intervention in Nicaragua.
His David and Goliath exploits are the theme of Nicaraguan
songs and ballads. On January 5, 1928, eight months after Sandino began his heroic struggle, Villard cabled journalist Carleton Beals in Mexico City requesting that he find and interview
Sandino for *The Nation*.

Five weeks later, when Beals filed the first installment of his
exclusive interview with Sandino, *The Nation* ran this editorial
note: "One American correspondent has got through to Sandino. . . . For almost two weeks he has been with Sandino's
troops, riding with them on horseback nearly halfway across
Nicaragua. With good luck he has escaped the bullets of the
marines and the bombs from the airplanes and has made his
way safely across the lines into "American" territory. Now, safe
in Managua he is sending the story of what he saw and what he
heard on that extraordinary journey. Against Lindbergh's
good-will flight, we match the good-will mission of Mr. Beals,
who toiled through the jungles instead of flying above them.
. . . He is the only foreign correspondent who has been behind Sandino's lines; the only American who has interviewed
that stubborn leader of a forlorn hope . . . *The Nation*'s desire
for full reports from both sides of the lines, and our correspondent's courageous readiness to undertake an uncertain and
hazardous mission, will, we hope, result in a new degree of
understanding of the State Department's 'war' in Nicaragua and
its purposes in waging it."

By cable from Managua, Nicaragua, February 11, 1928

Several days ago I rode out of the camp of General Augusto C. Sandino, the terrible "bandit" of Nicaragua who is holding the marines at bay. Not a single hair
of my blond, Anglo-Saxon head had been injured. On the contrary, I had been
shown every possible kindness. I went, free to take any route I might choose, with
permission to relate to anybody I encountered any and every thing I had seen and
heard. Perhaps my case is unique. I am the first and only American since Sandino
began fighting the marines who has been granted an official interview, and I am
the first bona fide correspondent of any nationality to talk to him face to face.

"Do you still think us bandits?" was his last query as I bade him goodby.

"You are as much a bandit as Mr. Coolidge is a bolshevik," was my reply.

"Tell your people," he returned, "there may be bandits in Nicaragua, but they
are not necessarily Nicaraguans."

It was the high hour of a cold night when I galloped in the teeth of an icy wind with three Sandinista officers into the main Sandino camp at San Rafael. It marked the climax of months of effort. It marked the climax of two weeks spent in establishing proper contacts all the way from Mexico City through Guatemala and San Salvador to Tegucigalpa, the capital of Honduras. It marked the climax of more than two weeks of hardship and the danger of being shot or bombed by both sides. Riding horseback from Tegucigalpa halfway across Nicaragua with Sandino troops through the almost impassable mountains of Nueva Segovia, through the jungles of the Coco River basin, occasionally within a few rods of the American lines, I finally reached my goal at San Rafael. There Sandino had been considerate enough to await me before marching south to Matagalpa. . . .

February 20, 1928
Grippe had me nailed to a cross; my bones were cracking with fever, but at eight o'clock at night we set out in a driving storm. We wove in and out of the back alleys of the town, took to the meadow, and sought at full gallop the southeast trail. Dogs barked, doors flashed open, but we vanished, leaving many to wonder what travelers were doing on the road at such an hour in such a storm. . . .

Bluefields, Nicaragua, February 27, 1928
Our Odyssey had begun. From the San Pedro ranch, the point where our connections with the next Sandino outpost were broken and we lost track of the route taken by General Sandino after his evacuation of El Chipote, our way led us even deeper into the mountains in an ever-widening inland circle about the scene of operations of the American marines. On every hand loomed height after height, crags and ridges, profound valleys, enormous precipices, all blanketed with the most dense tropical vegetation. On some days the earth simmered under a hot, tropical sky; at other times it was almost invisible while tropical storms deluged it. These would have been difficult mountains to cross even if we had known the exact direction of the trail we had to follow in order to reach Sandino. . . .

San Jose, Costa Rica, March 4, 1928
Though the wind howled over Remango we spent the night snugly in the long barracks. The soldiers were as free and easy as if the enemy were a thousand miles away instead of on the next ridge. . . .

After too few hours of sleep the blast of the bugler brought me to, fumbling for matches and shoes at the grim hour of four, according to schedule. In less than half an hour, Sandino received me in his office in the rear main barracks by the light of a lantern.

Sandino was born on May 19, 1893, in the village of Niquinohomo. He is short, not more than five feet five. When I saw him he was dressed in a uniform of dark brown with almost black puttees, immaculately polished; a silk red-and-black handkerchief knotted about his throat; and a broad-brimmed Texas Stetson hat, pulled low over his forehead and pinched shovel-shaped. Occasionally, as we conversed, he shoved his sombrero to the back of his head and hitched his chair forward. This gesture revealed straight black hair and a full forehead. His face makes a straight line from the temple to the jaw-bone. His jaw-bone makes a sharp angle with the rest of his face, slanting to an even, firm jaw. His regular, curved eyebrows are arched high above liquid black eyes without visible pupils. His eyes are of remarkable mobility and refraction to light—quick, intense eyes. He is utterly without vices, has an unequivocal sense of personal justice and a keen eye for the welfare of the humblest soldier. "Many battles have made our hearts hard, but our souls strong" is one of his pet sayings. I am not sure of the first part of the epigram, for in all the soldiers and all of the officers I talked to he has stimulated a fierce affection and a blind loyalty and has instilled his own burning hatred of the invader.

"Death is but a tiny moment of discomfort not to be taken seriously," he repeats over and over to his soldiers. Or he will say: "Death most quickly singles out him who fears death."

There is a religious note in his thinking. He frequently mentions God—"God the ultimate arbiter of our battles;" or "God willing, we go on to victory;" or "God and our mountains fight for us." His sayings run from tongue to tongue through his little army.

In our interview with Sandino he first mentioned some battles fought near Chipote. He claimed that all told nearly four hundred marines had lost their lives. This, of course, was an obvious exaggeration. General Feland insisted that only seventeen have died, but I am convinced after talking with many marine officers that the American casualties total between forty and sixty.

After describing the manner in which several American airplanes were brought down, Sandino in rapid fire gave me the basis of his demands in the present struggle: first, evacuation of Nicaraguan territory by the marines; second, the appointment of an impartial civilian President chosen by the notables of the three parties—one who has never been President and never a candidate for the Presidency; third, supervision of the elections by Latin America.

"The day these conditions are carried out," declared Sandino, "I will immediately cease all hostilities and disband my forces. In addition I shall never accept a government position, elective or otherwise. I shall not accept any government salary or pension. No position, no salary—this I swear. I will not accept any personal reward either today or tomorrow, or at any time in the future."

He left his chair and paced to and fro to emphasize this point. He stated vehemently: "Never, never will I accept public office. I am fully capable of gaining a livelihood for myself and my wife in some humble, happy pursuit. By trade I am a mechanic and if necessary I will return to my trade. Nor will I ever take up arms again in any struggle between the Liberals and Conservatives, nor, indeed, in any other domestic struggle – only in case of a new foreign invasion. We have taken up arms from the love of our country because all other leaders have betrayed it and have sold themselves out to the foreigner or have bent the neck in cowardice. We, in our own house, are fighting for our inalienable rights. What right have foreign troops to call us outlaws and bandits and to say that we are the aggressors? I repeat that we are in our own house. We declare that we will never live in cowardly peace under a government installed by a foreign Power. Is this patriotism or is it not? And when the invader is vanquished, as some day he must be, my men will be content with their plots of ground, their tools, their mules, and their families." . . .

February 29, 1928

. . . "We are not protesting against the size of the invasion," [said Sandino,] "but against invasion. The United States has meddled in Nicaragua for many years. We cannot merely depend upon her promise that she will some day get out. Every day intervention is more pronounced. The United States promised to give the Philippines their independence, but American troops still remain in the Philippines; they are still a subject people.

"You tell me that the governments of Honduras and El Salvador are hostile to me. Tomorrow they will regret such an attitude. All of Central America is morally obliged to help us in this struggle. Tomorrow each may have the same struggle. Central America should stand together against the invader instead of with the governments that ally themselves with the foreigner.". . .

"What," I asked Sandino, "do you consider the motives of the American Government?"

"The American Government," he said with a lurking smile, "desires to protect American lives and property. But I can say that I have never touched a pin belonging to an American. I have had respect for the property of everybody. And no American who has come to Nicaragua without arms in his hands has been injured by us.". . .

Managua, March 6, 1928

. . . When later we crossed into the Coco River basin, the cry was the same: "The Machos are coming!" "They will burn our houses." Here again, part of the region had lost many inhabitants.

Whatever the rest of Nicaragua may think of us, this little corner knows only bitterness and hatred. We have taken a place in the minds of these people with the hated Spanish conquerors of other days. The password runs among the people and it echoes in their songs: "We must win our second independence, this time from the Americans, from the Machos, the Yankees, the hated Gringos." Names enough they have for us.

My personal opinion is that if Sandino had arms he could raise an army of ten thousand men by snapping his fingers; that if he marched into Managua, the capital, tomorrow, he would receive the greatest ovation in Nicaraguan history. America's friends in Nicaragua are the politicians who have bled the country for so many decades, they are the politicians who wish to stay in power or to get into power with our help. I would not advise any American marine to walk lonely roads at night in Nicaragua.

FREDA KIRCHWEY

Out of Bondage
November 21, 1928

In the 1920s, *Nation* editor Freda Kirchwey wrote frequently about a woman's right to a planned pregnancy and urged the dissemination of birth control information.

Before me lies one of the most revolutionary documents ever published. It is, on its face, a collection of letters chosen from among the quarter-million or more received by the American Birth Control League, assembled here as a demonstration of the need of rescinding the laws which now forbid even the medical profession from giving information about the prevention of conception. It is called "Motherhood in Bondage" and is introduced by an appeal for sense and decency by Margaret Sanger. If you read one or two of the letters and feel the ignorance and panic that lie behind them you will undoubtedly be moved to a warm pity for human beings so desperately ensnared. If you read them all you will be stirred to wrath and shame. Taken separately each letter is a plea for help; together they become a shout of protest. The dynamic effect of hundreds and thousands of emotional outbursts gathered into a single explosion is terrifying and hopeful. Such feeling, so strong and so despairing, rooted in the deep centers of energy and life, pushing up and bursting out under such irresistible pressure—this, it seems certain, must finally shatter the forces that oppose it, backed though they are by gods and hobgoblins and all the more genteel forms of fear.

Those who read André Siegfried's lively and penetrating volume, "America's Coming of Age," can hardly have forgotten his picture of a civilization in which repression and standardization, accepted without undue protest by the vast complacent majority, rob individuals of an opportunity to live and move according to their personal desires. Americans—he said in effect—are people who love to pass laws, especially restrictive laws. Americans are people who wish to make their neighbors do things they would not do themselves. Americans are people who consider "the needs of the community supreme." Hence prohibition, hence restricted immigration, hence—even more particularly—eugenics. "If you visit the United States," said M. Siegfried, "you must not forget your Bible, but you must also take a treatise on eugenics. Armed with these two talismans, you will never get beyond your depth." He discussed the influence of Lothrop Stoddard and the Ku Klux Klan, and very specifically sought to identify the birth-control movement with these advocates of the supremacy of the Protestant Nordic.

But here, I believe, M. Siegfried was betrayed by his eagerness to make everything fit smoothly and evenly into his pattern of repression. Undoubtedly many eugenists support birth control; for all I know Mr. Lothrop Stoddard may make an annual contribution to the League. But when we consider M. Siegfried's "typical American"—he who elected Herbert Hoover and defeated Al Smith; who instinctively and indiscriminately dislikes Irish Catholics, communism, Jews, Italians, beer, and labor unions; the pious hillsman of the South, the Methodist minister in a Kansas town, the New England farmer—we find him solidly against birth control. This may astonish M. Siegfried, for he is a Frenchman and a logician. Obviously, if the domination of the Nordic is to be perpetuated, he must somehow seduce the "undesirables" and the aliens into reducing their birth-rate. If reason were to prevail the Birth Control League would be able to count on the solid backing of the fundamentalist majority.

But logic is not a vice of the fundamentalist. He is against birth control. He detests the very words. He shrinks from the thought behind the words. Birth control can hardly be considered without considering sex, and sex should be suppressed and ignored as far as possible. If children are born, let us not dwell on the incidences of their origin; let us presume that God sent them to bless our homes, and leave the matter there. Besides, says the fundamentalist under his breath, what will become of morals if people can sin without fear? And so, if pushed to the choice, the conventional and pious Nordic Protestant will refuse even the fundamental logic of self-preservation, which seems to him to imply, not regimentation and coercion as M. Siegfried would maintain, but new and alarming forms of freedom. By his different route, he arrives at the same attitude toward birth control as that maintained by the Catholic Church.

And the bigots of both faiths are right; they do well to fear the effect of a widespread knowledge of birth control methods. At present such knowledge is in the hands of the upper classes—through bootleggers—and the effect of it has been to change the habits and morals and economic status of middle-class women, and to modify almost beyond recognition the middle-class home. Some of this knowledge gets through to the poorer classes. But, like bootlegged liquor, it is apt to be poisonous—the more so, the cheaper the bootlegger. So the women of the working class are dying from the effects of drugs and abortions, when they are not dying from the effects of too many children; and a bitter, passionate clamor for fair treatment is beginning to sound through muffling layers of poverty and repression. Not for the sake of the dwindling Nordic, but for their own health and happiness and security and freedom and for their children's future, these women are going to have what they want. If you doubt it, read "Motherhood in Bondage."

HEYWOOD BROUN

It Seems to Heywood Broun *January 2, 1929*

Heywood Broun's column, "It Seems to Heywood Broun," ran from 1927 to 1937. In 1928 Broun, journalist and critic, had used his *Nation* page to express editorial disagreements with his main employer, the *New York World*, for which he wrote a daily column; its editor fired him for "disloyalty." Nine years later, Broun left *The Nation* for *The New Republic*, ostensibly because that magazine published articles criticizing President Roosevelt's plan to enlarge the Supreme Court. The first news Freda Kirchwey had of Broun's move was when *The New Republic* sent copy for an exchange advertisement in *The Nation* announcing the acquisition of Broun. Here Broun, who organized the American Newspaper Guild in 1933 and was its first president, relishes the freedom to criticize his employer.

I am asked to write a piece on "What's the matter with *The Nation*." Once I lost a job for something much like that, but easy come easy go. Accordingly, I hazard the opinion that *The Nation* suffers chiefly from the fact that it is edited by gentlemen and, almost I fear, by ladies. These are not terms of approbation in my vocabulary. I think a journal of opinion serves the community best if it is not too finicky. Naturally one hopes to find it honest. Few have ever questioned the sincerity of *The Nation*. Nor am I contending that the magazine should go completely yellow. But I would like more gusto. Often *The Nation* moves speedily enough in the defense of good causes, but there is no one on the board of control who gives me the impression of actually enjoying the business of fighting. There is too much regard for the Queensberry tradition. I like to see a liberal journal get aroused to the point of yodeling into battle and of biting in the clinches when it gets there.

This has happened in the history of *The Nation*, but all too infrequently. After the execution of Sacco and Vanzetti the magazine carried across its front page the screaming slogan "Massachusetts the Murderer." It would be hard to justify completely this title which Mr. Villard chose for his article. It was at any rate an overstatement. But surely there is historical precedent for the use of hyperbole by all who would steer the world out of its current courses. The scheme of *The Nation* seems to be to intellectualize mankind closer to Utopia. That can't be done. Even the most logical scheme for betterment gets nowhere unless it is expedited by the oil of emotion.

I am not contending that Mr. Villard and his associates constitute a bloodless crew. There's marrow in them but over the entire organization there clings the malarial mist of good taste. This, of course, is a term which needs defining. Fashions in taste vary from year to year. *The Nation* abides by the standards which animated the old *Evening Post* in the days of Mr. Villard's leadership. Clearly it is his intention to be both radical and respectable. And this, I hold, is a difficult combination. In justice to *The Nation* it must be admitted that patriotic organizations here and there have regarded it as inflammable and as undoubtedly in the pay of Soviet Russia. But such compliments are not deserved. For the most part *The Nation* has spoken softly and carried a swagger stick.

If it could have been married to the old *Masses* something of great quality might have been derived from the union. From the radical rag a necessary rowdiness could have been inherited, while on the other side Mr. Villard's prejudices against the newer art and poetry for once would not have been amiss. I am aware that the marriage of which I speak would have entailed great difficulties. *The Nation,* to be sure, is a liberal rather than a radical weekly. To me liberalism is by no means a burnt-out political philosophy, but all liberal leaders in America must face the charge that they have done little more than take radicalism and dilute it with cold water. My advice to *The Nation* would be to go ahead every now and then and be outrageously unfair and violent and decidedly ribald. No journal of protest is doing its job unless it gets barred from the mails once and so often.

The Nation is in special need of ribaldry. Here is a reform magazine in which the canons of good taste are almost as rigorous as those of the Boston *Transcript.* When Mr. Villard first gave me sanctuary within his pages and promised that I should have my say without let or hindrance I was grateful. I may have also been a little suspicious, for such promises are more easy to make than to keep. But a close friend of the magazine informed me I need have no fear. This time liberty did mean license. One warning he gave me. "You and Mr. Villard think sufficiently alike," he told me, "not to clash. There is only one point upon which you are likely to get into trouble. It is quite possible that you may write something which he will regard as dirty. Mr. Villard has an extremely conservative point of view with respect to obscenity."

But, as a matter of fact, the issue never came up. Soon after beginning on the paper I made a test case. In reviewing "The President's Daughter" I strove to be a little rowdy in my language. Nothing was altered and nobody told me not to do it again. Rather sadly Mr. Villard showed me several letters from old subscribers who complained that for the first time they had seen something in the pages of *The Nation* calculated to bring a blush to any proper cheek. Mr. Villard had gone through with his part of the bargain and I never tried him in this way again. Although I knew that he would allow me I, too, have my inhibitions and it is not possible for me to hurt a friend too much.

At this point I must digress a moment to avoid the charge of smugness. In saying that *The Nation* lacks gusto and ribaldry I have no intention of suggesting that I am just the proper person to supply these missing ingredients. I have a phobia in open places and vastly fear to find myself beyond the usual fences. I was thinking of somebody about like Mike Gold but less windy. However, I hope it will not be considered swanky if I maintain that I am much less the gentleman than Oswald Garrison Villard. It is a curious piece of casting which finds him head, and also body, of the most effective rebel periodical in America. It seems to me that *The Nation* deserves the title even though it is far less than the journal of a dream. In so many respects Mr. Villard is an extremely conservative man.

Once at a conference, I remember, the managing editor asked him if he could write a piece on Charles E. Hughes and turn it in on the following morning. He pleaded an engagement which would keep him busy through the evening. Pressed as to the nature of the date which took him away from *The Nation's* business he finally admitted that he had tickets for the Winter Garden. And the managing editor, with a shrewdness one would not have expected in a girl so young, replied, "Well, never mind the article in that case. I think it would be better for the magazine to have Mr. Villard go to the Winter Garden than sit up with Charles E. Hughes."

But Oswald Garrison Villard has not yet paid a sufficient number of visits to the Winter Garden. In fact his schedule ought to include as well the Dizzy Club, the Whoopee, and the Jungle Room. These are not the wells of wisdom but such contacts do belong as post-graduate work in the curriculum of any integrated personality. I regard it as sheer tragedy that one of the ablest progressive editors in America is a total abstainer. Or thereabouts. This fact does influence certain important decisions of *The Nation*. For instance in the last campaign there were many logical reasons why the magazine should support Thomas rather than Smith. Still, Mr. Villard leaned toward Smith. That, in my opinion, was the way *The Nation* should have gone. It never did, or at any rate not in whole-hearted fashion and I believe the hitch lay in the fact that Oswald Garrison Villard could not quite bring himself to enthusiastic support of a man who was said to drink highballs. Put vine leaves in Villard's hair and the circulation of *The Nation* would reach 200,000 before the year was out.

This article may seem to be less "What is wrong with *The Nation*" than "Why

Villard is less than Lincoln." I don't see how that can be avoided. *The Nation* is Oswald Garrison Villard. No other personality animates it. Even if we could make the boss a bit more rakish one other important reform would still be necessary. Intrenched capital he would tear down. All the pat slogans of militaristic patriotism he abhors. Where the Constitution pinches human liberty Villard would amend it. But he won't change type styles. A font is a shrine to him and though *The Nation* may preach what seems to some little less than red rebellion it will always appear in a frock-coated form.

This may not be a defect. I'll grant that the point is debatable. Possibly it is not necessary to get down to shirtsleeves in order to ascertain what is wrong with the world. But I think it is. I take issue with Chesterton who once maintained that in order to be a successful radical a man should be 90 per cent conservative. In the matter of editors the reverse appeals to me. The boss of a progressive weekly might be allowed a dislike for modern music or painting or he could be a slave of tradition in the matter of his stamp collection. In all other respects I should like to see him go the whole hog. Political radicalism in America has been for the most part carried on by personalities split in twain. Bryan who headed the Middle-Western revolt was always a stern fundamentalist in his religious views. Roosevelt who created the Bull Moose Party could not abide the thought of birth control. This may seem to some not inconsistent, but I feel that political action is never more than half the problem of reform. A rebel must be a man dissatisfied with many things in addition to the law of the land.

So far Oswald Garrison Villard has been treated as a static personality. As a matter of fact I never expect to find him addicted to big headlines or flamboyant pictures on the cover of his magazine. But old associates tell me that he changed enormously within the last few years in his views about the younger generation — to use a convenient phrase. It may be that the visit to the Winter Garden did accomplish something. I still think he should go again.

LIONEL TRILLING

Is Literature Possible?

October 15, 1930

Lionel Trilling, critic, writer and teacher, was a frequent contributor to the magazine in the 1930s and 1940s.

I

In the last twenty years, critical writing about American literature has successively occupied four main positions: first, the declaration of the non-existence of
any literature worth the name; second, about 1915, the acclamation of a new literature, fresh in kind and spirit; third, the discovery, some five years ago, of an
immaturity and insufficiency in the new writers; and fourth, now current, a sociological explanation of the failure of American writing and a prediction of the inevitable doom of all American art.

This last position is Spenglerian in derivation and tendency. The hope of the
last generation, that the machine would make for a great improvement in human
life, has ended in disappointment. That the machine, far from raising the plane
of human life, exercises an intolerable tyranny over it has become one of the commonplaces of modern thought. Upon it the exponents of Spenglerian literary criticism base their explanation of the present inferiority of American art and their
prediction of its eventual disappearance. They find that this tyranny of the machine over life affects art in three ways. It works on the artist himself, on the
material of his art, and on the social validity of the very function of art.

At the very beginning of his career – so the argument runs – the artist is in danger. For in our age the rewards of business are far greater than the rewards of
art, so that men of talent and of sufficient energy to make this talent effective are
drawn off from pursuits that in previous ages they might have blindly followed,
and are used in commerce and in technical pursuits. Or, if the artist is not tempted
away from his art, to continue in it under our economic system is so difficult that
he has not the equanimity to pursue it fruitfully. Further, he is forced to live in
an environment that oppresses his spirit – an environment without joy, without
gaiety, refusing him encouragement or fertilization.

This in itself would not be insupportable. But – continues the argument – not
only is it difficult to possess the simple necessities of the artistic life: what is worse
is that there is no important subject matter with which the American artist can
deal. American life, reduced to a sordid uniformity by the machine, offers no
break in its surface by which art can grasp it. The machine has impressed the individual into the mob. And with the mob art has never dealt and cannot deal.

Then, too, that sense, which every writer of considerable genius has had, of influencing and directing, in some measure, his world, cannot be enjoyed by the American artist. He must feel the arrogant imperturbability of the social structure he inhabits; he knows that his word can have no part in changing its habits or form.

And finally — the argument concludes — not only is it difficult for the artist to survive; not only does he lack a reasonable subject matter for his art and the feeling that he occupies a place in a society which, in some degree, is resilient to his touch; but art itself becomes less and less a necessary function or instrument of life. For mechanism regiments the emotions and categorizes the problems of living; mechanism supplies in itself a satisfaction to emotional needs and an answer to all questionings. It supplants the old human values with new mechanical ones. Emotional desires are satisfied — or deadened — by minor mechanisms: an inclosed shower, a squad of drilled flunkies, a washing-machine, a new car. Or sometimes the means of emotional satisfaction take deceptively the forms of art, the mass-produced amusement of the magazines and movies. By mechanism, all the subtle problems of one's relation to one's fellow-men and the momentous ones of one's relation to the universe are reduced to the simple but insistent one of relationship to an economic state which is not a means but an end. And in such an order art can have no use.

II

This position, attractive with a sort of grim sentimentality and sealed with the seven irrefrangible seals of sociological logic, has become widely current. It is based undeniably on truth, but the conclusions which it draws are far from demanding an inevitable assent.

Beginning with the situation of the artist himself, we may reject at once the assertion that the artist is being diverted from art to commerce and technical pursuits. Not only are the rewards of art — even admirable art — still possibly attractive, but we may recognize, in the old romantic fashion, the existence of a distinct artist-type, incapable of choosing freely among the professions the one that will most practically reward his devotion, a man predestined to art. Undoubtedly, the American artist has a sufficiently difficult economic struggle, frequently having to devote too much of his time to pursuits unrelated to art. But this struggle is certainly not materially greater than that of many men in England's nineteenth century. The presence in America of so great a body of writing of not debased, although assuredly mediocre, quality must indicate the possibility of the artist's economic survival.

In regard to his spiritual survival we must be less sanguine. It cannot be denied that even for the non-artistic citizen the conditions of our environment are in many respects far too strenuous not only for spiritual but even for physical health. And it would seem that the great effort expended to support the conditions of our life must inevitably divert energy from the artist's creation. The answer to this must be a simple one, even a puritanic one. Now, as always, we have the right to expect of the artist that he will so order his life that, although he keep himself always sensitive to his environment, he will provide himself with sufficient insulation to keep from being done in by it. The nature of the artistic process is such that the artist can make as good use of repulsive as of attractive material, and since the beginning of the nineteenth century it has been the repulsive rather than the attractive that has been the preoccupation of art. Lawrence and Joyce, to name only two Europeans, have based the great part of their work on the simple theme of repulsive environment. That they were forced to flee from this environment so that they might fully exploit it is of no consequence, just as, on the whole, the emigration and "expatriation" of the American artist is of no essential consequence. The question of whether America is an inhabitable country is not immediately relevant to the present point. The question that concerns us is whether Americans can produce an art comparable in quality to that of Europe since the beginning of the last century—an art of revolt, produced, we must remember, by men who were constantly fleeing from their native land.

But even if it be granted that it is possible for the American artist to survive, has he a scene which will yield fertilely to artistic treatment? Our Spenglerian critics will admit the validity of repulsive environment as an artistic theme, but they will assert that American life is of such a sort that even its repulsiveness cannot be treated. That is, it is so mechanized that nothing can be isolated for art. But this view is scarcely an accurate one, if only because it implies the existence of a kind of order and perfection. And perfection and order of even so debased a form as here implied do not exist in America; what we have is rather disorder under a superficial regimentation.

The material of art has always been the relation of man to himself, of man to fellow-man, of man to the universe. This material still exists, it is still the natural material of art, and in America it is being made both more subtle and more momentous.

If the existence of such material in America be admitted, it becomes impossible to deny the validity of an art which uses it. The indifference of the American public, for whom interest in art is not the major activity it conceivably should be, cannot invalidate it. The validity of art's function does not depend on the breadth or immediacy of its reception; we do not deny validity to Jeremiah's writing because it was not heeded.

If, then, the artist can survive in America, if he has a scene superbly ripe for artistic exploitation, if art still can have validity in America, why has so little art of major importance come out of us? Within limits, the process of the artistic mind reduces every environment to a common denominator, so that the philosophic worlds of Joyce, of Thomas Mann, of D. H. Lawrence, of Gide and Proust are substantially our philosophic world. And yet we have not had men who could treat our actual world in terms comparable to any of these.

It is difficult to state an all-inclusive reason for this failure. Perhaps there is no reason; perhaps in the last decade we have, by mere bad luck, lacked talent. But of this we can be certain: there can be no more disastrous critical move than to lift the blame for this failure from the artist and to place it on the environment. Such a shift, it is true, is in accord with a habit of modern thought in other fields, for example, criminology. But if there is one class of modern man that may be held accountable for its acts, it is the artist class. Nothing could more surely hasten the extinction of the artist than to convince him that he is a mere creature of his immediate environment.

This being the case, the function of the American critic becomes clear. He must cease making obeisance to "environment" and teach the artist that he too must heed his own god. He must make clear to the artist what the function of the artist is — which is not to be a mere literal expression of the life of his race but the imaginative understander, the wise investigator, the angry revolutionist. In short, the critic must help to restore to the artist something of his old function of seer and teacher. It does not much matter if the seer's vision or the teacher's precept be disregarded at the time of its utterance. It is a fate in which history will provide a fine array of colleagues.

Once art was synonymous with social rebellion and was therefore a cause of dread to the respectable. But now in America — if we may judge by any of our critics — the artist is deeply hurt because he cannot be at one with the establishment, because he cannot be a folk-artist whose art evolves, through the accidental medium of himself, out of the consciousness of the folk. But the salvation of American art certainly lies not in a greater rapprochement with the environment, but in its becoming subversive and dangerous to the social order.

The implications of this must not be mistaken. The art of simple realism and naive propaganda is essentially never dangerous. Inevitably it betrays itself in the half-truths which are the sure results of that lack of clear perception and precise expression which we call bad style. How true this is, the social literature of America in the past fifteen years will show. Two great tasks confront the American writer — the acquisition of considerable knowledge and the construction of a completely efficient style. One thinks of men — Mr. Dos Passos comes to mind, Mr. Edward Dahlberg — who understand the problem in large part and who are attempting, with a very fair measure of success, to solve it. They perceive the madness and hysteria in our life and they are rendering it admirably. Such writers should not be badgered with the insistence that their work is of no avail.

ALBERT EINSTEIN

The 1932 Disarmament Conference

September 23, 1931

Scientist-philosopher Albert Einstein's 1931 plea for disarmament augurs his 1949 warning to President Truman, in the wake of the Soviets' detonation of an atomic device. Einstein, who had originally called Roosevelt's attention to the potentialities of nuclear fission, warned that "the armament race between the U.S.A. and the U.S.S.R. . . . assumes hysterical character. On both sides, the means to mass destruction are perfected with feverish haste, behind respective walls of secrecy. . . . In the end, there beckons more and more clearly general annihilation."

Berlin, September 4, 1931

What the inventive genius of mankind has bestowed upon us in the last hundred years could have made human life care free and happy if the development of the organizing power of man had been able to keep step with his technical advances. As it is, the hardly bought achievements of the machine age in the hands of our generation are as dangerous as a razor in the hands of a three-year-old child. The possession of wonderful means of production has not brought freedom—only care and hunger.

Worst of all is the technical development which produces the means for the destruction of human life, and the dearly created products of labor. We older people lived through that shudderingly in the World War. But even more terrible than this destruction seems to me the unworthy servitude into which the individual is swept by war. Is it not terrible to be forced by the community to deeds which every individual feels to be most despicable crimes? Only a few have had the moral greatness to resist; they are in my eyes the true heroes of the World War.

There is one ray of hope. It seems to me that today the responsible leaders of the several peoples have, in the main, the honest will to abolish war. The opposition to this unquestionably necessary advance lies in the unhappy traditions of the people which are passed on like an inherited disease from generation to generation because of our faulty educational machines. Of course the main supports of this tradition are military training and its glorification, and not less important, the press which is so dependent upon the military and the larger industries. Without disarmament there can be no lasting peace. On the contrary, the continuation of military armaments in their present extent will with certainty lead to new catastrophies.

Hence the Disarmament Conference in Geneva in February, 1932, will be decisive for the fate of the present generation and the one to come. If one thinks back to the pitiful results achieved by the international conferences thus far held, it must be clear that all thoughtful and responsible human beings must exercise all their powers again and again to inform public opinion of the vital importance of the conference of 1932. Only if the statesmen have, to urge them forward, the will to peace of a decisive majority in their respective countries, can they arrive at their important goal. For the creation of this public opinion in favor of disarmament every person living shares the responsibility, through ever deed and every word.

The failure of the conference would be assured if the delegates were to arrive in Geneva with fixed instructions and aims, the achievement of which would at once become a matter of national prestige. This seems to be universally recognized, for the meetings of the statesmen of any two states, of which we have seen a number of late, have been utilized for discussions of the problem of disarmament in order to clear the ground for the conference. This procedure seems to me a very happy one, for two persons, or two groups, ordinarily conduct themselves most sensibly, most honorably, and with the greatest freedom from passion if no third person listens in, whom the others believe they must consider or conciliate in their speeches. We can only hope for a favorable outcome in this most vital conference if the meeting is prepared for exhaustively in this way by advance discussions in order that surprises shall be made impossible, and if, through honest good will, an atmosphere of mutual confidence and trust can be effectively created in advance.

Success in such great affairs is not a matter of cleverness, or even shrewdness, but instead a matter of honorable conduct and mutual confidence. You cannot substitute intellect for moral conduct in this matter—I should like to say, thank God that you cannot!

It is not the task of the individual who lives in this critical time merely to await results and to criticize. He must serve this great cause as well as he can. For the fate of all humanity will be that fate which it honestly earns and deserves.

OSWALD GARRISON VILLARD

The Pot and the Kettle
On Throwing Away Your Vote

October 5, 1932

As the 1932 election approached, editor Oswald Garrison Villard wrote a series of articles entitled "The Pot and the Kettle," in which he attacked the two major parties. Between Hoover and Roosevelt, the Republicans and the Democrats, *The Nation* saw no real choice, and it urged readers to vote for Socialist Party candidate Norman Thomas. The magazine did, however, endorse Roosevelt in the next three elections.

Norman Thomas has put it well: "The only way to throw your vote away is to cast it for somebody you don't really want, and then get him." There are literally millions of men who despise Herbert Hoover and don't like Franklin Roosevelt who are none the less going to vote for one or the other, thus doing their best to fasten upon all of us the shackles imposed upon us by the present corrupt and worthless political parties. Never in my experience has there been so little enthusiasm for either candidate. As has been well said, almost nobody is voting for anybody in this campaign. Everybody is voting against somebody or something. But that does not advance us one single bit. The impending election of Roosevelt gives little assurance that there will be anything like far-reaching, deep-seated, and thoroughgoing grappling with the problems which confront us. Even if Franklin Roosevelt had some heroic remedies to apply—I don't deny his power proposals are good as far as they go—what guaranty is there that he would have a Congress to uphold him? I am aware, of course, that all the indications are that the Democrats will easily control both houses. But when was a Democratic President able to control his own party? Certainly never on the tariff. The tariff revision put through at the insistence of President Cleveland was ruined by a Democratic Senator, Gorman of Maryland. The Wilsonian tariff revision was also knifed in the home of its friends. Since neither party has any principles nowadays upon which all its representatives in public life stand, you never can tell what will come to pass after a party takes power. Especially is this true of the Democrats. There is no certainty whatever that a man who plumps his ballot for Roosevelt will get what he wants if he is interested in water power, or desires a radical revision of the tariff, or wants to have the farmer freed from all tariff burdens, or believes in a small army and rapid disarmament on the seas. And heaven knows what the Republican voters will get if they reelect Herbert Hoover. There are no pledges in the Republican platform that will not be violated; that is what a platform is there for, to be violated.

*   *   *

So, I insist, the man who votes for either Hoover or Roosevelt is the one who is throwing away his vote. He is again turning the country over to the "bosses, or their owners, the great capitalists." He is again postponing the peaceful revolution which Woodrow Wilson said in 1912 was on the horizon. Look at the news from Wisconsin. There is a case of the failure of another effort to reform one of the major parties from within. How many failures have there not been since the days when the young Henry Cabot Lodge and Theodore Roosevelt walked out of the Republican convention of 1884 and declared to Horace White that they never, never would stand for the nomination of James G. Blaine—only to decide that they would stick by their party and reform it from within. Well, forty-eight years have passed since then, nearly half a century, and the Republican Party is still nominating unfit men for the Presidency, and is not a whit better than it was in 1884. But how many efforts have there not been during that period to reform both the parties from within? Were we not assured that Woodrow Wilson would purify the Democratic Party by the greatness of his spirit and his statesmanship, and by his silver tongue? Philip La Follette has worked hard to make his branch of the Republican Party in Wisconsin the dominant one; so has his brother, and so did his father. He has gone down to defeat. What is the earthly use of his remaining in the Republican Party? I do not know how Bob La Follette is going to vote in this campaign, for he has refrained from telling the public, but I feel very sure that these two fine young men ought to be in the forefront of a radical party rather than trying to profit by working under the shadow of the name of the Republican Party, from which spiritually and politically they are utterly separated. A vote for the Republican nominees in Wisconsin will certainly be throwing away one's vote.

*   *   *

The only way to make one's vote really count in the coming election is to cast it for a new and square deal. Throw away your vote when you put it in a box for Norman Thomas? I deny that with all possible warmth. No one can put his ballot to higher or better use than to cast it according to the highest dictates of his mind and his conscience. If one does that, one cannot throw it away. To protest against intolerable evils when they arise is the chief reason why we have the ballot. To use it in this way is not to be impractical and visionary, but in the best sense patriotic. Certainly no one can deny that we shall not take a step toward any new order with either Mr. Hoover or Governor Roosevelt in the White House; we shall merely again be asked to be content with a little patching here and a little patching there, on a machine which cannot be made to work efficiently. But a vote for Norman Thomas means another vote of protest, another serving of notice that the voter is through with both the old parties; that he wants something different, some promise that there will be a genuine attempt some day to

113

rebuild our social and political system in a way really to return the government to the people. Let no man think that he is not going to have a lot of company if he votes for Thomas. One of the foremost practical Democratic politicians in the East has gone on record as saying that there will be at least three million votes for Norman Thomas in November. If that is the case, it will be a protest vote which will make both the old parties sit up and take notice, and encourage those who desire a third liberal party without the Socialist name.

JAMES THURBER

The "Odyssey" of Disney   *March 28, 1934*

The writer, illustrator and humorist James Thurber was a staff writer at *The New Yorker* when he wrote this article. T.S. Eliot, reviewing Thurber's work, described it as "a form of humor which is also a way of saying something serious."

I have never particularly cared for the "Odyssey" of Homer. The edition we used in high school—I forget the editors' names, but let us call it Bwumba and Bwam's edition—was too small to hide a livelier book behind, and it was cold and gray in style and in content. All the amorous goings on of the story were judiciously left out. We pupils might, at that age, have taken a greater interest in T. E. Shaw's recent rendering, the twenty-eighth, by his count, in English; for bang-off in Book I the third sentence reads: "She craved him for her bed-mate: while he was longing for his house and wife." But there wasn't any such sentence in old Bwumba and Bwam. It was a pretty dull book to read. No matter how thin Mr. Shaw has sliced it, it is still, it seems to me, a pretty dull book to read.

The fact that the "Odyssey" is the "oldest book worth reading for its story and the first novel of modern Europe" makes it no more lively—to me, anyway—than does the turning of it into what Mr. Shaw's publishers call "vital, modern, poetic prose." There are too many dreary hours between this rosy-fingered dawn and that rosy-fingered dawn. The menaces in ancient Jeopardy were too far apart, the hazards prowled at too great distances, the gods maundered and were repetitious. Ulysses himself is not a hero to whom a young man's fancy turns in any season. The comedy of the "Odyssey" is thought by some students to be unintentional and by others to be intentional, and there must not be any uncertainty about comedy. But whatever may be said about it, the "Odyssey" will always keep bobbing up, in our years and in the years to follow them. The brazen entry into the United States of Mr. Joyce's "Ulysses" has most recently brought the "Odyssey" again into view; as the magazine *Time* points out to its surprised readers, "almost every detail of the 'Odyssey's' action can be found in disguised form in 'Ulysses.' " So, many a reader might naturally enough ask, what? So nothing—that is, nothing of real importance in so far as the "Odyssey" or "Ulysses" itself is concerned. The ancient story just happened to make a point of departure for Mr. Joyce. He might equally well have taken for a pattern Sherman's campaign in Georgia. Nevertheless, here is the old tale before us again not quite two years after Mr. Shaw went over the whole ground for the twenty-eighth time in English.

My purpose in this essay is no such meager and footless one as to suggest that it is high time for some other ancient tale to be brought up in place of the "Odyssey"—although, if urged, I would say the "Morte d'Arthur." My purpose is to put forward in all sincerity and all arrogance the conviction that the right "Odyssey" has yet to be done, and to name as the man to do it no less a genius than Walt Disney. A year or two ago Mr. Disney made a Silly Symphony, as he too lightly called this masterpiece, entitled "Neptune." Those who missed seeing it missed a lusty, fearsome, beautiful thing. Here was a god and here were sea adventures in the ancient manner as nobody else has given them to us. The thing cannot be described; it can be rendered into no English. But it was only a hint of what Mr. Disney, let loose in the "Odyssey," could make of it.

The dark magic of Circe's isle, the crossing between Scylla and Charybdis, the slaying of the suitors are just by the way; and so are dozens of other transfigurations, mythical feats of strength, and godly interventions. Mr. Disney could toss these away by the dozen and keep only a select few. For one: Ulysses and his men in the cave of the Cyclops. That would be that scene as I should like my daughter to know it first, when she gets ready for the "Odyssey," or when she is grimly made ready for it—I presume one still has to read it in school as I did, along with "The Talisman" and "Julius Caesar." Picture Mr. Disney's version of the overcoming of the giant, the escape tied to the sheep, the rage of Polyphemus as he hurls the tops of mountains at the fleeing ship of Ulysses and his men!

But I think my favorite scene will be (I'm sure Mr. Disney will do the "Odyssey" if we all ask him please) that scene wherein Menelaus and his followers wrestle with the wily Proteus on the island of Pharos. You know: the Old Man of the Sea comes up out of the dark waters at noon to count his droves of precious seals all stretched out on the beach. In his innocence of treachery or of any change in the daily routine, he unwittingly counts Menelaus and his three men, who are curled up among the seals trying to look as much like seals as possible. It doesn't come out, by the way, in any rendering I've read, and I've read two, just what the Old Man thought when he found he had four seals too many. Anyway, at the proper moment Menelaus and his followers jump upon Proteus. In the terrific struggle that ensues the Old Man changes into—here I follow the Shaw version—"a hairy lion: then a dragon: then a leopard: then a mighty boar. He became a film of water, and afterwards a high-branched tree."

How only for Walt Disney's hand and his peculiar medium was that battle fought! His "Odyssey" can be, I am sure, a far, far greater thing than even his epic of the three little pigs. Let's all write to him about it, or to Roosevelt.

EMMA GOLDMAN

The Tragedy of the Political Exiles

October 10, 1934

In 1934, anarchist and feminist Emma Goldman returned to America, bitter and pessimistic after living for fifteen years in exile. Of Russian birth, Goldman had been deported to the Soviet Union in 1919, at the height of the Red Scare. Goldman's views about the Soviet Union were not shared by *Nation* editor Freda Kirchwey, who wrote Goldman, after receiving the piece published below, "While I do not quarrel with your right to say what you believe, I feel that at a time when fascist dictatorship is the dominant instrument of oppression in Europe, you have been at least guilty of a lack of proportion in the emphasis you place on Russia's sins."

During my ninety days in the United States old friends and new, including people I had never met before, spoke much of my years in exile. It seemed incredible to them that I had been able to withstand the vicissitudes of banishment and come back unbroken in health and spirit and with my ideal unmarred. I confess I was deeply moved by their generous tribute. But also I was embarrassed, not because I suffer from false modesty or believe that kind things should be said about people only after their death, but rather because the plight of hosts of political exiles scattered over Europe is so tragic that my struggle to survive was hardly worth mentioning.

The lot of political refugees, even prior to the war, was never free from stress and poverty. But they could at least find asylum in a number of countries. France, Belgium, Switzerland were open to them. Scandinavia and the Netherlands received them kindly. Even the United States was hospitable enough to admit some refugees. The real haven, however, was England, where political rebels from all despotic lands were made welcome.

The world carnage put an end to the golden era when a Bakunin and a Herzen, a Marx and a Kropotkin, a Malatesta and a Lenin, Vera Sazulich, Louise Michel, and all the others could come and go without hindrance. In those days who cared about passports or visas? Who worried about one particular spot on earth? The whole world was one's country. One place was as good as another where one could continue one's work for the liberation of one's autocratic native land. Not in their wildest dreams did it occur to these revolutionaries that the time might come when the world would be turned into a huge penitentiary, or that political conditions might become more despotic and inhuman than during the worst period of the Czars. The war for democracy and the advent of left and right dictatorships destroyed whatever freedom of movement political refugees had formerly enjoyed. Tens of thousands of men, women, and children have been turned into modern Ahasueruses, forced to roam the earth, admitted nowhere. If they are fortunate enough to find asylum, it is nearly always for a short period only; they are always exposed to annoyance and chicanery, and their lives made a veritable hell.

For a time expatriated Russians were given some protection by means of the Nansen, or League of Nations, passport. Most countries were supposed to recognize that scrap of paper, though few did, least of all when politically tainted individuals applied for admission. Still, the Nansen passport was better than nothing at all. Now this too has been abolished, and Russian refugees are entirely outside the law. Terrible as was the Czarist time, it was yet possible to bribe one's way across frontiers. That is possible no longer, not because border police have suddenly become honest, but because every country is afraid of the bolshevik or the fascist germ and keeps the frontier hermetically sealed, even against those who hate every form of dictatorship.

I have already stated that political exiles are sometimes lucky enough to find an abode, but that by no means includes the right to work. Anything they do to eke out a wretched existence, such as lessons, translations, or any kind of physical labor, must be done furtively. Should they be caught, it would again mean the wearisome round of seeking another country. Politicals are constantly at the beck and call of the authorities. It is almost a daily occurrence for them to be pounced upon suddenly at an early morning hour, dragged out of bed, taken to the police station, and then expelled. It is not necessary to be guilty of any offense, such as participation in the internal political affairs of the country whose hospitality they have accepted.

A friend of mine is a case in point. He was expelled from a certain country merely for editing a small bulletin in English in order to raise funds for the Russian political prisoners. After we succeeded in bringing him back, he was three times ordered to leave, and when he was finally allowed to remain, it was on condition that he apply for a renewal of the permit every three months. For days and weeks he had to camp at the police station and waste time and health running from department to department. While waiting for the renewal he could not leave the city of his domicile. Every new place he might want to visit implied new registration, and as he was left without a single document while his renewal was pending, he could nowhere be registered. In other words, my friend was virtually a prisoner in one city until the renewal was granted. Few there are who could have survived such treatment. But my friend had been steeled in American prisons for sixteen years, and his had always been an indomitable will. Yet even he had almost come to the end of his endurance when the three months' renewal period was extended to six.

However, these miseries are by no means the only tragedies in the present plight of most political refugees. There are many more that try their souls and turn their lives into hideous nightmares. No matter how great their suffering in pre-war times, they had their faith and their work to give them an outlet. They lived, dreamed, and labored incessantly for the liberation of their native lands. They could arouse public opinion in their place of refuge against the tyranny and oppression practiced in their country, and they were able to help their comrades in prison with large funds contributed by the workers and liberal elements in other parts of the world. They could even ship guns and ammunition into Czarist Russia, despotic Italy, and Spain. These were certainly inspiring and sustaining factors. Not less so was the solidarity that existed among the politicals of different schools. Whatever their theoretical differences, there was mutual respect and confidence among them. And in times of important issues they worked together, not in a make-believe but in a real united front.

Nothing of that is left. All political movements are at each other's throats — more bitter, vindictive, and downright savage against each other than they are against their common enemies. The most unpardonable offender in this respect is the so-called Union of Socialist Soviet Republics. Not only is it keeping up a process of extermination of all political opponents in and outside its territory, but it is also engaged in wholesale character assassination. Men and women with a heroic record of revolutionary activity, persons who have consecrated themselves to their ideals, who went through untold sufferings under the Romanovs, are maligned, misrepresented, dubbed with vile names, and hounded without mercy. It is certainly no coincidence that my friend was expelled for a bulletin designed to raise money for the Russian politicals.

To be sure the Mussolinis and Hitlers are guilty of the same crime. They and their propaganda machines mow down every political opponent in their way. They also have added character assassination to the butchery of their victims. Human sensibilities have become dulled since the war. If the suffering of the German and Austrian refugees had failed to rekindle the dying embers of sympathy, one would have had to lose all faith in mankind. The generous response to their need is indeed the only ray of light on the black social horizon.

The Anarchists and Anarcho-Syndicalists have, of course, been forgotten. Or is it ignorance that causes the deadly silence about their plight? Do not the protesters against German atrocities know that Anarchists also are in Göring's dreadful concentration camps, subject to the brutalities of the Storm Troop barbarians, and that some of them have undergone more heinous punishment than most of the other Nazi victims? For instance, Erich Mühsam. Poet and social rebel, he paid his toll to the German Republic after the Bavarian uprising. He was sentenced to fifteen years in prison, of which he served five. On his release he immediately threw himself into the work of showing the inhuman conditions in the prisons under the Socialist and republican government. Being a Jew and an Anarchist and having a revolutionary past, Erich Mühsam was among the first to be dragged off by the SA gangsters. He was repeatedly slugged and beaten, his teeth were knocked out, his hair and beard pulled, and the swastika cut on his skull with a penknife. After his death in July, announced by the Nazis as "suicide," his widow was shown his tortured body, with the back of the skull crushed as if it had been dragged on the ground, and with unmistakable signs of strangulation.

Indifference to Mühsam's martyrdom is a sign of the sectarianism and bigotry in liberal and radical ranks today. But what I really want to stress is this: the barbarity of fascism and Nazism is being condemned and fought by the persons who have remained perfectly indifferent to the Golgotha of the Russian politicals. And not only indifferent; they actually justify the barbarities of the Russian dictatorship as inevitable. All these good people are under the spell of the Soviet myth. They lack awareness of the inconsistency and absurdity of their protesting against brutalities in capitalist countries when they are condoning the same brutalities in the Soviet Republic. A recent appeal of the International Workingmen's Association gives a heart-breaking picture of the condition of Anarchists and Anarcho-Syndicalists in Stalin's stronghold. Renewed arrests in Odessa, Tomsk, Archangel, and other parts of Russia have taken place. No charge whatever is made against the victims. Without hearing or trial they have been sent away by the "administrative process." Those whose sentences, some as high as ten years, have expired, have again been sent to isolated parts; there is no hope of liberation during the much-praised Communist experiment.

One of the tragic cases is that of Nicholai Rogdayeve, an Anarchist for years and an ardent fighter for emancipation of the Russian people. During the reign of the Romanovs, Rogdayeve knew all the agonies meted out to politicals—prison, exile, and *katorga*. After the March revolution Rogdayeve came back to freedom and new activities. With hundreds of others of every political shade he worked untiringly—teaching, writing, speaking, and organizing the workers. He continued his labors for a time after the October revolution. Then the Bolshevik persecution began. Though Rogdayeve was well known and loved by everyone, including even Communists, he did not escape the crushing hand of the GPU. Arrest, exile, and all the other tortures the Russian politicals are made to suffer undermined his health. His giant body was gradually broken by tuberculosis, which he had contracted as a result of his treatment. He died a few months ago. What was the offense of Rogdayeve and hundreds of others? It was their steadfast adherence to their ideals, to their faith in the Russian revolution and the Russian masses. For that undying faith they went through a thousand purgatories; many of them, like Rogdayeve, were slowly done to death. Thus, Katherine Breshkovsky, at the age of ninety and blind, has just ended her days in an alien land. Maria Spiridonova, broken in health, if not in spirit, may not go abroad to seek a cure from scurvy developed in the inner Cheka prison; Stalin's sleep might be marred were she at large. And Angelica Balabonov, what about her? Not even the henchmen of Stalin have dared to charge her with having made common cause with the enemies of the revolution. In 1917 she returned from Italy to Russia, joined the Communist Party, and dedicated herself to the Russian Revolution. But eventually, when she realized the intrigue and the corruption in the Third International, when she could no longer accept the ethics of the GPU, she left Russia and the Communist Party. Ever since, Angelica Balabonov has been used as a target for villainous attacks and denunciations from Moscow and its satellites abroad. This and years of malnutrition have left her ill and stranded.

The Russian refugees are not the only rebels whose dream of a new world has been shattered. Enrico Malatesta, Anarchist, rebel, and one of the sweetest personalities in the revolutionary ranks, was also not spared the agony of the advent of fascism. Out of his great mind and his loving heart he had given lavishly over a period of sixty years to free the Italian workers and peasants. The realization of his dream was all but within reach when the riffraff of Mussolini spread like a plague over Italy, destroying everything so painfully built up by men like Malatesta, Fabri, and the other great Italian revolutionists. Bitter indeed must have been the last days of Malatesta.

Within the last year and a half hosts of Austrian and German rebels have been added to the list of radicals from Russia, Italy, Poland, Hungary, Rumania, Jugoslavia, and other lesser countries. All these lands have become the graveyard of revolutionary and libertarian ideals. Few countries are left where one can still hold on to life. Indeed, nothing that the holocaust and its aftermath have brought to humanity can compare with the cruel plight of the political refugees. Yet undying are their faith and their hope in the masses. No shadow of doubt obscures their belief that the workers will wake up from their leaden sleep, that they will once more take up the battle for liberty and well-being.

MARGARET BOURKE-WHITE

Dust Changes America

May 22, 1935

> In the 1930s, photographer Margaret Bourke-White traveled
> through the Midwest and the South (with her soon-to-be hus-
> band Erskine Caldwell), documenting the victims of the Dust
> Bowl and the hardships of southern sharecropping families.
> Their book about southern tenant farmers, *You Have Seen Their
> Faces*, was published in 1937.

Vitamin K they call it—the dust which sifts under the door sills, and stings in the
eyes, and seasons every spoonful of food. The dust storms have distinct personalities, rising in formation like rolling clouds, creeping up silently like formless fog,
approaching violently like a tornado. Where has it come from? It provides topics
of endless speculation. Red, it is the topsoil from Oklahoma; brown, it is the fertile earth of western Kansas; the good grazing land of Texas and New Mexico
sweeps by as a murky yellow haze. Or, tracing it locally, "My uncle will be along
pretty soon," they say; "I just saw his farm go by."

The town dwellers stack their linen in trunks, stuff wet cloths along the window
sills, estimate the tons of sand in the darkened air above them, paste cloth masks
on their faces with adhesive tape, and try to joke about Vitamin K. But on the
farms and ranches there is an attitude of despair.

By coincidence I was in the same parts of the country where last year I photographed the drought. As short a time as eight months ago there was an attitude
of false optimism. "Things will get better," the farmers would say. "We're not as
hard hit as other states. The government will help out. This can't go on." But this
year there is an atmosphere of utter hopelessness. Nothing to do. No use digging
out your chicken coops and pigpens after the last "duster" because the next one
will be coming along soon. No use trying to keep the house clean. No use fighting
off that foreclosure any longer. No use even hoping to give your cattle anything
to chew on when their food crops have literally blown out of the ground.

It was my job to avoid dust storms, since I was commissioned by an airplane
company to take photographs of its course from the air, but frequently the dust
storms caught up with us, and as we were grounded anyway, I started to photograph them. Thus I saw five dust-storm states from the air and from the ground.

In the last several years there have been droughts and sand storms and dusters,
but they have been localized, and always one state could borrow from another.
But this year the scourge assumes tremendous proportions. Dust storms are
bringing distress and death to 300,000 square miles; they are blowing over all
of Kansas, all of Nebraska and Wyoming, strips of the Dakotas, about half of

Colorado, sections of Iowa and Missouri, the greater part of Oklahoma, and the northern panhandle of Texas, extending into the eastern parts of New Mexico.

Last year I saw farmers harvesting the Russian thistle. Never before had they thought of feeding thistles to cattle. But this prickly fodder became precious for food. This year even the Russian thistles are dying out and the still humbler soap weed becomes as vital to the farmer as the fields of golden grain he tended in the past. Last year's thistle-fed cattle dwindled to skin and bone. This year's herds on their diet of soap weed develop roughened hides, ugly growths around the mouth, and lusterless eyes.

Years of the farmers' and ranchers' lives have gone into the building up of their herds. Their herds were like their families to them. When AAA officials spotted cows and steers for shooting during the cattle-killing days of last summer, the farmers felt as though their own children were facing the bullets. Kansas, a Republican state, has no love for the AAA. This year winds whistled over land made barren by the drought and the crop-conservation program. When Wallace removed the ban on the planting of spring wheat he was greeted by cheers. But the wheat has been blown completely out of the ground. Nothing is left but soap weed, or the expensive cotton-seed cake, and after that—bankruptcy.

The storm comes in a terrifying way. Yellow clouds roll. The wind blows such a gale that it is all my helper can do to hold my camera to the ground. The sand whips into my lens. I repeatedly wipe it away trying to snatch an exposure before it becomes completely coated again. The light becomes yellower, the wind colder. Soon there is no photographic light, and we hurry for shelter to the nearest farmhouse.

Three men and a woman are seated around a dust-caked lamp, on their faces grotesque masks of wet cloth. The children have been put to bed with towels tucked over their heads. My host greets us: "It takes grit to live in this country." They are telling stories: A bachelor harnessed the sandblast which ripped through the keyhole by holding his pots and pans in it until they were spick and span. A pilot flying over Amarillo got caught in a sand storm. His motor clogged; he took to his parachute. It took him six hours to shovel his way back to earth. And when a man from the next county was struck by a drop of water, he fainted, and it took two buckets of sand to revive him.

The migrations of the farmer have begun. In many of the worst-hit counties 80 per cent of the families are on relief. In the open farm country one crop failure follows another. After perhaps three successive crop failures the farmer can't stand it any longer. He moves in with relatives and hopes for a job in Arizona or Illinois or some neighboring state where he knows he is not needed. Perhaps he gets a job as a cotton picker, and off he goes with his family, to be turned adrift again after a brief working period.

We passed them on the road, all their household goods piled on wagons, one lucky family on a truck. Lucky, because they had been able to keep their truck when the mortgage was foreclosed. All they owned in the world was packed on it; the children sat on a pile of bureaus topped with mattresses, and the sides of the truck were strapped up with bed springs. The entire family looked like a Ku Klux Klan meeting, their faces done up in masks to protect them from the whirling sand.

Near Hays, Kansas, a little boy started home from school and never arrived there. The neighbors looked for him till ten at night, and all next day a band of two hundred people searched. At twilight they found him, only a quarter of a mile from home, his body nearly covered with silt. He had strangled to death. The man who got lost in his own ten-acre truck garden and wandered around choking and stifling for eight hours before he found his house considered himself lucky to escape with his life. The police and sheriffs are kept constantly busy with calls from anxious parents whose children are lost, and the toll is mounting of people who become marooned and die in the storms.

But the real tragedy is the plight of the cattle. In a rising sand storm cattle quickly become blinded. They run around in circles until they fall and breathe so much dust that they die. Autopsies show their lungs caked with dust and mud. Farmers dread the birth of calves during a storm. The newborn animals will die within twenty-four hours.

And this same dust that coats the lungs and threatens death to cattle and men alike, that ruins the stock of the storekeeper lying unsold on his shelves, that creeps into the gear shifts of automobiles, that sifts through the refrigerator into the butter, that makes housekeeping, and gradually life itself, unbearable, this swirling drifting dust is changing the agricultural map of the United States. It piles ever higher on the floors and beds of a steadily increasing number of deserted farmhouses. A half-buried plowshare, a wheat binder ruffled over with sand, the skeleton of a horse near a dirt-filled water hole are stark evidence of the meager life, the wasted savings, the years of toil that the farmer is leaving behind him.

MARY McCARTHY and MARGARET MARSHALL

Our Critics, Right or Wrong
Literary Salesmen

December 18, 1935

> Mary McCarthy, novelist and critic, was a frequent contributor
> to *The Nation* in the 1930s. Margaret Marshall was *The Nation's*
> literary editor from 1937 until 1953. This article, the last in a
> five-part series, could be published today with only minor
> alterations.

In the past four articles of this series the *Herald Tribune Books,* the *Saturday Review of Literature,* the New York *Times Book Review,* and the literary section of the *New Masses* have been examined in respect to their usefulness as critical guides to literature during the past ten years. It would be pleasant to drop the matter here and to ignore the book columnist of the New York daily newspaper, since he is, after all, such an easy mark. Unfortunately, he is influential; his column is scanned (at least) by millions of readers a day. It is therefore vital that we take a brief look at him.

It must be acknowledged at the outset that it would be absurd to expect profound literary criticism from any writer whose job demands that he read and review one or more books in a single day. John Chamberlain may assert airily: "As a daily reviewer I am not momentously conscious of believing very differently than I did as a weekly reviewer or free-lance writer . . .": and it is quite probable that Mr. Chamberlain's general views of life and literature have undergone no striking change during his two years' tenancy of his column on the *Times.* His practice, however, *has* altered. It is extremely doubtful that Mr. Chamberlain, given a few days to think it over, would have said, for instance, that Robert Briffault's "Europa" "may lack one or two of the elements of great fiction but it . . . will probably stand up as the most useful novel that has come to light"; and the first sentence of his review of November 19 is the rather desperate remark of the typical newspaper reviewer: "One finishes Frederic Prokosch's 'The Asiatics' with a helpless tongue-tied feeling born of the fact that no critical clichés seem to fit this astonishing novel."

Lewis Gannett, who is disarmingly frank, put his finger on the difficulties of the trade he and Mr. Chamberlain now follow in his comment on Sholom Asch's "Three Cities": "It may be remembered when 'Anthony Adverse' is forgotten; but I never got well started. There were good books and shorter out that day." Each of the newspaper critics, with the exception of Mr. Chamberlain, has, on some

124

occasion, inveighed against the exigencies of time and mass circulation which hamper him in the exercise of his craft. A certain amount of this fretfulness is justified; but the book columnists overdo it when they offer the daily pressure to which they are subjected as a kind of blanket alibi for errors in judgment. Harry Hansen, for instance, simply does not make sense when he presents the following excuse for his erratic critical behavior:

> Now and then I hear that we are too enthusiastic . . . I don't share this view. The enthusiasm in newspaper reviewing comes, I believe, because we write after the first impact; if we had weeks and months to devote to a book we might cool off.

If this statement means anything at all, it means that Mr. Hansen fears that his first reactions to literature are usually wrong; and if Mr. Hansen really doubts the reliability of his first reactions he has no business running a daily book column. In a different way Lewis Gannett apologizes for his work in the *Herald Tribune:*

> My own column must reveal my lamentable ignorance of the eternal principles of criticism; a review of my own reviews would, I suspect, disclose little but an autobiography. Well, why not? Why pretend more? Anatole France called criticism the adventures of a soul among masterpieces; our daily columns are the adventures of our modern minds in the modern world as reflected in its books.

It is not necessary or even possible for the newspaper reviewer to write brilliant or subtle criticism. Still, it seems odd that a "lamentable ignorance of the eternal principles of criticism" should qualify a man for the position of book columnist, especially since he does not by any means restrict himself to reporting the evidence but is continually handing down critical decisions. Mr. Gannett sums up his own case adequately. He has had no special training in literature or criticism. He came to the *Herald Tribune* from *The Nation,* where he was a first-rate writer on foreign affairs. William Soskin of the *American* has an equally non-literary background. He was a law student at Columbia University, a reporter on Wisconsin and Chicago newspapers, managing and news editor of several New York newspapers, before he was appointed book columnist on the *Evening Post.* Harry Hansen was a war and peace-conference correspondent for the Chicago *Daily News* shortly before he became the literary editor of that paper and thence graduated to the New York *World.* Only John Chamberlain, who worked for some years on the literary section of the Sunday *Times,* and for a short period on the *Saturday Review of Literature,* seems to have served an apprenticeship in criticism. It is significant that Mr. Chamberlain today so far outshines his fellow book columnists that we tend to overestimate his talents.

If we wish to know why it is that a man so patently ill at ease in the critical chair as Mr. Gannett, say, or Mr. Soskin, is allowed to conduct a book column in an important New York newspaper, we need only to inquire into the book columnist's real function to discover the answer. The book columnist's job is not to evaluate literature, for at that he is woefully inefficient; his job is, to put it bluntly, to sell books. Since the *Herald Tribune*, for instance, does not print newspapers for art or typography's sake, Mr. Gannett's column must, at the very worst, pay for itself; and across the page from Mr. Gannett's column we find the publishers' advertising which supports it. Literature is art; but it is, at the same time, merchandise. Publishers cannot print only good books, even if they want to, for there are not in one season enough to go even once around. Publishers' lists, then, are substantially composed of mediocre books, heavily advertised as "good" or "great." Many or most of these books a newspaper columnist helps to sell. The average mediocre novel will draw from him a favorable review, warm enough in tone to send little trickles of cash customers into the city's bookstores. He writes favorable reviews, not because he is crooked, not because he is the conscious tool of the publishers whose advertising eventually pays his salary, but because he is a pleasant, generous man with no literary training, very little discrimination, and a vague "love of books." As one might expect, he professes contempt for "highbrows"; it is indeed his favorite rationalization when he is confronted with his own critical shortcomings. "The simple way of avoiding superlatives," says Mr. Brickell, neatly avoiding the issue, "and one that is often followed by the reviewers of the highbrow weeklies, is not to like anything, and particularly not to like anything that anybody else likes."

It is not to be imagined that Gannett, Brickell, Soskin, *et al.* are the only literary salesmen disguised as critics who function in the book world of today. The reviewers on the *Herald Tribune Books,* the *Saturday Review of Literature,* and the New York *Times Book Review* are performing precisely the same service for the publishing houses. Among the literary weeklies *Books* is most conscious of its role as a book-selling medium. There was a time, in the middle and late twenties, when *Books* was a moderately respectable literary journal. Its back pages were filled with reviews of trivial pieces of fiction and non-fiction, but its cover and front section were often devoted to articles by important men and women of letters. Virginia Woolf, Rebecca West, Paul Valéry, and Lytton Strachey were making in *Books* stimulating contributions to critical thought. Today any Sunday's *Books* looks like a trade journal. No distinguished critical name adorns its cover; an entire page in the back section is devoted to a tabulated account of the best-sellers as reported by bookstores all over the country; a downright unfavorable review, particularly of a work of fiction, is a rare and disturbing phenomenon, though some harassed reviewers have learned how to insert a hint of their real feelings between the favorable or equivocal lines.

The causes of this change in policy are readily perceived. *Books,* of course, subsists on advertising. Book publishers were among the first to feel the pinch of the depression. Lowered sales meant a lowered budget for newspaper advertising. What was more natural than that *Books,* recognizing the publishers' plight, should do what it could to get a larger slice of the reduced advertising budget. Before the realities of depression literary pretensions faded. The effort to make the date of its review coincide with the date of publication of the book reviewed was intensified until at present *Books* frequently appears, with its consistently favorable review, several days before the book is actually on sale. It began to feature lists solicited from well-known persons of "Books I Have Liked," "Good Reading," "Books I Have Read Recently," "Books I Expect to Like This Season," "Books I Wish I'd Read." Later it introduced a Popular Fiction Number and a Mystery Story Number. Its latest and most successful stroke in its campaign to endear itself to the publishers resulted in the publication of its tabulated list of best-sellers. This was the consummation of a deal with the booksellers. The *Herald Tribune* today distributes about thirty thousand copies of *Books,* at a nominal cost, to bookstores in all the key cities of America. The booksellers mail these on, free of charge, to thirty thousand customers; and, in return, *Books* every Sunday prints its lists of the booksellers' weekly accomplishments in the sale and propagation of culture.

Useful as all these sales stunts must have been to the financial welfare of *Books,* by themselves they would have availed virtually nothing. To cement the friendly relations between criticism and advertising, *Books* needed and got favorable reviews of new books. This it has achieved in various ways. Reviewers who were obviously second-string in the old days (and for some reason the majority of these are tender-hearted ladies) were moved up to take the place of more stringent commentators. Again, *Books* may hand out a doubtful book to the author's best friend, as when it invited Malcolm Cowley to review the work of his familiar, Matthew Josephson, and intrusted the latest effort of Branch Cabell to Ellen Glasgow. It encourages a specialist in one field to review a bad book in another, where his ignorance will make him timid. Stuart Chase, for example, was called upon to consider "The Glories of Venus," a novel about Mexico by Susan Smith. Mr. Chase, naturally, could only report: "Whether it is a good novel I cannot say, for I am an economist . . . Susan Smith can write." Sometimes it finds hidden virtues in hitherto neglected authors. In 1930, for instance, a whole page in *Books* was devoted to proving that Harold Bell Wright's works—which the reviewer admitted had had scant notice from *Books* in the past—are folk literature. No wonder the publishers found it worth while to insert, two pages later, a half-page advertisement of Mr. Wright's latest opus. Reviewers on *Books* are hand-picked, but if *Books* makes a mistake, there are ways of rectifying it. Sometimes the review is pulled out at the last minute and another substituted, as was the case with Benjamin Stolberg's review of Ida Tarbell's "Owen D. Young," which was subsequently published in *The Nation*, while Gannett's review of the same book took its place in *Books*. Sometimes, *Books* reviewers complain, the offensive (that is, critical) lines are cut; and whatever unfavorable reviews appear are usually printed some time after the book's publication. To insure perfect results, the selling power of the reviewing staff of *Books* has recently, we hear, been gone over by an efficiency expert. The expert, we understand, frowns on "negative" reviewers and smiles on Sinclair Lewis, who leads the list, though Lewis's most enthusiastic admirer, H. L. Mencken, once pronounced him "a dreadful ham as a critic."

The *Herald Tribune* is occasionally hypocritical about its activities, now and then candid. The editor of *Books,* instructing one young reviewer in the practice of her art, assured her that "there is something good in every book that must be brought to the attention of every reader." On the candid side are the quotations from booksellers which the *Herald Tribune* occasionally prints to the effect that Lewis Gannett is their favorite (best book-selling) critic, and the advertisement in *Books* which announced: "Every day Lewis Gannett writes on books. . . . Every day, too, timely advertisements and news stories keep you abreast of developments in the realm of books."

The *Herald Tribune's* book policy has had its effect on its competitors, the *Times Book Review* and the *Saturday Review of Literature.* Neither of these publications has gone to such extremes as *Books* has in its quest of advertising. The *Times,* as we pointed out in an earlier article, usually merely "covers" books as it would news events; while the editors of the *Saturday Review* are of so benign and uncritical a habit of mind that their opinions would scarcely disturb a publisher. Both of these periodicals have throughout the depression grown a little more kindly, but unlike *Books* they are not psychopathically antipathetic to unfavorable reviews. They have, however, resorted to other measures to keep pace with *Books.* The *Saturday Review* now gives out to booksellers a small rack with a place in the middle for the current *Saturday Review* and a place on each side for the display of two books reviewed in its pages. The *Times* has but lately introduced its own tabulated report from American booksellers. It also furnishes to publishers small cards to be inserted in new books, asking the book buyer what review inspired him to purchase the book. The *Times* tabulates the information received and issues it in pamphlet form to publishers. Naturally, the *Times'* book reviews lead all the rest in sales appeal.

The pressure which such sales devices must inevitably bring to bear upon reviewing is apparent. Booksellers are not interested in distributing among their customers or displaying in their windows a weekly literary supplement in which unfavorable reviews predominate. Whether or not the attempts on the part of the *Times* and the *Saturday Review* to compete with *Books* presage an era in which reviewing in the literary weeklies will have become merely a branch of advertising it is impossible to tell. Certainly, the publishers themselves are well aware of the growing benevolence of the critical brotherhood. An amusing advertisement by Coward-McCann for "Brassbound," by Mary Bickel, makes this quite clear.

> Book reviewers are optimists, turning on the adjectives at the slightest provocation. But book *sellers* are hard-boiled. . . . To rate a kindly adjective from a book *seller* a book must be way up in the stratosphere.

An examination of criticism in America today indicates that criticism is healthiest where it is farthest removed from publishers' advertising. *The Nation* and the *New Republic,* if they are in some cases a little stodgy, make a genuine attempt to maintain critical standards. The *New Masses,* for all its errors, is vigorous. These periodicals carry some advertising – not much. In the quarterlies – the *Yale Review,* the *Virginia Quarterly,* the defunct *Symposium* and *Hound and Horn* – none of which carries or carried advertising, some of the most independent criticism has been written. Unfortunately, these publications, removed as they have been from advertising, are also removed from mass circulation, and the criticism, therefore, though good, has been stylistically academic. During the last ten years in America criticism has been only sporadically interesting. Edmund Wilson, Joseph Wood Krutch, Rebecca West, Frances Newman, Louis Kronenberger, Clifton Fadiman, and Robert Morss Lovett have seemed, in varying degrees, perspicacious, but their faint catcalls have been drowned out by the bravos of the publishers' claque. Moreover, none of these critics, with the exception of Mr. Wilson, has made any extended effort to relate what is valuable in modern literature to the body of literature of the past. Really vital criticism will probably not come until genuinely critical and independent minds can somehow communicate unhampered with the vast body of the reading public.

JAMES T. FARRELL

The Fall of Joe Louis June 27, 1936

> Novelist James T. Farrell was best known for his Studs Lonigan trilogy, which depicted the Chicago of the 1920s with realism and bitterness. Here Farrell describes, in gritty detail, the Joe Louis–Max Schmeling fight of 1936.

Over forty thousand people were smeared about the Yankee Stadium to witness the predicted murder of the century. Half-interested, they watched preliminary boxers maul for pork-chop money, and they booed when one decision went to an overgrown Argentine battler. Those in the ringside section glanced around to see and to be seen. Photographers swarmed about, the bulbs attached to their cameras flashing like a miniature electric storm. When asked by cops whom they were shooting they tossed off names from Jack Dempsey down. One policeman remarked that the fight wouldn't last long, that he ought to be getting home early. Everybody waited to see Joe Louis, the "Human Python," slug Max Schmeling into a coma.

Both fighters received loud ovations when they entered the ring. They sat in their corners while celebrities were introduced. Champions past and present lightly leaped over the ropes, shook hands all around, and took their bows. Jack Dempsey received a bigger hand than Gene Tunney, whom the announcer characterized as "an inspiration to the youth of America." Mickey Walker, along with others, was revealed as a "thrill-producer." This formality settled, the fighters were presented, and the announcer exhorted everybody "to cast aside all prejudice regarding race, creed, or color." I suspected a note of patronage in the responding wahoo.

The crowd waited, keen, alert eyes riveted on the green-roped ring. Nervous conversation popped on all sides like firecrackers. On all sides, too, people were asking each other how long before they would see Schmeling, the "dark Uhlan," stretched out. The ring was cleared. Handlers whispered final words to the fighters. The gong! A loud cheer!

Dark-skinned Joe Louis danced and pranced cautiously about the ring facing a man who seemed clumsy. Louis, feinting with the snap of a trained, perfectly coordinated boxer, seemed to possess an almost insolent confidence. He maneuvered to let go with that deadly one-two punch, a left to the body, and a murderous right cross to the jaw, which was calculated to sink Schmeling quickly into a state of retching if temporary paralysis.

"Fight, you bums!" someone yelled from the grandstand behind me.

They sparred and shifted in a first round which went to Louis by a harmless margin. The crowd seemed to be with Schmeling. It coached him, loudly yelling advice and confidential instructions: "Get in there, Max! Bob and weave! That's right! Don't stand up straight! Duck his left, Maxie!"

Near me, there was a thin, cynical-faced chap in a checked grey suit. Peering through binoculars he made himself an unofficial broadcaster for a large area of ringside seats.

"Don't be a bum, Maxie! You're yellow, Max! Fighting the kind of a fight Joe wants you to! Down, there! Bob and weave, bob and weave! . . . Jesus Christ, look at him, standing up straight! Bob and weave! Use that right! Bob and weave!"

Others joined in. "Fight, you Dutch bum!" "Get going, Maxie!" "Make it fast, Louis!" Negroes sprayed through the ringside section and the grandstand shouted, some with hysterical confidence. A frail Negro lad wearing brown trousers and a checked gray coat, kept telling Louis, in a mild voice, to hit him. The second round was cautiously fought. Louis boxed, poised and graceful. Swaying and weaving, Schmeling still seemed clumsy, a man with no right to be in the ring with this black giant.

"He's feeling the Uhlan out. He'll tear in in a round or two."

"He's giving us a run for our money!"

The gong. The lights going on all over the arena. The high-pitched conversation. The seconds expertly working over the men. Again the gong. All lights off except those over the ring. Matches flashing on all sides as cigarettes were lit in the darkness. A loud and long Oh, and everyone leaping up. Schmeling had bounced Louis back with a powerful right.

"Oh, what a bum! He's yellow, Max! Get in there, Max! Polish him off! Dempsey would have killed him!" the gray-suited fellow with the binoculars yelled.

"Retaliate, Louis, retaliate!" the frail Negro, with the gray-checked coat called out. His voice was lost in the shrieks for a knockout.

The fellow with the opera glasses kept yelling that Louis was mad and swinging wild now. Louis was no longer the graceful, panther-like animal prancing around in sure expectation of a kill. The fourth round came up. The crowd yelled for blood. Many were asking about Schmeling's eye, which Louis had nicked in the early rounds. Louis went down. He was up immediately, punching wildly. He swung low with his left, landed. He was booed loudly and nastily.

"Hey! Hey! Watch it! Watch it, you!" the fellow with the opera glasses shrieked threateningly.

"Kill him, Max!" a woman cried hysterically from the grandstand.

Now the crowd cheered and exhorted Schmeling. Shaken by surprise at the unexpected turn of the fight, it wanted blood. Here and there Negroes began showing concern. Some were silent; others pleaded with Joe to win. The frail lad with the gray-checked coat meekly begged Louis to retaliate, his words drowned out by successive roars.

And the heart seemed utterly gone out of Joe Louis. Hurt, he floundered. Missing punches, he revealed the manner in which the German's plan of battle was working effectively. Drawing Louis to lead with his left, Schmeling ducked under the Negro, and pegged in solid right-hand smashes. Now many yelled that Louis couldn't take it. After each gong he wobbled about, scarcely able to find his own corner. Loud and gleeful voices announced that the black boy was out on his feet. The superman of pugilism had been turned into a "bum" by one knockdown and a pounding succession of drives from Schmeling's right hand.

Groggy for two rounds, Louis seemed to recover in the seventh round. He attacked and the mob was on its feet, ready to shift its allegiance as he banged at Schmeling.

"He ain't hittin' Max! He's hittin' Maxie's gloves! Louis's face is hamboiger! It's hamboiger! He's a sucker for a poifict right! Go in with the right, Maxie, and you'll kill the yellow bum!" the smart Aleck with the binoculars crowed.

"Retaliate, Louis, retaliate!"

For eight rounds Schmeling punched Joe Louis into a state of bewildered, rubbery-legged semi-helplessness. Louis swung wildly, feebly. Before the end Schmeling was laughing at him. The German continued to fight cautiously, ploddingly, slugging away until he grew arm-weary. A few called to the referee to stop it. One fellow began yelling that Schmeling was a bum because he was taking so much time to knock out a thoroughly beaten man.

The roaring grew in volume. From behind, there came petulant repetitive cries for those in front to sit down. Schmeling was exhorted to polish Louis off; to kill him. Louis, utterly confused and swinging aimlessly, landed several low punches. He was booed. Then finally Schmeling straightened Louis up and bounced a last needless right off his face. Louis fell into the ropes, relaxed, slid on to the canvas, quivered, turned over. A long and lusty roar acclaimed the end of one superman and the elevation of another superman to supplant him in the sports columns.

The beaten heavyweight was led off, half dragged half carried, his face smothered in a towel. A last pitying but friendly cheer followed him. Schmeling departed, guarded by an aisle of policemen, waving and grinning at the plaudits which acknowledged him the hero of the evening.

In the dressing-room Schmeling stood under a spraying shower, surrounded by reporters, his dark hair sopped, answering questions with a heavy German accent. His middle covered with a towel, he crushed his way out of the shower to dress. Photographers clambered on chairs, and flashed his picture continuously. Reporters asked the winner how he had won, and solemnly copied his statements down on note paper. He said that Louis was a good boxer, but could be hit, and that Louis's punches had not hurt him seriously, except for the low ones.

"Hey, Max, please smile! I want you smiling and I'm finished," one of the photographers pleaded.

Again Schmeling was asked how he won, and his answers were noted. The experts described the statements as fine and excellent. He spoke of the "shampionship." He was congratulated tumultuously on all sides. His manager, a corpulent, slack-faced little man, was chewing a cigar, wiping oceans of perspiration from his brows, and chiding the experts who had picked Louis. A sweating radio announcer with a handkerchief strung around his neck was concluding his broadcast in a thick, insinuating, histrionic voice.

"Hey, Maxie, please smile! Hey, tell him to smile! I can't go home till I get a shot of him smiling. Hey, Max, smile for just a second!"

Schmeling was dressed now, gay, not worrying over his bruised eyes. He has dark hair, heavy brows, a long, bony face. He is an ox-like, genial, stupid-looking German, his features from some angles almost suggestively animalistic.

"Hey, please, get Max to smile. For Christ sake, I can't go home until I get him smiling!"

A few minutes later Schmeling broadcast a statement to Germany, where the Nazis will make political capital of the fight and claim that Max Schmeling's victory is a triumph for Hitler and Wotan.

Dressed in a loud gray suit, with a straw hat askew on his enormous head, Joe Louis sat bowed. The son of exploited Alabama cotton pickers, he had in two years earned around a million dollars in his so-called "meteoric" rise in the prize ring; he had just earned well over one hundred thousand dollars. Now he sat like a sickened animal. He is a large Negro boy with blown-out cheeks, fat lips, and an overdeveloped neck. His face was puffed and sore. He dabbed his eyes with a handkerchief, revealing bruised knuckles. His trainer bent down and whispered to him, calling him Chappie. A second massaged his neck. He sat dazed, stupefied from punishment. Again he dabbed his eyes. A Negro boxer who had won a preliminary bout on a technical knockout dressed in an outer room, explained how he had gone into the fight to win; he entered Louis's quarters, talked condolingly with him, departed. Photographers stood on chairs, awaiting Louis's exit, begging for just one picture. Loud cheers echoing from outside heralded Schmeling's departure. Louis sat, still punch drunk. He went out like a drunken man, surrounded by cops and members of his retinue, his face hidden behind a straw hat and the collar of his gray topcoat. Unsupported, he would have fallen. The helpless giant was pushed into a taxicab and hustled away while a crowd fought with the police to obtain a glance at him.

JOHN DOS PASSOS

Big Parade—1936 Model

October 3, 1936

> John Dos Passos, author of the trilogy of novels *U.S.A.* and chronicler of American life, was a regular contributor to the magazine in the 1930s and 1940s. Here Dos Passos describes the transformation of the American Legion.

Cleveland, September 24, 1936

Through the swirl of dust and torn strips of last year's phone books and old mail-order catalogues that fly into your eyes and mouth and find their way down the back of your neck, they come, marching between hedges of faces, sweating in the cheap shimmery costumes out of old romantic musical comedies—the bands, the bands, the junior bands, cowboy bands, the redskin bands, the ladies' auxiliary bands (every lady has a fresh permanent frizzle, every lady sucks in in front and sticks out behind); cheeks puff, snare drums rattle, cymbals clash, and in front of every band stalks, minces, goose-steps, hobblewalks the inevitable drum major. There are tall drum majors, short fat drum majors, male and fairy drum majors, tiny-tot drum majors, pretty-girl drum majors. Their pants are tight, they suck in in front and stick out behind. There are the natty police bands, and cops, more cops than you can imagine, cops on motor cycles, cops on horseback, cops afoot, cops in radio cars; plenty of firemen, too, and the cheerful little locomotives and freight cars of the Forty and Eight societies; painted-up cars with bells and saluting cannon; various automotive whimsies—and it takes them eleven and a half hours to pass a given point.

On the sidewalks behind the ranked backs of the gazing public, in front of the plate-glass windows the storekeepers have protected with lattice and chicken wire, in the boom and tinkle of the old marching tunes, the boys keep up the traditional Legion whoopee now nineteen years stale; but all the same, in an intonation or a wisecrack, in the gesture of a man in shirt sleeves carefully measuring the contents of a pint into paper cups and at the same time popping his eyes at a girl, a trace remains perhaps of the old Battle of Paree, the kidding, the feeling of being on the loose in a town full of food and drink and women and comic adventures when next week you're just as likely as not to have your block blown off, and looking forward to telling tall stories to the guys in the outfit when they come back from leave—whatever it was that made the A.E.F. bearable nineteen years ago. Two men, each a little high, are wrangling about whether something happened at St. Quentin or in the Argonne. In the way they look now you can see how they looked then, nineteen years ago. "You better keep still till you find out what you're talkin' about, buddy." "Hell, boy, twenty years from now you'll be tellin' 'em you won the war."

In the convention hall it's not so much fun. There's a prayer. A bald-headed representative of the Legion of Valor refers to some communistic business (the C. L. U. pamphlet it must have been) that he found on the seats, and says he'd be sorry for them if they showed their ugly heads in this crowd, and goes on, amid ill-suppressed titters and finally hearty laughter, to a long-winded account of how the legionnaires had given him a royal welcome just like he'd entertained the Duke and Duchess of Kent when he was on a government post in Haiti. He was led away from the mike with difficulty. More addresses. The head of the Veterans' Bureau. A traffic-safety expert. Representative Rankin, white-haired, silver-tongued, from Alabama, quotes Tennyson on peace. A letter from Josephus Daniels, signed your old shipmate. Mr. Pratt of the American Educational Association makes a sensible conservative speech on the schools which is received with little enthusiasm except when he says that teachers should not teach subversive doctrines in the schools. He gets a big hand before he has time to continue that, nevertheless, in the opinion of American school teachers, it is their duty to give their pupils a fair picture of the pros and cons of social change. Then comes William Green, looking more like Uncle Wiggly than ever with his pink cheeks and gleaming glasses, to make a vague plea for peace in general and for cooperation between the A. F. of L. and the American Legion in particular.

The speeches, except for Mr. Pratt's unexpected note of good sense, were cut-and-dried occasional oratory. The main business of the day was the choosing of the next convention city. In spite of the pleas of Los Angeles, Denver, and Montreal (where, a little prematurely it turned out, they had named a street for Ray Murphy, the retiring national commander), New York, represented by Governor Lehman, Mayor LaGuardia, and 90,000 first-class hotel rooms, won the day. Then everybody hurried out to lunch in spite of the fact that the committees on Americanism and National Defense were reporting resolutions. A voice droned off a long set of vaguish resolutions in favor of a big navy, officers' training, a better army, aviation, a return to dirigibles, that were passed by acclamation without any comment by the few delegates left. The Americanism Committee came out with resolutions against relief for aliens, for cutting down immigration, against sedition, and home loans to non-citizens, for deportation of reds and jailing of subversive influences, but the hall was getting emptier and emptier. Finally merely the titles of the resolutions were read off and they were passed in bunches. It's lunch time. Sure, Mr. Hearst, it's O. K. by us — but the boys' hearts don't seem to be in their work.

What has happened is that in spite of the hopes of the founders that the Legion would be an aggressive arm against labor unionism and dangerous thoughts and a defense for the vested interests, it has settled down in this its year of greatest membership, of its biggest parade and smoothest convention — not a controversial matter reared its head from the floor — to being just another fraternal organization with its clubrooms and bridge parties and social work and poker evenings and fascinating internal politics. As such it is the field for the careers and supplies the meal tickets of thousands of professional organization workers. The legionnaires' interests, and those of the increasingly important women's auxiliary, lie in the bands and the parades and the junior baseball teams and in the comfortable feeling of belonging so necessary to people now that small-town life is broken up and the family is crumbling and people live so much by themselves in agglomerated industrial masses, where they are left after working hours with no human contact between the radio and the car and the impersonal round of chain stores and picture palaces. The fraternal organizations give people a feeling of belonging to something outside themselves. They are the folk life of America. We've got to have it. It's lonely being a unit in a parade that takes eleven and a half hours to pass through the public square. Makes you feel too small. Until something else more urgent arises to draw people together and as long as the little fellow can pay his dues, the professional organizers will continue to lead Elks and Redmen and Veiled Prophets and Mystic Shriners and legionnaires and their wives and little ones in brainless antics, decked in fatuous costumes, behind really excellent marching bands (that's one thing we do well) from convention city to convention city across the country. And steadily the American passion for a smooth-running machine, if nothing else, will tend to eliminate troublesome ideas, outstanding personalities, and dissenters who ask awkward questions about how and in what direction the parade is being led.

BERTRAND RUSSELL
On Being Modern-Minded
January 9, 1937

Beginning in the 1920s, the philosopher Bertrand Russell, recipient of the 1950 Nobel Prize in Literature, wrote frequently for *The Nation* on changing morals, on disarmament and on literature. In 1965, he wrote that the magazine "has been one of the few voices which has been heard on behalf of individual liberty and social justice consistently throughout its existence."

Our age is the most parochial since Homer. I speak not of any geographical parish: the inhabitants of Mudcombe-in-the-Meers are more aware than at any former time of what is being done and thought at Praha, at Gorki, or at Peiping. It is in the chronological sense that we are parochial: as the new names conceal the historic cites of Prague, Nijni-Novgorod, and Pekin, so new catchwords hide from us the thoughts and feelings of our ancestors, even when they differed little from our own. We imagine ourselves at the apex of intelligence, and cannot believe that the quaint clothes and cumbrous phrases of former times can have invested people and thoughts that are still worthy of our attention. If "Hamlet" is to be interesting to a really modern reader, it must first be translated into the language of Marx or of Freud, or, better still, into a jargon insistently compounded of both. I read lately a contemptuous review of a book by Santayana, mentioning an essay on Hamlet "dated, in every sense, 1908" — as if what has been discovered since then made any earlier appreciation of Shakespeare irrelevant and comparatively superficial. It did not occur to the reviewer that his review was "dated, in every sense, 1936." Or perhaps this thought did occur to him, and filled him with satisfaction. He was writing for the moment, not for all time; next year he will have adopted the new fashion in opinions, whatever it may be, and he no doubt hopes to remain up to date as long as he continues to write. Any other ideal for a writer would seem absurd and old-fashioned to the modern-minded man.

The desire to be contemporary is of course new only in degree; it has existed to some extent in all previous periods that believed themselves to be progressive. The Renaissance had a contempt for the Gothic centuries that had preceded it; the seventeenth and eighteenth centuries covered priceless mosaics with white-wash; the Romantic movement despised the age of the heroic couplet. Sixty-five years ago Lecky reproached my mother for being led by intellectual fashion to oppose fox-hunting: "I am sure," he wrote, "you are not really at all sentimental about foxes or at all shocked at the prettiest of all the assertions of women's rights, riding across country. But you always look upon politics and intellect as a fierce race and are so dreadfully afraid of not being sufficiently advanced or intellec-tual." But in none of these former times was the contempt for the past nearly as complete as it is now. From the Renaissance to the end of the eighteenth century men admired Roman antiquity; the Romantic movement revived the Middle Ages; my mother, for all her belief in nineteenth-century progress, constantly read Shakespeare and Milton. It is only since the war that it has been fashionable to ignore the past *en bloc*.

The belief that fashion alone should dominate opinion has great advantages. It makes thought unnecessary and puts the highest intelligence within the reach of everyone. It is not difficult to learn the correct use of such words as "complex," "sadism," "Oedipus," "bourgeois," "deviation," "left"; and nothing more is needed to make a brilliant writer or talker. Some, at least, of such words represented much thought on the part of their inventors; like paper money they were originally convertible into gold. But they have become for most people inconvertible, and in depreciating have increased nominal wealth in ideas. And so we are enabled to despise the paltry intellectual fortunes of former times.

The modern-minded man, although he believes profoundly in the wisdom of his period, must be presumed to be very modest about his personal powers. His highest hope is to think first what is about to be thought, to say what is about to be said, and to feel what is about to be felt; he has no wish to think better thoughts than his neighbors, to say things showing more insight, or to have emotions which are not those of some fashionable group, but only to be slightly ahead of others in point of time. Quite deliberately he suppresses what is individual in himself for the sake of the admiration of the herd. A mentally solitary life, such as that of Copernicus, or Spinoza, or Milton after the Restoration, seems pointless ac-cording to modern standards. Copernicus should have delayed his advocacy of

137

the Copernican system until it could be made fashionable; Spinoza should have been either a good Jew or a good Christian; Milton should have moved with the times, like Cromwell's widow, who asked Charles II for a pension on the ground that she did not agree with her husband's politics. Why should an individual set himself up as an independent judge? Is it not clear that wisdom resides in the blood of the Nordic race or, alternatively, in the proletariat? And in any case what is the use of an eccentric opinion, which never can hope to conquer the great agencies of publicity?

The money rewards and widespread though ephemeral fame which those agencies have made possible places temptations in the way of able men which are difficult to resist. To be pointed out, admired, mentioned constantly in the press, and offered easy ways of earning much money is highly agreeable; and when all this is open to a man, he finds it difficult to go on doing the work that he himself thinks best and is inclined to subordinate his judgment to the general opinion.

Various other factors contribute to this result. One of these is the rapidity of progress which has made it difficult to do work which will not soon be superseded. Newton lasted till Einstein; Einstein is already regarded by many as antiquated. Hardly any man of science, nowadays, sits down to write a great work, because he knows that, while he is writing it, others will discover new things that will make it obsolete before it appears. The emotional tone of the world changes with equal rapidity, as wars, depressions, and revolutions chase each other across the stage. And public events impinge upon private lives more forcibly than in former days. Spinoza, in spite of his heretical opinions, could continue to sell spectacles and meditate, even when his country was invaded by foreign enemies; if he had lived now, he would in all likelihood have been conscripted or put in prison. For these reasons a greater energy of personal conviction is required to lead a man to stand out against the current of his time than would have been necessary in any previous period since the Renaissance.

The change has, however, a deeper cause. In former days men wished to serve God. When Milton wanted to exercise "that one talent which is death to hide," he felt that his soul was "bent to serve therewith my Maker." Every religiously minded artist was convinced that God's aesthetic judgments coincided with his own; he had therefore a reason, independent of popular applause, for doing what he considered his best, even if his style was out of fashion. The man of science in pursuing truth, even if he came into conflict with current superstition, was still setting forth the wonders of Creation and bringing men's imperfect beliefs more nearly into harmony with God's perfect knowledge. Every serious worker, whether artist, philosopher, or astronomer, believed that in following his own convictions he was serving God's purposes. When with the progress of enlightenment this belief began to grow dim, there still remained the True, the Good, and the Beautiful. Non-human standards were still laid up in heaven, even if heaven had no topographical existence.

Throughout the nineteenth century the True, the Good, and the Beautiful preserved their precarious existence in the minds of earnest atheists. But their very earnestness was their undoing, since it made it impossible for them to stop at a halfway house. Pragmatists explained that Truth is what it pays to believe. Historians of morals reduced the Good to a matter of tribal custom. Beauty was abolished by the artists in a revolt against the sugary insipidities of a philistine epoch and in a mood of fury in which satisfaction is to be derived only from what hurts. And so the world was swept clear not only of God as a person but of God's essence as an ideal to which man owed an ideal allegiance; while the individual, as a result of a crude and uncritical interpretation of sound doctrines, was left without any inner defense against social pressure.

All movements go too far, and this is certainly true of the movement toward subjectivity, which began with Luther and Descartes as an assertion of the individual and has culminated by an inherent logic in his complete subjection. The subjectivity of truth is a hasty doctrine not validly deducible from the premises which have been thought to imply it; and the habits of centuries have made many things seem dependent upon theological belief which in fact are not so. Men lived with one kind of illusion, and when they lost it they fell into another. But it is not by old error that new error can be combated. Detachment and objectivity, both in thought and in feeling, have been historically but not logically associated with certain traditional beliefs; to preserve them without these beliefs is both possible and important. A certain degree of isolation both in space and time is essential to generate the independence required for the most important work; there must be something which is felt to be of more importance than the admiration of the contemporary crowd. We are suffering not from the decay of theological beliefs but from the loss of solitude.

NORMAN THOMAS

The Pacifist's Dilemma
January 16, 1937

Beginning in 1936, the magazine's pages were filled with editorials on what Freda Kirchwey considered "the most crucial of all issues" — the Spanish civil war. In 1937 America debated how best to respond to the threat posed by fascist dictatorships. The debate, between advocates of pacifism and collective security, was most clearly expressed by Norman Thomas, who was the Socialist Party's candidate for president in 1928 and in 1932 (when he received *The Nation*'s endorsement). From 1922 to 1932, Thomas was a contributing editor of the magazine.

New Year's bells rang in the definite and open beginning of a naval race which is immediately of staggering cost and potentially far more likely to prepare the way for new war than for peace. But as the old year closed, the great American protagonist of that race, President Roosevelt, fresh from a considerable triumph for international good-will on the Western Hemisphere, waxed caustic in condemning the sale of certain implements of war to the recognized Spanish government. Those who defended that sale were for the most part bitter opponents of the naval race and long-time foes of the international trade in armaments. This is but one example of the inconsistencies, or seeming inconsistencies, in a mad world. Rarely, if ever, has the struggle for peace been so complicated, or have the lovers of peace been more sharply divided. They are caught in the confusion of a world more keenly aware than ever before of the suicidal costs of world war, yet more inclined to accept it as inevitable.

The whole issue has been immensely complicated by the triumph of fascism in Italy and more especially in Germany. Fascism glorifies both militarism and war. It is as surely a menace to the peace as to the liberty of mankind. One may be against both war and fascism, and yet find in every dispatch from Spain grim proof that practically, under conditions all too likely to occur again and again, resolute and effective opposition to fascism means war. Is it any wonder that in this kind of world consistency among peace lovers is not a common virtue?

Among the enemies of both war and fascism are two groups which at first sight seem more consistent than the rest of us. There are on the one hand those pacifists who hold that the great commandment can be summed up in this: "Thou shalt take no part in any kind of war." On the other hand there are those advocates of collective security who proclaim a holy crusade of democratic nations against fascist aggressors. Both groups are more successful in criticizing their extreme opponents than in supporting their own positions. For neither group have we invented an accurate name. To the first I shall apply the word "pacifist," pausing only to remind my readers that there are pacifists and pacifists. The best *pacifists* are not passivists, individuals concerned only with their own soul's salvation or believers in divine intervention in behalf of the martyrs of peace. The pacifists can point out that history furnishes melancholy justification for their successive contentions: (1) that the right sort of America could have used its immense social and moral power to bring about a negotiated peace instead of entering the World War; (2) that the peace of Versailles was a peace to end peace; and (3) that reasonable concessions in the days when Stresemann and the Social Democrats were still strong in Germany would have greatly increased the chances of victory for the republic against militarism and fascism. Today these pacifists can make no equally practical suggestion in the struggle against fascist aggression, but at least we owe them something for their constant challenge to the method of war and their constant reminder of its bitter cost.

Nevertheless, the pacifism which makes mere abstention from war the supreme command will not deliver mankind from new cycles of war and new dark ages of oppression. It is unrealistic and mad to say that it does not matter who wins in Spain if only the guns are stilled. It matters profoundly not only for Spain but for mankind that the fascist aggression of which Franco is the nominal and brutal leader be defeated. Persons who believe this must support the gallant resistance of the workers and other loyalists.

Those who cannot accept pacifism as the first and last commandment are not therefore the foes of peace. Indeed, the advocates of one form or another of "collective security" speak as its champions. Originally they sought to unite the world against the aggressor nation or nations. They reasoned that if the certainty of united action were great enough, a would-be aggressor would shrink from putting his fortunes to the test of war or even from facing those economic sanctions which the more optimistic believed might serve as a substitute for war. Now—and the change in itself signifies the historical failure of collective security through the League of Nations—those who consider themselves "realists" in contradistinction to the "pacifists" pin their hopes on an alliance of "democratic" states against realms ruled by dictators.

In a powerful and eloquent little book "We or They," an American citizen sees two worlds in conflict—the world of democracy and the world of dictatorship. In the second he places the Soviet Union. Hamilton Fish Armstrong is, to be sure, aware of differences as well as resemblances between fascism and communism. In my judgment he understates the differences, but certainly in terms of practical politics an organization of the democracies against the dictators which must begin with bitter controversy concerning the place of mighty Russia scarcely solves any major problem of world peace. Nevertheless, Mr. Armstrong and the school for which he is a persuasive spokesman make us face a dilemma which Americans cannot escape by mere opposition to war or any feasible degree of isolation.

What then? Shall intelligent Americans seek to build a league of non-fascist states with the definite object of checking fascist aggression, if necessary by preventive war, before German rearmament has gone farther and the continuous advance of science has made war even more deadly? There would be logic in that, but advocates of collective security usually reject it. It is a tribute to Mr. Armstrong's candor that he goes farther and doubts whether liberalism can stand the compulsions which war would put upon it. Yet he favors a form of "international insurance" which, if it means anything, means military alliance, actual or tacit, among the democratic nations.

Objections to this course of action fairly leap to one's mind. Why should such an alliance, especially if it tentatively places Russia outside its fold, succeed where the League of Nations has egregiously failed? The conduct of all nations, our own included, proves that such an alliance would not diminish the weight of competitive armament but would cause each nation to arm the more frantically, not only against fascism but to guarantee its position in the councils of its allies. Even without war this race in militarism would jeopardize whatever democracy we had left. The minute war was declared, America would become a fascist state or a military despotism. This is the calm assumption underlying the War Department's plans for military mobilization. Moreover, a declaration of war in capitalist America would not initiate a new struggle to make the world safe for democracy any more truly than when Congress declared war on April 6, 1917. Ideals would have their place in inducing the American people to accept a new war, but the primary motive would not be, as the Communists hope, a desire to protect Soviet Russia or, as Mr. Armstrong hopes, a desire to preserve democracy. It would be a desire, intelligent or futile, to further national economic interests.

The whole theory of an effective alliance of capitalist states in behalf of democracy is discredited by each day's news. It is not likely that any clearer case for joint action against fascism will ever present itself than the fascist rebellion in Spain. Yet Blum was afraid to act, partly because he feared a fascist rising at home and partly because he could get no support from the British Foreign Office. To this day that great "democracy" over which Stanley Baldwin presides has no clear policy. British mining interests in Spain were original supporters of Franco's revolt. The instinctive sentiment of the ruling class was on the side of the fascists. No abstract love of democracy moves the British government in its growing fear of fascism in Spain but rather reflection on the danger that would threaten the Empire and its precious life line through the Mediterranean should Italy or Germany, or both, gain a commanding position in Spain.

It is facts like these, added to the long and melancholy story of the failures of the League of Nations, which make us challenge the assumption of "two worlds in conflict." There is, indeed, a conflict between dictatorship and democracy — even the bourgeois democracy with which we are familiar. But fascism itself is not basically a conspiracy of wicked dictators against democracy. It is a logical stage of development of the ideals and institutions of capitalism and nationalism. They made the first world war. They made the peace of Versailles. They plowed the soil in which Hitler sowed the seeds of his tribal fascism. Loyalty to democracy, even bourgeois democracy, may well be invoked in the struggle against fascism. But at best it can only win a temporary victory. The essential struggle is still socialism against capitalism, not democracy against fascism. Power-driven machinery has forced a high degree of collectivism upon us. The great problem for workers throughout the world is whether they can make that collectivism cooperative and achieve the genuine democracy of socialism, or whether they must ultimately accept the rule of a dictator.

It is preposterous to think that the workers in the United States, in the supreme emergency of war, can maneuver the capitalist state and its military organization to gain their own ends. They may conceivably act as a brake on the state and mobilize effectively against war; they cannot utilize an international war to achieve a workers' victory unless first their country's military machine has met crushing defeat. But the practical conclusion from these considerations is not that the United States should seek ostrich-like isolation. It is that in capitalist America it is mad utopianism to believe that the government can be armed for international war against fascist aggression or can enter such a war at a price tolerable to the American people or to mankind. It is far more feasible for the workers and all lovers of peace to try to keep America out of the pursuit of war profits and hence out of war, and in the comparative sanity of this condition to see that it uses its influence for peace. This is the case for making neutrality and an embargo on the export of war supplies the American rule in all international struggles. It is the case against American participation in the new naval race.

The action of sincere and qualified volunteers who are willing to risk their own lives in the struggle in Spain is a different matter. They are investing their own lives, not conscripting others or involving the government. They are of a long line of men who have said with Tom Paine: "Where liberty is not, there is my fatherland." Those sanctions and economic pressures which can be applied by unofficial groups do not fall under the condemnation of the attempt to make capitalist America an armed guarantor of peace.

Moreover, a belief in the wisdom of neutrality as the fixed policy of the United States in international war—with exceptions to be made by Congress, not by the President—does not mean that a friendly, democratically elected government, such as that of Spain, must be denied access to supplies necessary to put down armed fascist rebellion. It is an ugly world in which anti-fascist forces must pay tribute to private profiteers for the arms of defense. Yet the one outstanding chance of changing that world lies for the moment in preserving for the Spanish government the right to those forms of help which under international law governments extend to one another. To preserve it does not compel the United States to use its navy directly or indirectly to guarantee shipments, nor does it involve this nation in risk of war. To deny it is not only a discriminatory act, deliberate support of the rebel cause; it is also a reversal of accepted American practice. The United States has not prevented the sale of arms to the Nanking government for use in the slaughter of workers and in civil war against the Chinese red army, or to Latin American dictators engaged in suppressing rebellions. It has invoked this policy for the first time in a civil war to keep arms from the government of Spain—a tragic misapplication of the principle of neutrality.

Not a method of keeping out of war but the establishment of a warless world must be our goal.

THOMAS MANN

I Stand with the Spanish People   *April 17, 1937*

Thomas Mann, novelist and recipient of the 1929 Nobel Prize in Literature, left Nazi Germany in 1933 and settled in the United States three years later. This piece, one of many he contributed to *The Nation* in the 1930s and 1940s, is a statement of solidarity with the Spanish republicans, at the height of the Spanish civil war.

Küsnacht, Switzerland

I was not born a political man, that is to say, a partisan whose will exercises restraints and limitations upon his intellect. Nor is it interest that bids me speak, but only my suffering and indignant conscience. It is interest that commits all the great rascalities in the world. As now in Spain. Then whose affair is it, if not the creative artist's—the man's whose emotions are free—to assert the human conscience against the baseness of interest, at once so presumptuous and so petty; to protest against the stultifying, all-embracing confusion made in our time between politics and villainy?

There is no lower kind of scorn than that visited upon the artist who "descends into the arena." And the ground of that scorn is interest—interest which prefers to gain its ends in darkness and silence, unchecked by the forces of the intellect or the spirit. Interest would confine artists to their proper domain of the cultural by telling them that politics is beneath their dignity. The result is that the cultural becomes the slave of interest, its accessory and accomplice, all for the false coin of a little dignity in return. The artist must not see that in this stately retreat to his ivory tower he is committing an act of anachronistic folly—must not see, yet today can hardly fail to see.

Democracy is a realized and intrinsic fact today to the extent that politics is everybody's business. Nobody can deny this; it stares us in the face with an immediacy never known before. Sometimes we hear somebody say, "I take no interest in politics." The words strike us as absurd, and not only absurd but egotisti-

144

cal and anti-social, a stupid self-deception, a piece of folly. But they are more; they betray an ignorance not only intellectual but ethical. For the politico-social field is an undeniable and inalienable part of the all-embracing human; it is one section of the human problem, the human task, which the non-political man thinks to set off, as the decisive and actual, against the political sphere. The decisive and the actual: it is indeed that, for in the guise of the political the problem of the human being, man himself, is put to us today with a final, life-and-death seriousness unknown before. Then shall the artist—he who by nature and destiny ever occupies humanity's farthest outposts—shall he alone be allowed to shirk a decision?

Life-and-death seriousness. I use these words to express the conviction that a man's—and how much more an artist's—opinions are today bound up with the salvation of his soul. I deliberately use a religious terminology; so convinced am I that an artist who in our time avoids the issue, shirks the human problem when politically presented, and betrays to interest the things of the spirit is a lost soul. He must be stunted; not only because he sacrifices his existence as an artist, his "talent," and produces nothing more which is available for life, but because even his earlier work, not created under the pressure of such guilt and once good, will cease to be good and crumble to dust before humanity's eyes. That is my conviction. I have instances in mind as I write.

I shall be asked what I mean by spirit and what by interest. Well, then, the spiritual, seen from the politico-social angle, is the longing of the people for better, juster, happier conditions of life, more adequate to the developed human consciousness. And interest—interest is all that which seeks to thwart this consummation because it would thereby be cut off from certain advantages and privileges. In Spain interest rages. Rages with a shamelessness such as the world has seldom seen. What has been happening there for many months is one of the most scandalous and mortifying pages which history has to show. Does the world see it, feel it? Only very partially. For murderous interest understands only too well how to besot the world and throw dust in its eyes.

Have we then no hearts? No understanding? Shall we let ourselves be unresistingly deprived of our last remnant of free human judgment by interest, which unfailingly appeals to the worst instincts, though it clothe itself in lying names such as order, culture, God, and native land? A people held down and exploited with all the instruments of the most obsolete reaction strives toward a brighter existence more compatible with human dignity, a social order more creditable to the face of civilization. There freedom and progress are conceptions not yet vitiated by philosophical irony and skepticism. For these people they are conditions of national honor, values to be striven for to the utmost. The government, with all the caution prescribed by the special circumstances, undertakes to remove the grossest abuses, to carry out the most imperative reforms. What happens? An insurrection of generals, occurring in the interest of the old exploiters and oppressors, concocted with the help of hopeful foreign interest, blazes up and misfires. When it is already as good as beaten, it is propped up by foreign governments inimical to freedom in return for promises of strategic and economic advantage in case of victory. It is supported by money, men, and material, fostered and prolonged, until there seems no end to the bloodshed, the tragic, ruthless, obstinate carnage. Against a people desperately fighting for its freedom and its human rights the troops of its own colony are led into battle. Its cities are demolished by foreign bombing planes, women and children are butchered; and all this is called a national movement; this villainy crying out to heaven is called God, Order, and Beauty. If the interested European press could have its way, the capital would have fallen long since; the triumph of Order and Beauty over the Marxist rabble would long since have been consummated. But the half-demolished capital is not yet conquered, and the "red mob," as the interested press puts it in referring to the Spanish people, is defending its life, its higher life, with a lion-like courage which must make even the most besotted slave of interest pause and consider the moral forces here engaged.

The right of peoples to self-determination enjoys high official honor throughout the world today. Even our dictators and our totalitarian states lay stress upon it, finding it important to show that they have 90 to 98 per cent of their people behind them. Well, so much is clear: the revolting military have not got the Spanish people behind them and cannot pretend that they have. They must do their best with Moors and foreign troops. It may not be quite settled what the Spanish people want. But what they do not want is abundantly clear – General Franco. Those European governments which are interested in the strangulation of freedom have recognized as legal the rebel junta, in the midst of a furious struggle which they support even if they did not connive at its inception. At home they betray a considerable degree of sensitiveness in the matter of high treason. In Spain they support a man who delivers up his country to the foreigner. At home they call themselves nationalists. In Spain they enforce the power of a man to whom his country's independence is naught if he can do to death freedom and the rights of humanity, who declares that rather shall two-thirds of the Spanish people die than that Marxism – that is to say, a better, juster, more humane order – shall triumph.

LOUIS FISCHER

Spain's Tragic Anniversary

July 30, 1938

> Between 1936 and 1938, the magazine ran hundreds of articles
> and editorials supporting the Loyalists' struggle against Fran-
> co's forces in the Spanish civil war. (The magazine also took
> more direct action: In 1937 *The Nation* sponsored a food ship
> to "send food to the innocent women and children and old peo-
> ple of republican Spain," and in 1938 it announced that its ap-
> peals for contributions to send an ambulance to the Loyalist
> forces had been over-subscribed.) Long into the 1940s, the
> magazine continued to document the illegality of the Franco re-
> gime and demand that it be kept isolated. Louis Fischer con-
> tributed first-hand reports to *The Nation* during the civil war.

Paris, July 12, 1938

On July 30, 1936, three Italian bombers landed by mistake near Oran, in French
Africa. The French High Commissioner at Rabat, reporting this incident to his
Paris superiors, stated that the pilots, who were en route to Spanish Morocco to
aid Franco, had received their flying orders from the Italian government on
July 15. The Spanish insurrection broke out on July 17.

The conflict was never a pure civil war. The Italian and German governments
participated in its advance preparations. From the very beginning it partook of
the nature of a foreign invasion abetted by the Spanish military, whose loyalty
to caste and property exceeded their love of country and progress. The war was
planned and started by oath-breaking generals with the support of domestic reactionaries and in collusion with outside powers bent on acquiring raw materials,
markets, and strategic positions.

This initiative has cost Spain dearly. On both sides almost a million men,
women, and children have been killed in battles, homes, and prisons. Some
Loyalist towns and villages have been completely pulverized by aerial bombs.
Every republican city has been partially destroyed in air raids or in fighting.
Three million persons, fleeing before the rebel forces, are refugees in Loyalist
territory. They and the rest of the civil population in the government zone suffer
from food scarcity. Life is full of torture for these ten million human beings. Be-
reaved and hungry, they undergo the additional trial of repeated and ubiquitous
bombardments from the air. Men and women whom the blood-chilling air-raid
siren may have called to the underground shelters two or three times a night for
a total period of several hours are expected to work with maximum intensity the
next day producing munitions and other goods. Children play air-raid games,
make classroom sketches of airplanes dropping bombs, and grow accustomed to

seeing flattened bodies, torsos, and limbs removed from debris by men who stand in pools of human blood. Time makes the sorrow, nervous and physical strain, and loss cumulative. When the effect was greatest, the fascists intensified their air war and sought to impose an air blockade.

The hate engendered in the surviving victims against the perpetrators of these cruelties and of the original crime of injecting war into a peaceful nation becomes a major political factor. Franco, if he should win, could never govern with these people. He would have to rule over them and despite them. There is no peace in Franco. He imported the Moors, the Germans, the Italians. He lacerated his native land. The contempt for him and his allies explains the resistance of the republicans. He stands for the old Spain of poverty and social stagnation. The fierceness of the Loyalists' opposition, against heartbreaking odds, to the fascist advance is a measure of their rejection of Spain's past and their hope for a better future. It warrants the prediction that the war will go on beyond most people's expectation. If and when Franco achieves a victory on the field of battle the struggle against the feudal land tenure, hierarchical darkness, and low living standards will continue. The republic heralded the possibility of a French revolution in Spain. The Francos demurred. Spain will never be content unless it can at least overtake Europe's nineteenth century.

On July 17, 1936, the republican government was weak and indecisive. That encouraged its enemies to strike. But the improbability of quick victory and resentment against the invader have given the republic strength and cohesion it never possessed in peacetime. Social programs which could only find permanent application after the war are relegated to the background. Fervid patriotism replaces the party feuds and ideological combats of pre-war politics. The reverse is happening in Franco's territory. When the rebels reached the coast in the March-April Aragon offensive and severed Catalonia from Central Spain, it seemed to the rebels and to their friends abroad that the end of the war impended. This belief released bitter inter-factional rivalry in the rebel camp. Monarchists, fascist Falange, and army chiefs made bids for power. Such strife, natural enough when peace follows war, cannot now be arrested, even though the war, surprisingly to some, proceeds with increasing fierceness. Falange leaders and many of their supporters are being jailed, and the Church and the other big estate owners brand them as "our Reds," probably because they evince some interest in the fate of the peasantry. The rebel zone is duplicating, roughly, the class struggle which rocked all of Spain before the war commenced.

Franco has never conscripted heavily in Castile, Andalusia, or Estremadura. For in these provinces the peasantry is land-hungry. But the manpower of Morocco is well-nigh exhausted. Franco has taken 100,000 Moors to Spain. They have borne the brunt of numerous battles. He cannot expect to recruit many more even though the frontier between Spain and France, in Africa, is open, and the rebels have been drawing French Moors into their services. Franco must get additional Italians or mobilize Spanish villagers of doubtful loyalty. The fighting in recent weeks on the Castellon-Teruel-Sagunto front is perhaps the bloodiest of the war. Losses on both sides have been extremely heavy, but Franco's human resources are limited, whereas the republic's are only now being tapped. The Loyalists have 700,000 soldiers today and plan to have a million under arms by the autumn. There are at present approximately 9,000 foreigners in the republican army. No more than 4,000 of these are at the front. The total of non-Spaniards who enlisted in the Loyalist army (International Brigade) since hostilities started is about 36,000. Thousands were killed, incapacitated, or repatriated. There were never more than 700 Soviet Russians serving under the republican colors, and the number now is unlikely to be over 300. Franco, observers estimate, has between 6,000 and 10,000 Germans and 60,000 and 80,000 Italians. The International Brigade consists of volunteers, some of whom came to Spain despite the obstructions of their governments. The Italians and Germans were sent by their governments.

The rebels have a vast superiority in equipment. Italian and German arms were available to Franco from the first day of the insurrection. The quantity has increased and their quality improved with time. The first Soviet material, on the other hand, arrived in the fourth week of October, 1936—three months after the outbreak. Its flow, which was never as broad as the fascist munitions stream, has been interrupted by submarine piracy in the Mediterranean and by the closing of the Spanish-French border. Moreover, all fascist airplanes fly into Spain, and some of the recent bombing of coastal cities and shipping has been carried out by Italian machines which rose from airdromes in Italy or Sardinia, dropped their missiles on Loyalist cities, and then returned to their bases. But no Soviet planes have been flown into Spain. They come by long and difficult sea and land routes. Barcelona pays for and acquires title to all the arms it imports from the U. S. S. R. and other countries. This is not true of Franco's imports from fascist states.

"Non-intervention" has worked to the disadvantage of the Spanish republic because England and France, the two nations whose national and imperial interests might normally impel them to help the Loyalists, have faithfully abided by the agreement. It works to the advantage of the rebels because Germany and Italy intervene. These regimes have included Spain in their expansionist schemes. They have set themselves military, political, and economic goals in Spain. They have invested armies, arms, air armadas, and the blood of thousands of their subjects in the venture. Parliamentary declarations and legal documents will not eject them. The stake is too important. They could be deterred only by their own exhaustion, of which there are faint signs and which, if it became more serious, might prevent them from undertaking other acts of aggression, or by a clear indication, backed by peaceful deeds, that the Western powers wanted the invaders to get out of Spain. But Mussolini and Hitler are entitled to believe that the British and French governments are reconciled to a Franco victory. That victory cannot be won without further intervention. The fascists will therefore continue to intervene. Hence the skepticism about the execution of the British plan for the evacuation of foreign combatants. It is not merely that the scheme offers a thousand technical difficulties, loopholes, and opportunities for procrastination. If it were really intended to make non-intervention real it would provide for the removal of foreign arms and the interdiction of their ingress. As it is, unlimited squadrons of fascist airplanes can still be brought in by air. The cordon around the Loyalists, however, is complete. Rome and Berlin, as well as Burgos, therefore, can only conclude that the plan is not calculated to rob them of their ultimate triumph. They will behave accordingly.

What is required of the democratic powers who wish to create or sustain a reputation of opposition to aggression — America waits for such signs — is simply not to strangle Loyalist resistance, which yet has tremendous potentialities. Spain ruined Napoleon. It can ruin lesser men, both interventionists and non-interventionists. The outcome of the Spanish war is by no means certain. Between 1914 and 1918 Germany won most of the battles. So far Franco has won most of the battles. Except one — the one for the support and loyalty of the Spanish people.

Spain is a second-rate country somewhat removed from the heart of Europe. But the Spanish conflict is determining the foreign policies and plays a gigantic role in the internal affairs of most of the major powers. Spain may decide the fate of ministers, of ministries, and, equally, of countries. The fate of Spain itself is important enough. But Spain is regarded by the fascist dictators as the beginning of bigger things. It would be one more conquest for totalitarianism and thus prejudice the issue against democracy in neighboring states. More immediately, the fascist victory in Spain would pave the way to further assaults on peaceful nations. Anti-fascists have been making this assertion and it has been regarded by the naive as propaganda. Here is how the Italian fascist *Resto del Carlino* put it on June 30, 1938:

> The solution of the Czechoslovak problem and of the colonial problem will be facilitated from the day when communism and its blind auxiliary, democracy, will have suffered a bloody defeat in the Iberian peninsula. On that day, France, before mobilizing on the Rhine, will have to think of its other frontiers: that of the Alps and that of the Pyrenees.

When the fascists launch other wars the democracies will not be able to complain that they were not warned. The democracies have ears and eyes — but Spain is a test. If the Western powers allow Spain to be submerged they will invite more trouble, perhaps nearer home.

GEORGE S. KAUFMAN

Einstein in Hollywood   *August 6, 1938*

> Pulitzer Prize–winning playwright George S. Kaufman wrote frequently for *The Nation* in the 1930s.

Warner Brothers have cabled Sigmund Freud, in London, asking him to come to Hollywood to assist in the preparation of the new Bette Davis picture, Dark Victory. —*News item.*

Sigmund Freud had been in Hollywood about a year, and was engaged to marry Merle Oberon, when the studio got another great idea. Louella Parsons broke the story, and her papers gave it a two-column head:

WARNER BROS. TO FILM THEORY OF RELATIVITY
Prof. Einstein Signed to Write Screen Treatment of Own Story—
Arrives in Hollywood Next Month

Einstein's arrival in Hollywood, of course, was the signal for a gay round of dinners and cocktail parties. The Basil Rathbones, who had given a party in Freud's honor to which everyone came as his favorite neurosis, gave one for Einstein in which the guests were got up as their favorite numbers. Needless to say, there were some pretty hot numbers.

The climax, however, was a dinner at the Trocadero, given by the film colony as a whole, at which Will H. Hays was the principal speaker. "The signing of Professor Einstein for pictures," said Mr. Hays, "is the greatest forward step that the industry has ever taken. American motion pictures appeal to people all over the world. I will be happy to okay Professor Einstein's contract just as soon as we get permission from Germany."

Next morning, on the Warner lot, Professor Einstein was assigned an office in the writers' building and a stenographer named Goldie. Promptly at twelve o'clock he was summoned to a conference. The producer received him with a flourish.

"Professor," he said, "allow me to introduce Sol Bergen and Al Jenkins, who are going to work with you on the picture. Now, I've been thinking this thing over, and we want this to be absolutely *your* picture. What you say goes. But of course we all want a hit, and I'm sure you're willing to play ball with us. Now, I've got some great news for you. I've decided to put Joan Blondell in it."

Sol Bergen let out a war whoop. "Gee, Boss, that's great. Her name alone will put it over."

"I want the Professor to have the best," said the producer, "because I'm sure he's going to give us a great picture. Now, Professor, here's the problem: how can we treat this theory of yours so as to keep it just as you wrote it—because this has got to be *your* picture—and still make it entertainment? Because first and foremost a motion picture has got to be entertainment. But of course we want your theory in it too."

"I'm not sure that I've got the Professor's theory exactly straight," said Al Jenkins. "Would you mind, Professor, giving me just a quick summary of it, in a sort of non-technical way?"

"I don't think we have to bother the Professor about that," said the producer. "I've been thinking it over, and I've got a great way to work it in. And here it is." He leaned back and looked at them. "The scene is a college where they *teach* this theory of the Professor's. Only it's a very *tough* theory, and there's never been a *girl* that's been able to understand it. Of course it's a co-ed college. And finally along comes a girl, attractive, of course, and says, '*I* am going to understand it.' "

"Blondell!" said Sol Bergen.

"Right!" said the producer. "So she pitches in and goes to work. She won't go to parties or dances or anything, and she wears horn-rimmed glasses, and the boys think she's a grind and hasn't got any sex appeal. Underneath, of course, she's a regular girl."

"There's got to be one guy in particular that falls for her," said Jenkins.

"Sure!" said the producer, "and I'll tell you who'd be great in the part. Wayne Morris. How's that, Professor? How'd you like to have Wayne Morris in your picture?"

"Let's make him the captain of the football team," said Bergen. "It'll give us a great finale."

"Fine!" said the producer. "Now, Blondell has got a girl friend that goes to college with her, only she's a different type. Flighty, and never does any studying, but a smart little kid when it comes to handling the boys. Knows 'em from A to Z. Now, there's a millionaire, an old grad that's just presented the college with a stadium, and his son is going to the college. Lots of money, and a racing car, and this kid sets her cap for him. We could have a crack-up on his way back from the roadhouse."

"Or else he could lead the college band," said Bergen. "That way you get your music in."

"Great! And we have a kid playing the girl that can handle a couple of numbers.

Here's an idea, Professor. How about Warren and Dubin for the score? How would you like that, huh?"

"And how's this?" asked Jenkins. "She has another girl friend that sort of likes the older boys—with dough, see? And she sets out after the rich father."

"I've got it!" said the producer. "I've got the title! 'Gold Diggers at College.' Yes, sir, 'Gold Diggers at College,' by Albert Einstein, Sol Bergen, and Al Jenkins, based on the Theory of Relativity, by Albert Einstein. Professor, you've done a great picture!"

I.F. STONE

Making Defense Safe for Alcoa   September 27, 1941

One of America's most celebrated independent journalists, "Izzy" Stone earned a place as the conscience of American journalism through his incisive intelligence and his investigative zeal. As *The Nation*'s Washington correspondent from 1941 to 1946, and founder of the legendary *I.F. Stone's Weekly*—the independent, iconoclastic newsletter of opinion that he edited for nineteen years (1953–71)—Stone specialized in publishing information ignored by the mainstream media.

Last Monday the Truman committee, a Senate committee investigating the defense program, heard two witnesses. One was Jesse Jones. The other was Arthur H. Bunker, executive vice-president of the Lehman Corporation, now chief of the aluminum and magnesium section in the materials division of the OPM [Office of Production Management]. Both were unwilling witnesses. The story drawn from them, painfully and piecemeal, was a sensational story and an important story, for it dealt with aluminum. Without enough aluminum we cannot make enough planes, and without enough planes we can neither help the British and the Russians to survive nor defend ourselves in the event of their defeat.

Some important stories are dull stories—full of statistics and complicated facts. "Pig iron" we used to call them. The story developed by the Truman committee hearing was hardly dull. The testimony showed that (1) Bunker, the dollar-a-year man in charge of aluminum and magnesium, is still drawing his $60,000-a-year salary from Lehman Corporation, which owns stock in the Aluminum Company of America and its sister corporation, Aluminum Ltd., of Canada; (2) after four months not a shovelful of dirt has been turned on the 600,000,000 pound aluminum expansion program announced by the OPM last May; (3) the first contract to be signed under that program obligates the government to spend $52,000,000 to finance new alumina and aluminum plants but leaves the Aluminum Company of America to build these plants when it chooses and to operate them as it pleases; (4) this one-sided contract was negotiated by Jesse Jones, who can be the country's most hard-boiled horse-trader in dealing with some small business man or municipality; (5) Jones signed the contract two days after the receipt of a letter from Secretary of the Interior Ickes protesting that the contract was unfair to the government and contrary to the public interest, and ought not to be signed; (6) Jones testified that the contract was written "in the first instance" by "Mr. Cliff Durr, our general counsel," but a moment later Durr was forced to admit that the first draft was written by Oscar Ewing, counsel for the Aluminum Company of America. I can add, as my own contribution to this story, that there was very little difference between the first draft of that contract and the last, and that Ewing is not only one of Alcoa's principal attorneys and local lobbyists but also vice-chairman of the Democratic National Committee. At this point the Truman committee pulled its punches.

I went over the contract between Alcoa and Jesse Jones last week-end and mentioned it in last week's letter because I was naive enough to think the press could hardly ignore the story and would squeeze all the juice out of it before a weekly could get around to covering it. I saw eight or nine newspapermen at the committee hearing on Monday, and I see a good many papers every day, but the only place I saw the story printed was in the Baltimore *Sun,* which ran a short Associated Press account. Until yesterday the only clipping the Truman committee had received on the hearing was from the Baltimore *Sun.* The Ewing angle is political dynamite, but the Republican *Herald Tribune* in New York charitably overlooked it. The New York *Times,* which is for all-out aid to Britain, seems to have failed to see the connection between aluminum and planes. It does not hate Hitler less; perhaps it merely loves Alcoa more. The Washington papers kept mum on the story, although the Washington *Post* on Monday ran a rewrite of an A. P. dispatch saying that Jones would be put on the griddle by the Truman committee.

I think the silence of the press on the matter is as shocking as the inactivity of the OPM. Together they present Mussolini with a fine example of what he calls a "pluto-democracy." They show how little the real controls of the defense program have been changed behind all the recent scene-shifting and shake-ups. This is the kind of thing that rots empires and prepares defeats, and it is time that Mr. Roosevelt woke up to what is going on in his own defense household instead of continuing the grandiose face by which a Stettinius—more responsible than any other man for the delay in expanding aluminum production—is placed in charge of "speeding up" the lend-lease program!

The darkest aspect of this aluminum story is its one bright spot. When William L. Batt appeared before the Truman committee last May 12, he was able to show by some strenuous arithmetic that the present production of aluminum plus the expansion planned would be just enough by the spring of 1942 to take care of our "direct" military needs. The new bomber programs—which remain headline hashish without aluminum—have since increased those "direct" military needs for the light metal. Four months have been lost, and the only contract signed covers but half the expansion planned. The new aluminum-producing facilities will not be ready by next spring. I learned from Truman committee investigators, however, that the consequences will not be as serious as might have been expected because the lag in aircraft production is greater than the lag in aluminum production. Aircraft production is now expected to hit its full stride by December of 1942 instead of next spring, and aluminum planning is in terms of the winter and spring of 1942–43.

Judging from the testimony last Monday and the contract, what we have to begin worrying about now is whether present expansion plans will materialize in time to take care of expanded plane production in the winter and spring of 1942–43. Unless Alcoa's grip on the OPM and the [Reconstruction Finance Corporation] RFC is loosened, I do not think we will get that aluminum in time. The contract with Alcoa provides for four new plants. One is for alumina, the intermediate product from which aluminum is made. This plant, to be erected in Arkansas, will supply 400,000,000 pounds of alumina a year, or enough to make only an additional 200,000,000 pounds of aluminum. The three other plants are aluminum plants, one with a capacity of 150,000,000 pounds a year, to be built near Massena, New York; the second, with 90,000,000 pounds' capacity, to be constructed "adjacent to deep water" in Washington or Oregon; the third, with a capacity of 100,000,000 pounds, to be set up in Arkansas. That is a total of 340,000,000 pounds of aluminum. No contracts have yet been signed for the rest of the 600,000,000-pound expansion promised in May, or for the additional alumina required to produce the aluminum, or for the additional fabricating facilities necessary. Aluminum ingots don't fly.

The contract is full of loopholes that lawyers will appreciate. No time is fixed for completion of the plants, and there is, of course, no penalty clause. Alcoa merely agrees to "use its best endeavors" to obtain the land necessary for construction of the plants, and it is doubtful whether the sites have yet been picked. The best Jones could say was, "I think the site at Massena, New York, has been picked. I am not certain about Arkansas. I think the site for the Northwest plant has been picked." Alcoa agrees to prepare plans, and if the plans are approved by the government, to complete the work "as soon as practicable." Jones said it was his recollection that Alcoa thought it would have the plants ready in less than a year's time. When Hugh Fulton, counsel to the committee, asked him why that wasn't put into the contract with a penalty clause attached, Jones said, "I can't tell you." Jones's testimony is a lexicographer's nightmare. At one point he inter-

DAVID LEVINE: *I.F. Stone* **(1982)**

preted the word "shall" in the contract as meaning "maybe," and at another he said "or" meant the same as "both." In the construction of the plants Alcoa is not obligated to exercise "good faith and reasonable care," the usual formula, but "good faith or that degree of care which they normally exercise in the conduct of Alcoa's business." The non-lawyer reader may take my word for it that the second clause would make proof of negligence, much less bad faith, very difficult. Fulton wanted to know why the term "reasonable care" wasn't used instead and why the contract said "or" instead of "and." I quote from the record:

JONES:. . . I don't agree with you that "or" means one or the other. "Or" means both.
FULTON: "Or" means "both"?
JONES: Certainly. . .

Aluminum is made from alumina and alumina from bauxite. Ninety per cent of the country's high-grade bauxite, the only kind being used, is controlled by Alcoa. After the bauxite is purchased, on Alcoa's terms, the government will still have to ask Alcoa's permission to make alumina from it in the government's own alumina plant. The contract says, "When the alumina plant is completed, production of alumina therein shall be at such rates within its capacity and for such periods as shall be agreed upon from time to time by Defense [Plant] Corporation and Alcoa." Fulton asked Jones, "Suppose Alcoa tells you it doesn't agree that that plant should be operated, even though you have a good many millions of government money in it? I don't quite see under this contract, how you could require it to be operated."

JONES: I suspect you could if you were to try.
FULTON: Under what provision of the contract?
JONES: You could do it without a contract. . . .
FULTON: Why sign a contract where they have a right such as that, Mr. Jones, when you have no right to control and operate the plant? Why not insert a provision authorizing you to operate the plant if they don't want to?
JONES: I think we are fully protected. . . .

Under the contract, after Alcoa has permitted alumina to be produced in the government plant, the government cannot use its own alumina to make aluminum in its own aluminum plants except at a price satisfactory to Alcoa. If any alumina is left over, which could be made available to other manufacturers of aluminum, it cannot be sold except on terms satisfactory to Alcoa. Alcoa gets a five-year lease on the aluminum plants. The lease begins either seven years from the execution of the contract or whenever production reaches 80 per cent of capacity, whichever is earlier. This allows two years for construction of the plants. Once they are in operation, production in the government-owned plants is to be at the same rate as in Alcoa's plants, and under the contract the government cannot cancel the lease unless production is restricted to less than 40 per cent of capac-

157

ity. . . . I wish some Senator would have the courage to ask Jesse Jones whether this contract was written to defend the United States or the Aluminum Company of America.

HENRY MILLER

Mother and Son

June 5, 1943

[*book review*]

> Henry Miller's first two novels, *Tropic of Cancer* (1934) and *Tropic of Capricorn* (1939), were banned in the United States until the early 1960s.

Thomas Wolfe's Letters to His Mother, Julia Elizabeth Wolfe. **Edited with an Introduction by John Skally Terry. Charles Scribner's Sons. $3.**

The letters of a genius are always interesting even when they are dull, and these letters of Wolfe, like his books, are dull. Every other letter seems to be about money and how it gets that way. And when finally money does begin to flow his way, then come the lawsuits. Poor Wolfe discovers that even a halfwit has the right, in a democracy, to sue you, bleed you, though he hasn't a leg to stand on. In the course of a short life Wolfe seems to have discovered many things which the ordinary schoolboy knows instinctively. One of the most amusing statements is the one concerning Professor Baker of Harvard. "I think he's bitterly disappointed because I began teaching, but he never told me by what means I could live." Aye, there's the rub. And there is something pathetic about the inability of editors and publishers, in a land that worships money, power, fame, and success, to keep alive a man of genius whose needs are few. To receive $250 for something like 30,000 words is the sort of encouragement which makes a writer wonder if he wouldn't be better off digging ditches or robbing banks.

There is also something amusing and pathetic about the valiant and, to my mind, misguided efforts of the good Max Perkins to whip the amorphous volume of Wolfe's writings into some acceptable form. The only book of Wolfe's I could ever finish was the little volume called "The Story of a Novel." I was violently moved by this account and convinced, moreover, that a crime had been committed against Wolfe by the very man who tried to help him. It is quite possible, to be sure, that without editorial assistance Wolfe might never have brought any of his books to a conclusion. But would that have mattered? Just as his mother tried to keep him a child, so his publishers tried to keep him readable. A child who is weaned at the age of three and a half is never weaned; a boy who is kept in curls until he is a young man never becomes a young man; a giant who sleeps with his mother until it is time to find a mate never finds a mate. And a young genius who begins like a Niagara can never be made into an acceptable wooden novelist such as publishers are constantly looking for. Left to his own resources, encouraged to do as he pleased, Thomas Wolfe might have committed suicide at an early age, leaving to posterity a grandiose unfinished opus which would have been the pride of American letters.

The saddest thing about Wolfe is the feeling he gives of being alone in the world. And though he was always tied to his mother by the umbilical cord, he gives the impression frequently that he had been abandoned even by her. In trying to tell her what his first novel is about, he writes: "It says that we are born alone — all of us who ever lived or will live — that we live alone, and die alone, and that we are strangers to one another, and never come to know one another." Quite naturally this feeling was accompanied by a mania to devour the world; it was the only means left him to connect with the world. Instead of incorporating the world, however, he dies of glut. In this he reminds one of Balzac. The pattern of his life is that of the treadmill. He becomes a victim of work. No death, no phoenix rising from the ashes. Just a huge machine waging a hopeless battle with time.

His malady was gigantism, in all its manifestations. His tentacles spread everywhere, but they never light upon the golden shears which will liberate him and give him atonement. He is a river with a blind mouth, a moving panorama which erases itself with every turn of the bend. He will remember everything from the day he was born, and record it with the exactitude of a physicist, but though he labor like a fiend he will never succeed in laying the cornerstone of the temple he longs to inhabit. He remains the infant Gargantua, stumbling through the world nursery and scattering débris everywhere. An utterly humorless prodigy to boot. Alone, misshapen, misunderstood. A misfit. A giant for whom a toothache assumes the proportions of a tragedy: something to write home about, something to wrest a tear from that monument to real estate who could have been a writer too — if she had had the training.

His admirers are right in regarding him as a genuine American. He had all their faults and all their virtues. "I could never be anything but American if I tried," he writes. Yet again and again he expresses his disgust with "the huge, loud, noisy madhouse" that America is. And then, like all genuine Americans, he can add: "We have it in us to be a really great people, I think, whenever we find what is sometimes called a soul." In this utterance we have an intimation of the real tragedy which confronts every great American artist. For, until that soul emerges, how are we ever going to stop killing off our creative spirits? What place is there for a poet in a garden where automobile parts are at a premium? With Wolfe's death we are left with at most two or three writers of unmistakable genius. The others are the successful writers whom the mothers worship.

I.F. STONE

For the Jews—Life or Death?   June 10, 1944

Since the earliest months of the Nazi regime, *The Nation* had been urging the liberalization of American immigration laws to admit refugees from Nazi persecution. But the U.S., shamefully, refused to lower immigration barriers in any substantial way. While the extermination of the Jews received very little coverage in Allied and neutral newspapers, *The Nation* published many articles and editorials about the horrors of the situation in Germany in an attempt to force American and world attention to the Holocaust.

At his press conference on June 2, after this article was written, the President indicated that he was considering the conversion of an army camp in this country into a "free port" for refugees. Unfortunately, as the New York Post *has pointed out, "his statement was conditional, indefinite. The check is still on paper and we don't even know what the amount is." In these circumstances Mr. Stone's analysis of the urgency of the situation and his plea for public pressure to secure action from the Administration are no less valid than they were before Mr. Roosevelt spoke.*
                                                       —ORIGINAL NOTE

Washington, June 1, 1944

This letter, addressed specifically to fellow-newspapermen and to editors the country over, is an appeal for help. The establishment of temporary internment camps for refugees in the United States, vividly named "free ports" by Samuel Grafton of the New York *Post,* is in danger of bogging down. Every similar proposal here has bogged down until it was too late to save any lives. I have been over a mass of material, some of it confidential, dealing with the plight of the fast-disappearing Jews of Europe and with the fate of suggestions for aiding them, and it is a dreadful story.

Anything newspapermen can write about this in their own papers will help. It will help to save lives, the lives of people like ourselves. I wish I were eloquent, I wish I could put down on paper the picture that comes to me from the restrained and diplomatic language of the documents. As I write, the morning papers carry a dispatch from Lisbon reporting that the "deadline"—the idiom was never more literal— has passed for the Jews of Hungary. It is approaching for the Jews of Bulgaria, where the Nazis yesterday set up a puppet regime.

I need not dwell upon the authenticated horrors of the Nazi internment camps and death chambers for Jews. That is not tragic but a kind of insane horror. It is our part in this which is tragic. The essence of tragedy is not the doing of evil by evil men but the doing of evil by good men, out of weakness, indecision, sloth, inability to act in accordance with what they know to be right. The tragic element in the fate of the Jews of Europe lies in the failure of their friends in the West to shake loose from customary war and bureaucratic habit, to risk inexpediency and defy prejudice, to be whole-hearted, to care as deeply and fight as hard for the big words we use, for justice and for humanity, as the fanatic Nazi does for his master race or the fanatic Jap for his Emperor. A reporter in Washington cannot help seeing this weakness all about him. We are half-hearted about what little we could do to help the Jews of Europe as we are half-hearted about our economic warfare, about blacklisting those who help our enemies, about almost everything in the war except the actual fighting.

There is much we could have done to save the Jews of Europe before the war. There is much we could have done since the war began. There are still things we could do today which would give new lives to a few and hope to many. The hope that all is not black in the world for his children can be strong sustenance for a man starving in a camp or entering a gas chamber. But to feel that your friends and allies are wishy-washy folk who mean what they say but haven't got the gumption to live up to it must brew a poisonous despair. When Mr. Roosevelt established the War Refugee Board in January, he said it was "the policy of this government to take all measures within its power . . . consistent with the successful prosecution of the war . . . to rescue the victims of enemy oppression."

The facts are simple. Thanks to the International Red Cross and those good folk the Quakers, thanks to courageous non-Jewish friends in the occupied countries themselves and to intrepid Jews who run a kind of underground railway under Nazi noses, something can still be done to alleviate the suffering of the Jews in Europe and some Jews can still be got out. Even under the White Paper there are still 22,000 immigration visas available for entry into Palestine. The main problem is to get Jews over the Turkish border without a passport for transit to Palestine. "Free ports" in Turkey are needed, but the Turks, irritated by other pressures from England and the United States, are unwilling to do for Jewish refugees what we ourselves are still unwilling to do, that is, give them a temporary haven. Only an executive order by the President establishing "free ports" in this country can prove to the Turks that we are dealing with them in good faith; under present circumstances they cannot but feel contemptuous of our pleas. And the longer we delay the fewer Jews there will be left to rescue, the slimmer the chances to get them out. Between 4,000,000 and 5,000,000 European Jews have been killed since August, 1942, when the Nazi extermination campaign began.

There are people here who say the President cannot risk a move of this kind before election. I believe that an insult to the American people. I do not believe any but a few unworthy bigots would object to giving a few thousand refugees a temporary breathing spell in their flight from oppression. It is a question of Mr. Roosevelt's courage and good faith. All he is called upon to do, after all, is what Franco did months ago, yes, *Franco*. Franco established "free ports," internment camps, months ago for refugees who fled across his border, refugees, let us remember, from his own ally and patron, Hitler. Knowing the Führer's maniacal hatred for Jews, that kindness on Franco's part took considerably more courage than Mr. Roosevelt needs to face a few sneering editorials, perhaps, from the Chicago *Tribune*. I say "perhaps" because I do not know that even Colonel McCormick would in fact be hostile.

Official Washington's capacity for finding excuses for inaction is endless, and many people in the State and War departments who play a part in this matter can spend months sucking their legalistic thumbs over any problem. So many things that might have been done were attempted too late. A little more than a year ago Sweden offered to take 20,000 Jewish children from occupied Europe if Britain and the United States guaranteed their feeding and after the war their repatriation. The British were fairly rapid in this case, but it took three or four months to get these assurances from the American government, and by that time the situation had worsened to a point that seems to have blocked the whole project. In another case the Bulgarian government offered visas for 1,000 Jews if arrangements could be made within a certain time for their departure. A ship was obtained at once, but it took seven weeks for British officials to get clearance for the project from London, and by that time the time limit had been passed. The records, when they can be published, will show many similar incidents.

The news that the United States had established "free ports" would bring hope to people who have now no hope. It would encourage neutrals to let in more refugees because we could take out some of those they have already admitted. Most important, it would provide the argument of example and the evidence of sincerity in the negotiations for "free ports" in Turkey, last hope of the Balkan Jews. I ask fellow-newspapermen to show the President by their expressions of opinion in their own papers that if he hesitates for fear of an unpleasant political reaction he badly misconstrues the real feelings of the American people.

ARCHIBALD MacLEISH

The People Are Indivisible *October 28, 1944*

In 1944, poet Archibald MacLeish was Librarian of Congress. He contributed several articles to *The Nation* during the war.

It has taken us a long time to agree on the precise words in which the issue of this war should be put, but we have always known in our bones what the issue was. We have always realized that what was at stake was the relation of individual men and women to the governments under which they lived. We have realized that the outcome of the war would determine how individual men and women would live under government for generations to come—and not only in fascist countries and in the countries conquered by the fascists but in other countries as well, even our own. We have known, that is to say, that the basic issue of the war was whether men were to live from this time forth as citizens of a nation or as subjects of a state.

And there was something else we knew also. We knew that this same issue would be the issue not only of the war but of the peace. For we realized—and it was this that made it difficult for us to put the issue of the war in definite and certain words—we realized that the war could not itself resolve the issue which produced it. Or rather the war alone could not decide that issue in our favor: it could, against us. If the fascists won, men everywhere, in this country as well as in other countries, would come to live, sooner or later, as subjects of a state. In a universe of ant colonies no ants can survive which do not organize and discipline themselves on the helot model. If we won, men would have at least a chance to live as citizens of a nation. There would be a chance to construct men's lives on the surface of the earth in the free light and sweet air, rather than underground in the mutually exclusive, darkly hateful, armed and ignorant corridors of the colonies of ants. It was, I think, because we saw very well that to win the war was not thereby to win the issue of the war, while to lose the war was to lose everything, that we found it so difficult to put our purpose in the war in words.

But now that our victory in the war itself is certain—now that the defensive victory in arms is sure—the difficulty of the declaration of our purpose disappears. We can declare a purpose in the making of the peace which we could not have declared with confidence in the waging of the war. And that purpose is not peace. Peace can never be a purpose in itself, for peace, like war, is a resultant, and those who try to seize it in itself, like those who grasp for images in water, will lose the gains they have. Our purpose is a world in which a peace will be conceivable. Which means a world in which the power will be held by those who do not wish for war. Which means, in turn, a world in which the people hold the power. Our purpose in the peace is the affirmation of our purpose in the war. In the war we fought to overcome the forces which would turn all citizens to subjects. In the peace we aim to make a world in which men everywhere shall live as citizens—a world in which no ant-hill state shall dig us down to slavery and darkness by the dread of war.

I say that is our purpose. I mean, it should be. If we intend the words we speak about the war, our purpose, now the war is ending, will be this. There is no possibility of peace but in the practice of democracy, and there is no possibility of the practice of democracy if any corner of the world is held by fascist power, armed and prepared for war—or arming and preparing. If we mean what we have said, if we mean to make a peace, then there is no stopping in our purpose short of this—this purpose: a world in which men everywhere shall live as citizens, a world in which the people shall possess the power. And not here alone, or in the countries of our allies in this war, but everywhere.

But do we truly mean this? Do our agents and our representatives in other countries mean this? Do party leaders, candidates for office, makers of opinion mean this? Do we ourselves, as a people, as a nation, mean this? To mean that the ant-hill state shall be destroyed throughout the world, we must intend that men shall rule themselves throughout the world. We must advance, not for ourselves alone but for the people everywhere, the great American proposition on which the founders of this nation stood. We must believe positively and not passively, literally and not as a figure of speech, that the people ought to govern themselves because the people *can* govern themselves, and because the government of the people by themselves will make for peace. And do we believe it? Do we believe it, now, in fact, of all men, everywhere—and mean it?

We have made a practice of dividing the parties to this war into democrats and fascists, ourselves and the dictators, white and black, good and evil. The division on this issue of the peace is not so simple. There are men other than the men now or lately in control of Germany and Italy and Japan who do not in truth and fact believe in the people and in their right to rule themselves. Some of them, like the masters of the fascist states, disbelieve in the people because they despise the people, or because they fear the people, or because they want what the people might not wish to let them have. But there are others, and they are not few, and they do not live in Germany only or in Italy or in Japan, who disbelieve in the people not because they despise the people, or hate the people, or fear them, but for an honest reason, a regretful reason—because they doubt the ability of the people to govern in the modern world, because they think the complexity of the modern world is such that the people cannot possibly comprehend it and cannot, therefore, govern it by their majorities or by their votes.

The real enemies in the struggle for the peace we say we want are these men, not our enemies in arms. It is because of them that the struggle for the peace is doubtful. The doubtful struggles are the struggles in which no one knows his adversary—in which the adversary may walk beside him as a friend—may even be himself. And this is such a conflict. If the division were clear, if we on our side were united in acceptance of the proposition that the people can and ought to govern, there would be no question about the making of a successful peace. If we and our principal allies in the war were so united, there would be no question. Indeed, if even we alone, we Americans who first advanced the proposition of the people, were united in a firm and fierce belief, the question would be answered.

But are we so united? I am not thinking, when I ask this, of the practical politicians who sneer and snigger at the notion that the Hottentots can rule themselves, or that the Chinese can, or the Negroes in Mississippi. I am not thinking of the cynical men, or the selfish men, or the interested men, or the evil men. I am thinking of the rest, who are not cynical or evil. I am thinking of those who describe themselves as realistic and disinterested observers of their time—those who have seen what they have seen, those who put realities above the rhetoric no matter who composed the rhetoric, even Lincoln.

I am thinking of the disinterested observers who will tell you that the proliferation of printed matter in our time has become so vast and measureless that it threatens to bury the libraries, and that no citizen, no matter how conscientious, can learn a fraction of the things he needs to know to know his duty; of the students of technical matters who remind you that the multiplication of skills and crafts in our epoch has become so great, and the elaboration of technologies so intricate, that few citizens of any degree of intelligence—to say nothing of the masses of the citizens—can comprehend how the things they use and need the most are made; of the economists who point out that ours is a period in which the operations of commerce and of banking are so delicately and mysteriously adjusted that the writing of a number on a blackboard in New York may shake the lives of men and women in Australia by means no common citizen can comprehend; of the scholarly persons who remark that science in our generation has given over the explanation of the mysteries that every man can see, and has disappeared instead into the invisible world beyond the magnifying glass and behind the mathematical symbols, whence far explorers send their messages in codes and symbols that only their fellow-voyagers, and not always they, are able to decipher; of the philosophers who observe that space in our world has been turned into time, and that debt has been turned into wealth, and that men no longer work to build but to buy, and that nothing is what it seems, and that even the thing that seems is past the common man's conception.

What endangers, what really endangers, the making of the peace is not contempt for the people in the propaganda of our open enemies but this skepticism of our friends—and of ourselves. Few Americans, however realistic and objective, will openly repudiate the proposition Mr. Jefferson advanced, or reject the words in which, at Gettysburg, it took the shape that men remember. Most of us give at least the service of our lips to the American doctrine that the people—not the American people only but the People—can govern themselves and of right ought to. Our doubts are only reservations. But there are times when reservations are as dangerous as denials, times indeed when they can be more dangerous. When the world demands an act of faith, the reservations which deprive belief of passion, faith of ardor, can be worse than open treason. For they are not spoken and cannot be fought.

This is our danger as we make the peace: that we wish it but with reservations; that we do not sufficiently desire what we must desire if a peace is to be made; that we do not sufficiently believe what we must believe if we want a world in which a peace is possible. Many of us, even of the best of us, are all too ready to condone the questioning of the people's right to govern, the open doubts of the capacity of the people, which cynical publishers and politicians have expressed in words at home, and agents of this government have expressed in deeds abroad. Many of us, though we resent that conduct and those sneers in words, believe in our hearts that the doubts they imply are justified. Many of us, far too many of us, though we use the words for peace and liberty and freedom, do not believe at bottom, or do not believe enough, that the one essential condition of peace and liberty and freedom can be realized in the actual world.

If this is true, and if we fail to make the peace our victory demands of us, our failure will not be a failure of our possibilities but of our faith. And such a failure would be very strange. For we of all the nations of the earth, and ours of all the generations that have talked of people's governments and power, have now most reason to believe. Faith in the people is the deep American faith, and our generation is the generation which has seen more reasons to accept that faith than any which have lived before us. We have the proof before our eyes. We have the proof not in our own people only but in the peoples of France, Greece, Spain, Poland, and other countries—the visible and unanswerable proof that the people are capable, in the face of every difficulty and every risk, of governing themselves, of disciplining themselves, of resisting to death and beyond death, that the people are capable of governing themselves in the highest and noblest meaning of the word govern.

Jean-Paul Sartre has said all this superbly in an article which has made a deep impression on the French, an article published in Paris in *Les Lettres Françaises*.

They did not fight in the daylight, like soldiers—in every circumstance they were alone, they were pursued and arrested in their solitude. And it was in their loneliness, in their complete nakedness, that they resisted torture, alone and stripped before their well-shaven, well-fed, and well-dressed executioners, who mocked their pitiful flesh and whose complacent consciences and incredible social power gave every evidence of their being in the right.

Alone. Without the help of a friendly hand or any encouragement whatsoever. However, in the very depth of this solitude there were the others, all the others, all the comrades of resistance, whom they were defending. One single word sufficient to provoke ten or a hundred new arrests. This total responsibility in total solitude – was not this the final revelation of our liberty?

Thus, in blood and shadows, a republic erected itself, the strongest of republics. Each of its citizens knew what he owed to every other, and that each could count on that alone. Each of them understood, in the completest loneliness, his historic role and responsibility. Each of them undertook to be himself freely, irremediably against the oppressors. And in his freedom in choosing himself, he chose the freedom of all. This republic, without institutions, army, or police, made every Frenchman affirm and maintain it against Nazism and at every moment. No one here failed it.

How, with the proof of France before us, with the proof of the whole resistance before us, can we doubt, how can we permit ourselves to question, the great declaration of faith and of belief which brought this nation also into being? How, with this proof before us, with the proof of our own tremendous effort in the war before us, can we fail to silence the doubts, the reservations, which say that a people's peace cannot be made because a people's government is now no longer possible, or is only possible here, or in a few more fortunate countries, or under the best and the most favorable conditions? How, in the face of the mobilization of our own people for the war, in the face of these "republics of silence and of the night," can we lack an answer to the doubts which tell us that a modern civilization is too complicated and intricate and arcane and vast for the people to understand and govern, or that only the Americans, or only the most exceptional peoples, can govern in such a world? Can it not be answered to these doubters, whether in ourselves, or beside us in the streets, or elsewhere, that the peoples of many nations have accomplished in the dark, and in the dread of death, and naked, what we say cannot be done? Can it not be answered that men and women who have conquered their own fears, and fought a revolution with their empty hands, and nourished a republic in their nakedness and silence, have proved that men can understand more complicated problems than the bankers ever thought of, and master mysteries no scientist has seen?

The act of faith is never easy. It is not easy now, for faith is an action in our generation as it has not been for centuries. More are hated for belief than for their deeds, and more are punished for it – many ways of punishment. Nevertheless, if one thing in this terrible time is certain it is this – that only an act of faith can win this war, can win the issue that this war was fought for. If we cannot find again the faith in the people which moved the founders of this republic, if we cannot capture the new-found faith in themselves which upheld the peoples of Europe, the war our arms will win will not be won beyond the ranges of our guns or the enlistment of our armies. But if we can read our own past and believe it, if we can read the present of the men of Europe and believe it, the war will be won in places where no gun could ever strike, and still be won long after the last army is disbanded.

One World or None

August 18, 1945

[*editorial*]

Two weeks after the atomic bomb was dropped on Hiroshima, editor-in-chief Freda Kirchwey called for a world government to control nuclear weapons and save the world from the threat of destruction.

The bomb that hurried Russia into the Far Eastern war a week ahead of schedule and drove Japan to surrender has accomplished the specific job for which it was created. From the point of view of military strategy, $2,000,000,000 (the cost of the bomb and the cost of nine days of war) was never better spent. The suffering, the wholesale slaughter it entailed, have been outweighed by its spectacular success; Allied leaders can rightly claim that the loss of life on both sides would have been many times greater if the atomic bomb had not been used and Japan had gone on fighting. There is no answer to this argument. The danger is that it will encourage those in power to assume that, once accepted as valid, the argument can be applied equally well in the future. If that assumption should be permitted, the chance of saving civilization—and perhaps the world itself—from destruction is a remote one.

Solemn official talk is going on in Britain and here about controlling the use of the new force. But the talk is unconvincing. The atomic bomb represents a revolution in science—the greatest revolution ever accomplished. It calls for a comparable revolution in men's thinking and in their capacity for political and social readjustment. Not a hint of that has so far emerged in high places, either here or in Britain. And so far no leader of one of the lesser states, from which the new knowledge has been withheld, has presumed to open his mouth. No one has spoken the simple truth that the exploding atom has exposed to the whole world.

President Truman announced that he would recommend to Congress "the establishment of an appropriate commission to control the production and use of atomic power within the United States." He has promised that the secret of the bomb will be kept by the three nations that hold it until "means have been found to control the bomb so as to protect ourselves and the rest of the world from the danger of total destruction." Secretary Stimson says that "substantial patent rights" have been assured to the American, Canadian, and British governments to prevent independent exploitation of the discovery. Do these plans and promises mean anything? Or are they conventional, official, high-sounding nonsense?

First, if anything is sure about the atomic bomb it is that no physical protection against it will ever be possible. The bomb dropped on Nagasaki was far more advanced than that dropped two days earlier on Hiroshima. Both were crude beginnings. We have already been promised that their successors will be enormously improved. Soon they will be propelled by rockets – similar to Hitler's V-2s – and directed exactly to their destination by radar. When this is achieved, not only will armies and fleets and island bases and strategic frontiers all have been made obsolete, but widespread annihilation can be accomplished by any power, or even group of men, that can command atomic energy.

And that leads to the absurdity of an attempt to limit control of this force to the nations that now hold it. President Truman is whistling to keep our courage up. He knows that other nations are working on atomic explosives. Before its defeat Germany was on the edge of success. Sweden and Denmark are carrying out intensive experimentation. It is not likely that Russia – which knows how to keep a secret better than any other country – has lagged behind the rest. Are we to be asked to believe that the Anglo-Saxon peoples have alone been granted the godlike power to crack atoms? The secret was guarded long enough to enable us to smash Japan. It will not last much longer. The present "trustees" of this force had better stop thinking in terms of control by themselves and begin to figure how a world is to be run in which every nation equipped for research and modern production will soon be able to make and propel atomic bombs.

So what sense is there in setting up an American commission "to control the production of atomic power"? Perhaps a little. Already certain private interests in this country have let it be known that, while they recognize the government's present right to monopolize the manufacture of atomic bombs, they are not prepared to accept government control over future use of the new energy. And Secretary Stimson's phrase, "substantial patent rights," is at best equivocal. It suggests that certain less substantial but perhaps highly valuable patents may already be in the hands of Du Pont or General Electric. And so a commission may be of some value, at least as an interim safeguard. But it will be well for us to remind Congress that the men it appoints will be dealing with a source of power discovered through the expenditure of $2,000,000,000 of public money – taxpayers' money. That power belongs to the people if no other ever did.

Suppose the United States, Canada, and Britain attempt, as they seem prepared to do, to corner the knowledge of atomic power even for a brief period. What will be the effect of this monopoly? First, it will convert the three Anglo-Saxon nations into a monstrous threat to the rest of the world. Are other countries likely to accept with equanimity the fact that we and the British hold the secret of total destruction? Who but ourselves is going to trust us with such fantastic power? It would be healthy if Americans, just for a moment, would put themselves in the position of, let's say, the Russians or the Chinese, and try to see what this "democratic trusteeship" looks like from the vantage-point of Moscow or Chungking. No nation shut out from our closely guarded knowledge can possibly do other than speed up its own collective effort to gain the same ground. The policy announced by the President is power politics raised to a cosmic degree; if continued it will insure an era of desperate competition in destruction, which can have only one outcome.

Atomic energy should no more be controlled by a few sovereign nations than it should be by a few private companies. "Free enterprise" for nations has been wiped out by the discovery. When President Truman went to the microphone to explain the agreement reached at Potsdam, the first atomic bomb had already exploded. So he discussed the Potsdam arrangements side by side with his proposal for controlling atomic energy. The fantastic incompatibility of the two items apparently did not strike him. But it is clear as water than no collective arrangements can stand in the face of the power held by America and Britain. Even the modest, halfway security measures adopted at San Francisco and written into the United Nations Charter can hardly be expected to survive such a situation. At the very minimum, the United Nations must be made trustee of the atomic bomb. Otherwise the idea of collective agreements to keep the peace may as well be abandoned.

But this minimum is far too small to provide any serious measure of safety. For the San Francisco charter is itself a collective agreement based on power. As Edward R. Murrow said the other day, the big nations have "created an organization and made laws from which they are exempt." In other words, there is no rule of law to which all nations are equally subject. The authority of the United Nations rests in the coalition of great powers which form its core. How much value can such an organization now have even if the control of the atomic bomb should be vested in it? It cannot dominate the world, for a single nation, small or large, possessed of the facilities to make the new explosive, would have as much power to threaten peace and terrorize other nations as one or all of the Big Three—or Four—or Five. And any one of the large nations, ruled by a new Hitler, could reduce the world to slavery—or to dust. In the space of a day the World Security Organization grew from childhood to senility. Now it must be replaced.

If we are to survive our new powers we must understand their full meaning. We shall have to move fast, both internationally and within each country. No longer can we afford a world organized to prevent aggression only if all of the great powers wish it to be prevented. No longer can we afford a social system which would permit private business, in the name of freedom, to control a source of energy capable of creating comfort and security for all the world's people. This seems self-evident, and so it is. But it calls for changes so sweeping that only an immense effort of will and imagination can bring them about. A new conference of the nations must be assembled to set up a World Government, to which every state must surrender an important part of its sovereignty. In this World Government must be vested the final control over atomic energy. And within each nation the people must establish public ownership and social development of the revolutionary force war has thrust into their hands. This program will sound drastic only to people who have not yet grasped the meaning of the new discovery. It is not drastic. We face a choice between one world or none.

HANNAH ARENDT

French Existentialism
February 23, 1946

Philosopher and political scientist Hannah Arendt was best known for her books *The Origins of Totalitarianism* (1951) and *Eichmann in Jerusalem* (1963). From 1946 to 1948, Arendt was chief editor of Schocken Books.

A lecture on philosophy provokes a riot, with hundreds crowding in and thousands turned away. Books on philosophical problems preaching no cheap creed and offering no panacea but, on the contrary, so difficult as to require actual thinking sell like detective stories. Plays in which the action is a matter of words, not of plot, and which offer a dialogue of reflections and ideas run for months and are attended by enthusiastic crowds. Analyses of the situation of man in the world, of the fundaments of human relationship, of Being and the Void not only give rise to a new literary movement but also figure as possible guides for a fresh political orientation. Philosophers become newspapermen, playwrights, novelists. They are not members of university faculties but "bohemians" who stay at hotels and live in the cafe—leading a public life to the point of renouncing privacy. And not even success, or so it seems, can turn them into respectable bores.

This is what is happening, from all reports, in Paris. If the Resistance has not achieved the European revolution, it seems to have brought about, at least in France, a genuine rebellion of the intellectuals, whose docility in relation to modern society was one of the saddest aspects of the sad spectacle of Europe between wars. And the French people, for the time being, appear to consider the arguments of their philosophers more important than the talk and the quarrels of their politicians. This may reflect, of course, a desire to escape from political action into some theory which merely talks about action, that is, into activism; but it may also signify that in the face of the spiritual bankruptcy of the left and the sterility of the old revolutionary élite—which have led to the desperate efforts at restoration of all political parties—more people than we might imagine have a feeling that the responsibility for political action is too heavy to assume until new foundations, ethical as well as political, are laid down, and that the old tradition of philosophy which is deeply imbedded even in the least philosophical individual is actually an impediment to new political thought.

The name of the new movement is "Existentialism," and its chief exponents are Jean-Paul Sartre and Albert Camus, but the term Existentialism has given rise to so many misunderstandings that Camus has already publicly stated why he is "not an Existentialist." The term comes from the modern German philosophy which had a revival immediately after the First World War and has strongly influenced French thought for more than a decade; but it would be irrelevant to trace and define the sources of Existentialism in national terms for the simple reason that both the German and the French manifestations came out of an identical period and a more or less identical cultural heritage.

The French Existentialists, though they differ widely among themselves, are united on two main lines of rebellion: first, the rigorous repudiation of what they call the *esprit sérieux;* and, second, the angry refusal to accept the world as it is as the natural, predestined milieu of man.

L'esprit sérieux, which is the original sin according to the new philosophy, may be equated with respectability. The "serious" man is one who thinks of himself *as* president of his business, *as* a member of the Legion of Honor, *as* a member of the faculty, but also *as* father, *as* husband, or as any other half-natural, half-social function. For by so doing he agrees to the identification of himself with an arbitrary function which society has bestowed. *L'esprit sérieux* is the very negation of freedom, because it leads man to agree to and accept the necessary deformation which every human being must undergo when he is fitted into society. Since everyone knows well enough in his own heart that he is not identical with his function, *l'esprit sérieux* indicates also bad faith in the sense of pretending. Kafka has already shown, in "Amerika," how ridiculous and dangerous is the hollow dignity which grows out of identifying oneself with one's function: In that book the most dignified person in the hotel, upon whose word the hero's job and daily bread depend, rules out the possibility that he can make an error by invoking the argument of the "serious" man: "How could I go on being the head porter if I mistook one person for another?"

This matter of *l'esprit sérieux* was first touched upon in Sartre's novel "La Nausée," in a delightful description of a gallery of portraits of the town's respectable citizens, *les salauds*. It then became the central topic of Camus's novel "L'Etranger." The hero of the book, the stranger, is an average man who simply refuses to submit to the serious-mindedness of society, who refuses to live as any of his allotted functions. He does not behave as a son at his mother's funeral—he does not weep; he does not behave as a husband—he declines to take marriage seriously even at the moment of his engagement. Because he does not pretend, he is a stranger whom no one understands, and he pays with his life for his affront to society. Since he refuses to play the game, he is isolated from his fellow-men to the point of incomprehensibility and isolated from himself to the point of becoming inarticulate. Only in a last scene, immediately before his death, does the hero arrive at some kind of explanation which conveys the impression that for him life itself was such a mystery and in its terrible way so beautiful that he did not see any necessity for "improving" upon it with the trimmings of good behavior and hollow pretensions.

Sartre's brilliant play "Huis Clos" belongs to the same category. The play opens in hell, appropriately furnished in the style of the Second Empire. The three persons gathered in the room—"Hell is the Others"—set the diabolical torture in motion by trying to pretend. Since, however, their lives are closed and since "you are your life and nothing else," pretense no longer works, and we see what would go on behind closed doors if people actually were stripped of the sheltering cover of functions derived from society.

Both Sartre's play and Camus's novel deny the possibility of a genuine fellowship between men, of any relationship which would be direct, innocent, free of pretense. Love in Sartre's philosophy is the will to be loved, the need for a supreme confirmation of one's own existence. For Camus love is a somewhat awkward and hopeless attempt to break through the isolation of the individual.

The way out of pretense and serious-mindedness is to play at being what one really is. Again Kafka indicated in the last chapter of "Amerika" a new possibility of authentic life. The great "Nature Theater" where everyone is welcome and where everybody's unhappiness is resolved is not by accident a theater. Here everybody is invited to choose his role, to play at what he is or would like to be. The chosen role is the solution of the conflict between mere functioning and mere being, as well as between mere ambition and mere reality.

The new "ideal" becomes, in this context, the actor whose very profession is pretending, who constantly changes his role, and thus can never take any of his roles seriously. By playing at what one is, one guards one's freedom as a human being from the pretenses of one's functions; moreover, only by playing at he what really is, is man able to affirm that he is never identical with himself as a thing is identical with itself. An inkpot is always an inkpot. Man is his life and his actions, which are never finished until the very moment of his death. He *is* his existence.

The second common element of French Existentialism, the insistence upon the basic homelessness of man in the world, is the topic of Camus's "Le Mythe de

Sisyphe; essay sur l'absurde," and of Sartre's "La Nausée." For Camus man is essentially the stranger because the world in general and man as man are not fitted for each other; that they are together in existence makes the human condition an absurdity. Man is the only "thing" in the world which obviously does not belong in it, for only man does not exist simply as a man among men in the way animals exist among animals and trees among trees—all of which necessarily exist, so to speak, in the plural. Man is basically alone with his "revolt" and his "clairvoyance," that is, with his reasoning, which makes him ridiculous because the gift of reason was bestowed upon him in a world "where everything is given and nothing ever explained."

Sartre's notion of the absurdity, the contingency, of existence is best represented in the chapter of "La Nausée" which appears in the current issue of the *Partisan Review* under the title The Root of the Chestnut Tree. Whatever exists, so far as we can see, has not the slightest reason for its existence. It is simply *de trop*, superfluous. The fact that I can't even imagine a world in which, instead of many too many things, there would be nothing only shows the hopelessness and senselessness of man's being eternally entangled in existence.

Here Sartre and Camus part company, if we may judge from the few works of theirs which have reached this country. The absurdity of existence and the repudiation of *l'esprit sérieux* are only points of departure for each. Camus seems to have gone on to a philosophy of absurdity, whereas Sartre seems to be working toward some new positive philosophy and even a new humanism.

Camus has probably protested against being called an Existentialist because for him the absurdity does not lie in man as such or in the world as such but only in their being thrown together. Since man's life, being laid in the world, is absurd, it must be lived as absurdity—lived, that is, in a kind of proud defiance which insists on reason despite the experience of reason's failure to explain anything; insists on despair since man's pride will not allow him the hope of discovering a sense he cannot figure out by means of reason; insists, finally, that reason and human dignity, in spite of their senselessness, remain the supreme values. The absurd life then consists in constantly rebelling against all its conditions and in constantly refusing consolations. "This revolt is the price of life. Spread over the whole of an existence, it restores its grandeur." All that remains, all that one can say yes to, is chance itself, the *hazard roi* which has apparently played at putting man and world together. " 'I judge that everything is well,' said Oedipus, and this word is sacred. It resounds in the ferocious universe which is the limit of man. . . . It makes of destiny an affair of men which should be settled among men." This is precisely the point where Camus, without giving much explanation, leaves behind all modernistic attitudes and comes to insights which are genuinely modern, the insight, for instance, that the moment may have arrived "when creation is no longer taken tragically; it is only taken seriously."

For Sartre, absurdity is of the essence of things as well as of man. Anything that exists is absurd simply because it exists. The salient difference between the things of the world and the human being is that things are unequivocally identical with themselves, whereas man—because he sees and knows that he sees, believes and knows that he believes—bears within his consciousness a negation which makes it impossible for him ever to become one with himself. In this single respect—in respect of his consciousness, which has the germ of negation in it— man is a creator. For this is of man's own making and not merely given, as the world and his existence are given. If man becomes aware of his own conscious- ness and its tremendous creative possibilities, and renounces the longing to be identical with himself as a thing is, he realizes that he depends upon nothing and nobody outside himself and that he can be free, the master of his own destiny. This seems to be the essential meaning of Sartre's novel "Les Mouches" ("The Flies"), in which Orestes, by taking upon himself the responsibility for the neces- sary killing of which the town is afraid, liberates the town and takes the Flies—the Erinyes of bad conscience and of the dark fear of revenge—with him. He himself is immune because he does not feel guilty and regrets nothing.

It would be a cheap error to mistake this new trend in philosophy and literature for just another fashion of the day because its exponents refuse the respectability of institutions and do not even pretend to that seriousness which regards every achievement as a step in a career. Nor should we be put off by the loud journalistic success with which their work has been accompanied. This success, equivocal as it may be in itself, is nevertheless due to the quality of the work. It is also due to a definite modernity of attitude which does not try to hide the depth of the break in Western tradition. Camus especially has the courage not even to look for con- nections, for predecessors and the like. The good thing about Sartre and Camus is that they apparently suffer no longer from nostalgia for the good old days, even though they may know that in an abstract sense those days were actually better than ours. They do not believe in the magic of the old, and they are honest in that they make no compromises whatever.

Yet if the revolutionary élan of these writers is not broken by success, if, sym- bolically speaking, they stick to their hotel rooms and their cafes, the time may come when it will be necessary to point out "seriously" those aspects of their phi- losophy which indicate that they are still dangerously involved in old concepts. The nihilistic elements, which are obvious in spite of all protests to the contrary, are not the consequences of new insights but of some very old ideas.

JEAN-PAUL SARTRE

Americans and Their Myths

October 18, 1947

> *The Nation* introduced Jean-Paul Sartre to its readers as "the
> leading French existentialist. His exposition of his philosophy
> has recently been published in this country under the title 'Ex-
> istentialism.' He is also the author of a play, 'No Exit,' which
> was produced on Broadway last year, and of *The Age of Reason*,
> a novel."

Everything has been said about the United States. But a person who has once crossed the Atlantic can no longer be satisfied with even the most penetrating books; not that he does not believe what they say, but that his agreement remains abstract.

When a friend tries to explain our character and unravel our motives, when he relates all our acts to principles, prejudices, beliefs, and a conception of the world which he thinks to find in us, we listen uneasily, unable either to deny what he says or entirely accept it. Perhaps the interpretation is true, but what is the truth that is being interpreted? We miss the intimate warmth, the life, the way one is always unpredictable to oneself and also tiresomely familiar, the decision to get along with oneself, the perpetual deliberations and perpetual inventions about what one is, and the vow to be "that" and nothing else—in short, the liberty. Similarly, when a careful arrangement of those melting-pot notions—puritanism, realism, optimism, and so on—which we have been told are the keys to the American character is presented to us in Europe, we experience a certain intellectual satisfaction and think that, in effect, it must be so. But when we walk about New York, on Third Avenue, or Sixth Avenue, or Tenth Avenue, at that evening hour which, for Da Vinci, lends softness to the faces of men, we see the most pathetic visages in the world, uncertain, searching, intent, full of astonished good faith, with appealing eyes, and we know that the most beautiful generalizations are of very little service: they permit us to understand the system but not the people.

The system is a great external apparatus, an implacable machine which one might call the objective spirit of the United States and which over there they call Americanism—a huge complex of myths, values, recipes, slogans, figures, and rites. But one must not think that it has been deposited in the head of each American just as the God of Descartes deposited the first notions in the mind of man; one must not think that it is "refracted" into brains and hearts and at each instant determines affections or thoughts that exactly express it. Actually, it is something outside of the people, something presented to them; the most adroit propaganda does nothing else but present it to them continuously. It is not in them, they are in it; they struggle against it or they accept it, they stifle in it or go beyond it, they submit to it or reinvent it, they give themselves up to it or make furious efforts to escape from it; in any case it remains outside them, transcendent, because they are men and it is a thing.

There are the great myths, the myths of happiness, of progress, of liberty, of triumphant maternity; there is realism and optimism—and then there are the Americans, who, nothing at first, grow up among these colossal statues and find their way as best they can among them. There is this myth of happiness: black-magic slogans warn you to be happy at once; films that "end well" show a life of rosy ease to the exhausted crowds; the language is charged with optimistic and unrestrained expressions — "have a good time," "life is fun," and the like. But there are also these people, who, though conventionally happy, suffer from an obscure *malaise* to which no name can be given, who are tragic through fear of being so, through that total absence of the tragic in them and around them.

There is this collectivity which prides itself on being the least "historical" in the world, on never complicating its problems with inherited customs and acquired rights, on facing as a virgin a virgin future in which everything is possible—and there are these blind gropings of bewildered people who seek to lean on a tradition, on a folklore. There are the films that write American history for the masses and, unable to offer them a Kentucky Jeanne d'Arc or a Kansas Charlemagne, exalt them with the history of the jazz singer, Al Jolson, or the composer, Gershwin. Along with the Monroe doctrine, isolationism, scorn for Europe, there is the sentimental attachment of each American for his country of origin, the inferiority complex of the intellectuals before the culture of the old Continent, of the critics who say, "How can you admire our novelists, you who have Flaubert?" of the painters who say, "I shall never be able to paint as long as I stay in the United States"; and there is the obscure, slow effort of an entire nation to seize universal history and assimilate it as its patrimony.

There is the myth of equality—and there is the myth of segregation, with those big beach-front hotels that post signs reading "Jews and dogs not allowed," and those lakes in Connecticut where Jews may not bathe, and that racial *tchin,* in which the lowest degree is assigned to the Slavs, the highest to the Dutch immigrants of 1680. There is the myth of liberty—and the dictatorship of public opinion; the myth of economic liberalism—and the big companies extending over the whole country which, in the final analysis, belong to no one and in which the employees, from top to bottom, are like functionaries in a state industry. There is respect for science and industry, positivism, an insane love of "gadgets"—and there is the somber humor of the *New Yorker,* which pokes bitter fun at the mechanical civilization of America and the hundred million Americans who satisfy their craving for the marvelous by reading every day in the "comics" the incredible adventures of Superman, or Wonderman, or Mandrake the Magician.

There are the thousand taboos which proscribe love outside of marriage – and there is the litter of used contraceptives in the back yards of coeducational colleges; there are all those men and women who drink before making love in order to transgress in drunkenness and not remember. There are the neat, coquettish houses, the pure-white apartments with radio, armchair, pipe, and stand – little paradises; and there are the tenants of those apartments who, after dinner, leave their chairs, radios, wives, pipes, and children, and go to the bar across the street to get drunk alone.

Perhaps nowhere else will you find such a discrepancy between people and myth, between life and the representation of life. An American said to me at Berne: "The trouble is that we are all eaten by the fear of being less American than our neighbor." I accept this explanation: it shows that Americanism is not merely a myth that clever propaganda stuffs into people's heads but something every American continually reinvents in his gropings. It is at one and the same time a great external reality rising up at the entrance to the port of New York across from the Statue of Liberty, and the daily product of anxious liberties. The anguish of the American confronted with Americanism is an ambivalent anguish, as if he were asking, "Am I American enough?" and at the same time, "How can I escape from Americanism?" In America a man's simultaneous answers to these two questions make him what he is, and each man must find his own answers.

JAMES AGEE

Film

January 31, 1948

[The Treasure of the Sierra Madre]

James Agee, author of *Let Us Now Praise Famous Men* (with photographer Walker Evans), was *The Nation*'s film critic from 1942 to 1948. Margaret Marshall, then literary editor, gave him free rein to cover what he wanted and to write as he pleased. In a letter to the editor in 1944, W.H. Auden wrote, "In my opinion, Agee's column is the most remarkable regular event in American journalism today."

Several of the best people in Hollywood grew, noticeably, during their years away at war; the man who grew most impressively, I thought, as an artist, as a man, in intelligence, in intransigence, and in an ability to put through fine work against difficult odds, was John Huston, whose *San Pietro* and *Let There Be Light* were full of evidence of this many-sided growth. I therefore looked forward with the greatest eagerness to the work he would do after the war.

His first movie since the war has been a long time coming, but it was certainly worth waiting for. *The Treasure of the Sierra Madre* is Huston's adaptation of B. Traven's novel of the same title. It is not quite a completely satisfying picture, but on the strength of it I have no doubt at all that Huston, next only to Chaplin, is the most talented man working in American pictures, and that this is one of the movie talents in the world which is most excitingly capable of still further growth. *The Treasure* is one of very few movies made since 1927 which I am sure will stand up in the memory and esteem of qualified people alongside the best of the silent movies. And yet I doubt that many people will fully realize, right away, what a sensational achievement, or plexus of achievement, it is. You will seldom see a good artist insist less on his artistry; Huston merely tells his story so straight and so well that one tends to become absorbed purely in that; and the story itself—a beauty—is not a kind which most educated people value nearly enough, today.

This story and Huston's whole handling of it are about as near to folk art as a highly conscious artist can get; both also approach the global appeal, to the most and least sophisticated members of an audience, which the best poetic drama and nearly all the best movies have in common. Nominally an adventure story, this is really an exploration of character as revealed in vivid action; and character and action yield revelations of their own, political, metaphysical, moral, above all, poetic. The story unfolds so pleasurably on the screen that I will tell as little as possible of it here. Three American bums of the early 1920s (Walter Huston, Humphrey Bogart, Tim Holt) run into lottery luck in Tampico and strike into the godforsaken mountains of Mexico in search of gold. The rest of the story merely demonstrates the development of their characters in relation to hardship and hard work, to the deeply primitive world these modern primitives are set against, to the gold they find, and to each other. It is basically a tragic story and at times a sickeningly harsh one; most of it is told as cheerfully brutal sardonic comedy.

This may be enough to suggest how rich the story is in themes, semi-symbols, possible implications, and potentialities as a movie. Huston's most wonderful single achievement is that he focuses all these elements as simply as rays in a burning-glass: all you see, unless you look sharp, is a story told so truly and masterfully that I suspect the picture's best audience is the kind of men the picture is about, who will see it only by chance.

But this single achievement breaks down into many. I doubt we shall ever see a film more masculine in style; or a truer movie understanding of character and of men; or as good a job on bumming, a bum's life, a city as a bum sees it; or a more beautiful job on a city; or a finer portrait of Mexico and Mexicans (compare it with all the previous fancy-filter stuff for a definitive distinction between poetry and poeticism); or a crueler communication of absolute desolateness in nature and its effect on men (except perhaps in *Greed*); or a much more vivid communication of hardship, labor, and exhaustion (though I wish these had been brutally and meticulously presented rather than skillfully sketched); or more intelligent handling of amateurs and semi-professionals (notably the amazing character who plays Gold-Hat, the bandit leader); or a finer selective eye for location or a richer understanding of how to use it; or scenes of violence or building toward violence more deeply authentic and communicative (above all in Huston's terrific use of listlessness); or smarter casting than that of Tim Holt as the youngest bum and that of Bruce Bennett as an intrusive Texan; or better acting than Walter Huston's beautiful performance; or subtler and more skillful collusions and variations of tempo (two hours have certainly never been better used in a movie); or a finer balance, in Ted McCord's perfect camera work, in every camera set-up, in every bit of editing, of unaffectedness, and sensitiveness. (As one fine example of that blend I recommend watching for the shot of Gold-Hat reflected in muddy water, which is so subtly photographed that in this noncolor film the hat seems to shed golden light.) There is not a shot-for-shot's sake in the picture, or one too prepared-looking, or dwelt on too long. The camera is always where it ought to be, never imposes on or exploits or over-dramatizes its subject, never for an instant shoves beauty or special meaning at you. This is one of the most visually alive and beautiful movies I have ever seen; there is a wonderful flow of fresh air, light, vigor, and liberty through every shot, and a fine athlete's litheness and absolute control and flexibility in every succession and series of shots. Huston shows that he is already capable of literally anything in movies except the profoundest kind of movie inventiveness, the most extreme kind of poetic concentration, artiness, soft or apathetic or sloppy or tasteless or excessive work, and rhetoric whether good or bad. His style is practically invisible as well as practically universal in its possible good uses; it is the most virile movie style I know of; and is the purest style in contemporary movies, here or abroad.

I want to say a little more about Walter Huston; a few thousand words would suit me better. Rightly or wrongly, one thing that adds to my confidence that the son, so accomplished already, will get better and better, is the fact that the father has done that, year after year. I can think of nothing more moving or happier than every instance in which an old man keeps right on learning, and working, and improving, as naturally and eagerly as a child learns the fundamentals of walking, talking, and everything else in sight until his parents and teachers destroy his appetite for learning. Huston has for a long time been one of the best actors in the world and he is easily the most likable; on both counts this performance crowns a lifetime. It is an all but incredible submergence in a role, and transformation; this man who has credibly played Lincoln looks small and stocky here, and is as gaily vivacious as a water bug. The character is beautifully conceived and written, but I think it is chiefly Walter Huston who gives it its almost Shakespearean wonderfulness, charm, and wisdom. In spite of the enormous amount of other talent at large in the picture, Huston carries the whole show as deftly and easily as he handles his comedy lines.

There are a few weaknesses in the picture, most of which concern me so little I won't even bother to mention them. Traven's Teutonic or Melvillean excitability as a poet and metaphysician sometimes, I think, misleads him — and John Huston; magnificently as Walter Huston does it, and deeply as he anchors it in flesh and blood, the Vast Gale of Purifying Laughter with which he ends the picture strikes me as unreal, stuck-onto-the-character, close to arty; yet I feel tender toward this kind of cliché, if I'm right that it is one. One thing I do furiously resent is the intrusion of background-music. There is relatively little of it and some of it is better than average, but there shouldn't be any, and I only hope and assume that Huston fought the use of it. The only weakness which strikes me as fundamental, however, is deep in the story itself: it is the whole character of the man played by Bogart. This is, after all, about gold and its effects on those who seek it, and so it is also a fable about all human life in this world and about much of the essence of good and evil. Many of the possibilities implicit in this fable are finely worked out. But some of the most searching implications are missed. For the Bogart character is so fantastically undisciplined and troublesome that it is impossible to demonstrate or even to hint at the real depth of the problem, with him on hand. It is too easy to feel that if only a reasonably restrained and unsuspicious man were in his place, everything would be all right; we wouldn't even have wars. But virtually every human being carries sufficient of that character within him to cause a great deal of trouble, and the demonstration of that fact, and its effects, could have made a much greater tragi-comedy — much more difficult, I must admit, to dramatize. Bogart does a wonderful job with this character as written (and on its own merits it is quite a character), miles ahead of the very good work he has done before. The only trouble is that one cannot quite forget that this is Bogart putting on an unbelievably good act. In all but a few movies one would thank God for that large favor. In this one it stands out, harmfully to some extent, for everything else about the picture is selfless.

It seems worth mentioning that the only thing which holds this movie short of unarguable greatness is the failure of the story to develop some of the most important potentialities of the theme. In other words, "Hollywood," for once, is accountable only for some minor flaws. This is what it was possible to do in Hollywood, if you were talented enough, had standing enough, and were a good enough fighter, during the very hopeful period before the November Freeze. God knows what can be done now. But if anybody can hope to do anything, I count on Huston, who made *San Pietro* and *Let There Be Light* as an army officer and *The Treasure of the Sierra Madre* as a Hollywood writer-director.

STEPHEN SPENDER

Writers in America *December 3, 1949*

British writer and poet Stephen Spender's comments on American writers were based on his observations during an eighteen-month visit to the United States. This is the second of two articles.

The American writer is the most isolated in the world. Unless he happens to come from Boston or New York, he is isolated in his youth in the West or Midwest or South, and his isolation amid a kind of society which does not recognize the values of the artist may remain throughout his life as the valid basis of his work; he may always secretly remain ashamed of being a writer and not a "tough guy." He is isolated by the lack of cultural centers, corresponding to Paris and London, in which he may find a spiritual home. At a certain epoch, indeed—after 1920— Paris was a far truer center of American literary life than any city in America. He is isolated by success, which exploits his literary reputation and at the same time lifts him socially and economically both out of literature and out of his early sensitive experiencing, and he is isolated by failure, which may tie him down to academic and critical work and make him wish to intellectualize his talents to a point which is dangerous to his creativeness.

Yet the greatest achievements of American writing come out of this very isolation, this original loneliness within a deeply experienced environment where literature is derided, this later isolation within a success or unsuccess where it is still misunderstood. Intense loneliness gives all the great American literature something in common, the sense of a lonely animal howling in the dark, like the wolves in a story of Jack London, the White Whale chased across a waste of seas in Melville, the sensitive and exploitable young American, seeking his own soul through ruined European palaces, of James. The recurrent theme of American literature is the great misunderstood primal energy of creative art, transformed into the inebriate, the feeling ox, the sensitive, the homosexual, the lost child.

When W. H. Auden explained that the reason he lived in America was because he could be alone, he was at his most profound. The matey, the democratic country is the natural home of homeless wanderers, incommunicable voices pouring themselves out without hope of reaching an audience, on reams of paper. In passages of "Finnegans Wake" there is a kind of reaching out of the Irish wanderer to America, and perhaps the great, passionately formed yet formless masterpieces of this century, of James and Proust and Joyce, have a kinship with American literature. The loneliness of the American writer is significant because it corresponds to a very deep American experience, the kind of experience which James touches on in his portraits of the millionaires dying side by side in the sketch of his last novel, "The Ivory Tower."

This isolation explains a perplexing feature of American writing – its emphasis on violence, brutality, decadence. Reading the novels of Faulkner, Hemingway, Steinbeck, and other contemporary American writers, one has the impression not of a vital, progressive society but of the Russia of Dostoevski and Chekhov. Yet one can hardly accept this as a witnessing of America. For America *is* vital, young, optimistic, and in this way opposed to tired and disillusioned Europe. Or rather one America is like this. There is another America which is after all very old, very much attached to Europe. A conflict is implicit in the civilization of America, which is not really a young nation growing up in virgin country but a collection of people with roots in very old countries living the life of a young country. Thus there is a tendency always in American culture to jump from the pioneering to the over-civilized: and within this tendency also a reaction against it. There is Walt Whitman, and there is Henry James. The scene of the drama of America and Europe which is the theme of Henry James is America itself, Boston and New York rather than Paris and Rome.

Someone once said that America was a country which has passed from primitive pioneering to decadence with no interval of cultivated civilization in between. It would be truer to say that primitivism, decline, and vital civilizing forces all exist side by side in America. Its literature reflects this coexistence of extremes, this loneliness of conditions which do not understand one another, this frustration and violence.

Europe has an intellectual life in which writers know themselves, and know one another, and are known. Formerly American writers went to Europe to enter into this state of awareness and self-awareness. But a time can come when there is a movement of Europeans away from European self-awareness toward the American loneliness. This happens if European awareness becomes terrifying, chaotic, and disillusioned rather than harmonious and poetic. It seems that we may have reached the stage when European awareness is awareness of a purpose which has gone out of life, an illusion which is lost. French existentialism is awareness of the meaninglessness of the real condition of being human and the arbitrariness of constructive and creative attitudes. But isolation is the only tolerable condition of work for the individual, whose motives in creating and constructing are of a heroic arbitrariness. There comes a stage when a *knowing* community is one which knows that no one believes in the mission of this civilization any longer.

In such conditions one may get little revivals—a sudden interest, let us say, of a group of English artists in the Pre-Raphaelites and nineteenth-century Gothic. But in England everything descends below the level of the arbitrary gesture of public and artistic "engagement" to the children's game, the walks with the governess on the downs.

It is better perhaps, then, to be alone. And for this reason the American loneliness has a great attraction for the European intellectual today. There has been a movement of English writers to America, and were it not for language difficulties, one can scarcely doubt that there would be an emigration of European literary life on a considerable scale. Translations of contemporary American literature have swept the Continent into a movement which is an invasion by external forces. American loneliness is now a magnet which pulls across the Atlantic as powerfully as Europe once pulled in the other direction. In America you are acquainted with everyone, but you are known by and get to know hardly anyone. There is no awareness of what you are up to; reputations, good or ill, are based on the most elementary and widely diffused misunderstandings.

So it would be wrong to condemn the American isolation of talent and to assert that it must be replaced by a literary community corresponding to the European one. At the same time, one must distinguish between two kinds of isolation for the writer, one creative and one sterile, and one must bear in mind that the existence of literature depends on a readers' as well as a writers' situation.

Productive loneliness perhaps expresses the American tragedy of a great continent without a center. It is a loneliness of clarity free of the insidious intellectual connections and commitments which now threaten to betray the individual European talent by involving it too much in the unbelief of a declining civilization.

The uncreative loneliness is a too facile acceptance of the separation of the writer's particular situation from all others. It is the loneliness of the successful who sneer at the unsuccessful, of the unsuccessful who reject every possibility of success, of the poets who retire early into university careers and concentrate on tremendous labors of literary criticism, of the editors and publishers who allow policy to be dictated to them by sales managers, and equally of the editors who have no wish to expand their circulation beyond a tiny clique, the loneliness of those who retire bitterly to the Midwest or the Pacific coast, or of those who accept alcohol as their fatality and write with it and about it. This acceptance of partial situations is mechanical because it is a reflection of the segregating, specializing, commercializing tendencies of the whole of America.

The creative loneliness is, of course, the solving by individuals within their own work of the problems which society presents, so that the successful rises above the mere fortune of his success, and within conventions which the society accepts manages to create extremely vital work, as did Balzac and Dickens. There is a great vitality in America and Americans which permits of these miraculous solutions, which somehow permit films that are masterpieces to be produced within the conditions imposed by Hollywood, novels that are masterpieces to be accepted by book clubs. Nevertheless, the individual's capacity to solve the problem within his own work and life does not prevent the problem from being grave. And in America the lack of a middle-sized reading public, independent of book clubs and capable of choosing for itself, is the main cause of the extraordinary situation by which talent is less capable of supporting itself for what it is, less able to do what it wants to do, than in most European countries. It is true that today the European writer is going through a very grave crisis, but it is a crisis largely induced by paper shortages and other difficulties of a purely material nature. The American malady is a spiritual one, the commercialization of spiritual goods on an enormous scale and in the same way as material things are commercialized. Everything which sells has to sell on advertised merits which are not its true quality; everything made is made to satisfy a demand artificially stimulated by sales propaganda. In the country where culture is "sold" enormously, it is sold as something other than culture and tends to become something else in the process. That real values nevertheless are maintained is the triumph of certain individuals who are able to enter into and survive this enormous success-machinery, and of others who reject it heroically.

GUY ENDORE

Life on the Black List   *December 20, 1952*

> Guy Endore was a successful screenwriter in Hollywood
> when he was blacklisted in 1951. Endore's next film credit was
> in 1963.

Hollywood

How does it feel to be blacklisted in Hollywood? How does it feel when a producer who has been discussing a job with you for some time suddenly calls you up and explains with embarrassment that it's all off? For a moment you are seized by sheer panic. You are lost. You have no country, no civil rights, no means of livelihood. And you have heard so much about guilt by association that you hesitate to go to see anyone. When you meet an acquaintance you wait to be recognized, not wishing to spread the infection. You feel that like the lepers of the Middle Ages you ought to tinkle a bell and cry out the old warning, "Unclean!" "Unclean!"

But after a while you realize it isn't that way at all. Like so many other things that threaten our freedom, the black list is half reality and half myth.

An actor who had appeared at a televised hearing of the Un-American Activities Committee and been pilloried as a subversive—linked with the betrayers of our atom-bomb secrets and with those who were killing American boys in Korea—went home trembling at the thought of what the half-million television viewers would do to him. He pictured his little bungalow in ruins and an infuriated mob waiting for him.

Nothing of the kind. His neighbor was out mowing the lawn—a burly man who up to this time had never even exchanged a good morning. Now he left his lawnmower and came up to shake the actor's hand. Of course this did not help the actor in his subsequent financial difficulties, but it helped his morale. He could still feel he was a member of the community. He was still an American.

The myth in the black list is the studios' unsupported claim that Americans refuse to patronize pictures in which alleged "Reds" have any part, that they are forced to fire "suspects" to avoid financial loss. Yet almost any evening we blacklisted people can see ourselves in our old movies on television. Do the companies have any difficulty in selling these pictures? And are they not putting us right into people's homes?

The effect of the black list is the real part. After my earning power was cut off, I was forced to cancel some of my insurance policies. My agent told me I could never get them back at the old rates. "Blacklisted people," he said, "are rated like steeplejacks and gangsters; they must pay an additional 50 per cent premium because their chances of living out a normal life are that much lower than the average."

A writer can continue to make a few dollars as long as his typewriter is not confiscated; actors and directors are really on the spot. They can't use pen names—not that a pen name solves everything. A friend of mine has written a novel that seems slated for success and sale to the movies. But to get the film companies to take it he will have to publish it under a pseudonym as a first novel, forfeiting the benefit of his established reputation. Another blacklisted writer took a new name when he began to write for television. His scripts were so good that he was asked to sign a contract. This would have required his appearance at headquarters, and he had to refuse in order to prevent his identity becoming known. Now he is starting all over again under still another name.

Last August the California branch of Amvets, following the lead of the American Legion, called on the heads of motion-picture studios to sign a pledge that they would not employ any person who refused to answer the questions of the House Un-American Activities Committee or any other duly constituted government agency investigating charges of alleged subversion.

How are these vicious attacks being combated? The sterility of the defense is graphically illustrated by a recent proposal of the Motion Picture Industry Council, an association of the guilds and unions working in films. The council's solution was to create a "services committee" which would examine the various black lists, inform the victims, investigate their explanations of past political connections and conduct, and if possible have their names removed from the lists. If the "offense" amounted to nothing more than having been duped into signing a Communist-inspired petition, the committee hoped to be able to get an exoneration. The Screen Writers' Guild, balloting by mail, turned down the proposal. Its president, Mary McCall, put the situation in a nutshell. "This 'services committee,' " she said, "sets up a black list by inference. These people are not being challenged by the government but by the Myron Fagans, the Jack Tenneys, and the Gerald L. K. Smiths. It is time the motion-picture industry refused to be pressured by these groups."

Actors who sit endlessly by a telephone that doesn't ring and never will ring because their names are on some list that they have never been told about know the reality of the black list. The myth is that the American people support the shenanigans of the witch-hunters. As Governor Stevenson said in a campaign speech, the best answer to communism is more democracy.

NELSON ALGREN

American Christmas, 1952 December 27, 1952

Novelist, essayist and journalist Nelson Algren received the first National Book Award in 1949 for *The Man With the Golden Arm.*

When the wise old kings of Egypt decided to have a ball, I'm assured, they placed a mummy at the head of the table to remind themselves, even at the height of the festivities, of their own mortality. We might today with equal wisdom, in this our own season of celebration, nod respectfully toward the head of our own high-heaped board. Lest we also prove too proud.

For ball or no ball, any season at all, we live today in a laboratory of human suffering as vast and terrible as that in which Dickens and Dostoevski wrote, the only real difference being that the England of Dickens and the Russia of Dostoevski could not afford the sound screens and the smoke screens with which we so ingeniously conceal our true condition from ourselves.

So accustomed have we become to the testimony of the photo-weeklies, backed by witnesses from radio and TV, establishing us as the happiest, healthiest, sanest, wealthiest, most inventive, fun-loving, and tolerant folk yet to grace the earth of man that we tend to forget that these are bought-and-paid-for witnesses and that all their testimony is perjured.

For it is not in the afternoon in Naples nor yet at evening in Marseilles, not in Indian hovels half sunk in an ancestral civilization's ruined halls or within lion-colored tents pitched down the Sahara's endless edge that we find faces debauched by sheer uselessness. Not in the backwash of poverty and war but in the backwash of prosperity and progress.

Here in the back streets and the boulevards of New York and Chicago and Los Angeles, unused, unusable, and useless faces, so purposeless yet so smug, harassed, or half-dehumanized, so self-satisfied yet somehow so abject—for complacency struggles strangely there with guilt. Faces of the American Century, full of such an immense irresponsibility toward themselves.

As though the human cost of our marvelous technology has indeed been much too great.

Do American faces so often look so lost because they are most tragically trapped between a very real dread of coming alive to something more than merely existing and an equal dread of going down to the grave without having done more than merely exist?

If so, this is truly the great American disease, and would account in part for the fact that we lead the world today in incidence of insanity, criminality, alcoholism, narcoticism, cancer, homicide, and perversion in sex as well as perversion just for the pure hell of the thing.

Never before till here and now have men and women been so divided by the discrepancy between life and the representation of life.

Nowhere has any people set itself a moral code so rigid while applying it so flexibly.

Never has any people been so outwardly confident that God is on its side while inwardly terrified lest He be not.

"It is as if we are being endowed with a vast and thoroughly appointed body," Walt Whitman prophesied, "and left with little or no soul."

A consideration recently emphasized by William Faulkner when he observed, in accepting the Nobel Prize for Literature, that "the young man or woman writing today has forgotten the problems of the heart in conflict with itself. They write not of life but of lust. Not of the heart but of the glands."

I purely doubt that the young man or woman writing today has forgotten a thing. More likely, he is simply so intimidated by our souped-up drive toward conformity that he declines any risk which might conceivably imperil his livelihood.

For how can he write of the heart and yet conform? There are no Broyles bills for the heart. Its loyalty cannot be bounded by precinct or ward. The heart has but one nationality and that humanity's.

Yet, precisely as the Russians drive blindly to penalize all independence of action and thought, our specialists press the stethoscope of constituted authority to the American breast in the hope of catching the faint murmur of dissent.

The condition of liberty is the capacity to doubt one's own faith and to doubt it out loud as well.

The Out-Loud Doubters who took American thought out of the vault where the McCarthys and McCarrans of their time had locked it – Dreiser and Mencken and Sinclair Lewis and Lincoln Steffens – are down in the dust of the '20's.

And again the anonymous little men in the clean white collars will assure us, through editorial and rotogravure, that only by superbazooka and thunderjet can our famous American way of life be saved.

That if we can but build a space platform before anyone else we shall thus insure national contentment for keeps.

A Carthaginian faith in the ships of trade and the chariots of war as sound as Whittaker Chambers. As misleading as MacArthur. As complacent as Capehart. As suicidal as Forrestal. As false as McCarthy.

"Now git out of the way," Mr. Dooley once doubted out loud, "for here comes Property, drunk 'n raisin' Cain."

But behind Property's billboards and Property's headlines and Property's pulpits and Property's arsenals, the people of Dostoevski and Dickens yet endure the ancestral problems of the heart.

It is there that the young man or woman seeking to report the American Century truthfully today will have to seek, if it is the truth he seeks.

A Merry Christmas to all. And to all a good night.

Bill of Rights Day *December 12, 1953*
[*editorial*]

> *The Nation* was an early and consistent foe of McCarthyism, documenting its impact on people and institutions. This editori-

al introduced "Freedom and The American Tradition," one of
several special issues the magazine published in the 1950s on
the threat Cold War anti-Communism posed to America's civil
liberties.

With civil-liberties issues breaking in thunderous headlines every week, an examination of the continued relevance and integrity of the American tradition
becomes a first order of business.

Today both individuals and institutions are afflicted with a form of creeping paralysis which is both an effect and a cause of the crisis of democracy. Organizations that could normally be relied upon to come to the aid of the victims of the
witch hunt often fail to act, for the welfare, indeed the very existence, of the organization is threatened by the same forces that have set the witch hunt in motion.
In such circumstances it is easy and natural for the bureaucrats to rationalize as
follows: the principles to which the institution is dedicated must be "reconsidered"
in "the light of new circumstances"; the influence of the institution must not be
"frittered away" or used to protect unworthy victims; resources must be hus-
banded, etc. Many individuals keenly distressed by the witch hunt hesitate to take
action for much the same reasons. At what point, the individual asks, am I justified in risking the security of my family to defend a principle in which I believe?

In consequence a leadership vacuum is created enabling a handful of book-
burners and other zealots, well organized and knowing precisely what they want,
to rack up a seemingly endless list of conquests. Most of these might easily have
been avoided if persons devoted to civil liberties had intervened in a timely, coordinated manner. Thus in Los Angeles a fourteen-year-old juvenile delinquent
induces the cancellation of an important radio program by gleefully composing
a dozen poison-pen letters, written in different hands and signed by different
names, which he sends to the sponsors and the station. Or witness the many situations in which giant corporations have capitulated to a handful of fanatics. But
this is not to minimize the crisis today confronting American democracy, which
has had tragic consequences for thousands of law-abiding citizens.

In such times as ours those who defend civil liberties—and they are always a
minority—must do so at considerable personal risk and against unpleasant odds.
But unfortunately principles never defend themselves; every social value implicit
in the American tradition has been forged in a fire which consumed the lives and
hopes of a great many individuals. Today as always the principal defenders of
civil liberties are the victims of bigotry; on their behavior, on their courage or
the lack of it, the outcome largely depends. In their wretched loneliness these unfortunate ones seek some source of support for the risks they run in defense of
principles in which they believe. And as men have always done under such circumstances, they fall back on tradition to sustain them.

And so today many people are thinking about the American tradition and its relevance to their moral and political dilemmas and about the price they may be asked to pay for its preservation. Is it adequate to the needs of the times? Will it sustain them? Has it become irrelevant? What is the meaning of Irving Dilliard's comment in this issue that the Bill of Rights would probably fail of adoption in a nation-wide referendum today? If so, is this because we fail to see what is happening or are we deliberately rejecting this tradition? Is it any wonder that the Germans are said to take great satisfaction in the spectacle of the American people, under stress, exhibiting much the same susceptibility to demagoguery and the same failure to take timely action against it that we found inexcusable and inexplicable in them not so long ago?

The crisis of democracy in America is perhaps best indicated by the growing realization of a self-evident but long-neglected fact – namely, that the American tradition is not one thing. Various elements have long been in conflict in this multi-faceted tradition; indeed, this has been its unique quality, for it has forced every generation and every American to affirm that aspect of the tradition which most closely approximates his concept of what it *should be*. For better or worse, we must acknowledge the bastards spawned by the tradition as well as its heroes. Joe McCarthy and Justice William O. Douglas are both products of the American tradition. And so were the Salem witch-burners and Roger Williams, the slave traders and Abraham Lincoln, Father Coughlin and Franklin D. Roosevelt, Whittaker Chambers and the late John Jay Chapman. The duality of the tradition – so much in evidence today – confuses the world and breeds confusion in many individuals. And the bigots have served notice that they intend to rewrite this tradition to their liking. The phrase "un-American" surely has quite different meanings for Senators Jenner and Lehman, both of whom are equally patriotic in the sense that both would die for their country – although they could never agree on an answer to that searching question raised in the title of a great book by Alexander Meiklejohn, "What Does America Mean?" The fact that the American tradition has never been given an orthodox definition or an authoritative interpretation has been a source of strength; but today it can be a major weakness, for what we decide to do in the world hinges in no small measure on the way a majority of Americans answer Dr. Meiklejohn's question.

There is also the danger that when we appeal to the "American tradition" we do so in too formal a sense and are then dismayed to discover that since this tradition has no fixed meaning, new meanings must constantly be given the words and phrases of the Bill of Rights if its spirit is to be preserved and made applicable to current needs. There is a real danger in not thinking of the American tradition as living, growing, changing, an attitude of mind and heart – not an aging parchment. More than one person has commented upon the ironies implicit in sending the Freedom Train out across the country, with its cargo of precious documents, during a period when civil rights and civil liberties were being disregarded in many of the cities in which the train stopped. Indeed, the train had to detour certain cities to avoid segregated showings. On Bill of Rights Day (December 15) last year, the Constitution, the Bill of Rights, and the Declaration of Independence were removed from the Library of Congress and placed, with great fanfare and ceremony, in a shrine under the dome of the National Archives Building in Washington. The emphasis placed on the "security" of the documents themselves—sealed in helium between sheets of glass and then lowered into a fifty-ton safe guaranteed to protect them against every hazard except the loss of meaning—painfully suggested the ritual of interment, as was noted in *The Nation* of December 27, 1952, under the heading: The Bill of Rights—Burial or Resurrection. Then and there we decided to devote an entire issue, as this year's observance of Bill of Rights Day, to the American tradition in all its vital complexity. . . .

EDGAR SNOW

Red China at Geneva   *April 24, 1954*
Diplomacy's First Glimpse

The Nation's opposition to intervention in Vietnam can be traced back to 1948, when it criticized French colonialism and attempted to describe the nature of Vietnamese resistance. In 1954, journalist Edgar Snow argued that the war against Ho Chi Minh's Vietnam could not be won.

The Geneva conference on the Far East, opening next week, may be a severe test of American foreign policy. Although past experience gives us odds greatly against the Reds' offering any workable method of stabilizing peace by mutual compromise, it is just possible this time over one issue. If they were to propose any way for the French to terminate hostilities in Indo-China without too much loss of face, then M. Bidault would almost certainly have to explore it. But that would mean defiance of the Administration and its Congressional policy-makers, who insist that the French must destroy Ho Chi-minh. Whether Franco-American relations and E. D. C. could survive the strain of the Congressional displeasure sure to follow a French compromise in Indo-China is not certain.

For one thing, such a development now could provide Senator McCarthy and company with a badly needed new set of spies and traitors to blame for "our betrayal of Bai Dai." For the same Congressmen who convinced themselves that they once owned China, before Dean Acheson and Owen Lattimore gave it to the Reds, are today obsessed with the notion that Vietnam is ours to keep or give away or perhaps blow away. It is hard to realize that we have so many H-bombs and megatons of power but still do not really possess Indo-China. In truth, the French themselves have never recovered more than a shadow of sovereignty over the Vietnamese people since the Vichy regime a decade ago surrendered it to Japan without a struggle.

Shortly after V-J Day the *Saturday Evening Post* published a report by a correspondent who was in Saigon when the British landed there and first cajoled and then forced the Vietnamese government out of that major city. In this British-secured base the French eventually landed, with American arms, and began the attempt to reconquer their lost colony. By early 1946 it was already clear that the French plan was to liquidate the war-born Vietnamese republic—which was not for four years to receive any aid from Chinese or Russian Communists—and to replace it with a puppet regime of French colonial design. Vietnam was not "ready" for independence.

"The question of Indo-China's 'readiness' for independence," concluded the *Post* report of that period, "will not be answered by theses built on moral grounds or the logic of justice. Nor will it be settled in this new era of American world leadership in accordance with President Truman's fourth commandment of foreign policy, 'that all peoples who are prepared for self-government should be permitted to choose their own government without any interference from any foreign sources in Asia as well as in the Western Hemisphere.' Rather, it may be determined, as issues of slavery versus freedom have always been settled in the past, by the sum of armed force the 'slaves' are able to mobilize, by the degree of fanaticism with which they resist, by the moral and political strength behind their struggle, and in the last resort by the preparedness of the revolutionaries not so much for self-government as to be machine-gunned, bombed, or perhaps atomized in defense of their inalienable rights as free men."

I wrote that report. The record has sadly confirmed the prophecy, until today the French admit how greatly they underestimated "the degree of fanaticism" behind Vietnamese nationalism. Many regret now that they did not follow the example set by the British in India and Burma. But it is eight years too late for "orderly withdrawal." For the Communists, who in 1945 were a small minority, now firmly control the leadership of what has become Vietnam's war of independence and long-overdue social revolution. Unfortunately it is Ho Chi-minh, and not the former emperor Bao Dai and his mandarins, who has united the Vietnamese people and is their national hero. Without Ho's resolute and costly resistance to reconquest the question of Vietnam's "readiness for independence" would probably have become academic.

Few French officials dispute that the Vietnamese understand this very well. What they do not understand is America. For now at the twelfth hour the Administration is in various ways preparing us for more direct American intervention, not excluding large-scale use of combat forces. Doubtless that is no more paradoxical than certain other means of defending the free world which we have accepted with apathy or frightened rationalizations, such as the rearming of the Iberian liberator who murdered the Spanish republic with the friendly aid of Hitler and Mussolini; the rearming of a German Reichswehr run by ex-Nazi genocide artists, and alliance with a German Foreign Office back under Ribbentrop's boys; the restitution of industrial ownership and power to Krupp, Thyssen, and other Hitler-loving munitions-makers whose products exterminated vast numbers of peaceable people, and so on.

Nevertheless, it is as yet only in Indo-China that we are really making war against people who never attacked us – to preserve their sovereign rights as free men of the free world.

Among the common symptoms of schizophrenia, say Maslow and Mittelman, are a kind of emotional excitement, "rigid and preoccupied, without keen and adequate contact with the external world," and "bizarre thinking, which manifests itself in delusions, preoccupations with curious inventions, plans, and mechanical devices." The delusion that we can settle our differences with people who disagree with us everywhere merely by "mechanical devices" seems manifest in much of our official thinking about Vietnam, as ventilated in recent public speeches and interviews.

Indo-China is not Korea. In the Korean tragedy American intervention had the sanction of international legal and moral doctrine. It is not China, where at least there was a sovereign government to aid. Of course ethical consistency may be of no consequence in dealing with Communists, but more than that is involved here. It is the prospect of tremendous additional waste of material and life in vain. For it is almost mathematically predictable that large-scale American intervention in this colonial war, which has already cost almost as much in casualties and treasure as Korea, could not accomplish its political aims.

It is not impossible to defeat communism. It is not impossible to defeat its leadership of a colonial revolutionary movement. Theoretically it is not even impossible to win a real political victory against Ho Chi-minh. But it is hardly possible to destroy Ho's leadership of the Vietnamese revolution by the practical means available to General Motors' political and military thinking. The war can certainly be enlarged. For instance, French sources state that China has been sending Vietminh forces about 5,000 tons of goods per month. That is a bagatelle compared to the million tons monthly going to the French there from the United States. But major commitments of American ground and air-force help—or even the "united action" of pro-Western powers led by the United States with which Dulles prematurely threatened China—would doubtless bring increased Sino-Russian assistance to Ho. The war could thus be prolonged indefinitely—and incidentally quite a few new private fortunes could be made at the American taxpayers' expense. Increased sympathy for Vietnam in India, Burma, and Indonesia could be aroused, with mounting hostility against the United States. But Ho would not be destroyed.

The first and basic reason is because Ho Chi-minh is leading a mass movement in which every human being is now or potentially a weapon forged by national revolutionary means to play an active part in guerrilla military tactics. Though Americans won their own freedom by comparable means, they have forgotten the terms of such a war. They do not understand that thermonuclear weapons are of no practical or tactical value here. For overwhelming political reasons "massive retaliation" simply cannot be used. And even modern arms of conventional types are in this war largely of defensive value only.

The second reason is that the most effective strictly military method of defeating a revolutionary force of this kind—the method of complete encirclement, strangulation and destruction of the enemy's cadres, and extermination or transportation of the politically "infected" population—is not a practical possibility in Indo-China.

The third reason is that total blockade of the enemy's line of supply—from cities and ports of Indo-China as well as across the Chinese frontier—is hardly possible without a major war. Even if the Chinese frontier could be closed, effective blockade would be elusive. Ho Chi-minh's forces now have "bases" among village people from end to end of an agrarian country much larger than France—or about the size of the North China plain, where in seven years of similar kind of warfare against Japan the Chinese Reds built up the power to seize China.

The fourth reason is that the French—the Americans still less—have no reliable bases in the hearts of the people. They are everywhere surrounded by hostile peasants whose language they do not speak, who give them no voluntary help, who are in effect unarmed combatants inside their own lines. It is next to impossible for foreigners to create from this peasantry—and there is no other class which can provide it—the material for reliable anti-Communist combat forces. Many can of course be armed and drilled, for good pay and good food, to handle and use superior fire power in strictly positional warfare. But basically anti-Western peasants cannot be made into soldiers to win and hold villages against their own politically "infected" people.

The truth is simply that Ho Chi-minh has now mastered the slogans and organizational methods which brought the Communists to power in China. These include the techniques of the land revolution—mass arming of the peasants to wrest ownership from the native landlord-gentry minority—combined with a national-liberation revolution, the union of patriots of all classes against the foreign overlord. Since the foreign overlord cannot lead an anti-landlord campaign—which would behead his only native allies—or a self-liquidating social and national revolution, he has no means of organizing the mass support which is bound, in the setting of Indo-China, to decide the outcome of the war.

Nobody knows this by now better than the French—unless it is the Chinese and Russians, who will attend the Geneva conference. Nevertheless, official Washington statements and most press comment here thus far suggest that the purpose of the meeting is to permit the Chinese to guarantee the liquidation of Ho Chiminh. That would be a simple and agreeable solution indeed; only nothing of the kind can happen. Both China and Russia now fully recognize and indorse Ho and the "Democratic Republic of Vietnam." And China is not a defeated state coming to the table to receive demands but has become the most formidable military power in Asia. Its army and air force are today capable of either a successful landing in Formosa or adequate counter-moves against the intervention of American armed forces in Indo-China.

China and Russia will thus enjoy a solid bargaining position at Geneva, as London and Paris plainly recognize. Mr. Dulles at first appeased Congress by virtually pledging to listen to nothing short of unconditional-surrender offers from the other side. During his weekend trip to London and Paris, however, he was obliged to contradict such pledges. For the statements issued jointly with our allies, which envisage the possibility of Indo-Chinese peace by negotiation—a diplomatic word for horse-trading—are clearly irreconcilable with Dulles's earlier threats of settlement by ultimatums. It will be instructive to see how this paradox is to be resolved—without serious political consequences on one side or the other of the Atlantic.

Mr. Dulles also promised an agenda strictly confined to Korea and Indo-China. His contention is that it is not even a "five-power" conference because the United States does not recognize Red China. But it is now clear that it will prove impossible to exclude related questions. China's seat in the U. N., the American protectorate over Formosa, the rearming of Germany and Japan, increased East-West trade, prohibition of atomic warfare, and control of thermonuclear energy are among the subjects which must arise.

Communist-American agreement on such matters is as remote as the political unification of Korea, but the British and French are not unwilling to examine all of them. Any Chinese intimation of a desire for restoration of normal trade and diplomatic relations, for example, would fall on receptive ears. Already enjoying a boom in revived trade with Russia, the British undoubtedly feel that the security of Hongkong and recovery of some lost commerce on the mainland would be well worth the price of a U. N. member's ticket for Red China. Molotov has already indicated one Red aim as a Far Eastern nonaggression pact with Britain and France—and presumably the United States also—provided the French accept Ho's offer to make a truce and open negotiations for a peaceful settlement. What if the Reds offered to use their "good offices" to persuade Ho Chi-minh to agree to a U. N.-supervised general election in Vietnam—which would leave the French some hope of holding on to Cochin-China and Cambodia? What if they actually turned up at Geneva with Ho himself or one of his deputies ready to discuss such a deal?

A few other bids of a similar nature could turn the conference into at least a propaganda triumph for the Communists, especially if Mr. Dulles remains tied by his "no-compromise" pledges to his Congressional audience. In this respect Mr. Molotov, it should be noted, will enjoy the new advantage of sharing the voice of the Communist world with an Asian nation for the first time sitting as a peer of the great powers. This will tend to cut the ground from under the argument that the Western powers represent strictly free states only, as against a Russian-ruled empire of slave states denied any semblance of sovereignty.

Speaking about Asia and itself Asian, the Chinese voice could carry more weight among people on both sides of Suez than that of Western statesmen talking about Asia without the help of any great Asian state to interpret and validate their claims as champions of Eastern freedom. In spite of these interesting opportunities, however, the odds of experience are, as observed at the outset, that Mr. Molotov will not create any trouble for Mr. Dulles by being reasonable—not if he can help it. It remains to be seen whether Chou En-lai will follow the Molotov tradition.

ARTHUR MILLER

A Modest Proposal
For Pacification of the Public Temper

July 3, 1954

AUTHOR'S NIGHTMARE
Arthur Miller, author of the Pulitzer Prize play "Death of a Salesman" and last year's "The Crucible," which won the Antoinnette Perry and Donaldson Awards, wrote us in connection with A Modest Proposal: "I have only one fear about it. I hope it is printed as a literary effort before it actually becomes a law; and

if it is enacted, I pray I will not be given credit. My satires have a way of coming to pass. . . ."

Last week we announced that A Modest Proposal would appear in our July 10 issue. In deference to the author's fears we advanced the date of publication one week. —ORIGINAL NOTE

There being in existence at the present time a universally held belief in the probability of treasonous actions;

And at the same time no certain method of obtaining final assurance in the faithfulness of any citizen toward his country, now that outright Treason, dallying with the Enemy, and other forms of public and private perfidy have been abundantly demonstrated in and among persons even of the highest office;

I herewith submit a Proposal for the Pacification of the Public Temper, and the Institution among the People of Mutual Faith and Confidence;

Having clearly in mind the Damages, both financial and Spiritual, which have already accrued due to the spread of Suspicion among Citizens, the said Proposal follows, namely:

THE PROPOSAL

1. That upon arriving at his eighteenth (18th) birthday, and every second year thereafter so long as he lives, providing said day does not fall upon a Sunday or nationally proclaimed Legal Holiday, in which case performance shall take place on the first regular day of business following, every Citizen of the United States of America shall present himself at the office of the United States Marshal nearest his place of residence;

Duties of Marshal

1. That said Marshal shall immediately place the Citizen under what is hereby officially described and determined as Patriotic Arrest or National Detention, which shall in every way conform to regular and ordinary incarceration in the prison, jail, or other Federal Detention Facility normally used in that locality;

Duties of Incarcerated Citizen

1. That without undue delay the citizen shall be informed that he may avail himself of all subpoena powers of the Government in order to secure for himself all documents, papers, manifolds, records, recorded tapes or discs, witnesses and/or other paraphernalia which he requires to prove his Absolute and steady Allegiance to this Country, its Government, Army and Navy, Congress, and the Structure, Aims, and History of its Institutions;

2. That upon assembling such documents and/or witnesses in support, he shall

be brought before a Judge of the United States Court of Clearance, which Court to be established herewith;

Duties of Judge in Court of Clearance

1. That said Judge shall hear all of the defendant's witnesses and examine faithfully all evidence submitted;

2. That said Judge shall, if he deems it necessary, call upon the Federal Bureau of Investigation to refute or corroborate any or all claims submitted by the Citizen in defense of his Loyalty;

3. That if said proofs then be found invalid, untruthful, immaterial, irrelevant, or inconclusive, the Citizen shall be so notified and may thereupon at his option demand a Second Hearing meanwhile being consigned by Warrant and Seal of said Judge within one of the three Classifications hereunder described as Class CT, Class AT, or Class U.

CLASSIFICATIONS

Classification CT (Class CT)

1. Classification or Class CT shall be deemed to signify Conceptual Traitor;

Classification CT (Class CT) Defined

1. Class CT signifying Conceptual Traitor is herewith defined as including, but not exclusively,

a. Any person otherwise of good character, without police record of felony, who has been adjudged at his or her Clearance Trial and/or Second Hearing as having engaged in Conversations, talks, public or private meetings, lectures, visits, or communications the nature of which is not illegal but on the other hand not Positively Conducive to the Defense of the Nation against the Enemy;

b. Any person who, on evidence submitted by the F. B. I., or in the Absence of Evidence to the Contrary, has shown himself to have actually expressed concepts, parts of concepts, or complete ideas or sentiments Inimical to the Defense of the Nation against the Enemy;

c. Persons who have not actually expressed such concepts in whole or part, but have demonstrated a receptivity to such concepts as expressed by others;

d. Persons who have neither expressed themselves, nor shown a receptivity to expressions by others of concepts or sentiments Inimical to the Defense of the Nation against the Enemy, but on the other hand have failed to demonstrate a lively, visible, or audible resentment against such concepts or sentiments as orally expressed or written by others;

All the above described, but not exclusively, shall be classified Conceptual Traitors by the duly constituted Court of Clearance.

Classification AT (Class AT)

1. Classification or Class AT shall be deemed to signify Action Traitor;

Classification AT (Class AT) Defined

1. Class AT signifying Action Traitor is herewith defined as including, but not exclusively,

a. Any person who has been proved to have actually attended meetings of any group, organization, incorporated or unincorporated body, secretly or publicly, whose title is to be found upon the Attorney General's list of proscribed organizations;

b. Any person who has committed any of the acts attributable to Conceptual Traitor as above defined, but in addition, and within hearing of at least one witness, has spoken in praise of such groups or affiliates or members thereof, or of non-members who have themselves spoken in praise of said groups or organizations so listed;

c. Any and all persons not falling under the categories above described who nevertheless have been summoned to testify before any Committee of Congress and have failed to testify to the Expressed Satisfaction of said Committee or any two members thereof in quorum constituted;

Penalties

1. Penalties shall be laid upon those classified as Conceptual Traitors, as follows, namely:

a. The Judge of the Court of Clearance shall cause to be issued Identity Card CT. Upon all correspondence written by said Class CT Citizen the words Conceptual Traitor or the letters CT shall be prominently displayed in print or in ink; as well upon any and all books, articles, pamphlets or announcements whatsoever written by said Citizen; as well, any appearance on radio, television, theatrical or other public medium by said Citizen shall be preceded by the clearly spoken announcement of his Classification; and in addition his calling or business cards shall be so marked as well as any other cards, (Christmas, birthday, New Year's, etc., but not exclusively), which he may mail to anyone beyond his own family so connected by blood;

b. Any organization or person employing said citizen with or without remuneration in money or kind, shall, upon agreeing to such employment, apply to the Federal Bureau of Clearance, to be established herewith, for a Conceptual Traitor Employment Permit;

c. It shall be an infraction of this Act to refuse employment to a citizen Classified as Conceptual Traitor, or to discriminate against said Citizen for having been so Classified, and the employer, upon receiving his Conceptual Traitor's Employment Permit, shall cause to be imprinted upon all his stationery,

vouchers, public circulars, and advertisements, the following words or legend—
"We Employ A Conceptual Traitor"—or the initials, "WECT."

Release of Incarcerated CT's

1. Conceptual Traitors, upon being duly classified by the Court of Clearance, shall be instantly released and guaranteed all the rights and privileges of American Citizenship as defined in the Constitution of the United States.

a. No Conceptual Traitor duly classified shall be detained in jail or prison more than forty-eight hours (48) beyond the time of his Classification;

b. No person awaiting Classification shall be detained more than one year, (1 year).

Penalities for Action Traitors

1. Persons classified Action Traitors shall be fined two thousand dollars and sentenced to serve not more than eight (8) years in a Federal House of Detention, nor less than five years, (5 years).

UNCLASSIFIED PERSONS

1. Persons who are neither Classified as Action Traitor nor Conceptual Traitor shall be classified as Unclassified, or "U."

Unclassified Persons Defined

1. Unclassified persons, (U), shall be defined, although not exclusively, as those persons who are:

a. Unable to speak or understand the English language or any language for which an accredited Interpreter can be found, or can be reasonably thought to exist within the Continental United States or its Territories, Possessions, or Territories held in Trust;

b. Able to speak the English language or any of the languages for which an Interpreter may be found, but unable to understand the English language or any of the languages for which an Interpreter may be found;

c. Committed to institutions for the Insane or Homes for the Aged and Infirm;

d. Accredited members of the Federal Bureau of Investigation;

e. Accredited members of any Investigating Committee of the Congress of the United States;

f. Officers of the United States Chamber of Commerce;

g. Persons who are able to read, write, and understand the English language but have not registered their names in any Public Library as Lenders or Borrowers; and persons who have been registered as Borrowers in Public Libraries, but whose cards have never been stamped;

h. Listless persons, or persons who cannot keep their minds attentive to the questions asked by the Judge of the Court of Clearance;

i. All Veterans of the War Between the States;

j. All citizens who have Contributed to the Walter Winchell Damon Runyon Cancer Fund or who have been favorably mentioned in the newspaper column written by Ed Sullivan;

k. Most children, providing:

That none of the entities above mentioned be constituted as exclusive; and that no abridgment is made of the right of Congress to lengthen or shorten any of the defining qualifications of any of the above categories.

Release of Unclassified Persons (Class U)

1. All Unclassified Persons shall be instantly released, but with the proviso that any and all Unclassified Persons may be recalled for Classification.

POSSIBLE OBJECTIONS TO THIS PROPOSAL

The author of the above proposal, or Act, is well aware of certain objections which are bound to be made. All argument will inevitably reduce itself to the question of Civil Liberties.

The author wishes to state that, as will soon become apparent, it is only his devotion to Civil Liberties which has prompted creation of this Proposal, and in order to Enlighten those who on these grounds feel a reservation about this Proposal, he states quite simply the most vital argument against it which is that it sends absolutely everybody to jail.

This, unfortunately, is true. However, the corollary to this objection, namely, that this is exactly what the Russians do, is emphatically not true. I insist that no Russian goes to jail excepting under duress, force, and unwillingly; hence, he loses his liberty. But under this Act the American Presents himself to the prison officials, which is a different thing entirely. Moreover, he Presents himself without loss of liberty, his most precious possession, because he Presents himself with Love in his Heart, with the burning desire to Prove to all his fellow-citizens that he Is an American and is eager to let everybody know every action of his Life and its Patriotic Significance. It may as well be said that if an American boy is good enough to fight he is good enough to go to jail for the peace of mind of his Country.

The author can easily Visualize that going to the local Marshal for his Patriotic Arrest will soon become a kind of Proud Initiation for the Young American. He can Visualize the growth among the Citizens of Coming Out Parties when the young member of the family is released, and there is no doubt that the national Radio and Television Networks will do their best to popularize this form of Patriotic Thanksgiving, and the entire process of Waiting, Classification, and ultimate Deliverance will eventually become a hallowed Ritual without which no young man or woman would feel Complete and At Ease. It is, after all, nothing more than the Winning of Citizenship, something we who were given the blessing of American Birth have come to take for granted.

I would go even farther and say that the psychological significance of Arrest is beneficial. At the age of eighteen, or thereabouts, a person is just getting out of his adolescence, a period marked by strong feelings of guilt due to Pimples and so forth. This guilt, or Pimples, leads many an individual of that age to feelings of high idealism at which point he is amazed to discover the presence of Evil in the world. In turn, the recognition of Evil is likely to cause him to scoff at the Pretensions of the Older Generation, his parents and teachers, who in his new and emotional opinion have Failed to make a decent world for him. He is then wide open to the Propaganda of the Enemy.

It is at this very moment, when his spiritual pores, so to speak, are open, that under this Act he is sent immediately to Jail, and then through a Court of Clearance, to which institution he may Open his Heart. Under this Act, in short, every American over the age of eighteen (18) is automatically regarded as technically and momentarily Guilty. This, of course, represents no profound novelty, but instead of making it possible for only Traitors to Be Discovered, as at present, under this Act everyone will have the opportunity of being, so to speak, Discovered, but as a Patriot, which after all is what most Americans are.

The simple and pervasive Logic of this proposal will be completely evident if one reflects on the fact that in almost every other sphere of human activity the Society does in fact "clear" and give its stamp of Approval beforehand rather than afterwards; in most states we have to renew our dog licenses every year, and no dog with, for instance, rabies, is entitled to a license; we inspect cattle, motorists, buildings, railroads, elevators, sprinkler systems, teachers, and fish markets, for instance; nor do we wait until any of these have caused damage to the community. On the contrary, you have no need of suspecting an elevator, for instance, upon entering it because you know that it has been cleared, in effect, Before you arrived and you may therefore repose in it your utmost Confidence, nor do you take a Driver's Test after you have killed a pedestrian, you take it Before.

It is necessary to imagine, or Project, as the psychologists say, the National Situation as it will be after this Act is operative.

a. When walking down the street, buying in a store, waiting for a street car or bus, getting gas, buying stocks, Meeting Someone hitherto unknown, answering the doorbell, listening to a lecture, seeing a movie or Television Show, the Citizen will automatically know where everybody around him Stands. A sense of Confidence and Mutual Trust will once more flow into the Land. The Citizen will need have no fear of reading anything, attending any meeting, or being introduced to anyone; instead of an atmosphere of innuendo, suspicion, aborted conversations and low vocal tones, we shall have a situation in which you know and I know that you were in jail and I was in jail and that we are therefore good Americans, and if there was anything Wrong one of us, or both of us, would not be out here talking like this. That is, by and large.

Aside from avowed enemies there are, unfortunately, Patriotic people who will unquestionably be found in opposition to this Act. Mothers, for instance, may shudder at the idea of sending their boys to Jail. But they will quickly see that a short stay in Jail will be the Hallmark of every Good American.

To sum up, then, it can be said that the current sensations of Confusion, Ferment, Distrust, and Suspicion are obviously not being dissolved by any present methods of Investigation and Exposure. A Permanent, Regular, and Uniform Clearance Procedure is vitally necessary, therefore. Everyone knows that a Man is Innocent until proved Guilty. All this Act is meant to provide is a means for securing that proof. God Forbid the day when in America a man is guilty without Proof. Once it was a Land that millions of Americans were trekking thousands of miles to find; later it was Gold; recently Uranium has been sought for at great effort and expense. But it is fair to say that with our characteristic energy we are devoting more time, more concentrated effort, and more Patriotic Concern with discovering Proof than any other material in our Nation's History. Now, in a dignified manner, in a Regularized and profoundly American manner, we shall all have it.

DAN WAKEFIELD

Justice in Sumner
Land of the Free

October 1, 1955

> In the summer of 1955, Dan Wakefield visited *The Nation* offices and offered to cover the Emmett Till murder case in Mississippi if the magazine would buy him a round-trip bus ticket. The reports he sent from the South were his first articles to be published in a national magazine. (Most of the material in Wakefield's later books *Revolt in the South* and *Between The Lines* first appeared in *The Nation*.)

Sumner, Mississippi

The crowds are gone and this Delta town is back to its silent, solid life that is based on cotton and the proposition that a whole race of men was created to pick it.

Citizens who drink from the "Whites Only" fountain in the courthouse breathe much easier now that the two fair-skinned half brothers, ages twenty-four and thirty-six, have been acquitted of the murder of a fourteen-year-old Negro boy. The streets are quiet, Chicago is once more a mythical name, and everyone here "knows his place."

When the people first heard that there was national, even worldwide publicity coming to Sumner and the murder trial they wondered why the incident had caused such a stir. At the lunch recess on the first day of the trial a county health-office worker who had stopped by to watch the excitement asked a visiting reporter where he was from, and shook his head when the answer was New York City.

"New York, Chicago, everywhere," he said. "I never heard of making such a mountain of a molehill."

The feeling that it all was a plot against the South was the most accepted explanation, and when Roy Bryant and J. W. Milam ambled into court September 19 they were armed not only with their wives, baby boys, and cigars, but the challenge of Delta whites to the interference of the outside world. The issue for the local public was not that a visiting Negro boy named Emmett Louis Till had been dragged from his bed and identified later as a body that was pulled from the Tallahatchie River with a seventy-pound cotton-gin fan tied around its neck with barbed wire—that issue was lost when people learned that the world was clamoring to have something done about it. The question of "nigger-killing" was coupled with the threat to the racial traditions of the South, and storekeepers set out jars on their counters for contributions to aid the defense of the accused murderers.

Donations to the fund disqualified several prospective jurors, as prosecutors Gerald Chatham, district attorney, and Robert B. Smith, special assistant attorney general appointed to the case, probed carefully at every candidate for a day and a half before accepting the jury. Judge Curtis Swango, a tall, quietly commanding man, combined order with a maximum of freedom in the court, and when he had Cokes brought in for the jury it seemed as appropriate courtroom procedure as pounding the gavel.

While the jury selections went on inside, the crowds outside the building grew—and were automatically segregated. Aging, shaggy-cheeked Anglo-Saxons with crumpled straw hats lined a long wooden bench. Negroes gathered across the way at the base of the Confederate statue inscribed to "the cause that never failed." The Negro numbers increased, but not with the Negroes of Sumner. A red-necked deputy whose pearl-handled pistol showed beneath the tail of his sportshirt explained that the "dressed-up" Negroes were strangers. "Ninety-five percent of them's not ours," he said. "Ours is out picking cotton and tending to their own business."

Moses Wright, a Negro locally known as a good man who tends to his business, was the state's first witness. He pressed his back against the witness chair and spoke out loud and clear as he told about the night two white men came to his house and asked for "the boy from Chicago—the one that did the talking at Money"; and how the big, balding man came in with a pistol and a flashlight and left with Emmett Till. Mose fumbled several times under cross-examination but he never lost his straightforward attitude or lowered his head. He still of course was "old man Mose" and "Uncle Mose" to both defense and prosecution, but none of that detracted from the dignity of how he told his story.

The rest of the week he was seen around the courthouse lawn with his pink-banded hat tilted back on his head, his blue pants pulled up high on a clean white shirt by yellow-and-brown suspenders. He walked through the Negro section of the lawn with his hands in his pockets and his chin held up with the air of a man who has done what there was to do and could never be touched by doubt that he should have done anything less than that.

When Mose Wright's niece, Mrs. Mamie Bradley, took the stand it was obvious as soon as she answered a question that she didn't fit the minstrel-show stereotype that most of Mississippi's white folks cherish. Nevertheless, the lawyers of both sides were careful to always address her as "Mamie," which was probably wise for the favor of the jury, since a Clarksdale, Mississippi, radio station referred to her as "Mrs. Bradley" on a news broadcast and spent the next hour answering calls of protest.

J. J. "Si" Breland, dean of the defense attorneys, questioned her while he remained in his seat, occasionally slicing his hands through the air in the quick, rigid motions he moved with throughout the trial. She answered intelligently, steadily, slightly turning her head to one side as she listened to questions, replying with a slow, distinct emphasis. "Beyond the shadow of a doubt," she said, "that was my boy's body."

At lunchtime recess the crowds around the soft-drink and sandwich concession debated her identification of her son, and many were relieved in the afternoon session when Tallahatchie County Sheriff H. C. Strider squeezed his 270 pounds in the witness chair and said the only thing he could tell about the body that had come from the river was that it was human.

Sheriff Strider, who owns 1,500 acres of cotton land, farms it with thirty-five Negro families, has the grocery store and filling station on it, and operates a cotton-dusting concern with three airplanes, is split in his commitments in a way that might qualify him as the Charles E. Wilson of Tallahatchie County. What's good for his feudal plantation is good for the county, and his dual role as law-enforcement officer and witness for the defense evidently didn't seem contradictory to him. His commitments were clear enough that prosecution lawyers once sent two state policemen to search a county jail for one Leroy "Too-Tight" Collins, a key witness for the prosecution who was missing (and never found).

There were still missing witnesses, dark, whispered rumors of fleeing men who saw the crime committed, when Gerald Chatham tugged the sleeves of his shirt and walked over to the jury Friday morning to make the summation of the case for the prosecution. Both he and Smith, who is a former F. B. I. man, had followed every lead and sent state policemen driving through the countryside in search of the Mississippi witnesses, but only two of the four who were named — Willie Reed and Mandy Brandley — were found. The time had come for Chatham to work with what he had.

In a matter of minutes from the time he started talking the atmosphere of the court was charged with tension as he raised his arm toward the ceiling and shouted that "the first words offered in testimony here were dripping with the blood of Emmett Till." The green plaster walls of the room had grown darker from the clouds of the rain that was coming outside, as Chatham went on with the tones, the gestures, the conviction of an evangelist, asserting that "the guilty flee where no man pursueth," and retelling the story of the boy's abduction in the dark of night.

J. W. Milam, the bald, strapping man who leaned forward in his seat during most of the sessions with his mouth twisted in the start of a smile, was looking at the newspaper. Roy Bryant lit a cigar. With his eyebrows raised and his head tilted back he might have been a star college fullback smoking in front of the coach during season and asking with his eyes "So what?"

When Chatham was finished, C. Sidney Carlton, the able attorney for the defense whose large, fleshy face was usually close to where the cameras were clicking, poured a paper cup of water from the green pitcher on the judge's desk, and opened his summation. He spoke well, as usual, but after Chatham's oratory he was doomed to anticlimax. There had been a brief rain and the sun was out with more heat than ever. Defense attorney J. W. Kellum, speaking briefly after Carlton before the noon recess, had the odds of discomfort against his chances of stirring the jury, but he did his best with the warning that the jurors' forefathers would turn in their graves at a guilty verdict. And then he asked what was undoubtedly the question of the week. If Roy and J. W. are convicted of murder, he said, "where under the shining sun is the land of the free and the home of the brave?"

The question was a fitting prelude to the harangue of John Whitten, the defense's last speaker. The clean-shaven, pale young man in a neatly pressed suit and white shirt that defied perspiration announced his faith that "every last Anglo-Saxon one of you men in this jury has the courage to set these men free."

Mr. Whitten went on to declare he had an answer for the state's most convincing evidence—the ring of Emmett Till that was found on the body discovered in the Tallahatchie River. The body really wasn't Emmett Till, Whitten said, and the ring might have possibly been planted on it by the agents of a sinister group that is trying to destroy the social order of the South and "widen the gap which has appeared between the white and colored people in the United States."

He didn't name any group, but the fondly nurtured local rumor that the whole Till affair was a plot on the part of the N. A. A. C. P. made naming unnecessary.

It took the twelve jurors an hour and seven minutes to return the verdict that would evidently help close the gap between the white and colored races in the land of the free and the home of the brave. Tradition, honor, God, and country were preserved in a package deal with the lives of Roy Bryant and J. W. Milam.

Reporters climbed tables and chairs to get a glimpse of the acquitted defendants, and the newspaper, magazine, and television cameras were aimed at the smiles of their wives and families in a flashing, buzzing finale. Then the agents of the outside world disappeared in a rush to make their deadlines and the stale, cluttered courtroom was finally empty of everything but mashed-out cigarettes, crushed paper cups, and a few of the canvas spectator chairs that the American Legion had sold across the street for two dollars each.

The trial week won't be forgotten here soon, and glimpses of the "foreign" Negroes who don't till cottonfields but hold positions as lawyers, doctors, and Congressmen have surely left a deep and uncomfortable mark on the whites of the Delta. But at least for the present, life is *good* again. Funds are being raised for separate-and-equal school facilities in Tallahatchie County and on Wednesdays at lunchtime four of the five defense attorneys join with the other Rotarians of Sumner in a club song about the glad day "When men are one."

JOSEPHINE HERBST

The Ruins of Memory   *April 4, 1956*

> In the 1950s Josephine Herbst, a contributor to *The Nation* since the 1920s, began writing her memoirs. This essay on literature and politics emerged as part of that process.

What seems to be missing in a good deal of contemporary writing is a sense of the world. The world around us. For some time we have had so many writers trailing their own nervous systems, premonitions, fantasies and horrors that perhaps the time has come to dig up man, the guilty worm, and to see him in relation to an actual world. It has gone so far that the word "actual" may start an argument. I mean it, just the same, in its Jane Austen sense, its Flaubert sense, its Tolstoian sense. To insist on this point of the actual is, practically speaking, avant garde. One thing is certain, we have no avant garde to flutter anybody at present. The one we had got stuck some time back in the pages of the little magazines when they went academic. Then the critics took over. This has been a long period for the critics and editors. The great authors to come up since the Second World War have mostly been dead a long time. Kafka, Melville, Hawthorne, Henry James should be with us always but their resurgence in the forties presaged more than recognition of their stature. It signified also a genteel retreat from a period too complicated to confront easily. The writings of the detached past became a kind of smokescreen to conceal the present dilemma, and the ruins.

But a ruin can be as good a point of departure as any. There is usually new life in the ruins as anyone who ever saw a population react from a bombing can testify. But the picker-uppers are not trying to salvage tender mementos only. They usually are looking for bricks and firewood.

In the twenties writers seem to have been valued above critics and when a critic really got under the skin he was apt to be a writer. If you were a young writer then and read Ezra Pound in the *Little Review* or *Poetry Magazine* you were fired to write to the limit of your skill. Today if a young writer reads too much criticism he may feel that there is no use manning the ship which is overmanned already and besides will the captains care for his particular skill?

If past history is any guide, the present phase that tends to the compulsive presentation of people as isolated moral atoms without any sensible relation to society or the ideas of their time ought to have departed before this. For literary epochs come and go but this wave seems to have frozen in the cold war. In the freeze more is paralyzed than anyone cares to admit; perhaps more than the writer dares admit. But there is no such thing as a writer untouched by his time. Even the most inner experience is a response to some outside. That response may lead Kafka to explore the dark region beyond human experience or explanation in *The Castle* or Sean O'Casey to write from a sense of mission *Red Roses for Me*. In a favorable period when the atmosphere is fluid there will be many varieties of response to experience and what emerges is creation in full flower. Not without flaws, the decade of the twenties approached such a time of creative flowering if only because it was relatively hospitable to the new and diverse.

Every period takes stock of the one preceding it and the past that was good enough for the fathers never seems good enough for the children no matter how idyllic it may seem to the great-grandchildren. Writers in the twenties reacted not only to the shock of the First World War but to the values held dear in the nineteenth century. The stock responses of good will and progressive enlightenment as an explanation of human behavior had failed Dreiser and Sherwood Anderson even before the First World War. The new attitudes were expressed not only in the realm of ideas but were implicit in the texture of the work, its language, its style, even in what came to be tagged "lack of style."

If the values of the nineteenth century failed the writers of the twenties they collapsed utterly in the thirties. What could liberal belief in rationality do against the irrationality which was spreading over Europe? In a period of demoralization and terror it was no bad thing to try to act, however mistakenly or inadequately, as the conscience of the age. If you can bear to lift the black cloth placed over the thirties by the revisionists, some of whom seem more infatuated with the revelation of their own private sense of guilt than in the situation as it *then existed,* you may be surprised to discover work not entirely marred by "innocence" nor requiring the afterthought of "shame." The reaction in the forties, the Second World War, the new cynicism, the new prosperity and the new smugness put the thirties, its work and the sources of its potential, into a time capsule where it has been effectively isolated. But the fact remains that work marked by vitality and venturing did emerge in the arts, the theatre and in the writing of that decade and found a new dynamic.

It is a new dynamic which is now conspicuous by its absence. Material prosperity can never answer the questions, why do we live, what does it mean? When the notion spreads that getting along may be the ultimate aim of man's efforts, the surface hardens and the writer, by nature more of a rebel than he may choose to admit, tries to burrow somewhere for a hidden meaning. If the rigidities set up make it dangerous truly to look at the world around us, the writer may be driven to look only at himself, unrelated to the actual world. But writing *should* be dangerous: as dangerous as Socrates. There should be no refuge for the writer either in the Ivory Tower or the Social Church.

Gissing, whose work Henry James admired, said that in all character there sits a mind, and that the mind of the dullest is not dull because, at its lowest, it will at least reflect the social dilemma. Perhaps the writers in the thirties were so hardpressed by the immediacy of the dilemma that they scratched around for characters to explicate it. But it was no longer a time when the Nick Adamses up in Michigan could feel the question of the hour as merely a choice between freedom or that "fat married look." Straws in the wind, out of jobs, out of luck, the Nick Adamses of the thirties might well ask, freedom for what? It was a time when the feelings of the individual might seem haphazard, trivial, inconsequent compared with his feelings experienced as a member of a particular group. As an experience this was not new; soldiers in war know it; European literature has reflected it, but in the thirties it seemed to have had special significance for a nation dedicated to individualism. Some of the writing of the decade reflected this special kind of comprehension. Not every writer was obsessed with "the way out" or the idealized "worker," but as man had become a political animal, whether he liked it or not, the writers most sensitive to the temper of the time were bound to reflect it.

When you read *Let Us Now Praise Famous Men,* you realize that James Agee was feeling his way into the lives of poor and rejected people from whom his normal fate as a writer might have isolated him. There was discovery here that reminds us of the nineteenth-century Russian literature when Tolstoy attempted to understand far beyond the boundaries of his estate, and the affairs of Dr. Chekhov informed the writer Chekhov.

It takes a true writer to show us what has been missing in our lives. No one can give the writer an assignment that his own impulse has not bespoken but more than his security should inform him. "The pen," said Kafka to Janouch, "is not an instrument but an organ of the writer's." But what if that organ suffer a fatty degeneration and come to resemble the diseased liver of a Strassburg goose? What has a writer to say if he agrees that this is the best of all possible worlds and all of our major problems have been solved on a miracle time belt of endless prosperity? Aren't all the Nick Adamses of today fairly courting that "fat married look"? The routine may become boring, and the writer who in his life may batten happily on his role in a priggish status quo, may revert in his writing to the exotic and cash in on a kind of romantic nihilism which never attempts to deal with more than the desperate *sensations* of a felt or imagined experience. Don't our modern Stavrogins tend to wallow luxuriously in their dreadful predicaments? Seen without any surrounding pattern to light the actuality, they emerge as little more than case histories. One pathological case confined to its pathology is not a subject for literary work. Dostoevsky's Stavrogin also struggled against his doomed nature; he killed himself because he had a vision of a human world, not because he saw inhumanity triumphant with himself in a stellar role. His reaction implied more than a blighted ego.

How did we get where we are? Perhaps if beating the breast in public confession had not become *sine qua non* we might find out. Guilt is real, it is serious, but when it becomes also a fashion, there is corruption. No one can seek for new clues or discover the actual world when it becomes clouded with the smoke of penitents burning the past.

We are not only what we are today but what we were yesterday and if you burn your immediate past there is nothing left but ashes which are all very well for those heads that like nothing better than to be sprinkled with ashes. But are these ash-covered heads really the spokesmen of our conscience? For conscience implies constant vigilance, inquiry, challenge, seeking, wonder. A conscience larded with complacency and self-righteousness is no longer a conscience. And we may well ask what has come out of all this in the way of writing and where and how is the writer facing up to the consequences of his knowledge. Are these frequent stories of innocents whose baffled illusions are made to seem important, oh far more important than life itself, really the expression of man's fate? Is the eccentric really our man of the hour? Life is shown up as a little shabby in comparison to some of this starry-eyed frustration. In fact, many writers seem intent on what D. H. Lawrence called "doing dirt on life."

May a conscience be time-clocked and serve one decade and not another? It is all very well to have pursued with vigilance the psychopaths of "radical conformity," minds hardened against any human plea or valid idea embarrassing to the Party. But a mind can harden while manning a power post, any time, any place, whether in politics, government, Hollywood, the university or an institute of art and letters. It can harden while it succumbs to prevailing fashion under any banner.

If the social criticism of the thirties seemed able to analyze the roots only by disparaging the flower, the new detective-critics seem able to admire the flower only by pulling it to pieces. Between the opposing factions of this modern War of the Roses the flower is victimized, and the writer without whom there would be no flower, seems relegated to a Nobody. If behind the leaders of one faction waved the banners demanding a deterministic construction of man's role, behind the leaders of the opposing faction rose the misty phantoms of a Southern feudal aristocracy. Excesses in one direction turned to excesses in another; in both instances we seem to see looming above us the stern father image of an arbitrary authority. It is not only in politics that the age has been thus marked.

The language of our new critics was seductive, called us to account on many basic literary issues; and since we were fed up with too much democracy in the thirties, the notion of an aristocracy, if only in the arts, made a telling point. Form and precision of language are all important but there is also a point of view and one may well ask in what origins it arises. What assumptions are made from which the elegant flower is to grow? It is not coincidence that most of the writing to please the new detective-critics came from Southerners, most of whom were emigrés living in the North, getting their livings in Northern cities but with all feeling, knowledge and creative source in the South.

If it is our privilege to admire a body of brilliant writing by Southerners, worthy of a lasting place in our literature, it is also pertinent to ask why, in general, it has become so static. If it succeeded in producing a renascence for which we should be grateful, why did its influence effect a stalemate and degenerate into the picturesque, the bizarre and the exploitation of the eccentric? The insistence on perfection may produce a Rimbaud, revolutionary in form *and* content, but it may also settle for an inverted romanticism, a kind of snobbish chastity, implying that the hurly-burly is really not good enough for these particular garments.

Then the will to perfection without the valid idea may proliferate into mere decay and tedium, descending into the language and the thought of journalism, relying finally on the violence of the "you-gotta-knock-'em-dead" school. The secret prince and dreamer of perfection may become lost in the glitter of honor, and his talent may then make of him an actor for life.

There is a distinction to be made between the actual writing of the group that produced the renascence and the effects which followed in their train. This is no challenge to that body of writing; its writers had their aim and had to fulfill it by the inner secret processes of all creative work. But it also seems true that the sights were set toward a traditional past to the extinction of a prevailing present and as a result precluded a dynamic for writers to follow. From the richest section of this country in the sense of a literary potential we have arrived at a dead level of little studies of general decay. But the fact is that the South is not so much decaying as *changing* and it is fair to ask what use other writers in other countries in other epochs made of similar situations of transition. And it seems also to the point to suggest that of all the Southerners, Faulkner, who has mostly stayed put, has been able to gouge deeper, range more widely and feel more intimately the pressure of Southern change and responsibility, and to be, so far as I know, the only writer of the South willing to put himself on record on the murder of young Till. As for earlier epochs the writer did not have to applaud in order to respond knowingly; Balzac, attached to the feudal past, could take in what was going on around him with everything thrown in; Stendahl could write of the business-king Louis Phillipe so incisively that *The Green Huntsman* could not be published in his lifetime. A response to change was inherent in every line of Jane Austen. As for the Russians whose serfs were liberated in the same decade as the Civil War what did they *not* do?

This discussion would fail to make its point if it appeared to set up new goals for more authority instead of more freedoms. The writer has suffered more than the Wars of the Roses in this period. He, like everybody else, seems to have been atomized and a waif on his own, to be shut off from many of the sources of knowledge more freely come by at an earlier period. If his road leads to the university and conformity, it is not altogether by choice, but by grim necessity in a society where the writer has never been a culture-hero. Roving was good for the writer; to have been a reporter undoubtedly informed Ring Lardner, Ernest Hemingway, Stephen Crane. To know far more than he may ever use is imperative for the writer.

We should not have to choose between Dreiser or Henry James. A writer must follow his bent but there are situations when pressures from without press so strongly that he hardly knows if he is bending to his own inner impulse or to some compulsive outside. In these days of specialization, when the scientist may be immured with his experiment without knowledge of what is going on in other laboratories, when he may even be in ignorance of the whole meaning of the cultural processes of which he is a part, it seems to me that the writer too is running a risk of falling back into his own little corner where his very isolation within himself is aiding a sterilization of creative powers. Or in another category, that he too often refuses to confront the implications of his own work, and intending to show the menace of the violent, secretly champions the force he would deplore. If we believe with Henry James that any theory which prevents a writer from seeing is a wrong one, we might also meditate on the words of Rilke: that "everything is gestation and then bringing forth. To let each impression and each germ of feeling come to completion quite in itself, in the dark, in the inexpressible, the unconscious, beyond the reach of one's own understanding, and wait with deep humility and patience the birth-hour of a new clarity; that alone is living the artist's life — in understanding as in work."

SARAH PATTON BOYLE

Spit in the Devil's Eye   *October 20, 1956*
A Southern Heretic Speaks

ABOUT THE AUTHOR:

One of the most ardent workers for desegregation in Charlottesville is a University of Virginia faculty wife named Sarah Patton Boyle. . . . The Yankee visitor was sitting in his hotel room when the telephone rang and a pleasant voice said: "This is Mrs. Boyle. I just thought you'd want to know, there was a big cross burning out in the yard here tonight. Son took some pictures of it, . . ."
—DAN WAKEFIELD in *The Nation*, September 15, 1956.
— ORIGINAL NOTE

Charlottesville, Va.

I am a white Southerner who crusades for acceptance of colored citizens. Living in one of the five states sworn to resist integration at any cost, I'm roundly hated by some people, solidly disapproved of by many and supported by very few. I would have been a fool not to expect this when I resolved to brandish my banner — and I did. Beyond that, I was prepared for almost nothing that happened to me.

In the light of the experience of others, I expected to receive many threats. My psychological factory probably could convert these into stimulation, I thought. Timidity being unpopular in my family, I was raised to feel that even looming danger isn't the least imminent, and I characteristically trip with gay stupidity to the dentist's chair—to meet each onslaught of his buzzer with incredulity. Therefore, I concluded, a deluge of threats probably would challenge rather than terrify me. I felt disgustingly secure.

But with superhuman cunning, evil refrained from attacking me in a form which I was qualified to use constructively. Unless one interprets as a threat (which I didn't) the six-foot cross which was burned a slipper's toss from my bedroom window, in half-a-dozen years of crusading I've only once been threatened with bodily harm—when a locally postmarked letter warned that if I didn't shut up, my house might be bombed. (I didn't shut up, and here sits the house.)

The deluge which actually descended was one for which I was not psychologically prepared. It consisted of contemptuous jeers and obscene insults. Raised in a country home, the daughter and granddaughter of Episcopal ministers, my gutter vocabulary has been so neglected that much that's said to me by letter and on the telephone I can grasp only through its context. To say I was aghast is to use insipid language.

Moreover, it hadn't occurred to me that my motivation might be misinterpreted. I expected to be called a sentimentalist, an impractical idealist and even a crackpot. But I wasn't prepared for accusations that I am a paid agent of Communists, that I am bribed by the NAACP to tell lies, that I oppose the status quo because of a perverted passion for publicity, and—hardly least—that I long for integration because of a psychopathic yearning for the special pornographic skills of black men. As I've firmly turned the corner of my first half century, the latter bit of biological warfare on me is the more amazing.

Once I fondly imagined that the long residence of my forebears in Virginia would move fellow Southerners to the admission that I had some right to speak in favor of changing customs. "Nobody on earth can call me a Yankee," I told myself smugly.

I was soon wishing that they could. Not only is it more comfortable to be resented as a meddling outsider than to be despised as a traitor, but also if segregationists can disqualify you merely by calling you a Yankee, they need go no further, and—their own estimation to the contrary—this is not universally regarded as a disgrace. But a dyed-in-the-wool Southerner can be disqualified only through defamation of character.

Another early illusion, soon to be dispelled, was that quarter would be given for maintaining a gentle, reasonable approach. I assumed (Jesus' own experience to the contrary) that when you turn the other cheek, nobody actually hauls off and slugs it. I have approximately two splintered jaw bones to show for this conviction.

I entered the struggle with not one ray of malice toward, or contempt for, any one. I still have none. I understand well that the segregation pattern is taken firmly for granted by many white and some colored Southerners who sincerely believe that no good can come to any one through integration. I therefore seek to help them to understand the need for integration, rather than to attack them for opposing it. Yet they could not feel toward me much more bitterly if my public utterances were vindictive condemnations. Discovery of the explanation of this was one of the greatest of my many shocks.

It's simply that so fixed is their conviction that integration can bring only degradation that they find it impossible to believe that any one who defends it is not either utterly ignorant of conditions or completely evil. The native Southerner is not adjudged to be ignorant. Looking into the eyes of staunch segregationists, I usually see not respectful hostility, but incredulous contempt. The names they call me are not merely empty insults, but are rather accurate descriptions of what they really think of me. Dressed for this contest in the highest principles I know, I wasn't prepared for eyes which could see me garbed only in filthy rags.

Nor did my surprises end with those outlined above.

A year and a half ago the *Saturday Evening Post* featured one of my articles on integration. It was an attempt to show through statistics and little publicized facts that Southerners are readier for integration than they think—a contention which I still maintain. Because the background of the article was Charlottesville, I expected a wide local reading. But I didn't expect that twenty-four hours after it appeared, nearly every retail dealer, delivery boy, store and postal clerk, taxi driver and shoe repair man I knew would regard me with hardened and disillusioned eyes. Overnight my little daily contacts became chill.

Did I have a similar experience in my own social group? Not at first. For two days I received a stream of telephone calls telling me how true my statements were, and how much they needed stating. Acquaintances stopped me on the street with similar comments. Surrounded by this warmth, I could be philosophical about the few who looked straight through me—taking care that I should know their action was deliberate.

But the wave of approbation, I soon learned with a sickening thud, was individual reaction. It reflected merely how each person felt as he read the article in his own home. Group reaction, however, like mob psychology, is not merely the sum of individual reaction. As attacks on the article started in the newspapers, as enthusiastic supporters were wet-blanketed by those who claimed the facts I reported were half tommy-rot and half lies, the warm social pond in which I bathed suddenly froze. Some of the same people who had clapped loudly at first now let me know from behind stiffened faces that, after all, they did disagree with me sharply on some points.

Silence began to obtrude itself into all my social contacts except my closest friendships. The topic of integration was taboo if I was near. Though I was violently attacked almost daily in the press, no one referred to it. This was probably thought tactful, but I felt cut off. I never knew whether the person I was talking to agreed with me or with my attackers. The reticence was like a soundproof wall. Real communication ended. I began to welcome unpleasant telephone calls — pleasant ones had ceased — as at least a genuine form of human contact.

Yet, curiously, it isn't heartache which brings you closest to internal defeat as Southern tensions heighten. It's fatigue. You feel as if you've run too hard and long to catch a bus, or that it's four o'clock on a day when you forgot to eat lunch. It's almost as though, without knowing it, you had been invisibly connected with other people, drawing from them nourishment, comfort and strength. Now the unseen connections are severed. And a puny thing you are when separated from the rest.

Your isolation is not so much the direct result of enemy action as of the fact that when you travel this road your experiences are shared by fewer and fewer people, until at last there's no one to whom you can make yourself understood. For words communicate only so far as they serve to remind friends of experiences and sensations of their own that resemble those which you recount. No more than you can share through description a sunset with a man blind from birth, can you share with another an experience which doesn't resemble any he has known.

And those who would like to give you moral support are quite helpless with no rules to guide them. If you lost a member of your family, anybody with a desire to help would know what he should do. Where his own experience failed, established custom would guide him. But books of etiquette lack rules for comforting those attacked for their principles.

Where can one learn that if a cross is burned for you, and it is "tactfully" ignored, you feel as if you have some unmentionable disease? Where can one learn that if you're publicly attacked and friends are silent, there builds up in your subconscious mind the conviction that you are utterly alone — even though you positively know better?

Because the Southern press blazes away in headlines and editorials which proclaim the successes and opinions of segregationists, with only parenthetical or derisive mention of those who disagree; because your side is cautious and silent while the opposition is stridently vocal; because your attackers hammer away; for all these reasons, if your friends are silent, you hear only evil.

Something similar to Russian brain-washing of prisoners takes place inevitably in your consciousness. Day after day, week after week, month after month, you are told that you're a fool, a blackguard, a worker of evil. In the press, on the telephone, in your mail box, the same refrain beats on, like water dripping on the granite of your convictions: You're wrong, *you're wrong,* YOU'RE WRONG!

Friends tell you that they wanted to call you but knew you were busy and didn't like to interrupt; others that they meant to write but didn't get to it. But Mrs. Opposition didn't mind interrupting, and Mr. Opposition got to it. And the drip-drip-drip goes on and on. Slowly, like creeping paralysis, you find yourself losing confidence.

You find yourself developing a brand of schizophrenia. There is an ever-increasing cleavage between what you think and what you feel. You *know* that much progress has been made, yet you *feel* that there's just no use carrying the banner any more. You know that justice moves irresistibly to eventual triumph, yet you feel that only evil and ugliness have stout roots. You know you are right, yet building up in you is an enormous sense of guilt. This is your final, sickening surprise.

From birth, good Americans are assured that if they are well-behaved, are kind, honest and industrious, they will inevitably be rewarded by social approval. Naturally, when you are publicly attacked, they—including you—are filled with the unformulated suspicion that you got what you somehow deserved.

Is a Southern crusader for the rights of man doomed to eventual breakdown? Many seem to think so, for the rate of retirement in this field of activity must approach the record. Watching, Southern Negroes have grown cynical about the short-lived efforts of the white liberal—thus adding the minority's mistrust to his other pressures.

But I think I've rediscovered a way for you to keep your sanity and still crusade. It's simply meekly to accept "out-moded theology." With its able aid your psychological factor can convert pressure, pain and disillusionment into power to persist. Our modern view of the world, I now think, is the outgrowth of soft lives. In hand-to-hand combat with raw evil this sensible view seems less realistic.

When the smell, taste, sound and touch of evil are a nightmare against which you constantly struggle, the personification of evil is an intelligent device. In facing evil squarely and calling it the Devil, some of your horrid helplessness before its magnitude departs. Then, too, you find yourself more able to be dazzled into spontaneous worship by the glory of evil's opposite, the shining purity of love.

Years ago, on seeing the title of an article, "Humanitarianism Is Not Enough," I recall thinking, "How could that be?" I wouldn't ask myself that question now. When evils swarm you like a mob of maniacs you know that you must have both Something and Someone to worship, or perish.

Against a background of accusing enemies and silent friends, I hungrily reclaim the "morbid" doctrine that unearned suffering is redemptive, and that only the patient pain of the innocent can dissolve some human sins. It's the futility of pain stiffens your weary spine. The early Christians went singing to ugly deaths. The Southern crusader, too, has need of forgotten virile Christian truths.

So I shan't break down, and I shan't retire. For I shall refresh myself by looking at a sparkling, ethereal King, and I shall know an easier yoke and a lighter burden, and I shall learn to say, "Forgive them, Father," and—after taking practiced, careful aim—I shall spit in the Devil's eye.

HAROLD CLURMAN

Theatre   *November 24, 1956*
[*Eugene O'Neill's* Long Day's Journey Into Night]

Critic, director, producer and author Harold Clurman was *The Nation*'s theatre critic from 1953 to 1980.

The late October and early November openings of new plays have so piled up that I cannot perform my journalistic task with a regularity that fits the calendar. I prefer the Old Vic's production of *Richard II* to its *Macbeth,* but I shall return to the Old Vic season (at the Winter Garden) after the opening of its most entertaining production—*Troilus and Cressida*—which I saw and made note of in London.

I shall undoubtedly have something to say in a later piece about Rosalind Russell in *Auntie Mame* (Broadhurst) which I like somewhat less than most of the reviewers, and about Michael Redgrave and Barbara Bel Geddes in *The Sleeping Prince* (Coronet), as well as Phoenix Theatre's production of Ostrovsky's *Diary of a Scoundrel,* which I like more. But important matters should come first. I refer to José Quintero's production of O'Neill's *Long Day's Journey Into Night* (Helen Hayes).

It is easy to say—and I hereby say it categorically—that *Long Day's Journey Into Night* is a play everyone should see and admire. No matter how one views it, it is impressive. It is not only unique among American plays, but in O'Neill's work itself. For it is an unabashedly autobiographical statement, something torn in agonized honesty from the memory and conscience of its author—who appears to have been compelled to set down this testament of his early home life to preserve his sanity. His chief, one might almost say his only, purpose was revelation of himself to himself. There is something moving, even great, in the impulse of the play, and no one can witness it without reverence for the *selflessness* of this extremely personal act.

The result, artistically speaking, is a solid (despite its length), unadorned and arresting piece of realism. What is remarkable about this is that O'Neill, reputedly the arch-realist of the American drama, was never wholly a realist: he was largely a romantic—even something of a mystic. He was a romantic struggling to wrest meaning out of the painful data of his life, hope out of the sadness that never ceased to overwhelm him. Yet in this play where he undertook to expose the core and cause of his melancholy—his overpowering, majestic father, his envenomed brother, his shattered, innocent babe of a mother—in this play which he wrote as a release from his torment, as an expiation, as an effort at compassionate understanding and finally to enable himself to forgive, the texture is harder, less evocative, less profound in mood or meaning than in his technically and intellectually more fumbling plays. One leaves *Long Day's Journey* with a sense of stunned awe, but not emotionally transfigured.

One reason for this, I suspect, is that in his determination to be utterly objective—to avoid pitfalls of sentimentality and self-pity—O'Neill, who was neither a thinker nor a sharply observant depicter of character (the portraits in this play are convincing but rudimentary), lost some of the intuitive feeling which informs nearly all his work with a brooding and penetrating power far greater than anything that can be measured by a rational yardstick. O'Neill, the romantic though only half-articulate poet, yielded himself to the fullness of life's turmoil. He could not entirely cope with it, but for all that it became intensely dramatic and palpitant in his presentation.

O'Neill's formative years, epitomized in the play's long day in 1912, were part of a period when the American experience—no longer a fresh adventure, a healthy exercise in discovery, pluck and epic struggle—hung heavy on the citizens of our big cities and towns. The massive wealth with its raw patches of hang-dog poverty, the overfed acquisitiveness and the depleted inner energies, the proud muscularity coupled with increasing enervation, went into making that murky brown, dejected yet glamorous gloom which enveloped a giant people. This was the later-day period of America's coming to consciousness and no one in the theatre ever expressed it nearly as well as O'Neill. But, strangely enough, there is less of this atmosphere in *Long Day's Journey,* which purports to be a forthright document, than in his dramatic inventions, which often range very far from home.

The production of the play may be another cause for my reaction to it. It is a faithful, thoroughly intelligent and professionally knowledgeable production, wholly devoted to the realistic letter of the play. But by being so literal an embodiment of the dramatist's text the production comes to share the play's limitations, whereas it should transcend them. Means might have been found to create from the climate of O'Neill's spirit a greater feeling of shadow and depth out of which the play's figures might emerge with a more poetic and grander stature.

Fredric March and Florence Eldridge, excellent and finely motivated actors though they are, provide rather more characterization than creative interpretation. They excite our interest but tell us little more than what O'Neill has set down verbally. For sheer virtuosity—taking the stage, as professionals say—Jason Robards as the elder brother in the best-focussed scene of the production—a drunken midnight exchange with his brother—makes the most vivid theatrical impression. A greater scene—the final confrontation of father and younger son—fails of its full possibilities because the actors (March and Bradford Dillman as the boy) concentrate more on the momentary situation and on the action of the words than on the over-all inspirational source which gives the scene its lyric essence and thematic inevitability. For what the play deals with is not so much the details of one family's misery as the submerged struggle against the dead weight of material pressures in a world where the needs of the human soul are clamorous yet barely recognized.

DALTON TRUMBO

Blacklist=Black Market
May 4, 1957

It was Dalton Trumbo, more than any other writer, who broke the blacklist by exposing its absurdity, and its unworkability in the face of an industry's appetite for money-making talent. In 1959 the Motion Picture Academy rescinded its bylaw prohibiting awards to those who refused to cooperate with the House Un-American Activities Committee and, after more than a year's hesitation, Universal Studies announced in August 1960 that Trumbo would be credited as the writer of the film *Spartacus*. That same year director Otto Preminger revealed that Trumbo had written the screenplay for his film *Exodus*. Trumbo won an Academy Award for the 1956 film *The Brave One* under the pseudonym of Robert Rich.

ABOUT THE AUTHOR:

The presently known works of screenwriter Dalton Trumbo—which include Thirty Seconds Over Tokyo, A Man to Remember *and* Kitty Foyle, *among many others—may one day be revealed as his least important and least successful. Since his blacklisting as a member of the Hollywood Ten in 1947, Mr. Trumbo has become a prolific and anonymous contributor to Hollywood's black market in scripts, and for all anyone knows (other than Mr. Trumbo and his producers, who aren't saying),*

Hollywood

As the year 1957 lurches toward its mid-point, Hollywood finds itself celebrating, willingly or unwillingly as the case may be, the tenth anniversary of a blacklist which began in 1947 when a producers' delegation composed of Messrs. Dore Schary, Walter Wanger and Eddie Mannix appeared before the Screen Writers' Guild to plead for acquiescence in the blacklisting of the Hollywood Ten.

Mr. Schary, who is probably the most civilized and certainly the most literate man ever to achieve executive leadership of a major motion-picture producing company, acted as reluctant spokesman for the producers: reluctant because some of the doomed men were his friends; reluctant because he had worked with others of them in the various Roosevelt campaigns; reluctant because he was and is a liberal who hated the idea of a blacklist and probably hates it even more today.

Despite assurances that ten heads would appease the gods, the guillotine has since claimed some 250 other artists and technicians. The most powerful man in Hollywood today is an inconspicuous, pleasant-mannered fellow named William Wheeler, who works as investigator for the House Committee on Un-American Activities. Upon his modest shoulders has fallen the glory that was Zanuck's and the power that was Mayer's.

The paradox of the tenth anniversary of the blacklist lies in the fact that while it finds most surviving members of the Hollywood Ten busily engaged in the practice of their professions, Mr. Schary, amidst a hideous outcry from avaricious stockholders, has just been ejected from his producership at M-G-M and presently, as the euphemism goes, is at liberty.

The reason for his discharge, Mr. Schary wrote in *The Reporter* of April 18, 1957, was "that I made too many speeches and wrote too many articles, and that my participation in the 1956 Presidential campaign on behalf of the Democrats had made for irritation and enmity." Mr. Schary, in a word, fell victim to the blacklist his own eloquence had inaugurated; the decade ends, as it began, with an absurdity.

The truth, of course, is that the blacklist was openly called for in 1947 by the House Committee on Un-American Activities (". . . Don't you think the most effective way is the payroll route?" ". . . Do you think the studios should continue to employ these individuals?") and that the producers opposed the idea. Eric Johnston, president of the Motion Picture Association of America, told the committee that for producers "to join together and to refuse to hire someone or some people would be a potential conspiracy, and our legal counsel advised against it."

Louis B. Mayer testified that "They have mentioned two or three writers to me several times. There is no proof about it, except they mark them as Communists, and when I look at the pictures they have written for us I can't find once where they have written anything like that. . . . I have asked counsel. They claim that unless you can prove they are Communists they could hold you for damages." Jack L. Warner declared under oath that he "wouldn't be a party with anyone in an association, especially where you would be liable for having a fellow's livelihood impaired; I wouldn't want to do that."

They did it, however, a few days later at a famous meeting in the Waldorf-Astoria. Depositions taken from persons present reveal a long and stormy session during which the Hollywood executives strongly opposed demands of the "Eastern people" for a blacklist. The "Eastern people," unfortunately, controlled the film corporations involved and the source of investment capital with which production is maintained. It was no contest. The meeting ended with a sullenly unanimous proclamation of the first blacklist in the history of motion pictures.

The Hollywood Ten, blacklisted and cursed with the worst press since Bruno Hauptmann, stood trial for contempt of Congress, drew maximum fines and sentences, wrangled their way through skeptical courts and finally were distributed throughout the federal penitentiary system. Ring Lardner, Jr., and Lester Cole landed in Danbury, Connecticut, where they renewed an old acquaintance with ex-Congressman J. Parnell Thomas, chairman of the 1947 hearings which had done them in. Thomas had been caught with his hand in the wrong cash drawer.

Jack Lawson, Adrian Scott and this correspondent, incarcerated under heavy guard in the grand old state of Kentucky, were thrown into intimate contact with its favorite son, ex-Congressman Andy May, who had celebrated the glory of American arms by snatching a few wartime defense bribes. Almost every jail in the country during that curious time found Congressman and contemptee standing cheek by jowl in the chow line, all their old malignities dissolved in common hunger for a few more of them there beans.

Meanwhile, sustained by an Appellate Court decision which confirmed its right and even its duty to investigate artists and their works, the committee embarked on a permanent career in Hollywood. Francis Walter, his chariot drawn by captive starlets, passed like Caesar through the lots attended by a chanting host of the repentent. Under the yelping attack of this stream-lined, sharp-toothed wolf pack, Communists, near-Communists, neo-Communists, proto-Communists, non-Communists and a few friends of anti-Communists fell like tenpins.

And then, imperceptibly at first, the uproar began to diminish. It faded off, about a year ago, into a stunned and terrible silence. There wasn't anybody left to investigate. The silence continues to this day, broken only occasionally by the contemplative licking of old wounds.

A blacklist, far from being a funny thing, is an illegal instrument of terror which can exist only by sufferance of and connivance with the federal government. The Hollywood blacklist is but part of an immensely greater official blacklist—barring its victims from work at home and denying them passage abroad—which mocks our government in all its relations with civilized powers that neither tolerate nor understand such repression. The shock of the blacklist produces psychic disorders among sensitive persons, from which result broken homes, desolate children, premature deaths and sometimes suicide.

It is not alone the loss of income or of property that hurts: the more terrible wound is the loss of a profession to which one's entire life has been dedicated. A director must have the facilities of a studio: denied them, he sells real estate. A violinist must appear in person for the concert: barred from admittance, he becomes a milkman and practices six hours a day against the unrevealed time when his music once more may be heard. The actor's physical personality, which is his greatest asset, becomes his supreme curse under the blacklist; he must be seen, and when the sight of him is prohibited he becomes a carpenter, an insurance salesman, a barber.

A writer is more fortunate. Give him nothing more than paper, a pencil and a nice clean cell, and he's in business. Dante, Cervantes, Rousseau, Voltaire, Ben Jonson, Milton, Defoe, Bunyan, Hugo, Zola and a score of others have long since proved that in jail or out, writing under their own names or some one else's or a pseudonym or anonymously, writers will write; and that having written, they will find an audience. Only fools with no knowledge of history and bureaucrats with no knowledge of literature are stupid enough to think otherwise.

And so it chanced in Hollywood that each blacklisted writer, after swiftly describing that long parabola from the heart of the motion-picture industry to a small house in a low-rent district, picked himself up, dusted his trousers, anointed his abrasions, looked around for a ream of clean white paper and something to deface it with, and began to write. Through secret channels, and by means so cunning they may never be revealed, what he wrote was passed along until finally it appeared on a producer's desk, and the producer looked upon it and found it good, and monies were paid, and the writer's children began contentedly to eat. Thus the black market.

In the meantime, quietly domiciled nearby with his stunningly beautiful wife and two infant daughters a young man of Irish descent named Michael Wilson sat down at his typewriter and went furiously to work writing scripts. By 1951 he had risen to a position of such prominence that he was subpoenaed by the committee. Appearing before it in good form, Wilson took the Fifth Amendment, ending his career at the very moment it seemed ready to flower. Four months later his screenplay of *A Place in the Sun,* adapted from *An American Tragedy,* was nominated for an Academy Award. He thus became the first American screenwriter to be nominated for an award after being blacklisted. A month later he chalked up another first for the blacklist by winning the Oscar.

Wilson apparently had a number of unproduced scripts lying around the studios, for the following year his screenplay of *Five Fingers* was produced, and once again he received the Academy's scroll of nomination for the Award. With two nominations and one Oscar under his belt, Wilson continued the quiet life of a blacklistee until some two years later, when Allied Artists decided to produce another of his old scripts, this one an adaptation of Jessamyn West's *Friendly Persuasion.*

When the time rolled around for screen credits, Wilson discovered that Miss West and Robert Wyler, brother of the film's director, were credited as sole authors of the screenplay. Wilson appealed to the Writers' Guild arbitration committee, which ruled in his favor. Allied Artists thereupon released the picture without screenplay credits of any kind.

The Academy of Motion Picture Arts and Sciences was now confronted with the horrid possibility that the picture might bring Wilson, who had been dead professionally for five years, still another Oscar. The man seemed to be getting out of hand; God alone knew how many more of his unproduced manuscripts were lying in studio files. So twenty-two members of the Academy's Board of Governors passed a by-law which was to remain secret unless "*Friendly Persuasion* receives a writing nomination as the best screenplay." It provided that no person who behaved as Wilson had before a Congressional committee was eligible for an Academy prize. That is why, when the screenwriters did nominate Wilson for *Friendly Persuasion,* there was appended to the listing the sad little note: "Achievement nominated, but writer ineligible for Award under Academy by-laws."

Wilson, who during World War II served as a Captain in the Fifth Amphibious Corps, U. S. Marines, under Major General Holland (Howling) M. Smith, doesn't scare too easily, and appears to take a dim view of secret by-laws designed to celebrate his professional demise. He is presently bringing suit against the Academy, in the course of which the patriots on the Academy's board who barred his work will be given an opportunity to explain under oath just how their unanimity was achieved.

With *Friendly Persuasion* barred, the Academy for the first time in its history offered four instead of five candidates for its Best Screenplay Award. The Oscar, shabby and compromised but quite as golden as its twenty brethren, went almost by default to James Poe, John Farrow and S. J. Perelman for the screenplay of *Eighty Days Around the World.* The Oscar for the Best Original Story, glowing with the virtue of a fair contest, went to Robert Rich for *The Brave One.* The remaining writer's Oscar, for Best Original Screenplay, fell into the foreign hands of Albert Lamorisse for the French film, *The Red Balloon.*

And then something happened. A young man named Robert Rich (but not the Robert Rich for whom a proxy had picked up the Oscar), thinking no doubt to make sport of the Academy, pretended to be the *real* Robert Rich and sought to receive from the Academy those courtesies and distinctions that seemed to lie without visible claimant. In some fashion not yet known he got tangled up with Miss Margaret Herrick, executive director of the Academy, or George Seaton, its president, or some other Academy factotum yet undiscovered, and confessed his deception.

The Academy, giddy by now with patriotism, flushed with its victory over Wilson, anxious to proclaim itself Cerberus of the blacklist and sensing that a second barbarian might have breached the defenses and profaned the sanctuary, rushed at once into print with the most disastrous publicity release of its twenty-nine year history. "Robert Rich," it announced ominously, "credited by the studio which produced *The Brave One* with authorship of the motion-picture story and winner of the Academy Award in this category, stated today he was not the author of the story."

There followed a series of dire warnings from Mr. Seaton and his underlings. The original story, it was hinted, wasn't original at all, or if so it was very likely a plagiarism, and the Academy would probably withhold the award, or punish the King Brothers by giving it to the owners of another story who were suing the Kings, or even declare Robert Rich, like Wilson, a non-person, and turn the Oscar over to the next highest man in the vote, or maybe shoot craps for its custody.

Engrossed in its fierce pursuit of the infidel, the Academy had overlooked the fact that there are literally hundreds of valid, free-born, no-Amendment Robert Riches scattered through practically every country in the Western world. The King Brothers said theirs was a goateed young photographer-writer from whom they had purchased the story in 1952 in Munich, and no one has yet disproved their claim. Overnight the New York *Post* turned up five Robert Riches. From San Francisco the nephew of a deceased Robert Rich announced he was arriving shortly to claim the trophy for his uncle. The large vacuum which now surrounded the Oscar was quickly filled with claims, counter-claims and disavowals on behalf of such disparate characters as the late Robert Flaherty, Orson Welles, Jesse Lasky, Jr., Willis O'Brien and Paul Rader.

The search even penetrated those cavernous depths wherein dwell the blacklisted and the anonymous. Among those flushed for questioning was this correspondent, who cannily refused to affirm or deny authorship. Suspicions then skittered like a starling from Albert Maltz to Michael Wilson, from Wilson to Carl Foreman, from Foreman to Paul Jarrico to others of the damned.

As the fourth day of turmoil dawned, the Academy took rueful stock of its coup. Someone with more perspicacity than president Seaton began to comprehend what had happened to the Immortals. First, they had flatly declared that Robert Rich wasn't the author of *The Brave One,* whereas there was a very good suing chance that Robert Rich was. Second, they had revealed themselves somewhat too nakedly as chief advocates and policemen of a blacklist that everybody else was fed up with. And third, they had cast a fatal shadow over the only other Oscar won this year by an American writer, the first having already been dishonored by the *ex post facto* annihilation of Michael Wilson. The Academy, retiring behind its own version of the Fifth Amendment, announced that "on advice of counsel we are going to keep out of this situation." Since then there has been nothing but blessed silence.

Meanwhile William Stout, a brilliant young news commentator for Los Angeles Station KNX-TV, casting bemused eyes at Mr. Seaton and his cohorts, began to have a funny feeling. He telephoned me suggesting lunch, and we discovered that we both had a funny feeling. There was a stillness over Hollywood that seemed to call for a little noise. We decided on the spot to make our feelings known to the world via a filmed interview about the blacklist and the black market it produces.

The next evening Mr. Stout put part of the interview on the Emmy-winning program called *The Big News.* The following day four more minutes went coast-to-coast on the Douglas Edwards CBS-TV news show originating in New York. Later that night Mr. Stout wrapped it up with a second interview over KNX-TV.

What I said during the interview was what everyone in Hollywood knew but no one had ever mentioned: that I had been working steadily since the blacklist began; that others of my kind had also been working; that the major studios were openly in the black market, purchasing plays and other material and releasing them without their authors' names; that the Academy had become official guardian of the blacklist; that it had launched against the producers of *The Brave One* an attack it would never have dared make against any major producer; that I myself had been nominated for Academy Awards and would not tell whether I had won any Oscars; that I intended to keep right on working, and that I assumed others would continue also.

Five years ago, two years ago, perhaps even six months ago, such an interview would have brought down upon my head maledictions from the committee, outraged denials from the producers and parading delegations from the American Legion.

But in this pleasant April of 1957 I heard not one yelp of anger nor a single denial. All over town publicity departments worked furiously and overtime at the job of saying nothing and making sure nobody else said anything either. For the first time in ten years I was the only man in Hollywood who could be heard. Feeling that my personal charm alone couldn't explain such amiable treatment, I glanced cautiously about for the real reason, and came across a legal action called *Wilson vs. Loew's, Inc.*

On three different occasions, members of the Hollywood Ten have won jury decisions in contract cases against the producers; but each victory has been reversed by higher courts who found little merit in the opinions of twelve good men and true. Thus when *Wilson vs. Loew's, Inc.* was filed, it seemed only another futile and expensive attempt to crack the impregnable structure of the blacklist, and was presumed doomed to fail like all the others.

The suit, filed by Michael Wilson, Ann Revere, Gale Sondergaard, Guy Endore and nineteen others, charged that the plaintiffs had been blacklisted and demanded $52,000,000 for the losses and damages inflicted upon them. Loew's, Inc., while not admitting the existence of a blacklist, argued from the assumption that if a blacklist does exist it is justified and therefore legal. The district court ruled that even if everything alleged were true, the defendants were not entitled to judgment, and hence there was no reason for a trial. The Circuit Court of Appeals sustained the lower court. And then, quite suddenly and without warning of any kind, the Supreme Court granted certiorari, indicating the suit involves more substantial questions of law than the lower courts suspected.

Wilson vs. Loew's, Inc. will be argued before the Supreme Court next autumn. If the court rules for the plaintiffs – and there is just as much reason to believe it will decide for them as against them – the ruling will declare, in effect, that if the facts charged are true the plaintiffs are entitled to judgment. Then the lower courts will be compelled to accept for trial an issue which juries thus far have invariably decided in favor of plaintiffs. Pondering the possibilities, I am inclined to believe that *Wilson vs. Loew's* accounts for a great deal of the silence that has settled over Hollywood. It might even be the reason why the Motion Picture Association of America, ordinarily so greedy for space, denied to readers of *The Nation* answers to the questions propounded by their correspondent (following pages.)

There is, of course, another reason, which lies in the fading power and the growing disrepute of the committee itself. Only a few weeks ago the Board of Governors of the eminently conservative State Bar of California charged that "the proceedings of the committee and the conduct of the committee's counsel . . . were improper and lacking in dignity and impartiality which should govern the conduct of agencies of the United States . . . and they were of such a character as to pose a threat to the right to appear by counsel and to the proper independence of the Bar."

Rumblings now are heard from another quarter. *The Hollywood Reporter,* a trade paper which has been the committee's staunchest friend, carried on March 14 an item by its leading reporter, Mike Connelly, to the effect that "The House Un-American Activities Committee plans holding executive sessions to probe a report that one of its members received money to clear a show-business personality of suspicions of being a Red."

Thus far no member of the committee has denied the report. The committee's own standards of evidence would seem to require that each of its members take the oath and swear that he isn't receiving bribes—or to tell how much and from whom. It seems inconceivable that future witnesses won't demand such testimony in return for their own.

In the meanwhile there is stillness at Appomattox, broken only by an occasional crack in the blacklist. The committee has no clothes, no honor, small power and practically no remaining candidates for oblivion. Far from being able to sell indulgences, it can scarcely give them away in the present declining market. The black market flourishes and the producers know it and dare not deny it and pray each night for a court decision, please God just one decision, that will give them an excuse to shake young Mr. Wheeler off their backs and regain control of the organizations they head. The "Eastern people," cocking a thoughtful eye at the Supreme Court and *Wilson vs. Loew's, Inc.,* begin to recall the glories of free enterprise, and to wonder whether those plaintiffs would really want $52,000,000 if they were given a chance to return openly to their professions.

Only George Seaton and twenty-two Immortals still like the blacklist; but even they, with the shadow of *Wilson vs. Academy Board of Governors* darkening their little patch of sky, may find it in their hearts to decide that ten years is punishment enough for any crime—especially when you can't be sure the criminal isn't anonymously undercutting you in the financial department.

There may come a time in this country when blacklists turn popular, and inquisitors are invited to dinner, and mothers at bedtime read to their children the story of the good informer. But just now the current runs in an opposite direction.

All things, as the man said, change.

THE CRASH OF SILENCE

Along with his manuscript, Mr. Trumbo sent us the following brief diary which records his attempts to get the Motion Picture Association of America to answer some pointed questions. —EDITORS

Hollywood
Thursday, April 18. Telephone C. H. (Duke) Wales, popular and capable press relations man for Motion Picture Association of America. Explain mission re *Nation*, et al., read him following list of questions:

1. *Would the MPAA deny that major studios are purchasing material from Fifth Amendment writers and removing their names from the screen?*
2. *Would the MPAA say there is no blacklist in Hollywood except that which applies to the Hollywood Ten?*
3. *Would the MPAA have any objections if a major studio openly hired a Fifth Amendment writer or a member of the Hollywood Ten?*
4. *Does the MPAA deal with the Committee on Un-American Activities, or any representative of that committee, in determining the employability of artists or other persons in the motion picture industry?*
5. *If there is a blacklist in the industry, to what persons or organizations does the MPAA attribute it?*

Wales copies list, reads it back. Hell of a copyist. Everything checks out. I suggest he may want a little time. Wales agrees. Will be in office from 2:30 p.m. on, call him then. Call at 2:40 p.m. Wales not back yet. Call 4:00 p.m. Wales gone for day. Troubled by this, but still have faith in Wales.

Friday, April 19. Call Wales 9:34 a.m. Not in yet. Send fast straight wire reminding him of situation and giving phone number. Call Wales 1:50 p.m. Not back from lunch. Three p.m., no call from Wales. Send following straight fast wire 3:02 p.m.

C. H. WALES
MPAA
8480 BEVERLY BOULEVARD
HOLLYWOOD, CALIFORNIA

HAVE ACCURATE RECORD OF OUR TELEPHONE CONVERSATION AND OF MY SUBSEQUENT CALLS. I DON'T BLAME YOU FOR DUCKING, BUT UNLESS I HEAR FROM YOU BEFORE MY DEADLINE SIX P.M. TONIGHT I SHALL NOTE THE EXTENT OF MY EFFORTS AND THEIR FAILURE AND ASSUME MPAA HAS TAKEN THE FIFTH. ALTHOUGH I HAVEN'T HAD THE PLEASURE OF INVOKING THE FIFTH, IT'S A GRAND OLD AMENDMENT AND I SHOULDN'T WISH TO DEPRIVE ERIC JOHNSTON OF ITS PROTECTION. CORDIALLY,

DALTON TRUMBO

Call Wales 5:14 p.m. Young man says Wales not available. Chill touches my heart: first time word "unavailable" has been used. Tell young man I'll stay by phone till 7 p.m. Wales doesn't get through. Sorry about Wales, but console self with Eric Johnston 1947 statement, "As long as I live I will never be a party to anything as un-American as a blacklist." Feel certain Eric's heart still in right place. Satisfied Wales will call tomorrow.

Saturday, April 20. No call from Wales. Hope he isn't ill. Mission uncompleted.

—D.T.

KENNETH REXROTH

Jazz Poetry

> *The Nation* often heralded what was new in the politics of cul-
> ture. Poet Kenneth Rexroth was one of the earliest supporters
> of the Beat movement.

A little short of two years ago, jazz poetry was a possibility, a hope and the memory of a few experiments. Today it runs the danger of becoming a fad. The life
of fads is most often intense, empty and short. I feel, on the contrary, jazz poetry
has permanent value or I would not have undertaken it.

When it is successful there is nothing freakish or faddish about it nor, as a matter of fact, is there anything specially new. At the roots of jazz and Negro folk
song, especially in the Southwest, is the "talking blues." It is not much heard
today, but if you flatten out the melodic line, already very simple, in Big Bill
Broonzy or Leadbelly, you have an approximation of it, and some of their records
are really more talked than sung. This is poetry recited to a simple blue guitar
accompaniment. Long before this, in the mid-nineteenth century, the French poet
Charles Cros was reciting, not singing, his poems to the music of a *bal musette*
band. Some of his things are still in the repertory of living *café chantant* performers, especially the extremely funny *Le Hareng Saur.* Even today some Rock 'n
Roll "novelties" are recited, not sung, and they are some of the most engaging,
with music that often verges into the more complex world of true jazz. It has become a common custom in store front churches and Negro revival meetings for
a member of the congregation to recite a poem to an instrumental or wordless vocal accompaniment. I believe Langston Hughes recited poems to jazz many years
ago. I tried it myself in the twenties in Chicago. In the late forties Kenneth
Patchen recited poems to records. Jack Spicer, a San Francisco poet tried it with
a trio led by Ron Crotty on bass. The result, more like the Russian tone color music of the first years of the century, was impressive, if not precisely jazz.
Lawrence Lipton has been working with some of the the the best musicians in Los
Angeles for almost two years. William Walton's "Façade," Stravinsky's "Persephone," compositions of Auric, Honneger, Milhaud, are well-known examples
of speaking, rather than singing, to orchestra in contemporary classical music.
Charles Mingus and Fred Katz, two of the most serious musicians in jazz—to narrow that invidious distinction between jazz and serious music—have been ex-
perimenting with the medium for some time. The music has been impressive, but
in my opinion, speaking as a professional poet, the texts could be improved.

What is jazz poetry? It isn't anything very complicated to understand. It is the reciting of suitable poetry with the music of a jazz band, usually small and comparatively quiet. Most emphatically, it is not recitation with "background" music. The voice is integrally wedded to the music and, although it does not sing notes, is treated as another instrument, with its own solos and ensemble passages, and with solo and ensemble work by the band alone. It comes and goes, following the logic of the presentation, just like a saxophone or piano. Poetry with background music is very far from jazz. It is not uncommon, and it is, in my opinion, usually pretty corny.

Why is jazz poetry? Jazz vocalists, especially white vocalists and especially in the idiom of the most advanced jazz, are not very common. Most Negro singers stay pretty close the blues, and there is more to modern jazz than blues. Frank Sinatra, Ella Fitzgerald, there are not many singers whom all schools of jazz find congenial. Curiously enough, the poet reciting, if he knows what he is doing, seems to "swing" to the satisfaction of many musicians in a way that too few singers do. I think it is wrong to put down all popular ballad lyrics as trivial; some of them are considerable poetry in their own right, but certainly most are intellectually far beneath the musical world of modern jazz, and far less honest. The best jazz is above all characterized by its absolute emotional honesty. This leaves us with the words of the best blues and Negro folk song, often very great poetry indeed, but still a limited aspect of experience, and by no means everything, translated into words, that modern jazz has to say. In other words, poetry gives jazz a richer verbal content, reinforces and expands its musical meaning and, at the same time, provides material of the greatest flexibility.

How is it done, in actual practice? Kenneth Patchen has been working with Allyn Ferguson and the Chamber Jazz Sextet. The music is composed; it is actually written out, with, of course, room for solo improvisation, but with the voice carefully scored in. There is nothing wrong with this. Far more of the greatest jazz is written music than the lay public realizes. Some of even the famous King Oliver and Louis Armstrong records of long ago were scored by Lil Hardin, a very sophisticated musician. Duke Ellington and his arranger, Billy Strayhorn, are among America's greatest composers. For the past year I have been working with my own band, led by Dick Mills, trumpet, and including Brew Moore, tenor, Frank Esposito, trombone, Ron Crotty, bass, Clair Willey, piano, and Gus Gustafson, drums. Recently in Los Angeles, I played a two-week engagement with a fine band led by Shorty Rogers. In each case we worked from carefully rehearsed "head arrangements." The musicians had each in front of them the text of the poetry, and the sheets were used as cue sheets, scribbled with "inners and outers," chord progressions, melodic lines and various cues.

I feel that this method insures the maximum amount of flexibility and spontaneity and yet provides a steadily deepening and thickening (in the musical sense) basis, differing emotionally more than actually from a written score. The whole thing is elaborately rehearsed—more than usual for even the most complicated "band number." I would like to mention that jazz, contrary to lay opinion, is not just spontaneously "blown" out of the musician's heads. Behind even the freest improvisation lies a fund of accepted patterns, chord changes, riffs, melodic figures, variations of tempo and dynamics, all understood by the musicians. In fact, they are there, given, as a fund of material almost instinctively come by. Even in a jam session, when a soloist gets as far out as possible, everybody has a pretty clear idea of how he is going to get back and of how everybody is going to go off together again. Then the major forms of common jazz are almost as strict as the sonata—the thirty-two bar ballad, the twelve bar blues—bridges, choruses, fillers, all usually in multiples of the basic four bar unit, in four-four time. Needless to say, the poetry is not "improvised" either. This has been tried, but with disastrously ridiculous results, and not by me. On the other hand, several poets have read over their things once with sensitive musicians and then put on a thoroughly satisfactory show. I have done this with Marty Paitch on piano or Ralph Pena on bass—both musicians with an extraordinary feeling for the rhythms and meanings of poetry. It all depends on the musician.

I hope the faddist elements of this new medium will die away. The ignorant and the pretentious, the sockless hipsters out for a fast buck or a few drinks from a Village bistro, will soon exhaust their welcome with the public, and the field will be left clear for serious musicians and poets who mean business. I think that it is a development of considerable potential significance for both jazz and poetry. It reaches an audience many times as large as that commonly reached by poetry, and an audience free of some of the serious vices of the typical poetry lover. It returns poetry to music and to public entertainment as it was in the days of Homer or the troubadours. It forces poetry to deal with aspects of life which it has tended to avoid in the recent past. It demands of poetry something of a public surface —meanings which can be grasped by ordinary people—just as the plays of Shakespeare had something for both the pit and the intellectuals in Elizabethan times, and still have today. And, as I have said, it gives jazz a flexible verbal content, an adjunct which matches the seriousness and artistic integrity of the music.

Certainly audiences seem to agree. Wherever it has been performed properly, the college auditoriums, the night clubs, the concert halls have been packed, and everybody—musicians, poets and audiences—has been enthusiastic.

In the past two years it has spread from The Cellar, a small bar in San Francisco, to college campuses, to night clubs in Los Angeles, St. Louis, New York, Dallas and, I believe, Chicago; to the Jazz Concert Hall in Los Angeles, where Lawrence Lipton put on a program with Shorty Rogers, Fred Katz, two bands, myself, Stuart Perkoff and Lipton himself, heard by about six thousand people in two weeks. Kenneth Patchen and Allyn Ferguson followed us, and played there for the better part of two months. Dick Mills and his band have performed with me at several colleges and at the San Francisco Art Festival, and we are now planning to take the whole show on the road.

If we can keep the standards up, and keep it away from those who don't know what they are doing, who have no conception of the rather severe demands the form makes on the integrity and competence of both musicians and poets, I feel that we shall have given, for a long time to come, new meanings to both jazz and poetry.

RALPH NADER

The Safe Car You Can't Buy   *April 11, 1959*

> In 1959, editor Carey McWilliams published consumer advocate Ralph Nader's first article, an exposé of poor automobile safety standards and the resulting hazards to drivers. The article, which led to Nader's 1965 book *Unsafe At Any Speed*, helped spark the consumer movement for health and safety reforms.

The Cornell Aeronautical Laboratory has developed an exhibition automobile embodying over sixty new safety concepts which would enable an occupant to withstand a head-on collision at 50 mph with at most only minor scratches. In its design, six basic principles of crash protection were followed:

1. The car body was strengthened to prevent most external blows from distorting it against the passengers.

2. Doors were secured so that crash impacts could not open them, thereby saving passengers from ejection and maintaining the structural strength of the side of the car body.

3. Occupants were secured to prevent them from striking objects inside the car.

4. Interior knobs, projections, sharp edges and hard surfaces have been removed and the ceiling shaped to produce only glancing blows to the head (the most vulnerable part of the body during a crash).

5. The driver's environment was improved to reduce accident risk by increasing visibility, simplifying controls and instruments, and lowering the carbon monoxide of his breathing atmosphere.

6. For pedestrian safety, dangerous objects like hood ornaments were removed from the exterior.

This experimental car, developed with funds representing only a tiny fraction of the annual advertising budget of, say, Buick, is packed with applications of simple yet effective safety factors. In the wrap-around bumper system, for instance, plastic foam material between the front and rear bumpers and the back-up plates absorbs some of the shock energy; the bumpers are smoothly shaped to convert an increased proportion of blows from direct to glancing ones; the side bumpers are firmly attached to the frame, which has been extended and reinforced to provide support. Another feature is the installment of two roll-over bars into the top of the car body as added support.

It is clear that Detroit today is designing automobiles for style, cost, performance and calculated obsolescence, but not—despite the 5,000,000 reported accidents, nearly 40,000 fatalities, 110,000 permanent disabilities and 1,500,000 injuries yearly—for safety.

Almost no feature of the interior design of our current cars provides safeguards against injury in the event of collision. Doors that fly open on impact, inadequately secured seats, the sharp-edged rear-view mirror, pointed knobs on instrument panel and doors, flying glass, the overhead structure—all illustrate the lethal potential of poor design. A sudden deceleration turns a collapsed steering wheel or a sharp-edged dashboard into a bone- and chest-crushing agent. Penetration of the shatterproof windshield can chisel one's head into fractions. A flying seat cushion can cause a fatal injury. The apparently harmless glove-compartment door has been known to unlatch under impact and guillotine a child. Roof-supporting structure has deteriorated to a point where it provides scarcely more protection to the occupants, in common roll-over accidents, than an open convertible. This is especially true of the so-called "hardtops." Nor is the automobile designed as an efficient force moderator. For example, the bumper does not contribute significantly to reduction of the crash deceleration forces that are transmitted to the motorist; its function has been more to reflect style than absorb shock.

These weaknesses of modern automobile construction have been established by the investigation of several groups, including the Automotive Crash Injury Research of the Cornell University Medical College, the Institute of Transportation and Traffic Engineering of the University of California and the Motor Vehicle Research of Lee, New Hampshire. Careful coverage of all available reports do not reveal a single dissent from these findings:

1. There are direct causal relationships between automotive design and the frequency, type and severity of injuries.

2. Studies of body tolerances to abrupt deceleration show that the forces in most

accidents now fatal are well within the physiological limits of survival under proper conditions.

3. Engineering improvement in safety design and restraining devices would materially reduce the injury and fatality rate (estimates range from twenty to thirty thousand lives saved annually).

4. Redesign of injury-causing automotive components is well within the capabilities of present engineering technique and would require no radical changes in present styling.

5. Many design improvements have already been developed but are not in production.

The remarkable advances in crash-protection knowledge achieved by these research organizations at a cost of some $6 million stands in marked contrast to the glacier-like movements of car manufacturers, who spend that much to enrich the sound of a door slam. This is not due to any dearth of skill — the industry possesses many able, frustrated safety engineers whose suggestions over the years invariably have taken a back seat to those of the stylist. In 1938, an expert had this to say in *Safety Engineering*:

> The motor industry must face the fact that accidents occur. It is their duty, therefore, to so design the interiors of automobiles that when the passenger is tossed around, he will get an even break and not suffer a preventable injury in accidents that today are taking a heavy toll.

In 1954, nearly 600,000 fatalities later, a U.C.L.A. engineer could conclude that "There has been no significant automotive-engineering contribution to the safety of motorists since about the beginning of World War II. . . . " In its 1955 annual report, the Cornell crash-research group came to a similar conclusion, adding that "the newer model automobiles [1950–54] are increasing the rate of fatalities in injury-producing accidents."

In 1956, Ford introduced the double-grip safety-door latch, the "dished" steering wheel, and instrument panel-padding; the rest of the industry followed with something less than enthusiasm. Even in these changes, style remained the dominant consideration, and their effectiveness is in doubt. Tests have failed to establish, for example, an advantage for the "deep-dish" steering wheel compared with the conventional wheel; the motorist will still collapse the rim to the hub.

This year, these small concessions to safety design have virtually been discontinued. "A square foot of chrome sells ten times more cars than the best safety-door latch," declared one industry representative. Dashboard padding remains one of a few safety accessories available as optional equipment. This is like saying to the consumer: "Here's a hot car. Now, if you wish to be safe in it, you'll have to pay more."

None of this should be construed as placing the increasingly popular mites from abroad in a more favorable light. Most foreign cars offer far less protection to the motorist than domestic ones.

Prevailing analyses of vehicular accidents circulated for popular consumption tend to impede constructive thinking by adherence to some monistic theory of causation. Take one of the more publicized ogres—speed. Cornell's findings, based on data covering 3,203 cars in injury-producing accidents, indicate that 74 per cent of the cars were going at a *traveling* speed under 60 mph and about 88 per cent involved *impact* speeds under 60 mph. The average impact speed on urban roads was 27 mph; on rural roads, 41 mph. Dangerous or fatal injuries observed in accidents when the traveling speed was less than 60 mph are influenced far more by the shape and structure of interior car components with which the body came into contact than by the speed at which the cars were moving. Many fatalities have been recorded which occurred in panic stops or collisions at a speed under 25 mph. Cornell's concluding statement:

> Statistical tests indicated that even if a top speed limit of 60 mph could be uniformly and absolutely maintained, 73 per cent of the dangerous and fatal injuries observed would still be expected to occur. . . . the control of speed alone would have only limited effect on the frequency of dangerous and fatal injuries.

In brief, automobiles are so designed as to be dangerous at any speed.

Our preoccupation has been almost entirely with the cause of accidents seen primarily in terms of the driver and not with the instruments that produce the injuries. Erratic driving will always be characteristic, to some degree, of the traffic scene; exhortation and stricter law enforcement have at best a limited effect. Much more significant for saving life is the application of engineering remedies to minimize the lethal effects of human error by designing the automobile so as to afford maximum protection to occupants in the event of a collision. In a word, the job, in part, is to make accidents safe.

The task of publicizing the relation between automotive design and highway casualties is fraught with difficulties. The press, radio and television are not likely to undertake this task in terms of industry responsibility when millions in advertising dollars are being poured into their coffers. Private researchers are reluctant to stray from their scholarly and experimental pursuits, especially when cordial relations with the industry are necessary for the continuation of their projects with the maximum of success. Car manufacturers have thought it best to cooperate with some of these programs and, in one case, when findings became embarrassing, have given financial support. The industry's policy is bearing fruit; most investigators discreetly keep their private disgust with the industry's immobility from seeping into the public limelight. They consider themselves fact-finders and leave the value judgments to others. This adherence to the rigid division of labor provides a convenient rationalization for the widespread amorality among our scholarly elite, who appear insensitive to the increased responsibility as citizens which their superior knowledge should require them to shoulder.

For the past three years, a Special Congressional House Subcommittee on Traffic Safety has been conducting extensive hearings on automobile design. The industry and research organizations have all submitted their testimony and reports. Some revealing facts came out of these hearings, but the press, by and large, has chosen to ignore them. In any case, the subcommittee is proceeding too cautiously for so urgent a matter. It has been too solicitous of recommendations for delay advanced by some academicians who see automotive design from the viewpoint of engineering perfection rather than as a national health emergency requiring immediate, even if not perfect, engineering remedy. Better techniques will be developed, but at least for the present, there will be added protection from remedying known design hazards. This has been the point that many safety engineers and physicians have vainly been urging.

Even if all the facts, laid before the public, did not increase consumer demand for safety design (which is unlikely), the manufacturers should not be relieved of their responsibility. Innumerable precedents show that the consumer must be protected at times from his own indiscretion and vanity. Dangerous drugs cannot be dispensed without a licensed physician's prescription; meat must pass federal inspection before distribution; railroads and other interstate carriers are required to meet safety standards regarding their equipment.

State motor-vehicle codes set minimum standards for certain vehicular equipment. This legislation has not compelled manufacturers to adopt known safety-design features (with the exception of safety glass), but has merely endorsed previous standards long employed by the car producers. Examples: brake requirements, headlight specifications, horns, mufflers, windshield wipers, rearview mirrors. Thus the impact of these requirements falls primarily on the operator, who has to keep this equipment functioning. The legislative purpose is directed to accident *prevention* and only peripherally to implementing standards that might *prevent injuries*.

But state laws do not begin to cope with design defects of the postwar car which increase the *risk of collision*. Examples: the terrific visual distortion of the wraparound windshield; leakage of carbon monoxide; rear-end fishtailing in hard turns; undue brake fade and the decreased braking area of the recent fourteen-inch wheel; the tinted windshield condemned as violative of all basic optical principles to the extent that visual loss at night ranges from 15 per cent to 45 per cent; and the fire hazard of the undercoating and some upholstery.

Motor vehicles have been found to be poorly designed with regard to human capacities and limitations both physical and psychological. For example, there are—especially in truck cabs—unnecessary difficulties in reaching and operating control levers, in reading half-hidden dials and gauges; there are seats that induce poor posture or discomfort, mirrors whose poor placement and size impair vision, visors inadequately shielding eyes from bright light, and uncomfortable temperature, humidity and noise levels. The cumulative effects lead to fatigue, deterioration of driving efficiency and reaction time, and frequently to an accident which cannot be attributed, in the light of such poor design, to the driver.

Recourse to the courts for judgment against a manufacturer by a plaintiff injured by the defective interior design of his car while involved in an accident stands a dim chance of success. While the courts have hung liability on manufacturers for injuries due to defectively designed products, the closest they have come in motor-vehicle cases has been to hold the producer liable for a design defect instrumental in causing the accident, e.g., the braking system. The question of automotive death-traps cannot be dealt with adequately by the limited authority and resources of the judiciary, although a few pertinent decisions would have a salutary effect.

By all relevant criteria, a problem so national in scope and technical in nature can best be handled by the legislative process, on the federal level, with delegation to an appropriate administrative body. It requires uniformity in treatment and central administration, for as an interstate matter, the job cannot be left to the states with their dissimilar laws setting low requirements that are not strictly enforced and that do not strike at the heart of the malady—the blueprint on the Detroit drawing board. The thirty-three-year record of the attempt to introduce state uniformity in establishing the most basic equipment standards for automobiles has been disappointing.

Perhaps the best summation of the whole issue lies in a physician's comment on the car manufacturer's design policy: "Translated into medicine," he writes, "it would be comparable to withholding known methods of life-saving value."

It's Only Nikita, After All   *September 12, 1959*
[*editorial*]

During the Middle Ages, cities, sometimes whole countries, were thrown into consternation by visitations of the Prince of the Powers of the Air—the Devil himself. It was noticeable that the Foul Fiend sought out the most devout members of the community for the purpose of tormenting and terrorizing them; the easygoing were relatively immune. Something of the sort seems to be happening in the United States as the modern incarnation of Satan, a short, stout Russian named Nikita Khrushchev, prepares to board his U.S.-bound jet plane. The experienced immunologists of Freedom House are busy advising us on ways and means of avoiding the psychic contagion which the Evil One is bringing to our shores. In the House of Representatives, the distinguished member from Wisconsin, Mr. Zablocki, urges that Americans of all major religious faiths—Protestant, Catholic, Jewish and Eastern Orthodox—observe a nation-wide minute of silence at 11 A.M. on the fateful day of arrival. Workers, businessmen and farmers are asked to cease their labors for the crucial minute "where this will not entail a great inconvenience"—but what inconvenience could be too great in a matter of such importance? All automobile, bus and truck traffic would halt on every road and street in America. Church bells and air raid sirens would sound at the beginning of the minute of silence and again at its expiration. The minute of silence would sweep across the nation in eight great waves, beginning on the East Coast and Puerto Rico, and continuing across the continent and on out to Hawaii and the Bering Strait.

Other members of Congress have joined in a call to the American people for a day of national mourning during the ineffable Khrushchev's visit. No doubt these demonstrations, if they occur, will assuage the anxiety of those who engage in them. But is it not strange that the Russians were unconcerned about the visit of Vice President Nixon and the witchcraft he might work on them and their institutions? Even stranger, many Americans look on Khrushchev in the same way. Of course, if emotionalism is to be equated with patriotism, these Americans are not patriotic. They may have learned, however, that the great crises of life are best surmounted by a matter-of-fact attitude, rather than histrionics. When the Geneva Conference approached stalemate, the President, advised by Secretary of State Herter, decided to invite Mr. Khrushchev for an informal visit in preference to a renewed Berlin crisis or to a summit conference without the preparatory progress the President had stipulated. The visit of a foreign statesman does not imply endorsement of his ideas or his policies. All it implies is that it is in the national interest to talk with him.

Are We Training Cuban Guerrillas?

[*editorial*]

November 19, 1960

> *The Nation* was the only publication in America to warn of CIA
> plans for the ill-fated Bay of Pigs invasion. Afterward, Presi-
> dent Kennedy complained that the rest of the press, including
> the *New York Times*, had withheld advance information that
> would have raised questions about the plans, saying, "Maybe if
> [it] had printed more about the operation [it] would have saved
> us from a colossal mistake."

Fidel Castro may have a sounder basis for his expressed fears of a U.S.-financed
"Guatemala-type" invasion than most of us realize. On a recent visit to Guatemala, Dr. Ronald Hilton, Director of the Institute of Hispanic-American Studies
at Stanford University, was told:

1. The United States Central Intelligence Agency has acquired a large tract of land,
at an outlay in excess of $1,000,000, which is stoutly fenced and heavily guarded. Dr.
Hilton was informed that it is "common knowledge" in Guatemala that the tract is being
used as a training ground for Cuban counter-revolutionaries who are preparing for an
eventual landing in Cuba. It was also said that U.S. personnel and equipment are being
used at the base. The camp is said to be located in Retahuleu, between Guatemala City
and the coast.

2. Substantially all of the above was reported by a well-known Guatemalan journalist,
Clemente Marroquin Rojas, in *La Hora,* a Guatemalan newspaper of which he is the
director. His article appeared in violation, it is said, of a Government prohibition against
any public discussion of the matter.

3. More recently, the President of Guatemala, forced to take cognizance of the persistent reports concerning the base, went on TV and admitted its existence, but refused
to discuss its purpose or any other facts about it.

The American press — even media with accredited correspondents on the
scene — has apparently remained unaware of the public commotion the subject has
aroused in Guatemala. Not even President Ydigoras' TV statement that a secret
base exists has been reported in the United States, so far as we know. We ourselves, of course, pretend to no first-hand knowledge of the facts; nevertheless,
we feel an obligation to bring the subject to public attention. If Washington is ignorant of the existence of the base, or, knowing that it exists, is nevertheless innocent of any involvement in it, then surely the appropriate authorities will want
to scotch all invidious rumors and issue a full statement of the real facts. On the
other hand, if the reports as heard by Dr. Hilton are true, then public pressure
should be brought to bear upon the Administration to abandon this dangerous and
hair-brained project.

There is a second reason why we believe the reports merit publication: they can, and should, be checked immediately by all U.S. news media with correspondents in Guatemala.

Meanwhile, Dr. Hilton informs us that he will publish additional details of his findings in Guatemala in the November issue of the *Hispanic-American Review,* publ..hed by the Institute of which he is the director. The sooner the truth emerges, the better for all concerned—the United States, which now stands accused; the Cubans, who assert fear of an imminent invasion, and the Guatemalans, who appear to be thrust into a perilous quarrel not of their making.

RICHARD CONDON

'Manchurian Candidate' in Dallas December 28, 1963

Richard Condon is the author of *The Manchurian Candidate* and many other books. He wrote this piece a few days after President Kennedy was assassinated.

Paris

I was reading about how Senator Thruston Morton of Kentucky absolved the American people from any guilt in the assassination of the President when a reporter from a South African press association telephoned from London to ask if I felt responsible for the President's killing, inasmuch as I had written a novel, *The Manchurian Candidate,* on which had been based a film that had just been "frozen" in the United States because it was felt that the assassin might have seen it and been influenced by it. I told the reporter that, with all Americans, I had contributed to form the attitudes of the assassin; and that the assassin, and Americans like him, had contributed to the attitudes which had caused me to write the novel.

The differences between Senator Morton's views on this and my own are vast. The man who shot John Kennedy, Senator Morton said, "was a stranger to the American heritage" and "his mind had been warped by an alien violence, not by a native condition."

Brainwashing to violence and assassination is the line taken in my novel. On its melodramatic surface, the book is a study of the consequences of "a mind warped by alien violence," but I had also hoped to suggest that for some time all of us in the United States had been brainwashed to violence, and to indicate that the reader might consider that the tempo of this all-American brainwashing was being speeded up.

I meant to call attention, through example, to the proved brainwashing to violence shown by the increased sale of cigarettes after they had been conclusively demonstrated to be suicide weapons. I meant to show that when the attention of a nation is focused upon violence—when it appears on the front page of all newspapers, throughout television programming, in the hundreds of millions of monthly comic books, in most motion pictures, in the rhythms of popular music and the dance, and in popular $5 novels which soon become 50¢ paperbacks, when a most violent example is set by city, state and federal governments, when organized crime merges with organized commerce and labor, when a feeble, bewildered set of churches cannot counteract any of this and all of it is power-hosed at all of us through the most gigantically complex overcommunications system ever developed—we must not be surprised that one of us bombs little girls in a Sunday school or shoots down a President of our republic. We can feign surprise, as we did with the murder of President Kennedy, but none of us seemed either surprised or moved by the murder of Medgar Evers, who was also a brave leader of his people, also a man who had a young wife and children, and whose assassin most certainly matched the basic, American psychological pattern of the killer of our President.

I was not surprised at the similarities between the two American products, Lee Oswald and Raymond Shaw, one all too actual, the other the fictional leading character of *The Manchurian Candidate*. Oswald's wife has said she married him because she felt sorry for him: absolutely no one had liked him, "even in Russia." The novel says, "It was not that Raymond was hard to like. He was impossible to like." Oswald spoke frequently of the hardships his mother had experienced in the depression, before he had been born, and his mother had been quick to say that "they" had always been against her boy. In the novel, I quoted Andrew Salter, the Pavlovian psychologist, ". . . the human fish swim about at the bottom of the great ocean of atmosphere and they develop psychic injuries as they collide with one another. Most mortal of these are the wounds gotten from the parent fish." The Associated Press dug up a truancy report on Oswald which said his resentment had been fixed on "authority." On the surface he was calm, but inside there was much anger. "The resenters," says the Chinese brainwasher in *The Manchurian Candidate*, "those men with cancer of the psyche, make the great assassins." Raymond Shaw's account of his past was confusingly dramatic, as was Oswald's. It all seemed to revolve around his mother, as did Oswald's.

The brainwasher who was describing Raymond Shaw to an audience in an amphitheatre might have been describing the murderers of John Kennedy and Medgar Evers. "It has been said that only the man who is capable of loving everything is capable of understanding everything. The resentful man is a human with a capacity for affection so poorly developed that his understanding for the motives of others very nearly does not exist. They are men of melancholic and reserved psychology. They are afflicted with total resentment."

Lee Oswald's indicated murder of Mr. Kennedy seems motivated only by his resentment against the most successful man in the world; resentment against a wonderfully intelligent, puissant, healthy, wealthy, witty and handsome man who was so rich in spirit that he made no effort to conceal his superiority, who dominated the world and outer space, and who had an inexpressibly fine wife and two lovely children. From the view of this resentment, as long as this fellow stayed out of Lee Oswald's path he would be all right, but when he came laughing into Dallas, and the newspapers printed a map that showed he would drive right past where Lee Oswald worked for a lousy fifty bucks a week, it was more than this classical resentment could bear.

It takes time to achieve such resentment and to fire it there must be careful nurturing by constant, unrelenting conditioning to violence. Oswald was not the only violence-packed American who was capable of murdering President Kennedy. The assassination was a wasteful, impersonal, senseless act, but the United States has undergone such a massive brainwashing to violence that such a senseless waste is *à la mode*.

Ralph Gleason wrote in the *San Francisco Chronicle* after the President's murder: ". . . we bred his murderer, our society produced him and he is, in one sense, a part of us all." Then Senator Morton said: ". . . let us not mourn the American soul . . . let the blame be on him who actually committed the crime . . . what happened was not America's fault."

John Hay Whitney, publisher of the New York *Herald Tribune* and thus a leading figure in the overcommunications industry, most hotly denied that the American people must share the guilt for President Kennedy's murder. He amplified his defense by saying: "It's true that there is hate in America, and violence, and brutality. There always has been. But violence has not been and is not now a dominant strain in our character."

To me, it seems certain that Mr. Gleason is right and Senator Morton and Mr. Whitney are mistaken. Neither saints nor assassins appear among us fully grown and wholly developed. All of us are nothing more than the result of our conditioning.

When the fanatic is a ruler, rather than the assassin of a ruler, the people who permitted him to take power must be blamed—whether they be the Germans of 1933–35 for Adolf Hitler, or the people of Chicago, Illinois, for their local government. But when the fanatic is the assassin, he emerges from the very fabric of the people. In answer to Senator Morton: if the American people are encouraging a mass educational system—the overcommunications industry—which instructs for the production of the highest crime rate and the most widely shared violence dependencies of any country in the world, is it not time to say, most particularly by our government, that each American is responsible for that state of affairs because he does nothing to change it? We are not, as some well-meaning European newspaper put it, a violent and unstable people because such "toughness" was required to tame the wild frontier 125 years ago. We are violent and unstable because we have been so conditioned to these responses that civilized, thoughtful conduct has become impossible for us.

It is a hell of a spot for a country to be in. Who, the least brainwashed among us, will cast the first redemptive thought?

HUNTER S. THOMPSON

The Motorcycle Gangs
Losers and Outsiders

May 17, 1965

In 1965 Hunter Thompson was living in San Francisco. He had recently quit the *National Observer* and was dead broke. When Carey McWilliams sent him a query, enclosing a report of the California Attorney General's office on motorcycle gangs and an offer of one hundred dollars for an article, Thompson accepted. He later expanded his *Nation* article into his best-selling book, *Hell's Angels*. Thompson, the founder of "gonzo" journalism, went on to write, among other books, *Fear and Loathing on the Campaign Trail '72* and *The Great Shark Hunt*.

San Francisco

Last Labor Day weekend newspapers all over California gave front-page reports of a heinous gang rape in the moonlit sand dunes near the town of Seaside on the Monterey Peninsula. Two girls, aged 14 and 15, were allegedly taken from their dates by a gang of filthy, frenzied, boozed-up motorcycle hoodlums called "Hell's Angels," and dragged off to be "repeatedly assaulted."

A deputy sheriff, summoned by one of the erstwhile dates, said he "arrived at the beach and saw a huge bonfire surrounded by cyclists of both sexes. Then the two sobbing, near-hysterical girls staggered out of the darkness, begging for help. One was completely nude and the other had on only a torn sweater."

Some 300 Hell's Angels were gathered in the Seaside-Monterey area at the time, having convened, they said, for the purpose of raising funds among themselves to send the body of a former member, killed in an accident, back to his mother in North Carolina. One of the Angels, hip enough to falsely identify himself as "Frenchy of San Bernardino," told a local reporter who came out to meet the cyclists: "We chose Monterey because we get treated good here; most other places we get thrown out of town."

But Frenchy spoke too soon. The Angels weren't on the peninsula twenty-four hours before four of them were in jail for rape, and the rest of the troop was being escorted to the county line by a large police contingent. Several were quoted, somewhat derisively, as saying: "That rape charge against our guys is phony and it won't stick."

It turned out to be true, but that was another story and certainly no headliner. The difference between the Hell's Angels in the papers and the Hell's Angels for real is enough to make a man wonder what newsprint is for. It also raises a question as to who are the real hell's angels.

Ever since World War II, California has been strangely plagued by wild men on motorcycles. They usually travel in groups of ten to thirty, booming along the highways and stopping here and there to get drunk and raise hell. In 1947, hundreds of them ran amok in the town of Hollister, an hour's fast drive south of San Francisco, and got enough press notices to inspire a film called *The Wild One,* starring Marlon Brando. The film had a massive effect on thousands of young California motorcycle buffs; in many ways, it was their version of *The Sun Also Rises.*

The California climate is perfect for motorcycles, as well as surfboards, swimming pools and convertibles. Most of the cyclists are harmless weekend types, members of the American Motorcycle Association, and no more dangerous than skiers or skin divers. But a few belong to what the others call "outlaw clubs," and these are the ones who — especially on weekends and holidays — are likely to turn up almost anywhere in the state, looking for action. Despite everything the psychiatrists and Freudian casuists have to say about them, they are tough, mean and potentially as dangerous as packs of wild boar. When push comes to shove, any leather fetishes or inadequacy feelings that may be involved are entirely beside the point, as anyone who has ever tangled with these boys will sadly testify. When you get in an argument with a group of outlaw motorcyclists, you can generally count your chances of emerging unmaimed by the number of heavy-handed allies you can muster in the time it takes to smash a beer bottle. In this league, sportsmanship is for old liberals and young fools. "I smashed his face," one of them said to me of a man he'd never seen until the swinging started. "He got wise. He called me a punk. He must have been stupid."

The most notorious of these outlaw groups is the Hell's Angels, supposedly headquartered in San Bernardino, just east of Los Angeles, and with branches all over the state. As a result of the infamous "Labor Day gang rape," the Attorney General of California has recently issued an official report on the Hell's Angels. According to the report, they are easily identified:

The emblem of the Hell's Angels, termed "colors," consists of an embroidered patch of a winged skull wearing a motorcycle helmet. Just below the wing of the emblem are the letters "MC." Over this is a band bearing the words "Hell's Angels." Below the emblem is another patch bearing the local chapter name, which is usually an abbreviation for the city or locality. These patches are sewn on the back of a usually sleeveless demin jacket. In addition, members have been observed wearing various types of Luftwaffe insignia and reproductions of German iron crosses.* Many affect beards and their hair is usually long and unkempt. Some wear a single earring in a pierced ear lobe. Frequently they have been observed to wear metal belts made of a length of polished motorcycle drive chain which can be unhooked and used as a flexible bludgeon. . . . Probably the most universal common denominator in identification of Hell's Angels is their generally filthy condition. Investigating officers consistently report these people, both club members and their female associates, seem badly in need of a bath. Fingerprints are a very effective means of identification because a high percentage of Hell's Angels have criminal records.

In addition to the patches on the back of Hell's Angels jackets, the "One Percenters" wear a patch reading "1%-er." Another badge worn by some members bears the number "13." It is reported to represent the 13th letter of the alphabet, "M," which in turn stands for marijuana and indicates the wearer thereof is a user of the drug.

The Attorney General's report was colorful, interesting, heavily biased and consistently alarming — just the sort of thing, in fact, to make a clanging good article for a national news magazine. Which it did; both barrels. *Newsweek* led with a left hook titled "The Wild Ones," *Time* crossed with a right, inevitably titled "The Wilder Ones." The Hell's Angels, cursing the implications of this new attack, retreated to the bar of the DePau Hotel near the San Francisco waterfront and planned a weekend beach party. I showed them the articles. Hell's Angels do not normally read the news magazines. "I'd go nuts if I read that stuff all the time," said one. "It's all bullshit."

Newsweek was relatively circumspect. It offered local color, flashy quotes and "evidence" carefully attributed to the official report but unaccountably said the report accused the Hell's Angels of homosexuality, whereas the report said just the opposite. *Time* leaped into the fray with a flurry of blood, booze and semen-flecked wordage that amounted, in the end, to a classic of supercharged hokum: "Drug-induced stupors . . . no act is too degrading . . . swap girls, drugs and motorcycles with equal abandon . . . stealing forays . . . then ride off again to seek some new nadir in sordid behavior. . . ."

Where does all this leave the Hell's Angels and the thousands of shuddering Californians (according to *Time*) who are worried sick about them? Are these out-

*Purely for decorative and shock effect. The Hell's Angels are apolitical and no more racist than other ignorant young thugs.

laws really going to be busted, routed and cooled, as the news magazines implied? Are California highways any safer as a result of this published uproar? Can honest merchants once again walk the streets in peace? The answer is that nothing has changed except that a few people calling themselves Hell's Angels have a new sense of identity and importance.

After two weeks of intensive dealing with the Hell's Angels phenomenon, both in print and in person, I'm convinced the net result of the general howl and publicity has been to obscure and avoid the real issues by invoking a savage conspiracy of bogymen and conning the public into thinking all will be "business as usual" once this fearsome snake is scotched, as it surely will be by hard and ready minions of the Establishment.

Meanwhile, according to Attorney General Thomas C. Lynch's own figures, California's true crime picture makes the Hell's Angels look like a gang of petty jack rollers. The police count 463 Hell's Angels: 205 around Los Angeles and 233 in the San Francisco-Oakland area. I don't know about L.A. but the real figures for the Bay Area are thirty or so in Oakland and exactly eleven—with one facing expulsion—in San Francisco. This disparity makes it hard to accept other police statistics. The dubious package also shows convictions on 1,023 misdemeanor counts and 151 felonies—primarily vehicle theft, burglary and assault. This is for all years and all alleged members.

California's overall figures for 1963 list 1,116 homicides, 12,448 aggravated assaults, 6,257 sex offenses, and 24,532 burglaries. In 1962, the state listed 4,121 traffic deaths, up from 3,839 in 1961. Drug arrest figures for 1964 showed a 101 percent increase in juvenile marijuana arrests over 1963, and a recent back-page story in the *San Francisco Examiner* said, "The venereal disease rate among [the city's] teen-agers from 15–19 has more than doubled in the past four years." Even allowing for the annual population jump, juvenile arrests in all categories are rising by 10 per cent or more each year.

Against this background, would it make any difference to the safety and peace of mind of the average Californian if every motorcycle outlaw in the state (all 901, according to the police) were garroted within twenty-four hours? This is not to say that a group like the Hell's Angels has no meaning. The generally bizarre flavor of their offenses and their insistence on identifying themselves make good copy, but usually overwhelm—in print, at least—the unnerving truth that they represent, in colorful microcosm, what is quietly and anonymously growing all around us every day of the week.

"We're bastards to the world and they're bastards to us," one of the Oakland Angels told a *Newsweek* reporter. "When you walk into a place where people can see you, you want to look as repulsive and repugnant as possible. We are complete social outcasts—outsiders against society."

A lot of this is a pose, but anyone who believes that's all it is has been on thin ice since the death of Jay Gatsby. The vast majority of motorcycle outlaws are uneducated, unskilled men between 20 and 30, and most have no credentials except a police record. So at the root of their sad stance is a lot more than a wistful yearning for acceptance in a world they never made; their real motivation is an instinctive certainty as to what the score really is. They are out of the ball game and they know it—and that is their meaning; for unlike most losers in today's society, the Hell's Angels not only know but spitefully proclaim exactly where they stand.

I went to one of their meetings recently, and half-way through the night I thought of Joe Hill on his way to face a Utah firing squad and saying his final words: "Don't mourn, organize." It is safe to say that no Hell's Angel has ever heard of Joe Hill or would know a Wobbly from a Bushmaster, but nevertheless they are somehow related. The I.W.W. had serious plans for running the world, while the Hell's Angels mean only to defy the world's machinery. But instead of losing quietly, one by one, they have banded together with a mindless kind of loyalty and moved outside the framework, for good or ill. There is nothing particularly romantic or admirable about it; that's just the way it is, strength in unity. They don't mind telling you that running fast and loud on their customized Harley 74s gives them a power and a purpose that nothing else seems to offer.

Beyond that, their position as self-proclaimed outlaws elicits a certain popular appeal, however reluctant. That is especially true in the West and even in California where the outlaw tradition is still honored. The unarticulated link between the Hell's Angels and the millions of losers and outsiders who don't wear any colors is the key to their notoriety and the ambivalent reactions they inspire. There are several other keys, having to do with politicians, policemen and journalists, but for this we have to go back to Monterey and the Labor Day "gang rape."

Politicians, like editors and cops, are very keen on outrage stories, and state Senator Fred S. Farr of Monterey County is no exception. He is a leading light of the Carmel-Pebble Beach set and no friend of hoodlums anywhere, especially gang rapists who invade his constituency. Senator Farr demanded an immediate investigation of the Hell's Angels and others of their ilk—Commancheros, Stray Satans, Iron Horsemen, Rattlers (a Negro club), and Booze Fighters—whose lack of status caused them all to be lumped together as "other disreputables." In the cut-off world of big bikes, long runs and classy rumbles, this new, state-sanctioned stratification made the Hell's Angels very big. They were, after all, Number One. Like John Dillinger.

Attorney General Lynch, then new in his job, moved quickly to mount an investigation of sorts. He sent questionnaires to more than 100 sheriffs, district attorneys and police chiefs, asking for information on the Hell's Angels and those "other disreputables." He also asked for suggestions as to how the law might deal with them.

Six months went by before all the replies were condensed into the fifteen-page report that made new outrage headlines when it was released to the press. (The Hell's Angels also got a copy; one of them stole mine.) As a historical document, it read like a plot synopsis of Mickey Spillane's worst dreams. But in the matter of solutions it was vague, reminiscent in some ways of Madame Nhu's proposals for dealing with the Vietcong. The state was going to centralize information on these thugs, urge more vigorous prosecution, put them all under surveillance whenever possible, etc.

A careful reader got the impression that even if the Hell's Angels had acted out this script—eighteen crimes were specified and dozens of others implied—very little would or could be done about it, and that indeed Mr. Lynch was well aware he'd been put, for political reasons, on a pretty weak scent. There was plenty of mad action, senseless destruction, orgies, brawls, perversions and a strange parade of "innocent victims" that, even on paper and in careful police language, was enough to tax the credulity of the dullest police reporter. Any bundle of information off police blotters is bound to reflect a special viewpoint, and parts of the Attorney General's report are actually humorous, if only for the language. Here is an excerpt:

> On November 4, 1961, a San Francisco resident driving through Rodeo, possibly under the influence of alcohol, struck a motorcycle belonging to a Hell's Angel parked outside a bar. A group of Angels pursued the vehicle, pulled the driver from the car and attempted to demolish the rather expensive vehicle. The bartender claimed he had seen nothing, but a cocktail waitress in the bar furnished identification to the officers concerning some of those responsible for the assault. The next day it was reported to officers that a member of the Hell's Angels gang had threatened the life of this waitress as well as another woman waitress. A male witness who definitely identified five participants in the assault including the president of the Vallejo Hell's Angels and the Vallejo "Road Rats" advised officers that because of his fear of retaliation by club members he would refuse to testify to the facts he had previously furnished.

That is a representative item in the section of the report titled "Hoodlum Activities." First, it occurred in a small town—Rodeo is on San Pablo Bay just north of Oakland — where the Angels had stopped at a bar without causing any trouble until some offense was committed against them. In this case, a driver whom even the police admit was "possibly" drunk hit one of their motorcycles. The same kind of accident happens every day all over the nation, but when it involves outlaw motorcyclists it is something else again. Instead of settling the thing with an exchange of insurance information or, at the very worst, an argument with a few blows, the Hell's Angels beat the driver and "attempted to demolish the vehicle." I asked one of them if the police exaggerated this aspect, and he said no, they had done the natural thing: smashed headlights, kicked in doors, broken windows and torn various components off the engine.

Of all their habits and predilections that society finds alarming, this departure from the time-honored concept of "an eye for an eye" is the one that most frightens people. The Hell's Angels try not to do anything halfway, and anyone who deals in extremes is bound to cause trouble, whether he means to or not. This, along with a belief in total retaliation for any offense or insult, is what makes the Hell's Angels unmanageable for the police and morbidly fascinating to the general public. Their claim that they "don't start trouble" is probably true more often than not, but their idea of "provocation" is dangerously broad, and their biggest problem is that nobody else seems to understand it. Even dealing with them personally, on the friendliest terms, you can sense their hair-trigger readiness to retaliate.

This is a public thing, and not at all true among themselves. In a meeting, their conversation is totally frank and open. They speak to and about one another with an honesty that more civilized people couldn't bear. At the meeting I attended (and before they realized I was a journalist) one Angel was being publicly evaluated; some members wanted him out of the club and others wanted to keep him in. It sounded like a group-therapy clinic in progress—not exactly what I expected to find when just before midnight I walked into the bar of the De Pau in one of the bleakest neighborhoods in San Francisco, near Hunters Point. By the time I parted company with them—at 6:30 the next morning after an all-night drinking bout in my apartment—I had been impressed by a lot of things, but no one thing about them was as consistently obvious as their group loyalty. This is an admirable quality, but it is also one of the things that gets them in trouble: a fellow Angel is *always right* when dealing with outsiders. And this sort of reasoning makes a group of "offended" Hell's Angels nearly impossible to deal with.

Here is another incident from the Attorney General's report:

> On September 19, 1964, a large group of Hell's Angels and "Satan's Slaves" converged on a bar in South Gate (Los Angeles County), parking their motorcycles and cars in the street in such a fashion as to block one-half of the roadway. They told officers that three members of the club had recently been asked to stay out of the bar and that they had come to tear it down. Upon their approach the bar owner locked the doors and turned off the lights and no entrance was made, but the group did demolish a cement block fence. On arrival of the police, members of the club were lying on the sidewalk and in the street. They were asked to leave the city, which they did reluctantly. As they left, several were heard to say that they would be back and tear down the bar.

Here again is the ethic of total retaliation. If you're "asked to stay out" of a bar, you don't just punch the owner—you come back with your army and destroy the whole edifice. Similar incidents—along with a number of vague rape complaints—make up the bulk of the report. Eighteen incidents in four years, and none except the rape charges are more serious than cases of assault on citizens who, for their own reasons, had become involved with the Hell's Angels prior to the violence. I could find no cases of unwarranted attacks on wholly innocent victims. There are a few borderline cases, wherein victims of physical attacks seemed innocent, according to police and press reports, but later refused to testify for fear of "retaliation." The report asserts very strongly that Hell's Angels are difficult to prosecute and convict because they make a habit of threatening and intimidating witnesses. That is probably true to a certain extent, but in many cases victims have refused to testify because they were engaged in some legally dubious activity at the time of the attack.

In two of the most widely publicized incidents the prosecution would have fared better if their witnesses and victims *had* been intimidated into silence. One of these was the Monterey "gang rape," and the other a "rape" in Clovis, near Fresno in the Central Valley. In the latter, a 36-year-old widow and mother of five children claimed she'd been yanked out of a bar where she was having a quiet beer with another woman, then carried to an abandoned shack behind the bar and raped repeatedly for two and a half hours by fifteen or twenty Hell's Angels and finally robbed of $150. That's how the story appeared in the San Francisco newspapers the next day, and it was kept alive for a few more days by the woman's claims that she was getting phone calls threatening her life if she testified against her assailants.

Then, four days after the crime, the victim was arrested on charges of "sexual perversion." The true story emerged, said the Clovis chief of police, when the woman was "confronted by witnesses. Our investigation shows she was not raped," said the chief. "She participated in lewd acts in the tavern with at least three Hell's Angels before the owners ordered them out. She encouraged their advances in the tavern, then led them to an abandoned house in the rear. . . . She was not robbed but, according to a woman who accompanied her, had left her house early in the evening with $5 to go bar-hopping." That incident did not appear in the Attorney General's report.

But it was impossible not to mention the Monterey "gang rape," because it was the reason for the whole subject to become official. Page one of the report—which *Time's* editors apparently skipped—says that the Monterey case was dropped because ". . . further investigation raised questions as to whether forcible rape had been committed or if the identifications made by victims were valid." Charges were dismissed on September 25, with the concurrence of a grand jury. The deputy District Attorney said "a doctor examined the girls and found no evidence" to support the charges. "Besides that, one girl refused to testify," he explained, "and the other was given a lie-detector test and found to be wholly unreliable."

This, in effect, was what the Hell's Angels had been saying all along. Here is their version of what happened, as told by several who were there:

252

One girl was white and pregnant, the other was colored, and they were with five colored studs. They hung around our bar—Nick's Place on Del Monte Avenue—for about three hours Saturday night, drinking and talking with our riders, then they came out to the beach with us—them and their five boy friends. Everybody was standing around the fire, drinking wine, and some of the guys were talking to them—hustling 'em, naturally—and soon somebody asked the two chicks if they wanted to be turned on—you know, did they want to smoke some pot? They said yeah, and then they walked off with some of the guys to the dunes. The spade went with a few guys and then she wanted to quit, but the pregnant one was really hot to trot; the first four or five guys she was really dragging into her arms, but after that she cooled off, too. By this time, though, one of their boy friends had got scared and gone for the cops—and that's all it was.

But not quite all. After that there were Senator Farr and Tom Lynch and a hundred cops and dozens of newspaper stories and articles in the national news magazines—and even this article, which is a direct result of the Monterey "gang rape."

When the much-quoted report was released, the local press—primarily the *San Francisco Chronicle,* which had earlier done a long and fairly objective series on the Hell's Angels—made a point of saying the Monterey charges against the Hell's Angels had been dropped for lack of evidence. *Newsweek* was careful not to mention Monterey at all, but *The New York Times* referred to it as "the alleged gang rape" which, however, left no doubt in a reader's mind that something savage had occurred.

It remained for *Time,* though, to flatly ignore the fact that the Monterey rape charges had been dismissed. Its article leaned heavily on the hairiest and least factual sections of the report, and ignored the rest. It said, for instance, that the Hell's Angels initiation rite "demands that any new member bring a woman or girl [called a 'sheep'] who is willing to submit to sexual intercourse with each member of the club." That is untrue, although, as one Angel explained, "Now and then you get a woman who likes to cover the crowd, and hell, I'm no prude. People don't like to think women go for that stuff, but a lot of them do."

We were talking across a pool table about the rash of publicity and how it had affected the Angel's activities. I was trying to explain to him that the bulk of the press in this country has such a vested interest in the *status quo* that it can't afford to do much honest probing at the roots, for fear of what they might find.

"Oh, I don't know," he said. "Of course I don't like to read all this bullshit because it brings the heat down on us, but since we got famous we've had more rich fags and sex-hungry women come looking for us than we ever had before. Hell, these days we have more action than we can handle."

MARTIN LUTHER KING, JR.

The Last Steep Ascent   *March 14, 1966*

> From 1961 through 1966, the Reverend Martin Luther King,
> Jr., wrote an annual essay for *The Nation* on the state of civil
> rights in the United States.

At the end of 1965 the civil rights movement was widely depicted as bewildered and uncertain, groping desperately for new directions. The substantial legislative accomplishments of the past several years, it was argued, dealt so extensively with civil rights problems that the movement had become stagnated in an embarrassment of riches. Negro leaders, we were told, did not know how to maintain their assembled armies nor what goals they should seek.

The dominant white leadership of the nation, in perceiving the civil rights movement as uncertain and confused, is engaged in political projection. The Negro freedom movement has a policy and a program; it is the white power structure that gropes in indecision. White America, caught between the Negro upsurge and its own conscience, evolved a limited policy toward Negro freedom. It could not live with the intolerable brutality and bruising humiliation imposed upon the Negro by the society it cherished as democratic. A wholesome national consensus developed against *extremist* conduct toward nonwhite Americans. That feeling found expression in laws, court decisions, and in the alteration of long-entrenched custom. But the prohibition of barbaric behavior, while beneficial to the victim, does not constitute the attainment of equality or freedom. A man may cease beating his wife without thereby creating a wholesome marital relationship.

The quality and quantity of discrimination and deprivation in our nation are so pervasive that all the changes of a decade have merely initiated preliminary alterations in an edifice of injustice and misery. But the evils in our society oppressing the Negro are not now so heavy a social and moral burden that white America cannot still live with them. That is the dilemma of 1966, for which the white leadership has no clear and effective policy. The logic of growth means that the civil rights odyssey must move to new levels in which the content of freedom is security, opportunity, culture and equal participation in the political process. Negro goals are clearly defined, their tactics are tested, suitable and viable. The lag is appearing in the white community which now inclines toward a *détente,* hoping to rest upon past laurels. The changes it must accept in the new circumstances, however logical, have not been faced nor accepted as compelling.

The period which has been completed, though attended by turmoil and spectacular events, was relatively easy to accomplish. Negroes not only furnished the drive but by disciplined adherence to nonviolence swiftly educated and won millions to the righteousness of their demands. For the white majority there were few hardships, and the lifting of some burden of guilt adequately compensated for any limited inconvenience.

The future is more complex. Slums with hundreds of thousands of living units are not eradicated as easily as lunch counters or buses are integrated. Jobs are harder to create than voting rolls. Harmonizing of peoples of vastly different cultural levels is complicated and frequently abrasive. It is easy to conceive of a plan to raise the minimum wage and thus in a single stroke extract millions of people from poverty. But between the conception and the realization there lies a formidable wall. Someone has been profiting from the low wages of Negroes. Depressed living standards for Negroes are a structural part of the economy. Certain industries are based upon the supply of low-wage, underskilled and immobile nonwhite labor. Hand assembly factories, hospitals, service industries, housework, agriculture operations using itinerant labor, would all suffer shock, if not disaster, if the minimum wage were significantly raised. A hardening of opposition to the satisfaction of Negro needs must be anticipated as the movement presses against financial privilege.

Beyond this, long-established cultural privileges are threatened in the next phase. We have seen in the effort to integrate schools, even in the more tolerant Northern urban centers, that many reasonably unbigoted persons assume a new posture with the introduction of unfamiliar problems into school systems where they have a personal interest. In the quest for genuinely integrated housing, the intensity of opposition from many who considered themselves free of prejudice has made it clear that this struggle will be attended by tenacious difficulties.

It is against this reality that the new period must be analyzed. Negroes have benefited from a limited change that was emotionally satisfying but materially deficient. As they move forward for fundamental alteration of their lives, a more bitter opposition grows even within groups that were hospitable to earlier superficial amelioration. Conflicts are unavoidable because a stage has been reached in which the reality of equality will require extensive adjustments in the way of life of some of the white majority.

There is no discernible will on the part of white leadership to prepare the people for changes on the new level. This is the program that is absent. No one has been told what slum elimination actually entails or what the transition from equality to opportunity really involves. One is forced to believe that the answers have not been forthcoming because there is no genuine conviction that such fundamental changes need be on any early agenda.

All profound social movements reach a plateau of this sort, short of the summit, and the presence of new opposition should not dismay us. Because we have accumulated substantial successes we have been able to reach the inner walls of resistance. That was our goal. The new obstacles should not be deplored but welcomed because their presence proves we are closer to the ultimate decision. These walls will yield to the same pressures that left the outer battlements in fragments behind us.

Government policy with respect to recent legislation reveals the contradictions that cloud the forward movement of civil rights. At the beginning of 1965, it was clear that the Administration was satisfied to rest on the legislation of the previous year. It felt the digestion of so heavy a feast of victories would occupy the civil rights movement for years. But our first step in February to employ these rights released the whirlwind. The attempt at Selma to brutalize Negroes once again stimulated decent Americans to a glorious moral moment of flaming indignation. President Johnson's passionate reaction made political history and his Administration moved with commendable dispatch to enact the Voting Rights Act of 1965. It was aided very significantly by the Goldwater debacle. The elections of 1964 broke the decades-old Congressional alliance of Dixie-crats and Northern conservatives, and sent to the Congress some fifty new Representatives who were receptive to fresh thinking.

With the passage of the memorable Voting Rights Act, the Administration once more proclaimed that the door to freedom had been flung open. Not since the promulgation of the Emancipation Proclamation had the hopes of Negroes been so high. But the year that came in like a lion went out like a lamb. There were increases in voting registration, there were some accretions to the list of token desegregated schools; but sweeping implementation nowhere appeared. Restraint and caution became public policy. The 1965 voting law applied to more than 500 Southern counties, but more than six months after its enactment only thirty-seven counties had received federal registrars. In the most important county of the South, where the city of Birmingham is located, every form of sophisticated evasion was employed. We had to organize daily demonstrations, to face again police brutality, and to arrive almost at the brink of another holocaust, before the Department of Justice finally acceded and appointed federal registrars. The open door to freedom turned out in practice to be but slightly ajar, and even after mass action only a sliver of freedom was sliced off and served to a desperately hungry people.

Title Six of the same act had armed the government with substantial power finally to force school desegregation. The Department of Health, Education and Welfare wrote militant letters to school boards explicitly declaring that federal muscle would be used to break the resistance of a decade. Yet when the sound and fury abated, school desegregation continued merely to crawl forward.

The poverty program, which in concept elated the Negro poor, became so embroiled in political turmoil that its insufficiencies were magnified by paralyzing manipulations. Big-city machines felt threatened by it and small towns, particularly in the South, directed it away from Negroes. Its good intentions and limited objectives were frustrated by the skillful maneuvers of experienced politicians. The worst aspect of these negative experiences was the doubt cast upon the program as a whole and the discredit sustained by those Negroes involved directly in its administration. To launch a program with high-minded goals and to fail to safeguard it from opportunists and enemies amounted to sabotage, whether deliberate or undeliberate. It should have been obvious that Negroes, who alone were under pressure for results, would encounter difficulties in administration. They were ill prepared to handle the complexities that attended any novel and wide-ranging program. Yet they would have been successful even with their limitations if their efforts had not been impeded in so many instances by hostile municipal officials. At almost every turn malevolent press reports and irresponsible charges denigrated the projects that Negroes headed. Rumors and suspicions of corruption and waste proliferated until it became a hazard to assume responsibility.

Only a few weeks ago the President presented a plan to Congress for rebuilding entire slum neighborhoods. With other elements of the program it would, in his words, make the decaying cities of the present into "the masterpieces of our civilization." This plan is imaginative; it embodies social vision and properly defines racial discrimination as a central evil. However, the ordinary Negro, though no social or political analyst, will be skeptical. He knows how many laws exist in Northern states and cities that prohibit discrimination in housing, in education and in employment; he knows how many overlapping commissions exist to enforce the terms of these laws—and he knows how he lives. The ubiquitous discrimination in his daily life tells him that more laws on paper, no matter how breath-taking their terminology, will not guarantee that he will live in a "masterpiece of civilization." Laws affirming Negro rights have in every case been circumvented by ingenious evasions which render them void in practice. Laws that affect the whole population—draft laws, income-tax laws, traffic laws—do work, even though they are unpopular; but laws passed for the Negro's benefit are so widely unenforced that it is a mockery to call them laws. The missing ingredient is no longer the will of governments to enact legislation; what is absent is the will to make it operative. There is a double standard in the enforcement of law, and a double standard in the respect for particular laws.

The Negro in 1966 now challenges society to make law real on the neighborhood level, down in the ghetto streets where he lives, works and seeks opportunity. Equal protection of the law is still substantially a national myth and a national disgrace in the reality of Negro life. In 1966, the Negro response is no longer a passive skepticism, nor is it expressed in the cynicism of inaction. A decade of sporadic and sometimes coordinated nonviolent action has educated him in the methodology of social change. He has learned how to compel the enactment of law, how to utilize to a degree some laws and how to expose spurious laws. He has learned that his adversaries are cunning, skillful and resourceful in obstruction and evasion. He has learned that governments do equivocate and retreat, no matter how exultant they are when they seek credit for legislation. Finally he has learned something about himself: *Negroes are not now merely a subject of change but an active organ of change.* This is the new political equation in contemporary society.

The regression of government after momentum has developed, the omission of the necessary planning and implementation to give reality to the law, are not accidental phenomena. The defaults merge into a pattern reminiscent of the period following the Civil War. Chattel slavery was abolished, but a program to transform slaves into citizens was omitted. Negroes left the plantations in hundreds of thousands expecting that the government that freed them would pursue the logic of its own act and create a structure into which they could fit. When this was not done, Negroes themselves improvised, sacrificed and struggled to gain a foothold on secure shores. However, the omissions inexorably caught up with them, and their enemies, only partially defeated, gained the breathing spell to reassemble and renew their power. The era of hope ended with the return of Negroes to a more sophisticated form of slavery that was to last nearly a century.

The danger of this period is not that Negroes will lose their gains. History will not repeat itself in a simple cycle. It can, however, fail to move forward and can become stalled on a higher plateau without prospect of reaching the summit.

The white power structure had to remake the South and Negroes seized the moment of change to fit the fabric to their needs. Evolving modern industrialism is being forced to reshape urban centers into which 70 per cent of the population is already absorbed. Once again Negroes will not allow change to flow around them, but will insistently demand to be elevated with the majority. The key question now confronting the nation is whether a swiftly transforming society is to be permitted to give tokens to the Negro, while the white population ascends to new levels of social development.

Historic decisions have yet to be made which will determine the context of the future. The dominant white majority appears to lack policy and sincere purpose, but the Negroes, contrary to common belief, have a policy and a program. Having driven a sharp wedge into the once solid wall of resistance, they plan to hammer it in with increased force and vigor. Already they have shaken the political foundations of the South. Where once Atlanta was a singular example of Negro political emergence, today tremors are shaking state-wide areas of segregation. Utilizing the 1965 Voting Act where it was implemented, and acting without it where it was nullified by inaction, Negroes have patiently built significant voting power. They are a major factor in the forthcoming gubernatorial race in Alabama, that symbol of implacable resistance. In six counties of the state Negro registration exceeded white by the end of 1965. The hallowed state capitol, from which the Confederate flag still flies, will be host to black legislators, estimated at not less than eight members in the House and one member in the Senate.

More important than this, however, is the transformation of the old segregationist official from a single-minded racist into something approximating a Northern style politician. In January, in Alabama, as the lines of black people stretched before registration offices day and night, the state Democratic Party removed the slogan of white supremacy from the party symbol. It may still live on in many hearts, but it is disappearing from tongues. Two years ago, I wrote in *The Nation* that the solid South was already fissuring along a seam that divided the industrializing regions from the old plantation South. Today the entire Old South is in dissolution. The momentum of change will not abate. Negroes are signing themselves into citizenship at the rate of thousands each day.

In the North, a new, more complex front is emerging. Neglected during the entire period of change, the slums are smoldering and seething. It would have been wiser for white America to have seen for itself that the slums were intolerable and dispersed them. But many white people of even reasonably good will simply know too little of the agony of ghetto existence to make slums as dispensable as segregated lunch counters. People of ill will still stubbornly cling to the determination to maintain a double standard of social and economic justice.

The experience of SCLC in Chicago already indicates that Negroes of the North are prepared to move and that token concessions will not blunt their drive. When 168 organizations representing all levels of the community are able to unite around a militant program to end slums, ghettos are on the way out even though for the moment they maintain their bleak existence.

When SCLC went into Birmingham in 1963, we said that if this capital of segregation suffered even a single defeat the effects would radiate across the South. Birmingham has met a succession of defeats and is influencing not only the South but the North as well. Chicago is the capital of segregation in the North; transformations of its slums will leave no Northern city secure with its own.

Mass nonviolent action continues to be *the* effective tactic of the movement. Many, especially in the North, argue that the maximum use of legislation, welfare and anti-poverty programs now replaces demonstrations, and that overt and visible protest should now be abandoned. Nothing could prove more erroneous than to demobilize at this point. It was the mass-action movement that engendered the changes of the decade, but the needs which created it are not yet satisfied. Without the will to unity and struggle Negroes would have no strength, and reversal of their successes could be easily effected. The use of creative tensions that broke the barriers of the South will be as indispensable in the North to obtain and extend necessary objectives.

These are partial elements of the Negro's program for freedom. Beyond these is one of singular importance which will be featured in the North—economic security. This is usually referred to as the need for jobs. The distinction made here between economic security and jobs is not semantic. A job in our industrial society is not necessarily equivalent to security. It is too often undercut by layoffs. No element of the working people suffers so acutely from layoffs as Negroes, traditionally the first fired and the last hired. They lack the seniority other workers accumulate because discrimination thwarts long-term employment. Negroes need the kind of employment that lasts the year through. They need the opportunity to advance on the job; they need the type of employment that feeds, clothes, educates and stabilizes a family. Statistics that picture declining rates of unemployment veil the reality that Negro jobs are still substandard and evanescent. The instability of employment reflects itself in the fragile character of Negro ambitions and economic foundations.

Whether the solution be in a guaranteed annual wage, negative income tax or any other economic device, the direction of Negro demands has to be toward substantive security. This alone will revolutionize Negro life, including family relations and that part of the Negro psyche that has lately become conspicuous—the Negro male ego.

Our nation is now so rich, so productive, that the continuation of persistent poverty is incendiary because the poor cannot rationalize their deprivation. We have yet to confront and solve the international problems created by our wealth in a world still largely hungry and miserable. But more immediate and pressing is the domestic existence of poverty. It is an anachronism in the second half of the 20th century. Only the neglect to plan intelligently and adequately and the unwillingness genuinely to embrace economic justice enable it to persist.

Social conflict is not the product of skilled agitation. The apathy from which Negroes suffered for so long was derived from their powerlessness and their acceptance of the myth that abundance was not available. They are now accumulating power; they are taught by every media of communication that we are so opulent we can enjoy both butter and guns. That is why they confront the white power structure with their program and challenge it to produce one of its own. The creative combining of both programs would unite social and economic justice into a single package of freedom.

The Negro in 1966 does not issue his challenge in isolation. Selma in 1965 made clear that there are white Americans who cherish decency and democracy; who will physically come to the scene of danger; who will fight for their nation not only on foreign battlefields but where its integrity is threatened within its borders. When 50,000 Americans, white and Negro, Protestant, Catholic, Jew and non-believer, assembled in haste from all corners of the land at Montgomery, there lived again in a luminous moment the spirit of the Minute Men who at Lexington and Concord electrified the world.

Negroes expect their freedom, not as subjects of benevolence but as Americans who were at Bunker Hill, who toiled to clear the forests, drain the swamps, build the roads—who fought the wars and dreamed the dreams the founders of the nation considered to be an American birthright.

JAMES BALDWIN

A Report from Occupied Territory   *July 11, 1966*

James Baldwin was born in Harlem. His first published novel, *Go Tell It On The Mountain*, appeared in 1953; in 1955, his volume of essays, *Notes Of A Native Son*, was published. After living in Paris for nearly ten years, Baldwin returned to the U.S. in 1957. Popular success came with the publication of *Nobody Knows My Name* (1961), the novel *Another Country* (1962), and *The Fire Next Time* (1963). Baldwin's first published piece was a review, "Maxim Gorky as Artist," in *The Nation* (April 12, 1947). He was a member of the magazine's editorial board until his death in 1987.

On April 17, 1964, in Harlem, New York City, a young salesman, father of two, left a customer's apartment and went into the streets. There was a great commotion in the streets, which, especially since it was a spring day, involved many people, including running, frightened, little boys. They were running from the police. Other people, in windows, left their windows, in terror of the police because the police had their guns out, and were aiming the guns at the roofs. Then the salesman noticed that two of the policemen were beating up a kid: "So I spoke up and asked them, 'why are you beating him like that?' Police jump up and start swinging on me. He put the gun on me and said, 'get over there.' I said, 'what for?' "

An unwise question. Three of the policemen beat up the salesman in the streets. Then they took the young salesman, whose hands had been handcuffed behind his back, along with four others, much younger than the salesman, who were handcuffed in the same way, to the police station. There: "About thirty-five I'd say came into the room, and started beating, punching us in the jaw, in the stomach, in the chest, beating us with a padded club—spit on us, call us niggers, dogs, animals—they call us dogs and animals when I don't see why we are the dogs and animals the way they are beating us. Like they beat me they beat the other kids and the elderly fellow. They throw him almost through one of the radiators. I thought he was dead over there."

"The elderly fellow" was Fecundo Acion, a 47-year-old Puerto Rican seaman, who had also made the mistake of wanting to know why the police were beating up children. An adult eyewitness reports, "Now here come an old man walking out a stoop and asked one cop, 'say, listen, sir, what's going on out here?' The cop turn around and smash him a couple of times in the head." And one of the youngsters said, "He get that just for a question. No reason at all, just for a question."

No one had, as yet, been charged with any crime. But the nightmare had not yet really begun. The salesman had been so badly beaten around one eye that it was found necessary to hospitalize him. Perhaps some sense of what it means to live in occupied territory can be suggested by the fact that the police took him to Harlem Hospital themselves—nearly nineteen hours after the beating. For fourteen days, the doctors at Harlem Hospital told him that they could do nothing for his eye, and he was removed to Bellevue Hospital, where for fourteen days, the doctors tried to save the eye. At the end of fourteen days it was clear that the bad eye could not be saved and was endangering the good eye. All that could be done, then, was to take the bad eye out.

As of my last information, the salesman is on the streets again, with his attaché case, trying to feed his family. He is more visible now because he wears an eye patch; and because he questioned the right of two policemen to beat up one child, he is known as a "cop hater." Therefore, "I have quite a few police look at me now pretty hard. My lawyer he axe (asked) me to keep somebody with me at all times 'cause the police may try to mess with me again."

You will note that there is not a suggestion of any kind of appeal to justice and no suggestion of any recompense for the grave and gratuitous damage which this man has endured. His tone is simply the tone of one who has miraculously survived—he might have died; as it is, he is merely half blind. You will also note that the patch over his eye has had the effect of making him, more than ever, the target of the police. It is a dishonorable wound, not earned in a foreign jungle but in the domestic one—not that this would make any difference at all to the nevertheless insuperably patriotic policeman—and it proves that he is a "bad nigger." ("Bad niggers," in America, as elsewhere, have always been watched and have usually been killed.) The police, who have certainly done their best to kill him, have also provided themselves with a pretext *derisoire* by filing three criminal charges against him. He is charged with beating up a schoolteacher, upsetting a fruit stand, and assaulting the (armed) police. Furthermore, he did all of these things in the space of a single city block, and simultaneously.

The salesman's name is Frank Stafford. At the time all this happened, he was 31 years old. And all of this happened, all of this and a great deal more, just before the "long, hot summer" of 1964 which, to the astonishment of nearly all New Yorkers and nearly all Americans, to the extremely verbal anguish of *The New York Times,* and to the bewilderment of the rest of the world, eventually erupted into a race riot. It was the killing of a 15-year-old Negro boy by a white policeman which overflowed the unimaginably bitter cup.

As a result of the events of April 17, and of the police performance that day, and because Harlem is policed like occupied territory, six young Negro men, the oldest of whom is 20, are now in prison, facing life sentences for murder. Their names are Wallace Baker, Daniel Hamm, Walter Thomas, Willie Craig, Ronald Felder and Robert Rice. Perhaps their names don't matter. They might be my brothers: they might also be yours. My report is based, in part, on Truman Nelson's *The Torture of Mothers* (The Garrison Press, 15 Olive Street, Newburyport, Mass., with an introduction by Maxwell Geismar). *The Torture of Mothers* is a detailed account of the case which is now known as the case of The Harlem Six. Mr. Nelson is *not,* as I have earlier misled certain people into believing, a white Southern novelist, but a white Northern one. It is a rather melancholy comment, I think, on the Northern intellectual community, and it reveals, rather to my despair, how little I have come to expect of it that I should have been led so irresistibly into this error. In a way, though, I certainly have no wish to blame Mr. Nelson for *my* errors; he is, nevertheless, somewhat himself to blame. His tone makes it clear that he means what he says and he knows what he means. The tone is rare. I have come to expect it only of Southerners—or mainly from Southerners—since Southerners must pay so high a price for their private and their public liberation. But Mr. Nelson actually comes from New England, and is what another age would have called an abolitionist. No Northern liberal would have been capable of it because the Northern liberal considers himself as already saved, whereas the white Southerner has to pay the price for his soul's salvation out of his own anguish and in his own flesh and in the only time he has. Mr. Nelson wrote the book in an attempt to create publicity and public indignation; whatever money the book makes goes into the effort to free The Harlem Six. I think the book is an extraordinary moral achievement, in the great American tradition of Tom Paine and Frederick Douglass, but I will not be so dishonest as to pretend that I am writing a book review. No, I am writing a report, which is also a plea for the recognition of our common humanity. Without this recognition, our common humanity will be proved in unutterable ways. My report is also based on what I myself know, for I was born in Harlem and raised there. Neither I, nor my family, can be said ever really to have left; we are—*perhaps*—no longer as totally at the mercy of the cops and the landlords as once we were: in any case, our roots, our friends, our deepest associations are there, and "there" is only about fifteen blocks away.

This means that I also know, in my own flesh, and know, which is worse, in the scars borne by many of those dearest to me, the thunder and fire of the billy club, the paralyzing shock of spittle in the face; and I know what it is to find oneself blinded, on one's hands and knees, at the bottom of the flight of steps down which one has just been hurled. I know something else: these young men have been in jail for two years now. Even if the attempts being put forth to free them should succeed, what has happened to them in these two years? People are destroyed very easily. Where is the civilization and where, indeed, is the morality which can afford to destroy so many?

There was a game played for some time between certain highly placed people in Washington and myself before the administration changed and the Great Society reached the planning stage. The game went something like this: around April or May, that is as the weather began to be warmer, my phone would ring. I would pick it up and find that Washington was on the line.

Washington: What are you doing for lunch—oh, say, tomorrow, Jim?

Jim: Oh—why—I guess I'm free.

Washington: Why don't you take the shuttle down? We'll send a car to the airport. One o'clock all right?

Jim: Sure. I'll be there.

Washington: Good. Be glad to see you.

So there I would be the next day, like a good little soldier, seated (along with other good little soldiers) around a luncheon table in Washington. The first move was not mine to make, but I knew very well why I had been asked to be there.

Finally, someone would say—we would probably have arrived at the salad— "say, Jim. What's going to happen this summer?"

This question, translated, meant: Do you think that any of those unemployed, unemployable Negroes who are going to be on the streets all summer will cause us any trouble? What do you think we should do about it? But, later on, I concluded that I had got the second part of the question wrong; they really meant, what was *I* going to do about it?

Then I would find myself trying patiently to explain that the Negro in America can scarcely yet be considered—for example—as a part of the labor unions—and he is certainly not so considered by the majority of these unions—and that, therefore, he lacks that protection and that incentive. The jobs that Negroes have always held, the lowest jobs, the most menial jobs, are now being destroyed by automation. No remote provision has yet been made to absorb this labor surplus. Furthermore, the Negro's education, North and South, remains, almost totally, a segregated education, which is but another way of saying that he is taught the habits of inferiority every hour of every day that he lives. He will find it very difficult to overcome these habits. Furthermore, every attempt he makes to overcome them will be painfully complicated by the fact that the ways of being, the ways of life of the despised and rejected, nevertheless contain an incontestable vitality and authority. This is far more than can be said of the middle class which, in any case, and whether it be black or white, does not dare to cease despising him. He may prefer to remain where he is, given such unattractive choices, which means that he either remains in limbo, or finds a way to use the system in order to beat the system. Thus, even when opportunities — my use of this word is here limited to the industrialized, competitive, contemporary North American sense — hitherto closed to Negroes begin, very grudgingly, to open up, few can be found to qualify for them for the reasons sketched above, and also because it demands a very rare person, of any color, to risk madness and heartbreak in an attempt to achieve the impossible. (I know Negroes who have gone literally mad because they wished to become commercial air-line pilots.) Nor is this the worst.

The children, having seen the spectacular defeat of their fathers — having seen what happens to any bad nigger and, still more, what happens to the good ones — cannot listen to their fathers and certainly will not listen to the society which is responsible for their orphaned condition. What to do in the face of this deep and dangerous estrangement? It seemed to me — I would say, sipping coffee and trying to be calm — that the principle of what had to be done was extremely simple; but before anything could be done, the principle had to be grasped. The principle on which one had to operate was that the government which can force me to pay my taxes and force me to fight in its defense anywhere in the world *does not have the authority* to say that it cannot protect my right to vote or my right to earn a living or my right to live anywhere I choose. Furthermore, no nation, wishing to call itself free, can possibly survive so massive a defection. What to do? Well, there is a real estate lobby in Albany, for example, and this lobby, which was able to rebuild all of New York, downtown, and for money, in less than twenty years, is also responsible for Harlem and the condition of the people there, and the condition of the schools there, and the future of the children there. What to do? Why is it not possible to attack the power of this lobby? Are their profits more important than the health of our children? What to do? Are textbooks printed in order to teach children, or are the contents of these textbooks to be controlled by the Southern oligarchy and the commercial health of publishing houses? What to do? Why are Negroes and Puerto Ricans virtually the only people pushing trucks in the garment center, and what union has the right to trap and victimize Negroes and Puerto Ricans in this way? None of these things (I would say) could possibly be done without the consent, in fact, of the government, and we in Harlem know this even if some of you profess not to know how such a hideous state of affairs came about. If some of these things are not begun — I would say — then, of course, we will be sitting on a powder keg all summer. Of course, the powder keg may blow up; it will be a miracle if it doesn't.

They thanked me. They didn't believe me, as I conclude, since nothing was ever done. The summer was always violent. And in the spring, the phone began to ring again.

Now, what I have said about Harlem is true of Chicago, Detroit, Washington, Boston, Philadelphia, Los Angeles and San Francisco—is true of every Northern city with a large Negro population. And the police are simply the hired enemies of this population. They are present to keep the Negro in his place and to protect white business interests, and they have no other function. They are, moreover—even in a country which makes the very grave error of equating ignorance with simplicity—quite stunningly ignorant; and, since they know that they are hated, they are always afraid. One cannot possibly arrive at a more sure-fire formula for cruelty.

This is why those pious calls to "respect the law," always to be heard from prominent citizens each time the ghetto explodes, are so obscene. The law is meant to be my servant and not my master, still less my torturer and my murderer. To respect the law, in the context in which the American Negro finds himself, is simply to surrender his self-respect.

On April 17, some school children overturned a fruit stand in Harlem. This would have been a mere childish prank if the children had been white—had been, that is, the children of that portion of the citizenry for whom the police work and who have the power to control the police. But these children were black, and the police chased them and beat them and took out their guns; and Frank Stafford lost his eye in exactly the same way The Harlem Six lost their liberty—by trying to protect the younger children. Daniel Hamm, for example, tells us that ". . . we heard children scream. We turned around and walked back to see what happened. I saw this policeman with his gun out and with his billy in his hand. I like put myself in the way to keep him from shooting the kids. Because first of all he was shaking like a leaf and jumping all over the place. And I thought he might shoot one of them."

He was arrested, along with Wallace Baker, carried to the police station, beaten—"six and twelve at a time would beat us. They got so tired beating us they just came in and started spitting on us—they even bring phlegm up and spit on me." This went on all day. In the evening, Wallace Baker and Daniel Hamm were taken to Harlem Hospital for X rays and then carried back to the police station where the beating continued all night. They were eventually released, with the fruit-stand charges pending, in spite of the testimony of the fruit-stand owner. This fruit-stand owner had already told the police that neither Wallace Baker nor Daniel Hamm had ever been at his store and that they certainly had had nothing to do with the fruit-stand incident. But this had no effect on the conduct of the police. The boys had already attracted the attention of the police, long before the fruit-stand riot, and in a perfectly innocent way. They are pigeon fanciers and they keep—kept—pigeons on the roof. But the police are afraid of everything in Harlem and they are especially afraid of the roofs, which they consider to be guerrilla outposts. This means that the citizens of Harlem who, as we have seen, can come to grief at any hour in the streets, and who are not safe at their windows, are forbidden the very air. They are safe only in their houses—or were, until the city passed the No Knock, Stop and Frisk laws, which permit a policeman to enter one's home without knocking and to stop anyone on the streets, at will, at any hour, and search him. Harlem believes, and I certainly agree, that these laws are directed against Negroes. They are certainly not directed against anybody else. One day, "two carloads of detectives came and went up on the roof. They pulled their guns on the kids and searched them and made them all come down and they were going to take them down to the precinct." But the boys put up a verbal fight and refused to go and attracted quite a crowd. "To get these boys to the precinct we would have to shoot them," a policeman said, and "the police seemed like they was embarrassed. Because I don't think they expected the kids to have as much sense as they had in speaking up for themselves." They refused to go to the precinct, "and they didn't," and their exhibition of the spirit of '76 marked them as dangerous. Occupied territory is occupied territory, even though it be found in that New World which the Europeans conquered; and it is axiomatic, in occupied territory, that any act of resistance, even though it be executed by a child, be answered at once, and with the full weight of the occupying forces. Furthermore, since the police, not at all surprisingly, are abysmally incompetent—for neither, in fact, do they have any respect for the law, which is not surprising, either—Harlem and all of New York City is full of unsolved crimes. A crime, as we know, is solved when someone is arrested and convicted. It is not indispensable, but it is useful, to have a confession. If one is carried back and forth from the precinct into the hospital long enough, one is likely to confess to anything.

Therefore, ten days later, following the slaying of Mrs. Margit Sugar in Mr. and Mrs. Sugar's used-clothing store in Harlem, the police returned and took Daniel Hamm away again. This is how his mother tells it: "I think it was three (detectives) come up and they asked are you Danny Hamm? And he says yes and right away—gun right to the head and slapping him up, one gun here and one here—just all the way down the hall—beating him and knocking him around with the gun to his head." The other boys were arrested in the same way, and, again of course, they were beaten; but this arrest was a far greater torture than the first one had been because some of the mothers did not know where the boys were, and the police, who were holding them, refused for many hours to say that they were holding them. The mothers did not know of what it was their children were accused until they learned, via television, that the charge was murder. At that time in the state of New York, this charge meant death in the electric chair.

Let us assume that all six boys are guilty as (eventually) charged. Can anyone pretend that the manner of their arrest, or their treatment, bears any resemblance to equal justice under the law? The Police Department has loftily refused to "dignify the charges." But can anyone pretend that they would dare to take this tone if the case involved, say, the sons of Wall Street brokers? I have witnessed and endured the brutality of the police many more times than once—but, of course, I cannot prove it. I cannot prove it because the Police Department investigates itself, quite as though it were answerable only to itself. But it cannot be allowed to be answerable only to itself; it must be made to answer to the community which pays it, and which it is legally sworn to protect; and if American Negroes are not a part of the American community, then all of the American professions are a fraud.

This arrogant autonomy, which is guaranteed the police, not only in New York, *by the most powerful forces in American life*—otherwise, they would not dare to claim it, would, indeed, be unable to claim it—creates a situation which is as close to anarchy as it already, visibly, is close to martial law.

Here is Wallace Baker's mother speaking, describing the night that a police officer came to her house to collect the evidence which he hoped would prove that her son was guilty of murder. The late Mrs. Sugar had run a used-clothing store and the policeman was looking for old coats. "Nasty as he was that night in my house. He didn't ring the bell. So I said, have you got a search warrant? He say, no, I don't have no search warrant and I'm going to search anyway. Well, he did. So I said, will you please step out of this room till I get dressed? He wouldn't leave." This collector of evidence against the boys was later arrested on charges of possessing and passing counterfeit money (he pleaded guilty to a misdemeanor, "conspiring" to pass counterfeit money). The officer's home in Hartsdale, N. Y., is valued at $35,000, he owns two cars, one a Cadillac, and when he was arrested, had $1,300 in his pockets. But the families of The Harlem Six do not have enough money for counsel. The court appointed counsel, and refused to allow the boys counsel of their own choice, even though the boys made it clear that they had no confidence in their court-appointed counsel, and even though four leading civil rights lawyers had asked to be allowed to handle the case. The boys were convicted of first-degree murder, and are now ending their childhood and may end their lives in jail.

These things happen, in all our Harlems, every single day. If we ignore this fact, and our common responsibility to change this fact, we are sealing our doom. Here is the boy, Daniel Hamm, speaking—speaking of his country, which has sworn to bring peace and freedom to so many millions: "They don't want us here. They don't want us—period! All they want us to do is work on these penny-ante jobs for them—and that's *it*. And beat our heads in whenever they feel like it. They don't want us on the street 'cause the World's Fair is coming. And they figure that all black people are hoodlums anyway, or bums, with no character of our own. So they put us off the streets, so their friends from Europe, Paris or Vietnam—wherever they come from—can come and see this supposed-to-be great city."

There is a very bitter prescience in what this boy—this "bad nigger"—is saying, and he was not born knowing it. We taught it to him in seventeen years. He is draft age now, and if he were not in jail, would very probably be on his way to Southeast Asia. Many of his contemporaries are there, and the American Government and the American press are extremely proud of them. They are dying there like flies; they are dying in the streets of all our Harlems far more hideously than flies. A member of my family said to me when we learned of the bombing of the four little girls in the Birmingham Sunday school, "Well, they don't need us for work no more. Where are they building the gas ovens?" Many Negroes feel this; there is no way not to feel it. Alas, we know our countrymen, municipalities, judges, politicians, policemen and draft boards very well. There is more than one way to skin a cat, and more than one way to get bad niggers off the streets. No one in Harlem will ever believe that The Harlem Six are guilty—God knows their guilt has certainly not been proved. Harlem knows, though, that they have been abused and possibly destroyed, and Harlem knows why—we have lived with it since our eyes opened on the world. One is in the impossible position of being unable to believe a word one's countrymen say. "I can't believe what you say," the song goes, "because I see what you do"—and one is also under the necessity of escaping the jungle of one's situation into any other jungle whatever. It is the bitterest possible comment on our situation now that the suspicion is alive in so many breasts that America has at last found a way of dealing with the Negro problem. *"They don't want us—period!"* The meek shall inherit the earth, it is said. This presents a very bleak image to those who live in occupied territory. The meek Southeast Asians, those who remain, shall have their free elections, and the meek American Negroes—those who survive—shall enter the Great Society.

Paradise Reagan-ed
[*editorial*]

December 5, 1966

In 1966, after Ronald Reagan was first elected governor of California, Carey McWilliams responded with the following editorial.

To understand the election of Ronald Reagan as governor of California, it is important to grasp the idea of that state as "paradise." The Eden image has led millions to move there; from the Okie migrations of the thirties to the present the state has swarmed with newcomers.

California has given us the first auto-dominated city, Los Angeles; and even within the "old and settled" city of San Francisco people move around as though in a frenzy. All this movement to California and within it suggests that Californians are strongly motivated to escape—from the cold blasts of the Midwest or the problems of the South, or lack of opportunity, or whatever.

Thus, when an election came up during a time of rapid social change and increasing problems, the people of California fled reality. Instead, they indulged in a ritual cleansing, and brought in a totally inexperienced man who campaigned *on the basis* of being a political innocent. Brown, who campaigned on his experience, was fated to emphasize the very thing that people held against him: he reminded them that they were human, that they were part of society and had responsibilities. But now all is simple and wonderful in a land where "thinking makes it so." There is no need for government and, led by an innocent, the Californians can look forward to eternities of joy, while the rest of America, in the land of Nod (East of Eden) must continue to struggle and sweat.

JACK NEWFIELD

One Cheer for the Hippies
June 26, 1967

As assistant editor of the *Village Voice*, Jack Newfield contributed dozens of pieces to *The Nation*. Most of the articles he wrote for the magazine were reprinted, in a somewhat different form, in his books *A Prophetic Minority* (1966) and *Bread and Roses Too* (1971).

> Politics is dead. Culture is dead. The world stinks.
> —EMMETT GROGAN, founder of the Diggers
>
> I am a Roman Senator, not a Digger.
> —PAUL GOODMAN

The hippies are happening. Ed Sanders of the Fugs is on a cover of *Life*. Tulsa, Okla., which went for Barry Goldwater by 30,000 votes, recently had its first love-in. Gray Line sight-seeing buses detour through Haight-Ashbury to display the local "freaks" to the Babbitts. Squares (not hippies) pay $4 to see the psychedelic Billy Graham — Dr. Timothy Leary — preach his "turn on, tune in, drop out" sermons. Hollywood has adopted the vibrating, "acid art" poster style of the Fillmore Auditorium, using it in ads to promote the big-budget James Bond film, *Casino Royale*. And the folk-rock group, Jefferson Airplane, has recorded a commercial for white Levi denims — even as 460 of that company's employees strike in Blue Ridge, Ga., against the chronically exploitive conditions of Southern textile mills.

Individually, the hippies are beautiful. They know a lot of things the squares don't. They know that marijuana is mildly pleasant and doesn't give you lung cancer; that Bob Dylan, John Lennon and Leonard Cohen are authentic poetic voices for all those who have grown up absurd; that it is better to make love than war; that most things taught in college must be unlearned later in life; that it is healthier to be spontaneous, communal and tolerant than repressed, materialistic and bigoted; and that it is groovy to read Herman Hesse, Snoopy and Allen Ginsberg.

All this being eagerly granted, the point must now be made that the hippies have been overrated. Their ultimate vision is in no way superior to that of the New Left, of Mailer, Camus or Pynchon. The hippies will not change America because change means pain, and the hippie subculture is rooted in the pleasure principle. They have an intellectual flabbiness that permits them to equate an original talent like Kenneth Anger with a put-on like Andy Warhol. For this reason they are vulnerable to the kind of exploitation symbolized by the Jefferson Airplane commercial. They lack the energy, stability and private pain to serve as the "new proletariat" that some in the New Left perceive them to be. Bananas, incense and pointing love rays toward the Pentagon have nothing to do with redeeming and renovating America; Leary's call to "drop out" is really a call to cop out.

The whole hippie contagion seems to be a recoil from the idea of politics itself; it is not merely apolitical but anti-political. "Civil rights is a game for squares," one hippie told me. "Why should I demonstrate to get the spades all the things I'm rejecting?" And the *Berkeley Barb*, one of the best of the dozen underground weeklies, scorned the April 15 anti-war Mobilization for being "deadly serious, militant and political."

The hippies, in fact, have more in common with the nihilism of the 1950 beats, than with the activism of their generational comrades in the New Left. The beats opted out of a repressive, materialistic society because they felt impotent to change it. Ike, McCarthyism, Korea, Madison Avenue, the cold war, the defeats of Stevenson, made politics appear impossible to the alienated young of the 1950s. Without hope, they sought escape by withdrawing into Eastern religions, sex, jazz, drugs and madness. It required foreign examples of effective student radicalism — in Korea, Japan, Cuba and Turkey, all in 1959 — to inspire the young here.

The New Left took root in 1960 and 1961 because social change through political activism suddenly seemed possible with the election of John Kennedy. There were sit-ins, and lunch counters were desegregated. There were freedom rides, and bus terminals were desegregated. There were heroism and death in the Deep South, and a Civil Rights Act was drafted. There was a free-speech movement at Berkeley, and educational reform of the dehumanizing multiversity became a fashionable symposium topic. SDS organized around the ideal of a participatory democracy, and the "maximum feasible participation of the poor" clause was written into the anti-poverty program. For a time there appeared to be in Washington a higher moral authority which would respond humanely to protest.

But just as the beats did not develop in a vacuum, neither have the hippies; their growth has been in direct correlation to the country's drift to the right since the Gulf of Tonkin "incident" and the Watts "rebellion." The young who once idolized JFK perceive his successor—correctly, I think—as an anti-democratic manipulator who has stultified the possibility of change through dissenting politics. Johnson has become a depressing Ike figure and Vietnam the monstrously swollen equivalent of the Korean police action. In 1963 Bob Dylan sang of changes "blowin' in the wind"; today he chants: "Although the masters make the rules/ for the wise men and the fools/ I've got nothin', Ma, to live up to." In 1962 more Harvard seniors wanted to volunteer for the Peace Corps than wanted to work for a large corporation; this is no longer the case. The Haight-Ashbury scene jumped into national prominence in the same month that the voters were sanctioning Reagan, Wallace and Maddox, and the Vietnamese War turned a corner into its present open-ended escalation. Suddenly, it seemed more possible to change private reality with LSD than America's reality with SDS.

My own quarrel with the hippie ethic can be summarized in five arguments.

The first is that I don't think it will be permanently impossible to alter America through radical political action. The hippies seem to side with Sade when he says: "And why should you care about the world outside? For me the only reality is imagination, the world inside myself. The revolution no longer interests me." But the New Left is closer to Marat, who answers (in Peter Weiss's *Marat/Sade*): "Against nature's silence I use action. . . . I don't watch unmoved; I intervene and say this and this are wrong, and I work to alter and improve them. The important thing is to pull yourself up by your own hair, to turn yourself inside out, and see the whole world with fresh eyes."

What the hippies forget is how unlikely social change seemed in 1957 and 1958. It took a new generation of kids, who had not read *On the Road*, to prove that America had not congealed into a static cage. Reform will become possible again, especially once the Vietnamese War ends. What the pleasure-oriented hippies can't accept is that political action is a painful, Sisyphean task that includes sacrifice, boredom and defeat.

My second point against the hippies is that precisely because they are *not a real threat to anything* they are used to goose a lifeless middle class, and are even widely imitated. Thus they create the illusion of influence when the jet set adopts their fashions, slang and music. But it is huckster America that profits by merchandising everything from "psychedelic salami" to "psychedelic earrings."

Third, the hippies think their vision of a drug-induced, homogenized love is an original panacea. One hippie even told me: "Man, I love everything. That fire hydrant, LBJ, Wallace, all them cats."

America is surely short on love, but the love the hippies invoke is so generalized and impersonal as to be meaningless. And as an observer I don't detect any greater love content in relations within the hippie subculture; they are just as exploitive and ego-centered and neurotic as the rest of us.

Fourth, the philosophical rationale the hippies cite for dropping out is that life is essentially absurd anyway, and since it has no meaning, it is pointless to try to change events. It is better, they say, again echoing Sade, to savor all possible personal experience instead.

Evidence certainly mounts to support an absurdist interpretation of recent history, beginning with the assassination in Dallas, through the CIA's secret life, up to Byron de la Beckwith now running for lieutenant governor of Mississippi. Yet both Sartre and Camus accepted—and then transcended—absurdity, and were able to embrace an even deeper engagement and commitment. Sartre and Camus did not "turn on and drop out" when the Nazis marched across France; they both joined the underground

Finally, there is the dilemma of LSD. I have read several research papers and find much of the evidence is contradictory. Clearly, LSD has been useful, in a therapeutic sense, in treating problems like homosexuality, impotence and alcoholism. But LSD has also caused plenty of mental damage, recurring hallucinations, freak-outs and visits to hospital emergency wards by teeny-boppers who think they are giraffes. And, in general, the effect of acid on activists is to make them fugitives from the system, instead of insurgents against the system. Acidheads tend to withdraw from politics (as Dr. Leary recommends), pursue private or politically unrealistic goals, and become disruptive if they remain inside activist organizations. They lack the patience and stability for the drudgery of organizing and scholarship.

The alternative to the hippies remains the New Left, which contrary to some reports, seems still to be growing. The spring semester indicated how deep the roots of student discontent have penetrated, with major campus rebellions at Long Island University, Texas, Drew University, Catholic University, Howard, Jackson State and Oklahoma. In May, card-carrying SDS members were freely elected student body presidents at Indiana and Northwestern. More than 350 students have signed an ad in the *Harvard Crimson* asserting that they will defy the draft. Vietnam Summer claims to have 2,000 organizers in the field.

Undeniably, the hippies represent an important break with the past and have considerable merit. Their musical innovations will, I suspect, ultimately prove as rich as the bop revolution forged by Bird, Dizzy and Monk in the 1940s. The diggers, who run the indigenous mission halls for their hippie brethren, are closer to St. Francis than to Cardinal Spellman.

But, finally, Dylan, pot and bright colors are the *hippies'* liberation. The poor, the voteless, the manipulated, the spiritually undernourished – they are oppressed by injustice that is crystallized in institutions. Only a radical political movement can liberate *them*. I want to save the squares too.

As We See It

[*editorial*]

> *The Nation* has engaged in a continuing struggle with major party politics. On the eve of the 1968 elections, the magazine argued that the choice between Nixon and Humphrey was such a bad one that people should just stay home – an interesting prelude to *The Nation*'s endorsement of Jesse Jackson in 1988.

Most voters are understandably unhappy with the three leading Presidential contenders, Nixon, Humphrey and Wallace. An appalling percentage of ballots this November are going to be cast "against" rather than "for." Even many of those who vote for Wallace and LeMay – at least outside the Deep South – will be casting protest votes.

Comments on the choice offered voters range from "dismal" (Walter Lippmann) and "distasteful" (Tom Wicker of *The New York Times*) to the unprintable. Apart from the Wallace constituency, those who have decided to vote despite their dismay and distress will be influenced in the main by one or the other of the following arguments. Some feel, as Mr. Lippmann does, that the Republican Party, even with Nixon at the helm, is better able to govern than the tired, discredited, sharply divided Democratic Party. Others argue – David Broder is one – that in the unhappy situation in which most voters now find themselves the man is more important than the party. Mr. Broder is impressed by the fact that "from the rich array of talent in the Republican Party, Richard Nixon chose Spiro

T. Agnew for his Vice Presidential candidate," while "in the supposed ruins of the Democratic Party, Hubert Humphrey found Edmund S. Muskie."

While *The Nation* is inclined to agree with much of what Mr. Lippmann has to say about the Republican Party, if we were to make a selection on the basis of likability, we could discover in ourselves a preference for Humphrey and Muskie. But a central issue in this year's election transcends parties and personalities. In the 1964 campaign the electorate was offered what it had every right to assume was a choice—not an echo—on the vital issue of the war in Vietnam. The choice seemed clear-cut: a military victory through escalation (Goldwater) or "no wider war" (Johnson), which implied an honest effort to seek settlement through negotiation. The electorate gave Johnson an overwhelming mandate to pursue the policy he had unambiguously stated, but even before Election Day he had quietly set in motion preparations for escalation. In retrospect, the dubious Gulf of Tonkin resolution, so frequently cited as the basic authorization, appears to have been part of the President's advance planning for the unannounced course of action he had determined to follow. A self-respecting electorate would be most unwise to permit such a deliberate deception on a matter involving the honor and security of the United States to go unrebuked. We recognize, with Lincoln, that an element of moral ambiguity may be inherent in politics, but there are limits beyond which ambiguity cannot be made to stretch. We consider the President's deception about his intentions in 1964 to be an affront to the ethics of political leadership in a democratic society.

We could not possibly have endorsed President Johnson if he had sought re-election, regardless of whom the Republicans might have nominated. Nor can we endorse Vice President Humphrey, even though Richard Nixon is his principal opponent. We have not forgotten that when the Administration—with the cooperation of N.B.C.—decided to rebuke Martin Luther King after he had come out against the Vietnamese War, it was Mr. Humphrey who undertook the unsavory assignment. We have never thought of the Vice President as merely a loyal lieutenant serving a general of whose policies he disapproved. On the contrary, we have always assumed that the Vice President agreed with the President's policies, including the decision to escalate the war; his own statements over the last four years, delivered with characteristic fervor, make his position quite clear. To assume otherwise would be to place a very low evaluation indeed on the Vice President's courage, intelligence and integrity.

Nor can we endorse the Nixon-Agnew ticket—not even as a protest, not even to offset the possibility that Wallace may tumble the election into the House. As we have said many times, while we regard Nixon as an intelligent, hard-working, astute politician, we also regard him as a man without settled principles, values or convictions—a view that finds striking confirmation in his egregiously irresponsible selection of Spiro T. Agnew for a running mate. If Nixon gets to the

White House (a prospect we do not relish), he will owe his election to the performance of the Johnson-Humphrey Administration, capped by the disgraceful spectacle of the Chicago convention. We see no need to say what we think about the Wallace-LeMay ticket. In deciding to make no endorsement, we have considered the possibility that the election may be thrown into the House, but we do not think this likely.

It has been urged that failure to endorse the Humphrey-Muskie ticket will injure the chances of some excellent Democratic nominees, but in our view these nominees will fare better to the extent that they can separate their campaigns from the national ticket. Humphrey not only has no coattails to offer them; he is trying to ride on Muskie's. We are impressed by the fact that many of the Congressional leaders of the Democratic Party who were for Humphrey before and during the Chicago convention are now unwilling to give his candidacy active support, although most of them would welcome the support of Senator McCarthy. If the Vice President had spoken out against what happened at Chicago, in the convention and on the streets, he might have been able to restore a measure of unity. Critics within the party, Humphrey complains, have not rallied to his support. The fact is that the Johnson-Meany-Daley axis has done nothing to help these critics and is, in a variety of ways, conniving at their defeat. In Illinois, for example, the Democratic Senatorial nominee, William Clark, is not receiving the party support to which he is clearly entitled.

It is said, also, that if the Democratic nominees for President and Vice President are defeated, the party will fall apart and the pieces will be picked up by the old guard. But the Democratic Party is not going to fall apart, and the forces of the "New Politics" have a good chance in 1972 to win the victory they did not win this year. Time is running out on such bosses as Barr, Tate and Daley, and on such "labor leaders" as George Meany. Even though the All-Negro National Committee of Inquiry has voted not to endorse Humphrey (he notified Rep. John Conyers on September 25 that he did not have time to meet with the committee, a broadly based group of Negro moderates and militants with 1,000 members in thirty-two states, to discuss issues of interest to Negroes!), those Negroes who do vote, North and South, will probably be for Humphrey and Muskie. In many states the effect may well be to make Negroes the base of the Democratic Party, which this year has been deserted by so many of the elements that made up the New Deal coalition. Julian Bond, the Rev. Channing Phillips, Charles Evers, Aaron Henry and others are campaigning for the Humphrey-Muskie ticket—not with an excess of enthusiasm but to preserve the position that Negroes have won in the party. It is reasonable to assume, therefore, that the party will be refashioned between now and 1972 through pressures operating from within, such as the New Democratic Coalition and from without, such as the New Party, the Wallace adherents and the various new national constituencies.

It is said, finally, that citizens are always under an obligation to vote, even though they may not like the proffered choices. But this ignores the fact that abstaining is a kind of vote—a vote of no confidence (Wisconsin provides a place on the ballot to register such a protest)—and that under present circumstances it can be a very effective way of using the franchise. Old coalitions are falling apart, new coalitions are trying to form. As long as the electorate dutifully lines up behind the candidates whom the Democratic and Republican Party professionals see fit to run, the professionals will continue to offer candidates whose chief virtue is that they defer to the professionals. But let it be seen that a significant segment of the public has emancipated itself from a fanciful duty to vote for someone— anyone—and is reserving its endorsement for a candidate it likes, then the parties will find such men. (That they would not be hard to find was evidenced this year by the presence of Governor Rockefeller in Miami and Senator McCarthy in Chicago.) A "lesser evil" is still an evil (usually a hack). What this country must seek is a greater good. Whereas reasons can be cited for voting for Nixon or voting for Humphrey, there are at least as good reasons this time around for passing: the country might get a new deck of cards.

We hope nonetheless that there will be a large turn-out of voters on November 5. The feeling of distaste expressed by many voters for the Presidential nominees gives added importance to the contests in the Senate and House. Here is where voters sharing our point of view should invest their time, money and energy. . . .

ERNEST GRUENING

On Vietnam
May 5, 1969

In 1964, Senator Ernest Gruening of Alaska, a former *Nation* editor, was one of two senators to vote against the fateful Gulf of Tonkin resolution.

It is, and for some time has been, obvious that the most important issue facing our nation is to get out of the war in Southeast Asia. All our other issues and problems are slighted, impaired and unresolved until we halt the fighting, stop the concomitant continuing drain of blood and treasure, and turn to the long-neglected and pressing needs at home.

During his election campaign Richard Nixon told the American people that he had a plan to end the war, but did not want to disclose it for fear of interfering with the negotiations in Paris. After three months in office President Nixon gives us no indication of any formula or proposal for achieving that widely desired objective.

On the contrary, draft calls are undiminished, casualties mount and we continue, as we have for the last five years, to be winning the war only in the optimistic pronouncements of our military leaders and their supporting newspaper columnists. The President has shown a commendable restraint in not re-escalating the battlefield activity, having no doubt learned that every time our military propose just one more upmanship we get in that much deeper. But the prospect is for continued warfare.

A new approach is desperately needed, and I offer it in the fervent hope that President Nixon who, I doubt not, would like to rid his Administration of the albatross bequeathed him by President Johnson, will lay aside his preconceptions and the assumptions that have underlain our policies to date. For that purpose a review of what has happened is appropriate.

Five years ago, on March 10, 1964, I delivered the first major opposition speech on this issue made in Congress. It was entitled, "The United States Should Get Out of Vietnam." With exhibits, it occupied 30 pages in the *Congressional Record*. It would have been easy for President Johnson to accept that counsel and to withdraw at that time, since no United States units had been committed to combat, and the casualties had been very few.

The opening sentence of that March 10 address was: "The mess in Vietnam was inherited by President Johnson." That holds true for President Nixon today; he is under no more obligation than was President Johnson to perpetuate his predecessor's policies.

That we have lost some 34,000 young Americans killed in action, several thousand more through other causes, more than a quarter of a million wounded, some horribly crippled for life, have killed tens of thousands of innocent noncombatants, created more than a million homeless refugees, sunk in excess of $125 billion unrecoverably in the Asian quagmire, and sacrificed our moral standards before the conscience of mankind, does not lessen but increases the need for an alternative course. To continue to permit our men to die in vain—as they all have died in this war—is not short of criminal.

The extent of our folly, despite official propaganda and the ever optimistic and misleading reports of military and diplomatic experts in the scene, has dawned increasingly on the American people. The desire and need to disentangle ourselves have been widely expressed, and as widely countered with the hopeless and unimaginative retort: "Well, maybe we shouldn't have gone in but we're *there* now," with the accent on the "there," implying that we have to keep on with what we have been doing.

More recently, this has been refined by acknowledgments that, while we must find a way out, it must be an "honorable" way—which can be translated to mean victory for our position. The "unthinkable" proposal that we withdraw unilaterally (why not, since we barged in unilaterally and in violation of all our treaty commitments?) is met with the loaded cliché, "You wouldn't scuttle and run, would you?" I'll examine that in a moment.

Let me urge that *any* way out would be more honorable than to continue the needless slaughter, and the ever deepening submergence of our nation's interests and values. But actually the most honorable way out would be to repudiate the whole dishonorable episode (made even more demonstrably so, since the Fulbright committee hearings last year revealed that the Tonkin Gulf incident was spurious), to make an "agonizing reappraisal" and confess error.

Defense Secretary Laird has recently revived the shop-worn proposal that we strengthen the South Vietnamese army and turn the war over to it—Congress to appropriate additional millions of dollars for that purpose. This would mean merely further subsidy to the corrupt and dictatorial Saigon regimes which have been successively self-imposed by military coups or by electoral fraud, thereby justifying the struggles of the anti-Communist opposition, as well as of the Vietcong against puppet regimes which have no popular support and are maintained solely by American armed might and financial aid.

On February 26 of last year, addressing the Senate shortly after the rigged South Vietnamese elections and the sentencing to years at hard labor of the defeated non-Communist opponents of the Thieu-Ky ticket (it was as if President Nixon after his victory had ordered Mr. Johnson and Mr. Humphrey to the chain gang!), I made a specific recommendation to the President. It appeared in the *Congressional Record* under the heading, "One Possible Solution to the Vietnam Dilemma," and follows:

Recommendations for extrication of the United States from its Vietnamese folly are not the responsibility of those who for years have dissented from United States policy in Vietnam. It is the responsibility of those who got us into the Southeast Asia mess.

However, if President Johnson really wants to get the United States out of the morass in Vietnam, and save us from ever-mounting and ever-deepening disaster and the increasing slaughter of the flower of our youth and of thousands of Vietnamese noncombatants, his opportunity is here and now.

He could go on nationwide radio and television and, in effect, say to the American people:

My fellow citizens, I have tried for four years and my predecessors have tried for a decade previously to bring a semblance of self-government and democracy to the people of South Vietnam. It has become clear beyond peradventure that it is not their desire, and that the United States, despite its prodigious efforts in manpower and money, and the sacrifice of thousands of American lives, cannot achieve these desired results for them.

I have today ordered the unconditional cessation of all bombing of North Vietnam and of all offensive operations in South Vietnam. In addition, I have directed there be an immediate in-place cease-fire in South Vietnam on the part of the United States and I have requested the South Vietnamese Armed Forces to do likewise, with only defensive action authorized. I have called upon the forces of the National Liberation Front and of North Vietnam in South Vietnam to do the same. It is my purpose, which I now declare, to initiate a phased military withdrawal which should be completed within a year. In the meantime, behind the shield of American military forces with the leverage afforded by U.S. military and economic aid, U.S. representatives in South Vietnam will insist that the Thieu-Ky government broaden the base of its government to include their non-Communist opponents, represented in large measure by those whom they have now jailed and put in protective custody, and that this broadened South Vietnamese Government begin immediate negotiations with the National Liberation Front so that all these Vietnamese components can work out their own destinies.

In addition, I have directed our Ambassador to the United Nations to work with other nations there to find places of refuge in other lands for those who would not want to live in South Vietnam under the new regime which will be formed and I will ask the Congress for such additional authority as may be needed to admit such refugees to the United States and to assist in their resettlement elsewhere.

Further, I have instructed our Ambassadors to Great Britain, the Soviet Union, Canada, India and Poland to propose a greatly strengthened International Control Commission to supervise any elections to be held in South Vietnam to obtain an expression of the people's will.

The United States will assist in the reconstruction and rehabilitation of the burned villages, destroyed buildings and defoliated fields, and give suitable fiscal assistance to economic development. But our military efforts will cease. We will make every effort to assist the people of both North and South Vietnam to establish whatever form of government they can develop.

Here lies a solution which both Americans and Vietnamese, I am confident, will welcome.

This proposal in substance — with a few minor emendations because of changed conditions and its enunciation by a different President — is as valid for President Nixon today as when I proposed it to President Johnson fourteen months ago. President Johnson, of course, turned a deaf ear to it as to all other proposals for U.S. extrication. Instead, he extricated himself by announcing his withdrawal from office, a move which averted his certain defeat at the November elections.

This withdrawal was a confession of error even if he could not bring himself to admit such. He was lucky to have escaped impeachment proceedings which might have been his not undeserved fate, because of his betrayal of his campaign pledges, but was never a possibility because a supine Congress with its Democratic majority was a *particeps criminis* in the whole Southeast Asian affair.

Johnson's withdrawal, however, diminished the tension at home and allayed the mounting opposition to the war based on the hope that the "peace talks" in Paris could bring peace. This is an utterly vain hope because the premises of the two adversaries are diametrically opposed and irreconcilable. We have proceeded on the premise that we are there to repel aggression. Our adversaries maintain that the United States is the aggressor—a view substantiated by an objective review of the facts, many of them kept from the American people. That being so, our adversaries will naturally insist that we withdraw from Asia and let Asians settle their own problems. I doubt whether this proposition is negotiable and that peace by negotiation will be achieved. We should ask ourselves by what right we are there: what we have to gain by maintaining that presence, and whether the price is worth the costs—human, material and spiritual—which will haunt us for generations.

As for the secondary justification for our military intrusion to Southeast Asia— we must halt communism—it should be clear by now that we are actually aiding communism; that if the rulers of Communist Russia and Communist China desire our nation's debilitation and downfall, they could not devise a policy more likely to achieve that objective than the one our country is pursuing. To date, neither the Russians nor the Chinese have committed a single soldier to combat. And if our aim was to prevent the southward expansion of mainland China we have pursued the worst possible policy: we have weakened and sought to destroy Vietnam, which has been hostile to the Chinese for centuries and would fight their aggression as it has successively fought that of the French, the Japanese and the Americans.

What would be the consequences of a unilateral American withdrawal? It would not be "scuttle and run." A phased withdrawal would require months and could be replaced by a nation-wide coalition government more responsive to the Vietnamese Nationalist aspirations.

Would there be a blood bath? One is going on now and it will continue as long as the United States clings to its present policies. We can be confident that long before our withdrawal was far advanced the few hundred corrupt Vietnamese officials would have retired to Paris or the Riviera, to enjoy in luxury and ease the fortunes they have filched from our bounty. If some thousands of others would prefer to leave Vietnam, it would pay handsomely to arrange for their relocation and sustenance, if necessary for life, in other climes. It would be far less costly and more humane than the present $3 billion monthly military bill.

The others—the peasantry—would be absorbed and return to the life they had anticipated in the independent countries of Laos, Cambodia, and reunited Vietnam which the Geneva Agreements predicated and we had agreed to support.

President Nixon has the opportunity to end the war and end it honorably by readherence to principles upon which our nation was founded and through which it grew to greatness until a faulty leadership began to abandon them and got us into the present tragic disaster. That disaster – already great – will only be magnified and intensified unless President Nixon reverses the policy that has brought our nation to unfathomable depths. The Congress, too, has a responsibility to change its course and stop voting the military authorization and appropriations which have supported Presidential misleadership.

WILLIAM L. SHIRER

The Hubris of a President January 22, 1973

William Shirer, a foreign correspondent in Europe for two decades, was reporting in Berlin during the time he recalls in this piece. The best known of his many books are *Berlin Diary* and *The Rise and Fall of the Third Reich*.

Though Richard Nixon does not have the dictatorial power of Adolf Hitler – at least, not yet – he has shown in Vietnam that he has the awesome means, unrestrained by any hand, and the disposition to be just as savage in his determination to massacre and destroy the innocent people of any small nation which refuses to bow to his dictates and which is powerless to retaliate.

And apparently the majority of the American people, like the Germans under Hitler, couldn't care less. While Nixon was celebrating the festivities of the Prince of Peace by his reckless, bloody, paranoiac bombing of Hanoi, our God-fearing citizens were preoccupied with the Washington Redskins and the Miami Dolphins fighting their way to the Super Bowl, and seemed unmoved by the barbarism of their President and its horrible consequences for his victims.

I lived through a similar barbarism in Germany, when Hitler unleashed his terror bombing to force certain foreign peoples to do his bidding. I never thought it could happen here at home – even under a Nixon. No one of any consequence in Nazi Germany publicly protested, but at least the Germans had some excuse. To have spoken out might have cost a man his head – or at the very least the horrors of a concentration camp. But no American, watching the results of this President's violence over the Christmas holidays, viewing on his TV tube the shattered hospital in Hanoi, reading in his newspaper of the devastation Nixon was unleashing on the homes and streets of peaceful citizens, could have been restrained by such fears.

Yet, who, at no personal risk, denounced the monstrous crime? Not a single official in government, very few in the Congress, a few from labor and no one from big business, and not one notable churchman, Protestant or Catholic. There was not a peep from the President's friends among the clergy: no sound from the Rev. Billy Graham, the Rev. Norman Vincent Peale, or Cardinal Cooke (not even after the Pope had raised his voice against the bombing).

Perhaps this unconcern is due in part to the peculiar luck of Americans. Unlike the inhabitants of every other major country and scores of small ones, we have never been bombed, and hence cannot feel in our own flesh and minds the sufferings of those on whom our President wreaks his vengeance. As one who experienced to some extent in Germany the bombing by the British, and later in England the bombing by the Germans – it was minor, compared to what we have done in Indochina – I rejoiced that Americans had been spared that ordeal.

But no longer. It now occurs to me that, until we go through it ourselves, until our people cower in the shelters of New York, Washington, Chicago, Los Angeles and elsewhere while the buildings collapse overhead and burst into flames, and dead bodies hurtle about and, when it is over for the day or the night, emerge in the rubble to find some of their dear ones mangled, their homes gone, their hospitals, churches, schools demolished – only after that gruesome experience will we realize what we are inflicting on the people of Indochina and especially what we did over Christmas week to the common people of Hanoi.

Does one American in 1,000 or in 100,000, realize that, whereas the Germans dropped 80,000 tons of bombs on Britain in more than five years of war (and we thought it was barbaric), *we* dropped *100,000* tons on Indochina in the single month of last November, when Nixon restricted the bombing because of the Paris "peace" talks; and that under Lyndon Johnson and Richard Nixon we have dropped a total of *7 million* tons of bombs on Vietnam, Cambodia and Laos – vastly more than we and the British let loose on Germany and Japan together in World War II? It was done in the name of "a just peace," of course. Has not Nixon said it dozens of times, his face on the TV screen frozen in unctuousness, as he sent his troops to invade a new country – Cambodia, Laos – or as he ordered his bombers to resume unloading tens of thousands of tons of more lethal bombs on a country which had no Air Force with which to defend itself?

Hitler, a bully also, mouthed the same hypocrisy. As François-Poncet, the French ambassador in Berlin, remarked after the Fuehrer sent his warriors out on the first of his conquests at the very moment when he was showering Europe with a new offer of peace: "Hitler struck his adversary in the face, and then declared: 'I bring you proposals for peace!' "

Is that not what Nixon has done in Vietnam? Where else, since Hitler, has the head of government of a supposedly civilized people declared through a spokesman to his own people (on the eve of an election, to be sure) that "peace is at hand," that 99 per cent of the issues have been negotiated and that only three or four more days of talks are needed to tidy up the agreement, and then (after he is elected) struck the people he has been negotiating with "in good faith" with the most savage bombing in history—and put the blame on them?

I said that after experiencing at first hand the Nazi terror toward others, it never occurred to me that it could happen at home. Has it? To a certain extent? Just a beginning perhaps? Has Nixon shown that you don't need a totalitarian dictatorship like Hitler's to get by with murder, that you can do it in a democracy as long as the Congress and the people Congress is supposed to represent don't give a damn?

It can be extremely misleading to compare the Nazi regime in Germany with our own situation today. We are not a totalitarian dictatorship. The press, despite the Administration's assaults upon it, is still relatively free. Dissent, despite all the attempts of Nixon and his aides to silence it, is still heard. This article could never have been published under the Fuehrer. Nixon is no Hitler, though with his Christmas bombing he acted like one. The Americans could have thrown him out of office in November. The Germans, after the death of President Hindenburg in 1934, were stuck with Hitler. They had had a parliament, the Reichstag, which, if its members had showed any guts or wisdom, might have restrained him or even overthrown him in his first months of power in 1933, before he tricked it into committing suicide. We have an elected Congress, which had the constitutional power to prevent our Presidents from taking the nation into war in Vietnam and the power to take it out quickly. It abdicated that power. Like the Reichstag, its members were partly tricked (by such things as the Tonkin Gulf frame-up and other Presidential deceits) and like the Germans parliament its members have thus far lacked the guts or the wisdom to exercise the power the Constitution gave them.

Here begin the similarities. Are there others? One, I think, is in the attitude of Nixon toward the people. "The average American," he told a Washington *Star* reporter on the eve of his re-election, "is just like the child in the family." The implication was that the average citizen could easily be manipulated by Papa. It is, of course, a form of contempt for the common people. Disraeli, to whom Nixon compared himself in the same interview, had it, but surely the great Presidents —Jefferson, Lincoln, Wilson, Roosevelt, Truman, even Eisenhower—did not. Hitler, for all his professed love of the German people and his attempt to make of them the Master Race, had a profound contempt for them. He thought they were simpletons, at least politically—you could do anything with them. He called them, as Trevor-Roper has pointed out, *Dickshaedel, Querschaedel, Dummkoepfe*—blockheads and ninnies without political sense. But he would add: "Even stupid races can accomplish something, given good leadership." Once at a Nuremberg party rally, when asked to explain why the German masses became so delirious at these pageants, especially when he spoke, Hitler told a group of American correspondents – off the record – in words almost identical to Nixon's, that it was because they were children at heart. "What luck for rulers," he exclaimed on another occasion, "that men do not think!"

And in these days I cannot help recalling an opinion vouched by one of Hitler's woman secretaries after his death. "Though Hitler," she recalled, "ranged over almost every field of thought, I nevertheless felt that something was missing. . . . It seems to me that his spate of words lacked the human note, the spiritual quality of a cultivated man. In his library he had no classic work, no single book on which the human spirit had left its trace."

There were other things in Nazi Germany which recent happenings in this country have forced me, at least, to recall:

(1) *Justice and the courts.* One day in 1936 Hans Frank, the Nazi Minister of Justice (who was later sentenced to death at Nuremberg and hanged), called in the members of the bench and gave them a little advice: "Say to yourself at every decision that you make: 'How would the Fuehrer decide in my place?'" One wonders sometimes – I mean no disrespect to our judges – if some of the eminent jurists appointed by the President, especially those on the Supreme Court, do not at the moment of decision say to themselves: "How would President Nixon decide in my place?" Nixon's Front Four on the High Court, Burger, Blackmun, Rehnquist and Powell – joined often by "Whizzer" White, Kennedy's only contribution to that bench – have shown a teamwork that must be the envy of Coach Allen's fearsome Front Four, and they have used it increasingly to limit freedoms supposedly guaranteed by the First Amendment, to take but one example. In doing so they cannot have failed to please Nixon. Did he not boast that he appointed only those who shared his philosophy? Most other Presidents have been proud of trying to keep a balance on the Court.

(2) *Assaults on the freedom of the press, First Amendment guarantees, dissent.* Obviously we have not fallen as far as Nazi Germany, but are we not on our way? Have not Nixon and his minions carried on for four years an assault on our press freedoms and on the right to dissent – and not without success? They have intimidated the networks, threatened TV station owners with loss of their licenses if they do not, in effect, censor network news critical of the Administration, and successfully gone to court to induce the Supreme Court to rule by 5 to 4 that the First Amendment does not give reporters the right to protect their confidential sources – a telling blow to our press freedoms. On the other hand, the Administration, by propaganda, deceit, evasion, playing favorites, and by expert use of the power of the White House to make news and control it, has done very well in putting its own story over in the press. But this has not satisfied Nixon.

I sometimes wonder if he, and Klein, would envy the way the press was handled in Berlin in the days when I was working there. Every morning the editors of the capital's newspapers and the correspondents of out-of-town German journals were made to assemble at the Propaganda Ministry and told by Goebbels or one of his aides what news to print and what to suppress, how to write the news and headline it, and what editorials were to be written that day. To avoid any misunderstanding, a daily written Directive was furnished at the end of the oral instructions. For smaller provincial papers and periodicals without representatives in Berlin, Directives were sent by wire or mail. Radio (there was no TV then) was handled separately but similarly. Every editor, reporter, newscaster and commentator knew each day exactly what to write or say, and did it. Very simple and effective. Nixon's task obviously is more difficult, but he keeps plugging. As one of our great historians, Henry Steele Commager, wrote recently: "Never before in our history . . . has government so audaciously violated the spirit of the constitutional guarantee of freedom of the press."

(3) *Terror bombing, "targeting military objectives only," and the lies about them.* Here we come closer to the Nazi example. Hitler invented terror bombing (unless you count Mussolini's puny effort in Ethiopia), starting with Guernica in Spain and going on to Warsaw, Rotterdam and Coventry. Nixon has been an apt pupil, increasing the terror by more and bigger bombs, but sticking to the same lies about "targeting military objectives" and the same denials of damage to non-military objectives. Nixon's aides, Ronald Ziegler at the White House and Jerry Friedheim at the Pentagon, seem more adept at this business than even Joseph Goebbels. More adept and just as arrogant.

Ziegler, speaking for Nixon, offered two justifications for the Christmas resumption of the bombing—both offensive to the truth and to an American's intelligence. First, he linked the bombing to the threat of another Communist offensive: "We are not going to allow the peace talks to be used as a cover for another offensive." But he offered no evidence of an offensive, and the American Command in Saigon admitted it knew of none pending, nor did anyone in Washington. Next, Ziegler, speaking for his silent boss, declared that Nixon was "determined" to continue his bombing until Hanoi decided to resume negotiations "in a spirit of good will and in a constructive attitude." In the Hitler-Nixon double-talk that meant, "until Hanoi agrees to accept a peace that we dictate."

Jerry Friedheim at the Pentagon was worse—he was pure Goebbels. Twice, on December 27 and 29, he denied that we had damaged Hanoi's Bach Mai Hospital and attributed the reports to "enemy propaganda." The effrontery of this staggered a man who had listened to Goebbels' lies time after time. That was because, two days before the first denial, Telford Taylor, a distinguished lawyer, a retired brigadier general and our chief prosecutor at Nuremberg, had cabled *The New York Times* from Hanoi an eyewitness description of the bombed-out hospital. Moreover, millions of Americans had seen on TV Japanese and Swedish films of the hospital's devastation. Even when Friedheim finally admitted, on January 2, that "some limited accidental damage" had been done to the hospital, he suggested that it might have been caused by "North Vietnamese ordnance or aircraft."

I say Friedheim was pure Goebbels (and like him probably lying at the master's orders) because, after a German submarine had torpedoed the British liner *Athenia* on the first day of World War II, I heard Goebbels, first at a press conference and then over the air, deny categorically that the Germans had sunk the boat and then accuse the British of having done it. I will pass over Friedheim's bland assertion that if an American POW camp had been hit, as reported, Hanoi would be held responsible—"under the Geneva Convention." But it did remind me of Hitler's declaration on the mornings he attacked Norway, and later Holland and Belgium, that if they resisted they would be held responsible for the bloodshed. After Friedheim's performance, according to *The New York Times* of January 5, he was awarded the Defense Department Medal for Distinguished Public Service, with the citation: "He has provided with faultless professionalism clear, concise, accurate and timely information concerning the worldwide activities of the Department of Defense."

Did the President become enraged when Henry Kissinger returned from Paris without the agreement he had demanded and in his fury ("You can't do that to Richard Nixon!") order the resumption of the murderous bombing—Christmas or no? We do not know for sure, and probably never will, though Washington seethed with rumors, unconfirmed, that such was the case. Perhaps "high-ranking U.S. officials in Saigon," as an A.P. dispatch called them, were, for once, telling the truth when they said, according to the news agency, that "the ultimate purpose of the bombing was to punish Hanoi," and that "President Thieu had been told that President Nixon's strategy is to devastate North Vietnam."

It recalled a scene, which *was* confirmed, on the night of March 26, 1941, when news reached Hitler that the pro-Nazi government of Yugoslavia had been toppled and replaced by one that might not do the Fuehrer's bidding. The news, according to some of those present in the chancellery, threw Hitler into one of the wildest rages of his life. He took it, they said, as a personal affront—you couldn't do that to Hitler. He called in his generals and ordered them "to destroy Yugoslavia militarily and as a nation"—a stenographer noted down his words. "Yugoslavia," he added, "would be crushed with unmerciful harshness." He ordered Goering to "destroy Belgrade in attacks by waves" of bombers. That was done; the town was razed. Like large parts of Hanoi these past days.

It could have been, of course, that Nixon made his Yuletide decision to devastate Hanoi in a completely different mood—in a moment of icy calculation. Hitler was in that kind of mood on September 29, 1941 as his armies neared Moscow and Leningrad. His Directive to his army commanders that day began: "The

Fuehrer has decided to have Leningrad wiped off the face of the earth. The intention is to raze it to the ground by artillery and continuous air attack. The problem of survival of the population (3 million) is one which cannot and should not be solved by us." He issued a second Directive to the same effect for Moscow. Is it possible that Nixon issued a similar Directive for Hanoi in the same cold-blooded mood? The A.P. report from Saigon indicates the possibility.

(4) Hitler got by with murder because there was no restraining hand upon him—from any source. Did any hand in Washington try to restrain Nixon when he ordered the invasion of Cambodia and Laos, and especially when he ordered the devastating Christmas bombing of Hanoi? We do not know. But we know he did not consult the Congress. He did not confide in it or in the people.

Perhaps we are experiencing here what the Greeks called *hubris*, the sin of overweening pride. It has brought the downfall of so many conquerors—of the Greeks themselves, the Romans, the French under Napoleon, the Germans under Wilhelm II and then Hitler. And we are seeing in Washington what I saw in Berlin in the Nazi time—how power tends to corrupt and absolute power corrupts absolutely.

BARBARA L. BAER and GLENNA MATTHEWS

The Women of the Boycott   February 23, 1974

As a young lawyer in Los Angeles in the 1930s, Carey McWilliams had tried to improve the living and working conditions of migrant farm laborers. It was natural, therefore, that during his years as editor, *The Nation* published some of the earliest pieces about Cesar Chavez and the struggle to establish United Farm Workers.

Los Altos, Calif.
Dolores Huerta, vice president of the United Farm Workers, was standing on a flat-bed truck beside Cesar Chavez. She didn't show her eight-and-a-half months' pregnancy, but she looked very tired from the days and nights of organizing cross-country travel plans for the hundreds of people who were now waiting in the parking lot alongside the union headquarters at Delano, Calif. She leaned down and talked with children, her own and others. Small children held smaller ones, fathers carried babies on their shoulders.

The parking lot was filled with cars, trucks and buses, decorated with banners and signs. People sang strike songs and Chavez spoke to them about the boycott. Dolores listened intently, nodding, brushing her straight black hair away from her face from time to time and smiling softly at the children. A priest blessed the cars and buses whose destinations read like a history of the great American migrations—in reverse: *"Hasta la Victoria*—Miami!"; *"Viva la Huelga*—Cleveland!"; *"Hasta La Boycott*—Pittsburgh!"

Five years ago there would have been nothing unusual about hundreds of families assembling to move out with the crops, but this time the decision to pull up roots was different. The people on the dusty blacktop were UFW members and until a week earlier they had had a commitment to stay in the area. The union had made it possible for most to have a house or rent one, send their children to a school all year, get medical care. Most of these people had spent the summer on strike lines or in jails. Then, within one week of Cesar Chavez's announcement of a second national boycott of grapes, they had sold their houses and everything they could not carry with them to buy the cars, winter clothing, whatever else they might need for years outside the San Joaquin Valley. They were ready to leave by the last day in August.

We had come to Delano specifically to meet Dolores Huerta. As we waited for the caravan to leave, she told us to look well at the other women. These women were "nonmaterialistic." They packed up their families and pledged them to stay out on the boycott until the union got its grape and lettuce contracts back. If the woman of a family refuses, Dolores said, the family either breaks up or is lost to the union. Families are the most important part of the UFW because a family can stick it out in a strange place, on $5 a week per person, the wage everyone in the union is paid (plus expenses). Often the leaders would be women because women were strong in the home and becoming stronger in the union. The women decided the fate of the union, Dolores told us.

Chavez and Dolores Huerta knew the people they were talking about—and what they were asking of UFW members they asked of themselves first. All summer the union had fought to win second contracts from the grape growers in southern and central California valleys who had signed with them first in 1970. But as each contract expired, the Teamsters signed up the growers immediately—thirty at once around Delano. Chavez called the contracts illegal, "sweetheart agreements," because the workers had not voted on their representatives. Chavez called for pickets on the Teamsters-contracted fields. County courts, sympathetic to the growers, enjoined the UFW strikers from effective picketing. Thousands of clergy and students came to support the farm workers and some were jailed. Jailings and trials went on all summer.

Farm workers have never won a major strike in the fields because they are not protected by the National Labor Relations Act, whose provisions guarantee the right to picket; because growers and their allies have used violence and, most important, because there is an unlimited scab labor force across the Mexican border. There is no way to win a strike when men will scab at any price.

Toward the end of the summer the picket lines became violent. In separate incidents in the town of Arvin, two union men were killed. A sheriff struck Nagi Daifullah, a Yemenite, on the head with a flashlight. Juan de la Cruz was shot as he came off the picket line.

The United Farm Workers would not fight violence with violence. When the funerals were over, Chavez called for all strikers to get ready to leave on a second national boycott. The first had lasted five years. This one, though better organized, was more complicated: there were now grapes, wines, lettuce and Teamsters as well as the growers.

By noon the dust had settled in a low haze on this crossroads between vineyards—the stucco buildings the UFW calls "Forty Acres." The union offices were nearly empty, though telephones kept ringing. We went into a bare room with a long table to talk to Dolores Huerta.

Dolores was the first person Chavez called upon to work with him organizing farm workers into a union. That was more than a dozen years ago. She became the UFW's first vice president, its chief negotiator, lobbyist, boycott strategist and public spokeswoman. And in partnership, Dolores and Chavez formulated the UFW's nonviolent and democratic philosophy.

In 1955, Fred Ross brought Dolores Huerta to a meeting of the Community Service Organization in Stockton, and she has been in political action ever since. Ross, working in San Jose with Saul Alinsky, had taken Cesar Chavez to his first CSO meeting there. Both Dolores and Cesar say they owe their present lives to Fred Ross, and they keep drawing the thin, spare man, now 60, away from his book about the union and back into UFW struggles.

When Dolores began organizing, she already had six children and was pregnant with a seventh. Nearly twenty years later, there are ten children, and Dolores is still so slim and graceful that we find it hard to imagine her in her youth, the age of her daughter. She has not saved herself for anything, has let life draw and strain her to a fine intensity. It hasn't made her tense, harsh or dry. She shouts a lot and laughs with people. She tells us she has a sharp tongue but it seems to us she has an elusiveness of keeping her own counsel, mixed with complete directness and willingness to spend hours talking. Her long black hair is drawn back from high cheek bones, her skin is tanned reddish from the sun on the picket line, and in her deep brown eyes is a constant humor that relieves her serious manner.

Contradictions in her life must have taken, and continue to take, a toll: her many children, Catholic faith and a divorce, her high-strung nerves and the delicate health we know she disregards. It must be that her work, the amount she has accomplished and the spirit she instills in others, have healed the breaks. We talked to Dolores Huerta for several hours in the union offices when the last cars had left Delano.

"I had a lot of doubts to begin with, but I had to act in spite of my conflict between my family and my commitment. My biggest problem was not to feel guilty about it. I don't any more, but then, everybody used to lay these guilt trips on me, about what a bad mother I was, neglecting my children. My own relatives were the hardest, especially when my kids were small; you know, they were stair steps—I had six and one on the way when I started—and I was driving around Stockton with all these little babies in the car, the different diaper changes for each one. It's always hard, not just because you're a woman but because it's hard to really make that commitment. It's in your own head. I'm sure my own life was better because of my involvement. I was able to go through a lot of very serious personal problems and survive them because I had something else to think about. Otherwise, I might have gotten engulfed in my personal difficulties and, I think, I probably would have gone under.

"If I hadn't met Fred Ross then, I don't know if I ever would have been organizing. People don't realize their own worth and I wouldn't have realized what I could do unless someone had shown faith in me. At that time we were organizing against racial discrimination—the way Chicanos were treated by police, courts, politicians. I had taken the *status quo* for granted, but Fred said it could change. So I started working.

"The way I first got away from feeling guilty about neglecting my family was a religious cop-out, I guess. I had serious doubts whether I was doing the right thing, giving kids a lousy supper to go to a council meeting. So I would pray and say, if what I was doing wasn't bearing fruit, then it would be a sign I shouldn't be doing it. When good things came out of my work, when it bore fruit, I took that as a sign I should continue and that the sacrifices my family and I were making were justified.

"Of course, I had no way of knowing what the effects on my kids would be. Now, ten years later, I can look back and say it's O.K. because my kids turned out fine, even though at times they had to fend for themselves, other people took care of them, and so on. I have a kind of proof: my ex-husband took one of my kids, Fidel, during the first strike. We didn't have any food or money, there was no way I could support him. He was eating all right, like all the strikers' kids, but on donations. So my ex-husband took the boy until he was 11. I got him back just last year. He had a lot of nice clothes and short hair, but he was on the verge of a nervous breakdown. When my ex-husband tried to take another boy, the judge ruled against him. You could see the difference when you compared the two kids—one was skinny and in raggedy clothes and with long hair, but real well, happy. Fidel is coming back now to the way he used to be, and he's got long hair too.

"We haven't had a stable place to live—I haven't been anywhere for more than two months, except in New York on the boycott—since 1970. But taking my kids all over the states made them lose their fear of people, of new situations. Most of us have to be mobile. But the kids are in school, they go to school and work on the boycott. Even the 10-year-olds are out on the boycott in the cities.

"My kids are totally politicized mentally and the whole idea of working without materialistic gain has made a great difference in the way they think. When one of our supporters came to take my daughter to buy new clothes in New York, she was really embarrassed. We never buy new clothes, you know, we get everything out of the donations. She said, 'Mama, the lady wanted to buy me a lot of new things, but I told her they didn't fit me.' You know, she came home with a couple of little things to please the lady, but she didn't want to be avaricious. Her values are people and not things. It has to be that way—that's why everyone who works full-time for the union gets $5 a week, plus gas money and whatever food and housing they need to live on, live on at the minimum they can."

How has it happened, we asked, that in the very culture from which the word *"machismo"* derives, the women, have more visible, vocal and real power of decision than women elsewhere? Dolores told us that the union had made a conscious effort to involve women, given them every chance for leadership, but that the men did not always want it.

"I really believe what the feminists stand for. There is an undercurrent of discrimination against women in our own organization, even though Cesar goes out of his way to see that women have leadership positions. Cesar always felt strongly about women in the movement. This time, no married man went out on the boycott unless he took his wife. We find day care in the cities so the women can be on the picket line with the men. It's a great chance for participation. Of course we take it for granted now that women will *want* to be as involved as men. But in the beginning, at the first meetings, there were only men. And a certain discrimination still exists. Cesar—and other men—treat us differently. Cesar's stricter with the women, he demands more of us. But the more I think of it, the more I'm convinced that the women have gotten stronger because he expects so much of us. You could even say it's gotten lopsided . . . women are stronger than the men.

"Women in the union are great on the picket line. More staying power, and we're nonviolent. One of the reasons our union *is* nonviolent is that we want our women and children involved, and we stay nonviolent because of the women and children.

"One time the Teamsters were trying to provoke a fight to get our pickets arrested. Forty, fifty police were waiting with paddy wagons. We had about 300 people. The Teamsters attacked the line with 2 X 4 boards. I was in charge of the line. We made the men go to the back and placed the women out in front. The Teamsters beat our arms but they couldn't provoke the riot they wanted, and we didn't give in. The police stood there, watched us get beaten; the D.A. wouldn't even let us sign a *complaint*. But we had gained a lot of respect from our men. Excluding women, protecting them, keeping women at home, that's the middle-class way. Poor people's movements have always had whole families on the line, ready to move at a moment's notice, with more courage because that's all we had. It's a class not an ethnic thing."

We knew that the women of the UFW found themselves in a unique situation. Unlike the sex-determined employment of the urban poor, the jobs of farm worker women and men had always been the same. They *had* to work, but it wasn't housework or even factory work, separating them from men. Women had picked, pruned and packed in fields, cannery and shed side by side with men. But would the women decide to let the men organize the union? Dolores Huerta had spoken for herself alone; the resolution of conflicts between family and political, union action, would come to each UFW woman in her own terms.

Lupe Ortiz has been an organizer in a union field office since she left school. She is about 25, a natural leader, with a quality of making people laugh to get work done. Yet for all her big voice and humor, she didn't know how women could assert themselves at home as they did at work. What she told us seemed the reverse of our more familiar, middle-class feminism; here, by contrast, a woman insisted on work equality, and in large part received it, but she wouldn't challenge the traditional order of the family.

As Lupe directed her male co-workers in Spanish, she expounded to us in English the differences between "Anglo" and Chicano women. "You Anglo women, you do it your way, but I don't ever want to be equal to my husband."

"You get the same salary; don't you want the same voice at home?"

"In work, but not at home. No, at home you have to know when to open your . mouth and when not to. You have to learn you can't go places men go, like bars."

"Don't you want it to change? For men to act as though you're equal?"

"It's not exactly equality. It's our culture. I don't want our Chicano culture to change. Let men have the say-so." Lupe laughed, this time openly, as she looked at the men in the office. "I bet *you* split up with your husbands more often than we do because you make head-on conflicts."

Ester Yurande, a generation older than Lupe, showed a generation difference in her appearance: she was as carefully, femininely dressed, with lovely long hair and glittering earrings, as Lupe had been rugged in jeans, sweatshirt and close-cropped curls. Ester had worked in the fields until she became the bookkeeper for the Medical Clinic at Forty Acres. She had been a UFW member from the start, been jailed in the early 1960s. How, we asked her, had the union changed the lives of the women who came to the clinic?

"A doctor treats us with dignity now. We don't get charity when we're having a baby, we get care. It's to do with pride. Mexican women around here used to do what the men said, but Dolores Huerta was our example of something different. We could see one of our leaders was a woman, and she was always out in front, and she would talk back. She wasn't scared of anything."

Dolores herself had told us that she didn't hesitate to argue. "You know, Cesar has fired me fifteen times, and I must have quit about ten. Then, we'll call each other up and get back to work. There have been times when I should have fought harder. When he tells me now, 'you're getting really impossible, arguing all the time,' I say, 'you haven't seen anything yet. I'm going to get worse.' Because from now on I'm going to fight really, really hard when I believe something. There have been times I haven't. I can be wrong, too, but at least it will be on the record how I felt."

When we asked Ester how she felt about fighting back herself, she didn't want to answer. We had become outsiders once more, women who didn't comprehend her way. Men have accepted strong women in the union, but there remains deeply engrained in these women a respect for their men's *machismo*.

There is a religious fervor about the union, which has made its members call it La Causa. Perhaps the closeness of the Catholic Church to the movement is one more reason women have been able to identify with its goals. The UFW women have brought their personal strength and their faith to the union; the union in turn has reinforced and completed their lives by giving them a direct form of action and an ideal.

Dolores, very religious herself, told us that women were most important to the union because a woman determined the fate of a whole family. If a *wife* was for the union, Dolores said, then the husband would be, too. If she was not, if she was afraid or too attached to her home and possessions, then the family usually stayed out of the union, or it broke up. There had been a number of broken marriages that had cost the union the strength of a united family.

Maria-Luisa Rangel did not want to go out on the first boycott. At that time—in 1968—many women were staying in California while the men lived together in boycott houses in Eastern cities. The Rangels, parents of eight children, had saved enough money to own part of a family store, and they owned their home in the small town of Dinuba, near Fresno. They would have to part with both if they went to Detroit for two years. Hijino Rangel was determined to go. So Maria-Luisa went. Looking at her unsoftened features, her inaccessible but not unfriendly black eyes, we sensed the strength that had enabled her then to wrench herself away from everything she owned and keep her family together. She had a hard time in Detroit; she didn't know much English, the climate was completely strange and she had two operations in the city. But when they returned to the valley in 1970, the Rangels knew that they had helped win the boycott that secured the 180 union contracts with grape growers of the Coachella and San Joaquin Valleys. And the experience had worked on Maria-Luisa. She spoke out as a representative of the union about the present boycott. "It's just like it was then. The struggle is for the people to win, not the growers but the people. I know it, and *they* — the growers — know it."

Women have paid different prices for making the union part of their lives. The 100 women who spent many weeks in Fresno jails last summer (for violating anti-picket injunctions) ranged from minors to great-grandmothers. There were field workers and nuns, lay religious women and union officials. For some of the Chicano women, it was a reminder of previous jailings when no nuns had been present and the guards had beaten "the Mexicans." For others, it was the first time, and almost a vacation from their daily lives. Work-hardened baked hands became almost soft. All the women shared their experiences — the farm workers told city women like Dorothy Day, editor of the *Catholic Worker*, about their struggle, and learned from her about women's movements in the cities and in the Church.

Maximina de la Cruz and her husband, Juan, were born around 1910 in Mexico. Juan entered America on the bracero program, picked crops in Texas, and then in New Mexico, where Maximina worked in a clothing factory. They married, moved with their son to the San Joaquin Valley in 1960, and joined the union during the first strikes in 1965. Juan de la Cruz was killed last summer by a man who fired his .22-caliber rifle into the picket line from a truck. Maximina told us she remembers that many times the growers or the Teamsters put on deputy badges, joined in beating the farm workers, and then arrested them on grounds of self-defense. The man who shot de la Cruz has entered a plea in the valley courts that he shot defending himself from the picket line.

Maximina was observing the thirty-day mourning period when we came to her home in Arvin. Hearing us arrive, she and her mother, Porfiria Coronado, met us at their gate, and without a word, in the dark, she took us, with hands that felt like warm, worked clay, into her living room. Candles beneath pictures of saints and near a wedding photograph were the only light. As the night went on, she told us of her early life of hardship, the many moves, purchase of their small house, and the changes the UFW had made in their lives.

"We *know* the growers. They want to go back to the old days, the way it was before we had a union, when we got a dollar an hour, no toilets or water in the fields, no rest periods, and they could kick you out without any pay for not picking fast enough. A whole family earned less than one union man today. They fought us hard and dirty each time, but we didn't give in. We won't. This time we're out in the cities again to tell the good people what it is like to work here. I'm staying on here, and I'll be back at work in the fields, but not until the union gets its contracts back. I might have to wait a while but I know people will understand and help us win back our union. I'm proud to be a woman here. Juan was proud of the union. You know, on the picket lines, we were so gay, peaceful and *attrativas,* even the grandmothers. Until *they* shot their gun."

Except for the Catholic Church, the powerful and wealthy institutions of California have opposed the UFW at one time or another. Grower-biased central valley law enforcement and the courts have made a mockery of legal institutions; agri-business has never given up trying to break the union through legislation; Gov. Ronald Reagan has been photographed eating scab grapes; even the U.S. Government helped the growers by buying non-union lettuce in great quantity to ship to troops in Vietnam. Yet the greater the odds, the more the union has come to represent poor people against the rich and mighty. Dolores Huerta fights best when the situation looks bleakest. She attributes her refusal to give up to her mother's influence.

"My mother was one of those women who do a lot. She was divorced, so I never really understood what it meant for a woman to take a back seat to a man. My brothers would say, 'Mama spoiled you,' because she pushed me to the front. When I was first involved in organizing, my mom would watch the kids for me, but then she got involved herself and she couldn't baby-sit any more. She won the first prize in Stockton for registering voters and increasing membership.

"To tell the truth, I was prejudiced against women for a long time and I didn't realize it. I always liked to be with men because I thought they were more interesting and the women only talked of kids. But I was afraid of women, too. It was in the union that I lost my fear of being around women. Or put it this way, I learned to respect women. Cesar's wife, Helen Chavez, helped me more than anyone else. She was really committed to home. Actually, Cesar's toughest organizing jobs were on Helen, his wife, and Richard, his brother. They wanted to lead their own lives. Helen kept saying she wouldn't do anything, and she's so strong and stubborn you couldn't convince her to change her mind. She took care of the food and the kids, and while Cesar was organizing she was supporting them, too, working in the fields. Cesar, keeping his *machismo* intact in those days, would make her come home and cook dinner.

"We wanted her to learn the credit union bookkeeping. We yelled at her one night into the kitchen, 'You're going to be the assistant bookkeeper.' She yelled back, 'No, I won't either,' but we voted her the job. Boy was she mad! But you should see her books. We've been investigated a hundred times and they never find a mistake."

The union had to teach its members – farm workers with almost no education or training – the professional skills it required. Marie Sabadado, who directs the R. F. Kennedy Medical Plan, Helen Chavez, head of the credit union, and Dolores, chief negotiator and writer of labor contracts, taught themselves. Dolores made it sound almost easy to learn very specialized skills in a week's time.

"When Cesar put me in charge of negotiations in our first contract, I had never seen a contract before. I talked to labor people, I got copies of contracts and studied them for a week and a half, so I knew something when I came to the workers. Cesar almost fell over because I had my first contract all written and all the workers had voted on the proposals. He thought we ought to have an attorney, but really it was better to put the contracts in a simple language. I did all the negotiations myself for about five years. Women should remember this: be resourceful, you can do anything, whether you have experience or not. Cesar always says that the first education of people is how to be people and then the other things fall into place.

"I think women are particularly good negotiators because we have a lot of patience, and no big ego trips to overcome. Women are more tenacious and that helps a great deal. It unnerves the growers to negotiate with us. Cesar always wanted to have an *all-woman* negotiating team. Growers can't swear back at us or at each other. And then we bring in the ethical questions, like how our kids live. How can the growers really argue against what should be done for human beings just to save money?"

We knew everyone was immensely proud of the union services. We also knew that the legal staff (as well as the doctors and nurses at the clinic) were volunteer lawyers from the outside. In the past, the growers got rid of nascent farm-worker organizations by breaking them in the courts. The UFW has an excellent, tough legal staff. But to stay permanently with the union doctors and lawyers need to come from the farm workers themselves. The union will have to send its men and women out of the community for training. There has never been the luxury of a few years in which to do so, and there is a certain fear of becoming "corrupted" by the universities.

The United Farm Workers headquarters are located in Delano, between Bakersfield and Fresno, and also at La Paz, a town no larger than a half-block of post office, store and gas station, east of Bakersfield in the Tehachapi range. Union field offices lie in small towns in the central valleys. From anywhere in these valleys it is about three hours, north to San Francisco, or south to Los Angeles on any of the state's three parallel freeways. Meeting only union people, in their austere but clean and bright offices, we hadn't seen what local field-worker conditions were like. We took a look at some company towns by leaving the freeways and taking side roads at random into the fields.

Company towns are wholly dependent for their income on the prosperity and good will of the growers. Since the big growers are the last employers in America to escape collective bargaining, one can judge their civic responsibility by the looks of the town: boarded-up or gutted buildings, cracked sidewalks, decaying stores – they all show that the growers spend their profits on themselves. Only the bars, preserves of the men, where the wine is sold, do business.

Livingston is a company town of Gallo wines near Merced on Highway 99. Outside the town, the Gallo brothers haven't hidden their wealth. They have splendid houses, isolated even from one another, surrounded by velvety slopes leading to pools, tennis courts and greenhouses. Not far away, but well hidden, the Gallo workers live in company camps lost at dusty terminals of country roads in the shadow of enormous vats guarded by armed men. When we were there, a determined nucleus of UFW strikers who had refused to work under Gallo's new Teamster contract, had also refused to obey the grower's eviction notices. For that, they had been deprived of garbage collection and water.

Downtown Livingston seemed only slightly less bleak than the camps. Fifty people had gathered in front of the local courthouse for a silent protest against the imprisonment of fellow strikers. Aggie Rose, a former elementary school-teacher of Portuguese ancestry, was head of the union office. As she spoke to the men and women forming the procession, encouraging and exhorting them in Spanish and Portuguese to keep their spirits up, the intensity of her light eyes, her constantly moving thin figure, momentarily brought life back into the town. The line of marchers circled the courthouse for a while. Police in squad cars hovered along dark streets. There was nothing to do but disperse.

Dolores would soon be back in New York directing the East Coast boycott. She was determined that we understand, before we left, why the union would not be defeated, not even in Livingston.

"One of the reasons the growers are fighting us so hard is that they realize we're changing people, not just getting a paycheck for them. Without our militancy we wouldn't have a union. So we keep pushing our people, getting them out on other issues, like the tuition rise in California colleges, or the Presidential campaign. We had farm workers out door to door for McGovern. And when our people come back from the boycott, they will be stronger than ever."

We asked Dolores whether she had ever been scared, or lacked confidence in her ability to organize people.

"Of course. I've been afraid about everything until I did it. I started out every time not knowing what I was to do and scared to death. When Cesar first sent me to New York on the boycott it was the first time we'd done anything like that. There were no ground rules. I thought, 11 million people in New York, and I have to persuade them to stop buying grapes. Well, I didn't do it alone. When you need people, they come to you. You find a way . . . it gets easier all the time."

TODD GITLIN

SDS Around the Campfire   *October 22, 1977*

Todd Gitlin, author of *The Sixties: Years of Hope, Days of Rage,* was president of Students for a Democratic Society from 1963 to 1964.

One of the few things that *Newsweek* (September 5) and *People* (September 12) got right in their accounts of the late August reunion of Students for a Democratic Society was the irresistible fact that we met in a camp on the far side of Hell, Mich.

History does like some crude symbols. There was scarcely a person at this reunion who had not some time in the last ten years traversed a private hell within the collective catastrophe. SDS started out as an articulate political community for a generation of radicals; within a few years it became the central organization of the New Left, mobilized community organizations and anti-war projects, then learned fast to speak Marxese and finally went up in factional smoke. It was only seven years from the Port Huron Statement of 1962 ("We are people of this generation, bred in at least modest comfort, housed in universities, looking uncomfortably to the world we inherit") to SDS's 1969 crackup into Weathermen ("We are already [a working-class movement] if we put forward internationalist proletarian politics"), Revolutionary Youth Movement II (also supporting "the People's Republics of Korea and Albania"), and Progressive Labor (insisting on *its* true title to the vanguard of the proletariat). By the end, most of the membership were left out in the cold. During that long night of Vietnam, hundreds of thousands of students had passed through this organization, dreamed a radical dream and then watched it curdle into a nightmare.

By the time SDS broke apart, the original activist core—along with counterparts who had worked elsewhere in the New Left—had already been cast adrift. If politics meant the mania of the left-wing sects, perhaps they were not political any longer. Many became therapists, mystics, carpenters, developing crafts with which to practice largely depoliticized versions of the spirit they had once found in the civil rights and anti-war movements. Through the 1970s they wondered what was the political meaning of their hard-learned work. Some resumed interrupted careers, became academics, doctors, lawyers, planners; now they wondered how to continue their political identities when it was simply *so hard* to slog along on that proverbial "long march through the institutions." A few moved toward one of the new Marxist-Leninist grouplets. Many more though, doubled and redoubled their commitments to local political projects, digging in for the long haul as nitty-gritty organizers for welfare and utility reform, for the Equal Rights Amendment, for this or that union or reform candidate.

From among these strands, 200 people were asked to the SDS reunion, and half came. Most had been active in SDS before 1967; some had worked in other New Left projects and fraternal groups, especially from areas where SDS had never amounted to much, notably California. Hundreds of others could have been invited.

Many needs, many agendas. The reunion seemed a sure setup for grandiose expectations, for recriminations, for traditional SDS arrogance, or, as a fallback, for that tiniest common denominator: the clumsy attempt by 100 old comrades to find some common ground for talk. Perhaps, like old vets, we would sing our patriotic songs and swap war stories. Do you remember when?

Indeed, one of the main subjects of discussion at the beginning of the reunion was how reluctant nearly everyone had been to attend. The summer-camp cabins and workshops were thick with fear: that the wretched mutual accusations of late SDS would recrudesce; that one would again have to confront the ex-friends who, last visit, last decade, were accusing one of sexist abuses, insufficient revolutionary zeal, *petit-bourgeois* attitudes. Some still-activists feared that this collection of aging, politically homeless, but (as ever) presumptuous veterans would deceive themselves that it was 1960 again, and in their arrogance lurch into a new, half-baked political organization whose program was camouflaged nostalgia. Others, half-unconsciously, longed for just that organization, and through the week kept referring to the reunion as an SDS *convention*. A Canadian activist said her Canadian nationalist friends had warned her not to go; a gay man said his gay friends had warned *him* not to go. Some dreaded the meeting would be their long-anticipated tribunal; others that it would turn out to be an improvised Esalen Institute, an exercise in nostalgia suffused with the touchy-feelie spirit of instant intimacy. Neither notion was auspicious.

Any recollection of this event begins with its culture: the New Left had always been a cultural presence before it was a political "tendency," and no less so now. There were fewer flickers of out-and-out nostalgia than I'd expected: a few old rituals (folk songs around the campfire, dancing in the small hours to oldies-but-goodies), but more powerful, new ones. A Jewish poet led the reunion in an Arapaho Indian round dance: this ethnic combination is perhaps not unusual nowadays. A group of us sang *We Shall Not Be Moved* as we resisted being drawn into such mawkishness that is less usual. A part-Indian Oklahoman sang a song of the Warsaw ghetto in *Yiddish*: less usual still.

But the choice of identities was more supple, less driven, less embattled than before. The obligatory women's caucus discovered, after a couple of meetings, that it was meeting simply because women were expecting one another to caucus; they decided not to meet further. If women felt that feminist concerns were being scanted, or that they were being cowed by male palaver, they were strong and legitimate enough—after how many years of bitter struggle?—to say so straight to the men. The writer Judith Coburn later told the reunion she had been avoiding mixed politics throughout the 1970s in favor of feminist projects, and now she'd seen what she'd been missing. Meanwhile, the one black present for the whole reunion (SDS had been almost entirely white) felt capable of leading a workshop on racism—not some glamorously distant Theory of Racism and Neocolonialism, not a Theory of Racism in the Working Class, but racism in SDS: and she made there the argument that SDS had abandoned the real civil rights struggle in the late 1960s, chasing instead after snazzy media-trade black gods.

Such things were thought in the late 1960s; they were not said. And never had an SDS meeting asked how many present were Jewish, although in the early 1960s more than one Jew looked at SDS and thought that a measure of its "reality" was that it had more gentiles than Jews—it was *American*. At the same time, some radical Jews outside SDS had thought SDS disconcertingly *goyish*. Now this was all out in the open. A Jewish workshop met twice during the week and it was full of shared cramp about that particular closet, of thirst to learn Jewish history and to explore and argue the ties between radicalism and Jewishness. Some wanted to put together a workshop on religion, but, as with other important subjects, no time was found. Born-again Baptists identified themselves as such. (So did Red-diaper babies: another unacknowledged issue of the 1960s.) These discussions were preliminary, but they were starting to dig deeply.

There were also planned workshops and formal panels of a more analytic cast. Space permits mentioning only a few topics: the meaning of participatory democracy; politics and culture (including some comparable problems of artists and carpenters); the politics of the media; social origins of the New Left; and, at greatest length, the causes of what some called the collapse of SDS and others called the late-1960s "transition." Various lines of argument about the shared past proved compatible. Bob Gottlieb, an organizer of the New York Movement for a Democratic Society in the late 1960s and now author of a book on the *Los Angeles Times,* argued that the New Left had represented part of a "new working class," and that it had gone under because it had fled from the painstaking work of building radical coalitions within that class, pursuing instead one or another phantasm of the True Revolutionary Agency, or, that failing, committing political suicide. Former National Secretary (now therapist) Greg Calvert spoke similarly of a collective "flight from class identity" that led to a loss of moorings. There was finer sociological imagination in these discussions than at most sociology meetings.

Political imagination was scantier—many were reluctant to join current political questions for fear of disrupting the hard-won community. But former President (now political writer) Carl Oglesby made an impression when he argued that, whatever social forces had played themselves out in the 1960s, one political force that had been at work in no small way was the American secret police: informers, *agents provocateurs,* the whole barely uncovered apparatus of the FBI's COINTELPRO, the CIA's domestic operations, and God knows what else. Enthusiastically, the reunion decided to try to retrieve all extant government files —as the Socialist Workers Party is in the process of doing, and as a Student Nonviolent Coordinating Committee (SNCC) reunion last year also decided to do.

The greatest animation was in the spirit that welled up in rituals and happenings, planned and unplanned. The second day, a workshop in homophobia grew tense when a few heterosexuals wanted to know just what gays thought about the family, and really why anyone wanted to be gay in the first place. One of the gay men said he had not encountered such collective hostility in years. Everyone was bristling. The workshop went on past the time set to begin the plenary, as more and more people came to sit on the fringes. Gays say they hadn't thought they needed to teach the alphabet at an SDS reunion. One gay man, sobbing loudly, said his friends had been right to counsel him against returning to his old hurtful scene, and he was going to leave.

But gradually the conversations broke up; the fringes pulled in toward the conversational center and paid attention; the workshop became the plenary. And one by one, other old, bitter divisions cracked open. Some people recalled their failure to cope with the Weatherpeople when they had started, as somebody said in 1969, turning themselves into bricks in order to hurl themselves. Two articulate men, neither of them partial to the "touchy-feelie" style, spoke with evident emotion about the agony of having come from working-class families and finding themselves simultaneously suspected by parents for collegiate snobbery, and denounced by SDSers from elite colleges for domination and elitism. SDS, with its highfalutin class theories, had never faced head-on the class origins of its own people. A mother summoned up her resentment of the full-time organizers who had sneered at the more settled, the more "straight" or "bourgeois," those who had maintained borders of private life as hedges against fanaticism. Artists complained of neglect by the too, too serious Philistines of SDS. The testimonies went on for hours. Who had not been knocked around by the season's definition of right-on revolutionism? The gays had made it possible to uncover more than one old and unhealed wound.

One might have thought that a whole evening of this would be pathetic or self-indulgent, a sign that the New Left was really the soft-headed collective failure that is now enshrined in media mythology. But the process produced a communal high. Even people who had not been active in SDS were shaken and moved; their own hesitations about SDS had been not only corroborated but transcended. It was possible now to move past the competition among victims, the more-oppressed-than-thou catechisms that so often constitute the experience of the 1970s Left. It was possible to move on now. But where?

The past had undergone three days of criticism, some catharsis, some joyful reconnection. A complex process of recollecting had located some of SDS's turning points: hubris and failures of leadership. Now what the reunion hungered for was a collective assertion of the stakes, the full gravity of that movement. Those emotional bonds, those successes and failures, had after all taken place *in the United States of America in the 1960s, in the course of political battles over white supremacy and war.* What had been planned for the third night was a memorial service.

It had been planned, appropriately, by Alan Haber, the founder of SDS in 1960. It was Haber, now in a carpentry collective, who had brought together a group of old SDSers living in the San Francisco Bay Area to organize this reunion fifteen years after Port Huron. (The reunion affectionately dubbed them "the Gang of Six," respecting their initiative and foresight even when wanting this or that discussion to be given more space.) Haber had posted a piece of blank cardboard and asked us to record the names of fallen co-workers, comrades we wished to have publicly remembered. At nightfall, candles flickered on the floor as Haber stood up to read the names of our people. As the night went on, memories got jolted, more names were added.

Haber read the names one by one. "Remember A.J. Muste." "Remember Paul Goodman." People who'd known them stood up to say a few words about A.J. Muste, about Paul Goodman. "Remember Herbert Lee." Who? Herbert Lee was a black Mississippi farmer shot down for "uppityness" in 1961 by a white man during a voter-registration campaign in Amite County. Spontaneously, we sang the civil rights anthem written for Lee: *We'll Never Turn Back.* There were those more easily remembered: Martin Luther King, Malcom X, Andrew Goodman, Michael Schwerner, James Chaney; the Kent State and Jackson State dead; SDS organizer Carol McEldowney, dead in an auto wreck in 1973. Victims of more obscure massacres: an Austin, Texas Communist organizer murdered in 1967; three blacks murdered in Orangeburg, S.C. in 1968; Ralph Featherstone of SNCC killed by an (unsolved) bomb blast on his way to Rap Brown's trial in 1970. How many blacks, mostly forgotten? The litany cascaded on: suicides of the burned-out: the 1970 townhouse dead; Norman Morrison, Roger LaPorte, Alice

Herz, who had immolated themselves in protest against the war; the Rosenbergs, gays. Our own. *So many*. Not the sanctioned ideological heroes, not the mass-cultural gurus affixed onto our generation by the eager promoters of the cultural apparatus: not Mao Tse-tung, not Elvis Presley. In that cascade of names we refigured the terror, the surging emotion of the previous few days. In all the glib after-assessments of the 1960s, in all the myths and smugness of the media, all the famous quietude of the campuses, all the Dylan-quoting of a new President, it is easy to forget what has been out there to be overcome.

After a long, unmeasured time of eulogies, Mickey Flacks of Santa Barbara arose to remind us that there is a time to gain as there is a time to lose: we should now speak the names of our children. "Charles Wright Flacks." "Mark A.J. Flacks." Parents spoke those names. But this remembrance passed in an appalling rush. There were not nearly so many of those brought to life as those who had lost it. The shock of that discovery, coupled with the shock of the other losses, reverberated long and deeply. Who are "we" who shall overcome?

The final two days were, had to be, emotional anticlimax; the reunion wanted to move toward more definite discussion of political goals, work being done and work to be done. A couple of panel discussions on politics now flushed out some few of the differences that had been simmering under the surface. There were dedicated community organizers who believed, as SDS used to say, in "organizing people where they're at"; there were people working in the New American Movement; there were a few self-conscious, defensive Marxist-Leninists. There were some people active in the Mobilization for Survival, a coalition of groups against nuclear bombs and nuclear reactors; there were a few who thought it was distracting or demoralizing for local groups to consider the possibilities of nuclear war. Tom Hayden tried to put many of the strands together, and got a respectful hearing for his lucid presentation on principles of radical transformation. Hayden stressed the Left-scorned values of patriotism, nonviolence and wide reach, and declared that a radical movement with definite leadership is an absurdity. All week, in fact, at the edges of workshops and panels the old slogan about "no leaders" was under fire; it seemed to be generally acknowledged that leadership is not *ipso facto* tyranny. The evident intelligence of the Gang of Six was in this respect exemplary, a good advertisement for the possibility of sensible leadership.

But all in all, political positions were more staked out and suggested than thoroughly debated—there wasn't time for more, and the Gang of Six had wisely decided to emphasize unities over potential divisions. The quite considerable divisions in the American Left are both causes and consequences of its slightness and disorganization, and most of those divisions were lurking in Michigan. It required energy and tact to evade or postpone them. There was a complaint that the hard work of political clarification was being suppressed by the rituals of "love-tyranny and voodoo." The task-minded current activists were probably more frustrated by the brief attention given to current political questions, but they were also the most pleasantly surprised by the force of the process-minded reunion. It promises well for our larger political fortunes that, on this occasion, ideological antagonists could listen well.

As Greg Calvert said for the general will, there were evidently "networks" of common interest—community organizers, academics, feminists, gays, therapists —who should remain in touch and find ways to explore the hitherto unacknowledged bonds. On the last day Calvert proposed that a newsletter be published to carry these discussions forward, and that the Gang of Six be empowered to organize another conference within a year—this one not a reunion, but directed more to the future. There was much sentiment that this next meeting not be limited to the same SDS alumni. Whatever is to follow must be planned with great sensitivity and finesse, but the participants in Michigan seemed to agree there was no point in trying to repeat the spontaneous emotional bonding of the SDS elders, let alone SDS itself.

The motion passed by acclamation. What was also extraordinary was that Calvert credited the inspiration for his proposal to something said that afternoon by one of the first-generation SDSers. That "old guard" had been generally more intellectual, more Eastern, more Jewish—"junior achiever types," somebody said, though actually ambivalent about leadership. It had been displaced in 1966 by a more radical, more militant, more Great Plains and Southwestern "prairie power" group, of which Greg Calvert had been a mainstay. In 1967, a last-ditch attempt by the old guard to rally SDS graduates into a new organizational form had been smothered by, among other things, antagonisms between the old guard and the prairie people. I'd never thought I'd live to see leaders of the two groups proposing something together.

But what does this have to do with mass unemployment or the Equal Rights Amendment? With Anita Bryant or the cruise missile? What does an SDS reunion say to radicals who were never deeply involved in SDS, and why should anyone else care? The mass media have their answers already packaged: they are full of excited chatter about the death of the New Left. *People* (September 12) crows that at the SDS reunion "the old familiar faces were scarce," that the meeting's failure was evident in the fact that five of the Chicago 7 "skipped such a significant reunion" because "they have moved on to other things." Hype feeds on hype. The noisy 1960s were far out, the silent 1970s are far in. The Chicago 7, of course, were named movement celebrities by the Daley regime and the media; only four of the seven were in fact even invited to the SDS reunion, and the two who didn't come had personal reasons. Catch-23: name the leaders, then parade their names as symbolic tokens. *People* went on to trumpet in a headline: "Their Anger Behind

Them, the Chicago 7 Declare Peace in the '70s." Likewise, the papers are making John Froines's new Occupational Safety and Health job in the Carter administration into a surrender. And when Mark Rudd, unrelated to the reunion, surfaced from the Weather underground last month, Walter Cronkite chuckled beneficently, as if to say he'd known all along that at 30 one outgrows revolution. Kirkpatrick Sale, by far the best historian of SDS, points out accurately that Rudd was never as much national SDS's man as he was the cameras', but then media-made heroes serve nicely as anti-heroes when the mood changes. None of the myth makers is interested in the community organizers, the minority rights and peace campaigners, the radical doctors and lawyers and carpenters who have been working steadily for years outside what *Newsweek* disingenuously calls "public view," down off those photogenic barricades. The media obituaries are partly expressions of wish, partly sighs of relief, partly arguments against a resurrection.

The fact is that not only are the ideals of the New Left alive, not only do its intellectual projects continue and ramify, but the forms of activity it embodied are widespread. This is why the SDS reunion has, I think, a larger implication. *There may well be more active, even full-time radical organizers at work in the United States today than at the peak of the 1960s*. And the coming of a Democratic administration, with its galvanizing but unfulfilled promises of change, has begun to stoke up (as John Kennedy's did) a new round of direct actions. Since they are not usually seen in relation, let me simply itemize some signs:

The April-May occupation of the Seabrook, N.H. nuclear reactor site by the Clamshell Alliance was the largest, best-organized, perhaps most participatory nonviolent direct action in American history. Very little has been reported about the working of the remarkably persistent Kent State protests of the spring and summer, but I have been told they also combined "affinity group" organization with clear political vision. Eastern media largely missed the major demonstrations last spring at several California campuses (including more than 400 arrests at Santa Cruz) against university complicity in South African investments. The work begun twelve years ago by SDS and civil rights groups against American financial support of the South African dictatorship has been continued manifold under church and lay auspices, with considerable success in convincing American banks to cut those ties. Activists against nuclear weapons and nuclear power have federated for the first time in the Mobilization for Survival that is organizing teach-ins nationwide this fall, and will be staging demonstrations through 1978. Former SNCC activists and others have been organizing demonstrations for full employment and, with the Hawkins-Humphrey bill stalled, there will probably be more. New Left veterans have put together organizer training schools in Chicago and San Francisco. Radical and anti-Meany trade union insurgency is widespread. In all these projects there are continuities between the activists of the 1960s and those of the 1970s.

What is lacking needs little comment. There is precious little deliberate connection among these tendrils, and little of a unifying spirit. SDS's early 1960s slogan, "the issues are interrelated," is always hard to embody in a politically fragmented, interest-group culture. The ecological, feminist and gay movements are all meeting heavy resistance, and the student activists have still not learned how to reach toward unions and minorities without either submerging their identity or playing at vanguardism. It is a long way from one-at-a-time demonstrations to a common political program, and a long way from program to forms of serious, rooted, cross-class, cross-race, cross-sex, cross-generation organization and leadership that can do right by that program. It is exhausting even to contemplate that prospect. And the world does not wait.

The SDS reunion was not the place to find the roots for that development. By interest and recent experience it was too diverse; by class, by race, by age and 1960s experience, too narrow. It remains to be seen how (if at all) the bonds of collective ritual among one-time intimates can be inserted into the thick, messy, divisive stuff of political work, and what SDS's history has to do with that of anyone else. The many directions taken by old SDSers after 1969 — community organizing, professions, countercultural and therapeutic culture, to name only three major strands — are all continuations of the New Left's political identity and culture, but it would be foolhardy to predict that without the old camaraderie they are automatically compatible. Still, it is worth dwelling on the fact that, in Michigan, what began with eyes backward, a *re*-union, came to seem, however incompletely, an intimation. Perhaps this is *one* root of a politics for the 1980s, at least a sign of possibilities.

The *Newsweek* and *People* reporters, after poking uninvited into one reunion meal, made the obligatory snide reference to our "austere radical cuisine." Well, it was no doubt less carcinogenic than the usual expense-account stuff. It was also much praised, lavish and consistently delicious food, cooked by several University of Michigan undergraduates who, as it happened, had been wondering before this job whatever happened to the New Left. They'd felt deserted, even betrayed. They'd believed the media aftermyth: our whole political generation was played out, smashed.

At our last meal, they came out to thank us. The reunion had thrilled them. They'd attended workshops, they'd hung out: they saw not our past but a common present. They treated the old folks to ice cream and a rendition of a Presley song of the 1950s. Later, as each of us was saying where he or she would be heading from the reunion, one of the undergraduate cooks said he would be going home to Ann Arbor — "to revolt." The New Left is over. Long live the New Left.

ARTHUR H. SAMUELSON

The Dilemma of American Jewry   *April 1, 1978*

In the aftermath of Egyptian President Anwar Sadat's journey
to Jerusalem and the subsequent hardline stance of the Israeli
government, Arthur Samuelson interviewed a cross-section of
American Jewish leaders. In 1978, Samuelson was one of the
few writers, and *The Nation* one of the few American magazines, willing to document dissension in the ranks of the American Jewish community over Israel's settlement policies.

The American Jewish community has been confused and made tense by President
Sadat's sudden and dramatic journey to Jerusalem, followed by Prime Minister
Begin's decision to proceed with settlements in the disputed territories, and the
subsequent clashes between the Israeli and American Governments over his
insistence that United Nations Resolution 242 does not apply to the West Bank.
Carter's proposal to sell supersonic jets to Israel's enemies has temporarily
remobilized the community; the recent PLO attack on civilians in Tel Aviv and
Israel's retaliation in Lebanon may have unified it. But, the uneasiness that became manifest in the weeks after Sadat's visit, bringing with it the fear of a rupture
in American-Israeli relations, remains and promises to sharpen.

Speaking with Jewish leaders during the past month, I found that many had become privately alarmed over the hard-line positions taken by the Israeli Government in response to Sadat's peace initiative. Along with many Israelis, they
question the wisdom of establishing new settlements in the West Bank and the
Gaza Strip, just at the time when these territories have become the subject of
difficult negotiations. They have looked with great anxiety at public-opinion polls
which reveal that, for the first time in the history of the Arab-Israeli conflict,
Americans believe that Egypt is more sincere in its desire for peace than Israel.
They hesitate to express themselves publicly in the United States, lest their words
should further damage Israel's already-weakened position. Some have quietly
warned Israeli officials of the damage done by policies that many Americans believe were designed to anger the Egyptians and embarrass the Carter administration. In a time of increasingly stiff American-Israeli relations, many Jewish leaders wonder what role they should play. There is friction as to who is entitled to
speak for American Jewry, and what they should be permitted to say. Talking
with me, Jewish leaders expressed their concerns in terms that rarely reach the
American public or its Jewish segment.

Until recently, American Jews had little difficulty explaining and defending Israeli policy to the larger American public because American and Israeli interests

were widely perceived as compatible. The last major trial by fire came in 1956, when Israel took part in the Anglo-French Suez campaign and the Eisenhower-Dulles administration threatened to eliminate the United Jewish Appeal's tax-deductible status and to enforce sanctions against Israel if it did not withdraw from occupied Sinai. At that time, many Jews in this country who were active on behalf of the Jewish state felt themselves caught between their responsibilities as American citizens and as supporters of Israel. Few Jewish leaders want to be caught in the middle again. As the hour of a new American-Israeli showdown draws near, they are struggling to define a role that will allow them to influence both Carter and Begin toward positions that will prevent a head-on collision. There is as yet, however, no agreement as to how that might be done.

Thus far, the American Jewish Committee and the American Jewish Congress have avoided any public position on the settlements issue. Publicly, their general line has been to blame the stalemate in the negotiations on the Egyptians, "who do not want to negotiate a settlement but want to dictate the terms of surrender," as an official of one of these organizations put it. But privately, staff members told me that their leaders have notified Israeli officials of their concern for Israel's eroding position in the United States. "When looking for signs of discontent in the Jewish community with a specific Israeli policy or action," advises one highly placed official, "a good rule to follow is to look for silence, not public statements." The fear is that such statements would only make it easier for the administration to pressure Israel, and the feeling is that the Israelis are more receptive to private representations.

But most Jewish leaders are uncertain whether they have any right to an independent position on Israeli policy, believing that the country's needs must be defined by its own citizens. A staff member of one organization explains:

> There is a central irony in Jewish life whereby Menachem Begin will make a claim to the West Bank in the name of the Jewish people, but American Jews will be reluctant to take a stand on Israel's right to the West Bank because they believe that only those who are willing to pay the price with their own blood have the right to hold an opinion. Basically, the American Jewish community takes an advertising-agency approach. An agency never tells its client that its product is dangerous; it only asks that the client package the product a bit differently, so as to be able to sell it better. In our strategy meetings, most of my colleagues have been unwilling to say, "We will not sell this policy to the American people because we think it is not in Israel's interest." Instead, with only a few exceptions, they say, "We are going to have a hard time selling this policy because we do not believe it will work, but it is Israel's policy and we have the duty to support it no matter what."

Most Jewish leaders, however, feel no inhibition in telling the Begin government of their fears for Israel's reputation in the United States. One leader told me that, on the eve of a visit to Israel, he was urged by Israeli Embassy officials who shared his assessment of the damage being done, to bring his concerns before key members of Israel's governing coalition. *Ha'aretz,* the Israeli daily that has editorialized against the settlements policy, has told its public that such prominent Jews as historian Barbara Tuchman and novelist Elie Wiesel, well respected for their support of Israel's cause, are unhappy with the direction that Begin's policy has been taking. Yoel Marcus, the paper's Washington correspondent, recently interviewed Larry Tisch, president of Loews hotel and theatre group, and one of those who contribute more than $500,000 a year to the United Jewish Appeal. Marcus reports this interview as being representative of the feelings of most of the UJA leaders he spoke with in late February. Mr. Tisch was unavailable for comment when I phoned to record his opinions for *The Nation.* Excerpts follow from his *Ha'aretz* interview:

> There never was such an idiotic approach taken by an Israeli Government toward the settlements in the occupied territories. The Jews will always support Israel, even when they do not agree with her, but the American public is a different story. The average American lives between the hours of 6 and 7 P.M., between Cronkite and Chancellor, and he only knows that Sadat wants peace and Israel wants settlements in the territories. Begin does not seem to understand what is happening here. The administration wants a deal in the Middle East and the weak link in the deal is Israel because the Arabs have oil, markets and petrodollars. The Western world is leaning heavily in favor of the Arabs and the administration is listening carefully to what Japan, Germany and France are saying. The administration hopes to remove Israel from all of the occupied territories; Begin is wrong if he thinks he can do whatever he wants as if nothing has happened here.
>
> Certainly, the administration is using the settlements issue to pressure Israel, but that is no reason for Israel to play into the administration's hands and give it the rope to hang her with. The only thing that Israel has to offer is the justness of her cause. American Jews can influence American public opinion only when they can prove they are fighting for a just cause. We can fight for border adjustments or a fair settlement, but when Israel is wrong, we lose our power. If Begin insists on pressing the settlements issue, he will lose every last American. There is no justification for his position and Carter would not have dared propose the arms deal to Congress without the backdrop of the settlements. [The arms deal included sales to Egypt and Saudi Arabia as well as Israel.]

Rabbi Alexander Schindler, chairman of the Conference of Presidents of Major Jewish Organizations, an umbrella group embodying thirty-two Jewish organizations, has also told the Israelis he is disturbed by the state of Israel's image in the United States. Addressing the political committee of the World Zionist Congress in Jerusalem in late February, he reported that Israel had suffered a major setback in its battle for public support in the United States. Israel's image has become "untruthful, conniving" Schindler said, opening a "credibility gap" in the United States. On the other hand, he noted, the American public "by and large" accepted Sadat's messages: that Egypt gave much and received almost nothing in return, that Egypt took "the high road to peace" while Israel "quibbled over peripheral issues," and that Egypt was on the verge of giving up hope and "chucking in" its entire peace initiative. According to Schindler, Israel's sagging image in the United States was due partly to the cumulative effect of the State Department's assertions that Israel's settlements in the occupied territories were "illegal," and to the "double standard" the U.S. news media applied to Israel and the Arabs.

While American-Jewish newspapers and periodicals reflect little of the disquiet among Jews over Israeli policy, the *Jerusalem Post* has carried letters from U.S. Jews expressing indignation at that policy. One letter read: "Your statesmen have always contended that Israel's deepest wish is to be accepted in dignity and peace by its Arab neighbors. Judging from Begin's statements, it now appears that what Israel wants far more fervently than peace is to re-create what he considers to be the heyday of Israel's Biblical period, plus a few pieces of the Sinai for good measure." He hastened to add, lest he be misunderstood, that "I am not an American New Left-type Jew who has always been against Israeli policy (and even existence) on ideological grounds. I have almost always supported Israel's policies in the past, feel culturally, historically and emotionally linked to Israel, and deeply want Israel to survive and prosper."

Little of this sort of reaction has thus far been heard in this country, but a few U.S. Jews are tiring of private representations and communications and are beginning to speak out. They are usually intellectuals who do not depend on the Jewish community for either their livelihood or their reputation. One who has spoken out recently is the literary and social critic, Irving Howe, author of the best-selling history of American Jewish immigrant life, *World of Our Fathers.* Howe has stood up for Israel in the past, and is not reluctant to express his criticisms of Israeli policy now. When I interviewed him recently for *Politicks,* he said:

> I think that the Israeli position on the settlements is absolutely indefensible. Except for those people who have received word from heaven that Judea and Samaria belong to the Jews — and with such people it is impossible to argue — supporters of Israel have to recognize that if there is to be peace in the Middle East, sooner or later — and with all kinds of cautions and qualifications — Israeli domination of the West Bank has to end. That means that the Israeli Government has to give up the idea that it has a right to the domination of the West Bank, let alone to sovereignty over the West Bank. . . . As far as the settlements themselves are concerned, I do not think there is any objection to having Jewish settlements in Arab countries any more than there is objection to having Arabs within Israel, but that's a different issue. Clearly, Begin and his friends do not think of settlements in the West Bank as a Jewish enclave in an Arab society. As long as there is ambiguity on the part of the Israelis, there cannot be peace in the Middle East.

As is the case with almost all ethnic minorities, no one central agency represents the American Jewry, and that fact contributes to the present confusion and rancor as to who is entitled to convey "Jewish opinion" to the government and the public at large. However, the body often regarded by the press as authoritative is the Conference of Presidents of Major Jewish Organizations. Established after the Suez war by American-Jewish leaders with the encouragement of Israeli officials who sought an efficient way to manage Israel's information campaign in the United States, the conference is not a policy-making body but a coordinating council. Uniting the largest Jewish organizations – from the religiously and politically most conservative to the most liberal – it is an unwieldy body. Since its chairman is not elected (the position is rotated annually among member groups), he is required to communicate consensus to the outside world. From Israel's point of view, the conference provides a single platform from which its officials may speak to American Jewish leaders. From the Jewish point of view, it provides a means for coming to decisions on how Israel's case should be presented to American officials and the public. It also provides Jewish leaders with a forum at which to speak their minds to the Israelis.

But it is not expected, nor is it equipped, to determine which Israeli policies American Jews should support and this has made some of its member groups, usually those strongly advocating one position or another, dissatisfied with its circumscribed role. As one leader, known for his dovish proclivities put it:

> We American Jews have no real political strategy of our own when it comes to Israeli-American relations. The Presidents' Conference does not deal with substantive political issues, only with public relations difficulties which arise in defending Israeli policy. The conference has never gone to President Carter and said, we believe this and this as Americans and this is the policy we would like you to pursue. Instead, it acts like a third-rate messenger boy for the Israeli Embassy, only providing the Israeli reaction to events, never proposing alternatives. Schindler spends most of his time trying to convince the Israelis that Carter is not so bad and the Americans that Begin is not so bad. It is hard to take such a role seriously.

Another Jewish leader pointed to an article in which the *The New York Times* reported that Schindler had called the paper to complain that National Security Adviser Zbigniew Brzezinski was urging Carter to place pressure on Israel to give up the occupied territories. "To influence the administration," he said, "you have to have some credibility, and to be credible you have to be independent. Why should Carter or anyone listen to Schindler when they can get it straight from the Israeli Embassy?"

The issue of independence from Israel's policies became heated in February when it was learned that the Conference of Presidents was not prepared to accept President Sadat's offer to meet with them during his visit to Washington. In a statement explaining the decision, it was said that such a meeting might be misinterpreted to suggest that the Jewish community was "seeking to take part in these [Egyptian-Israeli] negotiations." One organization after another denounced

Sadat's invitation and his "Open Letter" in the *Miami Herald* (January 29), calling upon American Jews to support his peace efforts. They accused him of attempting to weaken Jewish support for Israel. Alexander Schindler welcomed Sadat "as a man of peace," but cautioned that "peace can only come if the parties that fought the wars sit together and negotiate in a spirit of good will and compromise. It can neither be imposed by outside powers nor arranged through intermediaries. We have no role in such negotiations as a Jewish community."

Schindler had visited Sadat in Cairo a month earlier, when the peace talks were still flourishing, but when the talks broke down, he was asked by Israeli officials not to lend a hand to Sadat's attempt to blame Israel for the collapse by meeting him in Washington. Chaim Herzog, Israeli Ambassador to the United Nations, expressed his country's position at an Israel Bonds dinner on February 4: "In our negotiations with Egypt, we will succeed only if we are strong as a united people, only if the Jews of America and the rest of the world stand with Israel without compromise. For the first time in history," he said, "an Arab leader is going over the head of Israel to negotiate with the Jewish public." He predicted that the Egyptian leader would not succeed in dividing American Jews and that eventually he would have to return to the business of negotiating with Israel.

But while the Conference of Presidents adhered to the Israeli request, a number of prominent American Jews, some of whom are leading members of the Conference of Presidents, decided that they would in fact attend such a meeting. The group included Phillip Klutznick, a 70-year-old real estate man from Chicago, who recently succeeded Dr. Nahum Goldmann as president of the World Jewish Congress. Under Goldmann, an Israeli citizen, the Congress had maintained an independent position on Israeli Government policy. Goldmann, who often angered Israeli officials with his outspokenly dovish criticism of their foreign policy, was invited to meet Egyptian President Nasser in 1970, but was refused permission to travel to Egypt by then-Prime Minister Golda Meir. In much the same language as Begin's government uses today, she insisted that Nasser's invitation, regarded by some as a critical breakthrough, was a ploy to divide the Jewish world from Israel and that only Israeli officials had a role to play in negotiating any settlement.

Known to share some of Goldmann's dovish views, Klutznick was a signer of the 1976 Brookings Institution report, "Toward Peace in the Middle East," in which Brzezinski had a major hand. Few were surprised, though many were dismayed, when Klutznick did not adhere to the Conference of Presidents' decision that Jewish leaders should stay away from Sadat. He said: "President Sadat has come here as a guest of the President of the United States on a mission that is vital to the whole world—peace in the Middle East. If he invites me as an American Jew to meet him, I would consider it demeaning not to accept the invitation."

To calls for his resignation from leaders of the Zionist Organization of America and the Religious Zionists of America (counterparts of the present governing coalitions in Israel) and from members of the American section of the World Jewish Congress, Klutznick replied that he had accepted the invitation in his private capacity and not as the leader of a Jewish organization. In a *Jerusalem Post* interview he answered those who had charged him with "dividing" American Jewry:

> As a former officeholder under United States Presidents [Klutznick had been a federal housing administrator under Roosevelt and Truman, and was appointed by Eisenhower and Kennedy to the U.S. delegation to the United Nations], I appreciate that one can influence thinking but one cannot initiate it. I am not interested in substituting for the duly elected officials of Israel. . . . Upon assuming my duties as president of the World Jewish Congress, I have accepted limitations on my freedom of expression. Though obliged to be inhibited, I will fight like hell for my principles. And I won't be stopped from seeing people. I intend to go on meeting my coffee-drinking friend Ghorbal [Egyptian Ambassador to the United States] whenever I damn well feel like it, as well as the Romanians and other Eastern bloc diplomats who cultivate my acquaintance.

While recognizing the need for Jewish solidarity, Klutznick told the Israeli paper that "it is a vain hope to have unity in the Diaspora if Israel is not united. I have found considerable debate in Israel. . . ."

While Sadat's invitation caused some confusion as to the political role that American Jews should take in the pursuit of peace, the Synagogue Council of America (SCA), the umbrella organization for the rabbinical and congregational bodies of the three branches of American Judaism, has taken advantage of the opening provided by Sadat to initiate a long-anticipated Muslim-Jewish religious dialogue, akin to the ecumenical movement that has brought Jews and Christians closer together around the world. A beginning was made when the Synagogue Council's executive director, Rabbi Henry Siegman, invited Egyptian Ambassador Ashraf Ghorbal to address a council meeting on December 7. Thereafter the Synagogue Council was invited to meet with Muslim scholars and Sadat in Cairo. It accepted, but when Israeli-Egyptian negotiations had been suspended, it found itself under fire from the Conference of Presidents and from some of its own Orthodox constituent groups. After an initial postponement—"We did not want to be seen arriving in Cairo as the Israelis were leaving," explains Siegman—the meeting in Cairo took place in February. The trip produced plans for a Jewish-Muslim meeting to be held under the auspices of Cairo University later this year, and Siegman reports that the president of the university offered to invite Jewish scholars from America, and possibly Israel, to teach Judaic studies as visiting professors at his university. The Egyptians also agreed to allow scholars to collect and catalogue the archival material and historic treasures of Egypt's millennium-old Jewish community.

Siegman has a firm answer for those who say the SCA has unwittingly aided Sadat's public relations drive: "The kind of relationship that we set out to build cannot possibly hurt Israel. Through religious and cultural dialogue, we are trying to build the infrastructure on which a lasting peace settlement can be built. Religion is supposed to bring people together and the Muslim-Jewish dialogue we began must continue, regardless of the state of the political negotiations." Siegman concedes that "open dialogue was impossible before Sadat went to Israel, because the Egyptians were not willing"; but, he adds, "we would not have been able to move so quickly when the time was right if we had not established prior personal contacts. Regardless of the political situation in the Middle East, we are determined that the religious dialogue will go on."

Throughout February and March, as relations between the United States and Israel became colder, one sensed a growing frustration on the part of some Jewish leaders because the system of private communications was not working. In early February, a delegation representing the Union of American Hebrew Congregations, the American Jewish Committee, the American Jewish Congress, the Anti-Defamation League and the National Jewish Community Relations Advisory Council met to discuss how best to inform visiting Foreign Minister Moshe Dayan of their assessment of the damage being done Israel's cause by the planting of new settlements in the Sinai and the West Bank. Expecting to confer with Dayan privately, they found to their dismay when they arrived that the press had also been invited. In response to a question, Dayan said with some bitterness that his concern was not for public relations but for Israeli lives, "I have more respect for settlers from Gush Emunim in the West Bank than I do for Israelis who leave to settle in Canada, or for American Zionists who stay in New York," he told his visitors. *"We* were the American Zionists he was talking about," says one of them, with some embarrassment. Later, a small delegation managed to meet privately with Dayan, but they did not emerge with any great hope that he would heed their advice. "Yes, we have regular channels of communication with the Israelis, but we have little conviction that the message gets through," reports one man who was at the Dayan meeting.

One of those most depressed by the "advertising-agency" approach is Rabbi Balfour Brickner, co-director of the Social Action Commission of the Union of American Hebrew Congregations: "There is a basic schizophrenia in American Jewry. We hide behind the argument that it is not for us to speak our minds, because the Israelis have to pay the price, but I think that is precisely why we have to speak out when we spot trouble—to save Jewish lives." He asks:

> Why is it that Israeli schoolchildren can write an open letter to Begin, saying his policy raises doubts in their minds as to Israel's sincerity for peace; and why is it that 300 vet-

315

eran officers can publish an advertisement in the Israeli press, saying that if Begin persists on the settlements issue they will have to draw conclusions as to the justness of Israel's cause; and Defense Minister Ezer Weizman can threaten to resign if work on the settlements is not terminated immediately—why, in that case, do I get called a traitor if I say the same thing? The Israelis have answers for everything, but they never have any solutions. What we need is for several big givers to the UJA to threaten to stop contributing if Israel does not retreat from its suicidal position. That is the only language the Israelis understand.

Recently, the *Jewish Post and Opinion,* one of the most independent of American Jewish publications, editorialized in a similar vein:

> If what the polls show is true, that a drastic drop in Israel's position in public opinion has occurred, then we are reaping the harvest of the role adopted by the American Jewish leadership which considers opposition to any Israeli actions as treason. Had U.S. Jewish leaders spoken up on the question of the new settlements in the occupied territories and had they reflected what we believe are the feelings of the average American Jew, Israel might not be in danger of losing the confidence of American popular opinion. The lesson is that we serve Israel best when we are honest with her, honest in our praise, honest in our criticism. It is treason when we refuse to speak up, not treason when we differ.

On February 23, when Elie Ben-Elissar, Begin's chief aide, told a meeting of the Conference of Presidents that Israel had no intention of surrendering control of the West Bank and that his government did not regard U.N. Resolution 242 as being relevant to the West Bank, it became clear for the first time to a majority of Jewish leaders that the head-on collision they had hoped to avoid was about to happen. American Jews, therefore, would have to decide whether or not to support this new interpretation of the U.N. resolution, for Israel was not going to back down. Elissar's candid remarks left Jewish leaders in shock.

As one Jewish official confided, "Our interpretation of U.N. 242 is the same as that of the United States Government and of the former Labor governments of Israel. If Begin insists on his interpretation of U.N. 242, then I am afraid we will have to come out of the closet to oppose him." His organization, like most of the Jewish groups in the United States that are not aligned to the parties of the Likud coalition, has for years trumpeted the importance of U.N. 242 as being the one international document that requires the Arabs to make peace with Israel. As long as such an undertaking was not offered by the Arab side, the resolution's balancing provision that Israel withdraw from the occupied territories did not require much discussion. Most Jewish leaders could live with Golda Meir and Yitzhak Rabin's interpretation that Israel would make withdrawals from all three fronts, holding on only to those areas vital to its security.

Begin had walked out of Golda Meir's national unity government in 1970 when U.N. 242 was accepted as the basis for negotiations with Egypt. Upon his election, he dispatched his close adviser, Shmuel Katz, to Washington to assure leaders there that the new Likud government intended to abide by all international agreements, including U.N. 242, signed by former governments. Initially fearful lest Begin, the hawk of hawks, should force a confrontation with the United States because of his promise to the electorate that "the West Bank would never be returned to foreign rule," Jewish leaders in this country were pleased and reassured by Begin's subsequent moderation and generosity in the peace negotiations with Egypt.

But if Israel now shows itself really determined to hold on to the West Bank for nationalist and religious reasons, it will probably encounter difficulties in the American Jewish community. There are, of course, many in that community who are willing to back whatever Begin attempts to do in the West Bank. But even some of Israel's staunchest defenders are finding it hard to give Begin's policies their unqualified support. "I am in favor of the Labor Party's interpretation of U.N. 242," says Norman Podhoretz, editor of *Commentary*. "When it is an issue of security," he predicts, "then most Jews will leave it up to the Israelis to decide what is best for them and how much territory they need to remain secure, but if it is a matter of ideology—that the West Bank belongs to Israel through Biblical prophecy—then there will be disagreements."

Seymour Martin Lipset, professor of sociology at Stanford University and president of the American Professors for Peace in the Middle East, says:

> If Begin and his government insist on this new interpretation of U.N. 242, it will mean the end of the negotiations. The Arabs will not accept Begin's interpretation and the United States will stick to its own interpretation. I do not think Carter can do very much to get Israel to agree to it, other than take the position, which he has already taken, that Israel is wrong. The basic decision has to be made within Israel. There is the beginning of an opposition within Israel on this issue and should the United States be seen as a source of strong pressure, it will hold up this conflict. I would think there is a majority in the Knesset which disagrees with Begin on U.N. Resolution 242 and my personal hope is that Begin will be forced to resign.

Lipset, who was co-author of an important article in last November's issue of *Commentary* which claimed that, should Carter pressure Israel, the polls show he would lose public support, is no longer so sure. "That was before Sadat. Now we have a different ball game."

The editor of an important Zionist magazine says:

> I am in a quandary and a dilemma. It is pretty clear to me that Begin is more interested in territory than peace. I cannot accept Begin's claim to the West Bank, but I do not feel I have the right to speak out against Israel in this country. And what do I need to do that for anyway? Carter will do it all for me by pressuring Begin and I can show my support for his policy by not saying anything at all. I predict that you will see a lot of

sudden apathy among Jews if there is a confrontation between Carter and Begin over the West Bank.

Leonard Fein, editor of *Moment*, a Jewish monthly published in Boston, is not so sure:

> Carter could split the Jewish community, but it depends on how the issue is presented. I have no confidence that the administration will be clever enough to make the confrontation with Israel appear to be over an issue of sovereignty, not security. If the administration is really clever, however, it could fracture the community and outmaneuver Israel entirely. It would have to spell out in considerable detail the security guarantees that it would offer in exchange for Israeli withdrawal from the West Bank—in other words, pressure Israel by giving something, not taking something away. But I do not think this will happen.

Few Jewish leaders doubt, however, that Carter is going to try to divide the community. "It is not Begin who has been pushing the issue of U.N. 242 but someone else," protests Rabbi Schindler in an interview.

Frustrated by Begin's refusal to desist from placing settlements in occupied territory, Carter appears to have chosen the issue of U.N. 242 to focus international and Jewish attention on Israel's desire for peace or territory. "My impression," writes Yoel Marcus in *Ha'aretz* "is that the administration is trying both to divide and convince the Jewish community of the soundness of its position. Primarily, it wants to learn, once and for all, the strength of Jewish power."

The issue is not one of power, as much as of cohesiveness and inner strength. If Jewish leaders doubt the wisdom of a particular Israeli policy, they rarely communicate it to their own membership. One is struck by the fact that many rank-and-file Jews are well versed on the relative merits of the military hardware Israel is requesting at the moment, but few are attuned to the range of discussion and debate taking place at the American Jewish leadership level, as well as in Israel. Many American Jews, even in the ranks of the established American Jewish leadership, feel that more discussion and debate is essential if they are to serve the real interests of both Israel and America. As Israeli-American relations deteriorate, one wonders whether any constructive role is possible for American Jewry in the absence of such an open dialogue within their own community.

JAMES PETRAS

White Paper on the White Paper   *March 28, 1981*

James Petras's piece was the first analytical review and critique
of the Reagan Administration's white paper on *Communist
Interference in El Salvador*, the document used to justify increased American intervention in El Salvador in the 1980s.

The State Department's white paper entitled *Communist Interference in El Salvador* purports to provide evidence demonstrating:

(1) "the central role played by Cuba and other Communist countries . . . in
the political unification, military direction and arming of insurgent forces in
El Salvador";

(2) that "the insurgency in El Salvador has been progressively transformed into
another case of indirect armed aggression against a small Third World country
by Communist powers acting through Cuba"; and

(3) that "Cuba, the Soviet Union and other Communist states . . . are carrying out what is clearly shown to be a well-coordinated, covert effort to bring about
the overthrow of El Salvador's established Government and to impose in its place
a Communist regime with no popular support."

The white paper fails to provide a convincing case for any of those proposi-
tions. On the contrary, its evidence is flimsy, circumstantial or nonexistent; the
reasoning and logic is slipshod and internally inconsistent; it assumes what needs
to be proven; and, finally, what facts are presented refute the very case the State
Department is attempting to demonstrate. The document, in a word, has the aura
of a political frame-up in which inconvenient facts are overlooked and innuen-
does and unwarranted inferences are made at crucial points in the argument. In
demonstrating this, I will follow the format of the white paper, discussing the
sections in order, under their original titles, and making cross-references to material in other sections where it is warranted; for example, when the authors
contradict themselves.

A CASE OF COMMUNIST MILITARY INVOLVEMENT
IN THE THIRD WORLD

The first technique that is employed in the white paper is to conflate what is happening in El Salvador with other alleged examples of Soviet and Cuban military
involvement. The political opposition is reduced to a group of extreme leftist
guerrillas manipulated by Cuba and in turn manipulating "small, non-Marxist-
Leninist parties" in order to deceive public opinion. Opposition activity is labeled

terrorist. Journalists who describe the U.S.-backed regime's behavior as terrorist are labeled as witting or unwitting dupes of an orchestrated Communist propaganda effort.

What is most striking about this description of the opposition to the junta Government is the complete absence of even a minimal account of the numerous social, political and civic movements that have developed in El Salvador over the past decade, which represent a wide range of political views and social strata. This collective omission on the part of the State Department is necessary if one is bent upon labeling the opposition as Soviet-Cuban manipulated and if one wishes to reduce the conflict to an East-West military confrontation.

The fact of the matter is that over the last decade an enormously rich variety of social organizations have emerged in El Salvador, embracing the great majority of professional and technical workers, peasants, labor and businesspeople. Their membership is in the hundreds of thousands and they are an integral part of the main political opposition group, the Revolutionary Democratic Front (F.D.R.). Almost all union members, peasant associations, university and professional people are members or supporters of social and civic organizations that are sympathetic to the front. The white paper clearly falsifies the political and social realities by excluding an account of the social forces involved with the opposition. Moreover, the origins of the opposition are clearly rooted in the social realities of the country—a point which the document admits in Section III in a politically vague and unspecified fashion when it notes that: "during the 1970's, both the legitimate grievances of the poor and landless and the growing aspirations of the expanding middle classes met increasingly with repression."

What the paper fails to acknowledge is that these "legitimate grievances" and "growing aspirations" found expression and were embodied in the mass organizations which are the essential components of the opposition groups that make up the F.D.R. The guerrilla movement is part and parcel of a larger political and social movement that has been and is repressed. Its activities stem from social realities of Salvadoran history, which the paper concedes is one of "repression, widespread poverty and concentration of wealth and power in the hands of a few families." Because it is intent on demonstrating that the problem is Soviet-Cuban intervention, the paper fails to examine the crucial relationship between the repressive nature of the state, social inequalities and the growth of opposition and guerrilla movements.

The "Non-Marxist" Opposition

The striking feature of the Salvadoran revolution is the broad array of political forces that have united to oppose this regime—Christian Democrats, Social Democrats and Liberal Democrats, as well as independent Marxist groups and pro-Moscow coalitions. What is particularly unique in the Salvadoran case is the substantial leadership and its popular base of support that has developed among Christian communities. In all areas of social and political organization, a plurality of political tendencies are represented – among peasants, workers, professionals and so on. The attempt by the white paper to reduce the opposition to a handful of Marxist guerrillas manipulating the "non-Marxists" is a crude oversimplification and gross distortion of reality. What is remarkable in the document is the systematic exclusion of any mention of the mass-based Christian opposition, the twenty-eight Christian priests, nuns and community leaders murdered by the regime for their opposition activities. A discussion of these facts would complicate the State Department's job of selling intervention to the U.S. public.

In describing the emergence of the guerrilla forces, the document downgrades accounts of repressive political conditions under the junta. Yet detailed descriptions are available from the Organization of American States, the United Nations and, most comprehensively, from the Legal Aid Commission of the office of the Archbishop of El Salvador, which has compiled a lengthy dossier of the regime's systematic violence against all legal public organizations opposed to it in any way. Churches, trade unions, independent newspapers and peasant co-ops have been assaulted and bombed, leaving almost 9,000 dead between January 1980 and January 1981. The precondition for the growth of guerrilla activity was the closing of political channels by the U.S.-backed regime – not Soviet intervention.

Shortly after the first junta was established in October 1979, and before the rightist military took over, the guerrillas and political opposition groups offered a cease-fire. The rightists in the armed forces responded by escalating the number of assassinations, which touched off renewed hostilities. The decision to seek a military-political solution was forced upon the opposition by the military regime when it murdered Archbishop Oscar Romero on March 24, 1980, and then the seven leaders of the F.D.R. meeting in San Salvador on November 27, 1980. The subsequent purge of the moderate Christian Democrats and reformist military officers from the first Government junta is further proof that political options had been taken away. The white paper overlooks this context of regime violence in order to invent a Cuban-inspired conspiracy and to impute the violence of the regime to its victims. The killings by the military regimes increased from 147 in 1978 to 580 between January and October of 1979 and to 8,952 between January 1980 and January 1981. This increasing reign of terror clearly was instrumental in lowering the rate of popular participation in public activity and swelling the numbers of clandestine groups. Oblivious to this reality, the white paper describes the increase in guerrilla activity as a willful act of the "extreme left."

In its attempt to cast doubt on the opposition's legitimacy, the paper omits any mention of centrist defections from the U.S.-backed junta to join the leadership of the Revolutionary Democratic Front. The shift of a significant body of centrist opinion to the opposition is described disparagingly in the following fashion: "For appearances' sake three small non-Marxist-Leninist political parties were brought into the front, though they have no representation in the D.R.U. [Unified Revolutionary Directorate]." These former Christian and Social Democratic allies of the U.S.-backed coalition had been described by U.S. officials a few weeks earlier as major political forces representing significant reform-minded sectors of Salvadoran public opinion. The fact that the pro-Moscow Communist Party of El Salvador is a marginal political force in the opposition coalition is never discussed by the white paper, nor is the fact that three of the four major leftist groups are critical of the Soviet Union.

Moreover, the paper's charge that Fidel Castro was responsible for unifying the left overlooks the fact that the unity of the leftist forces was under way prior to December 1979 as a result of increasing repression by the regime and pressure from the rank and file of all the groups. The F.D.R. was formed in El Salvador, not in Cuba, and was supported and promoted by European social-democratic forces. It was certainly not a product of the alleged machinations of Castro. As the participants stated at the time, the needs of the popular struggle, the limited options open to all opposition groups and the example set by the success of the Nicaraguan revolution were the main impulsions to unity.

Conspiratorial Hypothesis

The effort by the white paper to discredit the F.D.R. by describing it as a "front" disseminating propaganda for the guerrillas systematically ignores the popular support that these groups draw away from the junta, the internal political debates within the front and between the front and the guerrillas and the influence they have had in shaping the program in a reformist direction. The white paper's conspiratorial view requires that its authors overlook the importance of these moderates and their internal and external influence. The paper says nothing about the widespread international support for the front and the isolation of the junta. Indeed, it expands its conspiratorial hypothesis to find Cuban and Soviet-sponsored deception behind the front's success.

The numerous and detailed accounts of repression by the regime compiled by the Archbishop's Legal Aid Commission which have swayed world public opinion are not mentioned; nor are Amnesty International's publicized accounts of widespread systematic torture. In place of careful consideration of these documents, the white paper labels the 10,000 deaths attributed to the junta (13,000 by the time the paper appeared) an "extreme claim" of the guerrilla propaganda apparatus, which is parroted by the Cuban, Soviet and Nicaraguan media. Actually, the principal source of data collected on the regime's repression is non-Communist, Catholic and respected by most non-U.S. Government sources. In summary, through omissions and distortions, through labeling and simplification, the white paper early on fabricates a case against a broad-based popular revolutionary movement in order to prove "Communist military involvement." . . .

THE GOVERNMENT: THE SEARCH FOR ORDER AND DEMOCRACY

The massive propaganda effort to focus attention on outside Communist intervention is a way of diverting attention from the repressive regime that the United States is supporting. The Reagan Administration's tactic is to win backing for the junta not because of what it stands for (few democratic governments would support a government whose army has killed 13,000 civilians) but to "draw the line" against "outside intervention." . . .

The "Progressive" Coalition

The white paper describes the governing coalition that took over after the coup in October 1979 as being made up of progressive civilian and military officers. Yet the great majority of these progressives defected to the F.D.R. or were killed by the rightist faction which is now in control. The "three small non-Marxist-Lennist political parties" that the white paper earlier dismisses as window dressing in the F.D.R. leadership are later portrayed as significant progressives when they were in the first coalition. The white paper's inconsistency is apparent in the way it attempts to reclaim the progressive character of the original junta while discrediting the genuine progressives who resigned from it in protest or were pushed out. The systematic purge of the progressives by the rightist faction within the junta between October 1979 and March 1980 is described in the same vacuous, euphemistic language that is used throughout the white paper when the authors wish to cover their tracks: "After an initial period of instability, the new Government stabilized around a coalition that includes military participants in the October 1979 coup, the Christian Democratic Party and independent civilians." The white paper leaves out the purge of the Majano reformists, and the bulk of the Christian Democrats who are now in opposition, along with university faculty and students, Social Democrats and the other forces of reform. It does not say that ultra-right forces deeply involved in repressive actions are all that remain of the original junta that took power in October 1979.

The white paper claims that "since March 1980, this coalition has begun broad social changes." Actually, the number of peasants killed and co-ops that fell under military occupation rose sharply: peasants killed increased from 126 per month in February, to 203 in March, to 423 in July, totaling 3,272 for the glorious year of agrarian reform! The paper then repeats the falsehood that the opposition to this "reform" consists of Marxist-Leninist guerrilla terrorists and the three insignificant non-Marxist-Leninist political parties operating outside of the country.

Once again, the authors omit mention of the absence of any political rights in El Salvador, and the state of war that the junta has declared against all opposition.

Extremist Symbiosis

The white paper then proceeds to argue that the Government "faces armed opposition from the extreme right as well as from the left. . . . A symbiotic relationship has developed between the terrorism practiced by extremists of both left and right." This notion has been systematically refuted by the Archbishop's Legal Aid Commission report on repression, which adduces evidence showing that in 1980, 66 percent of the assassinations were committed by Government security forces, and 14 percent were committed by right-wing death squads. Moreover, voluminous testimony, documents and photographs have emerged to substantiate the frequent and close collaboration between the death squads and the regime's security forces. The "symbiosis" causing most of the violence is between the regime and the death squads, not the right and left.

In this regard it is important to note that not one right-wing death squad assassin has ever been apprehended, let alone prosecuted, despite the public nature of most of the killings. This in itself should dispel any notion that the regime is innocent in the activity of the death squads. The Legal Aid Commission study further demonstrates that the bulk of the victims were poor peasants, students and wage workers—the groups in whose names the purported reforms were carried out. In fact the reforms were mere facades for the militarization of the country. The escalation of regime terror against the peasants is the surest indication of this.

The white paper voices concern about the murder and rape of the U.S. nuns, but it fails to mention the fact that the nuns were opposed to U.S. policy, and were murdered by the junta along with more than a score of other church people working for the poor. While the white paper claims to be interested in a complete investigation of these killings, former Ambassador White stated emphatically that Washington has not made any effort to pressure the junta and has effectively collaborated with the regime in covering up the murders—rewarding its perpetrators with additional arms and economic aid.

In one of its more cynical statements, the paper notes that "few Salvadorans participate in anti-Government demonstrations"—implying that they support the Government. The scores of dead protesters, including mutilated and decapitated corpses that appeared in the wake of every protest march, have no doubt had a dampening effect on demonstrations. But to equate a terrorized population with one that approves the Government is a grotesque distortion which only indicates how out of touch this Administration is with the political reality in El Salvador and the rest of the Third World. There is not only an absence of political protest in El Salvador, there is an absence of all forms of political expression; the dictatorship is total. The support for the front and the guerrillas has not diminished—it has gone underground. The white paper's claim that U.S. aid "has helped create jobs and feed the hungry" is belied by the accounts of Church sources. U.S. economic aid has contributed to massive military corruption; military aid hardens the resolve of the military dictators and increases the rate of killing. U.S. economic aid does not keep up with the massive flight of private capital estimated at more than $1.5 billion during the past year. The collapse of the Salvadoran economy and the massive exodus of refugees from repression in rural areas hardly testifies to the "success" of what the paper describes as the "Duarte Government." The latter is a figment of the State Department's imagination, for real power continues to be vested within the military—a point emphasized by a military official in an interview in *Le Monde* recently.

Conclusion

The white paper is a thin tissue of falsifications, distortions, omissions and simplifications directed toward covering up increased U.S. support for a murderous regime. It has sought to transform a war between the regime and its people into an East-West struggle and to deny the internal socioeconomic and political roots of the struggle. The purpose of these distortions is to mobilize U.S. public opinion behind the new Administration's policies not only in El Salvador but throughout the Third World. The hypocrisy suffusing the white paper is vice's tribute to virtue, for it tacitly recognizes that if the truth were presented, the American people would balk at supporting a regime that is rewarded for killing its noblest sons and daughters who seek social justice in El Salvador.

E.P. THOMPSON

East, West—Is There a Third Way? *July 10-17, 1982*

E.P. Thompson, a social historian, writer and leader of the European Nuclear Disarmament movement, has been a frequent contributor to *The Nation* since 1981. He is the author of *The Making of The English Working Class* and many other books.

What, we must ask as we proceed into the 1980s, is the cold war all about? The answer to this question can give us no comfort at all. If we look at the military scene, nothing is receding. On the contrary, the military establishments of both superpowers continue to grow each year. The cold war, in this sense, has broken free from its historical moorings and has acquired an independent inertial thrust of its own. What is the cold war now about? It is about itself.

We face here, in the grimmest sense, the "consequences of consequences." The cold war may be seen as a show put on the road by two rival entrepreneurs in 1946 or 1947. The show has grown bigger and bigger; the entrepreneurs have lost control of it, as it has thrown up its own managers, administrators, producers and a huge supporting cast, all of whom have a direct interest in its continuance, in its enlargement. Whatever happens, the show must go on.

The cold war has become a habit, an addiction. But it is a habit supported by very powerful material interests in each bloc: the military-industrial and research establishments of both sides, the security services and intelligence operations, and the political servants of these interests. These interests command a large (and growing) allocation of the skills and resources of each society; they influence the direction of each society's economic and social development; and it is in the interest *of* these interests to increase that allocation and to influence that direction even more.

It is in the very nature of this cold war show that there must be two adversaries: each move by one must be matched by the other. This is the inner dynamic of the cold war which determines that its military and security establishments are *self-reproducing*. Their missiles summon forward our missiles which summon forward their missiles in turn. NATO's hawks feed the hawks of the Warsaw Pact countries.

For the ideology of the cold war is self-reproducing also. That is, the military and the security services and their political servants *need* the cold war. They have a direct interest in its continuance.

Yet a contradiction has arisen. Today's military confrontation has been protracted long after the reasons for it have vanished into history. I share the view of an editorial in *The Times* of London (October 2, 1981):

> The huge accumulations of weaponry which the two [super-powers] brandish at each other are wholly out of proportion to any genuine conflict of interests. There is no serious competition for essential resources, or for territory that is truly vital to the security of either, and the ideological fires have dwindled on both sides. In strictly objective terms a reasonable degree of accommodation should be easily attainable.

If the cold war is at once obsolete and inexorable—an ongoing, self-reproducing road show that has become necessary to ruling groups on both sides—can we find, within that contradiction, any resolution short of war?

Perhaps we can. But the resolution will not be easy. A general revolt of reason and conscience against the instruments which immediately threaten us—a perception, informing multitudes, of the human ecological imperative—this is a necessary part of the answer. Such a revolt, such a shift in perception, is already growing across Europe. But this cannot be the whole answer. For if the cold war has acquired a self-generating dynamic, then as soon as public concern is quieted by a few measures of arms control, new dangers and new weapons will appear. We must do more than protest if we are to survive. We must go behind the missiles to the cold war itself. We must begin to put Europe back into one piece.

And how could that be done? Very certainly it cannot be done by the victory of one side over the other. That would mean war. We must retrace our steps to that moment in 1944 before glaciation set in, and look once again for a third way.

If I had said this two years ago I would have despaired of holding your attention. But something remarkable is stirring in this continent today: movements which commenced in fear and which are now taking on the shape of hope; movements which cannot yet, with clarity, name their own demands. For the first time since the wartime Resistance there is a spirit abroad in Europe which carries a transcontinental aspiration. The Other which menaces us is being redefined not as other nations, nor even as the other bloc, but as the forces leading both blocs to auto-destruction—not Russia or America but their military, ideological and security establishments and their ritual oppositions.

And at the same time, as this Other is excluded, so a new kind of internal bonding is taking place. This takes the form of a growing commitment, by many thousands, to the imperative of survival and against the ideological or security imperatives of either bloc or their nation-states. In the words of the Appeal for European Nuclear Disarmament of April 1980:

> We must commence to act as if a united, neutral and pacific Europe already exists. We must learn to be loyal, not to "East" or "West," but to each other.

This is a large and improbable expectation. It has often been proclaimed in the past, and it has been as often disappointed. Yet what is improbable has already, in the past year, begun to happen. The military structures are under challenge. But something is happening of far greater significance. The ideological structures are under challenge also, and from *both* sides.

The cold war placed the political culture of Europe in a permanent double bind: the cause of "peace" and the cause of "freedom" fell apart. What is now happening is that these two causes are returning to one cause—peace *and* freedom—and as this happens, so, by a hundred different channels, the transcontinental discourse of political culture can be resumed.

The peace movements which have developed with such astonishing rapidity in Northern, Western and Southern Europe—and which are now finding an echo in the East—are one part of this cause. They have arisen in response not only to a military and strategic situation but to a political situation also. What has aroused Europeans most about the deployment of weapons whose target would be the "theater" of Europe is the spectacle of two superpowers arguing above the heads of the people who live there. These movements speak with new accents. They are, in most cases, neither pro-Soviet nor manipulated by the Communist-influenced

World Peace Council. Their objective is to clear nuclear weapons and bases out of the whole continent, East and West, and then to roll back conventional forces. Nor is it correct to describe them as "neutralist" or "pacifist." They are looking for a third way. A third way is an active way: it is not "neutral" between the other ways, it goes somewhere else.

The Western peace movements bring together traditions—socialist, trade unionist, liberal, Christian, ecological—which have always been committed to civil rights. They extend their support to the Polish renewal and to Solidarity, and to movements of libertarian dissent in the Warsaw Pact countries. And from Eastern Europe also, voice after voice is now reaching us—hesitant, cautious, but with growing confidence—searching for the same alliance: peace *and* freedom.

These voices signal that the whole thirty-five-year-old era of the cold war could be coming to an end: the Ice Age could give way to turbulent torrents running from East to West and from West to East. And within the peace movements, and also within movements of lower profile but of equal potential in Eastern Europe, there is maturing a further—and a convergent—demand: to shake off the hegemony of the superpowers and to reclaim autonomy.

The question before Europeans today is not how many NATO forward-based systems might equal how many Soviet SS-20s. Beneath these equations there is a larger question: in what circumstances might *both* superpowers loosen the military grip which settled upon Europe in 1946 and which has been protracted long after its origins have receded into history? And how might such a retreat of hegemonies and loosening of blocs take place without endangering peace? Such an outcome would be profoundly in the interests not only of the peoples of Europe but of the peoples of the Soviet Union and the United States—in relaxing tension and in relieving them of some of the burdens and dangers of their opposed military establishments. But what—unless it were to be our old enemy "deterrence"—could monitor such a transition so that neither one nor the other nation turned it to advantage?

We are not, it should be said, describing some novel stage in the progress known as détente. For in the early 1970s, détente signified the cautious tuning-down of hostilities between states or blocs, but without altering the cold war status quo. Détente (or "peaceful coexistence") was licensed by the superpowers; it did not arise from the client states, still less from popular movements. The framework of East-West settlement was held rigid by deterrence: in the high noon of Kissinger's diplomacy, détente was a horse trade between the leaders of the blocs, in which any unseemly movement out of the framework was to be discouraged as "destabilizing." Czechs or Italians were required to remain quiet in their client places, lest any rash movement should disturb the tetchy equilibrium of the superpowers.

But what we can glimpse now is something different: a détente of peoples rather than of states—a movement of peoples which sometimes dislodges states from their blocs and brings them into a new diplomacy of conciliation, which sometimes runs beneath state structures, and which sometimes defies the ideological and security structures of particular states. This will be a more fluid, unregulated, unpredictable movement than in the past. It may entail risk.

The risk must be taken. For the cold war can be brought to an end in only two ways: by the destruction of European civilization, or by the reunification of European political culture. The first will take place if the ruling groups in the rival superpowers, sensing that the ground is shifting beneath them and that their client states are becoming detached, succeed in compensating for their waning political and economic authority by engaging in a more and more frenzied militarization. This is exactly what is happening now. The outcome will be terminal.

But we can now see a small opening toward the other alternative. And if we think this alternative to be possible, then we should—every one of us—reorder all our priorities. We should invest nothing more in missiles, everything in the skills of communication and exchange. All I can do here is indicate, briefly, programs which are already in the making.

One such program is that of limited nuclear-free zones. A Nordic nuclear-free zone is now under active consideration. And in southeast Europe, the Greek government has pledged to initiate discussions with Bulgaria and Rumania in the Warsaw Pact, and with nonaligned Yugoslavia, for another nuclear-free zone.

Such zones have political significance. Both states and local authorities can enlarge the notion to include exchanges between citizens in direct, uncensored discourse. In Central Europe a zone of this kind might also take in measures of conventional disarmament and the withdrawal of both Soviet and NATO forces from both Germanys. This proposal is now being actively propagated in East Germany as well as in West—the late East German civil rights supporter Robert Havemann raised the question directly in an open letter to Chairman Brezhnev—and it is now being discussed, in unofficial circles, in Poland and Czechoslovakia too.

The objectives of such larger zones are clear: to make a space of lessened tension between the two blocs; to destroy the menacing, symbolic affront of nuclear weapons; to bring nations both East and West within reciprocal agreements; and to loosen the bonds of the bloc system, allowing more autonomy, more initiative to the smaller states.

But at the same time there must be other initiatives, through a hundred different channels, by which citizens might enlarge this discourse. It is absurd to expect the weapons systems of both sides to de-weaponize themselves, the security systems of both sides to fall into each other's arms. It is, precisely, at the top of the cold war systems that deadlock, or worse, takes place. If we are to destructure the cold war, then we must destabilize these systems from below.

I am talking of a new kind of politics which cannot (with however much good will) be conducted by politicians. It must be a politics of peace, informed by a new internationalist code of honor, conducted by citizens. And it is now being so conducted by the international medical profession, by churches, by writers and by many others.

Music can be a "politics" of this kind. There is today some generational cultural mutation taking place among the young people of Europe. The demonstrations for peace—in Bonn, London, Madrid, Rome, Amsterdam—have been thronged with the young. The young are *bored* with the cold war. There is a shift at a level below politics—expressed in style, in sound, in symbol, in dress—which could be more significant than any negotiations taking place in Geneva. The PA systems of popular music bands are already capable of making transcontinental sounds. The bands may not be expert arms negotiators, but they might blast the youth of Europe into each others' arms.

It has been proposed that there might be a festival—it might be called "Theater of Peace"—somewhere in Central Europe in the summer of 1983. Young people (although their elders would not be excluded) would be called to assemble from every part of the continent, bringing with them their music, their living theater, their art, their posters, their symbols and gifts. There would be rallies, workshops and informal discussions. Every effort would be made to invite youth from "the other side," not in preselected official parties but as individual visitors and strays. The project may be too ambitious for 1982; but as a primer for this, plans are now afoot for a popular music festival in Vienna early in August.

In conclusion, how do we put the causes of freedom and of peace back together? This cannot be done by provocative interventions in the affairs of other nations. And it certainly cannot be done by the old strategy of cold war "linkage." If we look forward to democratic renewal on the other side of our common world, then this strategy is plainly counterproductive. No popular movements in the East will ever obtain civil or trade union rights because the West is pressing missiles against their country's borders. On the contrary, this only enhances the security operations and the security-minded ideology of their rulers. The peoples of the East will seek their rights and liberties themselves and in their own way—as the Portuguese, Spanish, Greek and Polish people have shown us. What is needed, from and for all of us, is a space free from cold war crisis in which we can move.

There might, however, be a very different kind of citizens' linkage in which, as part of the people's détente, the movements for peace in the West and for free-dom in the East recognized each other as natural allies. For this to be possible, we in the West must move first. As the military pressure upon the East begins to relax, so the old double bind will begin to lose its force. And the Western peace movement (which can scarcely be cast convincingly as an "agent of Western imperialism" by Soviet ideologists) should press steadily upon the state structures of the East demands for greater openness of exchange, both of persons and of ideas.

A transcontinental discourse must begin to flow, in both directions, with the peace movement—a movement of unofficial people with a code of conduct which disallows the pursuit of political advantage for either side—as the conduit. We cannot be content to criticize nuclear missiles. We have to be, in every moment, critics also of the adversary posture of the powers. For we are threatened not only by weapons but by the ideological and security structures which divide our continent and which turn us into adversaries. Thus the concession which the peace movement asks of the Soviet state is not so much these SS-20s and those Backfire bombers but its assistance in commencing to tear these structures down. And in good time one might look forward to a further change in the Soviet Union itself, as the long-outworn ideology and structures inherited from Stalin's time give way before internal pressures for a Soviet renewal.

What I have proposed is improbable. But, if it commenced, it might gather pace with astonishing rapidity. There would not be decades of détente, as the glaciers slowly melt. There would be very rapid and unpredictable changes: nations would become unglued from their alliances; there would be sharp conflicts within nations; there would be successive risks. We could roll up the map of the cold war and travel without maps for a while.

I do not mean that Russia would become a Western democracy, nor that the West would go communist. Immense differences in social systems would remain. Nations, if unglued from their alliances, might—as Poland and Greece have shown us—fall back into their own inherited national traditions. I mean only that the flow of political and intellectual discourse, and of human exchange, would resume across the whole continent. The blocs would discover that they had forgotten what their adversary postures were about.

Our species has been favored on this planet, although we have not always been good caretakers of our globe's resources. Our stay here, in the spaces of geological time, has been brief. No one can tell us our business. But I think it is something more than to consume as much as we can and then blow the place up.

We have, if not a duty, then a need, deeply engraved within our culture, to pass the place on no worse than we found it. Those of us who do not expect an afterlife may see in this our only immortality: to pass on the succession of life, the succession of culture. It may even be that we are happier when we are engaged in matters larger than our own wants, larger than ourselves.

We did not choose to live in this time. But there is no way of getting out of it. And it has given us as significant a cause as has ever been known, a moment of opportunity which might never be renewed. If these weapons and then those weapons are added to the huge sum on our continent, if Poland drifts into civil war and if this calls down Soviet military intervention, if the United States launches some military adventure in the Middle East—can we be certain that this moment will ever come back? I do not think so. If my analysis is right, then the inertial thrust of the cold war, from its formidable military and ideological bases, will have passed the point of no return.

The opportunity is *now,* when there is already an enhanced consciousness of danger informing millions. We can match this crisis only by a summoning of resources to a height like that attained by the greatest religious or political movements of Europe's past. I think, once again, of 1944 and of the crest of the Resistance. There must be that kind of spirit abroad in Europe once more. But this time it must arise, not in the wake of war and repression but before these take place. Five minutes afterward, and it will be too late. Humankind must at last grow up. We must recognize the Other in ourselves.

ANDREW KOPKIND

The Return of Cold War Liberalism April 23, 1983

Andrew Kopkind, associate editor of *The Nation* since 1983, reports in this piece on the revival of a Cold War in American political and cultural life.

"Liberalism is out of fashion," Arthur Schlesinger Jr. wrote from the lower depths of the 1950s, "and liberals are out of office." The cold war of that decade did more than freeze East-West relations. It produced a profound chilling effect on the exercise of progressive politics on the home front. Excluded from power and denied prestige, the liberal brokers of the New Deal generation had to scramble merely to stay alive. And out of their isolation and insecurity—and their struggle for survival—came a new category of political behavior: cold war liberalism. It was both a sensibility and a strategy, a defensive posture toward the warriors of the right and an aggressive attack on the rebels of the left. Looking right, the cold war liberals affirmed the end of ideology, the vitality of the center, the failure of the socialist god. Looking left, they baited the hell out of Reds, fellow travelers and "progressives."

Now a new chill is in the air. The powerful producers of the plays of history have opened a sequel to their old cold war hit, and many of the cultural props that supported the first run are coming back into style. There's a retro look to the political landscape, the feel of the Dulles days. Rebellion, utopias and tender-mindedness are *out*; conformity, realism and hard-heartedness are *in*. Liberals—who always manage to mediate the terms of discourse—are out of high office and high fashion; and once more many of them have enlisted in a cold war, with their familiar postures and attacks.

The liberal media are in the forefront. CBS's *60 Minutes*, that exemplar of electronic liberalism, hounds the National and World Councils of Churches for allegedly supporting Marxism, revolution and lesser heresies, with a ferocity its correspondents usually reserve for corrupt politicians and quacks. *The New York Times* baits the Old Left, the New Left and lefts yet unborn for a variety of political sins and ideological errors; see, to give a few examples, recent harangues on the plot to defame Jerzy Kosinski, the slander of U.S. diplomats in Chile by the film *Missing*, the dolorous effects of the Vietnam War protests on foreign policy, the moral complexity of McCarthy-era anti-Communist investigations.

The Washington Post's editorial page is suddenly strident in its attacks on certain leftist organizations within the nuclear freeze and disarmament movement. *The New Republic* lets hardly a week go by without detecting the rebirth (or the persistence) of Stalinism in all the old familiar places on the left. Similar seizures occur with increasing frequency in the editorial chambers of *Harper's*, *Newsweek*, even *The New York Review of Books*, and at the major television networks.

There are more examples every day, but the new cold war liberalism goes far beyond a simple series of journalistic attacks on leftist positions in a few *causes célèbres*. It is a wide, deep and diffuse campaign against the left itself, a contest to define history, to capture political icons, terms and totems. It is a battle for legitimacy, waged by leading lights of liberalism against those on their political and cultural left flank. It is the first wave of an advancing cold war culture, propelled by the neoconservative and New Right tides of the recent past, which will touch all that we think and do in the period ahead.

It is Susan Sontag, in a speech at a Solidarity rally at Town Hall in New York City in February 1982, accusing many of her former comrades (including those here at *The Nation*) of countenancing Communist authoritarianism and aggression. It is Irving Howe, in his recently published book, *A Margin of Hope, An Intellectual Autobiography*, berating the New Left of the 1960s for its immature tolerance of Stalinism. It is David Horowitz and Peter Collier, in *Rolling Stone*, trashing the Students for a Democratic Society and the Weather Underground as orgies of sex and violence, without regard or sympathy for the radical movement's historical context or political analysis. It is Timothy Garton Ash, in *Harper's*, comparing the antinuclear Green Party to the Nazis because of its idealism. It is the *CBS Evening News* insinuating that President Mitterrand's compact with the Communist Party has brought a wave of terrorism to France. It is the uncritical broadcasting of rumors about K.G.B. plots, Libyan hit squads, Bulgarian conspiracies. It comes from Flora Lewis, Ronald Radosh, David Denby, the brothers Kalb, Morley Safer: liberals all, to some degree, writing and speaking in ideological phrases and accusatory tones not heard in this country since the end of the 1950s.

Anyone with an eye and an ear for the nuances of a new sensibility should be able to detect the telltale signs of the new cold war culture. Political discourse has shifted rightward; whole topics are excluded; fundamental arguments—about revolution, for example—have been dropped from conversation. There is an inordinate amount of talk these days about national security, military strategy, subversion and terrorism. The Soviet Union, after a period of relatively benign treatment in the press as well as in political conversations, is again a pariah state. Throughout, discussions of public issues have an ideological spin, and criticisms are hurled with a prosecutorial power that is strongly suggestive of the 1950s. Politics *feels* different.

The new cold war liberals are not to be confused with the New Right or the neoconservatives, who are illiberal across the board—on social welfare, civil liberties, racial and sexual equality, the environment and cultural styles. The cold war liberals are still left of center on most of these issues most of the time. CBS is committed to "soup-line journalism" and devotes precious air time to the downside of Reaganomics. *The New Republic* is staunchly civil libertarian. *The New York Times* is for clean air and pure water, even at corporate expense. *The Washington Post* speaks out strongly for civil rights.

What unites these still-liberal voices is a concern with loyalty, subversion and national security reminiscent of that displayed by the old cold war liberals of the 1950s. The issues are defined with more sophistication than they were three decades ago, but the objectives are basically the same.

THE LOYALTY PERPLEX

Take the matter of loyalty. In the 1950s, the working definition was simple: allegiance to the United States and not to the Soviet Union. The cold war liberals justified the expulsion of Communists and fellow travelers from American institutional life—from labor unions, veterans' groups, political parties, civil liberties organizations, universities, the media, the entertainment industry and, of course, government at every level—on the ground that the leftists were "under the discipline" of a foreign, hostile power. Communism had to be outlawed, and it was Hubert Humphrey, the compleat cold war liberal politician, who sponsored the necessary legislation, in 1954. C.P. membership was considered prima facie proof of disloyalty, and non-card-carrying fellow travelers had only to be shown to be adherents of the "party line" to be outlawed as well. An enormous effort went into the drawing of lines between "disloyal" leftists and "loyal" liberals. Constitutional rights were guaranteed only to those who were loyal to the Constitution, Q.E.D.

The loyalty issue in the 1980s is more ambiguous than it was in the 1950s because the limits of the left are not coterminous with the membership of the Communist Party (or *any* radical party), or even with an identifiable conspiracy of Communists-cum-fellow travelers who slavishly follow Moscow's orders. (To be sure, there is a small—almost minuscule—group of "official" Communist Party members who are once again feeling the sting of liberal swords, after a spell of laissez-faire tolerance or even camaraderie shown by liberals in the coalitions of the 1960s and 1970s.) The new loyalty battle is being fought largely in a single arena—the nuclear freeze and disarmament movement. Some of its liberal sympathizers call for the expulsion of Communists and their fellow travelers, "stooges" and "dupes" from the movement.

Sometimes the attacks are made with disarming sincerity, as when *The Washington Post* charged (in an editorial written by Stephen Rosenfeld) that the international peace circuit is riddled with "creatures of the K.G.B." Such statements are customarily accompanied by the sharp, screeching sounds of lines being drawn on slate, demarcating the bad guys on the left and the good ones from the center rightward.

Some of the critics, however, are less ingenuous. These sophisticates (who often have personal histories of radical activism in the 1960s) claim that the Communists, by dint of their single-minded dedication and demonic energy, will "take over" peace coalitions and "subvert" them to their own ends, thus weakening the potential for mass mobilization. For example, Ronald Radosh reported in *The New Republic* that a Communist member of the executive committee of the June 12 Rally Committee wanted last year's profreeze demonstration in New York City to endorse "such demands as a call for an end to U.S. intervention in Central America." That and similar appeals to "mushy logic," he warned, would drive out clear-thinking types who might otherwise demonstrate against nuclear war.

Here is a classic case of the "mush shift," a deft maneuver practiced by the old cold war liberals. The purpose, then and now, is to deflect the right-wing accusations of being muddle-headed and tender-minded onto the far left. It was practiced in antiquity by Arthur Schlesinger, who drew the line between the tender and the tough in his 1949 book, *The Vital Center*, the bible of cold war liberal thought.

The maneuver was part of the larger process of blame-shifting that became the liberals' standard technique of cold war survival. Of course, they insisted that their motives were moral rather than self-interested, patriotic rather than protective. They saw the evil of Communism and the perfidy of Communists, they said, and it was their duty to condemn wrong thinking and wrong doing. But while their intentions may indeed have been high-minded, their actions subverted their motives. What they did was destroy the left while hardly denting international Communism (that fight was carried on by the generals of capitalism, not their liberal lieutenants). Cold war liberalism's pre-eminent preoccupation — and its primary target — was the American left, and it succeeded mightily in its destructive work.

THUNDER ON THE RIGHT

Why has that preoccupation returned, like a long-buried fear-fantasy in the still of the night? Why are the new cold war liberals so concerned with loyalty, legitimacy and limpness of mind? It cannot be that a handful of American Communists pose a clear and present danger to Reagan's republic by their putative disloyalty, even if all the dupes, stooges and fellow travelers are lumped with them. Nor does their presence in the peace movement seem to be having any deleterious effect on its organizing efforts, or on its success in recruiting Middle Americans, from Vermont town meetings to the U.S. Congress. In fact, the cold war liberals are more worried about pressure from the right than any danger to the disarmament movement from the left. The calumny originates with President Reagan: The peace movement is "inspired by not the sincere, honest people who want peace, but by some who want the weakening of America and so are manipulating honest people and sincere people." From Senator Jeremiah Denton: Four groups advising Peace Links, the women's organization sponsoring National Peace Day, "are either Soviet controlled or openly sympathetic with, and advocates for, Communist foreign policy objectives." From *Reader's Digest*: The "patriotic, sensible people who make up the peace movement have been penetrated, manipulated and distorted to an amazing degree by people who have but one aim — to promote Communist tyranny by weakening the United States."

And how do the new cold war liberals respond? By blame-shifting, just like in the old days — calling the dogs off themselves by sicking them on the left. To be sure, critics like Radosh are careful to make a distinction between "Red-baiting and anti-Communism," but it is all in the eye of the attacker — a distinction without a difference. The objective effect of such attacks, whatever the claimed motive, is to undermine the left, to destroy both radical consciousness and radical activity as legitimate parts of political life.

Loyalty as an issue is now more complex. The left of the 1930s, which became the "generation on trial" of the 1950s, had an alien cast — in origin or allegiance — whereas the contemporary left has an all-American look. It was spawned on native soil, largely derived from the New Left of the 1960s, nurtured in the civil rights and antiwar campaigns and multiplied by the myriad movements of the succeeding years. It is hardly alien, and attempts to brand it disloyal require more elegant arguments than those used before.

Irving Howe, perhaps the greatest living arbiter of acceptable and unacceptable styles of leftism, unveiled some of the arguments against the New Left in a land-

336

mark article, "The Decade That Failed," which was published in *The New York Times Magazine* last September. In this excerpt from *A Margin of Hope*, he looked back in sorrow for the movement and in anger at those who did the damage: the "self-styled revolutionists," the "rigid" authoritarians, the white Marxist-Leninists, the black "Mau Maus," the naïve utopians, the student Stalinists—all the familiar terms in the arsenal of charges that liberals now use against the New Left.

Describing a decade as "failed," as Howe does the 1960s, is rather like calling a generation "lost." It is an expression of one's own disappointment and despair rather than a description of historical reality. Certainly there are arguments enough for those who would maintain that the social and political upheavals of the 1960s had enormously positive as well as negative consequences, even measured against the rigorous standards of a social democrat like Howe. But the inquests on the 1960s performed by Howe, by David Horowitz and Peter Collier and by others who have taken to baiting the New Left radicals are not primarily efforts to understand history; they are attempts to write it in their own terms, for their own ends.

RECAPTURING VIETNAM

The decade of the 1960s is a cultural artifact up for grabs—just as other decades were on the block when the earlier cold war liberals began grading their own loyalty tests. The far right of the McCarthy period thought the 1930s a season of treason perpetrated by Communists and New Dealers; the old cold war liberals then made their favorite distinction: the decade had failed because of the Reds, and the loyal New Dealers were not to blame. The new cold war liberals make an analogous distinction: the 1960s failed because of the aforementioned intellectual crimes and political treasons of the radicals, but the true "democrats" should be spared in the general disgrace.*

The battle to define the history of the 1960s is nowhere more noisy than in the contest for the hearts and minds of scholars and students of the Vietnam War. A

---

* There seems to be a contest for the definition of the struggles of every decade. The fight for the 1940s was over two issues: the historical meaning of World War II and the politics of the origins of the cold war. Radicals saw the war primarily as a resistance to fascism which turned into a vehicle for the expansion of the American empire. They perceived the cold war as an extension of the American imperial drive, now waged against its only serious opponent, the Soviet Union.

The fight for the history of the 1950s was over the issue of McCarthyism and the role of the various actors in that episode. Cold war liberalism is the ideological name for the middle position in that contest. The McCarthyites saw the 1950s as a time when Russia was preparing to subvert America and take over the world; the enemy was stopped by vigilant military and investigative measures. The left saw the time as a period of assault on both civil liberties and the radical presence in the United States. The cold war liberals agreed that McCarthyism was a menace, but they insisted that an anti-left campaign was necessary. However, their anti-Communism merged with Red-baiting to a point of indistinguishability.

fight has been brewing for some time, but it burst into public debate and into print just this year, at the Vietnam Reconsidered conference at the University of Southern California, and in an exhaustive cover article in *The New York Times Magazine*, "The New Vietnam Scholarship," by that paper's former Saigon correspondent Fox Butterfield. The antecedent of the contest was the right wing's indiscriminate assault on the whole antiwar movement, from the quagmire theorists who believed that the war was simply not winnable to the anti-imperialists who hoped the Vietcong revolutionaries would, in the words of one Vietnam veteran who spoke at the U.S.C. conference, "kick the U.S. in the ass." In response to the right, the liberal "revisionists" have declared the antiwar movement another failure of the left because it enabled Communists to win in Indochina (with the usual blood baths and re-education camps) and because it weakened the power of the United States to work its good will elsewhere in the world. To give native color to the argument, *The New York Review of Books* published a rather bizarre complaint from the first major defector from the National Liberation Front of South Vietnam—the broad revolutionary organization that fought the Americans and their Saigon clients. Truong Nhu Tang said that the N.L.F. had all along wanted the United States to leave behind a neutralist, liberal Vietnam, but that the Tet offensive and the American antiwar movement had delivered his country over to the Communists. Tang now lives in Paris.

Naturally, the liberals absolve themselves from blame for events after the war in Vietnam; it was the fault of the other guys—the radicals who tripped to Hanoi, who waved N.L.F. banners at antiwar rallies, who expressed solidarity with the "enemy." That is, the ones who were disloyal to flag and country.

What's wrong with the liberal blame-shifting in this case is that it revises history in such a way as to make it fantastic. The antiwar movement had only one objective: the disengagement of the United States from Indochina. There was no disagreement between liberals and radicals (or anyone else in the movement) on that score. It was a movement in America, not in Vietnam; its targets were the policy makers in Washington, not in Hanoi. It did not demand of Presidents Johnson and Nixon that the United States disengage itself from the war only if social democracy were installed in Saigon; it was for the reign of peace, not for the establishment of a parliament in Vietnam or the victory of the Communist Party. The sympathies, the rhetoric and even the behavior of many radicals may have been tasteless or provocative, but that was irrelevant to the shape of the peace. Nor could the radicals conceivably have delayed the ultimate American withdrawal or damaged the antiwar movement; the radicals *made* the movement. Insofar as American policy was shaped by domestic pressures (rather than by the situation in Vietnam), the disruption of the social fabric on the home front was certainly critical to stopping the war.

There is another struggle taking place over the right to define current history.

The new cold war liberals have seized on the revolt of the Polish workers, for example, and entered it in the books as another failure of the American left. Susan Sontag sounded the theme of this effort in her Town Hall speech, in which she warned leftists against ignoring the Solidarity movement because of the same sentimental attachment to Communism that had led them astray in the 1950s. They could have learned "the truth" about Communism, she said, by reading *Reader's Digest*. Movie critic David Denby made a similar charge in the course of a roundhouse swing at *Village Voice* columnist Alexander Cockburn in an article in *The New Republic*. Denby observed that while Cockburn could get worked up about the plight of the Palestinians, he had hardly a word to say about the tragedy of the Polish workers.

One could debate the truth of this accusation (actually, Cockburn had written in defense of Solidarity), but such specifics were secondary to Denby's main purpose, which was to blame the American left for betraying the Polish workers' movement and thus contributing to its failure. Liberals love failure because they can blame it on the left.

THE SUBVERSION-TERRORISM EQUATION

Subversion as an issue in the culture of the new cold war liberalism has surfaced in somewhat the same way as loyalty: in response to repeated rumblings on the right. And like the loyalty issue, subversion has an antiquated as well as a contemporary aspect.

The subversion problem in the 1950s was stated to be that Russian spies, or spies for the Russians, were stealing secrets (the Rosenbergs), manipulating policy (Alger Hiss in the State Department) and brainwashing the masses (the Hollywood Ten). Subversion was the objective act; it was produced by disloyalty, the subjective state. The great subversion trials of the cold war era were meant to provide proof that disloyalty had a perilous predicate. When cold war liberals bore witness against leftists before Congressional committees, or when they enforced blacklists, or when they voted to outlaw Communism, they tacitly (or loudly) accepted the theory, enshrined in the Smith Act of 1940, that American Communists posed a danger to America.

In time, and with the cold war thaw, the operative sections of the Smith Act were declared unconstitutional, after which espionage, when it was discovered, was treated as a criminal act, not an ideological statement. Now, as the new cold war settles in, there is a revival of interest in the old spy stories. Two books about the Rosenbergs are due this year (the thirtieth anniversary of their execution), Alger Hiss's case is flaring up again in the courts and the British cold war spies are forever popping up in one connection or another. Michael Straight comes out in his book, *After Long Silence*. Donald Mclean and Anthony Blunt die, and the obituary writers celebrate their contributions to Soviet espionage. It all serves to create a credible context for cold warriors: what happened once could happen again.

But subversion has a different face in the 1980s. Just as the right is more worried about the disloyalty of native New Leftists, so it is fearful of a new kind of home-grown subversion: the name is terrorism. The right is apt to lump everyone it doesn't like into one terrorist group, so it has fallen to the cold war liberals, again, to take cover and direct the fire to their left. The far right, for instance, figures that mainline Protestant churches in the United States and abroad are fomenting revolution on every continent. *60 Minutes*, however, does a two-part special on the peculiar perfidy of the leadership of the National and World Councils of Churches (as opposed to the loyal, conservative membership) and their grants to such groups as the North American Committee on Latin America and the Committee in Solidarity with the People of El Salvador. Various shots of "leftist" church people are intercut with shots of Fidel Castro, unidentified marching Asians and unnamed black Africans carrying (according to correspondent Morley Safer) revolutionary rifles.

It is not a very great leap from there to the conclusion that those who support revolution in the Third World are soft on terrorism, or worse. Since we know, or have been told by Alexander Haig, Jeane Kirkpatrick and President Reagan, that terrorism is international, that the Palestinians who kill innocent people in Jerusalem are allied with the Black Liberation Army and Weather Underground guerrillas who kill bank guards in Nyack, New York, it must follow that anyone who holds the politics of insurrection is a potential terrorist.

There is a perdurable debate within the left, and between liberals and leftists, over both the morality and the efficacy of nonviolence, revolution, guerrilla warfare and even standard-brand terrorism. The debate has cropped up in hundreds of political upheavals, from the French Resistance and the Warsaw uprising in World War II, through the anticolonial wars in Asia and Africa, to Cuba and Nicaragua, and to the black liberation movement in the United States. But the kind of treatment *60 Minutes* gave to the subject was quite different from the old debate: it was a prosecutorial campaign. "Terrorism" as a term thus becomes an ideological weapon, like "Marxism" (which Safer also hurled at the church leaders) or "Stalinism." The words are not meant to have descriptive value, only firepower.

RETURN OF THE RED MENACE

Like loyalty and subversion, national security has made an unexpected comeback on the list of liberal concerns. After the fearful 1950s, it seemed that the question of American military security was dead and buried; its last gasp came during the

Kennedy Administration, with its apocalyptic vision of a missile gap, the Cuban missile scare and the Berlin crisis. J.F.K.'s "Ich bin ein Berliner" were famous last words of the old cold war. After that came a period of concentration on internal social problems (poverty, racism), the war in Vietnam, détente and Watergate. And *voilà*! The missiles are bristling once again, the bomb looms large and militarism is in command.

After the setback in Vietnam, the New Right and the neoconservatives set out to kill détente and restore American military supremacy. Their method was to raise the specter of the "Soviet threat," that is, the Red menace in Russian uniform. But their strategy could never have succeeded without the participation of liberals in a revived cold war discourse.

The liberal reaction to pressure from the right worked on two levels. The ideological groundwork was laid by placing communism—as an ideology—outside lawful limits of thought. "Communism *is* fascism," Sontag said at Town Hall. If that is true, then communism in any national accent—Russian, Cuban, Ethiopian, Nicaraguan—is dangerous, and must be destroyed before it destroys us. (Communism in countries that happen to be soft on America can be redefined as something else, such as Yugoslav "Titoism," or Chinese "revisionism," and need only be patronized, rather than liquidated.) Marxism—when it wears a guerrilla uniform or a kaffiyeh—is simply communism waiting to shoot its way into a government. The cold war liberals can thus condemn Salvadoran rebels and Palestinian fighters with the same fervor they display toward Soviet soldiers.

On the second level, the new cold war liberals offered a political platter of fine distinctions and sophistries about the arms race and the nuclear freeze and disarmament movement. These were most cogently stated by Leon Wieseltier, in his exhaustive rumination in the January 10 & 17 issue of *The New Republic*, entitled "Nuclear War, Nuclear Peace." Wieseltier's very comprehensiveness defeats analysis, let alone characterization; but it is fair to say that after demonstrating that both the "hawks" and the "doves" are neither all wrong nor all right, he concludes that there is indeed a Soviet military threat and that nuclear deterrence is the only possible political and moral method for meeting it.

This is an important conclusion for cold war liberals, similar in significance to the decision of their predecessors thirty years ago to stand behind, or under, Dullesian "massive retaliation," and to sanction containment, brinkmanship and the various permutations of confrontational policy in that era. And while Wieseltier and like-minded theorists begin by responding to the fears of the right about Russian domination, they end up by attacking the left—the freeze movement, the disarmament prophets (Jonathan Schell and E.P. Thompson) and the naïve, sentimental, tender-minded troops in the ranks.

ROBERT GROSSMAN *"Cold War II"* (1983)

A COLD WAR IS REBORN

Culture, like history, is dialectical; it develops in response to the interplay of political and intellectual forces on a scale of time in the real world. Cultural developments do not appear out of nowhere, or float free of the basic relationships of power and privilege that they reflect. The culture of the new cold war has a history and a reason which are related to its times. And it has a future which can be presumed, though not precisely predicted.

In its current phase, the cold war began, or resumed, at the moment détente was declared – whichever date one may care to name: when President Nixon announced his mission to Moscow in 1971, when he signed the SALT I arms treaty in May 1972, when Congress authorized its approval in September. In any case, six months later, the Coalition for a Democratic Majority – soon to be renamed the Committee on the Present Danger – was in business, plotting a campaign to restore the *status quo ante* détente.

The coalition was composed of Vietnam hawks from the Johnson wing of the Democratic Party, who had lost power to the McGovern wing in the wake of the war. Later, the committee was broadened to include Republicans, former New Dealers and freelance anti-Communists who agreed with the group's manifesto calling for aggressive opposition to the "Soviet drive for dominance based upon an unparalleled military buildup."

What started as a letterhead listing Democrats on the outs gained the support of those disaffected from détente: Jewish neoconservatives worried about Israel's security in a depolarized world, corporate politicians concerned about the safety of petroleum supplies, old cold warriors who refused to die or fade away and ambitious young men seeking a hook for their hopes for power in government, the universities or one or another social or intellectual set. Match these names with any of those categories: Norman Podhoretz, Zbigniew Brzezinski, Henry Jackson, George Will, Paul Nitze, Eugene Rostow, Daniel Moynihan, Leon Keyserling.

In the mid-1970s, the infant cold war campaign was run for the most part by neoconservatives; it flourished in the world of the formerly liberal. There were historical reasons for that, particularly the long memories from the 1950s. But there were practical reasons as well. The neoconservatives were closest to power, and they used the cold war threat as a means to consolidate their position. It had, after all, worked before.

There was another source of heat on the issue of Communism and national defense. The old right had been utterly out of power, office and fashion since the McCarthy days. In the post-Vietnam political trough the New Right – McCarthyism rehabilitated – was making its bid. Eventually, these far rightists would merge into the Reagan campaign (and Administration). In the late 1970s,

343

they were still outside the political mainstream, firing away at the liberals and the left with indiscriminate enthusiasm, while the neoconservatives—a more tasteful, pin-striped bunch—were more precise in their aim.

Their target was the tender-minded liberalism of the Vietnam period, now embodied in the McGovern wing of the Democratic Party and in what journalists called the "left" of the Carter Administration. They were particularly hostile to Carter's disarmament chief, Paul Warnke, to U.N. representative Andrew Young and to Secretary of State Cyrus Vance. Their principal policy demand was the scrapping of the SALT II treaty; their main military objective was the authorization of the MX missile.

The jousting that had gone on between 1974 and 1978 was a preliminary to the main event: Carter's capitulation to the new cold warriors halfway through his term. It was at that point that cold war liberalism was born, a brand-new political baby, the product of—but distinct from—a set of neoconservative and right-wing forebears.

CARTER MOVES RIGHT

If there is one episode that can be identified as the historical fulcrum between détente and the new cold war, it was the small tempest over the existence—never proved—of a "Soviet combat brigade" in Cuba, which Senate Foreign Relations Committee chairman Frank Church announced had been detected in the summer of 1979. Over the determined opposition of Vance, who actually offered to resign because of the specious charges (which were endorsed by national security adviser Brzezinski), Carter grossly exaggerated this Soviet "threat" in order to co-opt his right-wing critics and to move to the patriotic high ground from the slough of post-1960s defeatism.

Then in November came the Iranian hostage affair, followed by the Soviet invasion of Afghanistan in December. Warnke, Young and Vance fled into the descending night. Carter reinstituted draft registration; he imposed sanctions on trade and "technology transfers" and stopped grain sales to the Russians; he opted for the MX and its absurd subterranean shell-game siting plan; he pulled America out of the Olympics; and he scrapped SALT II. Détente was dead.

As much as anything, Carter's surrender to the New Right and the neoconservatives on defense and national security issues deprived his Administration of an independent foreign policy that liberals could support. It may well have led to his defeat in 1980. For the liberal members of the Vietnam generation, whom Carter had courted and who had helped provide his small margin of victory four years earlier, were demoralized and disillusioned—and bored, to boot. Carter had given the left a declaration of amnesty for Vietnam-era draft resisters and deserters. He had tried to curb the most rapacious imperial instincts of American policy in Africa and Latin America. He had gone all gooey for human rights. But then he changed tack, and his Administration offered the left only an echo of a right-wing foreign policy, not a meaningful choice.

Thus, the new cold war liberalism is a consequence of pressure from both neoconservatives and the New Right, the changelings and the hard core. This dynamic is very much like the one that produced the cold war liberalism of the 1950s, which was a response to the Republican far right and the new conservatives who became ensconced in the last years of the Roosevelt regime. They had engineered the dumping of Henry Wallace in 1944, and had advised Truman to assume his cold war positions in the early postwar period.

THE GREAT RECANTATION

But there was another dynamic at work in the return of cold war liberalism, which had its origins in the personal history of a generation, the evolution of its ideas and the development of its consciousness.

History, Hegel said, is the problem of consciousness. The generation of the 1960s cut its consciousness on a liberationist, activist, sometimes utopian vision of the world. Only a few members of the 1960s cohort actually acted out that vision in a purposeful, dedicated way. The great majority watched, sympathized or dabbled with the passing radical causes and countercultural styles: civil rights, antiwar protest, Third World revolution, sexual liberation, communalism, high times, working-class militancy.

Their sympathies were based, for the most part, on sentiment rather than ideology. They felt a shiver of excitement when civil rights organizers raised their fists for "black power," even though the slogan—and the politics behind it—contradicted the ideal of integration, which they affirmed when challenged. Many secretly approved of the most violent expressions of social protest and personal rage, even if they stated their opposition to violence as a matter of policy. I remember lunching in Washington with a leading black official in the Johnson Administration during the bloody Detroit riots of 1967. His job was to keep the lid on racial conflict, to defuse tensions and maintain social peace. But he told me that he and his wife watched the news every night and cheered, "Burn, baby, burn!" as Detroit went up in flames. There were other cheers for the Vietnamese Communists' victory of Tet, for various Weather Underground exploits, for blows against the American empire struck throughout the world.

Many of the cheering liberals on the broad fringes of the radical issues never stopped to think that what was happening in the movement and in the streets would be inimical to their own class and career interests. For example, the defeat of the United States in Vietnam and the victory of the Vietnamese Communists would over the long run jeopardize the liberals' privileged position in the center

345

of imperial society. And the growing counterculture of alienated, adventurous, dropout and potentially explosive youths would later subvert the liberals' image as responsible members of the mainstream.

The followers of the radical political and social movements of the 1960s joined in celebrating the great moments of the period without worrying much about the inevitable problems down the road. They reveled in the sit-ins and the freedom marches, the campus strikes and the smoke-ins, the cane-cutting expeditions to Cuba and the encounters with the Vietcong in Canada and Czechoslovakia. Now, however, they feel guilty about—or have been made to take the blame for —a rigid Communist regime in Vietnam, murderous black cults like the Symbionese Liberation Army, the desperate junkie society that replaced the pot-and-flowers communes.

When the right wing—both the neoconservatives and the New Right—began its attack on the politics and lifestyles of the 1960s, many members of the vast liberal fringe, now grown-up and settling into conventional jobs and marriages, realized they had to fight for their own legitimacy. Their loyalty, broadly defined, was questioned in the context of a new cold war which was revived for that very purpose—to delegitimize the radical consciousness of a generation. Without many second thoughts, the liberal fringe turned right—and pointed left, with accusing fingers and hostile words.

The new cold war liberals were prepared to disown their history for both a personal and a practical reason. Many members of that generation found themselves facing choices in their own lives that required them to deny or redefine their earlier experiences. Whatever else the 1960s did, the decade seemed to promise its children an honest, humane, useful and communitarian life. Those promises were always exaggerated, and when they could not be fulfilled, the aging children labeled them "lies," and the whole decade a "failure." It was tempting for them to condemn the expectations when confronted by their own accommodations to a competitive, individualistic, illiberal and often inhumane world. And those who feared they had "sold out" resented those whose continued activity according to the old patterns of thought presented a constant reproach.

The practical reason for the turnaround was simple: the 1960s no longer sells. Liberals in government, the media and academe are the ideological entrepreneurs of the American system. Their power is that of the broker. In the last two decades they brokered peace in Vietnam and social tranquility, racial harmony and economic opportunity at home. It worked this way: liberals delivered the support, the votes and the good behavior of their constituents "at the base" to the political and corporate governors "at the top." The payoff, which the liberals negotiated, was civil rights legislation, a Vietnam settlement, antipoverty transfer payments to the underclass and relaxation of social and sexual norms.

Today the currency of payoffs is in short supply—or no supply at all. What the people at the top have to offer is national security, patriotism and good feelings about America: cold war values. And liberals must adapt to this new marketplace. The hysterical popular response to the Iranian hostage affair and the reception accorded the returning hostages, the celebration of the U.S. hockey team's Olympic victory over the Russians in 1980 and the great fear of Soviet military "superiority" all helped create an aggregate demand which the cold war liberals' entrepreneurial skills are now devoted to meeting.

50S' ISSUES AND ICONS

The personal and practical dynamic in the rise of the new cold war liberalism is also identifiable in the old version. The left of the 1930s also had a broad liberal fringe, which sympathized with the radical causes of the era in a vague, sentimental, nonideological way. Liberals then were generally approving of militant labor fights, the Spanish Civil War, resistance to fascism and the activities of the artistic avant-garde. After World War II, the liberals, now grown-up and settled in, pulled back, first into a self-absorbed apathy and privatism which anticipated the "personal liberation" and "human potential" movements of the 1970s, then into downright hostility to their past sympathies and to those who still maintained the old ideals. The liberals' transformation was accompanied by name-calling ("Stalinist") and name-naming ("fellow traveler"); they beat a retreat from the concerns of the radical decades to the safety of the cold war issues.

As the cold war culture spread across the land, the liberals began addressing new questions, or redefining old ones. They fought for the ownership of icons and issues. They began a debate over Freud: Is psychoanalysis a panacea for the individual or a means to social change? Over Marx: dead determinist or live methodologist? Over sociology: prescriptive or descriptive? Over philosophy: concerned with words or things?

The liberals sought to depoliticize all aspects of culture, to emphasize technique over ideology, the instrument over the idea. Daniel Bell's book *The End of Ideology* decreed the cessation of class struggle in America. The surviving form of liberalism was "managerial" rather than ideological; it offered a method for adjusting social imbalances rather than a blueprint for reforming society. The technical approach became the Democratic Party's "program" in the 1950s. Liberalism is, of course, nonrevolutionary by definition, and even in the headiest days of the New Deal, liberals opposed the transformation of the capitalist system. But with the death, or dormancy, of the radical left in the 1950s, liberalism lost even its reformist character, and it, too, became depoliticized.

Militarism, individualism and consumerism invaded the cultural life of the 1950s. The emblematic cold war television program was *Victory at Sea*, a Churchillian celebration of World War II, minus the politics. The representative novelists were J.D. Salinger, James Gould Cozzens and Ayn Rand. The dominant market icons were the TV set and the tail-fin automobile. Social criticism was aimed at the tasteless or debilitating effects of the political and economic system, not the system itself: Vance Packard on advertising (*The Hidden Persuaders*), David Riesman on alienation (*The Lonely Crowd*), William Whyte on suburban conformity (*The Organization Man*).

THE NEW COLD WAR CULTURE

The new cold war of the 1980s has already had similar success in reframing cultural discourse. A rapid and radical depoliticization has seized the country; it is obvious in the media, in the universities, in literature, in social criticism. There is even a depoliticization of politics itself. Public issues are not discussed in terms of power, justice, idealism and morality, as they were in the 1960s, but as a kind of theater, or a category of esthetics. Compare, for example, Joan Didion's *Salvador*, published this year, with the "literary" reportage of the Vietnam era: Susan Sontag's *Trip to Hanoi*, Mary McCarthy's *Vietnam*, Norman Mailer's *Armies of the Night*. Less high-flying reports are similarly depoliticized, and they evince a "pendulum" theory of history: things are one way, then the other, but nothing really changes. In the more starkly politicized journalism of the 1960s there was a sense of movement rather than stasis, of evolution (or revolution) rather than termination, of optimism rather than cynicism.

There are clashes over the issues and icons of the 1980s, corresponding to the cultural battles of the 1950s. Now there is a fight for Foucault and semiotics: tool for change or for analysis? For the Holocaust: failure of the human spirit or tragedy of the war against fascism? For Poland: working-class struggle or anti-Communist revolt? Even for peace: disarmament or deterrence? And for the history of decades and wars gone by: the 1930s, World War II, Vietnam, the McCarthy era, the 1960s.

Ever ready to grasp new issues and broker them to their customers, the liberal media have picked up on the new cold war culture and are selling it by the pound. Only a while ago, magazines were weighty with discussion of black oppression and insurgency, of youth's search for fulfillment through social transformation, of the Third World's valiant revolts, of women's quest for liberation through sexual politics. Now the journals are weighted with heavy metal subjects: missile deployment, weapons development, war strategy. Magazine covers are likely to feature figures of authority and success—Defense Secretary Caspar Weinberger, Chrysler chairman Lee Iacocca, French Cardinal Lustiger—rather than images of insurgency. Stories about the Third World conclude that revolutions have failed or will soon do so; stories about students say they are more interested in careers than in mindless rampage; stories about women report that they have rediscovered the delights of family life and are concerned about good salaries and fringe benefits; stories about crime focus on the need for more jails; stories about espionage rehearse old tales of Russian treachery rather than expose the misdeeds of C.I.A. agents.

Overall, there is a new cold war "spin" to the discussion of public policy and social issues. Militarism, individualism and consumerism are back in fashion. The first great TV show of the emerging culture was *The Winds of War*, a (long) brief for the cold war liberals in the contest for intellectual property rights to World War II, the Holocaust and attendant events. The debate over the role of the left in the McCarthy era has flared anew with the publication of William L. O'Neill's *A Better World*, which is subtitled *The Great Schism: Stalinism and the American Intellectuals*. O'Neill (and his sympathetic reviewers in *The New Republic* and the daily *New York Times*) argues once again that C.P. members and leftist intellectuals who refused to denounce American Communism were doing Stalin's work under the cloak of constitutional liberties. No historical debate can ever be finally settled, especially one in which the historical participants are still alive. But the O'Neill book arrives as an offensive weapon in a political fight: to discredit the left, to link what leftists thought with what Stalin did, to prove past guilt by association.

The world-shaking movements connecting personal and political change— feminism and gay liberation— have been transformed into little more than support systems for getting ahead and having it all. Betty Friedan, who inspired the first wave of militant feminism twenty years ago, now, in *The Second Stage*, argues for the traditional values of family life in a home full of upscale appointments. The impetus toward retrenchment in liberation ideology is rationalized in the name of realism or pragmatism— those reborn cold war virtues from the earlier age. Contempt for idealism and blindness to the visions of utopia are hallmarks of the emerging culture, for both idealism and utopianism are necessary for radical change.

THE SECOND TIME AROUND

Analogies are logically imperfect. When historical events happen for the second time, as Marx remarked, they are likely to make farcical what was initially deadly tragic. The first cold war culture not only imposed a stultifying, conformist creed on creative work and thought. People really suffered. There were purges of leftists from unions, political parties, public organizations, the news media, academe, show business, publishing, government. The woods are full of "McCarthy victims" who survived. But a lot of them did not survive. They were all victims of the cold war liberals as well as of the McCarthyites. The liberals were well placed to do the hatchet jobs, the dirty work, for they were in charge of the great institutions sheltering the left.

Can it happen here, and now? In a very small sense, it may be happening already. Journalists who consider themselves (or are considered) leftists say that many publications that once welcomed their work for its trendiness have shut tight in recent months. The big corporate publishers, often subsidiaries of vast conglomerates, are showing less interest in issues as leftists frame them. Hollywood, which has not been markedly political since the 1940s, is extremely sensitive to the current ideological crosscurrents. One film released this year, *The Lords of Discipline*, which takes place in a Southern military academy, was set in 1964 — pre-Gulf of Tonkin — rather than in 1966, when the novel on which it was based was set. The change was made to avoid any mention of the war in Vietnam, though it was crucial to the author's theme. It's a wonder *Reds* wasn't set in 1904. The unexpected success of the Academy Award-winning *Gandhi* seems like another symptom of cold war fever. The Mahatma, after all, was the favorite foreign rebel of Americans after World War II, the liberal alternative to China's revolutionary Mao Zedong.

As mentioned, the fiercest fighting is centered in the nuclear freeze and disarmament movement — the only place where an organized left politics is highly visible and active. In response to pressure from President Reagan and the Far Right, some moderate members of the movement have attempted to exclude Communists and radicals from the coalition groups. So far, the left is holding its own. But it is precisely in such coalitions that the new cold war liberals can be expected to move against the left.

Outside of the peace movement, the left today is dispersed, fragmented and isolated. It is even difficult to speak of "a left," a unitary, self-conscious political cohort such as existed before the old cold war. So the destructive tactics of the cold warriors — both the right-wing and liberal varieties — are inappropriate in the current situation.

But if there is not a left, there are leftists — that is, there are countless heirs to the political and countercultural traditions of the 1960s, as well as older radicals and newly organized sympathizers — who occupy positions (generally in the lower ranks) in the established liberal institutions: unions, schools and colleges, social welfare agencies, service organizations, the media and even government. They also can be found in thousands of activist organizations — tenant unions, environmental lobbies, labor insurgencies, legal aid offices, health groups, women's and homosexuals' support groups, foreign policy study and action projects. These, and many more, represent a largely innovative development in American institutional life. Their members are not always aware that they are playing a wider political role — that they constitute an ad hoc left or radical presence. At least, they do not function that way. But the presence is there, it is important, and it is felt.

In a sense, the emergence of the new cold war is logically connected to the development of a new class of post-1960s activists. It is this new political class, however incoherently its politics and class demands are expressed, that the cold war liberals are engaging.

How successful the liberals will be in determining the course of the conflict is impossible to gauge. Cold war liberalism, in its new form, is a phenomenon whose meaning has only begun to "mean itself"; events that have yet to happen, developments that have yet to develop and consequences that have yet to occur will make the determination.

But at the core of the process is war—the militarization of American society, the obsession with national security, the preoccupation with loyalty, patriotism and power. War, Orwell said, is the engine that drives society. It is certainly the motivation for neoconservatism, the New Right and, now, cold war liberalism. The issue of war and peace has shaped every aspect of American policy in this century, from highway construction to education to economic strategies to the preservation of civil liberties. If the country moves toward war, the pressure will increase on all the forces in the land that seek to open institutions to popular participation, change and equality. If we move toward peace, the space for freedom will begin to expand again.

The Long Shadow
[editorial]

October 22, 1983

> The Nation's commitment to civil liberties is exemplified by the magazine's continuing attention to the injustices of the Hiss and Rosenberg cases. Editor Victor Navasky wrote this editorial in preparation for a 1983 debate at New York City's Town Hall, "Were the Rosenbergs Framed?" (co-sponsored by The Nation and The New Republic).

Last week the Supreme Court denied Alger Hiss's request to set aside his 1950 perjury conviction. This week 1,500 people will gather at Town Hall in New York City to hear a debate sponsored by The Nation and The New Republic on the subject "Were the Rosenbergs Framed?" Why, more than three decades after the fact, do these infamous cold war cases refuse to die?

They are, of course, different in critical ways. Hiss was convicted of perjury, the Rosenbergs of conspiracy to commit espionage. Hiss was vaguely accused of stealing policy-oriented papers from the State Department, the Rosenbergs of stealing the secret of the atomic bomb. Hiss lost his career, the Rosenbergs their lives. But there are fundamental similarities that help account for the continuing interest in, and importance of, these cases.

First, in the overheated atmosphere of the cold war, neither Hiss nor the Rosenbergs received fair trials. Possibilities of fabricated evidence and frame-ups aside, materials made available under the Freedom of Information Act, as well as the independent findings of journalists, lawyers and scholars, suggest that through the use of wiretaps, informers, ex parte communications, break-ins and other extrajudicial methods, the defendants were deprived of their basic rights, in violation of the American promise of justice for all.

Second, the cases have come to symbolize cold war politics. The Hiss case was cynically used by the right to taint a generation of New Deal liberals, and to prove that Communists and their agents had infiltrated the policy-making apparatus of the U.S. government at the highest levels. The Rosenberg case served to reinforce the myth that there *was* a domestic Red menace sufficiently menacing to justify intrusions on fundamental rights and liberties.

The way the political culture responded to these cases at the time and subsequently has profoundly influenced the lives of liberals and those on the left. The film *Daniel*, from E.L. Doctorow's *The Book of Daniel*, which was inspired by the Rosenberg case, has generated controversy because so many of us are, in a sense, children of these cold war cases.

Thus the debate at Town Hall and the ongoing attempts of scholars and journalists (if not the courts) to set the record straight in the Hiss case are not exercises in nostalgia. For the liberal left, in particular, establishing the facts where they can be known, accepting what cannot be known and focusing on how the political process worked in relation to these cases — how it was used and misused for ideological purposes — may be the prelude to a generation's coming to terms with its own identity.

But debates are adversarial by their nature, and historians lack subpoena power and investigative staffs. Enough is now known about the injustices connected with the Hiss and Rosenberg cases to warrant an official inquiry by a body modeled after the Royal Commissions of Britain.

KURT VONNEGUT

The Worst Addiction of Them All

December 31-January 7, 1984

Kurt Vonnegut's novels include *Welcome to the Monkey House,*
Slaughterhouse Five, and Breakfast of Champions.

What has been America's most nurturing contribution to the culture of this planet
so far? Many would say jazz. I, who love jazz, will say this instead: Alcoholics
Anonymous.

I am not an alcoholic. If I was, I would go before the nearest A.A. meeting
and say, "My name is Kurt Vonnegut: I am an alcoholic." God willing, that might
be my first step down the long, hard road back to sobriety.

The A.A. scheme, which requires a confession like that, is the first to have any
measurable success in dealing with the tendency of some human beings, perhaps
10 percent of any population sample anyone might care to choose, to become addicted to substances that give them brief spasms of pleasure but in the long term
transmute their lives and the lives of those around them into ultimate ghastliness.

The A.A. scheme, which, again, can work only if the addicts regularly admit
that this or that chemical is poisonous to them, is now proving its effectiveness
with compulsive gamblers, who are not dependent on chemicals from a distillery
or a pharmaceutical laboratory. This is no paradox. Gamblers, in effect,
manufacture their own dangerous substances. God help them, they produce
chemicals that elate them whenever they place a bet on simply anything.

If I was a compulsive gambler, which I am not, I would be well advised to stand
up before the nearest meeting of Gamblers Anonymous and declare, "My name
is Kurt Vonnegut. I am a compulsive gambler."

Whether I was standing before a meeting of Gamblers Anonymous or Alcoholics Anonymous, I would be encouraged to testify as to how the chemicals I had
generated within myself or swallowed had alienated my friends and relatives, cost
me jobs and houses and deprived me of my last shred of self-respect.

Not every member of A.A. or G.A. has sunk quite that low, of course—but
plenty have. Many, if not most, have done what they call "hitting bottom" before
admitting what it is that has been ruining their lives.

I now wish to call attention to another form of addiction, which has not been
previously identified. It is more like gambling than drinking, since the people
afflicted are ravenous for situations that will cause their bodies to release exciting
chemicals into their bloodstreams. I am persuaded that there are among us people
who are tragically hooked on preparations for war.

Tell people with that disease that war is coming and we have to get ready for it, and for a few minutes there, they will be as happy as a drunk with his martini breakfast or a compulsive gambler with his paycheck bet on the Super Bowl.

Let us recognize how sick such people are. From now on, when a national leader, or even just a neighbor, starts talking about some new weapons system which is going to cost us a mere $29 billion, we should speak up. We should say something on the order of, "Honest to God, I couldn't be sorrier for you if I'd seen you wash down a fistful of black beauties with a pint of Southern Comfort."

I mean it. I am not joking. Compulsive preparers for World War III, in this country or any other, are as tragically and, yes, as repulsively addicted as any stockbroker passed out with his head in a toilet in the Port Authority bus terminal.

For an alcoholic to experience a little joy, he needs maybe three ounces of grain alcohol. Alcoholics, when they are close to hitting bottom, customarily can't hold much alcohol.

If we know a compulsive gambler who is dead broke, we can probably make him happy with a dollar to bet on who can spit farther than someone else.

For us to give a compulsive war-preparer a fleeting moment of happiness, we may have to buy him three Trident submarines and a hundred intercontinental ballistic missiles mounted on choo-choo trains.

If Western Civilization were a person—

If Western Civilization, which blankets the world now, as far as I can tell, were a person—

If Western Civilization, which surely now includes the Soviet Union and China and India and Pakistan and on and on, were a person—

If Western Civilization were a person, we would be directing it to the nearest meeting of War-Preparers Anonymous. We would be telling it to stand up before the meeting and say, "My name is Western Civilization. I am a compulsive war-preparer. I have lost everything I ever cared about. I should have come here long ago. I first hit bottom in World War I."

Western Civilization cannot be represented by a single person, of course, but a single explanation for the catastrophic course it has followed during this bloody century is possible. We the people, because of our ignorance of the disease, have again and again entrusted power to people we did not know were sickies.

And let us not mock them now, any more than we would mock someone with syphilis or smallpox or leprosy or yaws or typhoid fever or any of the other diseases to which the flesh is heir. All we have to do is separate them from the levers of power, I think.

And then what?

Western Civilization's long, hard trip back to sobriety might begin.

A word about appeasement, something World War II, supposedly, taught us not to practice: I say to you that the world has been ruined by appeasement. Appeasement of whom? Of the Communists? Of the neo-Nazis? No! Appeasement of the compulsive war-preparers. I can scarcely name a nation that has not lost most of its freedom and wealth in attempts to appease its own addicts to preparations for war.

And there is no appeasing an addict for very long.

"I swear, man, just lay enough bread on me for twenty multiple re-entry vehicles and a fleet of B-1 bombers, and I'll never bother you again."

Most addictions start innocently enough in childhood, under agreeable, reputable auspices — a sip of champagne at a wedding, a game of poker for matchsticks on a rainy afternoon. Compulsive war-preparers may have been encouraged as infants to clap their hands with glee at a campfire or a Fourth of July parade.

Not every child gets hooked. Not every child so tempted grows up to be a drunk or a gambler or a babbler about knocking down the incoming missiles of the Evil Empire with laser beams. When I identify the war-preparers as addicts, I am not calling for the exclusion of children from all martial celebrations. I doubt that more than one child in a hundred, having seen fireworks, for example, will become an adult who wants to stop squandering our substance on education and health and social justice and the arts and food and shelter and clothing for the needy, and so on — who wants us to blow it all on ammunition instead.

And please understand that the addiction I have identified is to *preparations* for war. I repeat: to *preparations* for war, addiction to the thrills of de-mothballing battleships and inventing weapons systems against which there cannot possibly be a defense, supposedly, and urging the citizenry to hate this part of humanity or that one, and knocking over little governments that might aid and abet an enemy someday, and so on. I am not talking about an addiction to war itself, which is a very different matter. A compulsive preparer for war wants to go to big-time war no more than an alcoholic stockbroker wants to pass out with his head in a toilet in the Port Authority bus terminal.

Should addicts of any sort hold high office in this or any other country? Absolutely not, for their first priority will always be to satisfy their addiction, no matter how terrible the consequences may be — even to themselves.

Suppose we had an alcoholic President who still had not hit bottom and whose chief companions were drunks like himself. And suppose it were a fact, made absolutely clear to him, that if he took just one more drink, the whole planet would blow up.

So he has all the liquor thrown out of the White House, including his Aqua-Velva shaving lotion. So late at night he is terribly restless, crazy for a drink but proud of not drinking. So he opens the White House refrigerator, looking for a

Tab or a Diet Pepsi, he tells himself. And there, half-hidden by a family-size jar of French's mustard, is an unopened can of Coors beer.

What do you think he'll do?

CALVIN TRILLIN

Uncivil Liberties

January 11, 1986

> When he was approached about writing a column for *The Nation* in 1978, Trillin asked editor Victor Navasky for only one guarantee: that he would be allowed to make fun of the editor.

When the editor of *The Nation*, the wily and parsimonious Victor S. Navasky, said he was going to double my pay, I did the only honorable thing: I resigned. Maybe I should start at the beginning. Here are some milestones in our relationship since the aforementioned Navasky asked me if I'd be interested in writing a column for *The Nation*:

March 18, 1978. The wily and parsimonious Victor S. Navasky and I have lunch in the Village to talk about his grand vision for transforming *The Nation* from a shabby pinko sheet to a shabby pinko sheet with a humor column and a large office for the editor. I pick up the check. I ask what he plans to pay for each column. He says, "Somewhere in the high two figures."

March 20, 1978. I refer the offer to my high-powered literary agent, Robert (Slowly) Lescher, together with instructions for the ensuing negotiations: "Play hardball."

April 8, 1978. Slowly gets him up to $100.

September 5, 1978. The W. & P. Victor S. Navasky questions the authenticity of some quotations used in my column. He asks if John Foster Dulles really said, "You can't fool all of the people all of the time, but you might as well give it your best shot." I say, "At these rates, you can't expect real quotes."

May 14, 1980. Executive editor Richard Lingeman, who would probably be described by one of those hard-nosed post-Watergate reporters as "a longtime Navasky operative," sends me a Table of Organization chart that gives me pause: it lists me under Casual Labor."

November 10, 1981. The W. & P. Victor S. Navasky says that although he would never try to exert any pressure to influence what I write, he might just point out that columns devoted to ridiculing him are less likely to be sold for republication in newspapers because they are considered "inside" and (although he doesn't say this) perhaps a bit distasteful. I say not to worry: since *The Nation* never gets around to paying me my share of the republication fees, I feel no pressure at all. To show there are no hard feelings on my part, I write a column revealing him to be a klutz on the basketball court. To show there are no hard feelings on his part, he continues to hold onto my share of the republication fees.

May 29, 1982. I receive a letter from a reader who asks, "Is it true that employees of *The Nation* are forced to sell flowers and candy in airports and turn the proceeds over to Victor S. Navasky?" I publish the letter in my column, along with my strongly worded reply ("Not exactly").

October 25, 1985. The wily and parsimonious Victor S. Navasky and I have lunch in the Village. He picks up the check. I am instantly put on my guard. He says he is going to double my pay. I figure he has to be up to something. I resign. He tells me my share of the check is $13.38.

"I've quit," I told my wife when I returned from lunch. "That'll show him."

"Why didn't you just tell him you got a better offer from the newspaper syndication people?" she said.

"Because I prefer to resign on a matter of principle."

"What, exactly, is the principle involved?"

"Worker solidarity."

"Worker solidarity!" she said. "I never heard you talk about worker solidarity before."

"I never got a better offer before," I said.

"I think it's terrible that all you can talk about, even now that you're leaving *The Nation*, is money," she said.

"That's what the owners of the textile mills in Yorkshire in the nineteenth century used to say about the workers who complained that a family couldn't be supported on two and six a day: 'All they ever talk about is money.' "

"Aren't you going to miss *The Nation*?" my wife asked.

Well, of course. It was sort of comforting to know that whenever I'd show up at the office the fellow we call Harold the Committed would ask me if I'd like to see civilization as we know it destroyed in a nuclear holocaust: it's *The Nation*'s equivalent of having an elevator operator who can be counted on to say "Have a nice day." And I do feel solidarity with my fellow workers. I feel kinship with the ancient bookkeepers who have been convinced by Navasky that 10 percent of their salary is going directly into a legal defense fund for the Scottsboro Boys. I feel comradeship with the college interns Navasky has managed to lure into *The Nation*'s slave/study program. I feel brotherhood with Richard Lingeman, who, finding himself in 1956 with a strong hand but no cash during a poker game in New Haven that included Victor S. Navasky, covered a raise by signing a paper for thirty-five years of indentured editorial service, and then failed to fill out his flush. For that matter, I feel a communal bond with all those *Nation* employees selling flowers and candy in airports.

"And how about Victor Navasky?" my wife said.

"Oh, he'll get along without me.

"No doubt," she said. "But will you get along without him? Every time you haven't been able to think of a column idea, you've attacked poor Victor—just the way Ronald Reagan, whenever he was stuck for an answer, used to mention that woman who picked up her Aid for Dependent Children check in a Cadillac."

I hadn't thought of that. Navasky has been, in a manner of speaking, my welfare cheat. Doing the column for the newspapers I wouldn't have Navasky to kick around anymore. I could imagine editors from Midwestern dailies sending queries back to the syndication people: "Who's this Navasky anyway?" they'd ask, or "What's this mean here—'There's no gonif like a left-wing gonif'?"

"Yes, I will miss the old W. & P.," I said to my wife.

"Well, it would be nice if you did something to show that," she said.

Fine. But what? "I've got it," I said, after a while. "I'll attack him for trying to double my pay."

GORE VIDAL

Requiem for the American Empire *January 11, 1986*

Gore Vidal's most recent books are *Lincoln, The Second American Revolution* and *Hollywood*.

The following article is adapted from a speech Gore Vidal delivered this past November at an "author's evening" sponsored by PEN American Center in New York City. Appearing on the same program and largely agreeing with him was Norman Mailer. But newspaper reports of the affair focused on the two writers' past tiffs rather than the substance of their remarks, which contained some political proposals. Here is what Vidal said.
—ORIGINAL NOTE

On September 16, 1985, when the Commerce Department announced that the United States had become a debtor nation, the American Empire died. The empire was seventy-one years old and had been in ill health since 1968. Like most modern empires, ours rested not so much on military prowess as on economic primacy.

After the French Revolution, the world money power shifted from Paris to

London. For three generations, the British maintained an old-fashioned colonial empire, as well as a modern empire based on London's primacy in the money markets. Then, in 1914, New York replaced London as the world's financial capital. Before 1914, the United States had been a developing country, dependent on outside investment. But with the shift of the money power from Old World to New, what had been a debtor nation became a creditor nation and central motor to the world's economy. All in all, the English were well pleased to have us take their place. They were too few in number for so big a task. As early as the turn of the century, they were eager for us not only to help them out financially but to continue, in their behalf, the destiny of the Anglo-Saxon race: to bear with courage the white man's burden, as Rudyard Kipling not so tactfully put it. Were we not—English and Americans—all Anglo-Saxons, united by common blood, laws, language? Well, no, we were not. But our differences were not so apparent then. In any case, we took on the job. We would supervise and civilize the lesser breeds. We would make money.

By the end of World War II, we were the most powerful and least damaged of the great nations. We also had most of the money. America's hegemony lasted exactly five years. Then the cold and hot wars began. Our masters would have us believe that all our problems are the fault of the Evil Empire of the East, with its Satanic and atheistic religion, ever ready to destroy us in the night. This nonsense began at a time when we had atomic weapons and the Russians did not. They had lost 20 million of their people in the war, and 8 million of them before the war, thanks to their neoconservative Mongolian political system. Most important, there was never any chance, then or now, of the money power (all that matters) shifting from New York to Moscow. What was—and is—the reason for the big scare? Well, World War II made prosperous the United States, which had been undergoing a depression for a dozen years; and made very rich those magnates and their managers who govern the republic, with many a wink, in the people's name. In order to maintain a general prosperity (and enormous wealth for the few) they decided that we would become the world's policeman, perennial shield against the Mongol hordes. We shall have an arms race, said one of the high priests, John Foster Dulles, and we shall win it because the Russians will go broke first. We were then put on a permanent wartime economy, which is why a third or so of the government's revenues is constantly being siphoned off to pay for what is euphemistically called defense.

As early as 1950, Albert Einstein understood the nature of the rip-off. He said, "The men who possess real power in this country have no intention of ending the cold war." Thirty-five years later, they are still at it, making money while the nation itself declines to eleventh place in world per capita income, to forty-sixth in literacy and so on, until last summer (not suddenly, I fear) we found ourselves close to $2 trillion in debt. Then, in the fall, the money power shifted from New

York to Tokyo, and that was the end of our empire. Now the long-feared Asiatic colossus takes its turn as world leader, and we—the white race—have become the yellow man's burden. Let us hope that he will treat us more kindly than we treated him. In any case, if the foreseeable future is not nuclear, it will be Asiatic, some combination of Japan's advanced technology with China's resourceful landmass. Europe and the United States will then be, simply, irrelevant to the world that matters, and so we come full circle. Europe began as the relatively empty uncivilized Wild West of Asia; then the Western Hemisphere became the Wild West of Europe. Now the sun has set in our West and risen once more in the East.

The British used to say that their empire was obtained in a fit of absent-mindedness. They exaggerate, of course. On the other hand, our modern empire was carefully thought out by four men. In 1890 a U.S. Navy captain, Alfred Thayer Mahan, wrote the blueprint for the American imperium, *The Influence of Sea Power Upon History, 1660–1783*. Then Mahan's friend, the historian-geopolitician Brooks Adams, younger brother of Henry, came up with the following formula: "All civilization is centralization. All centralization is economy." He applied the formula in the following syllogism: "Under economical centralization, Asia is cheaper than Europe. The world tends to economic centralization. Therefore, Asia tends to survive and Europe to perish." Ultimately, *that* is why we were in Vietnam. The amateur historian and professional politician Theodore Roosevelt was much under the influence of Adams and Mahan; he was also their political instrument, most active not so much during his Presidency as during the crucial war with Spain, where he can take a good deal of credit for our seizure of the Philippines, which made us a world empire. Finally, Senator Henry Cabot Lodge, Roosevelt's closest friend, kept in line a Congress that had a tendency to forget our holy mission—our manifest destiny—and ask, rather wistfully, for internal improvements.

From the beginning of our republic we have had imperial tendencies. We took care—as we continue to take care—of the indigenous population. We maintained slavery a bit too long even by a cynical world's tolerant standards. Then, in 1847, we produced our first conquistador, President James K. Polk. After acquiring Texas, Polk deliberately started a war with Mexico because, as he later told the historian George Bancroft, we had to acquire California. Thanks to Polk, we did. And that is why to this day the Mexicans refer to our Southwestern states as "the occupied lands," which Hispanics are now, quite sensibly, filling up.

The case against empire began as early as 1847. Representative Abraham Lincoln did not think much of Polk's war, while Lieut. Ulysses S. Grant, who fought at Vera Cruz, said in his memoirs, "The war was an instance of a republic following the bad example of European monarchies in not considering justice in their desire to acquire additional territory." He went on to make a causal link, something not usual in our politics then and completely unknown now: "The Southern rebellion was largely the outgrowth of the Mexican War. Nations, like individuals, are punished for their transgressions. We got our punishment in the most sanguinary and expensive war of modern times."

But the empire has always had more supporters than opponents. By 1895 we had filled up our section of North America. We had tried twice—and failed—to conquer Canada. We had taken everything that we wanted from Mexico. Where next? Well, there was the Caribbean at our front door and the vast Pacific at our back. Enter the Four Horsemen—Mahan, Adams, Roosevelt and Lodge.

The original republic was thought out carefully, and openly, in *The Federalist Papers*: we were not going to have a monarchy and we were not going to have a democracy. And to this day we have had neither. For 200 years we have had an oligarchical system in which men of property can do well and the others are on their own. Or, as Brooks Adams put it, the sole problem of our ruling class is whether to coerce or to bribe the powerless majority. The so-called Great Society bribed; today coercion is very much in the air. Happily, our neoconservative Mongoloids favor only authoritarian and never totalitarian means of coercion.

Unlike the republic, the empire was worked out largely in secret. Captain Mahan, in a series of lectures delivered at the Naval War College, compared the United States with England. Each was essentially an island state that could prevail in the world only through sea power. England had already proved his thesis. Now the United States must do the same. We must build a great navy in order to acquire overseas possessions. Since great navies are expensive, the wealth of new colonies must be used to pay for our fleets. In fact, the more colonies acquired, the more ships; the more ships, the more empire. Mahan's thesis is agreeably circular. He showed how little England had ended up with most of Africa and all of southern Asia, thanks to sea power. He thought that we should do the same. The Caribbean was our first and easiest target. Then on to the Pacific Ocean, with all its islands. And, finally, to China, which was breaking up as a political entity.

Theodore Roosevelt and Brooks Adams were tremendously excited by this prospect. At the time Roosevelt was a mere police commissioner in New York City, but he had dreams of imperial glory. "He wants to be," snarled Henry Adams, "our Dutch-American Napoleon." Roosevelt began to maneuver his way toward the heart of power, sea power. With Lodge's help, he got himself appointed Assistant Secretary of the Navy, under a weak Secretary and a mild President. Now he was in place to modernize the fleet and to acquire colonies. Hawaii was annexed. Then a part of Samoa. Finally, colonial Cuba, somehow, had to be liberated from Spain's tyranny. At the Naval War College, Roosevelt declared, "To prepare for war is the most effectual means to promote peace." How familiar that sounds! But since the United States had no enemies as of June 1897, a contemporary might have remarked that since we were already at peace with everyone, why prepare for war? Today, of course, we are what he dreamed we would

361

be, a nation armed to the teeth and hostile to everyone. But what with Roosevelt was a design to acquire an empire is for us a means to transfer money from the Treasury to the various defense industries, which in turn pay for the elections of Congress and President.

Our turn-of-the-century imperialists may have been wrong, and I think they were. But they were intelligent men with a plan, and the plan worked. Aided by Lodge in the Senate, Brooks Adams in the press, Admiral Mahan at the Naval War College, the young Assistant Secretary of the Navy began to build up the fleet and look for enemies. After all, as Brooks Adams proclaimed "war is the solvent." But war with whom? And for what? And where? At one point England seemed a likely enemy. We had a boundary dispute with it over Venezuela, which meant that we could invoke the all-purpose Monroe Doctrine (the invention of John Quincy Adams, Brooks's grandfather). But as we might have lost such a war, nothing happened. Nevertheless, Roosevelt kept on beating his drum: "No triumph of peace," he shouted, "can equal the armed triumph of war." Also: "We must take Hawaii in the interests of the white race." Even Henry Adams, who found T.R. tiresome and Brooks, his own brother, brilliant but mad, suddenly declared, "In another fifty years . . . the white race will have to reconquer the tropics by war and nomadic invasion, or be shut up north of the 50th parallel." And so at century's end, our most distinguished ancestral voices were not prophesying but praying for war.

An American warship, the Maine, blew up in Havana harbor. We held Spain responsible; thus, we got what John Hay called "a splendid little war." We would liberate Cuba, drive Spain from the Caribbean. As for the Pacific, even before the Maine was sunk, Roosevelt had ordered Commodore Dewey and his fleet to the Spanish Philippines — just in case. Spain promptly collapsed, and we inherited its Pacific and Caribbean colonies. Admiral Mahan's plan was working triumphantly.

In time we allowed Cuba the appearance of freedom while holding on to Puerto Rico. Then President William McKinley, after an in-depth talk with God, decided that we should also keep the Philippines, in order, he said, to Christianize them. When reminded that the Filipinos were Roman Catholics, the President said, Exactly. We must Christianize them. Although Philippine nationalists had been our allies against Spain, we promptly betrayed them and their leader Aguinaldo. As a result it took us several years to conquer the Philippines, and tens of thousands of Filipinos died that our empire might grow.

The war was the making of Theodore Roosevelt. Surrounded by the flower of the American press, he led a group of so-called Rough Riders up a very small hill in Cuba. For this proto-photo opportunity he became a national hero, Governor of New York, McKinley's running mate and, when McKinley was killed in 1901, President.

Not everyone liked the new empire. After Manila, Mark Twain thought that the stars and bars of the American flag should be replaced by a skull and crossbones. He also said, "We cannot maintain an empire on the Orient and maintain a republic in America." He was right, of course. But as he was only a writer who said funny things, he was ignored. The compulsively vigorous Roosevelt defended our war against the Philippine population, and he attacked the likes of Twain. "Every argument that can be made for the Filipinos could be made for the Apaches," he explained, with his lovely gift for analogy. "And every word that can be said for Aguinaldo could be said for Sitting Bull. As peace, order and prosperity followed our expansion over the land of the Indians, so they will follow us in the Philippines."

Despite the criticism of the few, the Four Horsemen had pulled it off. The United States was a world empire. And one of the horsemen not only got to be president but for his pious meddling in the Russo-Japanese conflict, our greatest apostle of war was awarded the Nobel Peace Prize. One must never underestimate the Scandinavian wit.

Empires are restless organisms. They must constantly renew themselves; should an empire start leaking energy, it will die. Not for nothing were the Adams brothers fascinated by entropy. By energy. By force. Brooks Adams, as usual, said the unsayable. "Laws are a necessity," he declared. "Laws are made by the strongest, and they must and shall be obeyed." Oliver Wendell Holmes Jr. thought this a wonderful observation, while the philosopher William James came to a similar conclusion, which can also be detected, like an invisible dynamo, at the heart of the novels of his brother Henry.

According to Brooks Adams, "The most difficult problem of modern times is unquestionably how to protect property under popular governments." The Four Horsemen fretted a lot about this. They need not have. We have never had a popular government in the sense that they feared, nor are we in any danger now. Our only political party has two right wings, one called Republican, the other Democratic. But Henry Adams figured all that out back in the 1890s. "We have a single system," he wrote, and "in that system the only question is the price at which the proletariat is to be bought and sold, the bread and circuses." But none of this was for public consumption. Publicly, the Four Horsemen and their outriders spoke of the American mission to bring to all the world freedom and peace, through slavery and war if necessary. Privately, their constant fear was that the weak masses might combine one day against the strong few, their natural leaders, and take away their money. As early as the election of 1876 socialism had been targeted as a vast evil that must never be allowed to corrupt simple American persons. When Christianity was invoked as the natural enemy of those who might limit the rich and their games, the combination of cross and dollar sign proved — and proves — irresistible.

During the first decade of our disagreeable century, the great world fact was the internal collapse of China. Who could pick up the pieces? Britain grabbed Kowloon; Russia was busy in the north; the Kaiser's fleet prowled the China coast; Japan was modernizing itself, and biding its time. Although Theodore Roosevelt lived and died a dedicated racist, the Japanese puzzled him. After they sank the Russian fleet, Roosevelt decided that they were to be respected and feared even though they were our racial inferiors. For those Americans who served in World War II, it was an article of faith—as of 1941, anyway—that the Japanese could never win a modern war. Because of their slant eyes, they would not be able to master aircraft. Then they sank our fleet at Pearl Harbor.

Jingoism aside, Brooks Adams was a good analyst. In the 1890s he wrote: "Russia, to survive, must undergo a social revolution internally and/or expand externally. She will try to move into Shansi Province, richest prize in the world. Should Russia and Germany combine . . ." That was the nightmare of the Four Horsemen. At a time when simpler folk feared the rise of Germany alone, Brooks Adams saw the world ultimately polarized between Russia and the United States, with China as the common prize. American maritime power versus Russia's landmass. That is why, quite seriously, he wanted to extend the Monroe Doctrine to the Pacific Ocean. For him, "war [was] the ultimate form of economic competition."

We are now at the end of the twentieth century. England, France and Germany have all disappeared from the imperial stage. China is now reassembling itself, and Confucius, greatest of political thinkers, is again at the center of the Middle Kingdom. Japan has the world money power and wants a landmass; China now seems ready to go into business with its ancient enemy. Wars of the sort that the Four Horsemen enjoyed are, if no longer possible, no longer practical. Today's conquests are shifts of currency by computer, and the manufacture of those things that people everywhere are willing to buy.

I have said very little about writers because writers have figured very little in our imperial story. The founders of both republic and empire wrote well: Jefferson and Hamilton, Lincoln and Grant, T.R. and the Adamses. Today public figures can no longer write their own speeches or books; and there is some evidence that they can't read them either.

Yet at the dawn of the empire, for a brief instant, our *professional* writers tried to make a difference. Upton Sinclair and company attacked the excesses of the ruling class. Theodore Roosevelt coined the word "muckraking" to describe what they were doing. He did not mean the word as praise. Since then a few of our writers have written on public themes, but as they were not taken seriously, they have ended by not taking themselves seriously, at least as citizens of a republic.

After all, most writers are paid by universities, and it is not wise to be thought critical of a garrison state which spends so much money on so many campuses.

When Confucius was asked what would be the first thing that he would do if he were to lead the state — his never-to-be-fulfilled dream — he said *rectify the language*. This is wise. This is subtle. As societies grow decadent, the language grows decadent, too. Words are used to disguise, not to illuminate, action: you liberate a city by destroying it. Words are used to confuse, so that at election time people will solemnly vote against their own interests. Finally, words must be so twisted as to justify an empire that has now ceased to exist, much less make sense. Is rectification of our system possible for us? Henry Adams thought not. In 1910 he wrote: 'The whole fabric of society will go to wrack if we really lay hands of reform on our rotten institutions." Then he added, "From top to bottom the whole system is a fraud, all of us know it, laborers and capitalists alike, and all of us are consenting parties to it." Since then, consent has grown frayed; and we have become poor, and our people sullen.

To maintain a thirty-five-year arms race it is necessary to have a fearsome enemy. Not since the invention of the Wizard of Oz have American publicists created anything quite so demented as the idea that the Soviet Union is a monolithic, omnipotent empire with tentacles everywhere on earth, intent on our destruction, which will surely take place unless we constantly imitate it with our war machine and its secret services.

In actual fact, the Soviet Union is a Second World country with a First World military capacity. Frighten the Russians sufficiently and they might blow us up. By the same token, as our republic now begins to crack under the vast expense of maintaining a mindless imperial force, we might try to blow them up. Particularly if we had a President who really was a twice-born Christian, and believed that the good folks would all go to heaven (where they were headed anyway) and the bad folks would go where *they* belong. Fortunately, to date, we have had only hypocrites in the White House. But you never can tell.

Even worse than the not-very-likely prospect of a nuclear war — deliberate or by accident — is the economic collapse of our society because too many of our resources have been wasted on the military. The Pentagon is like a black hole; what goes in is forever lost to us, and no new wealth is created. Hence, our cities, whose centers are unlivable; our crime rate, the highest in the Western world; a public education system that has given up . . . you know the litany.

There is now only one way out. The time has come for the United States to make common cause with the Soviet Union. The bringing together of the Soviet landmass (with all its natural resources) and our island empire (with all its technological resources) would be of great benefit to each society, not to mention the world. Also, to recall the wisdom of the Four Horsemen who gave us our empire, the Soviet Union and our section of North America combined would be a match, industrially and technologically, for the Sino-Japanese axis that will dominate the future just as Japan dominates world trade today. But where the horsemen thought of war as the supreme solvent, we now know that war is worse than useless. Therefore, the alliance of the two great powers of the Northern Hemisphere will double the strength of each and give us, working together, an opportunity to survive, economically, in a highly centralized Asiatic world.

CARLOS FUENTES

Land of Jekyll and Hyde

March 22, 1986

Much of Carlos Fuentes' life has been closely bound to the United States, but his perspective is uniquely international. He was born in Washington, where his father was a member of the diplomatic corps. In the 1950s he worked in Mexico's Foreign Ministry and later served as Mexican Ambassador to France. He is the author of several novels, including *Terra Nostra*, *The Old Gringo* and most recently, *Constancia and Other Stories for Virgins*. In 1984 he won Mexico's National Prize in Literature.

The perception of the United States in Latin America has undergone enormous variations ever since history brought us together as inevitable neighbors. The American Revolution inspired our own founding fathers to draw political legitimacy from revolt. The Constitution of the United States became the model for our own republics, but the limitations proved to be fictional ones, whereby a legal country disguised a real country. Latin American conservatives in the early nineteenth century were the militant foes of the United States. They saw it as an uncompromisingly revolutionary state, unwilling to reach any kind of conciliation with exiled Tories, ready to repel their *contra* attacks and to send them expeditiously to face firing squads.

Latin American conservatives saw the United States as a multiple menace to their interests: it was a Protestant power in the hemisphere, and it was a modernizing, democratic, capitalist and egalitarian power. Those were the worst sins in the conservative book, where virtue spelled Catholicism, Counter Reformation, royal absolutism, the divine right of kings, patrimonialism and privilege. But most of all, conservatives from Mexico to Argentina feared the expansionist policies of the new American republic.

They were soon joined in this fear by Latin American liberals, who initially idenfified with all those U.S. virtues that the conservatives regarded as vices. But the annexation of Texas and the entire Southwest after the Mexican War of 1846, and the interventionist policies following the Spanish-American War of 1898, convinced liberals that the conservatives were right: the gringos were the enemy.

Admiration changed to fear and fault finding. At the turn of the century most Latin Americans readily adopted the views expressed in "Ariel," the enormously influential essay by the Uruguayan writer José Enrique Rodó. The United States stands for progress and material achievements, Rodó wrote, but it is a barren spiritual landscape. Cultural primacy in this hemisphere belongs to the Latins, who may be materially poor but are spiritually rich. The brutality of U.S. interventions in Nicaragua, Mexico, Haiti, Honduras, Cuba and the Dominican Republic during the first three decades of this century magnified and justified this attitude.

I believe that, by and large, it was my generation that upset Rodó's perception. Pablo Neruda had sung with and to Whitman; Octavio Paz made us conscious of Pound, Cummings and Crane, whom he translated. Julio Cortázar not only translated the complete stories of Poe; he brought jazz to Latin America. Gabriel García Márquez proclaimed his admiration for Hemingway and Faulkner, and Jorge Luis Borges translated *The Wild Palms* in 1956. I wrote on Melville and movies. And indeed, a great deal of the work of Guillermo Cabrera Infante and Manuel Puig is an ironic extension of the Hollywood dream.

Having grown up in the United States, I was willing and able, in spite of catcalls from my compatriots, to praise the democratic process of the United States, its capacities for self-criticism, self-government, self-negotiation, even self-flagellation and self-consciousness. In the New Deal era I witnessed the best in the United States: the value it set on its human capital, its energy and enthusiasm for solving problems, its choice of dialogue instead of confrontation on Latin American issues. When the United States joined the effort to win World War II, Roosevelt's noninterventionist policies in Latin America had already won the support of most of the people there. We were finally willing to admit that there was a conjunction of the actions and the ideals of the North Americans.

This illusion has been painfully shattered over the past thirty years. Two democratically elected governments in this hemisphere — Guatemala's in 1954 and Chile's in 1973 — were overthrown with the full connivance of U.S. administrations. Who could then believe that the United States truly favored the democratic process in the continent? Washington placed two indigenous Latin American revolutions — Cuba's in 1959 and Nicaragua's in 1979 — in the context of the East-West conflict and then forced them to live up to that self-fulfilling prophecy. The lesson was clearly understood by Latin Americans: the United States does not care about democracy in Latin America. It worries more about the independence of formerly dependent Latin American republics and will risk anything — including the stability of other, friendly republics — to realign its client states.

The perversion of language that accompanies this perversion of politics is best illustrated by Reagan's rhetoric on the Nicaraguan *contras*. By calling them "freedom fighters" and "the moral equivalent of our Founding Fathers," he may hoodwink members of Congress and part of the media, but he merely reminds Latin Americans that the *contras* are paid and manipulated by the United States government, that they are recruited and commanded by Somoza's former National Guardsmen and that they are criminals who not only kill Nicaraguan farmers, women and children but are also particularly adept at killing one another. Their internal brutality is perfectly documented by Christopher Dickey in his recent book, *With the Contras*.

So we are left with this final image of the United States: a democracy inside but an empire outside; Dr. Jekyll at home, Mr. Hyde in Latin America.

We will continue to praise the democratic achievements and the cultural values of the society of the United States. But we will continue to oppose its arrogant and violent policies in Latin America. We will do so painfully, because we love so many things in the United States. We will not confuse the United States and the Soviet Union, or indeed accept their moral equivalence. The problem is far more tragic: the Russians act as an empire inside and outside. They are perfectly coherent. The United States, by acting like the Russians in its sphere of influence, becomes profoundly incoherent and hypocritical.

Latin Americans must not simply ship Mr. Hyde back to Washington. We must defeat him in his old stamping grounds, the Caribbean and Central America. Then we can all sit down and talk with Dr. Jekyll, his alter ego having been exorcised by his friends in this hemisphere.

The Revenge of Ahab
[editorial]

May 31, 1986

In only a few lines, this editorial by Andrew Kopkind provides
a metaphor for the destructive sensibility and random violence
of contemporary American life.

What did the killer say as he pumped four .22 caliber bullets into the body of a young female Beluga whale cavorting in New Haven Harbor? "You've had it, pal"? "Go ahead, make my day"? What insult was avenged, what crime punished, what principle upheld? B.W., the ten-foot, 950-pound cetacean, dropped out of her school a year ago and took up residence along the Connecticut coast, amusing herself and delighting the nearby humans in playful encounters. She nuzzled small boats, tickled swimmers and performed such self-taught tricks that many terrestrial mammals came to believe their marine relative possessed an intelligence comparable to their own. B.W. was not, scientifically speaking, a great whale, but she was a very good one, a veritable Girl Scout. She was trustworthy, loyal, friendly, brave and perhaps even reverent. She was certainly harmless. She cruised the waters unarmed, she never demanded spare change, she did not sponsor terrorism or export revolution, she did not come ashore to take someone's job or go on welfare.

Whoever killed B.W. one fine day in May must have seen her as a symbol suitable for slaughter. Whales have been problematic partners of men at least since Jonah, and long after Moby Dick. Whale catching was the economic foundation for the flowering of New England, and although whale watching is now a peaceful pastime, it may be simply a sporting sublimation rather than a moral equivalent of the cruel hunt.

As a beast, B.W. was perhaps too good, too intelligent and too trusting to survive in man's jungle. The will to kill has never been stronger, and a complete catalogue of means and motives are retailed in the media, in the proud boasts of politicians, in the triumphant toasts of national heroes. The trick is to keep from becoming a target, which is one B.W. did not learn.

MOLLY IVINS

Tough as Bob War and Other Stuff   *June 7, 1986*

Molly Ivins is a political columnist for the *Dallas Times Herald*, a contributing writer to *Mother Jones* and a contributing editor of *The Nation*.

Austin

We've just survived an 'her political season largely unscathed. I voted for Bobby Locke for governor: he's the one who challenged Col. Muammar el-Qaddafi to hand-to-hand combat. In the Gulf of Sidra. On the Line of Death. At high noon. Next Fourth of July. "Only one of us will come out of the water alive," said Locke. Locke thinks the trouble with America is that we've lost respect for our leaders and this would be a good way to restore same. Me too. Besides, you should have seen the other guys.

The Republicans had a Congressman running who thinks you get AIDS through your feet. That's Representative Tom Loeffler of Hunt, who is smarter than a box of rocks. His television advertisements proudly claimed, "He's tough as bob war" (bob war is what you make fences with), and also that in his youth Loeffler played football with two broken wrists. This caused uncharitable persons to question the man's good sense, so he explained he didn't know his wrists were broken at the time. Loeffler went to San Francisco during the campaign to make a speech. While there, he wore shower caps on his feet while showering lest he get AIDS from the tile in the tub. He later denied that he had spent the entire trip in his hotel room. He said: "I did walk around the hotel. I did see people who do have abnormal tendencies. I'd just as soon not be associated with abnormal people." If that's true, what was he doing running for governor of Texas?

Perhaps Loeffler's most enduring contribution to Texas political lore was a thought that seemed to him so profound he took to repeating it at every campaign stop and during televised debates as well: "As I have traveled around this state, many people have said to me, 'Texas will never be Texas again.' But I say they are wrong. I say Texas will *always* be Texas." Hard to add anything to that.

On the Democratic side, the nerd issue was dominant. The ugly specter of nerditude was raised by A. Don Crowder, a candidate from Dallas. Crowder's platform consisted of vowing to repeal the no-pass, no-play rule on account of it has seriously damaged high-school football and is un-American, un-Texan and probably communist inspired. No pass, no play was part of the education reform package enacted last year by Governor Mark White and the State Legislature. If you don't pass all your school subjects, you can't participate in any extracurricular activities, including—football. Quite naturally, this has caused considerable resentment and could cost White the governorship. So A. Don Crowder holds this press conference in which he says the reason Mark White favors no pass, no play is because White was "one of the first nerds in Texas." As evidence, Crowder produces White's high-school annual, and there it was; the guy was zip in extracurricular activities in his school days. We're talking, not even Booster Club. Not Glee Club or Stage Crew. Not even the Prom Poster Committee. According to Crowder, this explains "the psychological reasoning behind White's dislike of football."

There were headlines all over the state: "Gov. White Called 'Nerd' By Yearbook Wielding Foe." "Nerd Charge Merits Scrutiny." Meanwhile, we tracked down Donnie Crowder's high-school annual and guess what? He was captain of the football team. Played baseball. Ran track. And was in the French Club. French Club! Need I say more? *Quel fromage.*

White's initial response to this slanderous aspersion was to whine about how tacky it was for Crowder to be so ugly right after the explosion of the shuttle Challenger. Nerd City. Then his campaign manager tries to pull it out by saying, So the guy was not real active in high school—but he was super-involved in after-school activities at the Baptist Church. Nerd! Nerd! Finally White gets his act together, comes out and says, Look, I grew up poor. His daddy had an accident when the guy was just a sophomore and he couldn't work after that, so the guy spent his high-school years working summers and after school. While A. Don Crowder was in French Club, doubtlessly conjugating highly irregular verbs with busty cheerleaders over the pâté and vin rouge, our Governor was out mowing lawns, frying burgers and pumping gas to help his dear old silver-haired mother. Great stuff. Besides, Bubba never joined no French Club.

Marko Blanco, as we call him in South Texas, will meet former Governor Bill Clements for a rematch in November. Clements was defeated by White four years ago on account of he's an awful grouch. Grumpy versus the Nerd—what a match-up.

Also contributing to the political festivities of late is that peerless, fearless commie-hater Charlie Wilson of Lufkin. When folks started calling from around the state, and indeed the nation, a month or so back saying, "My God, do you realize there's a Texas Congressman over in Afghanistan killing Russians? And he's wearing black monogrammed cowboy boots, and he's got a former Miss World with him?"—I, of course, replied, "Must be Charlie Wilson." What else can you say at a time like that?

It's possible to get used to Charlie. He has a certain charm. When I called him to verify some of the more bloodthirsty quotations attributed to him in *The Houston Post*'s account of his latest trip to the Afghanistan border, the first thing he said was, "The only thing those cocksuckers understand is hot lead and cold steel." I was especially pleased that he took his lady friend, Annelise Ilschenko, a former Miss World U.S.A., along on the Afghan jaunt. According to *The Houston Post*, she is a "dark-haired and sloe-eyed beauty," and you hardly ever find a good case of sloe-eyed beauty in the newspapers anymore. *The Post* said, "[She] went everywhere with Wilson, not even flinching as she sank her high-heeled white leather boots into the thick brown ooze [of] Darra's main street." No sacrifice is too great when you're fighting for freedom.

Charlie told *The Post* reporter he went over there hoping to "kill Russians, as painfully as possible." Myself, I think it had more to do with an observation he made after he got back: "Hell, they're still lining up to see *Rambo* in Lufkin." Patriotism is always in good smell in East Texas. The night El Presidente started bombing Libya, the deejay at Benny B's, a honky-tonk in Lufkin, made all the patrons stand on their chairs and sing "The Star-Spangled Banner." He said if anybody refused to do it, "We'll know you're a commie faggot." Of course, they do the same thing at Benny B's for David Allan Coe's song "You Never Even Called Me By My Name." Sometimes living in East Texas can be a real challenge.

Living anywhere in Texas is getting to be a challenge as the price of oil slides gracefully toward single digits. Texas-bashing seems to be a popular new national pastime. "Let 'Em Rot in the Sun" said a cordial headline in *The New Republic*. Some Northern papers ran stories on our oil woes with heads the likes of "Sorry

About That, J.R." I don't see that we've got any cause to whine about this vein of snottiness: some of the Bubbas did put bumper stickers on their pickups a few years back that said, "Let the Yankee Bastards Freeze in the Dark." Somehow I forebode that Yankees going and doing likewise is not going to teach Bubba any manners. The rest of us down here been having poor luck at it for a long time.

I would point out, though, that Texas is not a rich state, never has been. Never even made it up to the national average in per capita income until the tail end of the oil boom, and then we slid right down again. Poverty level here is always among the nation's highest and, according to a recent study by a team from Harvard University, Texas has more counties beset by hunger and malnutrition than any other state. Our second-biggest industry after oil is agriculture, and you've maybe read something about how it's going for farmers these days. Citrus crop in the Rio Grande Valley was wiped out by a freeze three years ago. Now they got drought and 40 percent unemployment, and the peso is still going down. Our banks had their money in oil, agriculture and Mexico. We're losing a lot of banks.

There is no social support system for the poor in Texas. Adults get nothing; children get $57.50 a month. Bubba's got a beer gut he can let shrink some and not be hurting, but almost half the children in this state are black or brown and they have no cushion. If Eddie Chiles goes broke, it's Don't Cry for Me Texarkana; John Connally and Ben Barnes on hard times, search me for sympathy; and I could give a shit about J.R. But that's not who's hurting.

Good thing we've still got politics in Texas—finest form of free entertainment ever invented.

KATHA POLLITT

The Strange Case of Baby M   *May 23, 1987*

In March 1987, in the first test of the legality of a surrogate mother contract, New Jersey Superior Court Judge Harvey Sorkow ruled that the contract was "constitutionally protected" and awarded custody of the child, hitherto known as "Baby M," to her biological father. Katha Pollitt's essay lays out all the inconsistency, irony and orthodoxy which attached itself to the Baby M case. Pollitt is a poet, writer and contributing editor of *The Nation*.

I think I understand Judge Harvey Sorkow's ruling in the Baby M case. It seems that a woman can rent her womb in the state of New Jersey, although not her vagina, and get a check upon turning over the product to its father. This transaction is not baby selling (a crime), because a man has a "drive to procreate" that deserves the utmost respect and, in any case, the child is genetically half his. The woman he pays for help in fulfilling that drive, however, is only "performing a service" and thus has no comparable right to a child genetically half hers. Therefore, despite the law's requirements in what the layperson might think are similar cases (women who change their minds about giving up a child for adoption, for example), a judge may terminate a repentant mother-for-money's parental rights forever without finding that she abused or neglected her child—especially if he finds her "manipulative, exploitive and deceitful." In other words, so-called surrogacy agreements are so unprecedented that the resulting human arrangements bear no resemblance to adoption, illegitimacy, custody after divorce, or any other relationship involving parents and children, yet, at the same time, bear an uncanny resemblance to the all-sales-final style of a used-car lot.

The State Supreme Court will hear Mary Beth Whitehead's appeal in September and has meanwhile granted her two hours of visiting time a week—a small sign, perhaps, that in jettisoning the entire corpus of family law, Judge Sorkow may have gone a bit too far. (*The New York Times* had trouble finding a single legal scholar who supported the judge's reasoning in full.) Maybe not, though. Despite the qualms of pundits, the outrage of many feminists and the condemnation of many religious leaders, every poll to date has shown overwhelming approval of Judge Sorkow's ruling. Twenty-seven states are considering bills that would legalize and regulate bucks-for-baby deals. What on earth is going on here?

Some of this support surely comes from the bad impression Mrs. Whitehead made every time she opened her mouth—most damningly, in her tape-recorded threat to kill Baby M and herself. And some comes from the ineptitude of her lawyer. (Where was the National Organization for Women? Where was the American Civil Liberties Union?) The Sterns said they would drag the Whiteheads through the mud, and they did. We learned as much about the Whiteheads' marital troubles, financial woes and quarrelsome relatives as if they were characters on *All My Children*. Distinguished experts testified that Mrs. Whitehead, who has raised two healthy, normal kids, is a bad mother and emotionally unbalanced; she was "overenmeshed" with her kids, disputed the judgment of school officials, gave Baby M teddy bears to play with instead of pots and pans (*pots and pans?*) and said "hooray" instead of "patty-cake" when the tot clapped her hands. I know that, along with two-thirds of the adult female population of the United States, I will never feel quite the same about dyeing my hair now that Dr. Marshall Schechter, professor of child psychiatry at the University of Pennsylvania, has cited this little beauty secret as proof of Mrs. Whitehead's "narcissism" and "mixed personality disorder." Will I find myself in custody court someday, faced with the damning evidence of Exhibit A: a half-empty bottle of Clairol's Nice 'N' Easy?

Inexplicably, Mrs. Whitehead's lawyer never challenged the Sterns's self-representation as a stable, sane, loving pair, united in their devotion to Baby M. And neither did the media. Thus, we never found out why Dr. Elizabeth Stern claimed to be infertile on her application to the Infertility Center of New York when, in fact, she had diagnosed herself as having multiple sclerosis, which she feared pregnancy would aggravate; or why she didn't confirm that diagnosis until shortly before the case went to trial, much less consult a specialist in the management of M.S. pregnancies. Could it be that Elizabeth Stern did not share her husband's zeal for procreation? We'll never know, any more than we'll know why a disease serious enough to bar pregnancy was not also serious enough to consider as a possible bar to active mothering a few years down the road. If the Sterns's superior income could count as a factor in determining "the best interests of the child," why couldn't Mary Beth Whitehead's superior health?

The trial was so riddled with psychobabble, class prejudice and sheer callousness that one would have expected public opinion to rally round Mrs. Whitehead. Imagine openly arguing that a child should go to the richer parent! (Mr. Whitehead drives a garbage truck; Dr. Stern is a professor of pediatrics, and Mrs. Stern is a biochemist.) And castigating a mother faced with the loss of her baby as hyperemotional because she wept! But Mrs. Whitehead (who, it must be said, did not help her case by perjuring herself repeatedly) made a fatal mistake: she fell afoul of the double standard of sexual morality. Thus, in the popular mind, Mrs. Whitehead was "an adult" who "knew what she was doing," while Mr. Stern, presumably, was not an adult and did not know what he was doing. Mrs. Whitehead was mercenary for agreeing to sell, but not Mr. Stern for proposing to buy. That victim-as-seducer mentality hasn't got such a workout since a neighborhood matron decided to stop for a drink at Big Dan's bar in New Bedford, Massachusetts.

The personalities of the Whiteheads and the Sterns, so crucial during the custody phase of the trial, will soon fade from public memory. The extraordinary welter of half-truths, bad analogies, logical muddles and glib catch phrases that have been mustered in defense of their bargain are apparently here to stay. If we are really about to embark on an era of reproductive Reaganomics – and most Americans seem to be saying, Why not? – we at least ought to clear away some of the more blatantly foolish things being said in support of it. For example:

Mary Beth Whitehead is a surrogate mother.

"Mother" describes the relationship of a woman to a child, not to the father of that child and his wife. Everything a woman does to produce her own child Mary Beth Whitehead did, including giving it half the genetic inheritance regarded by the judge as so decisive an argument on behalf of William Stern. If anyone was a surrogate mother, it was Elizabeth Stern, for she was the one who substituted, or wished to substitute, for the child's actual mother.*

What's in a name? Plenty. By invariably referring to Mrs. Whitehead as a surrogate, the media, the courts and, unwittingly, Mrs. Whitehead herself tacitly validated the point of view of the Sterns, who naturally wanted to render Mrs. Whitehead's role in producing Baby M as notional as possible, the trivial physical means by which their desire – which is what really mattered – was fulfilled. And if Mrs. Whitehead was the substitute, then Dr. Stern must be the real thing.

Oddly enough, Mr. Stern, whose paternity consisted of ejaculating into a jar, was always referred to as the father or natural father or, rarely, biological father of Baby M, except by Mrs. Whitehead, who called him "the sperm donor." Although that is a far more accurate term for him than "surrogate mother" is for her (let alone "surrogate uterus," which is how the distinguished child psychologist Lee Salk referred to her), her use of it was widely taken as yet another proof of her irrational and cruel nature. Why was this harpy persecuting this nice man?

Surrogacy is a startling new technological development.

This claim is a favorite of columnists and other instant experts, who, having solemnly warned that reproductive science is outstripping society's ability to deal with it, helplessly throw up their hands because – what can you do? – progress marches on. But a maternity contract is not a scientific development; it is a piece of paper. Physically, as Mary Beth Whitehead pointed out, it involves merely artificial insemination, a centuries-old technique which requires a device no more complicated than a turkey baster. And artificial insemination itself is a social contrivance, the purpose of which is to avert not infertility but infidelity.

What is new about contract motherhood lies in the realm of law and social custom. It is a means by which women sign away rights that, until the twentieth century, they rarely had: the right to legal custody of their children, and the right not to be bought, sold, lent, rented or given away. Throughout most of Western history and in many countries even today, there has been no need for such contracts because the father already owned the child, even if the child was illegitimate (unless the child's mother was married, in which case her husband owned the child). If a father chose to exercise his right to custody, the mother had no legal standing. In most societies, furthermore, a man in William Stern's position could have legally or semilegally acquired another female whose child, as per above, would be legally his: a second (or third or tenth) wife, a concubine, a slave, a kept woman. This is the happy state of affairs to which the maternityh contract seeks to return its signers.

---

*In this article I will use the terms "contract mother," "maternity contract" and their variants, except where I am indirectly quoting others.

Those who comb history, literature and the Bible for reassuring precedents ignore the social context of oppression in which those odd little tales unfold. Yes, Sarah suggested that Abraham impregnate Hagar in order "that I may obtain children by her," but Hagar was a slave. What's modern about the story is that once pregnant, Hagar, like Mary Beth Whitehead, seemed to think that her child was hers no matter what anyone said. The outcome of that ancient domestic experiment was, in any case, disastrous, especially for Baby Ishmael. So perhaps the Bible was trying to tell us something about what happens when people treat people like things.

Surrogacy is the answer to female infertility.

It has widely and properly been noted that only the well-to-do can afford to contract for a baby. (The Sterns, with a combined income of more than $90,000, paid $25,000 all told for Baby M, with $10,000 going to Mrs. Whitehead.) Less often has it been remarked that contract maternity is not a way for infertile women to get children, although the mothers often speak as though it were. It is a way for men to get children. Elizabeth Stern's name does not even appear on the contract. Had Mr. Stern filed for divorce before Baby M was born, had he died or become non compos, Dr. Stern would have been out of luck. Even after she became Baby M's primary caretaker, until the adoption went through, she had no more claim on the child than a baby sitter. Rather than empower infertile women through an act of sisterly generosity, maternity contracts make one woman a baby machine and the other irrelevant.

And there is no reason to assume that contracts will be limited to men married to infertile women — indeed, the Sterns have already broken that barrier — or even to men married at all. I can hear the precedent-setting argument already: Why, your honor, should a man's drive to procreate, his constitutional right to the joys of paternity, be dependent on the permission of a woman? No doubt, this further innovation will be presented as a gesture of female altruism too ("I just wanted to give him the One Thing a man can't give himself"). But take away the mothers' delusion that they are making babies for other women, and what you have left is what, in cold, hard fact, we already have: the limited-use purchase of women's bodies by men — reproductive prostitution.

So what? A woman has the right to control her body.

The issue in contract motherhood is not whether a woman can bear a child for whatever reason she likes, but whether she can legally promise to sell that child — a whole other person, not an aspect of her body — to its father. Judge Sorkow is surely the only person on earth who thinks William Stern paid Mary Beth Whitehead $10,000 merely to conceive and carry a baby and not also to transfer that baby to him.

Actually, maternity contracts have the potential to do great harm to the cause of women's physical autonomy. Right now a man cannot legally control the conduct of a woman pregnant by him. He cannot force her to have an abortion or not have one, to manage her pregnancy and delivery as he thinks best, or to submit to fetal surgery or a Caesarean. Nor can he sue her if, through what he considers to be negligence, she miscarries or produces a defective baby. A maternity contract could give a man all those powers, except, possibly, the power to compel abortion, the only clause in the Stern-Whitehead contract that Judge Sorkow found invalid. Mr. Stern, for instance, seemed to think he had the right to tell Mrs. Whitehead's doctors what drugs to give her during labor. We've already had the spectacle of policemen forcibly removing 5-month-old Baby M from the arms of Mrs. Whitehead, the only mother she knew (so much for the best interests of the child!). What's next? State troopers guarding contract mothers to make sure they drink their milk?

Even if no money changed hands, the right-to-control-your-body argument would be unpersuasive. After all, the law already limits your right to do what you please with your body: you can't throw it off the Brooklyn Bridge, or feed it Laetrile, or even drive it around without a seat belt in some places. But money does change hands, and everybody, male and female, needs to be protected by law from the power of money to coerce or entice people to do things that seriously compromise their basic and most intimate rights, such as the right to health or life. You can sell your blood, but you can't sell your kidney. In fact, you can't even donate your kidney except under the most limited circumstances, no matter how fiercely you believe that this is the way you were meant to serve your fellow man and no matter how healthy you are. The risk of coercion is simply too great, and your kidney just too irreplaceable.

Supporters of contract motherhood talk about having a baby for pay as if it were like selling blood, or sperm, or breast milk. It is much more like selling a vital organ. Unlike a man, who produces billions of sperm and can theoretically father thousands of children at zero physical risk to himself, a woman can bear only a small number of children, and the physical cost to her can be as high as death. She cannot know in advance what a given pregnancy will mean for her health or for her ability to bear more children. (Interestingly, both the Sterns, who delayed parenthood until they found pregnancy too risky, and the Whiteheads, who foreclosed having more children with Mr. Whitehead's vasectomy, show just how unpredictable extrapolations from one's reproductive present are as guides to the future.) How can it be acceptable to pay a woman to risk her life, health and fertility so that a man can have his own biological child, yet morally heinous to pay healthy people to sacrifice "extra" organs to achieve the incomparably greater aim of saving a life? We're scandalized when we read of Asian sterilization campaigns in which men are paid to be vasectomized—and not just because of the abuses to which those campaigns are notoriously subject but because they seem, by their very nature, to take advantage of people's shortsightedness in order to deprive them forever of something precious. Why is hiring women to have babies and give them away any better?

The question of payment is crucial because although contract mothers prefer to tell the television cameras about their longing to help humanity, studies have shown that almost nine out of ten wouldn't help humanity for free. (Well, it's a job. Would you do your job for free?) But women to whom $10,000 is a significant amount of money are the ones who live closest to the economic edge and have the fewest alternative ways of boosting their income in a crisis. Right now contract motherhood is still considered a rather *outré* thing to do, and women often have to talk their families into it. But if it becomes a socially acceptable way for a wife to help out the family budget, how can the law protect women from being coerced into contracts by their husbands? Or their relatives? Or their creditors? It can't. In fact, it can't even insure uncoerced consent when no money changes hands. *The New York Times* has already discovered a case in which a family matriarch successfully pressured one relative to produce a child for another.

If contract motherhood takes hold, a woman's "right to control her body" by selling her pregnancies will become the modern equivalent of "she's sitting on a fortune." Her husband's debts, her children's unfixed teeth, the kitchen drawer full of unpaid bills, will be her fault, the outcome of her selfish refusal to sell what nature gave her.

A deal's a deal.

This is what it's really about, isn't it? To hear the chorus of hosannas currently being raised to this sacred tenet of market economics, you'd think the entire structure of law and morality would collapse about our ears if one high-school-dropout housewife in New Jersey was allowed to keep her baby. "One expects a prostitute to fulfill a contract," intoned Lawrence Stone, the celebrated Princeton University historian, in *The New York Times*. (Should the poor girl fail to show up at her regular time, the campus police are presumably to tie her up and deliver her into one's bed.) Some women argue that to allow Mrs. Whitehead to back out of her pledge would be to stigmatize all women as irrational and incapable of adulthood under the law. You'd think she had signed a contract to trade sow bellies at $5 and then gave premenstrual syndrome as her reason for canceling.

But is a deal a deal? Not always. Not, for instance, when it involves something illegal: prostitution (sorry, Professor Stone), gambling debts, slavery, polygyny, sweatshop labor, division of stolen goods and, oh yes, baby selling. Nor does it matter how voluntary such a contract is. So if your ambition in life is to be an indentured servant or a co-wife, you will have to fulfill this desire in a country where what Michael Kinsley calls "the moral logic of capitalism" has advanced so far that the untrained eye might mistake it for the sort of patriarchal semi-feudalism practiced in small towns in Iran.

Well, you say, suppose we decided that contract motherhood wasn't prostitution or baby selling but some other, not flatly illegal, transaction: sale of parental rights to the father or some such. Then a deal would be a deal right? Wrong. As anyone who has ever shopped for a co-op apartment in New York City knows, in the world of commerce, legal agreements are abrogated, modified, renegotiated and bought out all the time. What happens when contracts aren't fulfilled is what most of contract law is about.

Consider the comparatively civilized world of publishing. A writer signs up with one publisher, gets a better offer from another, pays back his advance — maybe — and moves on. Or a writer signs up to produce a novel but finds she'd rather die than see it printed, although her editor thinks it's a sure-fire best seller. Does the publisher forcibly take possession of the manuscript and print 100,000 copies because it's his property and a deal's a deal? No. The writer gives back the advance or submits another idea or persuades her editor she's such a genius she ought to be given even more money to write a really good book. And, somehow, Western civilization continues.

The closer we get to the murky realm of human intimacy the more reluctant we are to enforce contracts in anything like their potential severity. Marriage, after all, is a contract. Yet we permit divorce. Child-support agreements are contracts. Yet a woman cannot bar the father of her children from leaving investment banking for the less lucrative profession of subway musician. Engagement is, if not usually a formal contract, a public pledge of great seriousness. Yet the bride or groom abandoned at the altar has not been able to file a breach of promise suit for almost a hundred years. What have we learned since desperate spouses lit out for the territory and jilted maidens jammed the courts? That in areas of profound human feeling, you cannot promise because you cannot know, and pretending otherwise would result in far more misery than allowing people to cut their losses.

When Mary Beth Whitehead signed her contract she was promising something it is not in anyone's power to promise: not to fall in love with her baby. To say, as some do, that she "should have known" because she'd had two children already is like saying a man should have known how he'd feel about his third wife because he'd already been married twice before. Why should mothers be held to a higher standard of self-knowledge than spouses? Or, more to the point, than fathers? In a recent California case a man who provided a woman friend with sperm, no strings attached, changed his mind when the child was born and sued for visitation rights. He won. Curiously, no one suggested that the decision stigmatized all his sex as hyperemotional dirty-dealers.

Fatherhood and motherhood are identical.

It is at this point that one begins to feel people have resigned their common sense entirely. True, a man and a woman contribute equally to the genetic makeup of a baby. But twenty-three pairs of chromosomes do not a baby make. In the usual course of events the woman is then pregnant for nine months and goes through childbirth, a detail overlooked by those who compare maternity contracts to sperm donation. The proper parallel to sperm donation is egg donation.

Feminists who argue that respecting Mrs. Whitehead's maternal feelings will make women prisoners of the "biology is destiny" arguments should think again. The Baby M decision did not disclaim the power of biology at all; it exalted male biology at the expense of female. Judge Sorkow paid tribute to Mr. Stern's drive to procreate; it was only Mrs. Whitehead's longing to nurture that he scorned. That Baby M had Mr. Stern's genes was judged a fact of supreme importance — more important than Mrs. Whitehead's genes, pregnancy and childbirth put together. We might as well be back in the days when a woman was seen merely as a kind of human potting soil for a man's seed.

Speaking as a pregnant person, I find the view of maternity inherent in maternity contracts profoundly demeaning. Pregnancy and delivery are not "services" performed for the baby's father. The unborn child is not riding about inside a woman like a passenger in a car. A pregnant woman is not, as one contract mother put it, "a human incubator"; she is engaged in a constructive task, in taxing physical work. Some of this work is automatic, and no less deserving of respect for that, but much of it is not — an increasing amount, it would appear, to judge by doctors' ever-lengthening list of dos and don'ts.

Now, why do I follow my doctor's advice: swill milk, take vitamins, eschew alcohol, cigarettes, caffeine, dental X-rays and even the innocent aspirin? And why, if I had to, would I do a lot more to help my baby be born healthy, including things that are uncomfortable and wearisome (like staying in bed for months, as a friend of mine had to) or even detrimental to my own body (like fetal surgery)? It's not because I want to turn out a top-of-the-line product, or feel a sense of duty to the baby's dad, or have invested the baby with all the rights and privileges of an American citizen whose address just happens to be my uterus. I do it because I love the baby. Even before it's born, I'm already forming a relationship with it. You can call that biology or social conditioning or a purely emotional fantasy. Perhaps, like romantic love, it is all three at once. But it's part of what pregnancy is — just ask the millions of pregnant women who feel this way, often to their own astonishment, sometimes under much less auspicious circumstances than Mrs. Whitehead's. It makes my blood boil when it is suggested that if contract mothers delivered under anesthesia and never saw their babies they wouldn't get a chance to "bond" and would feel no loss. I suppose the doctor could just tell them that they gave birth to a watermelon.

And so we arrive at the central emotional paradox of the Baby M case. We accept a notion that a man can have intense fatherly emotion for a child he's never seen, whose mother he's never slept with, let alone rubbed her back, or put his hand on her belly to feel the baby kick, or even taken her to the hospital. But a woman who violates her promise and loves the child she's had inside her for nine months, risked her health for, given birth to . . . She must be some kind of nut.

Women need more options, not fewer.

To suggest that female poverty can be ameliorated by poor mothers selling their children to wealthy fathers is a rather Swiftian concept. But why stop at contract motherhood when there's still a flourishing market for adoptive babies? Let enterprising poor women take up childbearing as a cottage industry and conceive expressly for the purpose of selling the baby to the highest bidder. And since the law permits parents to give up older children for adoption, why shouldn't they be allowed to sell them as well? Ever on the reproductive forefront, New Jersey recently gave the world the sensational case of a father who tried to sell his 4-year-old daughter to her dead mother's relatives for $100,000. Why he was arrested for doing what Mary Beth Whitehead was forced to do is anybody's guess.

Even leaving aside the fact that maternity contracts involve the sale of a human being, do women need another incredibly low-paying (around $1.50 an hour) service job that could damage their health and possibly even kill them, that opens up the most private areas of life to interference by a pair of total strangers, that they cannot get unless they first sign an ironclad contract forgoing a panoply of elementary human rights? By that logic, working in a sweatshop is an option, too—which is exactly what sweatshop employers have always maintained.

But people are going to do it anyway. Shouldn't they be protected?

There are some practices (drinking, abortion, infidelity) so entrenched in mass behavior and regarded as acceptable by so many that to make them illegal would be both undemocratic and futile. Contract motherhood is not one of them. In ten years only about 500 women have signed up. So the argument that we should legitimize it because it's just human nature in its infinite variety is not valid—yet.

Now, it's probably true that some women will bear children for money no matter what the law says. In the privacy of domestic life all sorts of strange arrangements are made. But why should the state enforce such bargains? Feminists who think regulation would protect the mother miss the whole point of the maternity contract, which is precisely to deprive her of protections she would have if she had signed nothing. If the contracts were unenforceable, the risk would be where it belongs, on the biological father and his wife, whose disappointment if the mother reneges, though real, can hardly be compared with a mother's unwilling loss of her just-born child. The real loser, of course, would be the baby-broker.

(Noel Keane, the lawyer who arranged for Baby M, made about $300,000 last year in fees for such services.) And that would be a very good thing.

But most surrogates have been pleased with their experience. Perhaps the Baby M trial is just a hard case making a bad law.

It's possible to be horrified by what happened to Mary Beth Whitehead and still think that contract motherhood can be a positive thing if carefully regulated. If there had been better screening at the clinic, if the contract had included a grace period, if actual infertility had been required of Elizabeth Stern, we would never have heard of Baby M. If, if, if.

Regulation might make contract motherhood less haphazard, but there is no way it can be made anything other than what it is: an inherently unequal relationship involving the sale of a woman's body and a child. The baby-broker's client is the father; his need is the one being satisfied; he pays the broker's fee. No matter how it is regulated, the business will have to reflect that priority. That's why the bill being considered in New York State specifically denies the mother a chance to change her mind, although the stringency of the Stern-Whitehead contract in this regard was the one thing pundits assured the public would not happen again. Better screening procedures would simply mean more accurately weeding out the trouble-makers and selecting for docility, naïveté, low self-esteem and lack of money for legal fees. Free psychological counseling for the mothers, touted by some brokers as evidence of their care and concern, would merely be manipulation by another name. True therapy seeks to increase a person's sense of self, not reconcile one to being treated as an instrument.

Even if the business could be managed so that all the adults involved were invariably pleased with the outcome, it would still be wrong, because they are not the only people involved. There are, for instance the mother's other children. Prospective contract mothers, Mrs. Whitehead included, do not seem to consider for two seconds the message they are sending to their kids. But how can it not damage a child to watch Mom cheerfully produce and sell its half-sibling while Dad stands idly by? I'd love to be a fly on the wall as a mother reassures her kids that of course she loves them no matter what they do; it's just their baby sister who had a price tag.

And, of course, there is the contract baby. To be sure, there are worse ways of coming into the world, but not many, and none that are elaborately prearranged by sane people. Much is made of the so-called trauma of adoption, but adoption is a piece of cake compared with contracting. Adoptive parents can tell their child, Your mother loved you so much she gave you up, even though it made her sad, because that was best for you. What can the father and adoptive mother of a contract baby say? Your mother needed $10,000? Your mother wanted to do something nice for us, so she made you? The Sterns can't even say that. They'll have to make do with something like, Your mother loved you so much she wanted to keep you, but we took you anyway, because a deal's a deal, and anyway, she was a terrible person. Great.

Oh, lighten up. Surrogacy fills a need. There's a shortage of babies for adoption, and people have the right to a child.

What is the need that contract motherhood fills? It is not the need for a child, exactly. That need is met by adoption—although not very well, it's true, especially if parents have their hearts set on a "perfect baby," a healthy white newborn. The so-called baby shortage is really a shortage of those infants. (Shortage from the would-be adoptive parents' point of view; from the point of view of the birth mothers or Planned Parenthood, there's still a baby surplus.) What William Stern wanted, however, was not just a perfect baby; the Sterns did not, in fact, seriously investigate adoption. He wanted a perfect baby with his genes and a medically vetted mother who would get out of his life forever immediately after giving birth. That's a tall order, and one no other class of father—natural, step-, adoptive—even claims to be entitled to. Why should the law bend itself into a pretzel to gratify it?

The Vatican's recent document condemning all forms of conception but marital intercourse was marked by the church's usual political arrogance and cheeseparing approach to sexual intimacy, but it was right about one thing. You don't have a right to a child, any more than you have a right to a spouse. You only have the right to try to have one. Goods can be distributed according to ability to pay or need. People can't.

It's really that simple.

STEPHEN F. COHEN

Sovieticus

June 13, 1987

Stephen Cohen, a professor of Soviet politics and history at Princeton University, started writing his monthly column "Sovieticus" for *The Nation* in October 1982.

Why do so many American commentators still insist that no significant improvements in the Soviet system are possible, despite more than two years of evidence that Mikhail Gorbachev is determined to introduce far-reaching reforms?

A *Miami Herald* columnist crudely dismisses the Soviet leader with the proverb

"Dress a monkey in silk, and he'll still be a monkey." A *Washington Post* editorial concludes that Gorbachev's proposed changes in the system will not "make it less of a police state but a more efficient police state." Henry Kissinger assures *Time* readers that the Soviet Union "will be a totalitarian state even after the reforms are completed." And a *Wall Street Journal* columnist flatly maintains that Soviet ideology "makes genuine reform a practical impossibility."

Denying that the Soviet Union can change for the better, or that it ever has, is a longstanding tradition in the United States. Such assertions were frequent even when the de-Stalinization policies of Nikita Khrushchev were under way. Indeed, the favored cliché of many pundits, including some alleged experts, holds that "nothing meaningful has changed" since Stalin.

A full explanation of this wrongheaded tradition would require a large book exploring both American political thinking and the nature of the Soviet system, but five important factors can be briefly identified.

§ Only one is rooted primarily in the Soviet system. In all countries political change is generated by struggles between opposing social demands, ideological convictions, group interests and leadership factions. Those dynamics in the Soviet Union have usually been concealed by official censorship, which has misled Americans into believing that they do not exist, that "all Communists think alike," that the Soviet establishment is politically uniform and, therefore, that no leader or faction can emerge to challenge the status quo. In reality, that establishment, including the Communist Party, has long been deeply divided over fundamental political and ideological issues, and especially over the desirability of large-scale change in the system inherited from Stalin. How could it be otherwise in a nation whose history has been so traumatic and whose recent transition from a predominantly rural society to an urban one has created so many new demands and problems? The extent of that conflict remains out of public view, but much of it now has surged into the Soviet press because of Gorbachev's proposed reforms and the opposition to them.

§ The second factor is indigenously American, a kind of national conceit produced in our own relatively benign political experience. It is the widespread opinion that nothing short of democratization qualifies as "meaningful" change in the Soviet Union. Khrushchev's abolition of the Stalinist mass terror did not lead to democracy, but it liberated millions of people from Gulag labor camps and exile and reunited them with their families. If successful, Gorbachev's economic and social policies will improve the lives of tens of millions of Soviet citizens. And yet many American commentators dismiss the significance of such changes because, to cite A.M. Rosenthal of *The New York Times*, they are not "even faintly good enough for you and me." We may wish for democracy in the Soviet Union, but to deny that lesser improvements are meaningful is a profound failure of analysis and of compassion.

§ The third factor is the instinctive American practice of judging Soviet internal developments largely by objectionable Soviet behavior abroad, which is the main focus of U.S. media coverage. Most Americans still remember Khrushchev not as a great reformer but as a menacing leader who put Soviet missiles in Cuba. Similarly, much American commentary today implies that Gorbachev will be a real reformer only if he ends the Soviet Union's role as a super-power and capitulates to the United States in world affairs. A nation's foreign policy does reveal something about its political system, but it is not the only criterion. If it were, we would have to judge the American system solely by its behavior in Vietnam and Nicaragua.

§ In that connection, there is also the important role played by American institutions and groups that for years have zealously promoted and thrived on the popular image of an unchanged and unchangeable Soviet Union. They include the military-industrial complex, legions of professional cold-warriors and self-described national security intellectuals, certain Jewish organizations and an array of other special interests. Any acknowledged improvement in the Soviet system threatens their political, economic and ideological well-being. In fact, for many such groups and individuals, the necessity of eternal cold war against the Soviet Union is theological rather than analytical, and thus can never be diminished. If one reason is removed—if a Sakharov or a Shcharansky is released, a weapons "gap" closed, an international problem ameliorated—they will always find others. Ever vigilant against any "illusions" of Soviet change, they incant ritualistically, as did a *New York Post* editorialist last year, "There's nothing new at all going on over there." Collectively, these cold war forces exercise enormous influence on American perceptions and politics, and there are virtually no anti-cold war lobbies strong enough to offset them.

§ Finally, there is another, more complex, legacy of the decades-long cold war. America, it seems, has developed a deep psychological need for an immutably ugly Soviet Union in order to minimize or obscure its own imperfections. How often do we say, for example, that while we may practice some social injustices at home, everything is much worse in the Soviet Union? Or while we may be behaving badly in Nicaragua, the Russians are doing much worse in Afghanistan? Or that our nuclear plants are not as unsafe as Soviet ones? If America does need an evil empire in the East to feel better about itself, nothing that Gorbachev or any Soviet reformer may do is likely to matter. Indeed, future historians, if there are any, may wonder how authoritarian Soviet behavior came to be a moral and political standard for democratic America.

CHRISTOPHER HITCHENS

Minority Report
August 29, 1987
[the death penalty]

Christopher Hitchens started contributing "Minority Report,"
his biweekly column on political affairs in Washington, D.C.
and around the world, in 1982.

State Penitentiary, Parchman, Mississippi
I had to come this far to see my first gas chamber. The apparatus is encased in
a flagon-shaped container, rather like a man-sized version of the killing bottles
used by lepidopterists. The killing bottle in turn is housed in a shed. And the shed
is adjacent to a row of cells, in which the human specimens are kept for the bottle's
convenience.

It ought to be the work of a moment to take a man out of a cell, whisk him into
the bottle, and put him beyond the reach of earthly cares. But in some peculiar
way the process is a protracted one. The man I had come to see, Edward Earl
Johnson, had been kept waiting for eight years. During those eight years, which
began shortly after his eighteenth birthday, he had seen and heard other men being fed into the bottle. When the bottle is being readied, the sound of the guards
and technicians going about their tasks is clearly audible. They tend to whoop,
with excitement or disappointment, when they "do the bunnies." "Doing the bunnies" involves inserting some experimental rabbits into the bottle and observing
the effect of cyanide gas upon them. Sometimes the bunnies check out very rapidly. Other times, they linger. If you are in a cell waiting to be gassed yourself,
you can gauge the probable speed of your own demise by the noises coming from
the shed.

The last man to enter the bottle before Johnson was Jimmy Lee Gray. Even
the prison authorities admit that his death was low on dignity and lacking in
dispatch. Shortly after midnight on September 2, 1983, a switch was thrown,
causing lethal fumes to rise from the cyanide crystals. Gray went into convul-
sions, which lasted for eight minutes. He was observed to gasp deeply eleven
times and to smash his head repeatedly on the metal pole behind him. After those
eight minutes, the guards lost their nerve and hustled the witnesses from the
shed, where they had been gaping through the bottle's glass flanks. So nobody
really knows how long it took Jimmy Lee to pay his ultimate debt to society.
Johnson, who was gassed a few days after I said goodbye to him, survived in
the bottle for a full fifteen minutes.

Jimmy Lee Gray was white and had pleaded guilty to the murder of a white child. Edward Earl Johnson was black and denied to the end that he had shot a white policeman. According to evidence recently accepted by the Supreme Court, a black man who kills a white is three times more likely to suffer the penalty of death than a white man who kills a white. A black man who kills a white is eleven times more likely to be slain by the state than a white man who kills a black. In my idealistic youth, this was known as racial discrimination or even racism. Now, says the majority on the Supreme Court, it is "a discrepancy that appears to correlate with race." However, as the justices went on to say, such "apparent disparities in sentencing are an inevitable part of our criminal justice system." If that last statement is true, it is rather a condemnation.

If you get hold of Amnesty International's report *The United States of America: The Death Penalty* (322 Eighth Avenue, New York, N.Y. 10001, $6), you can read a meticulous account of the operations of the capital-punishment system. The gas chamber, the firing squad, and the electric chair are employed on the mentally ill, on juveniles, on racial minorities, and, of course, on those who have committed no crime. State and regional variations in sentencing make a mockery of consistency and therefore of even the vaguest utility of that incoherent concept "the deterrent." The fashion for allegedly more humane execution by lethal injection has resulted in obscenely painful and grotesque episodes, and involves the corruption of the Hippocratic code of medical ethics. Yet, under the Reagan Administration, this death cult has been given every encouragement to spread.

Two additional objections struck me during my stay at Parchman. The first was so obvious that it took me some time to realize it. Edward Earl Johnson was not merely rotting under sentence of death; he was being tortured. I had never actually seen anyone being tortured before. Perhaps, as a member of the post-Nuremberg generation, I had naïvely supposed that the practice had been at least officially done away with. But if I was confined in a windowless cell shortly after my eighteenth birthday, and was kept waiting for eight years to know if I would live or go to the bottle, I would believe that I was in prison not *as* punishment but *for* punishment. That is torture. The state of Mississippi makes a big thing of the last-minute reprieve, or stay. (Justice Earl Warren once telephoned Parchman at midnight, only to be told that it was too late; now they wait a ritual extra ten minutes.) So you don't know, even when the men with masks and rubber gloves enter your cell, that it is really the end. And then it can take you quite a long time to die, with strangers watching. The tableau is made complete by the representatives of my two least favorite professions—the lawyer and the priest. These have been essential fixtures at the stake and the scaffold since medieval times. But we have no right to consider torture medieval while it is still legally practiced in the New World.

My second objection is that capital punishment strikes directly at democracy and due process. It can't be coincidence that it is used most frequently in countries that consider the citizen to be the property of the state. In a caste-bound or dictatorial system, the condemned can be taken from the dock to the execution yard, and that's that. At least the relatives of the victim (if the system has picked the right culprit) have the paltry satisfaction of swift justice. But democracy requires appeal procedures, mature consideration, review, and the possibility of clemency and revision. This, in the strict sense, is incompatible with the death penalty and, when combined with it, makes a charade of the legal system, turning ostensibly humane review into a protracted humiliation.

Racist, brutalizing, antidemocratic, sadistic, and thoughtless—is it any wonder that this special symbol of primitivism is undergoing a recrudescence in the era of Edwin Meese?

JOHN LEONARD

Delirious New York   *November 28, 1987*

John Leonard's spirited essay rolls together *Dissent* magazine's special issue on New York with Tom Wolfe's modish New York slumming in *The Bonfire of the Vanities* to form the quintessential statement on what it was like to be in this place at this time.

The Bonfire of the Vanities. **By Tom Wolfe. Farrar, Straus & Giroux. 659 pp. $19.95.**

In Search of New York. **A Special Issue of *Dissent*. Edited by Jim Sleeper. 240 pp. $5.**

I. THE WAY WE ARE

We live in this imaginary city, a novel that needs a rewrite, where the only politicians not in jail probably ought to be, except for Ruth Messinger, and all of them are Democrats; where the unions don't care, and the schools don't work, and the cops deal drugs, and the Mayor has his own foreign policy and I can't leave home without stepping over the body of a runaway or a derelict. We didn't elect Felix Rohatyn to anything, but the Municipal Assistance Corporation is more important than the City Council. Nor did we vote for Steinbrenner, Trump or the rest of the bullies and crybabies who bray on our battlements and wave the bloody pennants of their imperial omophagous selves—and yet Mort Zuckerman will have his Zuckermandias at Columbus Circle, his finger in the sun, on the same Coliseum site from which Robert Moses before him dispossessed an entire neighbor-hood; and because none of these heroes ever takes the subway, there's no one to shoot them. Maybe we need Jeremiah more than we need Tom Wolfe or a bunch of disappointed intellectuals.

But Wolfe and *Dissent* have written their New York City novels anyway. Wolfe, the parajournalist, looks pretty much the same as always, still grinning at us out of the nimbus of his double-breasted signature white suit, a vanilla-colored Mau Mau. *Dissent*, on the other hand, has had a format face-lift and for the first time in thirty-three years you can read the socialist quarterly without an O.E.D. magnifying glass. In both their novels, the underclass is the stuff of dreams, the return of the repressed, a history-making black magic. They dis-agree, of course, on whether this is a good thing. Listen to Wolfe:

> You don't think the future knows how to cross a *bridge*? And you, you WASP charity-ballers sitting on your mounds of inherited money up in your co-ops with the twelve-foot ceilings and the two wings, one for you and one for the help, do you really think you're impregnable? And you German-Jewish financiers who have finally made it into the same buildings, the better to insulate yourselves from the *shtetl* hordes, do you really think you're insulated from the *Third World*?

Dissent wants this very same Third World—2.5 million "newcomers" since 1965—to be an energizing principle. In diversity we've always found our jumping beans. From the abrasions of culture on culture, we rub up a public philosophy and a civic space. Surely these new immigrants, this ethnic muscle, will rescue us from a mood grown "sullen, as if in contempt of earlier feelings and visions" and "a peculiar kind of social nastiness" (Irving Howe); a "trained incapacity to see the city as a human environment, or as anything more than a machine for generating money" (Marshall Berman); "a way of life that is not much better than jungle warfare" (Ada Louise Huxtable); and "a world devised in its entirety by Dostoevski's Smerdyakov" (Paula Fox).

It's odd that Wolfe is so much better than *Dissent* on the details of class animus. Whereas *Dissent* can barely bring itself to mention the cops, Wolfe goes under-ground into the criminal justice system, where the hatred is naked. If *Dissent* is too polite these days to call anybody an out-and-out racist, Wolfe has been to some fancy dinner parties and taken notes, like Saint-Simon, and bites the hand that scratches his ears, like Truman Capote. It's equally odd that Ed Koch, who certainly deserves it, is all over the pages of *Dissent*, while Wolfe entirely ignores him. A New York novel without Koch is like a court without a Sun King. Even Danny Ortega took time out to rub Crazy Eddie's lucky hump.

But there are many oddities. Neither New York novel has much of anything to say about drugs or organized crime. Both mention Alexander Cockburn.

II. VANITIES

Sherman McCoy is a 38-year-old Yalie who decided to sell bonds on Wall Street instead of going into his father's good-bones law firm. He made almost $1 million last year, but when he sits down in his Ox-blood Moroccan leather swivel chair in front of the tambour door of his *faux*-Sheraton TV cabinet, he's still broke, because of his $2.6 million tenth-floor Park Avenue duplex, a Southampton house on Old Drover's Mooring Lane, a wife who decorates her interiors with Thomas Hope chairs, three servants, a handyman, club dues, car insurance for the Mercedes and private-school tuition for cute little Campbell, who, "supremely ladylike in her burgundy Taliaferro jumper and blazer and white blouse with a buttercup collar," bakes bunny rabbits in the kitchen and writes short stories about sad koala bears.

Sherman also has a bimbo. Wolfe's no better than Bill Buckley at heavy breathing, but he knows enough to borrow from his betters. Poor-white Southern-trashy Maria—the faithless wife and merry widow—slinks right out of a 1940s detective novel into Sherman's nerveless arms. "Her medium was men . . . the way a . . . dolphin's medium is the sea." At the wheel of Sherman's Mercedes, at night on an off-ramp in darkest Bronx, Maria will hit, run down and run away from a young, black, fatherless "honor student" from the nearby bombed-out projects, and Sherman of course will be blamed.

This malefaction will excite a black demagogue, the Rev. Reginald Bacon of Harlem; a white, Kunstler-like attorney, the radically chic Albert Vogel; an English reporter for a Murdoch-minded tabloid, the alcoholic Peter Fallow; a Jewish D.A. up for re-election in a Bronx that's 70 percent black and Hispanic, the publicity-hungry Abe Weiss; a Jewish assistant D.A. who'd rather be an Irish cop, the horny and impoverished Lawrence Kramer; and assorted Communists, "the lesbos and the gaybos," welfare bums and fluffy-headed TV nightly news anchorpeople.

Poor Sherman. In his rent-controlled love nest, he's menaced by the landlord's hired Hasidic muscle ("These . . . unbelievable people . . . could now walk into his life"). When the cops ("insolent . . . Low Rent . . . *animals*") come to take him to the Bronx for his arraignment ("*the brutes* from the outer boroughs"), they are driving an Oldsmobile Cutlass! When he looks down from his tenth-floor co-op, a black mob is howling for his blue blood. (The *Other* is gaining on *him!*)

Only Tom Wolfe could descend into the sewers of our criminal justice system and find for his hero a *white* victim in a city where Bernie Goetz gets six months, John Gotti and Ray Donovan walk, Robert Chambers blames the victim and Eleanor Bumpers and Michael Stewart are still dead. Only Wolfe could want to be our Balzac and yet not notice the real estate hucksters and the homeless nor send a single one of his characters to a concert, movie, play, museum, Chinese restaurant or all-night delicatessen. So the women are Tinkertoys, the blacks corrupt cartoons, the sex silly and the homophobia tedious, the politics a surly whelp of Evelyn Waugh and Joseph de Maistre and the author less amusing than he was when he trashed modern art. Nobody's perfect.

But on several subjects, all but disdained by *Dissent*, Wolfe can really sweat our socks.

III. THE "DELIRIOUS PROFESSIONS" . . .
FEAR . . . AND . . . SHOES

By the "delirious professions," Paul Valéry meant "all those trades whose main tool is one's opinion of one's self, and whose raw material is the opinion others have of you." In other words, Creative People, who in New York are not merely artists, writers, actors, dancers and singers but journalists, editors, critics, TV and radio producers, anchorpeople and talk-show hosts, noisy professors of uplift or anomie, vagabond experts on this week's Rapture of the Deep at the 92nd Street Y, even (gasp) advertising account execs and swinging bankers and yuppies in red suspenders on the stock exchange. Each is asked every minute of the day to be original; *unique*. Only then will they be lifted up by their epaulets to Steinbrenner's box in the stadium sky, there to consort with city presbyters the likes of the late Roy Cohn, where you can't tell the pearls from the swine.

Dissent isn't interested in these people, these vanities and their white suits and their bonfires. When *Dissent* nods at the market, it's merely to observe that "a multi-billion dollar, cost-plus, militarized economy virtually guaranteed spectacular profits to investors in the West and South" (Berman). When it mentions the media at all, it's only to complain of their role in a "bipartisan incumbent-protection society" and their " 'objective' contempt" for politics as anything other than "sport" (Jim Chapin), or to make fun of *Manhattan, inc.* and *Spy* (Brian Morton). Where, for heaven's sake, is an analysis of *The Times*? How come *Newsday* was the only daily to oppose the re-election of Al d'Amato (whom Irving Howe calls "picklehead")? For *Dissent* the delirious professions belong merely, anonymously, to a "service sector" as remote from the new Third World as Mars.

Yet these are the people, making images and taste and deals, who write the city's *Zeitgeist*, the heat waves and cold fronts and snow jobs and acid rain of our emotional weather. Without their complicity, there will be no change. Change needs better P.R. Dazzle them — mostly male and mostly pale — into a militant sentience. At least take seriously their many failures of intelligence and character.

And Wolfe can't get enough of them. "They were moving about in an agitated manner and sweating early in the morning and shouting, which created the roar. It was the sound of well-educated young white men baying for money on the bond market." Pre-staggered cash flows! Convertible asset management! Capital-sensitive liquidity ratios! He's got their number: "He was wearing a covert-cloth Chesterfield topcoat with a golden brown velvet collar and carrying one of those burgundy leather attaché cases that came from Mädler or T. Anthony on Park Avenue and have a buttery smoothness that announces: 'I cost $500.' " He obviously knows his way around *The New York Post*, where he decided that the press are "fruit flies," the TV types are print-dependent bubble-brains (although demonstrators only show up to protest the latest outrage when they're sure the camera's rolling) and "dancers, novelists, and gigantic fairy opera singers [are] nothing but court jesters" to the bond-selling "Masters of the Universe."

Wolfe knows, too, that his delirious professionals—"frisky young animal[s] . . . of that breed whose natural destiny it was . . . to have what they wanted!"—are scared to death, especially on the subway: "Into the car came three boys, black, fifteen or sixteen years old, wearing big sneakers with enormous laces, untied but looped precisely in parallel lines. . . . They walked with a pumping gait known as the Pimp Roll. . . . They drew closer, with the invariable cool blank look. . . . Such stupid self-destructive macho egos."

It's the attitude. Compare Wolfe's to a lovely riff from Wesley Brown in *Dissent*: "a display of bravado by a young, indigo-skinned black male, moving through a crowded subway car like a point guard bringing the ball up the court, sporting a haircut that makes the shape of his head resemble a cone of ice-cream, and wearing barge-sized sneakers with untied laces thick as egg noodles, is immediately considered a dangerous presence whether he is or not." By whom? By delirious professionals. On the subway, the First World and the Third coincide, at least until the express stop at Columbus Circle.

They are afraid, too, that what they do is make-believe; that their luck and their charm will run out; that they will look in the mirror one morning and see, if not the other side of the room, then maybe something no longer brand-new and unique, someone *found out*, like Sherman. They will lose their co-op and our good opinion. As cops and press and mob close in on Sherman, his megabucks Paris deal on Giscard bonds is also falling apart and his panic is palpable. (Nobody writing for *Dissent* seems to be afraid; angry, maybe, or tired, or sad or contemptuous, but not scared.) Wolfe makes us sweat. As bad as he is on sex, he's terrific on money, and hangovers, and . . . *shoes*.

There are no shoes in *Dissent*. There are two references to "shoemakers," but that's just left wing atavism. Whereas shoes are Wolfe's big story, from "the Boston Cracked Shoe look" to Maria's "electric-blue lizard pumps with white calf caps on the toes" to Sherman's infamous $650 bench-made half-brogued English New & Lingwoods with the close soles and beveled insteps. Shoes for Wolfe are character. Sherman's dandified defense attorney wears brown suede shoes. Assistant D.A. Kramer wears Johnson & Murphy "clodhoppers." A witness for the prosecution is partial to snow-white Reeboks, but they make him change into leather loafers for the grand jury. Ballet slippers or "go-to-hell" sneakers with Velcro straps, Wolfe's gone that extra mile and worn them.

What does this mean? More than you think. I've consulted Krafft-Ebing's *Psychopathia Sexualis*, Sacher-Masoch's *Venus in Furs* and Kurella's *Naturgeschichte des Verbrechers*. I know more than I ought to about high-buttoned patent-leather boots, "Hungarian high-heels," the legend of Aschenbrödel, the toe-sucking (and later beatified) Marie Alacoque, foot fetishists East (Junichiro Tanizaki) and West (Restif de la Bretonne), not to mention vampirism, anthropophagy and coprolagnia, and not even to think about "shoes of the fisherman" Christian symbolism. On one level, the meaning of shoes in Wolfe is upward mobility—we are what we feet—but there is of course a subtext. Not one, but two Primal scenes in *Bonfire* make this obvious.

The young men baying for money on the bond market spend most of their time with their mouth on a telephone and their shoes in a stirrup. Sherman loves it: Felix, the middle-aged black shoeshine man,

> was humped over . . . stropping Sherman's right shoe, a New & Lingwood half-brogue, with his high-shine rag. . . . Sherman enjoyed the pressure of the rag on his metatarsal bones. It was a tiny massage of the ego, when you got right down to it—this great strapping brown man, with the bald spot in his crown down there at his feet, stropping, oblivious of the levers with which Sherman could move another nation, another continent, merely by bouncing words off a satellite.

But the Master of the Universe will be punished. Shoes in Wolfe's novel are like the guns in Chekhov's plays, that have to go bang. Before Sherman is fingerprinted in the Bronx, he is made to stand outside in the rain and soak his New & Lingwoods. And before he's tossed in the holding pen, where surly men of color want to wrinkle his friskiness, he is made to remove his belt *and his shoelaces*, "like two little dried dead things." His pants fall down and his shoes fall off and he has to *shuffle*: "The shoes made a squishing sound because they were so wet." At the end of *Bonfire* he changes into hiking boots and we know why. Shoes are sex.

IV. THERE ARE MORE THAN THREE WORLDS

From Wolfe, you wouldn't know that we've got one big problem with real-estate developers and another with the homeless. For *Dissent*, these are strophe and antistrophe, as in an old Greek choral ode, with everybody moving right to left and back again. To be sure, Deborah Meier, the heroine of District 4, has important things to say about "teaching for testing" and alternative schools; and Maxine Phillips would like to pay for the care of our 60,000 children who are abused or neglected each year by taxing cooperative apartments like Sherman McCoy's; and

Theresa Funicello is furious at "workfare," wondering why "a black woman hired as a nanny for an upper-class white family is a 'worker,' [while] a mother struggling under adverse conditions to raise her own children on welfare . . . is a parasite on society"; and Anthony Borden points out that 55 percent of all our AIDS victims are black or Latino, and so are 90 percent of our AIDS children, who never had a chance to say no to anything; and Gus Tyler looks at what happened to labor-intensive light manufacturing in this city (it went to Korea and Taiwan); and Michael Oreskes follows the garment industry to nonunion sweatshops in Chinatown or Queens; and Jewel Bellush explains "room at the top" for black women in organizing hospital, school and clerical workers; and John Mollenkopf can't find a "good government" reform movement anywhere.

Moreover, *Dissent*'s a lot more cultured than Wolfe. This novel has a chapter by Paul Berman on the sexual confusion and political ambivalence of those "prisoner[s] of culture" who live below Fourteenth Street and therefore have to read Kathy Acker, look at David Salle, listen to Peter Gordon and go to plays by Albert Inauratto; and a chapter by Juan Flores on the convergence of black and Puerto Rican cultures in "hip-hop," by way of Bo Diddley, Joe Cuba, Frankie Lymon, doo-wop, *capoeira*, break-dancing and rap; and a chapter by Ellen Levy on group theater versus performance art. And then it's Memory Lane: Michael Harrington, who may have less to be ashamed of than any other man of the left I know, admires Ruth Messinger and tries hard to remember when Crazy Eddie was a liberal. Morris Dickstein and Robert Lekachman feel bad and write agreeably about the Upper West Side and our favorite slumlord, Columbia University. Rosalyn Drexler and Leonard Kriegel go back to the Bronx (all that Art Deco on the Grand Concourse), and Kriegel finds a whole new *Irish* community Wolfe must have missed while soaking Sherman's shoes. Alfred Kazin has fun spanking such avatars of agitprop as N. Podhoretz, A. Cockburn, H. Kramer and G. Vidal, and then he gets serious: "When the great Reagan counterrevolution is over, what I shall remember most is the way accommodating intellectuals tried to bring to an end whatever was left among Jewish intellectuals of their old bond with the oppressed, the proscribed, the everlasting victims piled up now in every street."

Which brings us back to the grubby and the brutish. Marshall Berman itemizes everything Tom Wolfe never noticed:

spectacular giveaways to real estate developers; the attacks on the poor, depriving them of industrial work, low-income housing, public hospitals. . . . the casual brutality that has come to permeate our public life, as in the recent wave of mass arrests to drive homeless people out of the railway terminals that the city's own development policies have driven them into; the triumphal march of the city's rejuvenated political machines, whose movers . . . have made the 1980s one long carnival of white-collar crime; the rescue of the city from the clutches of a hostile federal government, by selling it (or giving it away) to rapacious real estate empires that will tear down anything or throw up anything, if it pays; the long-term transformation of New York into a place where capital from anywhere in the world is instantly at home, while everybody without capital is increasingly out of place.

In this corner: the Cross-Bronx Expressway, the Coliseum, Lincoln Center, Westway, Zuckermandias, Trump Television City, Times Square as Alphaville and Disney World. In the opposite corner: the homeless—the usual ghosts, of course, on the brownstone stoop with the little green bottles, and the bag lady who reads *Vogue* and the portly sociopath with the green beret and the 8-inch pigsticker, as well as the ambassador of this month's designer-zombie mushroom, nodding off on his way to where the action isn't. But they were our regulars, and they've been overwhelmed by a deindustrialized proletariat, a ragged army of the dispossessed, a supply-side migratory tide of angry beggars and runaway refugee children and almost catatonic nomads. Have you seen the cold-water, crime-ridden, disease-spreading shelters in which we warehouse these dropouts and castaways? They are safer on the streets, except for Crazy Eddie and his net. In the parks, of course, we burn them alive.

There are an estimated *100,000* homeless in the imperial city today. In the last 20 years—the years of the 2.5 million "newcomers"—housing production has *decreased* from 60,000 new units in 1966 to 7,000 in 1985 (Huxtable). Twenty-five percent of us live below the poverty line. At the end of World War II there were a million jobs in New York City light industries; today it's down to 400,000. White unemployment is 7.2 percent; for blacks, 11.5 percent; for Hispanics, 13.4 percent; among the white young, 22.5 percent; and for the black young, 47.9 percent (Tyler)—*47.9*, all of them Pimp Rolling on Tom Wolfe's subway.

Meanwhile, why do you suppose that real-estate developers, brokerage houses and their law firms forked out over $4 million in 1985 campaign contributions to Koch and the other seven members of the Board of Estimate? Maybe because Koch and the board have given these same people $1.3 billion on property tax breaks and zoning variances since 1978 (Jim Sleeper). Since 1981, we have as much new commercial space—45 million square feet—as the total commercial space of Boston and San Francisco combined (Sleeper), and yet there's still no room for the homeless. There isn't even any room for a simple idea like San Francisco's: in San Francisco you can't put up new commercial space downtown unless you pay for day-care for the children of the people who will work there (Messinger). Of course the Reagan Administration won't invest in permanent housing for New York's poor: *that* would be socialism, the dreaded "S word." But Crazy Eddie doesn't want unions or churches or foundations or grass-roots community groups or anybody else (except his favorite developers) in the business of rehabilitating the 100,000 vacant properties the city already owns. Nor are a big developer's tax breaks available to these groups. Why not? Maybe because this kind of low-cost community initiative is bad for the Profit Motive and the Power Base. Certainly permanent housing for the poor—the ever-unpopular "free ride"—is bad for the Work Ethic, like Aid to Families with Dependent Children.

It's not just the money. It's a social philosophy which is at the same time greedy and punitive. We might scrounge the money. Messinger reminds us of that mysterious $500 million in unspent revenues—most from "Big MAC," World Trade Center and Battery Park City surpluses—that the city "rolls over" every fiscal year until it disappears whenever anyone wants to spend it on basic decencies. Dan McCarthy can find another half-billion in a capital-gains tax on real estate. If we tax cooperative apartments for mortgage-recording and real-property transfers, as Phillips suggests, that's another $60 million. Just suppose we killed off "gratuitous tax abatements to Smith-Barney or A.T.&T.," decided to use the city's zoning clout to insist on social services, and helped low-income communities "establish themselves in properties the marketplace has abandoned" (Sleeper). We aren't talking here about anything so radically Scandinavian as income redistribution. But we *are* talking about more than anybody now in power has the conscience and commitment to attempt. What we need, of course, is a change of philosophy and philosophers.

For this change, *Dissent* looks to those 2.5 million "newcomers" with mixed feelings. We've been a "minority-majority" city since the middle of this decade—blacks and Puerto Ricans joined by Dominicans, Cubans and other Caribbeans and South Americans, plus Africans and 350,000 Asians. (The indefatigable Sleeper tells us that by 1995, "with revolution in Korea and the defenestration of Hong Kong," our Asian population will have tripled.) To this "Third World" of Tom Wolfe's swamp-fever dreams—Koreans in the fruit and vegetable trade, Indians in the newstand business, Arabs in neighborhood groceries and head-shops, Senegalese street vendors—add 200,000 Russian Jews, Israelis, Poles, Italians, Greeks and the Irish in Kriegel's Bronx. That's a lot of clout waiting to be mobilized.

But Sleeper, Chapin and Philip Kasinitz are also cautionary tale-tellers. Blacks and Hispanics haven't got their act together, except in "hip-hop," even in Brooklyn. Many newcomers can't speak English, aren't citizens, aren't registered or aren't old enough to vote. Why should Korean shopowners in Washington Heights or Cuban doctors in Jackson Heights join a coalition that cares about the interests of welfare mothers in Bedford-Stuyvesant? It isn't Popular Front-romantic when blacks resent Koreans, the Russians are "rednecks," the Chinese won't join unions and the unions are mostly right-wing anyway. Chapin is cold-eyed: "Immigrant insurgencies are generally pluralist rather than radical in nature. Some are even regressive." He asks the left—census figures on this minority have been unavailable since the Molotov-Ribbentrop pact—to "stop mistaking ethnicity for politics;

while ethnicity may be more important than class to voting, economics is more important to governing policy than ethnicity."

This doesn't exactly sing, but we'd better learn to hum it. To be sure, even the broadest coalition—of immigrants and intellectuals, teachers and preachers, limousine liberals and Republican "good government" types, low-income community organizers and "delirious professionals"—can't save the city all by itself. Even the Federal government (another bunch of once and future jailbirds) can't control oil prices or the dollar or the deficit or international drug traffic. No government in the world, says Marshall Berman, knows how to regulate "the vastly accelerated mobility of capital, propelled by breakthroughs in information technology" that "is fast bringing about the deindustrialization of America." But if we begin by being ashamed of ourselves and then start working the streets, we might find enough conscience and will to make over again the city Randolph Bourne once called "a federation of cultures."

On the other hand, tourism is up, from 3.3 million in 1975 to 17.5 in 1987. Just like Venice: a theme park. See the pretty Winter Palace.

ALEXANDER COCKBURN

Beat the Devil   *March 26, 1988*
[*the legacy of My Lai*]

Alexander Cockburn began writing "Beat The Devil," his bi-weekly column on the press and politics, for *The Nation* in February 1984.

He Did Not Stand Idly By

The trench filled with 583 bodies—Vietnamese men, women and children systematically killed by soldiers in Charlie Company over a number of hours starting at 7:30 A.M., March 16, 1968, recorded later that day by U.S. Army photographer Ron Haeberle—has not figured much this year in retrospectives of the 1960s. And, in fact, set against the backdrop of the maniacal B-52 bombings in the South and the free-fire clearances conducted by the United States through 1968 and 1969, My Lai was nothing special in the way of war crimes. Operation Speedy Express saw at least 5,000 noncombatant Vietnamese killed. (I should also say that all these numbers are speculative; almost certainly underestimates.) The United States didn't just threaten to bomb Vietnam back to the Stone Age; it went right ahead and did so. But My Lai became the war crime of choice, and its ultimate exposure in the United States was due entirely to the courage of one man, Ron Ridenhour. Without Ridenhour there would have been no Army investigation, no Seymour Hersh breaking the story through a small news service, nothing; except perhaps the memorial in Vietnam listing the 583 victims by name, for the N.L.F. had reported the massacre right away, but no one in America paid any attention.

"Did we learn anything?" Ridenhour said the other day. "A lot of Americans learned, a lot of middle-class people learned, 'Gosh, these guys will do anything.' I learned that. The motherfuckers will do anything. There really are no limits."

These days Ridenhour is working in New Orleans for a magazine called *City Business*. He just won a George Polk Award for local reporting, on graft in the city government. Back in March of 1967 he was 20, living in Arizona, and had just been drafted. He was shipped to Hawaii in September and trained in long-range reconnaissance with men who ended up being assigned to Charlie Company, under the command of Lieut. William Calley. Ridenhour was assigned to helicopter observation in Vietnam and later to a reconnaissance unit.

"Right after My Lai," Ridenhour recalled for me last week, "a lot of these guys in Charlie Company started to transfer back into long-range reconnaissance. The first guy I ran into, I said, 'Hey, what have you guys been doing?' And they said, 'Oh man, did you hear what we did at Pinkville?'

"I said, 'No, what's Pinkville?' It was a village; that's what they called My Lai at the time, Pinkville. He tells me this story about how they went in and massacred all those people. When I heard that, I was horrified; my response was pretty much instantaneous. I wanted to get away from it, and I thought the only way I could do that, get away from it, not be part of it, would be to discover whether it was true, and if it was true, to denounce it. To act against it in some way.

"I proceeded to do that. Every time I ran into someone who had been with that unit, I'd say, 'Hey man, what happened?' These young men were traumatized and horrified that they had been involved in this. Now, all the time I was compiling this information I didn't have anyone I could—it was a very precarious situation, as you can imagine."

"Did you think someone might just kill you?"

"Well, I didn't know. I mean, these guys had just been involved in a massacre."

"You were making notes?"

"I was keeping a notebook in my head. I did go down to Twenty-third Division office and obtain the official account of that action, which of course was quite different from what actually occurred. I took some notes on that. Everything else I just kept in my head. Do you know what a LRRP mission is? Well, they'd bring you out by helicopter in five- and six-man units, out into the jungle, way back in the mountains, and you'd watch trails and count enemy soldiers. It was considered a pretty risky business. Whole recon teams went into the jungle and were never heard from again.

"For my first five missions four of the people I went out with were veterans of My Lai. Two were good friends and two not such good friends, and I didn't know what their reaction would be if they knew what I was intending to do, so I just didn't tell anybody. About two weeks before I left, I ran into a friend who had been in the unit in Charlie Company. I'd heard from other friends that he had been opposed to what had happened, had seen what was coming and had not participated. He was in a hospital with a terrible case of jungle rot, waiting to go home. I went over to the hospital and we conversed for a while until we sort of decided we were both coming from the same place. We agreed that we would try to get an investigation going, that we would stay in touch, and if they came and asked him questions, that he would tell the truth.

A few weeks later Ridenhour shipped home. He tried to figure out what to do and consulted friends. Most of them told him to forget it, but in the end someone suggested that he write a letter to his local Congressman. Ridenhour decided to write such a letter, detailing what he knew, how he came to know it; to demand an investigation; and to send the letter to a whole lot of people. In December 1968 he had a relapse of malaria. When he got out of the hospital he began to write. The letter took six weeks to complete. Someone proofread it; someone else typed it. Ridenhour made 200 copies and sent out thirty of them on March 29, 1969. One went to his Congressman, Mo Udall, whose office responded almost immediately. Udall's administrative assistant asked permission to circulate the letter to the House Armed Services Committee, of which Udall was a member. Its chair, Mendel Rivers, was requested to demand a Pentagon investigation.

By April 30 the Pentagon, which claims it was acting on receipt of a copy of Ridenhour's letter and not under pressure from Rivers, had appointed an investigating team, headed by a colonel.

"I was in Arizona, waiting to go to school and working in a popsicle factory," Ridenhour said. "They came and interviewed me, and then some of the people I mentioned in the letter—maybe five other soldiers—gave them more names. It sort of bumped and grinded along from late April to September, when they charged Calley. I was convinced there was a cover-up going on, that these guys were not sincere in pursuing the business. They stopped accepting my calls. Then they called me and said they had arrested Calley. I waited to see what would happen, and then, when no one else was arrested, I knew what they were going to do. They were going to flush Calley, claim that this was the act of a wild man and then let it go. That's when I started trying to get in touch with the press."

He talked to a man from *The Arizona Republic*. Nothing got published. The Army had put out a brief statement—two paragraphs long—saying that it had charged a lieutenant, Calley, with the murder of an unknown number of civilians.

The Associated Press carried the story, but no one picked it up. As Ridenhour tells it, a general who had worked on the Calley investigation became indiscreet at a cocktail party in Washington, let drop details of My Lai and the Calley arrest a relative of Seymour Hersh, who duly passed on the news. Hersh found the brief item mentioning Calley's arrest and interviewed Calley, who was being held at Fort Benning, Georgia. (Hersh says he had already been working on the story after a tip-off from a public service lawyer.)

Hersh's first story prompted *The Arizona Republic* to print its article, which Hersh, in turn, saw. He flew out to talk to Ridenhour, who gave him the names and addresses of the people who had been at My Lai. Hersh asked Ridenhour to hold the story from anyone else for three days and went about his business. "I was glad to give him the three days," Ridenhour said. "He was the first person to respond. He went off and started finding those other kids, and they told him those horrible stories."

Almost as soon as we started talking Ridenhour wanted to make a point. "The important thing is, this was an act of policy, not an individual aberration. My Lai didn't happen because Lieutenant Calley went berserk. There were similar acts of policy all over the country. I mean, every once in a while they decided they would make an example. If you read about the cover-up, you'll see that above My Lai were helicopters filled with the entire command staff of the brigade, division and task force. All three tiers in the chain of command were literally flying overhead all morning, while it was going on. It takes a long time to kill almost 600 people. It's a dirty job, you might say. These guys were flying overhead from 7:30 in the morning, when the unit first landed and began to move into those hamlets. I think the command units didn't get there till 9 A.M. They were there at least two hours, at 500 feet, 1,000 feet and 1,500 feet.

"So did we learn anything? Yes, we learned to have brown boys pull the trigger instead of good American boys. The policy continues. We continue to make war on civilians across the world. We've got black boys killing black people in Africa. It's our money that's paying for it. That's the lesson the Pentagon, the policymakers learned. Like I say, a lot of Americans learned, the motherfuckers will do anything."

'If I Had a Rocket Launcher . . .'

After Ridenhour finished, I talked to Kevin Buckley, a correspondent for *Newsweek* in Saigon at the time. Buckley had done a thorough investigation of Speedy Express, finally published in part in *Newsweek* in 1972. "My Lai," Buckley remembered, "was in the spirit of post-Tet. The saying was that the whole country had become a free-fire zone. The soldiers would say that either with relief or disgust, depending on which way their immortal souls were headed."

There was heavy fighting during June and July, when the Democratic convention was going on in Chicago. Candidates were taking out positions on a windup of the war. A peace negotiation in Paris was being envisaged. "Against the possibility of a cease-fire in place," Buckley said, "the pacification program became the Accelerated Pacification Program. They went at it with B-52s, everything. The idea was to create as many 'pro-government' places as possible." In Operation Bold Mariner there was saturation bombing of the Quang Ngai Province, where the survivors of My Lai had been relocated. By the end of 1968 the Ninth Division went into the delta and Speedy Express began.

"At that time the U.S. was stronger than it had ever been. The other side was on the ropes militarily. Tet had cost the N.L.F. its leading cadre. But U.S. policy equated peace with defeat. The idea was to destroy South Vietnam [and North Vietnam up to the 20th parallel]. The bombing ravaged so many things, like farming, timber, rubber, the natural commerce of the place. They attacked the coconut trees. 'The trees are our enemy,'" said one American commander at the time.

"Nixon and Kissinger decided to plunge on and 'win' the war. The result of this bloody folly was ignominy, uncounted Cambodians, Indochinese, dead and wounded. In certain areas, Vietnamese who were whole, who had all their limbs, looked strange. Such was the 'application' of U.S. firepower. The war could have ended in 1968 [actually, 1963 if it hadn't been for the United States]. So far as the U.S. was concerned the Vietnam Memorial would have been half as long."

This is the same Kissinger who recently said the uprising in the West Bank and Gaza should be put down, in the words of the memorandum recording his off-the-record session with American Jewish leaders, "brutally and rapidly." This is the same Nixon calling, in the March 13 *New York Times Magazine,* for "resolve" in dealing with Gorbachev. Such was their moral monstrosity, 1969–1974.

Sometimes people ask in a puzzled sort of way why bits of the antiwar movement freaked out in the late 1960s and demonstrated what one could call certain pathological symptoms. I remember reading about accelerated pacification, saturation bombing, strafing, slaughter, day after day after day. It was hard not to freak out. As the man sings, "If I had a rocket launcher, I'd make somebody pay." My Lai remains a symbol, just an intimation of what happened in that destroyed land where they made a desert and had the effrontery to call it defeat, thus requiring that "honor" be retrieved and "resolve" be demonstrated on battlefields elsewhere.

EDWARD SOREL: *"It's Only a Theory"* (1987)

For Jesse Jackson and His Campaign
[*editorial*]

April 16, 1988

> In 1988 *The Nation* endorsed Jesse Jackson for the Democratic
> nomination for president of the United States.

Jesse Jackson is a serious candidate for the presidency. He was always serious; it was just the press, the political scientists and the other politicians who belittled his campaign, trivialized his efforts and disdained his prospects. Despite the contempt and condescension of the media – or perhaps because of it – Jackson went to the most remote and isolated grass roots in the American social landscape to find the strength for a campaign that has already begun to transform politics. For five years his distance from the funders, the managers, the mediators and the consultants who manipulate the Democratic Party and legitimize its candidates has allowed Jackson to do unimaginable things and say unspeakable words – about race, about class, about equality and, indeed, about democracy. To an extent that may be unique in presidential elections in this century, he derives his power from the people. The enormous energy that his campaign releases has created a new populist moment, over-taking the languid hours and dull days of conventional politics and imagining possibilities for substantial change beyond the usual incremental transactions of the two-party system. It offers hope against cynicism, power against prejudice and solidarity against division. It is the specific antithesis to Reaganism and reaction, which, with the shameful acquiescence of the Democratic center, have held America in their thrall for most of this decade and which must now be defeated. For that reason, *The Nation* is endorsing Jesse Jackson for the Democratic nomination for President.

The Jackson campaign is not a single shot at higher office by an already elevated politician. Rather, it is a continuing, expanding, open-ended project to organize a movement for the political empowerment of all those who participate. In the beginning, Jackson identified his basic constituency as the most "dispossessed and disaffected" Americans of all, the blacks of the rural South and the Northern ghettos, people who seemed permanently disenfranchised from citizenship and thus denied entrance into the system of rewards and privileges that is every citizen's right. In a real sense, the campaign became a new civil rights movement with an added dimension of economic justice deriving in spirit from the last campaigns of Martin Luther King Jr. with the black working poor.

"We work every day," he reminds the crowds, which invariably respond with knowing assent. "And we are still poor. We pick up your garbage; we work

403

every day. We drive your cars, we take care of your children, we empty your bedpans, we sweep your apartments; we work every day. We cook your food, and we don't have time to cook our own. We change your hospital beds and wipe your fevered brow, and we can't afford to lie in that bed when we get sick. We work every day." He does not merely see the poor as victims; he calls them to struggle for their rights.

To include would-be followers in his new movement Jackson made a simple demand: that they register and vote. They responded with groundbreaking enthusiam. Millions of people who won the vote in the great civil rights efforts of the early 1960s exercised that right for the first time two decades later. The success of Jackson's long march through the cotton counties and ramshackle slums of America was evident before his current campaign commenced, and in ways outside the realm of presidential elections. The "new voters" he inspired joined with millions more, motivated by the stirrings of populist potential on many fronts, and helped break the conservative stranglehold on the Senate in 1986.

More than that, young black—and white—activists from the new movement challenged the legitimacy of cynical and sometimes corrupt leaders who for years had dominated racial and ethnic politics on the local level. Jackson felt compelled to deal with many of the anachronistic demagogues, ward bosses and machines that were in place in his field of operations. He had not yet built an independent force strong enough to present a credible alternative, and his 1984 campaign suffered from that weakness. The pool of available, authentic leaders who shared his vision was smaller then, and he chose some who did his project discredit. His perplexing association with the charismatic but divisive Nation of Islam firebrand Louis Farrakhan can be seen more clearly now in terms of the contradiction it expressed: the tactical acceptance of a powerful rival who had considerable authority over the hearts and minds of the very people Jackson meant to organize.

It is no longer necessary for Jackson to make such bad deals, if it ever was. His successful resolution of those earlier problems, by building his base and expanding his horizons, shows a skill and a sophistication that makes a powerful case for his candidacy. In Mississippi, in Vermont, in Maryland, in Michigan, California, Texas and across his sphere of operations a new breed of progressive leadership has penetrated and in some cases replaced the old power structures. In Detroit, the successful campaign is poised at Mayor Coleman Young's door. And not only in elective office: The campaign has already begun to have important consequences for restructuring leadership of work, social and religious institutions at the base—in labor locals, church groups, community organizations and academic associations.

As the Rainbow Coalition reaches beyond its primary constituency to include an array of new ones, the values espoused are incorporated into the growing movement. When unionists, feminists, Hispanics, Asian-Americans, students, civil libertarians and community activists join or endorse the Rainbow campaign, they contribute their ideals and their energies while they share the coalition's strength. And in the end, it is their participation that catches Jackson's attention and insures the campaign's integrity. Jackson has struggled to legitimize his own leadership above the Old Guard, and he is strong enough now to transcend most of the regressive elements and see the parts of his coalition actually coalescing in practice as well as theory. The results are startling. Farmers from Iowa campaign in black Chicago, white ethnic hard-hats and young gays and lesbians work together in northern Wisconsin, genteel peace activists and black hiphoppers leaflet in the projects of Hartford. The culture of American politics is being radically reformed.

The shape and substance of the Jackson campaign—in the long version—is essential to an understanding of his candidacy. For one thing, they offer evidence of Jackson's extraordinary conceptual powers and political skills and constitute just the kind of "experience" a President should have to organize the country around a transformative agenda. The argument that Jackson is unqualified for high office because he has never held one is bogus on its face. A modern President—or a postmodern one—is not primarily a business executive or even an engineer of a sterile consensus. There are plenty of managers, budgeters, policy analysts and public relations specialists who would love such jobs and can be hired to perform them. A seat in the Senate or an office in the statehouse has undoubted advantages in the electoral game, but neither has much to do with being President of the United States. A President who would bring real change must organize a social movement to do it, must recast the culture, must institutionalize a vision in politics from the grass roots to the halls of power.

Building a coalition "on the ground" is one thing; using it as a model for an Administration that would redistribute power, reorder priorities and extend democracy is another. The Jackson campaign is woven around a dream whose realization would bring into Washington such doers and dreamers as have not been seen since the first age of Jackson in the infancy of America. They propose to shift the direction of foreign policy from its costly and dangerous obsession with cold war relationships in a bipolar world to a new partnership with the dispossessed and disenfranchised. In this vision, Third World countries would no longer be appraised as mere bases to be contested and their populations as markets to be exploited, but as organic components of an economic and political order in which development and independence take precedence over profits and the paranoia of empire.

Jackson's shorthand on the stump for the new economic system he envisions is, "Stop jobs from going out." What that entails is exceedingly complex. For starters, it involves the C.I.A. and its old assets in labor ceasing to manipulate foreign trade unions; U.S. corporations and transnationals curtailing their most exploitative practices and redirecting the profits from their foreign operations to the development of independent local economies; and a change in monetary policies and debt management in this country to end the economic enslavement of America's clients.

At home, Jackson vows to end the "economic violence" evidenced everywhere—in the ravaged cities and crumbling factories and deserted farms, the homeless and the overcrowded and the underpaid, the uneducated and the sick and the alienated. Despite the blather of the social theorists, those conditions and those people did not just happen; they are the grist of a specific economic order that is supported up and down the line by government policy. Jackson's campaign proposes to confront corporate power with the challenge of populist power, something that sets him apart from the other candidates, who are still reeling from the corporate counterattack in full force since the early 1970s. He has consistently urged real tax reform to reverse the regressive Reagan legislation (passed with many Democratic votes) and, beyond that, to begin a program to redistribute wealth and power from the corporate class to the consuming and working class, on a magnitude that has eluded even the best-intentioned liberals since the New Deal.

Electing Jesse Jackson means endorsing an increase in the minimum wage; measures to end gender pay inequities and reward work on the basis of "comparable worth"; an attempt to reverse the systematic destruction of family farms by corporate agribusiness; Federal action to halt factory flight, of both the offshore and Sun Belt varieties, and ameliorate its consequences among workers and their communities. Jackson's Justice Department, free at last of the Meese curse, could begin to enforce and extend antitrust laws to deal with mergers, takeovers and acquisitions and their baleful effect on economic growth and employment.

In time, under such a presidency, the war economy that has defined the American Century for fifty years might begin to give way to a peace economy. Jackson's first step, and one that could be taken quickly, would be to freeze the defense budget, beginning to weaken apace the ideology of militarism that it has produced. The high-tech hardware firms that bankroll so many political campaigns—Democratic as well as Republican—would have to find new ways to invest their surplus capital. More ambitious still, substantial new investment in education, housing, transportation, community services and infrastructure would lay the foundation for a full-employment society, promised and postponed by Democrats since the end of World War II. Jackson asks that the national education budget be doubled. He proposes job training (and retraining) and a national child-care program to help people stay off welfare. And he seeks a complete revision of the social welfare system as a concept: assistance to the needy not as a necessary evil or noblesse oblige but as a matter of human rights. Finally, alone among presidential candidates now or in the past, Jackson proposes a national health-care plan that would end America's disgraceful attitude toward its sick and make preventive medicine and long-term treatment universally available.

All of Jackson's critics ask, How would you pay for it? He would annually save $60 billion by 1993 from a freeze in defense spending, $20 billion by restoring the maximum personal income tax rate to 38.5 percent (affecting the wealthiest 600,000 Americans) and $20 billion by returning corporate taxes to near their 1970 levels. The campaign has drawn up impressive budgets, and Jackson is offering ingenious new ways of liberating capital for public use, such as the investment of pension funds in federally approved projects. But the budget crunch that has deadlocked social development in America for a generation cannot be approached by limiting the range of possibilities to existing categories of revenue. Look at the wealth of America, weigh its resources, feel its power. There's enough money in this country to do everything Jackson asks, and more. The neoliberal formula manipulates available resources within the existing orders of priority; the progressive vision articulated by Jackson points to the country's vast wealth, and the waste of so much on militarism and imperial adventure. On one side lie the values of the market and the counsel of despair; on the other, the values of citizenship and the sense of possibilities.

But are we only dreaming? Jackson is leading a movement for reform, not a revolution, and he would occupy the presidency as a radical reformer atop an essentially liberal consensus with powerful—extremely powerful—conservative forces battering at the gates. Even in the best of situations, he does not have the means or power to hold the whole country in his hands. Washington's permanent government, which wakens all dreamers in the White House after their first night's sleep, would do its best to dash the fondest hopes of real reform.

The ability of the Chief Executive to act decisively remains immense, however: With a virtual stroke of the pen, Jackson could put an end to covert action, for example, or institute a nuclear test ban or restore diplomatic relations with Cuba. He could reinvigorate the Civil Rights commission, feminize family policy departments and end discrimination against gays and lesbians in Federal employment. The change in the political center of gravity that would make possible his election, plus the powers of the presidency, the arrival of new leaders in Congress and the city halls and state legislatures would give Jackson important strength to withstand an inevitable counteroffensive by the military and intelligence communities, the private banks, corporations and multilateral financial institutions— even, perhaps, a recalcitrant Democratic Congress. It is impossible to foresee the final outcome of these conflicts. There would be wounding skirmishes and bloody battles, retreats and compromises, but all in the direction of the sweeping visions that inspirit the movement. The ideals set forth in this campaign are important in themselves, apart from their enactment in a land under a far-off Rainbow. They should stand as a new agenda for progressive America, a yardstick against which all others must be measured. For, after all, it is this set of values and the campaign that has formed around them that are of historic importance to America; they must outlast even the best leaders who espouse them. The campaign contains the dream, which will not die with defeat or delay. It already has strongly influenced the other Democratic candidates, who have appropriated not only the themes but in many cases the images and the words Jackson has long been using. If winning the presidency isn't the only thing valuable about this interminable campaign, Jackson has already won something: He has set the tone and the terms of debate beyond anyone's predictions.

Jackson has neither diluted his principles nor altered his positions, even as representatives of the party elite offer him help and support with each new electoral success. When he consults with Bert Lance or Clark Clifford, he does so to seek what little protection they can provide in an increasingly furious campaign. Having failed, first, to get rid of Jackson by ignoring him, and then having failed to co-opt him as a good ol' boy of Democratic centrism, the political and corporate forces he threatens most have begun to bash him with unprecedented ferocity. "Wait until New York," one of his campaign workers said last week. "It's going to be a nuclear war."

Whatever happens in the big-state primaries still to come, Jackson cannot be counted the "front-runner" for the nomination, because the rich and powerful in the Democratic party fear not only his program but his prospects for election, and will do everything they can to stop him. Now that the euphoria of his Michigan landslide has been curtailed by three straight losses (Connecticut, Colorado and Wisconsin), the heat on him may abate. That old bugbear "electability" needs to be confronted head-on. By running and winning, Jackson has demonstrated that he is as electable as any candidate need be to get the nomination. The impetus and euphoria of his campaign in recent weeks lie in its ability, demonstrated repeatedly, to reach beyond the core that explicitly shares Jackson's ideological frame. There is evidence in the primaries of a broadening audience responding to the restoration of a politics that has profound roots in the American heartland; there is also a recognition that Jackson's candidacy does not emerge from nowhere but rather lies squarely within a tradition extending from the earliest part of nineteenth-century Democratic revivalism through Midwestern Populism, the labor wars, the New Deal and the civil rights movement.

At the end of the day, it may yet be that racism and conservatism, and Democratic defections, doom Jackson to defeat. There is that risk. There is always that risk, but both principle and a sudden, pragmatic sense of what may be possible dictate that the risk on this occasion is acceptable, not foolhardy. There are worse things in the world than losing. And anyway, moving closer to the Republicans in order to stave off a Democratic defeat yields not only a bad candidate but a low-energy campaign. The means to victory is in energizing the voters, offering real change and expanding and recapturing the party's base. In that respect, Jackson has already won more than anyone had hoped, and the longer and stronger his campaign continues, the more he can make over the political face of America.

Jackson is not the perfect candidate; many of us at this magazine see serious flaws in the man. The flamboyant manner, the flair for grandstand gestures and the evident temper and ego must all be calculated in any assessment of his candidacy. Questions remain about his past—his behavior in the aftermath of the assassination of Martin Luther King Jr., his careless financial management of the PUSH operation in Chicago and the provenance of some of its funding (which might eventually be raised against him). Nor has the intensely emotional issue of Jackson's relations with American Jews been resolved. Despite several heartfelt apologies—including one on the rostrum of the Democratic National Convention in San Francisco—he has not won the forgiveness of the organized Jewish community and many individuals for his insensitive "Hymietown" remark or his embrace of Farrakhan in 1984. Many Jews also fear his support for Palestinian self-determination and his willingness to talk to their chosen representative, the Palestine Liberation Organization. The first were serious errors, but the last is a matter of principle for Jackson, and he has no reason to apologize for it. Indeed, the mainstream of American politics—George Shultz, Jimmy Carter, even Richard Nixon—has caught up with his courageous recognition that the Palestinians must be dealt with directly. He may have had vestigial attitudes of prejudice that are rooted in American culture, but they are unlike the virulent racism that characterizes the present Administration in Washington, and he seeks to transcend them.

Jackson's roots in the rural, religious South and his distance from the development of contemporary movements of sexual liberation and personal autonomy also pose problems which must be overcome. He has made stopping drug use and teen-age pregnancy central issues in his campaign—for very good reasons—and he has never associated himself with a strong feminist position on abortion, for not so good ones. Too often Jackson's attacks on social evils sound moralistic and condemnatory, suggesting the preacher's sermon rather than the radical reformer's demands. But only candidate Jackson marched with lesbians and gays in Washington last October. He asks for women to become an institutionalized segment of the Rainbow, and he consistently looks at the economic basis of women's oppression.

On balance, we believe the importance of a black candidacy for President and a progressive movement for change in America overshadows any deficiencies in Jackson's résumé and the faults in his campaign. Racism may be as American as cherry pie, but it is a poisonous portion that fouls every dream and deforms every vision. It might have been that a candidate from the racial majority would lead a campaign to defeat racism, but that did not happen. History has come up with another and more fitting scenario: A candidate from the most oppressed minority will organize a national coalition to accomplish that end. In March, Texas Agriculture Commissioner Jim Hightower brought Jesse Jackson into the Senate Chamber of the State Capitol for his endorsement announcement. At the time, Hightower was the only white, elected state official in America publicly to support the black candidate. Under a portrait of Jefferson Davis, flanked by full-length paintings of Lyndon Johnson and Barbara Jordan, Hightower read a short speech that caught the historic meaning—and illustrated the essential ironies—of this extraordinary year.

"Frankly, it had not occurred to most populist leaders like me that our movement might become black-led, reaching out to whites," Hightower drawled, "but there it is." He added, "I would not escape the inner voice of integrity saying that the Rev. Jesse Jackson was forcefully, proudly and successfully carrying the populist program that I espouse."

For us at *The Nation,* too, the Jackson campaign now embodies what we believe is necessary and just for America, and we are proud to stand with it.

DANIEL SINGER

In the Heart of Le Pen Country   *June 18, 1988*

Daniel Singer has been *The Nation*'s European correspondent since 1982.

Marseilles, France

"It cries in my heart as it rains on the town," wrote Verlaine, and it was pouring over Marseilles as I arrived just before the Whitsun holiday. Then the mistral cleared the sky and the sun shone on all the celebrated landmarks: the vast avenue of the Canebière descending to the Old Harbor, the Vieux Port itself, with its armada of small boats in white or blue, and the bigger ones taking the tourists to the Château d'If of Monte Cristo fame. But for all the fine weather, the time was for tears rather than smiles in Marcel Pagnol's country. With 102,541 of its 361,804 voters picking Jean-Marie Le Pen in the first presidential round in April, Marseilles, the old melting pot, the gateway to Africa and the Orient, has become the racist capital of Europe.

As last week's national elections approached, all the main leaders of Le Pens' xenophobic National Front swooped over the region, the department of Bouchesdu-Rhône, like vultures in search of parliamentary seats. Le Pen himself picked the eighth district of Marseilles (where in April he had polled nearly 30 percent). But attention is already being focused beyond the current election, toward the Ides of March, the likely date of next year's poll for the Town Hall. Can a neofascist become the mayor of France's second city? The very fact that the question can be raised requires a lot of explanation.

The Thug and the Politician. If you want to see a folkloric image of the danger, take the left side of the Old Harbor, move beyond the restaurants whose enterprising owners solicit you to taste their bouillabaisse, to the Bar des Yachts. You can't miss it: Posters of the leader are plastered all over with the now-obsolete stickers "Le Pen—president." On the left-hand side there is a symptomatic kitsch painting: A priest with a holy cross is exorcising a devil painted in red. So that the point should not be missed, the devil has 1789—the date of the French Revolution— scribbled on his back. The bar's owner, Dedé (short for Andrew), a man well known for his exploits with fists or gun, is well in line with the painting: "It's the Alamo here. Only instead of being on the defensive, we shall attack." Then, changing periods and metaphors: "Charles Martel [who stopped the Arabs near Poitiers in the seventh century]—that's kid stuff. It's from here that the great anti-Islamic crusade will start." The customers, who look like a bunch of aggressive salesmen, nod approvingly. If the National Front attracted only such reactionaries, nostalgic for the King, Pétain and French Algeria, the threat would not be too great.

To measure its seriousness I have to go to the other side of the Old Harbor, beyond the seventeenth-century Town Hall, where the Socialists are still the masters, to a warehouse that had been turned into offices and plastered with portraits of Le Pen with or without a tie. There I meet the local leader of the National Front. Sixtyish and paunchy, Pascal Arrighi is one of the reactionary notables who rallied to Le Pen. A former high-level public servant, he is a clever politician and a smooth talker. Why does his party do well in this area? In addition to economic circumstances, there are two basic reasons—immigration and "its daughter, insecurity." Marseilles, he claims, is a hospitable city, but the Arabs are just too much. When I venture that the arguments used to explain their otherness— different race, different religion, they don't mix or intermarry—had been advanced to oppose Jews before the war, he weighs me up suspiciously then decides to play it safe: No, the Jews had "the gift of adaptation and the will to integrate," whereas the Arabs are unbearable. He takes me into his confidence: "A cousin of mine, a doctor, her name was not in the telephone book, but they found it to shout obscenities because she had refused to sign phony certificates for social security. They just get on everybody's nerves."

When he talks of local politics, the man can be quite witty. I asked him why he was so sure that candidates of the respectable right, the followers of Jacques

Chirac and Raymond Barre, would stand down for National Front men and vice versa, whatever the official orders from Paris. Because they don't want to commit political suicide, he replied: "On the fourth floor, faced with the choice between the window and the staircase, you obviously can jump, but . . . " Dedé is there for Arab-bashing and Arrighi for vote-catching—the Front, after all, is doing well here in both posh and popular districts—but when it comes to fundamentals their message is the same. It panders to the lowest prejudices and plays on the deepest fears, seeking the ultimate root of all evil in the outsider, the alien, in this case the Arab.

Mohammed the Scapegoat. Next to the names of National Front candidates on the billboards there are small posters. With a minaret in the background and a quotation: "In 20 years' time, it is sure, France will be an Islamic republic." It is not worth checking whether the Hezbollah leader to whom this is attributed really did make such an absurd forecast. All foreigners combined account for less than 7 percent of the French population, a proportion that has remained roughly stable for the past dozen years, and immigrants from North Africa represent 2.6 percent. Besides, it is estimated that only some 5 percent of the potentially Islamic population are practicing Moslems. But to give credence to such forecasts is no more irrational than the often-heard suggestion that if you want a job, a subsidized flat or a place in a kindergarten, you had better be called "Ben-something" than Dupont. This kind of whispering campaign is universal; only here it is unusually successful.

Is it because foreigners are so much more numerous here in Marseilles? Not really, since according to the 1982 census, they number 80,852—or 9.3 percent of the population; immigrants from North Africa, estimated at 56,784, account for 6.5 percent of the total. Admittedly, they are more visible, since the immigrant ghetto lies in the center of the city. The district stretching between the Canebière and the railway station with its monumental staircase, full of narrow streets and shady hotels, has always been a shelter for the poor of the planet. By now it has expanded and looks like a North African casbah. Arabs are thus to be found not only on the outskirts in the most overcrowded and derelict housing projects but also in the very heart of the town. On top of it all, there is the population afloat. The port of Marseilles is the main transit place and provisional stop for North Africans entering or leaving France.

Yet one cannot attribute the political explosion of racism to some optical illusion. Having once gone to school here, I can testify that Marseilles is an ethnic patchwork, the nearest thing to the United States with its successive waves of immigrants. The Arabs come after the Spaniards, Armenians and Greeks on the solid foundations laid by the Corsicans and, above all, the Italians. In 1931 foreigners accounted for a quarter of the town's population, so to talk now of a "threshold of tolerance" is nonsense. Besides, the proportion of foreigners has not grown perceptibly in the past seven years, during which the National Front has climbed from marginality to political pride of place in this city. To understand this rise, racism alone is not sufficient explanation; it is necessary to glance at the deeper crisis of this town, of its living conditions, its economy and its system of power.

La Rose in Concrete. The eighth electoral district of Marseilles, picked by Le Pen to test his strength, is a mixture of popular and middle-class sections. You can reach it by the new modern subway, getting off at La Rose station, the end of the line. Outside you have blocks and blocks of flats. Indeed, as you reach the suburbs of Marseilles you are struck by a series of high-rise, cheap housing projects, which have grown like mushrooms during the building boom. Those at La Rose are not among the worst and therefore not packed with immigrants. Yet here as elsewhere there are no cultural amenities, and community spirit has vanished. The blue- and, increasingly, white-collar workers feel insecure, worried about travel in their evenings, about their jobs, about the future. Marseilles seems to be surrounded by a concrete wall of crumbling expectations.

Experts on the spot confirm what is written in the few studies on the subject, namely that Marseilles has mismanaged its economic modernization. It is not just that the harbor was affected by the end of the French Empire; this was partly compensated for by the development of oil traffic. Marseilles failed to build an industrial hinterland, to diversify beyond its traditional activities connected with the harbor, or with the soap, oil and food manufacturing industries. The failure was concealed for a time by the building boom, linked with the jump in population — from 660,000 in 1954 to 882,000 in 1968 — spurred partly by the return of French settlers from North Africa. But beneath this bustle, the local bourgeoisie, satisfied with petty speculation, missed its opportunity during the postwar transformation of the French economy to more capital-intensive methods of production. Or, to be more accurate, the chance of regional expansion conceived of in the late 1960s through the Fos complex (i.e., petrochemicals and a steel industry based on imported ore) came too late. The "miracle" was over and the vast plan got bogged down in the international crisis.

As a result, Marseilles is a town whose population is dwindling and where industrial jobs are declining — a very partial explanation of the collapse of the local Communist Party, whose electoral strength declined in seven years from 25.8 to 10.9 percent. White-collar employment has not expanded sufficiently to compensate and is, on the whole, on the lower end of the pay and status scale. Marseilles, lagging behind the national average in higher or technical education, is well above it in unemployment. The North Africans, brought over during the boom years, particularly for work in the construction industry, provide their contingent of the jobless. The economic deterioration goes a long way to explain the melancholy mood of this town and coincides with the end of one man's political reign.

In Search of a Godfather. On arrival in Marseilles everybody tells you that this month's parliamentary elections are merely skirmishes for next year's big municipal battle, which will determine the choice of the new godfather. This mafia analogy is disrespectful – if not entirely unfair – to the Socialist Gaston Defferre, a well-off Protestant lawyer from neighboring Hérault who dominated local politics throughout the postwar period. He was Mayor of Marseilles for thirty-three years until his death in 1986, but his system lasted for thirty; it was set up in 1953, when, fearing a Communist takeover, the right – except for the Gaullists – made an alliance with the Socialists. The pact was based on the assumption that the bourgeoisie would get the profits and the Socialists the patronage. Thus, town planning, for example, was entrusted to the right, which explains the social segregation that has seen the poorer people driven from the city center to the new high-rises of the periphery. The Socialists were in charge of the allocation of lower-rent flats and also controlled jobs provided by the municipality and the harbor. Indeed, they turned the network of power and patronage into a fine art; hence the passion in the present struggle for the Town Hall.

Strained by the economic and social crisis, the pact collapsed under the impact of national politics. Defferre could not sit in government in Paris (where he was Minister of the Interior) together with the Communists and at the same time rule in Marseilles in alliance with the right. In 1983 he chose to fight the municipal election with a popular front. The two big parties of the respectable right, determined to defeat him, based their campaign on law and order. To their surprise, a completely unknown list called Marseilles-Security captured more than 5 percent of the poll. The way in which not only the right but the Socialists too wooed this jingoist electorate between ballots was one of the most shameful pages in the S.P.'s history.

While Defferre survived by the skin of his teeth, his system was in ruins. In the European elections a year later the National Front made a triumphant entry with 21.4 percent of the votes cast, grabbing support from all sides. In the parliamentary elections of 1986, which unlike this year's were run through proportional representation, it climbed to 24.4 percent, while the left, once an overwhelming power in the town, was reduced to about 40 percent. Le Pen's score in this April's presidential poll thus marks a steady rather than a spectacular advance. The swing is no longer from the left but from the classical to the extreme right. The loser is Jean-Claude Gaudin, the conservative bloc's crafty leader, rather than its strongman. He thought it clever to be elected president of the regional council with the support of the National Front, then to take neofascists as his assistants. He simply rendered the Front more respectable. With 28.3 percent of the poll, Le Pen won more votes in Marseilles than Chirac and Barre combined.

It was this showing that induced Le Pen to seek his fortune here. Yet he was taking quite a gamble. To get a parliamentary seat, let alone the Town Hall, Le Pen, who got 33 percent of the poll in the first ballot, on June 5, required the backing not just of some but of all the supporters of the respectable right to stand a chance of winning. Had we reached that stage, the situation would be desperate, which it is not. With Le Pen faltering, the Socialists will now present as their candidate for mayor Michel Pezet, the man who won the skin game for Defferre's succession. But they were playing it safe.

Le Pen was not the only "parachutist," as carpetbaggers are called in France, in this area. Bernard Tapie, the handsome tycoon and media personality, landed in Marseilles with the Socialists' blessing, promising to cure unemployment. That this capitalist champion of "restructuring" should be one of the few cases of *ouverture* is symptomatic. Come to think of it, Mitterrand's "opening" is really the Defferre system writ large on a national scale, a Socialist alliance with the bourgeoisie, with the respectable right renamed the "center" for the purpose. This will be the test in next year's municipal elections. In the polarized world of French politics, it will not be an easy one, either in Marseilles or the rest of the country.

The Thermometer and the Epidemic. I have written so far as if Marseilles were an island. Admittedly, this volatile port has some unhappy precedents: Simon Sabiani and his gangsters controlled the city in the early 1930s, and the Gaullist Rally at its worst conquered the Town Hall in 1947. But today Marseilles has ceased to be so distinctive. It has the same disease only in stronger or more advanced forms. It is not even very much ahead of the trend in the Midi. The electoral map of Southern France now looks pretty ghastly. Le Pen got a quarter of the vote in the regions around Marseilles, Nice and Toulon; a fifth in the Avignon, Nîmes and, further west, Perpignan areas. The greater success of the National Front in the southern regions is partly due to the presence there of French settlers from North Africa—adding to French racism their own anti-Arab brand—and possibly to a greater fear of European integration. But nobody likes to be squeezed in the name of economic progress, or to call "modernization" what is perceived as unemployment. Le Pen has reached close to 10 percent support in Brittany, for instance, where there are no foreign workers. The disease has become national.

What Marseilles does reveal is how the National Front has grown, and the timing of its growth. The economic crisis and a good number of immigrants were not sufficient on their own. The left had first to get into office—on the one hand to madden the right, and then, on the other, having failed to keep its promises, to disappoint its own supporters. It was in 1983–84, with those two preconditions fulfilled, that the National Front took off. Then, in the past two years, the respectable right had to get back into office and confirm its own inability to cope, giving a new boost to the Front.

Historians will probably describe this period as the end of an era for two major movements—the Gaullist Party, which had managed to harness the authoritarian trend of the French right, and the Communist Party, which had furnished hope and the semblance of a solution to left-wing protesters. Consensus politics will not exorcise the Front. If the crisis and unemployment continue, as they are likely to, and no section of the left provides a radical alternative, Le Pen has quite a future ahead of him.

Is this forecast not too gloomy now that the share of the National Front in the total vote has gone down from over 14 percent to less than 10 percent, and the party has been virtually deprived of deputies? No. A movement whose growth is so recent and which lacks well-known figures was bound to lose some ground in an election where local personalities matter, while the disappearance of deputies is purely the effect of a change in the electoral law from proportional representation to a winner-take-all system. The danger now is that those who have altered the way one reads the thermometer may convince themselves that the disease is cured. Yves Montand, the brilliant performer who now seldom misses the chance to say something politically silly, argued the other day that one cannot describe as fascists the people with whom he plays *pétanque* on the Riviera. Jackboots somehow do not fit into Pagnol's country.

But serious trouble does not begin when the men with jackboots or with cloven hoofs opt for fascism. It begins when the tinker and tailor, your neighbor and your cousin, are driven sufficiently mad by circumstances to vote for an admirer of Pinochet, a preacher of apartheid, a man for whom the gas chambers are a mere "detail." As I looked down from the steps of the station, on departing this outwardly still-warm and attractive town, I could not help feeling that moral pollution is not so easily perceived. All the more reason to probe below the surface, to sound the alarm and, above all, to seek a cure—unless we want to wake up one day, too late, in a fully contaminated city or country.

PENNY LERNOUX
Casting Out the 'People's Church'
August 27/September 3, 1988

Penny Lernoux began writing for *The Nation* in 1971. As the magazine's Latin American correspondent, Lernoux wrote frequently about the fight for the soul of the Catholic Church in Latin America.

Twenty years ago, in August in the Columbian city of Medellín, Latin America's Catholic bishops signed a remarkable document that would become a religious magna carta for political and social change. The "Medellín Conclusions" led to

416

a radical shift in religious attitudes among the Catholic masses, millions of whom joined church-sponsored organizations seeking economic and political justice. The post-Medellín Latin American church also had a profound influence on Catholic churches in other Third World regions as the philosophical nets of liberation theology spread. Ironically, while celebrations are in progress throughout the Catholic world in honor of the twentieth anniversary of "a historic monument," as Pope Paul VI called the Medellín Conclusions, Pope John Paul II is engaged in its destruction. If his efforts succeed, little will remain of Latin America's socially committed and theologically innovative church.

From the viewpoint of the Latin American poor the timing of the shift in Vatican policy could not be worse. Two decades of pastoral work and the martyrdom of thousands of Catholic activists have produced a network of some 300,000 Christian communities that are the seeds of a more democratic society. Composed primarily of poor people, these groups (known officially as ecclesial base communities) have for the first time in the region's history given voice to the voiceless on a local and national level. But they are fragile buds, still dependent on the institutional church for guidance and support, and the institution is rapidly losing its prophetic character because of the Pope's appointment of conservative bishops.

While the papal crackdown has affected churches around the world, Latin America has been singled out for attention because it is the most populous Catholic region (more than half the world's 907 million Catholics live in the Third World). Latin America is also the birthplace of liberation theology and the site of the first successful Christian-Marxist revolution, in Nicaragua. In addition, the National Conference of Brazilian Bishops, among the Catholic world's largest, leads the universal church's progressive wing, often clashing with Rome over the rights of local churches.

Like other socially committed church leaders, many of Brazil's bishops are adherents of the Second Vatican Council, or Vatican II, a watershed in the early 1960s that ended centuries of "holy isolation" by exhorting the church to participate in humanity's struggle for peace and justice. Vatican II triggered reforms throughout the universal church, among the most important being a greater respect for cultural diversity and pluralism and a modernization of rituals, such as the change from Latin to the vernacular in the Mass. The latter created new interest in the Bible and a more Christ-centered church, in contrast to the traditional caste system dominated by European clerics in Rome.

The council described this new church as the "People of God," a phrase that has become part of the Catholic vocabulary. The expression conveyed the biblical image of the Hebrew people in exodus, and for the church of Vatican II it symbolized a community on the move in search of a deeper understanding of faith. When translated into Portuguese and Spanish, however, "People of God" took on an even deeper meaning, for it became *Pueblo de Dios*—and *pueblo* has always been understood as the masses, the poor.

It was this reality of poverty that made the Medellín meeting different from earlier bishops' conferences to discuss directives from Rome. Instead of parroting what they had been told, the bishops took a hard look at political and economic conditions in Latin America, going beyond Vatican II by interpreting conciliar changes in light of the poverty and injustice in their underworld. Heretofore allies of the upper classes and the military, the bishops shocked the region's elites by denouncing the "institutionalized violence" of the rich against the poor and by committing the church to help the poor organize themselves to achieve greater political, social and economic equality.

Medellín's "preferential option for the poor" sent a strong message to the masses, who discovered that God had historically been on their side. In a culture imbued with Catholicism that discovery was—and still is—political dynamite. Whereas Catholicism had previously encouraged fatalism among the Latin American poor, the post-Medellín church taught that all people were equal in the sight of God and that the impoverished masses should take history into their own hands by seeking political and economic change. It was not God's will that their children die of malnutrition but the result of sinful man-made structures, the bishops said. Suffering, which had traditionally been endured in the expectation of a better life in the hereafter, gained a different symbolism through identification with the hope of Christ's death and resurrection: It suggested that a community of believers could overcome their wretched conditions by working together for the common good and a better future.

By the mid-1970s, when Catholic base communities had spread throughout Latin America, it had become clear to the upper classes and the military that the church of the poor was a threat to their entrenched privileges. At the time, most of Latin America was under the boots of military dictatorships determined to wipe out all dissent. But while they were able to destroy political parties, labor unions, a free press and other opposition, they failed to stop the growth of the base communities because the institutional church gave them its protection. Hundreds of priests and nuns, and even some bishops, were threatened, arrested, tortured, murdered and exiled; yet the church stood firm. Because of its institutional power—most dictators were Catholics, as was a majority of the population—the military regimes did not close the churches, and the churches, particularly the base communities, became a surrogate for democracy.

The experience of the 1970s, when tens of thousands of people were assassinated or "disappeared" and when the poor became even poorer, strongly affected the Latin American church. While the bishops' declarations at Medellín had shown intellectual and pastoral vision, it was only in the 1970s that the institution really became a church of the poor, by suffering along with and on behalf of the victims of repression. In such countries as Brazil the church's call for democracy in secular society was echoed in the church structure itself, which became more pluralistic, open and dedicated to such priorities of the poor as agrarian reform and a more equal distribution of national wealth.

Unfortunately, the trend toward a more pluralistic church is anathema to John Paul's Vatican, which, said a Brazilian cardinal, "thinks it can tell the colonies how to behave." Long before he became Pope, John Paul showed a clear preference for a hierarchical church. During Vatican II, which he attended while Archbishop of Krakow, he opposed a definition of the church as the "People of God," meaning a community of equals, each with a different charisma to share. He envisioned not a church of the people but a "perfect society" defined in all aspects—secular as well as religious— by a clerical class under which the laity worked. French theologian Marie-Dominique Chenu, one of the stars of Vatican II, put it bluntly: John Paul harks back to the "prototype of the church as an absolute monarchy."

The Pope's belief in such absolutisms derives from his Polish heritage. The church in Poland has survived and flourished in the midst of persecution because it functions as an absolute monarchy, ruled from the top by the cardinal primate and his fellow bishops. Unlike the South American church, which developed an internal democracy in response to external dictatorship, the Polish hierarchy has demanded and received absolute loyalty from its troops. The loyalty may be *pro forma* in some respects—abortion and divorce rates are surprisingly high—but the church is undoubtedly the principal mediating force in Polish society, whether for labor unions, peasant farmers or university students. It does not need its own political party because it has the political allegiance of a majority of the people.

It is this church that formed the Pope's zealous commitment, theological orthodoxy and belief in absolute obedience and absolute power. A man of great compassion, he understands the sufferings of the Poles and of the other peoples who live under Soviet domination, but democracy is an alien experience to him. In Polish terms the concept of a People of God—or a more democratic church that accepts diversity as a sign of unity—is suicidal, for it has only been by speaking with a single voice that the church in Poland has survived. As explained by Father Adam Boniecki, who worked for John Paul when the Pope was Archbishop of Krakow, "There is not, and cannot be, any difference of opinion in the Polish church."

Although the Pope has frequently spoken out against human rights violations and on behalf of the poor, his message is belied by the Vatican's actions in strengthening control from Rome to the detriment of local churches that work with the poor and on behalf of human rights. The appointment of conservative bishops and the emphasis on orthodoxy above all else have forced liberal church leaders into a defensive position. Rome's open disapproval of the Sandinista regime has also sent a message to socially activist church groups to avoid leftist politics. While church-state relations in Cuba have improved substantially in recent months – to the point that Fidel Castro has agreed to receive 10,000 nuns – the Vatican remains hostile to the Nicaraguan experiment. Despite its past opposition to organized religion, the Cuban government did not attempt to establish a parallel Catholic church. In Nicaragua, however, Christian revolutionaries, including priests in the government, have refused to take orders from Rome, while at the same time insisting that they, too, are members of the church. This so-called popular church presents a different challenge to the Vatican than the more familiar problems posed by Communism, because it symbolizes the fusion of Catholicism with left-wing nationalism. John Paul's experience in Poland has shown him that the church can survive and thrive alongside a Marxist government, so long as it represents nationalistic aspirations. But in Nicaragua nationalism is identified with Sandinismo.

The Vatican claims that the popular church has become a political tool of the Sandinistas, and it is true that priests and nuns identified with it are strong supporters of the government. At the same time, the pro-Vatican faction of the Nicaraguan church led by Cardinal Miguel Obando y Bravo has also played politics on behalf of the *contras*, with the Pope's blessing. While the Vatican has good reason to worry about the polarizing effects of church involvement in politics – the Nicaraguan church is effectively in schism – it is in no position to throw stones, because of its own association with the political right.

Yet stones Rome is throwing, and hard-hitting ones. Progressive Latin American church leaders who earlier championed the Sandinistas' cause have become less outspoken in the past year because support for the Nicaraguans means another black mark against them in Rome. Liberation theologians are writing about less controversial themes, such as spirituality, and many speak of a "time of hibernation." "Everyone is keeping his head down," admitted one theologian.

For example, in Peru, which is the birthplace of liberation theology, six bishops, or one-ninth of the hierarchy, belong to the extreme-right Catholic movement, Opus Dei, and the only remaining liberal archbishop is Lima's Cardinal Juan Landázuri Ricketts. But Landázuri must retire at the end of the year because of the church's mandatory age limit, and there is widespread fear that his replacement will be a conservative. Among those likely to suffer from the change is the Peruvian priest Gustavo Guitérrez, generally considered the father of liberation theology. Gutiérrez has been repeatedly targeted by Cardinal Joseph Ratzinger, the powerful head of the Congregation for the Doctrine of the Faith, a latter-day version of the Inquisition. Only Landázuri's intervention has protected Gutiérrez from Vatican sanctions.

Similarly, in Chile the pattern for the appointment of bishops has been uniformly conservative. Santiago's Cardinal Juan Francisco Fresno is a pale reflection of his outspoken predecessor, Cardinal Raúl Silva (the cautious Fresno is known as *renos,* or "Brakes," among inhabitants of the capital's shantytowns). Nevertheless, Fresno has occasionally spoken out against the Pinochet regime's acts, and his administrative style is low-key. But Fresno, too, is due to retire. Liberal Chilean Catholics worry that his replacement could be a right-wing hard-liner, such as Miguel Caviedes Medina, the Bishop of Osorno and a critic of liberation theology and the church of the poor. As in other countries, the Vatican's local representative will play a key role in the succession. Bishop Angelo Sodano, until recently the papal nuncio to Chile, was influential in the appointment of Medina and other conservative bishops and publicly showed his support for the Chilean dictator by attending a televised meeting of government sympathizers to promote Gen. Augusto Pinochet's plebiscite campaign.

Even in Brazil, where the church has strongly resisted Vatican encroachment, the pendulum is swinging to the right, threatening to end the prophetic leadership of the country's bishops. Thanks to the steady appointment of Vatican yes-men, conservative archbishops now outnumber progressives. Indicative of the consequences is the shift in church priorities in the country's impoverished northeast, which once led the Brazilian church in denouncing human rights abuses and economic injustice. Since John Paul's advent, conservative prelates there have come to dominate the region and are now in charge of the leadership of its regional bishops' conference. When Dom Hélder Cámara, the outspoken Archbishop of Recife, resigned on reaching the mandatory retirement age, he was replaced by a conservative, Archbishop José Cardoso Sobrinho, who has ceased church support for consciousness-raising work with the poor. He has also forbidden Dom Hélder to speak publicly in the Recife archdiocese. Meanwhile, Cardoso has reopened the local seminary to provide orthodox training for priests; the seminary competes with the Recife Theological Institute, which teaches liberation theology and encourages students to live in poor communities as part of their training. If the competition proves tough enough – the northeast's traditionalist bishops prefer to have their future priests trained by Cardoso's seminary – the theological institute could be forced to close. "At a time when church communities would like priests who are more familiar with their people," said one theologian, "there appears to be a growing tendency to form them behind closed doors, to make them more concerned with the internal institutional order than with the church's mission in the world."

Prayer and religious rituals have always been the glue that held the Catholic base communities together, but Medellín gave the religious vision an added social impulse through its emphasis on peace and justice. The rightward shift in the church threatens to alter that vision by reemphasizing piety at the cost of solidarity and by slowing the institutional momentum behind the base communities.

Nine years ago, when the region's bishops reaffirmed the commitment made at

Medellín during a follow-up meeting in Puebla, Mexico, the communities seemed likely to serve as a trampoline for other popular movements, such as women's clubs, slum theaters, unions and peasant federations. In many countries the lessons in democracy learned in the communities proved vital to the creation of other neighborhood groups that gave the poor a public voice. These spinoffs will continue to grow, but increasingly they will have to do without the support of the institutional church. Progressive church leaders say that a hierarchical church determined to reassert control over the laity and reduce tensions with right-wing governments may also help isolate activist base communities.

As the Rome representative of an international religious order pointed out, the ongoing appointment of conservative bishops will inevitably alter the pastoral direction of the Latin American church because the training given to its pastoral agents, particularly priests and nuns, will reflect the hierarchy's conservatism. Although some base communities have advanced to the stage that such pastoral agents are no longer needed, the majority depend on the organizational support and spiritual leadership of the local church. Then too, most poor Latin Americans remain in awe of their bishop. If there is a confrontation between the liberal leadership in the communities and a conservative bishop, said a Brazilian lay leader, the people "will always support their bishop. And we [progressives] will be seen as heretics." Still, the memory of Medellín cannot be entirely erased, for too many changes have occurred in Latin American Catholicism in the intervening two decades. As Archbishop Cámara says, those who seek a new path, whether in the church or secular society, should not expect roses but must be prepared to endure the prophet's life in the desert. Yet, as the Archbishop notes, "The desert also blooms."

ROBERT SHERRILL

White-Collar Thuggery
[book review]

November 28, 1988

Robert Sherrill has been writing for *The Nation* since 1964. He currently covers corporations for the magazine.

Corporate Crime and Violence: Big Business Power and the Abuse of the Public Trust. By Russell Mokhiber. Sierra Club Books. 450 pp. $25.

If the Bible were being rewritten today, and Russell Mokhiber were on the committee doing the work, I think he would insist (with every good reason) that in the future Romans 6:23 be updated to read: "For the wages of sin is death, except for corporations. But they should be included."

Mokhiber is editor of "Corporate Crime Reporter," a weekly newsletter published in Washington, D.C., at a subscription cost that, I regret to say, is so steep only corporate criminals can afford to read about their nefarious ways in its pages.

However, *Corporate Crime and Violence: Big Business Power and the Abuse of the Public Trust,* priced affordably, summarizes quite enough evil to last you the rest of the decade. This is repulsive, disgusting, infuriating, treasonous (in the true sense of betraying one's country) stuff—around which, I suspect, the Wharton and Harvard schools of business have not developed a course.

Mokhiber offers us thirty-six cases of corporate misconduct that killed people or destroyed the environment. Many of the episodes are several years old: Most of them were widely reported and commented on when they occurred, or shortly thereafter. No doubt the establishment press, being loath to force ethical conduct on its corporate peers in the fashion proposed by Mokhiber, will dismiss the book as "old stuff." But criticizing the age of the material misses the point entirely. Mokhiber is not dealing in "exposés." He is reviewing history for the purpose of suggesting reform. And he does it beautifully, masterfully. Some of these cases are so complex that a book could be written about them individually—books *have* been written about them. But Mokhiber condenses each case into about ten pages, and manages it so well that the core of each crime is saved for our thorough inspection.

I believe that what Mokhiber wants you to keep in mind more than anything else when reading his book is that these corporate crimes were not impersonal ones. When General Motors or McDonnell Douglas or J.P. Stevens did violence to their workers or to the public, it did not happen in the manner of a landslide or flood. It was not an accident, or an act of God. There was plenty of *mens rea* involved, which Mokhiber, a lawyer, will remind you is a "legal term used to identify the mental element in crime." The decision to risk lives, or to ignore warnings that people were dying or might die from company actions, or to fight attempts to help the victims—these decisions can't be nullified or neutered by the word "corporate." *Men,* thinking men, in those corporations, consciously made the decisions. In many instances, it seems to me, the deliberateness—the premeditation—that went into those decisions, given the results, would have made first-degree murder charges perfectly justified.

There are many, many murders done in these pages: sly, calculated, coldblooded and often (though, thank goodness, not always) highly profitable murders.

When I say calculated, I mean among other things that a common theme running through these cases is a conscious contempt for life. Mokhiber will introduce you to corporations that persisted in marketing a dangerous product and took no

423

thought for the consequences, even though they could have made the product safe very easily and cheaply.

The Ford Motor Company supplies two fine examples:

In the early 1960s, Ford began making cars that had a little problem: On its own, the transmission would often slip from park to reverse, triggering a release of the parking brake, and the car would be on its way, running into or over anything in its path—which very often was a person. By the time Ford quit making that particular transmission, in 1980, more than 400 persons had been killed and thousands injured by runaway Fords. Mokhiber says that midway through this slaughter, Ford engineers came up with a design change that would have eliminated 90 percent of the park-to-reverse failures. "It would have cost Ford only three cents per vehicle. But Ford refused to adopt it."

When Ford put the Pinto on the market, it knew that the car had been designed so poorly that its gas tank was a potential bomb, waiting to be touched off if hit from the rear by another vehicle going no more than 30 miles an hour. The design could have been changed to make the car safe at a cost of no more than $11 per vehicle. Ford decided against making the change, and hundreds of people were killed or injured.

Too bad there isn't space to touch on all these crimes, but, since we must limit ourselves, let's start with the biggest mass murder on Mokhiber's list and work down, as an easy way to see into the heart of corporate America.

Union Carbide. Union Carbide controlled a pesticides factory in Bhopal, India, a city of 800,000. Officials had had recent and ample notice that the Bhopal plant was burdened with so many defective instruments and "safety" valves, so many poorly trained workers and such lax management that, in the words of a secret report submitted to the company by a team of experts, the plant had "serious potential for sizable releases of toxic materials." In the previous six years, there had been six serious accidents at the plant that must have raised doubts about the quality of the operation. Union Carbide paid no attention.

Shortly after midnight on December 3, 1984, the accident occurred that started the methyl isocyanate leak. The gas poured across the city. Because some families buried victims before they were counted, there is no accurate number of the deaths, but best guesses are somewhere between 2,000 and 5,000. Possibly as many as 200,000 persons were harmed; at least 30,000 to 40,000 were *seriously* hurt—eyes, lungs, brains permanently damaged, etc. It was, as Mokhiber says, "the world's worst industrial disaster."

Stop to think what the results would have been if such a thing had happened in this country. But, as everyone knows, India is a nation of wogs, and wogs don't count, really. You can kill a great many wogs and not have to pay much, if anything. Union Carbide didn't.

Lawsuits could have fixed Union Carbide's hash, if they had been handled in this country. The company could have been wiped out. But a sympathetic Federal judge transferred the lawsuits to Indian courts, which simply are not equipped to handle such gargantuan litigation, and there the cases languish to this day, while the number of plaintiffs is thinned by death and migration.

Readers who feel that the willful indifference to plant conditions should have resulted in jail sentences for Carbide's top officials will be happy to know that when Union Carbide chair Warren Anderson visited India shortly after the leak, he was charged with criminal negligence and put in jail. They won't be so happy to learn it was merely a ceremonial incarceration of six hours. Says Mokhiber, "The charges were never pursued, which suggests that the arrests were made by the government to quell public outrage at the corporation, which became popularly known in Bhopal as 'Killer Carbide,' and at the government, which was widely perceived as ineffective in bringing medical relief to the victims."

Released from jail on $2,000 bail, Anderson flew home to say he was "proud of the way the corporation responded."

How exactly had it responded? Why, Union Carbide had said it was sorry it had killed and maimed so many people, and to demonstrate its sorrow, this corporation boasting a $5 billion equity had sent $1 million in disaster relief, which as Mokhiber reminds us, "came to about $5 a victim." A week after the accident, "Carbide sent one shipment of medicine, sufficient for 300 to 400 persons."

Dow Chemical. Long before the Vietnam War, Dow knew that the chemicals contained in Agent Orange (as the defoliant became known during the war) were extremely hazardous. But when the Pentagon ordered something to kill vegetation in the war zone to make it difficult for the enemy to hide, Dow did not hesitate to package Agent Orange and send it into battle. So far as is known, the corporation (and the six other firms contributing to the sale) did not warn the Pentagon of the dangers. Certainly the G.I.s in Vietnam were not warned, though they surely must have had some idea of the defoliant's potency when they saw that "a dose of the synthetic growth hormone would send tropical plants into a wild cancerous growth spree until they got so big they would explode into limp nothingness. Two-foot-long bananas, tree-sized weeds, and mangled mangroves would lie dead . . . in hundreds of acres of mutilated forests." Insects, birds, animals, fish, all gone. "The soldiers labeled Agent Orange-sprayed forests 'the land of the dead.' "

Never mind the bananas. What about people? What could it do to them? "Three ounces of dioxin (the chief killer in Agent Orange) placed in New York City's drinking water supply could wipe out the city's entire populace," writes Mokhiber. One hundred and thirty pounds of dioxin were scattered over Vietnam — and over civilian residents and soldiers and sailors.

Returning G.I.s discovered they were carrying a plague in their blood. Thousands began suffering a variety of physical ailments. But the ailments they sometimes passed on through their genes were even more terrible.

Dow officials still claim Agent Orange is "extremely safe." Furthermore, they insist that as a war contractor they were only following the government's orders. Dow chair Earle Barnes says that Dow's accusers are guilty of "Hitler-type propaganda."

But Elmo Zumwalt 3d, son of the admiral who ordered the Agent Orange campaign in the first place, said he was "convinced" that "all the medical problems — nervous disorders, cancer and skin problems — reported by Vietnam veterans, or their children's severe birth defects" were caused by Agent Orange.

When the younger Zumwalt served in Vietnam he was exposed to the defoliant. He died of cancer this August 13, at the age of 42. He left behind an 11-year-old son born with a congenital dysfunction that confuses his physical senses. Dow's denials notwithstanding, even *The New York Times* seemed to think the cause of Zumwalt's death was obvious enough to merit a headline description of him as a "Victim of Defoliation in Vietnam."

Many lawsuits have been filed. Dow and the six other companies have settled out of court for $240 million including interest — a conclusion that has been upheld by the U.S. Supreme Court — against the wishes of thousands of vets who feel that amount to be a total betrayal of their cause. "It is pin money," Mokhiber notes, "for a company as Dow which grossed $11 billion last year. Its payment is mostly covered by insurance. The day the settlement was announced, Dow's stock went up."

If the settlement is spread equally over the 250,000 people who could receive money, it would mean $960 per victim. Somehow, it doesn't seem likely that really would compensate, say, former jungle fighter Michael Ryan and his wife, Maureen, whose first daughter, Mokhiber tells us, was born with "no rectum. No urethra. Two vaginas. Four ovaries. Minus one elbow. Minus one wrist. Spine problems. Muscle problems. Limp arm. Missing fingers. A hole in the heart. Two cervixes."

Firestone. As early as 1972, Firestone knew that its "500" belted radial tires had a frightening rate of blowouts. It kept selling them even after tire tests in 1975 showed that none could even come close to meeting Firestone's own minimum standard of lasting 15,000 miles. No tire lasted longer than 1,385 miles.

Naturally, consumers were somewhat upset because driving on Firestone 500s resulted in such high garage, hospital and mortuary bills. Forty-six percent of the company's customers were raising hell. But still Firestone tried to bluff it out because a recall of the 500s would have busted the company. When Ralph Nader's investigators got hold of a government study that showed just how dangerous the tires were, and released it to the press, did Firestone burn its worthless 500s? No, no. It dumped them on the market through half-price sales.

That was ten years ago. Now and then an accident happens that shows some Americans are still barreling down the highways on those bargain tires, risking their necks with every turn.

The score so far is vague, but government investigators count "thousands of accidents, hundreds of injuries, and 34 known fatalities" from driving on Firestone 500s.

Punishment? Ho, ho ho. No Firestone official went to jail for killing people, but the company was fined $50,000 for selling a defective product — an amount 560 times smaller than its advertising budget for the year its tires were having a record number of blowouts.

Eli Lilly. This homicidal corporation is particularly worth noting because it is sort of George Bush's baby. He used to sit on its board of directors, and when he moved to Washington as Vice President he owned $180,000 worth of Lilly stock, which, we may assume, is one reason he told a drug industry convention in 1982, "Government shouldn't be an adversary. It ought to be a partner" with big business.

Lilly's reputation as a lawbreaker was well established, says Mokhiber, long before it got into trouble with its anti-arthritic drug Oraflex. Cynics called one of its previous drugs, Darvon, "less effective than aspirin in killing pain [but] more common than heroin in killing people." Then came Oraflex.

Oraflex was tested first overseas. It didn't do so well; in fact, several dozen persons had died after using the drug — a little matter that Lilly failed to mention when it sought, and with surprising speed won, approval from the Food and Drug Administration to market the drug in this country. But why allow ethics to get in the way of what Lilly (listening to financial analysts) believed would be quarter-billion-dollar sales within three years?

Alas, that golden future was not to be. Oraflex consumers overseas kept falling over at such a rate that Britain suspended the drug's sales in August 1982. Realizing that would trigger similar action by the F.D.A., Lilly pulled Oraflex from the market — something that probably would not have happened if Britain hadn't acted first. Knowing of the deaths overseas, Dr. Sidney Wolfe, head of Nader's health research group, had been hounding the Department of Health and the Justice Department for months to punish Lilly for its deadly cover-up. Public pressure finally mounted to the point that in August 1985 Justice cooked up a deal with Lilly by which the company would be charged with misdemeanors and fined $25,000 — a "punishment" that was 480 times smaller than the $12 million advertising campaign for Oraflex that year.

General Motors. The air in the Los Angeles basin is, as everyone knows, foul beyond belief. In four out of six categories, its air pollution exceeds acceptable limits set by the Environmental Protection Agency. Twelve and a half million people in that area have had their lives shortened by being exposed to smog and ozone pollution that, more often than not, is 200 to 300 percent above acceptable health standards.

There are many corporate murders involved in this pollution today—including, particularly, the operators of the dozen oil refineries in the basin—but, Mokhiber tells us, the original assassins, the folks who thought up the scheme that has ruined atmospheres and lives in this way, included: General Motors, Standard Oil of California, Mack Trucks and our old friend Firestone.

General Motors, the ringleader, decided in the 1930s to destroy the streetcar systems then operating all over urban America and replace them with bus lines. The details of the conspiracy are too complex to go into here, but the motivation of the corporations was simple enough: to sell vehicles, gasoline, tires. By the time the conspirators were through persuading—bribing?—city and county officials to go along with the scheme, a hundred electric transit systems in forty-five cities around the country had been wiped out: East St. Louis, Tulsa, Jackson, Montgomery, Port Arthur, Cedar Rapids and many et ceteras, including the biggies like New York City, Philadelphia, Baltimore, Oakland and Los Angeles.

Thirty-five years ago, 3,000 quiet, pollution-free electric trains transported 80 million people annually throughout the sprawling metropolis. Los Angeles was no hick town, either, but a fully developed city, a city developed by the trains, not by the automobile, and it prospered in a cleaner environment.

The clean, efficient train system, then owned by the Pacific Electric utility company, was the world's largest interurban electric railway system. Branching from Los Angeles east to San Bernardino, and south to Santa Ana, it carried thousands of commuters between Los Angeles and the area's fifty-six separately incorporated cities. Today this railway no longer exists. The tracks have been ripped out or paved over, the train cars destroyed; smog has replaced clean air.

The destruction was complete by the end of the 1950s. By the early 1970s, Los Angeles's so-called leaders saw what a catastrophe they had allowed to happen and thought of rebuilding the system. Too late. The replacement cost had risen to $6.6 billion, and they couldn't afford it.

So they are left with 8 million cars and G.M.'s buses pumping 26,000 tons of pollutants daily into the atmospheric septic tank.

Were G.M. and the other conspirators punished? Of course they were. You can't kill whole cities and get away with it. The corporate antitrust conspirators were fined $5,000 each. The individuals were fined $1 each. Nobody went to jail.

Pittston Corporation. For callous mass murder, this one, I think, is the saddest in the book. At least a quarter-million people will be killed by Johns Manville and the other asbestos companies. The textile industry has brought scores of thousands of people to an early grave via brown lung syndrome. The harvesting of the tobacco companies is seen around us every day. Infant formula manufacturers like Nestlé, Mokhiber says, have lured Third World mothers away from breast-feeding and into a bottle routine that in one recent year was blamed for killing one million infants. And then, of course, there was Bhopal.

Compared with those wide-screen wipeouts, the 125 people who died at Buffalo Creek, West Virginia, may seem relatively negligible. But there was something about the event that hit me the hardest.

Starting at the top of the mountain, where three tiny waterways converge to form Buffalo Creek, the water trickles down the hollow past the tiny coal towns of Kistler, Fanco, Becco, and Pardee, and 12 others, including Man, some 17 miles downstream, where Buffalo Creek empties into the Guyandotte River. Nestled in the western edge of the Appalachian mountains in West Virginia, Buffalo Creek hollow was home to 5,000 rugged Appalachian mountaineers—people who had a deep pride in home and neighborhood, who were committed to hard work and a rejection of every kind of welfare.

But they were coal miners, prisoners of the coal economy, vulnerable to every dangerous whim of the coal companies.

"Waste was a big problem for" the Buffalo Mining Company, owned by New York City-based Pittston Corp., one of the largest coal companies in the country. "With every four tons the company dug out of the ground came one ton of 'slag' or 'gob'—a black mixture of mine dust, shale, clay, and other impurities."

Coal companies, not having the slightest regard for the aesthetics of nature, dump their wastes wherever it suits them. Buffalo Mining dumped its waste in Middle Creek, one of the three streams that made up Buffalo Creek. A thousand tons a day were dumped into the stream, up at the top of the mountain. The people living down below could see it growing into an enormous dam, 200 feet deep, 600 feet wide, 1,500 feet long.

While the mining company was building the dam of slag, it was also dumping a half-million gallons of polluted waste water behind the dam, into the same stream. The people living below were scared. Every time it rained, they feared the dam would give. After all, it wasn't really a dam. No engineering had gone into its construction; it was just an enormous pile there at the top of the mountain, waiting to wash down on them. Every time it rained, many residents sought higher ground—just in case.

But officials of the company laughed at them, assured them everything was safe, told them not to worry. So the folks wrote the Governor, asking for help ("Please for God's sake have the dump and waters destroyed. Our lives are in danger"). He sent a couple of bureaucrats, but company officials soft-talked them, and nothing was done.

On the morning of February 26, 1972, the dam broke. The "black torrent of 132 million gallons of water and a million tons of solid waste" thirty feet high swept down, wiping out whole towns, not a stick left standing. One hundred and twenty-five people were killed; 4,000 of Buffalo Creek's 5,000 residents were left homeless. Three years later, "survivors were still living in makeshift huts and a team of 60 psychiatrists, psychologists, and social workers concluded that Buffalo Creek valley was virtually 'a village of the damned.' "

At first, Pittston Corporation claimed that it was an "act of God," hoping to avoid any financial responsibility. When its record of ignoring warnings came out, the corporation knew it would have to dodge the bullet another way. Dealing with incredibly poor and psychologically vulnerable people, Pittston's lawyers moved in, "canvassing the hollow offering money settlements to the dazed survivors if they would agree not to take Pittston to court." Many of the survivors, ignorant of what they could do in court, accepted the offers. But 625 banded together and sued for $64 million. They didn't do too well, settling out of court for a mere $13.5 million—$5.5 million for property losses and in wrongful death payments and $8 million for mental suffering.

We may assume that each of those 625 lost at least one family member and their home. The average settlement for home and death combined was $21,600.

The state of West Virginia sued Pittston for $100 million but, always craven in a showdown fight with coal companies, the state settled for one cent on the dollar.

Nobody at Pittston or its subsidiary went to jail.

What will be done to stop all this? Probably very little. In his landmark *White-Collar Crime,* Edwin Sutherland noted the difficulties of overcoming "the cultural homogeneity of legislators, judges, and administrators with businessmen. Legislators admire and respect businessmen and cannot conceive of them as criminals; businessmen do not conform to the popular stereotype of 'the criminal.' " What that really means is that rogues and thugs in the top 3 percent of the income scale stick together.

But Sutherland wrote that forty years ago. I'm not sure that the "popular stereotype of 'the criminal' " doesn't today include white-collar rogues and thugs, although our judges and legislators like to pretend the public hasn't progressed that far. A national *Washington Post*-ABC poll of 1,147 registered voters interviewed in July showed that to the statement "Large corporations have too much power for the good of the country," 73 percent registered a hearty Amen! Among Democrats, it was 79 percent; among Republicans, 66 percent. Granted, only 14 percent of the Republican delegates to their national convention said they agreed (versus 67 percent of Democratic delegates), and granted there has been an incredible tolerance among the general populace toward an Administration that has virtually abandoned the antitrust laws, antipollution laws, consumer protection laws and industrial safety laws. Still, it would seem from those figures that more than seven out of ten Americans today feel that they are being crapped on by big business and would welcome stiff enforcement of stiff laws to correct the situation.

Getting Congress to agree is, of course, another matter.

But if, on some road to Damascus, those spineless wonders should see the light, they have here in *Corporate Crime and Violence* the answers they need. Mokhiber lists fifty—it's a big, big problem, so fifty is none too many—steps that should be taken to subdue the wicked giant. I will name just a few of his ideas.

§"The trouble with using fines to control corporate crime . . . is that the amount paid is more than offset by the financial gain from the offense . . . four-fifths of the penalties levied against corporations were $5,000 or less." Furthermore, most criminal corporations (60 percent) simply don't pay their fines, and they get away with it. "At the end of fiscal year 1982 (the last data available), the amount of delinquent debt owed to the federal government was a staggering $38 billion."

So, along with the fines (and more vigorous ways of collecting them), a maximum sentence of fifteen years and a minimum of one year should be written into Federal corporate laws governing criminal executives. "In addition, sentencing guidelines for judges in the case of lesser offenses must be written so as to protect against the lenient sentences currently endemic."

§Treat criminal executives like criminals, by abolishing country club prisons and making the C.E.O. bunk in with an arsonist. "The price-fixer should be housed next to the burglar, the company official whose drug company knowingly marketed unsafe drugs that killed people should be housed with other murderers." Mokhiber adds, with a fine touch of humor, I think, "A side benefit of ending this separation will be the improvement of prison conditions for all inmates. The white-collar criminals will insist on improvement."

§We should have the death penalty for corporations that have committed the equivalent of premeditated murder. "Legislatures should adopt provisions to strip corporations of their charters for serious corporate violations or for recidivist behavior. Some states already have such provisions, although they are rarely invoked."

§In fact, it isn't safe to leave any of these penalties to the states, because most state legislatures and most state bureaucracies are totally in the thrall of big business.

So, force all corporations to get a Federal charter. Admittedly, the Federal government isn't the toughest police dog in the world, but it is one hell of a lot tougher than, say, the West Virginia or the Texas Legislature and perhaps more likely to revoke the charters of criminal corporations.

§Pass laws barring convicted executives from holding corporate office for a given number of years. "A federal law, the Landrum-Griffin Act of 1959, prohibits convicted felons from holding union office for five years following conviction. . . . When then should an executive of a drug manufacturing company who has been convicted of violating federal food and drug laws be allowed to return to work in the drug industry?"

I may not have mentioned the remedies on this intelligent list that Mokhiber wants to push the hardest. The thing for you to do is buy this book and read all these case histories and all his remedies. That should motivate you to go corner your senators and congressmen and threaten to tie them down and force-feed them coal dust, lint, baby formula, Oraflex and asbestos, if they don't agree to help us out. Now.

EDWARD W. SAID

Palestine Agenda   *December 12, 1988*

> Edward Said's piece on the declaration of a Palestinian state is especially interesting given the energetic role played by Freda Kirchwey and *The Nation* in the 1940s in securing the partition of Palestine and the creation of a Jewish homeland. In fact, in May 1948, just after President Truman's de facto recognition of the state of Israel, Kirchwey remarked that pressure from the magazine had had an impact on the decision. Said, a *Nation* music critic since 1987, is a professor of English literature at Columbia University, and the author of *The Question of Palestine* and *Orientalism*. He has been a member of the Palestine National Council.

The nineteenth session of the Palestine National Council, formally titled the "*Intifada* Meeting," was momentous and, in many great and small ways, unprecedented. There were fewer hangers-on, groupies and "observers" than ever before. Security was tighter and more unpleasant than during the 1987 P.N.C. session, also held in Algiers. Algeria had just had its own brutally suppressed *intifada,* so the presence of several hundred Palestinians and at least 1,200 members of the press was not especially welcomed by the Benjedid government, which paradoxically needed the event to restore some of its tarnished revolutionary luster. The three-and-a-half-day conclave also accomplished more than any Palestinian meeting in the post-1948 period. Above all, it secured for Yasir Arafat his place in Palestinian and world history.

None of the approximately 380 members came to Algiers with any illusion that Palestinians could again get away simply with creative ambiguity or solid affirmations of the need to struggle. The *intifada*'s momentum and its ability to created a clear civil alternative to the Israeli occupation regime necessitated a definitive statement of support by the P.N.C. This required an unambiguous claim for sovereignty over whatever Palestinian territories were to be vacated by the occupation. There also had to be an equally unambiguous statement on peaceful resolution of the conflict between Palestinian Arabs and Israeli Jews, based on U.N. Resolutions 181 (partition), 242 and 338. In short, the P.N.C. was asking of itself nothing less than an emphatic transformation: from liberation movement to independence movement. Jordan's recent withdrawal of claims for the West Bank made the need for transformation urgent and compelling.

Everyone gathering in Algiers knew that this profound step was Arafat's: first to define, then to persuade us to take, then finally to choreograph politically. When I arrived, he handed me the Arabic draft of the declaration of statehood and asked me to render it into English. It had been written by committee, then rewritten by Mahmoud Darwish, then, alas, covered with often ludicrously clumsy insertions and inexplicable deletions. Darwish later told me that the Old Man had struck the phrase "collective memory" because, we opined, he took it as poetic. "Tell him it has a serious and even scientific meaning," Darwish implored me; "maybe he'll listen to you." He didn't, and I didn't listen when Arafat wanted other, mistaken phrases inserted.

Perhaps the oddest thing about this P.N.C. – with its obsessive postmodern rhetorical anxieties – was that we discussed the two main documents (the declaration of statehood and the political resolutions) in public debates for hours on end without a piece of paper before us. After the opening ceremonies on Saturday, the Council divided itself into two committees, the political and the *intifada*. Arafat had the texts memorized, and Nabil Shaath, brilliantly adroit chair of the political committee, had them before him. All relevant discussion took place in the riveting atmosphere of that committee, with speaker after speaker sounding off on what after all was the most significant political moment in Palestinian life since 1948. Words, commas, semicolons and paragraphs were the common talk of each recess, as if this were a convention of grammarians.

The heart of the debate was articulated by George Habash and Abu Iyad (Salah Khalaf), the first an opponent of the by now well-known substance of the political program, the second Arafat's key supporter and one of the main leaders of Fatah. Habash's express reservations concerned the clear acceptance of 242 and 338, resolutions unfriendly to Palestinians not only because they treat us simply as "refugees" but also because they contain an implicit pre-negotiating recognition of Israel. This, Habash said, was going too far too soon; there had been agreement that such tough issues as recognition, 242, borders, etc., would be handled at the international conference. Why, Habash asked, must we go forward on everything *before* the conference? He spoke passionately, saying without hesitation that he and the Popular Front for the Liberation of Palestine wished to remain in the P.L.O. no matter what the outcome or the disagreements. To which, in a superbly meandering and yet fascinating speech, Abu Iyad said that decisions had to be made now, not only in the face of the discouraging realities of the Israeli elections but because our people needed an immediate, concrete statement of our goals. What clinched it for me was the logic of Abu Iyad's thesis that decisive clarity was necessary principally for ourselves and our friends, not because our enemies kept hectoring us to make more concessions.

By about 9:30 P.M. on Monday, November 14, the political program had been passed by a large majority in the political committee, and immediately afterward the whole P.N.C. was reconvened in plenary session. Habash and supporters fought each sentence almost word by word on the crucial 242/338 paragraph, which was voted on in different forms half a dozen times. The ungainly paragraph that resulted shows the effect of those battles, although the substance remains unmistakable. At one point Arafat stood up and recited the entire program from memory, indicating where the clause, sentence and paragraph breaks occurred, so that there could be no mistake about meaning, emphasis, conclusion. For the first time in P.N.C. history, voting by acclamation wasn't going to be enough; Habash had insisted on precise tallies, which emerged to his disadvantage: 253 for, 46 against, 10 abstaining. There was a sad nostalgia to what he represented, since in effect by voting against him we were taking leave of the past as embodied in his defiant gestures. The declaration ceremonies that closed the meetings were jubilant, yet somehow melancholy.

About this break with the past there could be no doubt whatever. To declare statehood on the basis of Resolution 181 was first of all to say unequivocally that an Arab Palestinian and an Israeli state should coexist in a partitioned Palestine. Self-determination would thus be for two peoples, not just for one. Most of us there had grown up with the reality (lived and remembered) of Palestine as an Arab country, refusing to concede anything more than the exigency of a Jewish state, one at our expense in the loss of our land, our society and uncountable thousands of lives. As we met, a million and a half of our compatriots were under brutal military occupation, fighting tanks and fully armed soldiers with rocks and an unbending will. For the first time also, we implicitly recognized a state that offered us nothing but the empty formulas of Camp David or the openly racist threats of "transfer." The declaration of statehood spelled out principles of equality, mutuality and social justice far in advance of anything in the region. Then too the *principle* of partition was asserted, not the territories specified in the 1947 U.N. resolution. All of us felt that since Israel has *never* declared its boundaries, we could not declare ours now; better to negotiate the question of boundaries with Israel and a confederal relationship with Jordan directly. There was no doubt, however, that we were discussing the territories occupied in 1967.

Secondly, there was absolute clarity in speaking of a peaceful settlement to the conflict. "Armed struggle" does not appear in the binding resolutions to the political program. Central to those resolutions is a long and awkward sentence endorsing an international peace conference based on 242 and 338. The language surrounding acceptance of the U.N. resolutions raises no reservations about that acceptance but simply states the obvious. Representation by the P.L.O. on an equal footing with other parties, the aegis of the Security Council, the *implementation* of 242 and 338, the centrality of the Palestinian-Israeli conflict, the inalienable rights of the Palestinian people—all these are mentioned as the *context*, the history, the Palestinian interpretation, of what we were accepting. This was crucial because 242 and 338 say nothing about the political actuality of the Palestinian people, which in 1967 seemed scarcely evident.

Thirdly, the rejection of terrorism (also affirmed in the declaration) emphatically distinguishes between resistance to occupation, to which Palestinians are entitled according to the U.N. Charter and international law, and indiscriminate violence against civilians by states or by individuals and groups. Note that there exists no all-purpose definition of terrorism, one that has international validity and impartiality of application. Also note that Israel has always arrogated to itself the right to attack civilians in the name of its security.

Finally and most important, all the resolutions clearly intend willingness to negotiate directly. There are no disclaimers about the "Zionist entity," or about the legitimacy of Israeli representatives. All the relevant passages about peace, partition and statehood in the 1964 Palestinian National Covenant are flatly contradicted by the 1988 P.N.C. resolutions. All the refusals, attacks and insults heaped on the Council's results, both by Israel and the usual array of U.S. "experts," signify consternation. Clearly, the more Palestinians take responsible and realistic positions, the less acceptable we become, not just because Palestinians want peace but because Israelis don't know what to do when peace is offered to them. There is a dispiriting continuity here between the early days of Israel's existence, when Ben-Gurion refused peace with the Arabs, and the all-out rejection trundled out today by Likud and Labor alike.

The point is not that the Council's documents are perfect and complete but that they must be interpreted as everyone in Algiers intended—as a beginning that signals a distinct break with the past, as an assertion of willingness to make sacrifices in the interests of peace, as a definitive statement of the Palestinian acceptance of the international consensus. A few days before the Algiers meeting Ariel Sharon appeared on Italian television vociferating about the need to kill Arafat. That no comparable sentiment was expressed in Algiers about an Israeli leader testifies eloquently to the real difference now between Israeli and Palestinian leaders. These are dangerous times for Palestinians; the occupation will get worse, and assassinations and full-scale political war will intensify. For once, however, the record is unmistakable as to who is for peace, who for bloodshed and suffering. But our campaign for peace must be joined.

What I cannot understand or condone is how the U.S. media—quite unlike that in the rest of the world—has internalized the rejectionism promulgated by the Israeli and U.S. establishments. Far from reading the texts as they were meant to be read, commentators persist in suggesting that whatever was said in the texts could not, by definition, be enough. Why is Israel not asked whether it is willing to co-exist with a Palestinian state, or negotiate, or accept 242, or renounce violence, or recognize the P.L.O., or accept demilitarization, or allay Palestinian fears, or stop killing civilians, or end the occupation, or answer any questions at all? Perhaps the media will break their silence, as Palestinians already have.

DARRELL YATES RIST

The Deadly Costs of an Obsession

February 13, 1989

Darrell Yates Rist's impassioned piece on AIDS sparked a debate, which is partially reflected in the two commentaries published on the pages that follow the article. Rist is a gay activist and co-founder of the Gay and Lesbian Alliance Against Defamation.

> In seasons of pestilence, some of us will have a secret attraction to the disease—a terrible passing inclination to die of it. And all of us have like wonders hidden in our breasts, only needing circumstances to evoke them.
> —CHARLES DICKENS
> *A Tale of Two Cities*

Not long ago, while I was researching a book on the lives of gay men across America, a writer friend offered me an unsettling view of gay San Francisco. Rob Goldstein had no use for the polish and smugness of the Castro, the Promised Land for homosexuals; he toured me instead through the disenfranchised Latino gay life of the Mission district and the destitution of the Tenderloin. In the Tenderloin, I met homeless gay men with AIDS and gay teen-age runaways who risked their lives bartering sex for meals and drugs, hustling on every street corner.

I had just spent a night among those abandoned adolescents when, at a dinner in the Castro, I listened to the other guests talk about nothing but AIDS, the dead, the dying—which to their minds included every gay man in the city: fashionable hysteria. "This," one of them actually said, "is the only thing worth fighting for." Not long before, I'd heard Larry Kramer, playwright and AIDS activist, say something like that too, and had felt, in that suffocating moment, that finally we'd all gone suicidal, that we'd die of our own death wish.

Though I tried above all to empathize with my tablemates' wretchedness, the other images of San Francisco kept importuning. I described what I'd seen in their hometown and recalled the gay youth agency I knew best, New York City's Hetrick-Martin Institute, its dreary facilities, small staff and paltry budget. "Shouldn't we start worrying again about all those issues we've forgotten in the epidemic? Gay kids?" I ventured—as though we'd ever really cared. "Even if they don't get AIDS, what are we giving them to *live* for?"

The guests fell silent. Across from me sat an elder of the city's gay community, a man of money and influence. He stared at me in utter disbelief, his face suspended above the pork roast. "How *can* we?" he rasped. "We're *dying!*"

There's an oily sentiment among gay men and lesbians these days that—amid the din of a culture that keeps us in our place—we've matured; that we've grown aggressive in defense of our lives since fate, with some harsh wisdom, sent us AIDS. We produce abundant evidence of sacrifice to prove the claim: For most of this decade we've frantically been building AIDS organizations, draining our pockets poor with AIDS donations, exhausting our strength as AIDS volunteers, doing battle with AIDS bigots, creating mayhem in the streets, nurturing, mourning, worrying about infection till we're sick, dying with a desperate hold on dignity. We've been full of AIDS—gay men, lesbians, our parents, our newly sympathetic heterosexual friends. We've all had heart, in fact, for nothing else.

Even lesbians, none of whom, according to the U.S. Centers for Disease Control (C.D.C.) have contracted AIDS making love to a woman, have taken to keening that the whole gay community is dying—so compulsive is the human need to partake in the drama of catastrophe. And this panicky faith that all of us are doomed cries down the sobering truth that it is only a minority of homosexuals who've been stricken or ever will be, leaving the rest of us to confront not so much the grief of dying as the bitterness, in an oppressive world, of staying alive.

No one has influenced (or parroted) the gay community's views on AIDS more than Larry Kramer and his organizational offspring, New York's AIDS Coalition to Unleash Power (ACT UP)—chic street protesters with clones, albeit autonomous ones, in nearly every major city. The numbers they use to pronounce universal death on the gay community's men are immoral because they are panic-mongering, insidious because they are specious. They fall within some extreme theoretical realm of possibility, and therefore prey on the frightened; they willfully propagate the worst that medical science can imagine, regardless of the improbability, regardless of maddening contradictions in epidemiologic definitions and data.

Neither Kramer nor anyone else has any hard national figures on the prevalence of infection with HIV, the virus assumed to cause AIDS. But most activists, and the media, seem to have swallowed the C.D.C.'s estimate of 1 million to 1.5 million men, women and children. These numbers, unchanged since 1986 despite the luridly publicized "spread" of HIV, ludicrously derive not from national seroprevalence surveys but in great part from mythical assumptions about the population size and sexual practices of gay men. Nevertheless, both Kramer's crowd and the media continue to broadcast the notion that HIV infection is uniformly fatal, even though the C.D.C.'s own Kung Jong Lui and William Darrow, on whose research the morbid dogma is based, have disavowed such sweeping prognoses as egregious misapplications of their work. Their San Francisco study, published in the June 3, 1988 issue of *Science*, suggested only that, among a small and very high-risk group of HIV antibody-positive men, there was a 90 percent probability that between 39 percent and 100 percent would develop AIDS – a crap shoot in statistics, one never intended to be a prediction.

More hopeful yet, the New York Blood Center's head epidemiologist, Dr. Cladd Stevens, has found that 20 to 25 percent of the HIV antibody-positive men she studied for ten years show no measurable immune dysfunction. Yet an article in *The Washington Post* on HIV infection, "AIDS Virus Likely Fatal to All Infected," chose, like most media reports to misinterpret hysterically Lui and Darrow's study. And it is such terrifyingly irresponsible misanalyses of the San Francisco numbers that Kramer and his disciples embrace. Members of ACT UP have even passed out copies of the *Post* article in the streets, like biblical tracts.

According to the Kinsey statistics – old, but the most reliable figures we have – American men whose homosexuality is "more than incidental" make up 13 to 38 percent of the male population. Today, that's between 11.2 million and 32.8 million men. For the sake of argument, let's accept the C.D.C.'s top figure of 1.5 million people who would test positive for HIV in the United States. Let's even assume that *all* of them are homosexuals – ignoring the hundreds of thousands who are heterosexual intravenous drug users, hemophiliacs, heterosexually infected women, infected babies. Even if all 1.5 million died off in a biologically improbable holocaust, a minimum of 9.7 million homosexually active men and 5.6 million lesbians (from Kinsey's minimum incidence of 6 percent homosexuality among women) would remain uninfected and sentenced to life.

Data on the homosexual population and AIDS will change in time and yield more truth – or less. But no imprecision in the numbers has sobered the gay apocalyptics for a moment. And their fantasy of wholesale mortality gives us yet a new excuse to desert the business of living and ignore the most vulnerable among us. Certainly when it comes to kids, even the homosexual heart for AIDS beats false; it beats only for men of a certain age, a certain color – in fact, a certain social class.

Since its founding in 1981, New York's pre-eminent AIDS service organization, the Gay Men's Health Crisis (G.M.H.C.), with an annual budget of almost $11 million – and $1 million more in material donations for new office furnishings last year – has never funded outreach of any kind to gay and lesbian youth. I've been told again and again the organization is fearful of being accused of proselytizing, that most vicious imputation afflicting homosexuals. So children die while we dance to the songs of bigots. The Hetrick-Martin Institute makes its services available to the 150,000 gay and lesbian adolescents that it estimates live in New York City. This group does provide AIDS outreach, but also administers a high school for homosexual kids harassed out of public schools, educates parents and teachers, runs support groups, conducts counseling, furnishes food, clothing and access to shelter to the adolescent homeless – almost all of whom are black or Latino. The institute had a staff last fiscal year of only twenty-four (including street counselors) and a mere $755,000 budget, most of which came from the city and state. Only 18 percent of the money came from the generosity of homosexual men and women and their friends, whereas nearly three-quarters of G.M.H.C.'s budget currently comes from private donations and interest on the investment of excess income.

But even concerns more immediate than gay children fail to engage our self-interest. The battle against anti-gay violence languishes while assaults have soared specifically as a backlash to the disease. According to the New York City Gay and Lesbian Anti-Violence Project (A.V.P.), in the city alone there were 609 reported queer-bashings last year, reflecting a more than 300 percent increase since 1984, when AIDS stories began to saturate the media. Moreover, the A.V.P. reports that 90 percent of anti-gay and -lesbian crimes nationwide are never reported: Victims are afraid of being forced from the closet and demeaned by the police or made to face, in many states, the legally sanctioned discrimination of sodomy laws. Despite New York's huge gay and lesbian population at risk of assault, the A.V.P. could muster a budget last year of a mere $150,000, just $10,000 of which was donated by the community.

The epidemic of violence has been long, brutal and often fatal. David Wertheimer, director of A.V.P., describes the hatred vented in anti-gay attacks as "unimaginable." Speaking about a series of murders in New York's Chelsea neighborhood that began in 1985, he said, "The victim is commonly found stabbed twenty or thirty times, sometimes with his castrated penis stuffed in his mouth." Yet there has not been a sustained outcry from the gay community against this violence.

Why are we so callous about these attacks? Can no threat but AIDS ignite our indignation? Why do we care so little, in fact, even for the sanctity of our relation-

439

ships? Why is there no ACT UP specifically to protest laws forbidding same-sex marriage, banned in every state? Why no marathon protests at marriage license bureaus, no sit-ins at state legislatures, no class action suits? Why doesn't such brutality against our love incite our anger? Are we such demoralized creatures that only the threat of extinction can stir our collective will? When a car wreck left Sharon Kowalski a quadraplegic, her homophobic father had her quarantined by a court from Karen Thompson, her lover. Is the murder of their relationship at the hands of American law less of a horror than losing one's lover to a virus?

For the first time since the onslaught of the AIDS epidemic in the early 1980s, one crucial organization, the National Gay and Lesbian Task Force, has begun to put AIDS in sane perspective. "We can't go on just living *through* AIDS," the task force's Urvashi Vaid has said. "We have to think in terms of living *beyond* it if this movement's going to survive." The organization has contained its AIDS expenditures at 15 percent of its total program budget and reinforced its primary work of gay liberation. Yet the task force has a staff of only ten, and some 400 occasional volunteers nationally. New York's G.M.H.C. has a staff of 105, plus 1,900 volunteers. The task force's 1988 budget was a humiliating $860,000—more than $10 million less than the budget of the G.M.H.C. This grotesque disparity is compounded over and over across the nation.

Even otherwise deeply closeted gay men and lesbians are avid in their testimonials about the need to wage war against the disease. But too many of these AIDS crusaders never go public over the right of homosexuals to something more than not dying. In my gym, a crossroads of Manhattan, a coterie of cultish gay men plastered ACT UP's "Silence=Death" logo everywhere in the facility and are given to working out in ACT UP or G.M.H.C. T-shirts—as though sporting such gym wear were a courageous act. But I've not seen one of that crowd so boldly advertise a more identifiably gay and therefore riskier issue. A certain interest in AIDS has become the trendy code for suggesting one's homosexuality without declaring it, what being a bachelor and an artiste used to suggest.

The ruse that comforts us is that the fight against AIDS and the struggle for gay rights are the same. Last year, a gay Chicago newspaper headlined, "Riverside [California] Supports Gay Rights." The story below read: "The Riverside City Council unanimously approved an ordinance that bans discrimination against people with AIDS." It's in this very sort of thing that we're deceived. What good do those laws do for most lesbians, who certainly are not suffering from AIDS? Or for the average homosexual or bisexual man, who, whatever our hysteria, would not test positive for HIV either? Or for those who have been exposed to the virus but are asymptomatic, not all of whom will sicken and die, however fantastic the latest rumors? What's the benefit of such legislation to gay men with AIDS themselves if the excuse to abuse their rights isn't AIDS but homosexuality?

Any benefit that gay men and lesbians get from the legislated rights of people with AIDS is second-handed grace: you have to claim to be dying to receive it.

But our failure is far more iniquitous than mere dereliction. For, though the constituencies of gay rights and AIDS activism may overlap, the politics—as conceived—are often violently incompatible. At the October 1987 National March on Washington for Lesbian and Gay Rights, an uncommon show of militant self-respect among homosexuals, at least a half-million of us paraded not just against AIDS but for all the rights and privileges that heterosexuals enjoy. Yet, even as we rallied, I sat in a meeting of national AIDS activists who fretted over the possibility that the event would become a political embarrassment for AIDS lobbyists. The symbolic public same-sex wedding the Saturday before the march, a demonstration for spousal rights, was a particular sore point. The director of a powerful national AIDS umbrella organization especially complained that when the wedding hit the news a disgusted Congress would renege on AIDS funding. She and her colleagues still hoped desperately that last-minute maneuvers would kill the thing—treachery bartering away gay liberation.

Some angry lesbians question whether bourgeois gay men ever wanted more than comfortably closeted sex anyway—and now wonder if they want more than a quick cure for AIDS in order to get back to the old days. Some ask more bitterly yet whether men, who demand center stage for AIDS, would sacrifice a pittance of their politics or pleasures if lesbians were the ones dying. Yet, there always have been gay men who've wanted more than sex and obsequious privacy, whose cause has been politically radical and impolite. They've been largely shouted down by the politics of this epidemic. And the more the AIDS movement divorces itself from the demands of gay rights, the more it becomes a route to respect for homosexuals not open to unapologetic gay activists. AIDS is the cause célèbre, and, insidiously, we are drawn in, chumming with the Liz Taylors and even the William F. Buckley Jrs. (who've contributed charitably to the fight against AIDS, though Bill has called for tattooing infected gay men's asses). Gossip columnists bold-face AIDS activists' names among mentions of the socially registered. New York's artsy Bessie Committee even gave ACT UP a performance citation last year for its street protests, unlikely applause for genuine revolutionaries.

But even homophobes who'd never want to see a homosexual holding a lover's hand, especially in front of the children, can cry (and contribute) at the thought of so many gay men dying. They're with us on AIDS: Dying and preoccupied with dying, we're less of a threat, our radical potential diverted to mere survival. Through a marriage with disease we've arrived. But to live with our apostasy we've also had to hide from the damning truth that our patrons in the fight against AIDS are seldom dear friends when we're not being sick, just homosexual.

It isn't a virus that for centuries has deprived us gay men and lesbians of our freedom, nor is it this epidemic that now most destroys our lives. Nor is it bigotry. It's our own shame, a morbid failure of self-respect and sane, self-righteous anger. If we care about nothing but AIDS now, it is because identifying with sexually transmitted death plays to some dark belief that we deserve it.

In the midst of death, we are confronted with a choice of life that so far we've only dallied with, the terrible responsibility of living free. For wholeness demands more than arguing with bigots, more than crying for acceptance, more than fighting against disease. It asks that we abandon selfishness, self-pity and every compromise of our self-worth. It insists that we nurture the dying, more selflessly than we ever have, but care as much for the promise of life. It compels us to understand that silence equals death not only in the middle of an epidemic, but that it always has killed us and will continue its genocide when AIDS is gone. And wholeness forces us to forsake AIDS as our dark obsession, as the sum of our lives. For this disease is at least as fatal to our hearts as to our blood. Our devotion to it will kill us more surely than a virus ever could.

[exchange] March 20, 1989

MARTIN BAUML DUBERMAN

I want to offer one bit of personal experience in support of Darrell Yates Rist's main contention, but then to disassociate myself from some of his secondary points.

First, the support. Three and a half years ago a group of gay and lesbian scholars banded together, at my invitation, to form a center for gay and lesbian studies, culminating two years later in our being welcomed to the Graduate Center of the City University of New York. Formal accreditation, however, still awaits our ability to raise a first-year budget of $50,000. Thus far we have been unable to obtain the needed funds from foundations. And the financial slack has not been taken up by the gay community itself—which *does* reflect, just as Rist claims, the near single-minded focus these days on fighting the scourge of AIDS.

Why is this so? I am not—on several grounds—content with Rists's answer. It is not "fashionable hysteria," as Rist would have it, but necessity that has led the gay community to focus on AIDS. If the straight world had shown more than a modicum of concern about those suffering from the disease, then gay people might never have felt thrown back so entirely on their own resources—which they have marshalled with extraordinary heroism. Even if the prevalence of HIV infection turns out to be lower than is sometimes claimed and the incidence of fatality among those infected less than 100 percent (which seems increasingly likely), the crisis was and remains profound; in explaining the alarm within the gay community, no recourse is needed to Rist's suspect theory that our "keening" reflects a "compulsive . . . need to partake in the drama of catastrophe." The catastrophe is real and the legions of the young in ACT UP who have stationed themselves on the front lines deserve something better than being characterized as "clones" and "chic street protesters."

When Rist further denounces them as "immoral because they are panic-mongering," I find myself angrily at odds with him. How can he call young men fighting for their lives "immoral" when he does not even pause to denounce a Federal government whose indifference made such a fight mandatory? This, I submit, is blaming the victim—and excusing the oppressor—with a vengeance. This, I further submit, is yet another instance of the internecine name-calling long characteristic of the organized gay movement—so inappropriate while our persecutors go unaccountable, so redolent of an internalized homophobia among our own people.

Like Rist, I am appalled that the needs of gay and lesbian adolescents go largely untended, that the Gay and Lesbian Anti-Violence Project is underfunded—and yes, that my own hope for establishing a gay and lesbian research center has thus far been stymied. But unlike Rist, I cannot ascribe this to the "callousness" of the gay community. Nor can I see that its current lack of interest in demanding a repeal of laws against same-sex marriage is anything but a proper allocation of priorities. (Radical gays, among whom both Rist and I count ourselves, might eventually want, I had thought, to insist upon the right of marriage—to insist on *any* rights that everybody else has—but would hardly want to recommend or proselytize for the imitative practice.)

Nor can I share Rist's analysis that AIDS is "yet a new excuse to desert the business of living." He is surely right to be concerned, as I am, that we have yet to build enough strong, life-affirming gay institutions. But gay involvement in the AIDS crisis is such a transparent necessity, given the indifference of the straight world, that it cannot fairly be viewed as an "excuse" of any kind. Moreover, we need to acknowledge—and it should be a matter of pity rather than scorn—that even before AIDS appeared we lacked those needed institutional arrangements; I mean pity for the large majority of gay people who lived on a daily basis with far too much terror to declare and mobilize themselves in their own behalf.

The paradox, unmentioned by Rist, is that *as a result* of the successful mobilization of our own people in the fight against AIDS, so many have for the first time discovered their anger at heterosexist oppression that we may emerge from this crisis with the needed legions—at last—to militantly insist on an end to our oppression.

Rist is surely right that until now our own low self-esteem has contributed to our lack of self-assertion. What he now needs to affirm is that our community's noble — yes, that is the word — mobilization in the AIDS crisis will come to be seen as the turning point in that struggle for self-esteem. Out of this terrible trial, paradoxically, may well come that very commitment to asserting the value of gay lives and gay life for which Rist so eloquently yearns. That, at least, is the hope; there are no guarantees.

Martin Bauml Duberman is distinguished professor of history at Lehman College, City University of New York, and the author of *Paul Robeson: A Biography*.

ACT UP

In this short space it is impossible to expose all of Darrell Yates Rist's ugly misrepresentations of the AIDS activist movement, especially regarding ACT UP. Certainly to indulge in the sort of divisiveness he does would only extend the insult done to us and the lesbian and gay community by printing his article in the first place. However, some clarification is in order.

ACT UP, the New York City-based AIDS Coalition to Unleash Power, was formed two years ago almost exclusively by gay white men as a direct-action group confronting the issues of discrimination against people with HIV infection and restricted access to experimental AIDS drugs. Since then, the growing involvement of women (predominantly lesbians) and people of color has caused ACT UP to expand our approach to the politics of health care and disfranchisement. The inequities endemic in the AIDS crisis have made clear to gay white men in the group that their marginality is akin to that of women, people of color, the poor and intravenous drug users, communities long aware of the life-threatening consequences of being ignored. The ensuing mix of concerns, as well as the changing demographics of the crisis, provoke constant consciousness-raising at ACT UP's Monday night meetings, pushing us to address the major issues of our day: racism, sexism, disablism, homophobia, economic disfranchisement, homelessness and unequal access to decent health care, among other issues.

We are, many of us, a new generation of political people coming out and being politicized around the AIDS crisis. We do not function hierarchically, but in an occasionally unwieldy, radically democratic forum of 200 to 400 activists packed, standing-room only, into the Lesbian and Gay Community Center, voting on just about everything. Anyone can speak, in turn. After attending two meetings, anyone can vote. All are welcome. Like the gay and lesbian liberation groups of the early 1970s, our goal lies both in the ends we seek and in the kind of movement we build in seeking them.

Unquestionably, lesbian and gay issues are a part of that goal — for most of us, a profoundly determining part. ACT UP has refused on two occasions to endorse or support AIDS demonstrations that did not also explicitly support the rights of gays and lesbians. Last August, ACT UP joined the Gay and Lesbian Alliance Against Defamation at their 103rd Street rally against anti-gay violence. In fact, it was three ACT UP members who first sat down in the intersection of 100th Street and Broadway during the subsequent march, and ACT UP civil disobedience expertise that organized legal support and coordinated the safe release of the 100 arrested that night. Further, after a recent Monday night meeting, 230 of us staged a same-sex kiss-in (our favorite form of legal public disruption) at St. Vincent's Hospital in protest of two reported incidents of anti-gay and -lesbian violence by hospital personnel. ACT UP sent a major contingent to the October 1987 civil disobedience protesting the Supreme Court's decision to uphold the Georgia sodomy law.

And for some of us the most moving, empowering and joyful demo was in support of Sharon Kowalski, a lesbian severely disabled in a car accident, who has been isolated by her parents, with a court order, from her lover, Karen Thompson. Organized by our Women's Caucus as a "zap," on August 5 of last year twenty-five same-sex couples, male and female, descended on the New York City Marriage License Bureau. When the first two lesbians were told same-sex couples were not allowed to marry in New York state, one of them protested "but I *love* her, I want to *marry* her," whereupon the group sat down and demanded an explanation from the person in charge. Singing, "We're goin' to the chapel and we're gonna get married," they were joined by many of the straight couples applying for licenses. The significant number of gay men at the "zap" and the subsequent rally is a measure of the deepening solidarity among lesbians and gay men in ACT UP. It was clear to all of us that Karen Thompson's plight is identical to that of same-sex partners denied access to their lovers with AIDS.

Today, we all live with AIDS. Each time a gay man puts on a rubber or a lesbian uses a rubber dam we live with AIDS. (There are at least three documented cases of woman-to-woman transmission and various cases of "uncertain transmission.") AIDS is more than a temporary interruption in the cultural flow of the gay and lesbian community. We in ACT UP see this not as an obsession with death, as Rist does in his revamping of an old homosexuality-as-sickness metaphor, but as a determination to celebrate life, health and self-empowerment. We fight AIDS because we have seen our various marginalities made perniciously manifest by it. As an ACT UP member on trial in February for committing an act of civil disobedience last summer to protest the irresponsible slashing of New York City's estimates of HIV-infected gay and bisexual men testified: "Gay people growing up in this society are made to internalize a system of repression that would render them invisible. Those of us in ACT UP who are gay are acutely aware that this invisibility and its companion, silence, have conspired in the deaths of many of our friends and lovers. We are fighting AIDS in an attempt to save lives, because truly, silence equals death." ACT UP! FIGHT BACK! FIGHT AIDS!

In slightly longer form, this statement was approved without dissension by 300 people at an ACT UP meeting on February 13, 1989.

ARTHUR C. DANTO

Art
April 3, 1989
[*Andy Warhol*]

Arthur Danto, a professor of philosophy at Columbia University, has brought the perspective of a philosopher to bear on the passing art scene since he began writing his biweekly column for *The Nation* in 1984.

It is possible—I would argue that it is necessary—to explain the history of art through the past century as a collective investigation by artists into the philosophical nature of art. The significant art of this extraordinary period accordingly has to be assessed as much on grounds of speculative theory as on those of aesthetic discrimination. "Beginning with van Gogh," Picasso said to Françoise Gilot, "however great we may be, we are all, in a measure, autodidacts—you might almost say primitive painters." It was as if each artist was at the beginning of a new era opened up by his own theories. Picasso had supposed that he and Braque had done something more important in Cubism than to have made some works of art: He believed they had created a style of art that would compose a new canon, sparing those who followed them the need to define the essence of art. For a time, neither of them even signed their works—one does not sign a theory—and when Cubism failed to bring back the sense of order, Picasso tried one thing after another, inventing whole art-historical periods that he alone occupied. I recall when Abstract Expressionism was deemed the new paradigm, destined to last for as long at least as the tradition which came to its end in Impressionism. It was the collapse of that faith with the advent of Pop, rather than the irreverence and brashness of Pop Art itself, that disillusioned so many artists in the early 1960s who believed that they knew what art was. Pop violated every component of their theory and somehow remained art. And so the quest went on.

"Art?" Warhol once asked in response to the inevitable question, "Isn't that a man's name?" Well, suppose we think of the century as Art's heroic-comic quest for his own identity, his true self, as it were, and the artworks of the century as Art's discarded theories, which may have had coincidentally some redeeming aesthetic merit. (Art's peradventurous history would resemble that of his second cousin Geist, as comically narrated in Hegel's side-splitting *Bildungsroman, Phänomenologie des Geistes.*) That would mean that no artist could be taken seriously who did not, as part of whatever he or she made by way of negotiable works, play a role in Art's stumbling search. So the history of Art proceeds on two levels: as a sequence of objects and as a sequence of enfranchising theories for those objects.

The story has its high and low moments, but it would not be easy to tell, always, from an inspection of the objects alone, without reference to the theories through which they must be interpreted, whether they marked high moments or low. Thus the objects might be pretty unprepossessing and yet specify important stages in Art's coming to philosophical terms with himself. Few aesthetes would be stopped dead in their tracks by certain of Duchamp's blank ready-mades—his grooming comb, his snow shovel—but they are climactic moments in the epic. And few would expect from the crashing tautologies of the 1950s—"Painting is painting, the action of spreading paint"—the opulent glory of the Abstract Expressionist objects they so inadequately characterize. Clement Greenberg's identification of painting with the flatness of their surfaces went perfectly well with the canonical works his theory championed (and in some cases generated). But except by denouncing as "not really art" everything that failed this austere and reductive definition, Greenberg was unable to characterize anything *except* the canonical work.

Bitter as the truth may be to those who dismissed him as a shallow opportunist and glamour fiend, the greatest contribution to this history was made by Andy Warhol, to my mind the nearest thing to a philosophical genius the history of art has produced. It was Warhol himself who revealed as merely accidental most of the things his predecessors supposed essential to art, and who carried the discussion as far as it could go without passing over into pure philosophy. He brought the history to an end by demonstrating that no visual criterion could serve the purpose of defining art, and hence that Art, confined to visual criteria, could not solve his personal problem through art-making alone. Warhol achieved this, I think, with the celebrated Brillo boxes he exhibited a quarter-century ago at Eleanor Ward's Stable Gallery in New York.

A great deal more was achieved through the Brillo boxes than this, to be sure, but what was most striking about them was that they looked sufficiently like their counterparts in supermarket stockrooms that the differences between them could hardly be of a kind to explain why they were art and their counterparts merely cheap containers for scouring pads. It was not necessary to fool anyone. It was altogether easy to tell those boxes turned out by Warhol's Factory from those manufactured by whatever factory it was that turned out corrugated cardboard cartons. Warhol did not himself make the boxes, nor did he paint them. But when they were displayed, stacked up in the back room of the gallery, two questions were inevitable: What was it in the history of art that made this gesture not only possible at this time but inevitable? And, closely connected with this, Why were *these* boxes art when their originals were just boxes? With these two questions posed, a century of deflected philosophical investigation came to an end, and artists were liberated to enter the post-philosophical phase of modernism free from the obligation of self-scrutiny.

Warhol was, appropriately, the first to set foot in this free moral space. There followed a period of giddy self-indulgence and absolute pluralism in which pretty much anything went. In an interview in 1963, Warhol said, "How can you say one style is better than another? You ought to be able to be an Abstract Expressionist next week, or a Pop artist, or a realist, without feeling you've given up something." Who can fail to believe that, in art at least, the stage had been attained that Marx forecast for history as a whole, in which we can "do one thing today and another tomorrow, to hunt in the morning, fish in the afternoon, rear cattle in the evening, criticize after dinner, just as I have a mind, without ever becoming hunter, fisherman, shepherd or critic." Its social correlate was the Yellow Submarine of Warhol's silver-lined loft, where one could be straight in the morning, gay in the afternoon, a transexual superstar in the evening and a polymorphic rock singer after taking drugs.

It has at times been urged as an argument against Warhol's extreme originality that Duchamp did it before, inasmuch as there also is little to distinguish one of his ready-mades from the mere object he transfigured by appropriation. But it is the shallowest order of art criticism to say that something has been done before. Two historical moments can resemble each other outwardly while being internally as different as the snow shovel that is a work of art is from one that is a mere tool for clearing sidewalks.

In the early days of Pop, artists were taking over images wherever they found them. Roy Lichtenstein was sued for using a diagram from a famous book on Cézanne. Warhol was sued by the photographer whose image he used and modified in his marvelous flower paintings of 1967. (And I think a suit was threatened by the artist, in fact an Abstract Expressionist, who designed the Brillo carton.) The flower paintings mark a later phase, but in the classic moment of Pop, it was essential to the enterprise that the images be so familiar that "stealing" them was impossible: they belonged to the iconography of everyday life, like the American flag, the dollar sign, the soup label, the before-and-after shots of transformed faces and physiques. These were wrenched out of their locus in the universal language of signs and given the power of art while retaining their own native power as symbols. Duchamp's objects were often arcane and chosen for their aesthetic blandness. Warhol's were chosen for their absolute familiarity and semiotic potency. It was not merely that Brillo pads were part of every household, as the Campbell's Soup can was part of every kitchen—the one item likely to be found in the barest cupboard, by contrast, say, with a can of artichoke hearts or of pickled quail's eggs—but beyond that, the cardboard container was ubiquitous, disposable and part of Americans' itinerant mode of life. It was the container of choice for shipping and storing books, dishes, clothing, or for bringing kittens home in. It was what everyone threw away.

Duchamp's gestures of 1913–17 were jokes. They were evidence that Art had evolved to a point where Anti-Art was his own doppelgänger. As part of Dada, the ready-made was a kind of thumbed nose at the pretentiousness of art in the scheme of exalted values that just happened to be responsible for World War I. But artistically, really, it was a snigger from the margins. With Warhol, the gesture was mainstream: This was what Art had evolved into by 1964, when his search reached its end. Moreover, it was a celebration rather than a criticism of contemporary life, which is partly why Warhol was so instantly popular. Everyone had been saying how awful contemporary culture was, and here was the most advanced artist of the time saying it was really wonderful—saying, as Warhol in effect did, "Hey, I like it here." Finally, it can be argued that the two moments of Duchamp and Warhol reverse the in-any-case arbitrary Marxian order—a farce the first time around, something deeper and more tragic the second.

There is a contingent of Brillo boxes at the great Warhol retrospective at the Museum of Modern Art in New York City (until May 2), and it was a joy to see them again after so many years. But I could not help but reflect, as I stood for a moment in contemplation (Aristotle is shown contemplating the bust of Homer, but Dante. . . .), how different it was to see them as part of an achieved corpus from what it had been to see them in 1964, when they defined the living edge of art history. I have the most vivid recollection of that show, and of the feeling of lightheartedness and delight people evinced as they marveled at the piles of boxes, laughing as they bought a few and carried them out in clear plastic bags. They didn't cost very much, and I believe it was part of Warhol's intention that it should be possible for people to own the art that so perfectly embodied the life it reflected: I bought one of the flower prints for $5 or $10 from a stack of them at Castelli's. (The opening night crowd at the retrospective evidently felt moved by this intention when they sought to walk away with some of the silver pillows that decorated MoMA's ceiling, to the consternation of the museum guards.)

Fascinated as he was by money, it must have shocked Warhol that his work became so pricey: The thought of a painting of Coca-Cola bottles going for $1.43 million at auction is a real-life cartoon, something that would have aroused some mild amusement had it been drawn for *The New Yorker* twenty years ago. Warhol was fairly tight, as might be expected of a Depression child, but he was not, like Dali, avid for dollars ("Salvador Dali = Avida Dollars" was the famous anagram). Arne Ekstrom once told me that he commissioned some art made with hat forms from a number of artists, and afterward decided to purchase some of the works. One artist, quite famous, wanted $5,000, a lot of money at the time. Warhol said he could have his for 2 cents, which he raised to 3 cents because of the arithmetic involved in paying his dealer a commission. (He cashed the check.)

For many of us, the excitement of the current Warhol show is in part the memory of the excitement of seeing the artist's amazing career unfold from exhibit to exhibit through the 1960s and 1970s. In compensation, seeing it all spread before us, synchronically, as it were, one has available the priceless gift of retrospection, through which we can see where Warhol was heading—invisible, of course, until he got there. I particularly cherish, for example, the fascinating transitional pieces from the early 1960s, such as the Dick Tracy paintings, in which there is a powerful tension between style and subject. There are unmistakable comic-strip personages, down to the word-balloons, but the hard commercial-style drawing wars with the Expressionist paint, as the commonplace imagery wars with the high romanticism of Expressionist art. Everyone is familiar with the story about Warhol showing Emile de Antonio two Coca-Cola bottles, one done in the flat laconic manner of the newspaper graphic, the other in the flamboyant brushy style, and asking which road he should follow when he had already, by presenting that choice, taken the road to Pop. Dick Tracy, like Warhol's Popeye or Nancy or Superman, belongs to that wonderful period of 1957–64, in which Art was putting aside his romantic phase and entering his minimalist-conceptual-philosophical phase. The Dick Tracy paintings belonged to a future no one could know about when they were shown, and experiencing them today is something like walking through one of those late Romanesque churches, like St. Severin in Paris—that church the Cubists so loved—built at a time when architects were evolving a still-not-well-understood Gothic style.

There is a further compensation. At the opening I had a moment's conversation with a young critic, Deborah Solomon. She expressed the view that Warhol had peaked in the early 1960s, precisely in the Dick Tracy paintings and their peers. I responded that Warhol always peaked, but on reflection it occurred to me that she was privileged in a way I was not, to be able to see Dick Tracy as a painting rather than as a transitional document, and hence aesthetically rather than historically. This show gives us perhaps our first glimpse of Warhol as an artist, and for the first time a perspective on his work is opened up from the standpoint of the future, so that we can see it as we see, for example, the work of the Impressionists or the Sienese masters. The organizers of this exhibition are displaying Warhol as if he had already passed the test of time, as he must have to the sensibility of young people who address his work simply as work.

In truth, I am not certain that I know what it is to view Warhol's creations disinterestedly and from across an aesthetic distance. Nor do I know to what degree an artist so vehemently part of the consciousness of his own time can be detached from that consciousness and held up for critical scrutiny. Lately, art historians have been seeking to restore the Impressionists to their own temporal situation, as if they have so completely stood the test of time that we can no longer see the life to which they were responsive and are blind to the deep human content of their work. The question for me is to what degree it is even possible to see Warhol now in the tenseless light of pure art. And this raises the further question of whether, when there is no longer an audience that shares beforehand the images that compose these works from the 1960s, that is in effect a community *because* it shares those images as part of itself, there really will be much left of the power of the work.

What Warhol had not computed into his fifteen minutes of fame was the curatorial obligation to regard artworks as eternal objects, subject to a timeless delectation. Warhol enjoyed making "time capsules," sweeping up into cardboard cartons the ephemera and detritus of common life. But really, his whole output is a kind of time capsule precisely because of those features that set it apart from the impulses of Dada, especially the celebration of the commonplace. How will all this be perceived when the commonplace is no longer commonplace — when the Brillo people, as they are certain to do, change the design of the packaging? Suppose the old familiar Brillo cartons get to be collector's items and a market emerges for unopened cartons with their original scouring pads intact. Or that corrugated paper becomes a camp item in its own right, like bakelite, the technology of packing having moved on to generalized bubble wraps with little stickers to identify content.

Warhol said, "The Pop artist did images that anybody walking down Broadway could recognize in a split second . . . all the great modern things that the Abstract Expressionists tried so hard not to notice at all." But privileging the commonplace depends upon its being ubiquitous, so that only an absolute stranger would not know what, if an image, it is an image of. All Warhol's images in the early works were of this order, and part of the pleasure of his art is in having these utterly banal forms lifted out of the plane of daily intercourse and elevated to the status of art, a kind of revolutionary reversal. The thought of the Brillo box in the art gallery connects with the American ideal of people in high places being still just folks (cf. Barbara Bush). But not only are these images instantly identified; they condense the whole emotional tone of life, of the consciousness in which those who know them participate. A person who has to have Marilyn — or Jackie or Elvis or Liz or Superman — identified is an outsider. Those faces belong with the Campbell's Soup label, the S&H Green Stamps, or Mona Lisa, since everyone knows her. But what happens when there is not this split-second recognition? Was Troy Donahue really the kind of icon Marilyn Monroe was? One panics in front of one of Warhol's iterated portraits of a man nobody knows, thinking one should know him when he was in fact selected for his anonymity. And how many, really, recognize Ethel Scull on sight? I think eventually people competed to be portrayed by Warhol because that appeared to give them an instant immortality, of the sort usually enjoyed only by the greatest of stars or the most celebrated products, as if they were also part of the common consciousness of the time.

The work from the 1980s is less complex from this point of view. It really does become, more or less, just art, connected to the culture only through being done by Warhol, who had by then become as much an icon or superstar as anyone he ever portrayed. When his *Last Supper* was displayed in Milan, in a kind of citywide two-man show with Leonardo, 30,000 people flocked to see it, hardly any of whom went on to see the "other" *Last Supper*. Perhaps, then, these late works can be viewed, even now, merely as art. But Warhol's greatest works come from the time when the boundaries between art and life were being exploded, everything was being redrawn and we were all living in history instead of looking backward at what had been history. The late work escapes me, but here is a prediction: When the final multivolume *Popular History of Art* is published, ours will be the Age of Warhol—an unlikely giant, but a giant nonetheless.

PAUL KRASSNER

Abbie

May 8, 1989

Paul Krassner, a founder of the Yippies, edits *The Realist*.

On April 14, the Los Angeles City Council voted unanimously to adjourn in memory of Abbie Hoffman. America's most prominent radical would have appreciated the irony of that gesture. Indeed, the title of his first book, *Revolution for the Hell of It* (1968) positively sparkled with irony. Although his style was wildly theatrical, he was earnestly committed to fighting dehumanization. As a charismatic organizer of the Youth International Party (Yippies), he articulated the consciousness of a counterculture that realized that the ultimate extension of arresting kids for smoking marijuana in this country was dropping napalm on other kids in Southeast Asia.

In 1967, Abbie imagined a sexual equivalent to MACE, the tear gas, which he christened LACE, ostensibly a combination of LSD and the transmission agent DMSO. When applied to the skin LACE would be absorbed into the bloodstream and serve as an instant aphrodisiac. The press was invited to his apartment to observe LACE in action. He wanted me to be there as a reporter who would "accidentally" be sprayed with LACE from a water pistol. I was then to take off my clothes and start making out with a lovely redhead who also had been "inadvertently" sprayed, along with another, deliberately sprayed couple, right there in the living room, while the journalists took notes.

But there was a scheduling conflict. On that same day, I was slated to speak at a literary conference at the University of Iowa. So instead Abbie assigned me to purchase cornmeal, with which he planned to encircle the Pentagon in a pre-levitation rite. The novelist Robert Stone drove me to a farm in Iowa, where I duly requested some cornmeal to go. The farmer asked, "Coarse or fine?" I looked at Stone. He shrugged. "Since it's for a magic ritual," he said, "I would definitely recommend coarse." So I flew back east with a sack containing thirteen pounds of coarse cornmeal. And the guy who substituted for me in that well-covered encounter with the lovely redhead ended up living with her. Romance among the Yippies.

In the novel *Cards of Identity* by Nigel Dennis, a character states, "You are most yourself when you are trying not to be yourself." This was certainly true of Abbie Hoffman on the lam in the 1970s to avoid a fifteen-year-to-life sentence for a coke bust. Under the name Barry Freed he became an activist in environmental causes. He felt "like a hunted animal" but, with the aid of plastic surgery, managed to keep a high profile. In fact, one day, in separate stories in the same issue of his local newspaper in upstate New York, there were photos of both Abbie and Barry. While Abbie was a fugitive, Barry was being honored.

During those underground years, I remained in contact with Abbie. I saw him and Johanna Lawrenson, his "running mate," one Christmastime in San Francisco. He stood next to a Salvation Army Santa Claus on Broadway, rang his bell and urged unsuspecting passersby to drop some cash into Santa's cauldron. Then he proceeded to take the place of a barker in front of a strip joint. "Come on in," he yelled. "Whatever you want, we got. You want ladies with stretch marks? We got 'em here!" Abbie was driven to squeeze adventure out of every moment.

I saw him in Washington at Jimmy Carter's inauguration. We were standing just a few yards away as the new President and his wife walked hand in hand down the street. "Hey, Jimmy!" Abbie shouted, knowing his voice was overwhelmed by the cheering of the crowd along the sidewalk. "Hey, Jimmy! Why don'tcha gimme a pardon as your first act in office?" Who could have dreamed that a decade later Abbie would be joining Amy Carter and about 200 other students protesting C.I.A. recruitment at the University of Massachusetts? Later he told her father of that inaugural scene. "I would've pardoned you," the former chief executive responded.

The last time I saw Abbie was in Chicago at a three-day conference last summer, celebrating the twentieth anniversary of the mass protest against the Democratic Convention. It was held in the same amphitheater that Hubert Humphrey was nominated in as skulls were smashed by billy clubs on Michigan Avenue and protesters chanted "The whole world is watching!" As I gave my talk, I couldn't help but notice that Abbie was sitting exactly where Mayor Richard Daley had sat and screamed obscenities at Senator Abraham Ribicoff for trying to call attention to what would later be officially labeled in the Kerner commission report "a police riot."

Abbie followed me to the stage and declared: "I believe that what happened here in the streets of Chicago energized [the nation], went beyond the left, cracked the barrier that the media had placed around how it covered the antiwar movement, how it covered Vietnam, and reached into the hearts and souls of Americans—in particular, Americans who were fighting in Vietnam." He said that of all the people he had met in the past twenty years, he was most touched by "soldiers who were in Vietnam, who were not privileged to attend all the conferences where the 'isms' debated the 'wasms' about whether we should go this way or that way in terms of revolutionary theory as defined by Marx or Mao or Bakunin or Avakian or J. Edgar Hoover." But these soldiers were well aware, he said, that "their contemporaries . . . [were taking] risks to go against the war machine."

It is hard to believe that Abbie committed suicide—especially so late in the day that he missed *The New York Times*'s deadline. But the autopsy report indicated that he had taken more than 150 phenobarbital capsules and drunk alcohol. I remember a conversation with him while he was working on his book opposing compulsory drug testing, *Steal This Urine Test*; he poked fun at Robert McFarlane, who during the Iran/*contra* investigations had feebly attempted suicide by downing "just a few measly tranquilizers."

It was during the trial of Oliver North that Abbie Hoffman died at age 52. By contrast, he shines with incredible brightness as a *real* national hero and, in death, revives the spirit of community that he inspired in life.

MEREDITH TAX

March to a Crossroads on Abortion   *May 8, 1989*

Writer Meredith Tax reported from Washington, D.C. on the largest abortion rights march in American history. *The Nation* has championed reproductive rights since 1918, when Oswald Garrision Villard became editor. In the 1920s, editor Freda Kirchwey wrote editorials advocating women's right to a planned pregnancy and the distribution of birth-control information. In 1932 the magazine published a special issue on birth control (Margaret Sanger contributed a piece on "The Pope's Position on Birth Control"), and in 1937 *The Nation* celebrated the legalization of the dissemination of birth-control information in the U.S. with a cover story, "Birth Control Wins."

I marched for abortion rights on April 9 with two high-school freshmen — my daughter Corey with her friend Kate — both so wide-eyed and excited they didn't even complain about being hungry. But of course, as Corey kept saying, she has been going on abortion marches since she was 3. That was the year of the Hyde amendment, which restricted public funding for abortions. She's 14 now; her whole life has been punctuated by this fight.

Though the end's not in sight, I think April 9 will prove to be a crossroads in this long struggle. Even if the Supreme Court does its damnedest, we know who we are now, and how strong. Many of us worried about the yuppies, fearing that, since they've always had abortion rights, they wouldn't know enough to fight for them until it was too late. We're not worried anymore. Half the people at this march must have been under 35. Three hundred thousand, six hundred thousand — after a certain number, who can count? The crowd was so thick I couldn't beat my way through it or find anyone I was looking for — but what a treat to go to a demonstration where I knew hardly a soul!

They came from everywhere: whole delegations from Texas and Maine and California; from Carleton College and Brandeis University and the University of Kentucky. Wisconsin and Vermont ran out of buses and couldn't meet the demand. There were lots of mother-daughter teams, and lots of men.

The spirit was calm determination, for the most part, with a little ferocity on the part of some, like the women who run the Dallas abortion clinic that supported the original Jane Roe suit; they wore cowboy hats with wire hangers stuck through them and carried a list of Operation Rescuers who've been busted. They are really on the line down there; Roe had her house shot at just the other day. It's war in Florida too; two clinics were torched the day of the demonstration, and doctors who perform abortions are regularly denied hospital privileges.

But after this march, there can be no doubt who's in the mainstream on this issue. I have never seen so many straight-looking people in one place in my life, let alone in a demonstration. This must have been the first march for an awful lot of them. Ann Snitow, who organized the No More Nice Girls delegation (they dressed in black and in chains, and were "pregnant" with pillow bellies) said, "It was the heartland — family and Kalamazoo and union. It was the solid Protestant core of America, who really do believe in individual rights and don't want anybody messing with theirs!"

It was a tolerant march, welcoming to difference. Despite the National Organization for Women's plea to wear virginal white like the suffragists (most of whom had other women do their laundry), nobody looked askance at the outlandish outfits of No More Nice Girls or the two punks in kilts with Vaselined hair who marched near us. Many people carried prefab pro-choice signs, but there were plenty of homemade ones, ranging from "There are More of Us Than You Think in Orange County" to "Equality, Planning, and Choice" to "Free Women, Free Bodies." There was the young man with his "Men Who Will Not Take Responsibility for Birth Control Should Fuck Themselves" and the two women proclaiming they were "Mormons for Choice." The latter would "probably be kicked out of the church by sundown," muttered Linda Nochlin, marching near me.

Everywhere people pushed strollers with placards declaring the occupants to be wanted babies. The delegation from the AIDS Coalition to Unleash Power bopped by in a conga line chanting, "Keep abortion safe and legal. Act up! Fight back!" The group from "Jane" got its own special cheers. Jane was the women's liberation abortion network in Chicago in the days of clandestinity, as they say in Latin America. You would call a number, ask for Jane and be passed along until you finally made contact with an abortionist. Jane's sign read, "We did it before, we can do it again."

It was a united march, with no separate agendas for once. This unity has been a long time coming, and the lack of it has hurt us. Of course, the main reason we are teetering on the brink of losing abortion rights is the right-wing offensive of the past twelve years, with church and state tripping over each other in their hurry to crush women. But we have had weaknesses—in the women's movement, the abortion rights movement and on the left—and we are paying for them.

The women's movement, having won the right to abortion, immediately demobilized. The left-wing women's organizations had begun to disintegrate by the mid-1970s and were in no shape to fight the right-to-lifers' onslaught when it began. Meanwhile, NOW singlemindedly pursued the Equal Rights Amendment and refused to work on anything else (or in coalition with anybody else) until 1985. Only with the defeat of the E.R.A. did NOW begin to understand that it must fight the right-wing backlash on a wider battlefield. Its 1986 march on Washington for abortion rights attracted 125,000 and was the largest pro-choice action up to that time. But 1986 was already late in the game, and the conservatives had the advantage of momentum.

One of the few women's groups that developed a strategy to meet the changing situation was the New York City-based Committee for Abortion Rights and Against Sterilization Abuse (Carasa). Its newly revised pamphlet, "Women Under Attack" (South End Press), provides a concise and readable account of the backlash and of other developments. Carasa developed a strategy of linking abortion rights and sterilization abuse as "two sides of the same coin, since poor women, denied funding for abortion [by the 1977 Hyde amendment], might be coerced into sterilization, which, by contrast, was funded 90 percent by the government." By making this link, Carasa and the reproductive rights groups that united with it in a national network tried to build unity across race and class lines, the lack of which "had been one of the failings of the family limitation movement."

This is an understatement. For years before the passage of the Hyde amendment, the National Abortion Rights Action League (Naral), as well as Planned Parenthood, had asked for support on the ground that giving women abortion rights would cost less money than supporting welfare babies. No wonder black activists saw a genocidal thrust in such campaigns for choice.

Carasa and its sister groups put abortion rights in the context of a program of reproductive freedom, which comprised a broad list of demands, including funding for the medical care and social services necessary to support poor women's right to have children. Struggling to redefine the problem in those terms, the reproductive rights groups gradually moved mainstream organizations like Naral away from population control rhetoric toward recognition of women's need for a wide range of reproductive choices. Without this change in the abortion rights movement, subsequent shifts in the black movement, reflected in the 1988 Jesse Jackson campaign's support of women's right to choose, would not have been possible.

Jackson was responding to the fact that poor women and women of color demand abortion rights: Poor women have already lost Medicaid funding in many states, and they and their children are most at risk if abortion is plunged into illegality. His presence on the speaker's platform, and the absence of population control slogans at the march, are signs that the movement has matured enough to see that unity is critical, despite the demise of many of the reproductive rights groups that originally fostered it. There were more women of color at this demonstration than at any other abortion march I have been in; many of them were teenagers.

Though the attack on women's liberation has been one of the most pronounced features of the conservative backlash, the left has not in general taken women's issues as its own, and it has been relaxed in its defense of abortion rights. Writers like Christopher Lasch and Jean Bethke Elshtain prefer to defend the family, attributing its disintegration to female selfishness and the power of the women's movement. (If the women's movement had that kind of power, we wouldn't have to worry about losing abortion rights.) Some coalitions have been willing to include demands for reproductive rights on their solidarity leaflets, but much of the left still sees women as just another special-interest group to be mollified or sacrificed as advantage dictates.

A recent example is Christopher Hitchens's column in the April 24 *Nation*, in which he criticizes feminists as proponents of "disposable fetuses" and, with sweet trust in the state, proposes that "we" address abortion in terms of social needs rather than individual rights. This is to be done via a National Health Service that will give free birth control and prenatal care. (Is it possible that he thinks he is the first person to propose this, and has done so little homework that he is ignorant of the work of the feminist health movement?)

I don't know what benign state Hitchens is talking about; it can't be the one I live in. As for utopian fantasy, mine does not include handing over the rights to my body to any state. As a woman, I can no more afford to feel Hitchens's contempt for what he calls " 'Me Decade' possessive individualism" than can the millions of Soviet citizens who want *glasnost*. Hitchens is one more example of the striking fact that men who can eloquently defend the individual right to free speech, as he did in the case of Salman Rushdie, can be completely out to lunch when it comes to women's individual rights—to the point where they can't even see the intimate connection between the right to free speech and the right to birth control and abortion, intertwined in the history of this country.

The right-to-lifers are more up-front; even while they use the language of social needs, their hatred and fear of women is plain on their faces. The last time I made an open-air speech on abortion, a right-to-lifer came up afterward, her fists clenched with the effort not to hit me, her mouth so contorted with rage she could barely speak. "People like you should be boiled alive in oil," she hissed. Rage like this does not spring from compassion. Despite the disclaimers of *The Village Voice*'s Nat Hentoff, the Berrigans and others who give the antiabortion movement its left cover, the motor power of this campaign is not love or compassion but rage—the rage of the repressed, who think sex is sin and must be punished. "Doesn't want a baby? She should have thought of that when she had her fun!" Such is the common coin of street-level right-to-lifers.

This is why it is so necessary to keep affirming the sexual aspect of the abortion issue and not let it dissolve into mainstream mush or let the issue be defined in terms of the extremes of rape and incest. Most women who get pregnant do so because of voluntary sex; and we cannot afford to abandon the hard-won ground of women's right to sexual pleasure and autonomy. On the other hand, we have to realize how temporary and fragile this right is without the social backups— health care, housing, day care, a decent income, all the rest—necessary to permit women a true choice, not only to have abortions but to have children, in the confidence that they can provide for them well.

The most radical slogan of all may still be the simple one: A woman has the right to a life. One of the women who came to the march was Kitty; ten years ago she was a high-school student in Somerville, Massachusetts. Born into poverty, brought up in the projects, she got pregnant at 15 like her sisters before her. But her teacher was in the women's movement and took her to have an abortion. Kitty now has a husband, a job and two kids she planned, unlike her sisters, one of whom had three kids before she was 17; the other recently died of AIDS. "That abortion gave me a life," Kitty says.

Abortion is as fundamental to women's liberation as is the right to work and it should be as central to any left-wing program. Full citizenship—the ability to participate in political movements, to work in the wage economy, to have an independent life—is impossible when a woman is a slave to her own fertility, trapped in an endless, unwilled round of pregnancy after pregnancy, exhausted by childbearing and child care, old at 35. Technological progress is never without ambiguity, but twentieth-century advances in fertility control have laid the basis for a new level of female participation in politics, society, culture and the work force. April 9 demonstrated that the strength of the women's movement is still growing and is largely untapped.

Sometimes I think of women's oppression as an enormous boulder that we are slowly pushing up a steep mountain. Most generations can push it only an inch. Weak generations, or those that hit a rock, may let it slip, and a few million women are crushed. Fortunate generations like mine may get up enough momentum or be helped by favorable terrain enough to go two inches instead of one.

The long escalator that carried us from the subway to the buses following the march brought this mountain image to mind. Laden with hundreds of women, it lumbered at a forty-five-degree angle toward daylight. Suddenly, I saw the faces of the women at the top light up, and as they began to cheer and wave I looked behind me and saw an endless, Dantesque stream of women, moving steadily out of the Metro and onto the platform, while other trains bearing more thousands were backed up behind, hidden in the shadow of the tunnel.

Tears came to my eyes, and I thought, What power. If only we used it more often. But we don't know how. Then I looked at my daughter and the other young girls around me and realized we don't have to figure that out alone anymore. A new generation is coming of age, our children, whose historical experience is different from ours; they can take up where we leave off. Together we can keep the boulder from slipping down and crushing those beneath. I think we can even push it a few more inches up the mountain.

ALICE WALKER

The Right to Life: What Can the White Man . . . Say to the Black Woman?   *May 22, 1989*

Alice Walker is the author of *The Temple of My Familiar*, *The Color Purple* and many other books.

> What is of use in these words I offer in memory and recognition of our common mother. And to my daughter.

What can the white man say to the black woman?

For four hundred years he ruled over the black woman's womb.

Let us be clear. In the barracoons and along the slave shipping coasts of Africa, for more than twenty generations, it was he who dashed our babies' brains out against the rocks.

What can the white man say to the black woman?

For four hundred years he determined which black woman's children would live or die.

Let it be remembered. It was he who placed our children on the auction block in cities all across the eastern half of what is now the United States, and listened to and watched them beg for their mothers' arms, before being sold to the highest bidder and dragged away.

What can the white man say to the black woman?

We remember that Fannie Lou Hamer, a poor sharecropper on a Mississippi plantation, was one of twenty-one children; and that on plantations across the South black women often had twelve, fifteen, twenty children. Like their enslaved mothers and grandmothers before them, these black women were sacrificed to the profit the white man could make from harnessing their bodies and their children's bodies to the cotton gin.

What can the white man say to the black woman?

We see him lined up on Saturday nights, century after century, to make the black mother, who must sell her body to feed her children, go down on her knees to him.

Let us take note:

He has not cared for a single one of the dark children in his midst, over hundreds of years.

Where are the children of the Cherokee, my great grandmother's people?
Gone.
Where are the children of the Blackfoot?
Gone.
Where are the children of the Lakota?
Gone.
Of the Cheyenne?
Of the Chippewa?
Of the Iroquois?
Of the Sioux?
Of the Mandinka?
Of the Ibo?
Of the Ashanti?
Where are the children of the "Slave Coast" and Wounded Knee?

We do not forget the forced sterilizations and forced starvations on the reservations, here as in South Africa. Nor do we forget the smallpox-infested blankets Indian children were given by the Great White Fathers of the United States government.

What has the white man to say to the black woman?

When we have children you do everything in your power to make them feel unwanted from the moment they are born. You send them to fight and kill other dark mothers' children around the world. You shove them onto public highways in the path of oncoming cars. You shove their heads through plate glass windows. You string them up and you string them out.

What has the white man to say to the black woman?

From the beginning, you have treated all dark children with absolute hatred.

Thirty million African children died on the way to the Americas, where nothing awaited them but endless toil and the crack of a bullwhip. They died of a lack of food, of lack of movement in the holds of ships. Of lack of friends and relatives. They died of depression, bewilderment and fear.

What has the white man to say to the black woman?

Let us look around us: Let us look at the world the white man has made for the black woman and her children.

It is a world in which the black woman is still forced to provide cheap labor, in the form of children, for the factories and on the assembly lines of the white man.

It is a world into which the white man dumps every foul, person-annulling drug he smuggles into creation.

It is a world where many of our babies die at birth, or later of malnutrition, and where many more grow up to live lives of such misery they are forced to choose death by their own hands.

What has the white man to say to the black woman, and to all women and children everywhere?

Let us consider the depletion of the ozone; let us consider homelessness and the nuclear peril; let us consider the destruction of the rain forests—in the name of the almighty hamburger. Let us consider the poisoned apples and the poisoned water and the poisoned air and the poisoned earth.

And that all of our children, because of the white man's assault on the planet, have a possibility of death by cancer in their almost immediate future.

What has the white, male lawgiver to say to any of us? To those of us who love life too much to willingly bring more children into a world saturated with death?

Abortion, for many women, is more than an experience of suffering beyond anything most men will ever know; it is an act of mercy, and an act of self-defense.

To make abortion illegal again is to sentence millions of women and children to miserable lives and even more miserable deaths.

Given his history, in relation to us, I think the white man should be ashamed to attempt to speak for the unborn children of the black woman. To force us to have children for him to ridicule, drug and turn into killers and homeless wanderers is a testament to his hypocrisy.

What can the white man say to the black woman?

Only one thing that the black woman might hear.

Yes, indeed, the white man can say, Your children have the right to life. Therefore I will call back from the dead those 30 million who were tossed overboard during the centuries of the slave trade. And the other millions who died in my cotton fields and hanging from my trees.

I will recall all those who died of broken hearts and broken spirits, under the insult of segregation.

I will raise up all the mothers who died exhausted after birthing twenty-one children to work sunup to sundown on my plantation. I will restore to full health all those who perished for lack of food, shelter, sunlight, and love; and from my inability to see them as human beings.

But I will go even further:

I will tell you, black woman, that I wish to be forgiven the sins I commit daily against you and your children. For I know that until I treat your children with love, I can never be trusted by my own. Nor can I respect myself.

And I will free your children from insultingly high infant mortality rates, short life spans, horrible housing, lack of food, rampant ill health. I will liberate them from the ghetto. I will open wide the doors of all the schools and hospitals and businesses of society to your children. I will look at your children and see not a threat but a joy.

I will remove myself as an obstacle in the path that your children, against all odds, are making toward the light. I will not assassinate them for dreaming dreams and offering new visions of how to live. I will cease trying to lead your children, for I can see I have never understood where I was going. I will agree to sit quietly for a century or so, and meditate on this.

This is what the white man can say to the black woman.

We are listening.

RICHARD J. BARNET
Bush's Splendid Little War   *January 22, 1990*

Richard Barnet is a senior fellow at the Institute for Policy Studies in Washington, D.C. and the author of *The Alliance*, *Real Security*, *The Giants* and, most recently, *The Rockets' Red Glare*.

It was a made-to-order occasion for muscle flexing: a central-casting villain, with a weakness for drugs, voodoo, pornography and pictures of Hitler, who made clumsy threats and shed American blood; a relatively low-cost military operation to convince taxpayers that the $300 billion military budgets of recent years actually buy something you can use; a military victory for a comander in chief who is still suspected of wimpishness; and a glorious moment in the war against drugs— Bush finally got his man.

At any time in the 1980s the U.S. invasion of Panama would have looked like a throwback to the era of gunboat diplomacy. But as 1989, that extraordinary year, was about to be added to the history books, this unilateral use of force without even the fig leaf of legality that Ronald Reagan's spin doctors contrived for the Grenada invasion struck a defiantly anachronistic note. Shelling civilian neighborhoods in search of the thug who was once a prize asset of the Central Intelligence Agency was not without historical precedent, but in the revolutionary year just ended the whirlwind invasion collided head-on with the fresh breezes of peaceful change and democracy blowing in from across the Atlantic.

In 1989 people in Eastern Europe, in an extraordinary display of the courage of nonviolence, threw off the shackles of repressive rule. Even as talk of secession spread within the Soviet Union, Mikhail Gorbachev sent no tanks to what used to be called its satellites. In this historic moment President Bush restored "peace and democracy" in the so-called U.S. backyard by shedding blood—at least twenty-four American soldiers and hundreds of Panamanian civilians died—all the while disregarding the world's opposition to the action.

Nineteen eighty-nine, like 1789, 1917, 1968 and other evocative dates of modern history, will be remembered because millions of people acted in ways that transformed the way we look at politics. In 1989 the myth on which Jeane Kirkpatrick built a second career—that Communist governments cannot be reformed or overthrown by their people—was confirmed as mere right-wing ideology. But the Bush Administration, while celebrating the democratic revolution in Eastern Europe, had so little faith in the people of Panama that it installed the elected government at gunpoint. In the process it made clear, as it had in the Philippines when U.S. planes scared off the plotters against Corazon Aquino, that the government was utterly dependent on American military power. It may be true, as news reports suggest, that all Panamanians except Noriega's henchmen are elated at being in U.S. receivership, but the memory of the invasion will feed anti-Americanism all over Latin America long after the former U.S. protégé is forgotten.

Members of Congress applauded this latest presidential war or elected to remain silent. Only Charles Rangel, Ted Weiss, Don Edwards and a few others dared to act like legislators and raise some of the legal, moral and practical objections that the news media almost totally ignored.

The network pundits and most editorial writers accepted Bush's premises justifying the Crusade for a Democratic and Drug-Free Hemisphere. The press told the American people once again that their nation was "standing tall," but the rest of the world believes that the spasm of violence in Panama indicates the reverse. The invasion did not impress the industrial nations with whom the United States will have to conduct its most important negotiations in the 1990s; the invasion was a show of impotence. Unable to use its still-considerable political and economic power in the hemisphere to get rid of a clever, outrageous con artist, the United States stages a blunderbuss attack with a heavy loss of civilian lives and property. Still remarkably passive and indecisive about the future arms levels and military arrangements it would like to see or about the future of Europe over which the nation fought two world wars, President Bush committed the power of the United States to a non-solution of a third-order problem. Even Richard Nixon thought it would have been better to let Noriega fall of his own weight.

This latest splendid little war will not help the United States in the crucial negotiations over the future of Europe that lie ahead. Gorbachev is struggling to redefine the meaning of being a great power; he understands that the basis of security in the 1990s is a strong economy and a productive and engaged society invigorated by democratic institutions. As the new decade opens it is not clear that he will succeed in making such a transition. The use of force by the United States is ammunition for the old-line Stalinist thinkers who believe that Soviet restraint feeds imperialist appetites. For twenty years the United States has been urging new rules of the game to limit superpower interventions. Improved relations between the United States and the Soviet Union appeared to herald at least the beginning of a new understanding that military interventions, including arms sales to warring Third World nations, produced more costs than benefits. The invasion was a blow to all this. Having taken on the responsibility, in the tradition of Woodrow Wilson, to teach the Panamanians to "elect good men," the United States is now stuck with policing the country. After spending billions in the 1980s on military operations in Central America, the United States is increasingly mired in a region that is a shambles.

But the greatest blows have been struck against the spirit of the new age waiting to be born. In Eastern Europe and in the Soviet Union millions of people risked their lives for an idea — the rule of law. No man or woman could be free if government was run at the whim of one man and his cronies. While people were dying for this principle in Rumania, the nation that was once the symbol of modern democracy violated its own Constitution as well as international law. The strictures against unilateral intervention enshrined in U.S. treaties, including the United Nations Charter, are the supreme law of the land, according to our Constitution. Scarcely a bow was made to Congress's war-making powers. The Speaker of the House was informed, not consulted, less than three hours before the invasion began. The provisions in the Panama Canal treaty specifying that U.S. intervention is permitted only when the operation of the canal is endangered were ignored, for no evidence that the canal was threatened was presented.

In Communist countries governments were swept away because entrenched party bosses had destroyed the last shreds of legitimacy; their lies fed popular rage. People went into the streets because they could not stand to see their own histories disappear into the mists of Orwellian propaganda or to lose all touch with truth. Selling the operation in Panama required not just the usual bodyguard of lies but the proclamation of an imperial world view to a world that is moving toward the rejection of imperialism. The lawyerly lie that the United States was engaged in "self-defense" against Panama, the suggestion that the United States has a writ to avenge on American life by risking the lives of thousands more, and the fantasy that this burst of war will make a dent in the drug problem undermine the credibility, the power and the security of the United States.

Behind the hollow rhetoric used to justify the invasion is a President stung by the charge of having been outwitted by a tinhorn dictator. Like Lyndon Johnson, George Bush has let a personal obsession dictate American foreign policy. Anthony Eden's obsession with Gamal Abdel Nasser in the 1950s led to the disastrous invasion of Suez and marked the end of the British Empire. It is characteristic of aging empires to act out the obsessions of frustrated leaders, but the historical precedents suggest that this is not a good way to arrest the processes of decline. In 1989 the United States missed the chance to show the world that it too understands the changed nature of national security. In the 1990s a nation cannot be strong by preparing for or fighting wars, even small ones, but by building a productive economy and democratic institutions grounded in law and respect for truth.

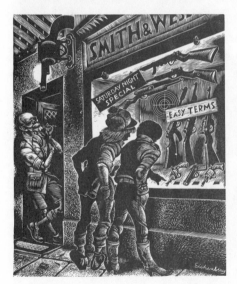

FRITZ EICHENBERG: *Woodcuts (1930-1980)*

Poetry

D.H. LAWRENCE

Bare Almond Trees

October 10, 1923

D. H. Lawrence's poems "Bare Almond Trees," "Tropic," "Peace" and "Humming-Bird" covered a full page of the "Fall Book Section" on October 10, 1923.

Wet almond trees, in the rain
Like iron sticking grimly out of earth;
Black almond trunks, in the rain
Like iron implements twisted, hideous, out of the earth,
Out of the deep, soft fledge of Sicilian winter-green
Earth-grass uneatable,
Almond trunks curving blackly, iron-dark, climbing the slopes.

Almond tree, beneath the terrace rail,
Black, rusted, iron trunk
You have welded your thin stems finer,
Like steel, like sensitive steel in the air;
Gray, lavender, sensitive steel, curving thinly and brittly up in a parabola.

What are you doing in the December rain?
Have you a strange electric sensitiveness in your steel tips?
Do you feel the air for electric influences
Like some strange magnetic apparatus?

Do you take in messages, in some strange code,
 From heaven's wolfish, wandering electricity, that prowls so constantly round
    Etna?
Do you take the whisper of sulphur from the air?
Do you hear the chemical accents of the sun?
Do you telephone the roar of the waters-over-the-earth?
And from all this, do you make calculations?

Sicily, December's Sicily in a mass of rain
With iron branching blackly, rusted like old, twisted implements
And brandishing and stooping over earth's wintry fledge, climbing the slopes
Of uneatable soft green!

ROBERT FROST

The Bear

April 18, 1928

Robert Frost's book of poetry *West-Running Brook* was published in 1928, the year this poem appeared in *The Nation*.

The bear puts both arms round the tree above her
And draws it down as if it were a lover
And its choke-cherries lips to kiss goodby,
Then lets it snap back upright in the sky.
Her next step rocks a boulder on the wall.
(She's making her cross-country in the fall.)
Her great weight creaks the barbed wire in its staples
As she flings over and off down through the maples,
Leaving on one wire tooth a lock of hair.
Such is the uncaged progress of the bear.
The world has room to make a bear feel free.
The universe seems cramped to you and me.
Man acts more like the poor bear in a cage
That all day fights a nervous inward rage,
His mood rejecting all his mind suggests.
He paces back and forth and never rests
The toe-nail click and shuffle of his feet,
The telescope at one end of his beat,
And at the other end the microscope,
Two instruments of nearly equal hope,
And in conjunction giving quite a spread.
Or if he rests from scientific tread,
'Tis only to sit back and sway his head
Through ninety-odd degrees of arc it seems,
Between two metaphysical extremes.
He sits back on his fundamental butt
With lifted snout and eyes (if any) shut
(He almost looks religious but he's not),
And back and forth he sways from cheek to cheek,
At one extreme agreeing with one Greek,
At the other agreeing with another Greek,
Which may be thought but only so to speak.
A baggy figure equally pathetic
When sedentary and when peripatetic.

EMILY DICKINSON

Four Poems

Emily Dickinson (1830–1886) published only seven poems in
her lifetime. She is thought to have composed the poems on this
page c. 1862–66. They were to appear in *Further Poems of
Emily Dickinson* (1929), edited by her niece, Martha Gilbert
Dickinson Bianchi.

Revolution is the pod
Systems rattle from;
When the winds of
Will are stirred,
Excellent is bloom.

But except its russet
Base
Every summer be
The entomber of itself;
So of Liberty.

Left inactive on the
Stalk,
All its purple fled,
Revolution shakes it
For
Test if it be dead.

There is a pain so utter
It swallows Being up,
Then covers the abyss with trance
So memory can step
Around, across, upon it,
As One within a swoon
Goes steady, when an open eye
Would drop him bone by bone.

I took one draught of life,
I'll tell you what I paid,
Precisely an existence —
The market price, they said.

They weighed me, dust by dust,
They balanced film with film,
Then handed me my being's worth —
A single dram of Heaven.

Color, Caste, Denomination —
These are Time's affair,
Death's division classifying
Does not know they are.

As in sleep — all here forgotten,
Tenets put behind,
Death's large democratic fingers
Rub away the brand.

If Circassian — He is careless —
If He put away
Chrysalis of Blonde or Umber,
Equal butterfly —

They emerge from His obscuring,
What Death knows so well,
Our minuter intuitions
Deem incredible.

FEDERICO GARCIA LORCA

Song of the Little Death

November 28, 1936

The Spanish dramatist and poet Federico Garcia Lorca was shot
by Franco's forces at the outbreak of the Spanish civil war in
1936, the year this poem was published in the magazine.

Mortal lunar meadow
And blood under the ground.
Ancient bloody meadow.

Yesterday, tomorrow.
Mortal grassy heaven.
Light and sandy darkness.

There I met with Death.
Mortal earthy meadow.
Tiny little Death.

The dog on the roof top.
And my lonely left hand
Crossing endless forests
Where the flowers wither.

Cathedral of the ashes.
Light and sandy darkness.
Tiny little Death.

Death and I, a man.
A man alone with her,
Tiny little Death.

Mortal lunar meadow.
The snow heaped high and sifted
Across the very doorway.

A man, and what? I told you,
A man alone with her.
Love, light, and sand, and meadow.

(Translated by Rolfe Humphries)

LOUISE BOGAN

The Dream

February 12, 1938

The Nation published several poems in the twenties, thirties and
forties by Louise Bogan, the poet, editor and critic.

O God, in the dream the terrible horse began
To paw at the air, and make for me with its blows.
Fear kept for thirty-five years poured through its mane,
And retribution equally old, or nearly, breathed through its nose.

Coward complete
I lay and wept on the ground,
When some strong creature appeared, and leapt for the rein.
Another woman, as I lay half in a swound,
Leapt in the air, and clutched at the leather and chain.

Give him, she said, something of yours as a charm.
Throw him, she said, some poor thing which you alone claim.
No, no, I wept. He hates me. He's out for harm,
And whether I yield or not, it is all the same.

But, like a lion in a legend, when I flung the glove
Pulled from my sweating, my cold right hand,
The terrible beast, that no one may understand,
Came to my side, and put down his head in love.

W.B. YEATS

Long-Legged Fly

April 15, 1939

On April 15, 1939, three months after the sudden death of William Butler Yeats, this poem was published in the magazine. It subsequently appeared in *Last Poems, 1936–1939*.

That civilization may not sink
Its great battle lost,
Quiet the dog, tether the pony
To a distant post.
Our master Caesar is in the tent
Where the maps are spread,
His eyes fixed upon nothing,
A hand under his head.

Like a long-legged fly upon the stream
His mind moves upon silence.

That the topless towers be burnt
And men recall that face,
Move most gently if move you must
In this lonely place.
She thinks, part woman, three parts a child,
That nobody looks; her feet
Practice a tinker shuffle
Picked up on the street.

Like a long-legged fly upon the stream
Her mind moves upon silence.

That girls at puberty may find
The first Adam in their thought,
Shut the door of the Pope's Chapel,
Keep those children out.
There on that scaffolding reclines
Michael Angelo.
With no more sound than the mice make
His hand moves to and fro.

Like a long-legged fly upon the stream
His mind moves upon silence.

WALLACE STEVENS

On an Old Horn

September 30, 1939

These poems by Wallace Stevens and W.H. Auden were among seven selected by poet John Berryman for the September 30, 1939 Issue, and published under the heading "Autumn Miscellany."

I

The bird kept saying that birds had once been men,
Or were to be, animals with men's eyes,
Men fat as feathers, misers counting breaths,
Women of a melancholy one could sing.
Then the bird from his ruddy belly blew
A trumpet round the trees. Could one say that it was
A baby with the tail of a rat?
                                  The stones
Were violet, yellow, purple, pink. The grass
Of the iris bore white blooms. The bird then boomed.
Could one say that he sang the colors in the stones,
False as the mind, instead of the fragrance, warm
With sun?
              In the little of his voice, or the like,
Or less, he found a man, or more, against
Calamity, proclaimed himself, was proclaimed.

II

If the stars that move together as one, disband,
Flying like insects of fire in a cavern of night,
Pipperoo, pippera, pipperum . . . The rest is rot.

W.H. AUDEN

Matthew Arnold

September 30, 1939

His gift knew what he was—a dark disordered city;
Doubt hid it from the father's fond chastising sky,
Where once the mother-farms had glowed protectively
Spread the haphazard alleys of the neighbors' pity.

Yet would have gladly lived in him and learned his ways,
And grown observant like a beggar, and become
Familiar with each square and boulevard and slum,
And found in the disorder a whole world to praise.

But all his homeless reverence, revolted, cried:
"I am my father's forum, and he shall be heard;
Nothing shall contradict his holy final word,
Nothing." And thrust his gift in prison till it died.

And left him nothing but a jailor's voice and face,
And all rang hollow but the clear denunciation
Of a gregarious optimistic generation
That saw itself already in a father's place.

CARL SANDBURG

Memory

February 10, 1940

Carl Sandburg's poem was published in *The Nation*'s seventy-fifth anniversary issue. In 1940, Sandburg received his second Pulitzer prize for the last of six volumes of his biography of Abraham Lincoln.

Memory is when you look back
And the answers float in
to who? what? when? where?

The members who were there then
are repeated on a screen
are recalled on a scroll
are moved in a miniature drama,
are collected and recollected
for actions, speeches, silences,
set forth by images of the mind
and made in a mingling mist
to do again and to do over
precisely what they did do once—
this is memory—
sometimes slurred and blurred—
this is remembering—
sometimes wrecking the images
and proceeding again to reconstruct
what happened and how,
the many little involved answers
to who? what? when? where?
and more involved than any
      How? how?

MARIANNE MOORE

The Mind Is an Enchanting Thing

December 18, 1943

In 1952, Marianne Moore received the Bollingen Prize for poetry and the Pulitzer Prize for her *Collected Poems*.

is an enchanted thing
   like the glaze on a
katydid-wing
       subdivided by sun
       till the nettings are legion.
Like Gieseking playing Scarlatti;

like the apteryx-awl
   as a beak, or the
kiwi's rain-shawl
       of haired feathers, the mind
       feeling its way as though blind,
walks along with its eyes on the ground.

It has memory's ear
   that can hear without
having to hear.
       Like the gyroscope's fall,
       truly unequivocal
because trued by regnant certainty,

it is a power of
   strong enchantment. It
is like the dove-
       neck animated by
       sun; it is memory's eye;
it's conscientious inconsistency.

It tears off the veil, tears
   the temptation, the
mist the heart wears,
       from its eyes—if the heart
       has a face; it takes apart
dejection. It's fire in the dove-neck's

iridescence; in the
inconsistencies
of Scarlatti.
Unconfusion submits
its confusion to proof; it's
not a Herod's oath that cannot change.

ROBERT LOWELL

The Death of the Sheriff

August 3, 1946

This poem by Robert Lowell is from *Lord Weary's Castle*, for
which he received a Pulitzer Prize in 1947.

> *"forsitan et Priami fuerint quae fata, requiras?"*

I
NOLI ME TANGERE

We park and stare. A full sky of the stars
Wheels from the pumpkin setting of the moon
And sparks the windows of the yellow farm
Where the red-flannelled madmen look through bars
At windmills thrashing snowflakes by an arm
Of the Atlantic. Soon
The undertaker who collects antiques
Will let his motor idle at the door
And set his pine-box on the parlor floor.
Our homicidal sheriff howled for weeks;

We kiss. The State had reasons: on the whole,
It acted out of kindness when it locked
Its servant in this place and had him watched
Until an ordered darkness left his soul
A *tabula rasa*; when the Angel knocked
The sheriff laid his notched
Revolver on the table for the guest.
Night draws us closer in its bearskin wrap
And our loved sightless smother feels the tap
Of the blind stars descending to the west

To lay the Devil in the pit our hands
Are draining like a windmill. Who'll atone
For the unsearchable quicksilver heart
Where spiders stare their eyes out at their own
Spitting and knotted likeness? We must start:
Our aunt, his mother, stands
Singing *O Rock of Ages*, as the light

Wanderers show a man with a white cane
Who comes to take the coffin in his wain,
The thirsty Dipper on the arc of night.

II
THE PORTRAIT

The whiskey circulates, until I smash
The candelabrum from the mantel-top,
And scorch Poseidon on the panel where
He forks the blocks of Troy into the air.
A chipmunk shucks the strychnine in a cup;
The popping pine-cones flash
Like shore-bait on his face in oils. My bile
Rises, and beads of perspiration swell
To flies and splash the *Parmachenie Belle*
That I am scraping with my uncle's file.

I try the barb upon a pencilled line
Of Vergil. Nothing underneath the sun
Has bettered, Uncle, since the scaffolds flamed
On butchered Troy until Aeneas shamed
White Helen on her hams by Vesta's shrine . . .
All that the Greeks have won
I'll cancel with a sidestroke of my sword;
Now I can let my father, wife and son
Banquet Apollo for Laomedon:
Helen will satiate the fire, my Lord.

I search the starlight . . . Helen will appear,
Pura per noctem in luce . . . I am chilled,
I drop the barbless fly into my purse
Beside his nickel shield. It is God's curse,
God's, that has purpled Lucifer with fear
And burning. God has willed;
I lift the window. Digging has begun,
The hill road sparkles, and the mourners' cars
Wheel with the whited sepulchres of stars
To light the worldly dead-march of the sun.

RANDALL JARRELL

A Game at Salzburg

January 1, 1949

Randall Jarrell was acting literary editor of *The Nation* in 1946.
This is one of five poems published by Jarrell in *The Nation* between November 1, 1947, and June 16, 1951.

A little ragged girl, our ball-boy;
A partner — ex-Afrika-Korps —
In khaki shorts, P.W. illegible.
(He said: "To have been a prisoner of war
In Colorado is a *privilege.*")
The evergreens, concessions, carousels,
And D.P. camp of Franz Joseph Park;
A gray-green river, evergreen-dark hills.
Last, a long way off in the sky,
Snow-mountains.

Over this clouds come, a darkness falls,
Rain falls.
        On the veranda Romana,
A girl of three,
Sits licking sherbet from a wooden spoon;
I am already through.
She says to me, softly: *Hier bin i'.*
I answer: *Da bist du.*

I bicycle home in my raincoat
Through the ponchos and pigtails of the streets,
Bathe, dress, go down four flights of stairs
Past Maria Theresa's sleigh
To the path to the garden, walk along the lake
And kick up, dreamily, the yellow leaves
Of the lindens; the pigeons are cooing
In the morning-glories of the gardener's house,
A dragonfly comes in from the lake.
The nymphs look down with the faces of Negroes,
Pocked, moled with moss;
The stone horse has sunk in marsh to his shoulders.

But the sun comes out, and the sky
Is for an instant the first rain-washed blue
Of becoming: and my look falls
Through falling leaves, through the statues'
Broken, encircling arms
To the lives of the withered grass,
To the drops the sun drinks up like dew.
Life, life everywhere.
In anguish, in expectant acceptance,
The world whispers: *Hier bin i'*.

WALLACE STEVENS

The Plain Sense of Things

December 6, 1952

Wallace Stevens won *The Nation*'s poetry prize in 1936 for his
poem, "The Men That Are Falling."

After the leaves have fallen, we return
To a plain sense of things. It is as if
We had come to an end of the imagination,
Inanimate in an inert savoir.

It is difficult even to choose the adjective
For this blank cold, this sadness without cause.
The great structure has become a minor house.
No turban walks across the lessened floors.

The greenhouse never so badly needed paint.
The chimney is fifty years old and slants to one side.
A fantastic effort has failed, a repetition
In a repetitiousness of men and flies.

Yet the absence of the imagination had
Itself to be imagined. The great pond,
The plain sense of it, without reflections, leaves,
Mud, water like dirty glass, expressing silence

Of a sort, silence of a rat come out to see,
The great pond and its waste of the lilies, all this
Had to be imagined as an inevitable knowledge,
Required, as a necessity requires.

LAWRENCE FERLINGHETTI

What Happened the Day a Poet Was Appointed Postmaster

April 19, 1958

Lawrence Ferlinghetti co-founded City Lights Books in San Francisco. *Pictures of The Gone World* (1955) was the first book published under the City Lights imprint.

With violet pencils
he wrote upon the back side
of returned love letters and lost light years
readdressing them
to eternity

Their cancelled postage stamps
wheeled away on round postmarks
and flew off like flying saucers
marked Moscow Los Angeles and New York

The moon turned to tenements
for lack of lovers

And a cancelled George Washington
flew over America

WILLIAM CARLOS WILLIAMS

A Brueghel Nativity

May 31, 1958

Williams's long poem *Paterson* was originally published in five
separate books between 1946 and 1958. This poem is from
Paterson V.

        Peter Brueghel, the elder, painted
a Nativity, painted a Baby
new born!
among the words.
                      Armed men.
savagely armed men
                  armed with
pikes,
halberds and swords
whispering men with averted faces,
get to the heart
              of the matter
as they talked to the pot bellied
greybeard (center)
the butt of their comments,
looking askance, showing their
amazement at the scene,
features like the more stupid
German soldiers of the late
war

—but the Baby (as from an
illustrated catalogue
in colors) lies naked on his Mother's
knees

—it is a scene, authentic
enough, to be witnessed frequently
among the poor (I salute
the man Brueghel who painted
what he saw —
           many times no doubt
among his own kids but not of course
in this setting)

The crowned and mitred heads
of the three men, one of them black,
who had come, obviously from afar
(highwaymen?)
by the rich robes
they had on—offered
to propitiate their gods

Their hands were loaded with gifts
—they had eyes for visions
in those days—and saw,
saw with their proper eyes,
these things
to the envy of the vulgar soldiery

He painted
the bustle of the scene,
the unkempt straggling
hair of the old man in the
middle, his sagging lips
— —incredulous
that there was so much fuss
about such a simple thing as a baby
born to an old man
out of a girl and a pretty girl
at that

But the gifts! (works of art,
where could they have picked
them up or more properly
have stolen them?)
—how else to honor
an old man or a woman?

—the soldiers' ragged clothes,
mouths open,
their knees and feet
broken from thirty years of
war, hard campaigns, their mouths
watering for the feast which
had been provided

Peter Brueghel the artist saw it
from the two sides: the
imagination must be served —
and he served
　　　　　dispassionately.

SYLVIA PLATH

Two Views of a Cadaver Room   *January 30, 1960*

"Two Views of a Cadaver Room" appeared in Sylvia Plath's first book of poems, *The Colossus*.

I

The day she visited the dissecting room
They had four men laid out, black as burnt turkey,
Already half unstrung. A vinegary fume
Of the death vats clung to them;
The white-smocked boys started working.
The head of his cadaver had caved in,
And she could scarcely make out anything
In that rubble of skull plates and old leather.
A sallow piece of string held it together.

In their jars the snail-nosed babies moon and glow.
He hands her the cut-out heart like a cracked heirloom.

II

In Breughel's panorama of smoke and slaughter
Two people only are blind to the carrion army:
He, afloat in the sea of her blue satin
Skirts, sings in the direction
Of her bare shoulder, while she bends,
Fingering a leaflet of music, over him,
Both of them deaf to the fiddle in the hands
Of the death's-head shadowing their song.
These Flemish lovers flourish; not for long.

Yet desolation, stalled in paint, spares the little country
Foolish, delicate, in the lower right hand corner.

ANNE SEXTON

The Starry Night

September 2, 1961

Anne Sexton received the Pulitzer Prize for poetry in 1967.

> "That does not keep me from having a terrible need
> of—shall I say the word—religion. Then I go out
> at night to paint the stars."
>
> VINCENT VAN GOGH
> *in a letter to his brother.*

The town does not exist
except where one black haired tree slips
up like a drowned woman into the hot sky.
The town is silent. The night boils with eleven stars.
Oh starry starry night! This is how
I want to die.

It moves. They are all alive.
Even the moon bulges in its orange irons
to push children, like a god, from its eye.
The old unseen serpent swallows up the stars.
Oh starry starry night! This is how
I want to die:

into the rushing beast of the night,
sucked up by that great dragon, to split
from my life with no flag,
no belly,
no cry.

LE ROI JONES

After the Ball

January 23, 1963

> Le Roi Jones, who changed his name in the late 1960s to Imamu
> Amiri Baraka, published his first book of poems, *Preface to a
> Twenty-Volume Suicide Note* in 1961.

The magic dance
of the second ave ladies,

    in the artificial glare
    of the world, silver-green curls sparkle
    and the ladies' arms jingle
    with new Fall pesos, sewn on grim bracelets
    the poet's mother-in-law thinks are swell.

    So much for America, let it sweep in grand style
up the avenues of its failure. Let it promenade smartly
beneath the marquees of its despair.
    Bells swing lazily in New Mexico
ghost towns. Where the wind celebrates
afternoon, and left over haunts stir a little
out of vague instinct,

    hanging their messy sheets
    in slow motion against the intrepid dust
    or the silence
      which they cannot scare.

ROBERT DUNCAN

Up Rising

September 13, 1965

Robert Duncan is the author of *Bending the Bow* (1968), *Roots and Branches* (1969) and *The Opening of the Field* (1973), among other books of poems.

Now Johnson would go up to join the great simulacra of men,
    Hitler and Stalin, to work his fame
    with planes roaring out from Guam over Asia,
all America become a sea of toiling men
    stirrd at his will, which would be a bloated thing,
    drawing from the underbelly of the nation
    such blood and dreams as swell the idiot psyche
    out of its courses into an elemental thing
    until his name stinks with burning meat and heapt honors

And men awake to see that they are used like things
    spent in a great hecatomb of youths, this Texas barbeque
        of Asia, Africa and all the Americas,
And the professional military behind him, thinking
    to use him as they thought to use Hitler
    without losing control of their business of war,

But the mania, the ravening eagle of America
    as Lawrence saw him "bird of men that are masters,
    Lifting the rabbit-blood of the myriads up into . . ."
    something terrible, gone beyond bounds, or
As Blake saw figures of fire and blood raging,
    . . . in what image? the ominous roar in the air,
the omnipotent wings, the all-American boy in the cockpit
    loosing his flow of napalm, below in the jungles
    "any life at all or sign of life" his target, drawing now
        not with crayons in his secret room
the burning of homes and the torture of mothers and fathers and children,
    their hair a-flame, screaming in agony, but
in the line of duty, for the might and enduring fame
    of Johnson, for the victory of American will over its victims,
releasing his store of destruction over the enemy,
in terror and hatred of all communal things, of communion,
    of communism;

has raised from the private rooms of small-town bosses and businessmen,
from the council chambers of the gangs that run the great cities,
        swollen with the votes of millions,
from the fearful hearts of good people in the suburbs turning the savory meat
    over the charcoal burners and heaping their barbeque plates with more
    than they can eat,
from the closed meeting-rooms of regents of universities and sessions of
    profiteers —

back of the scene: the atomic stockpile; the vials of synthesized diseases eager
    biologists have developed over half a century dreaming of the bodies of
    mothers and fathers and children and hated rivals swollen with new plagues,
    measles grown enormous, influenzas perfected; and the gasses of despair, con-
    fusion of the senses, mania, inducing terror of the universe, coma, existential
    wounds, that chemists we have met at cocktail parties, passt daily on the way
    to classes or work, have workt "to make wars too terrible for men to wage";

raised this secret entity of America's hatred of Europe, of Africa, of Asia,
the deep hatred for the old world that had driven him out,
and for the alien world, the new world about him, that might have been
    Paradise
but was before his eyes already cleard back in a holocaust of burning indians,
    trees and grasslands,
reduced to his real estate, his projects of exploitation and
        profitable wastes,

this specter that in the beginning Adams and Jefferson feard and knew
would corrupt the very body of the nation
        and all sense of our common humanity,
this black bile of old evils arisen anew,
takes over the vanity of Johnson;
and the very glint of Satan's eyes from the pit of the hell of America's
    unacknowledged, unrepented crimes that I saw in Goldwater's eyes
now shines from the eyes of the President
        in the swollen head of the nation.

ROBERT BLY

Johnson's Cabinet Watched by Ants *May 30, 1966*

This poem of opposition to the war in Vietnam, by Robert Bly, was published in *The Nation* in 1966 under the heading "Poetry of the Read-In Campaign."

As part of the continuing effort of the intellectual community to speak out on Vietnam, American writers have been appearing at group readings throughout the country in witness of their opposition to this war. Beginning with the first read-in at New York's Town Hall, these events soon spread to the campuses. Organized by a group of poets (Robert Bly, Galway Kinnell, David Ray) and student and faculty activists, read-ins have taken place at, among other institutions, Portland State, Harvard, Columbia, Cornell, Chicago, Reed, Wisconsin and Pennsylvania. In one ten-day period in May, a dozen read-ins took place in the East.

Although some question the effectiveness of the read-in as a protest gesture, there can be little question of the eagerness of a section of our leading writers to make public their position on Vietnam. Particularly the poets have responded virtually unanimously. Indeed, while local faculty members, prose writers and entertainers have also participated, to a great extent the heart of the read-in has been the poetry. A number of poets have managed to travel from one read-in to another. Among those who have participated are Paul Blackburn, Robert Bly, Robert Creeley, Alan Dugan, Lawrence Ferlinghetti, Edward Field, Anthony Hecht, George Hitchcock, X. S. Kennedy, Galway Kinnell, Stanley Kunitz, Denise Levertov, John Logan, Walter Lowenfels, Robert Lowell, David Ray, Vern Rutsala, Adrienne Rich, Muriel Rukeyser, Louis Simpson, William Stafford, George Starbuck and James Wright.

Not all the poems read are on political subjects. Some poets have chosen not to read from their own work at all, but from Thucydides, Walt Whitman, Rimbaud and even — with a terrifying aptness — from Hitler, Goebbels and the Japanese General Staff. But the situation in Vietnam — perhaps even the phenomenon of the read-in itself — is beginning to call forth its own poetry, and many poets for the first time in their careers, or after long silence, are striking what must be called a political note.

—ORIGINAL NOTE

I

It is a clearing deep in a forest. Overhanging boughs
Make a low place. Here the citizens we know during the day,
The ministers, the department heads,
Appear differently: the stockholders of large steel companies
In small wooden shoes: here are the generals dressed as gamboling lambs.

II

Tonight they burn the rice supplies; tomorrow
They lecture on Thoreau; tonight they move around the trees,
Tomorrow they pick the twigs from their clothes;
Tonight they throw the fire-bombs, tomorrow
They read The Declaration of Independence; tomorrow they are in church.

III

Ants are gathered around an old tree.
In a choir they sing, in harsh and gravelly voices
Old Etruscan songs on tyranny.
Toads nearby clap their small hands, and join
The fiery songs, their five long toes trembling in the soaked earth.

DENISE LEVERTOV

What Were They Like?
(questions and answers)

June 27, 1966

Denise Levertov was *The Nation*'s poetry editor in 1964.

1) Did the people of Viet Nam
   use lanterns of stone?
2) Did they hold ceremonies
   to reverence the opening of buds?
3) Were they inclined to rippling laughter?
4) Did they use bone and ivory,
   jade and silver, for ornament?
5) Had they an epic poem?
6) Did they distinguish between speech and singing?

1) Sir, their light hearts turned to stone.
   It is not remembered whether in gardens
   stone lanterns illumined pleasant ways.
2) Perhaps they gathered once to delight in blossom,
   but after the children were killed
   there were no more buds.
3) Sir, laughter is bitter to the burned mouth.
4) A dream ago, perhaps. Ornament is for joy.
   All the bones were charred.
5) It is not remembered. Remember,
   most were peasants; their life
   was in rice and bamboo.
   When peaceful clouds were reflected in the paddies
   and the water-buffalo stepped surely along terraces,
   maybe fathers told their sons old tales.
   When bombs smashed the mirrors
   there was time only to scream.
6) There is an echo yet, it is said,
   of their speech which was like a song.
   It is reported their singing resembled
   the flight of moths in moonlight.
   Who can say? It is silent now.

W.S. MERWIN

Gift

November 27, 1972

W. S. Merwin, a former poetry editor for *The Nation*, received
the Pulitzer Prize in 1971 for *The Carriers of Ladders*.

I have to trust what was given to me
if I am to trust anything
it led the stars over the shadowless mountain
what does it not remember in its night and silence
what does it not hope knowing itself no child of time

what did it not begin what will it not end
I have to hold it up in my hands as my ribs hold up my heart
I have to let it open its wings and fly among the gifts of the unknown

again in the mountain I have to turn
to the morning

I must be led by what was given to me
as streams are led by it
and braiding flights of birds
the gropings of veins the learning of plants
the thankful days
breath by breath

I call to it Nameless One O Invisible
O Untouchable O Free
I am nameless I am divided
I am invisible and untouchable
and empty
nomad live with me
be my eyes
my tongue and my hands
my sleep and my rising
out of chaos
come and be given

MARGARET ATWOOD

Marsh, Hawk

July 7, 1973

Margaret Atwood is the author of the novels *The Handmaid's Tale* and *Cat's Eye*, and several books of poems, including *The Circle Game* (1967) and *Power Politics* (1971).

Diseased or unwanted
trees, cut into pieces, thrown
away here, damp and soft in the sun, rotting and half-
covered with sand, burst truck
tires, abandoned, bottles and cans hit
with rocks or bullets, a mass grave,
someone made it, it spreads on the
land like a bruise and we stand on it, vantage
point, looking out over the marsh.

Expanse of green
reeds, patches of water, shapes
just out of reach of the eyes,
the wind moves, moves it and it
eludes us, it is full
daylight. From the places
we can't see the guttural swamp voices
impenetrable, not human,
utter their one-note
syllables, boring and
significant as oracles and quickly over.

It will not answer, it will not
answer, though we hit
it with rocks, there is a splash, the wind
covers it over; but
intrusion is not what we want,

501

we want it to open, the marsh rushes
to bend aside, the water
to accept us, it is only
revelation, simple as the hawk
which lifts up now against
the sun and into
our eyes, wingspread and sharp call
filling the head / sky, this,

to immerse, to have it slide
through us, disappearance
of the skin, this is what we are looking for,
the way in.

ERNESTO CARDENAL

The Arrival

November 1, 1975

> Ernesto Cardenal's books of poetry include *Apocalypse and
> Other Poems* (translated by Thomas Merton and others), and
> *With Walker in Nicaragua and Other Early Poems* (translated
> by Jonathan Cohn). In 1979, Cardenal became minister of cul-
> ture in the Sandinista government.

We get off the plane and we go, Nicaraguans and foreigners,
all mixed together toward the huge building all lit up—first stop
Immigration and Customs—and as we approach, passports in hand,
I think of how proud I am to be holding
the passport of my socialist country, and of my satisfaction
in arriving in a Socialist Nicaragua. "Comrade"
they will say to me—a revolutionary comrade welcomed
by the revolutionary comrades of Immigration and Customs—
not that there aren't any controls; there ought to be controls
so that capitalism and Somozaism never come back—
and the emotion of coming back to my country in revolution
with more changes, I hear of more and more decrees
of expropriation, changes more and more radical,
many surprises in the short time one has been away
and I see joy in the eyes of everyone—those that have stayed,
the others have already gone—and now we go into the brightness
and they ask nationals and foreigners for their passports . . .
but it was all a dream and I am in Somoza's Nicaragua
and they take my passport from me with the icy courtesy
with which Security would say to me: "Do come in"
and they take it inside and they don't bring it back (they surely
must surely be telephoning to Security
to the Presidential Palace or to somebody or other) and by now
all the passengers are gone and I don't know if they're going to arrest me
but no: at the end of an hour they come back with my passport,
the CIA probably knew that this time I didn't go to Cuba
and that I was just a single day in East Berlin
and so at last I can go through Customs
all alone in Customs with my old suitcase
and the kid that inspects just pretends to inspect
without inspecting anything and he murmurs to me: "Father"

and he doesn't dig down into the suitcase where he would find
the phonograph record with Allende's last appeal to the people
from the Palace, interrupted by the noise of bombs going off,
the record I bought in East Berlin, or Fidel's speech
about Allende's overthrow, the one that Sergio gave me,
and the kid says: "It's eight o'clock already and we haven't eaten,
we Customs workers get hungry, too"
"What time do you have supper?" I asked "Not until after the last plane lands"
and now I am moving towards the dark demolished city
where eveything is just the same and nothing happens but I have seen
his eyes and with his eyes he has said to me: "Comrade."

(Translated from the Spanish by Donald D. Walsh)

JAMES WRIGHT

To a Blossoming Pear Tree

October 18, 1975

James Wright was awarded the Pulitzer Prize in 1972 for his
Collected Poems.

Beautiful natural blossoms,
Pure delicate body,
You stand without trembling.
Little mist of fallen starlight,
Perfect, beyond my reach,
How I envy you.
For if you could only listen,
I would tell you something,
Something human.

An old man
Appeared to me once
In the unendurable snow.
He had a singe of white
Beard on his face.
He paused on a street in Minneapolis
And stroked my face.
Give it to me, he begged,
I'll pay you anything.

I flinched. Both terrified,
We slunk away,
Each in his own way dodging
The cruel darts of the cold.

Beautiful natural blossoms,
How could you possibly
Worry or bother or care
About the ashamed, hopeless
Old man? He was so near death
He was willing to take
Any love he could get,
Even at the risk
Of some mocking policeman

Or some cute young wiseacre
Smashing his dentures,
Perhaps leading him on
To a dark place and there
Kicking him in his dead groin
Just for the fun of it.

Young tree, unburdened
By anything but your beautiful
natural
    blossoms
And dew, the dark
Blood in my body drags me
Down with my brother
In pain.

MAY SWENSON

Teeth

May Swenson received the Bollingen Prize for poetry in 1981.
She is the author of *In Other Words: New Poems (1987)*.

Teeth are so touchy. They're part of your skeleton.
Laid out on the dentist's couch, you're being strummed.
Still vibrant. For how long? You're shown an X-ray

of the future: how the lower jaw has wandered away
into a neighbor's lot. The fillings glitter,
but it's glowworm's work by now.

A skull white as enamel,
the fontanelle's fine stitchery can be admired.
Does it remember being covered

with scraggly hair, like a coconut?
Bald as a baby, and with one wide bucktooth left,
you have the upturned grin of a carefree clown.

So you drool and spit up. That's only
temporary. There'll be just one big cavity soon.
You'll be dry—yes, dry as a bone.

OCTAVIO PAZ

Nightfall

June 23, 1979

Octavio Paz, a Mexican diplomat, writer and poet, is the author
of many books of poems, including *Configurations* (1971) and
The Bow and the Lyre (1973).

What sustains it,
The half-open
Clarity of nightfall,
The light let loose in the gardens?

All the branches,
Conquered by the weight of birds,
Lean toward the darkness.

Pure, self-absorbed moments
Still gleam
On the fences.

Receiving night,
The groves become
Hushed fountains.

A bird falls,
The grass grows dark,
Edges blur, lime is black,
The world is less credible.

(Translated from the Spanish by Eliot Weinberger)

PABLO NERUDA

Injustice March 28, 1981

Pablo Neruda, the Chilean Nobel Laureate, died in 1973.

Whoever discovers who I am will find out who you are,
and the why, and the where.
Early on, I discovered the range of injustice.
Hunger was not just hunger,
but rather the measure of man.
Cold and wind were also measures.
The proud man racked up a hundred hungers, then fell.
Pedro was buried at the hundredth cold.
The poor house endured a continuous wind.
And I learned that centimeter and gram,
spoon and tongue, were measures of greed,
and that the harassed man soon fell
in a hole, and knew no more.
Nothing more. That was the setting,
the real gift, the reward, light, life.
That was it, suffering cold and hunger,
not having shoes, feeling fear
in front of the judge, in front of the other one,
the other being with his sword or his inkwell,
and so, digging and cutting,
sewing, making bread, planting wheat,
hammering every nail the wood needed,
burrowing in the earth as in intestines
to drag out, blind, the crackling coal
and, even more, going up rivers and mountains,
riding horses, tending to ships,
baking tiles, blowing glass, washing clothes
in such a way as to make that seem
a kingdom brought newly into being,
grapes shining in their clusters,
when a man set his mind on being content,
and was not, and was not so. I was discovering
the laws of misery,
the throne of bloodstained gold,

the whore freedom,
the land with no overcoat,
the wounded, worn-out heart,
and talk of the dead ones, tearless,
dry, like fallen stones.
And then I left off being a child
because I learned that for my people
life was not allowed
and the grave was forbidden to them.

(Translated from the Spanish by Alastair Reid)

JOSEPHINE JACOBSEN

Tears

April 4, 1981

This poem was included in Josephine Jacobsen's collection of poems, *The Chinese Insomniacs* (1981). Jacobsen was poetry consultant at the Library of Congress from 1971 to 1973.

Tears leave no mark on the soil
or pavement; certainly not in sand
or in any known rain forest.
Never a mark on stone.
You would think that no one in Persepolis
or Ur ever wept.

You would assume that, like Alice,
we would all be swimming, buffeted
in a tide of tears.
But they disappear. Their heat goes.
Yet the globe is salt
with that savor.

The animals want no part in this.
The hare both screams and weeps
at her death, one poet says.
The stag, at death, rolls round drops
down his muzzle; but he is in
Shakespeare's forest.

These cases are mythically rare.
No, it is the human being who persistently
weeps; in some countries, openly, in others, not.
Children who, even when frightened, weep most hopefully;
women, licensed weepers;
men, in secret, or childishly; or nobly.

Could tears not make up a sea of their mass?
It could be salt and wild enough;
it could rouse storms and sink ships,
erode, erode its shores:
tears of rage, of love, of torture,
of loss. Of loss.

Must you see the future
in order to weep? Or the past?
Is that why the animals
refuse to shed tears?
But what of the present, the tears of the present?
The awful relief, like breath

after strangling? The generosity
in the verb *to shed*?
They are a classless possession
yet not to be found in the museum
of even our greatest city.
Sometimes what was human, turns
into an animal, dry-eyed.

Afterword

[E]very publisher has regarded the responsibility
as a public trust.

—CAREY McWILLIAMS

On close inspection the political history of a magazine like *The Nation* has more zigs and zags than one might suppose. At the same time, its publishing history— the relationship between owner and editor, the money and the words—tends to be invisible, underestimated as a factor in making possible the astonishing assortment of cultural and political treasures found in the preceding pages.

Anyone who has ever set foot in the offices of *The Nation*, whether at 20 Vesey Street or 333 Sixth Avenue or its current address, 72 Fifth Avenue (note the creeping uptownism!) can attest that its trouble-making politics have at best been inconsistent, an ever-shifting battleground usually—but not always—involving the radicals and the liberals. But anyone who has read *The Gilded Age of Letters of E.L. Godkin*, by *The Nation*'s founding editor; *Fighting Years*, the autobiography of Oswald Garrison Villard, who presided over *The Nation* from 1918 until December 1932 and stayed with it until 1940; Sara Alpern's biography, *Freda Kirchwey: A Woman of the Nation* (editor from 1937 until 1955) or *The Education of Carey McWilliams* by Carey McWilliams (editor from 1955 to 1975); will also tell you that we are talking about a magazine that—despite occasional innocent claims to the contrary—lost money for virtually 125 years. The key to understanding such a magazine's ability to survive as a dissenting, independent, trouble-making, idea-launching journal of critical opinion while hundreds of others—some more targeted, others vastly richer and with the benefit of Wharton School number-crunchers—went under, lies in the often overlooked matter of the editor-publisher relationship.

Personally, I agree with Carey McWilliams, who wrote on the occasion of *The Nation*'s 100th anniversary that there is a thread of consistency which has run through the magazine down through the years, but that it has less to do with partisan politics or ideology than with "the moral view." Its consistency, in a word, is to be found in its

refusal to buy "the official line," in its insistence on the hard critical view, in its honesty and in its idealism. "There is no force so potent in politics as a moral issue," *The Nation* pointed out in an editorial of June 18, 1908. "Politicians may scorn it, ambitious men may despise it or fight shy of it, newspapers may caricature or misrepresent it; but it has a way of confounding the plans of those who pride themselves on their astuteness and rendering powerless the most formidable enginery of party or boss."

This anthology, then, is predicated on the refusal to concede that idealism is irrelevant, and on a 125-year-old business ethic which is a corollary of that impractical principle. Consider as Exhibit A the document by which Hamilton Fish III, publisher of *The Nation* from 1978 to 1987, turned over the business responsibility of *The Nation* to Arthur Carter on December 20, 1985 (Fish didn't step down as publisher until almost two years later). Carter, a self-made multimillionaire who had founded the investment banking firm which eventually evolved into Shearson Lehman Hutton, a maverick in his personal style, and founder of a quality country weekly, came to *The Nation* with a healthy respect for its heritage of independence, despite no prior history of involvement in *Nation* causes or left-liberal politics. Ponder the instrument, not to mention the consternation on the face of the lawyers who were asked to draw it up:

> Seller and buyer desire to preserve the character and tradition of *The Nation* magazine . . . as stated in its original prospectus in 1865, viz: *"The Nation* will not be the organ of any party, sect or body. It will, on the contrary, make an earnest effort to bring to the discussion of political and social questions a really critical spirit, and to wage war upon the vices of violence, exaggeration and misrepresentation by which so much of the political writing of the day is marred . . . "
>
> Seller and buyer share the belief that *The Nation* has survived as America's oldest continuously published weekly precisely because it has been a voice of opinion and dissent. As the Magazine's founding editor stated in 1967: "We profess to supply opinions exactly as we have formed them, and not in the shape in which they will be likely to please or encourage or console."

The agreement went on to spell out in quasi-legalese the pointedly held theory of the principals that editorial independence and sound business practice were interwoven ideas.

Arthur Carter, in this perspective, is the latest in an impressively short line of publishers who intuitively held (or went along with) the peculiar belief that the owner's job (where he/she is not the editor) is to protect the principle of editorial independence rather than to visit his/her own views on the publication; and that the measure of success is not financial performance.

Looking backwards, nothing could have been clearer. Read again *The Nation*'s original prospectus—how it was not going to serve any sect, party or movement. The new weekly was going to be a conscience, a gadfly to "wage war upon the vices of . . . exaggeration and misrepresentation." The editorial formula— have the best thinkers of the day apply reason, logic, criticism, *moral* criticism, to the key problems of the day—entailed a business structure which would insulate these intellects from untoward interference. E.L. Godkin, the Anglo-Irish journalist who came to this country in 1856 had worked it all out. He had raised $100,000 in capital and signed on the elite and most thoughtful of the literary establishment, including Henry Wadsworth Longfellow, James Russell Lowell,

William James, Henry James, Henry Adams, and William Dean Howells. The first issue appeared on July 6, 1865 with a counter-trendy first sentence in its first story announcing, "The week has been singularly barren of exciting events." The subscriptions came pouring in. There seemed to be no stopping *The Nation*.

And then it was almost stopped. The largest single contributor to Godkin's $100,000 capital was the Boston abolitionist George Luther Stearns, a lead pipe manufacturer who supplied John Brown with the weapons that were used at Harper's Ferry. A second chunk of money had come from a Philadelphia group headed up by James Miller McKim, one of the founders of the American Anti-Slavery Society, who wanted to take up the cause of the newly emancipated slaves in the spirit of the great abolitionist William Lloyd Garrison's *The Liberator*, which went out of business when the Civil War was won. McKim was also looking for a job for his prospective son-in-law, the abolitionist's son, Wendell Phillips Garrison, who was made literary editor and invented the system of sending books out to reviewers with credentials relevant to the subject matter. Other monies had come from a Boston-based group affiliated with the Loyal Publication Society, which distributed broadsides on such subjects as Negro citizenship and financing the war, free of charge, to nearly 1,000 editors. It was a forerunner of the syndicated column, and also had an interest in dealing with the problems of the freedmen. Godkin's *Nation* went on to endorse the early Reconstruction program: the Freedman's Bureau, the Civil Rights Bill of 1866, the Reconstruction Acts of 1867 and the war amendments. But it balked at proselytizing on behalf of the radical reconstructionists, and even qualified its support for freedmen voting by proposing an education test for suffrage.

Stearns complained. The radical reconstructionist Wendell Phillips, in a speech before the Anti-Slavery Society in Boston, said, "look at this new journal, *The Nation*, which undertakes to represent these Freedman's Associations, and which all the subscribers of anti-slavery papers are advised to take instead of old anti-slavery journals. How uncertain its sound! How timid, vacillating, and noncommittal is its policy! . . . Are you willing such a neutral should represent us?"

Godkin, for his part, had more mundane matters to worry about. By the end of July 1865, circulation was up to 5,000 copies and forty new subscribers on average were coming in each day; but the magazine was losing nearly $5,000 a month and, as he saw it, his nearest competitor, *The Round Table*, benefitted by not having to concentrate primarily on the freedmen. "I am told," he wrote his Bostonian friend and *Nation* contributor Charles Eliot Norton, "they rely for success against us, on their freedom from any responsibility with regard to the Negro, and on being more sprightly." In another letter he added:

> When the editorship was offered me, I took it on the understanding, which was afterwards reduced to writing, that I was to be completely independent to any extent that an

honorable man could be. Of course, I could not call myself an honorable man, if, having been converted to proslaveryism or secession, I failed instantly to resign. But it was never understood or hinted that I was to be inspired by, or was to edit the paper under the supervision of Major Stearns, or of anybody else. . . . It was not to be a party paper. It was to devote a good deal of attention to the social and political condition of the blacks at the South, not as their organ, but as one of the great questions of the day. And it was to discuss this and all other questions in such a tone and style as to secure the attention of a class to which anti-slavery journals have never had access.

Godkin went on to say that he undertook to produce a paper that would be not a commercial success but one "whose influence on those who read it, and on the country papers, would be enlightening, elevating, and refining." He was concerned that *The Nation* was "degenerating into a mere canting organ of the radical wing, and argued that "too close identification with a factional or partisan cause was bad journalism as well as bad policy." When Stearns threatened to withdraw if Godkin didn't mend his ways, one Samuel G. Ward wrote Godkin that to make *The Nation*'s "assurance doubly sure," he would himself "take every share that had not been paid up," and he did so "on the spot." Whereupon with the help of Frederick Law Olmsted, architect of Central Park, who had put Godkin in touch with the money men in the first place, Godkin arranged for a new corporate structure which prevented anyone from telling him what to do.

Godkin was a Brahmin and his magazine gave voice to upper-middle-class protest — 'Brahmins from Boston to Brooklyn' as the historian William Armstrong wrote. "Beyond the Appalachians . . . his writ did not run." Godkin's *Nation* was pro-free trade (his backers were split on that too) and anti-imperialist, but it looked upon socialism as something to be stopped. "John Stuart Mill was our prophet," he wrote, "and Grote and Bentham were our daily food." It accepted the late-nineteenth-century synthesis of classical economics, Spencerian science and Protestant theology. As Margaret Marshall, literary editor in the 1940s, noted, "The great Godkin . . . allowed women to contribute to his paper, but opposed giving them the vote." His *Nation* attacked the trust and the railroad barons, but he was suspicious of labor, calling the striking Pullman railroad workers "Debs' Desperadoes." By 1880 he published an article on "The White Side of the Southern Question." He seemed oblivious to the fundamental changes wrought by the industrial revolution. His main preoccupation was civic reform — Boss Tweedism replaced racism as *The Nation*'s most covered subject — which caused one wag to dub *The Nation* "The Weekly Day of Judgement." The *Springfield Republican* wrote that Godkin's *Nation* functions "as a sort of moral policeman of our society, our politics, and our art . . . " In politics, he became a neo-mugwump, bolting from the Republican Party to support Grover Cleveland in the 1884 presidential campaign.

Yet, as William James wrote, "To my generation, Godkin was certainly the towering influence in all thought concerning public affairs, and indirectly his influence has certainly been more pervasive than that of any other writer of the generation, for he influenced other writers who never quoted him, and determined the whole current of discussion." Godkin's *Nation* is more quoted in the histories of the period than any other contemporary periodical. But his most admirable characteristic, as I.F. Stone has pointed out, was his independence. Don't forget he took the name *The Nation* (rather than the more passive "union") from a Dublin weekly described as "remarkable for its talent, for its seditious tendencies, and for the fire and spirit of its political poetry." His legacy had less to do with radical or even liberal politics than with journalistic integrity.

In 1881, when the railroad magnate Henry Villard purchased the *New York Evening Post* and offered him a job, Godkin built an editorially independent *Nation* into the deal. Villard, by the account of his son Oswald Garrison Villard, "gave his majority stockholding to my mother [a daughter of Lloyd Garrison] and then trusteed it, giving complete power to three trustees" in order that no one should say that the *Post* or *The Nation* "was dominated by a Wall Street man and also to assure to the editors their complete independence." Godkin turned over *The Nation*'s daily editorial chores to Wendell Phillips Garrison, Villard's brother-in-law. Oswald Garrison Villard, who had begun writing for the *Nation* in 1894, became a *Nation* editorial writer and president of The Nation Company in 1908, and took over as editor in 1918.

From 1881 to 1918, *The Nation* was an insert in or a weekly supplement to the *New York Evening Post*, and like Rip Van Winkle, it went to sleep. While the arrangement guaranteed the magazine's survival and Henry Villard's trust protected its editorial independence, it snoozed in the shadow of the daily paper. It reprinted Godkin's *Post* editorials, and became more a book review than anything else. Its subscriber circulation shrank to a few thousand, and after the retirement of Wendell Phillips Garrison it had a quick succession of editors. When Garrison was ready to retire, his idea was that *The Nation* should die because he could think of nobody "fit to carry it on who would respect it and its traditions." When Villard mentioned the name of Hammond Lamont, Garrison changed his mind—but alas, the talented Lamont died, during what had been expected to be a minor operation on his jaw, less than three years after becoming *The Nation*'s editor. His successor, beginning in May 1909, was Paul Elmer More.

Under More (1909–1914), a Sanskrit scholar, *The Nation* described itself as an "organ of thinking people, the exponent of sane progress, of wise conservatism." But even in these years of confused political identity, the editors cherished the magazine's high standards. Paul Elmer More's biographer, Arthur Dakin, wrote that "his intellectual conscience was as formidable a thing as were the religious consciences of his New England ancestors." He seemed, however, more interested in his own literary essays than in the magazine—but not so much that he didn't find time to write a trusted friend, "I am very much afraid (this, of course, is entirely *entre nous*) that Villard's influence will cheapen *The Nation* and deprive it of its unique quality." After More came Harold deWolf Fuller, whom Oswald Garrison Villard considered a "very dull person . . . stubbornly narrow [and] utterly unyielding in his prejudices."

H.L. Mencken captured this interlude in the magazine's history best when he wrote in the *Baltimore Sun* that "*The Nation*, since the passing of Godkin, had been gradually dying. It was, perhaps, the dullest publication of any sort ever printed in the world. Its content consisted on the one hand, of long editorials reprinted from the *Evening Post*, and on the other hand, of appalling literary essays by such pundits as Paul Elmer More. Villard, when he took it over, threw out the garbage and started printing the truth. The effect was instantaneous. His circulation increased four or five-fold in a few months." Actually, circulation jumped from 7,200 in 1918 to 38,087 by 1920.

As editor, of course, Villard was able to finesse any potential editor-owner tension by inheriting the thing. As he wrote some years later in 1937, "if the ownership and editorship of a journal can be combined it is by all odds the best arrangement. That was my fortunate situation from 1918 to 1932. Indeed, I have been favored beyond most journalists in that in all my forty years in newspapers I have never had to take orders from anybody . . . " Even Villard had to buttress his financial resources, diminished by the post-World War I depression, so he created a Nation Foundation, asking influential friends to help underwrite expenses, hoping the magazine would break even in three years—the perpetual optimist. Actually, life for Villard the editor-publisher wasn't all that tranquil. One scholar observed that had Villard—one part patrician, one part social reformer, by conviction a pacifist, by temperament a fighter—been less divided against himself, "*The Nation* from 1918 to 1933 might have been more consistent; but it is difficult to believe that it would have been equally interesting." As the irrepressible Heywood Broun put it in his weekly column, "Oswald Garrison Villard is the product of an interesting experiment. His grandfather was an abolitionist and his father a railroad magnate. As far as the researches of science have gone, the rule seems to be that when you cross abolitionist blood and railroad stock you get a liberal." But Villard was no ordinary liberal. If Godkin's legacy was the politics of mugwumpery and the journalism of social and moral responsibility, Villard's was the politics of lost causes and the journalism of the crusader.

Villard was a believer in non-violence, but was the sort of militant pacifist who could write that "President McKinley ought to have been shot with his entire cabinet for putting us into an unnecessary war with Spain." He was a founder of the anti-imperialist league and a friend of civil rights; his *Nation* fought for the formation of the NAACP in the summer of 1905, the release of conscientious objectors after World War I, an executive pardon for the unjustly jailed labor organizer, Tom Mooney, and a new trial for Sacco and Vanzetti; and his 1927 editorial ("A Decent Respect for the Opinions of Mankind") helped radicalize a young Bostonian named James Storrow, Jr. who thirty-eight years later became publisher of *The Nation*. Under Villard *The Nation* was staunch in its attack on the extension of the Monroe Doctrine to justify U.S. imperialism in Latin America, opposed the "theft" of the Panama Canal and the plan to annex Hawaii, and supported independence for the Philippines and self-determination for the Irish. It was against conscription on the eve of World War I, which Villard regarded as a war between rival imperial powers, and "The Madness at Versailles" in the war's aftermath. The thousands of cancellations which came in the wake of *The Nation*'s anti-war stance were recouped only when the postmaster seized as seditious the September 14, 1918 issue of the magazine because he objected to an editorial by Albert J. Nock criticizing the government's choice of American Federation of Labor president Samuel Gompers—who had "held labor in line" in deference to wartime patriotism—to report on labor conditions abroad. (Villard put the advertising value of the seizure at over $100,000.)

One of Villard's most successful innovations was a fortnightly sixteen-page "International Relations Section," which would print original documents. As Managing Editor Lewis Gannett recalled, the *[New York] Times* and the other papers were killing off Lenin and Trotsky and crushing the Russian revolution three times a week," but *The Nation* had its own reports. It was, for example, the first to print the new Soviet Constitution, among other scoops. Of the Bolsheviks, however, Villard had few illusions, writing that "with all their desire for peace, justice, liberty, and equality for a nation of workers, [they] offer side by side with tremendous benefits, the methods of a Caesar, a Cromwell, a Franz Joseph, a Nicholas, a Mussolini." He came to regard Stalin and Hitler as rival dictators and thought we should butt out.

Villard's improvisory style and willingness to back up his editorial instincts with his pocketbook—albeit in the non-extravagant style that has become *The Nation*'s trademark—may be gathered from his January 5, 1928 wire to Carleton Beals: "CAN YOU PROCEED IMMEDIATELY NICARAGUA FOR NATION SENDING EXCLUSIVE STORIES AMERICAN POLICY MARINE RULE POPULAR FEELING ETCETERA, REACHING SANDINO IF POSSIBLE. TRIP POSSIBLY OCCUPY A MONTH. CAN OFFER A HUNDRED A WEEK AND EXPENSES. WIRE COLLECT." The exclusive interview with Sandino, leader of the revolt against U.S. domination in that small country, and the series which grew out of it was reprinted worldwide (although not in Nicaragua). And reviewing *The Nation*'s lonely battle for justice in Haiti from 1915 on, Villard wrote: "I look back upon these crusades on behalf of our Caribbean neighbors with unbounded satisfaction. They also seem to me to have justified all the time and money I put into *The Nation*."

519

have backers, and since these backers are not in it for the money, they will periodically erupt over a matter of social policy. Thus it was that Francis Neilson—a former Canadian M.P., the husband of a meat-packing heiress, and a longtime patron of *The Nation*—came to feel that he had a call on its economics editorials. In addition to putting up $30,000 a year, Neilson was paying the salary of one of the magazine's more creative editors, Albert J. Nock. Not coincidentally, both of them were single-taxers. When Villard declined to endorse the single-tax—a formula aimed at eliminating land speculation and promoting economic equality—as the solution to the country's economic woes, Neilson withdrew his support and founded a new magazine, *The Freeman*, with Nock as its editor. The first issue appeared in the spring of 1920 and Villard welcomed it to the ranks of liberal journalism in an editorial, to which Nock quickly replied, "You make your appeal to the liberals; we make ours to the radicals."

In 1932, after nearly fifteen years, Villard retired as editor and put a committee of four (including Freda Kirchwey, thirty-nine years old) in charge, although he stayed on as majority owner and publisher. Meanwhile, the forces behind the rise of Hitler in Germany and the election of Franklin Delano Roosevelt in the U.S. had lent strength to *The Nation* as circulation hit 36,000. "Ironically, this brief and unwonted solvency almost wrecked the new set-up," Kirchwey later wrote in an unpublished memoir. "For Mr. Villard, who retained ownership, came within an ace of selling *The Nation*—with no warning to the board—to Raymond Moley who was looking for a political organ. The result was the resignation of two key editors . . . who concluded that if the penalty of success was the probable loss of one's job, it would be better to leave under one's own steam."

In 1934 Maurice Wertheim, an investment banker and longtime generous and non-interfering patron of the magazine, offered to buy it for $50,000, and Villard said no thanks. A year later, he was faced with a deficit, sons who had no interest in taking over, and estrangement from his editors over such matters as the extent of America's neutrality. When Wertheim again offered to buy the magazine—this time for $25,000—Villard accepted, with the understanding that Kirchwey would become the new editor and Villard would continue to write his weekly column, "Issues and Men.

Freda Kirchwey had spent virtually her entire working life at *The Nation*. She was a recent Barnard graduate (who had been voted "Most Famous in Future," "Best Looking" and "Most Militant") when she heard from a friend that there was an opening in the new International Relations Section, and wrote to her old economics professor Henry Raymond Mussey, a *Nation* editor, "If you think I'm the man for the job, will you put in a word for me?" She went on to become managing editor, literary editor, editor and, ultimately, publisher. She took a leadership role on issues such as sexual freedom, birth control, democracy vs. Fascism and Nazism, the Spanish civil war, pacifism and collective security, refugees,

McCarthyism and censorship, the peaceful employment of atomic energy, and Zionism. (After the war she went to Palestine as *The Nation*'s correspondent and her visit to Ein Hashofed, a kibbutz founded by Americans, turned up forty *Nation* readers.)

Wertheim and Kirchwey were good friends, and the magazine received a dividend during this period in the form of Maurice Wertheim's daughter Barbara (later Tuchman) who, still in her early twenties, reported for *The Nation* from Spain. But according to Kirchwey's notes at the time, Wertheim, "bound by an agreement guaranteeing complete editorial freedom . . . rapidly became worried and critical. Not to mention his growing hostility to the New Deal in general and his brother-in-law, the eminent Secretary of the Treasury [Henry Morgenthau] in particular." By early 1937 Maurice Wertheim was "fed up," his business partners had stopped talking to him and his annual loss was up to $35,000. When *The Nation* came out in favor of FDR's court packing plan he gave his ultimatum. He'd sell to Freda Kirchwey for $15,000 down and $15,000 later. She asked if she might have time to put together a syndicate and he said no, she could do it herself and let him know after the weekend or he would sell to the highest bidder.

What is remarkable is that here was a publisher who had an editorial disagreement with his editor, and instead of firing her or insisting that she follow his line or cajoling her, he first tried a modest end-run by putting people like Max Lerner on the payroll in the hopes that they would turn the magazine's pro-New Deal policy around; but when that didn't work—they all turned out to support it—he felt that the right thing to do where *The Nation* was concerned was to turn over the enterprise to its editor for a nominal sum. In the end, Wertheim's Civic Aid Foundation lent her the second $15,000. (And before he died he gave his three daughters one piece of advice: Never invest money in magazines. But two of them, Nan Werner and Jo Pomerance, ignored or overcame their father's warning and joined the consortium that Hamilton Fish put together in 1977 to purchase *The Nation* from James J. Storrow, Jr.)

It was perhaps inevitable—given Villard's volatile temperament and his strong anti-war, pro-neutralist position—that he and Kirchwey would quarrel. She started killing what she regarded as his more hysterical columns (one, anachronistically, seemed to say the Jews were behind the intervention movement). Eventually, Villard broke with *The Nation* over the issue which split the left-liberal community in the late thirties. As Norman put it in "The Pacifist's Dilemma," there were two total evils in the world—war and fascism—and it now began to seem, according to Thomas (and to Freda Kirchwey too, not incidentally), that "resolute and effective opposition to fascism means war."

"I have never been able to work happily with men or women who are incapable of hot indignation at something or other," Villard wrote in his memoir. "To minimize every evil is to my mind to condone it and in time to destroy one's influence."

Villard, ever faithful to his credo, did not go gently. On June 13, 1940, he wrote a letter to Freda Kirchwey:

> After reading your last two issues and particularly your coming out for universal military service, I want to notify you at once that I cannot continue to write for *The Nation* and I will wind up my connection of 46 years with a valedictory next week. It is, as you know, a complete and absolute break with all the traditions of *The Nation*, of which there is nothing left now but the name. Some day perhaps I shall have some explanation as to how Freda Kirchwey, a pacifist in the last war, keen to see through shams and hypocrisies, militant for the rights of minorities and the downtrodden, has now struck hands with all the forces of reaction against which *The Nation* has battled so strongly. There is now, of course, no reason for buying *The Nation* when one can read Walter Lippman, Dorothy Thompson, *The New York Times* or *The New York Herald Tribune*.
> . . . You have, according to my beliefs, prostituted *The Nation*, and I hope honestly that it will die very soon or fall into other hands.

After Villard's departure, Freda Kirchwey's *Nation* was deeply involved in the effort to rescue refugees, believed that a Jewish "homeland" was the best hope for democracy in the Middle East, and saw Jewish emigration to Palestine as a matter of "elementary Justice." It sided with the Loyalists in the Spanish civil war, supported the Free French against the U.S. pro-Vichy policy, opposed the China lobby and the backers of Chiang Kai-shek's mainland recovery schemes, and came to see the issue of collective security as critical. On the eve of World War II, Kirchwey saw the battle as between democracy and fascism. When the Nazi-Soviet pact was signed she called it "menacing," and correctly predicted that "the long range ambitions of Stalin and Hitler were bound to clash." Although she published criticism of the purge trials in the Soviet Union, the Spanish Loyalists' conduct of their cause, and the brutal Soviet invasion of Finland, and wrote, "To my mind the effort to promote unity on the left will fail if it is predicated on a categorical declaration of faith in the virtues of the Soviet Union," her biographer, Sara Alpern, concludes that she was a "moralist against fascism," but a relativist where the Soviet Union was concerned—probably a fair judgment.

Her fierce anti-fascism, further fueled by the exigencies of war, even led her to suspend *The Nation*'s traditional preference for the First Amendment absolutism when she demanded within months of our entry into World War II that the government "Curb the Fascist Press!" It was, she wrote, "a menace to freedom and an obstacle to winning the war." She resigned her membership in the American Civil Liberties Union. Yet after the war, as Carey McWilliams has written, "Nothing in its history does *The Nation* more credit than its resolute refusal, under Freda Kirchwey's editorship, to join the cold war or to chorus in on the domestic witch hunt." She was an unrelenting critic of McCarthyism.

Because of its anti-cold war stance, the magazine's financial problems became more acute. As a publisher without independent resources Kirchwey depended on fund raising to make up the annual deficit. In 1943 she had transferred title of ownership of *The Nation* to a non-profit entity, the Nation Associates, in which subscribers were asked to enroll as members at from ten to one hundred dollars a year. The Nation Associates supported the magazine through fund raising but also ran conferences and conducted research. (For example, it commissioned twelve studies on the Middle East, some documenting collaboration between the Nazis and the Mufti of Jerusalem.) Now, because of the cold war atmosphere, traditional-cause fund raising became almost impossible. In the late forties and early fifties, two serious rounds of merger negotiations actually took place with the magazine's friendly competitor, *The New Republic*—but they bogged down over the question of where the merged publication would be located, and who would be in charge of what.

Kirchwey described *The Nation* during her tenure as a "propaganda journal"—not in the sense that it omitted the inconvenient fact to make its point, but rather that it openly espoused many causes. Unlike Villard, she was not a particular champion of lost causes. Indeed, when the magazine described Henry Wallace's 1948 Progressive Party campaign as "Quixotic," J.W. Gitt, the publisher of the *York Pennsylvania Gazette and Daily*, wrote, "My God, woman, all my life I have been engaged in what some people have called 'Quixotic endeavors,' and if I may be pardoned for saying so, I fear that you have been too. At least I thought so."

Anti-fascism was her overarching cause to the end and it undoubtedly contributed to the mindset which led her to sue *The New Leader* magazine when it published former *Nation* art critic Clement Greenberg's letter accusing her friend and *Nation* political editor J. Alvarez Del Vayo, former foreign minister of the Spanish Republic from 1936 to 1939, of being an instrument of Stalin. Declining to publish Greenberg's attack in *The Nation*, she had written him that "if the letter is published or circulated anywhere, we will immediately bring suit for libel against you . . . [a periodical] has a public as well as a private duty not to spread untrue and malicious statements."

Kirchwey obviously didn't subscribe to *The Nation*'s current view that such suits constitute an infringement on political speech, contribute to a general chilling effect, and set a dangerous precedent. More pressing in her mind was Del Vayo's refugee status, which rendered him vulnerable to deportation. She also calculated—wrongly, as it turned out—that the lawsuit would stop the endless debate about whether *The Nation* should have printed Greenberg's letter in the first place, which she considered a diversion from more urgent matters. On advice of counsel, other letters in the case (including one from the embattled young historian, Arthur Schlesinger, Jr., accusing the magazine of printing "wretched apologies for Soviet despotism") also went unpublished; Robert Bendiner and Reinhold Niebuhr asked to have their names removed from the magazine's masthead; and the dispute festered for four years. The lawsuit was not dropped until Carey

McWilliams — whom Kirchwey had recruited to come east and edit a special civil liberties issue ("How Free is Free?") — agreed to replace Freda as editor only on condition that the case be abandoned. He had arrived in New York in 1951 and by 1955, in debt and exhausted and confident that McWilliams was "the right man for the job," Kirchwey retired.

McWilliams recruited his own publisher before he took the job — George Kirstein, a recently retired health insurance executive with *Nation* politics, a modest family inheritance, and few illusions about *Nation* economics. "Without exception," McWilliams would later write, "every publisher has regarded the responsibility as a public trust. Any publisher who thought of the magazine as a possible profit-making venture could not have been familiar with its history."

McWilliams had been privy to *The Nation*'s financial problems ever since late 1950, when Kirchwey had summoned him to New York for an emergency conference. The overheated political atmosphere of the cold war had suddenly made it virtually impossible to raise funds through the sort of public functions that Lillie Shultz, who directed the activities of Nation Associates, had made something of an art. One of the most prominent of these had been a 1946 conference in Los Angeles on "The Challenge of the Postwar World to the Liberal Movement." (Among other speakers was a young actor, Ronald Reagan.) But by 1948–49, many left liberals and radicals were upset with *The Nation* for not having supported the independent candidacy of Henry Wallace, and anti-Communist cold war intellectuals, some of them former Communists themselves, had targeted *The Nation* as un-American and pro-Soviet for its criticism of cold war policies (which, as McWilliams would later point out, led directly to the Vietnam disaster.)

This, of course, was not the first time *The Nation* was in the eye of the political storm. As Henry Raymond Mussey recalled in the sixtieth anniversary issue, back in 1918 "all about surged the roaring flood of public passion hell-bent on victory alone. [*The Nation*] stood for truth amid the raging storm of lies religiously whipped up by every possible agency of public and private mendacity, stood for tolerance and fair play amid a mob who called tolerance treason and labeled fair play pro-bolshevism."

At that time, Villard had the personal resources to see the magazine through and the magazine attracted the intellectual resources to nourish the progressive movement while it mobilized to return to power with the New Deal in 1932. In the late 1940s and 1950s, however, even publications with vast fortunes behind them, such as the progressive daily *PM*, went down. *The Nation*, McWilliams would write in his memoirs, "was lucky to stay alive." At one point its finances were so precarious that he had to arrange for the magazine to be published at the plant of Aubrey Williams's *Southern Farmer* in Alabama. Costs were lower and Williams was liberal in extending credit.

After ten years, Kirstein turned the publishership over to James J. Storrow, Jr., a fifth generation Harvard graduate and incidentally a classmate of Blair Clark, the *Harvard Crimson* editor who would succeed McWilliams as editor of *The Nation*. Like Kirstein, Storrow was a man of inherited wealth, a long-time sharer of *Nation* values; he was also an expert in microfilm and print technologies. His wife Linda became associate publisher. McWilliams served as editor until 1975 and the debt-free magazine that Storrow turned over to his successors was a tribute to McWilliams's editorial ingenuity, in the sense that in the hardest of times he continued to put out a magazine which became mandatory reading for a beleaguered constituency. A jotting from McWilliams's notebook: "It is always a question of finding that reader for whom a publication like *The Nation* is a lantern in the dark. Once he learns of *The Nation* he is a likely reader for life."

McWilliams always insisted that he was not an innovator—that *The Nation* he ran from 1955 to 1975 was informed primarily by his study of Godkin's conception of a journal of opinion. It may well have been true that McWilliams hitched Godkin's basic idea to his own rebel-radical politics, but the magazine he produced had a character uniquely attuned to the era in which it appeared. For example, at a time of extreme xenophobia he discovered William Appleman Williams, who went on to become the most influential of the cold war revisionist historians. In a typical piece, Williams decimated *Time* and *Life* publisher Henry Luce's delusional notions about the "American Century"—an era of unquestioned American hegemony. To Williams, Luce's "black and white austere certainty" prompted such decisions as the State Department cancellation of a projected visit by forty-seven American students to China because it "would be subversive of the United States foreign policy." Indeed, there were few revisionist historians whose first work did not appear in *The Nation*—Walter La Feber, Gabriel Kolko, Barton Bernstein, H. Stuart Hughes, Howard Zinn, and many others appeared week after week.

McWilliams also insisted that *The Nation* was not a "news" magazine, that its destiny and its strength had to do with ideas, with opinion journalism, with explaining the underlying meaning of events rather than reporting them. Yet Leonard Downie, Jr., in his book *The New Muckrakers,* correctly credits *The Nation* with "keeping the muckraking tradition alive in the decade from 1955 to 1965." It was not really *The Nation*'s beat, but the need and the opportunity were obvious, so *The Nation* kept the spotlight on the inquisitorial tactics of the U.S. Congress. In 1953 it also ran the first article by an acknowledged expert linking cigarette smoking to cancer. It took a chance on a Harvard law student and published "The Safe Car You Can't Buy," which launched Ralph Nader on his career as ombudsman and corporate muckraker.

McWilliams even sent Carleton Beals back to the jungles, and his 1960 reports foresaw the 1961 Bay of Pigs invasion. *The Nation* was the only American magazine to report on the CIA training camps in Guatemala before the invasion although the information was available to other journalists. Had the mainstream press not abandoned its adversary role on cold war issues, McWilliams believed, the "debacle might have been avoided."

By the late sixties, *Newsday* and the Associated Press got the idea and set up teams of investigative reports. "We could not compete once muckraking had become the new radical chic in American journalism, nor was there any reason why we should," McWilliams wrote in his memoir. "During a long arid season we had kept the tradition alive by demonstrating the need for investigative journalism and the interest in it. At the same time we had lifted taboos on subjects long regarded as sacrosanct and called attention to a wealth of new subjects in urgent need of critical media attention."

McWilliams understood that it was important to deal with taboo subjects simply because they were regarded as taboo—Fred Cook's issue-long exposes of the FBI and the CIA changed forever the way those previously inviolate institution were reported upon. And *The Nation*'s special issue "Juggernaut: The Warfare State" (1961) put the military-industrial complex on the nation's agenda so that other media found it hard to ignore.

Nobody ever accused McWilliams of putting out a humor magazine, but Dalton Trumbo's exposé of the Hollywood blacklist and former FBI agent Jack Levine's explanation of how the FBI was a financial backer of the Communist Party—one out of four members of the party's local central committees were agents or informants who regularly put party dues on their expense accounts—offered some sardonic comic relief.

McWilliams's idea that the function of the journal of opinion was to put new ideas on the national agenda found expression in such special issues as "The Wired Nation" by Ralph Lee Smith (1970), which first brought the policy implications and potential of cable television to national attention; and in "think pieces" like Christopher Lasch's meditation on the meaning of the cultural cold war as fought by the Congress for Cultural Freedom.

Under McWilliams, *The Nation* sounded the alarm on American involvement in Vietnam—it ran sixty-six pieces on the subject between January 1, 1954 and June 1, 1966. In 1962, the magazine called the conflict between the French and Ho Chi Minh's forces a "dirty war." In the September 14, 1963 issue, a *Nation* editorial called South Vietnam a "booby trap" for the U.S. and said that unless Washington changed its policies the war could soon involve "not thousands, but hundreds of thousands of men. The cardinal fallacy of American policy has been the idea that 'victory' could be achieved by personnel and methods as evil as any the Communists have employed, and that democracy can use tyranny as its shield."

McWilliams was also a frustrated publisher, and had forceful notions about how to fund the magazine and build its subscriber base at the same time: revive the idea of *Nation* dinners, hold them once a month around the country, and feature speakers like Martin Luther King, Jr., —who wrote an annual civil rights audit for *The Nation* and who, at a *Nation*-sponsored conference in Los Angeles in 1967, first came out unequivocally against the Vietnam War. McWilliams believed that each dinner could attract at least 1,000 people who would enroll as subscribers as part of their admission fee. 10,000 to 20,000 new subscribers a year for a magazine with an average of 30,000 in these years wouldn't be bad. But he and Storrow were still too busy dealing with the vestiges of McCarthyism—which persisted despite the Senate's censure of McCarthy in 1954—and figuring out how to meet the next week's payroll to implement these well-conceived schemes.

Came 1975, and McWilliams began to feel "I was writing a frenzied, never-ending serial on The Last Days of Richard Nixon with alternating notes on This Week in Vietnam." An era was coming to a close, he had books to write, and he told Storrow his time was up.

Blair Clark—who came to *The Nation* from stints as associate publisher of *The New York Post*, general manager and vice-president of CBS Television, and campaign manager of Eugene McCarthy's anti-Vietnam War independent presidential run of 1968—had barely gotten started as editor when Storrow, for reasons of ill-health, let it be known that he was ready to step down. Clark, who had helped arrange the financing for *The New York Review of Books*, and might have become *The Nation's* editor/publisher, had family obligations which led him, too, to retire. No fewer than twenty-four groups came forward to "buy" what Carey McWilliams had correctly identified as "not for sale." Storrow, who had each suitor prepare a memorandum on his/her plans for the future, chose a twenty-fifth: a consortium organized by Hamilton Fish III, a recent Harvard graduate with whom I had become friends in the course of a glorious losing cause—Ramsey Clark's 1975 run for the U.S. Senate from New York.

I had most recently worked as an editor on the Sunday *New York Times Magazine* and was finishing a book on the Hollywood blacklist and teaching a course on "Politics and the Press" at Princeton University when Hamilton Fish and I decided to enter the fray. I would prepare an editorial prospectus and Hamilton would do the fund raising. The goal was to raise $950,000: $150,000 was the purchase price, which was what Storrow had paid Kirstein. About $300,000 was to go toward severance obligations and subscription fulfillment. And the remaining $500,000 was supposed to guarantee that the new entity, which started with no capital of its own, would be solvent for at least three years. (As it happened, Clark was impelled to leave before the funding was in place, but happily for me, by mid-1977 Storrow had decided that I was the man for the job, and offered me the opportunity to edit the magazine I had come – through my researches on the McCarthy phenomenon – to admire more than any other.)

Here is not the place to record the unsung heroes in Hamilton's quest for gold, nor to document the perils of fund raising, except as they relate to *The Nation*'s larger story. The structure of the new consortium was the latest incarnation of Godkin's goal. Under the limited partnership agreement, the editor and publisher would be general partners, responsible for the day-to-day operations of the magazine (each having the final say in his own domain), and the investors would be limited partners, precluded by law from having any say in the operation of the magazine. My favorite meeting was with a Massachusetts man who agreed to make a substantial investment, but on two conditions: that the magazine adopt a subtitle which would be carried on the masthead, so that it would read *The Nation: And How to Change It,* and that at the end of every article there would be an italicized paragraph telling the reader what he/she could do to remedy the injustice or help solve the problem previously set forth. A marvelous idea for a magazine, but not *The Nation*. We declined the suggestion, he declined the investment. Then there was our encounter with the late Dorothy Schiff, formerly publisher of the *New York Post*. She first attempted to persuade Hamilton that she should be the sole investor, which she was prepared to do, provided that she have the traditional publisher's prerogatives. As she put it, she was reluctant to be a limited partner because "I don't believe in taxation without representation." In the end, Mrs. Schiff, a good sport, came around anyway, and made a substantial investment. A few years later, when she became disillusioned and impatient with the magazine's occasional editorial insults to her friends, she simply donated her stock back to the company.

Aside from *Nation* book reviewers, who seemed programmed either to ignore or assault the many books which were written by various of our twenty-odd silent partners, we had only one serious problem. We had been in business about three months when our young publisher came into my office holding a letter between his thumb and index finger, asking, "What do we do about this?" And he deposited on my desk a letter from one of our limited partners who objected to a newsmaking article in the previous week's issue deploring the Israeli arms trade with South Africa. When he agreed to invest in *The Nation*, he wrote, he hadn't intended to support a magazine which engaged in gratuitous Israel-bashing, and since presumably other nations were also sending arms to South Africa, why single out Israel, which had enough trouble already? It seemed to me that our shareholders had every right to disagree with our editorial content (although in this case I felt that any true friend of Israel would want it out of the arms-trading business with an apartheid nation), but because Mr. X had yet to put up his money, the complaint seemed improper and I said so. In effect, he was threatening to withhold his financial support over an issue of editorial policy, when the structure had been designed precisely to preclude this sort of pressure. We never saw the money, and although our attorneys advised us that the commitment was legally binding, we thought it inappropriate to sue. Investment in a magazine like *The Nation* has to be by free choice.

Apart from this one episode, the limited partnership device seemed perfectly suited to *The Nation*, although it did have one serious limitation. It required a built-in fund raiser with Fish's energy, enthusiasm and commitment. He stuck with it for almost ten years, but when the siren song of politics beckoned, he left *The Nation* to pursue a career of public service, long a Fish family tradition.

Luckily for *The Nation*, even before Hamilton realized how restless he was getting, Arthur Carter, our present publisher, appeared on the scene – although on reflection it was probably not luck at all. There is a theory, to which I only partly subscribe, that the magazine has survived for 125 years *because* rather than in spite of its failure to earn a profit. Had it made a profit and been seen as a potential money machine, it might have attracted proprietors determined to enhance its value by making it look and be like most money-making magazines – in other words, making it conform to the rules of the game. Were that to happen, *The Nation* would no longer be *The Nation*. Arthur Carter's view is that without changing a word, through imaginative, energetic and professional management, *The Nation* can be made to pay its own way. A maverick magazine, it has attracted maverick proprietors, which may be one of its survival secrets.

Let others assess *The Nation*'s performance during the years I and my various associates have been involved – too involved to pretend to any perspective. As we move towards the twenty-first century with an administration and especially a Supreme Court that has been Reaganized, an economy that has been globalized, a mass media that has become conglomerated and Murdochized, a Europe that has self-revolutionized, a Japan that has emerged as an imperial power, I would expect that *The Nation* would still be *The Nation*. If Godkin's writ extended only to the Hudson, and McWilliams expanded that all the way to the Mexican border and California, future *Nation*s will undoubtedly expand coverage of the global village, and invent a transnational journalism to cover the transnational corporation. We will continue to fight for causes, lost and found. There is something quite beautiful in J.W. Gitt's idea about the importance of lost causes. Indeed, someone once described *The Nation* as a magazine for the permanent minority. At first I was put off by that because one expects that from time to time a cause, no matter how apparently remote, will prevail. But a magazine for the permanent minority is an honorable undertaking, especially if that minority includes those who are ahead of their time. Political movements – and here I include the Rainbow Coalition and bioregionalists as well as Democrats and other less adventurous entities – will, and some even should, come to power. A magazine shouldn't come to power. It can nourish, it can prod, it can hector, it can educate, it can cajole, wheedle, expose, embarrass, inform, illuminate and inspire. And if it does all these things, as the pieces in this volume bear witness, the laws of capitalism notwithstanding, it will survive.

VICTOR NAVASKY
(EDITOR, 1978–   )
New York City
April 1990

Index to Authors

Agee, James, 178

Algren, Nelson, 187

Arendt, Hannah, 171

Atwood, Margaret, 501

Auden, W.H., 479

Baer, Barbara L. and
    Glenna Matthews, 288

Baldwin, James, 261

Barnet, Richard J., 463

Beals, Carleton, 96

Benchley, Robert C., 24

Bly, Robert, 497

Bogan, Louise, 476

Bourke-White, Margaret, 121

Boyle, Sarah, 214

Broun, Heywood, 102

Cardenal, Ernesto, 503

Cather, Willa, 49

Clurman, Harold, 219

Cockburn, Alexander, 397

Cohen, Stephen, 383

Condon, Richard, 242

Danto, Arthur, 446

Debs, Theodore, 32

Dickinson, Emily, 473

Doctorow, E.L., xi

Dos Passos, John, 133

DuBois, W.E.B., 62

Duncan, Robert, 495

Eastman, Crystal, 76

Einstein, Albert, 110

Eisenstein, Sergei, 89

Endore, Guy, 185

Farrell, James T., 129

Ferlinghetti, Lawrence, 488

Fischer, Louis, 147

Frost, Robert, 472

Fuentes, Carlos, 366

Garcia Lorca, Federico, 475

Garrison, W.P., 19

Gitlin, Todd, 299

Godkin, E.L., 2, 12, 15

Goldman, Emma, 116

Gruening, Ernest, 277

Hays, Arthur Garfield, 23

Herbst, Josephine, 208

Hitchens, Christopher, 386

Hitler, Adolf, 66

Hughes, Langston, 72

Ivins, Molly, 369

Jacobsen, Josephine, 511

James, Henry, 5

Jarrell, Randall, 485

Jones, LeRoi, 494

Kaufman, George S., 151

King, Martin Luther Jr., 254

Kirchwey, Freda, 100, 168

Kopkind, Andrew, 332

Krassner, Paul, 452

Lawrence, D.H., 471

Leonard, John, 388

Lernoux, Penny, 416

Levertov, Denise, 499

Lewis, Sinclair, 47

Lowell, Robert, 483

MacDonald, William, 27

MacLeish, Archibald, 163

McCarthy, Mary and
    Margaret Marshall, 124

McWilliams, Carey, 269

Mann, Thomas, 144

Mencken, H.L., 53

Menuhin, Moshe, 95

Merwin, W.S., 500

Miller, Arthur, 197

Miller, Henry, 158

Moore, Marianne, 481

Nader, Ralph, 234

Navasky, Victor, 351, 513

Neruda, Pablo, 501

Newfield, Jack, 270

Paz, Octavio, 508

Petras, James, 319

Plath, Sylvia, 492

Pollitt, Katha, 372

Pound, Ezra, 92

Rexroth, Kenneth, 231

Rist, Darrell Yates, 436

Russell, Bertrand, 136

Said, Edward W., 432

Samuelson, Arthur, 308

Sandburg, Carl, 480

Sartre, Jean-Paul, 176

Seldes, Gilbert, 41

Seligman, Herbert J., 36

Sexton, Anne, 493

Shaw, George Bernard, 61

Sherrill, Robert, 422

Shirer, William, 282

Sinclair, Upton, 80

Singer, Daniel, 410

Snow, Edgar, 192

Spender, Stephen, 182

Stevens, Wallace, 478

Stone, I.F., 153, 160

Swenson, May, 507

Tax, Meredith, 454

Thomas, Norman, 139

Thompson, E.P., 325

Thompson, Hunter S., 245

Thurber, James, 114

Trillin, Calvin, 356

Trilling, Lionel, 106

Trumbo, Dalton, 221

vanden Heuvel, Katrina, xv

Van Doren, Mark, 70

Vidal, Gore, 358

Villard, Oswald Garrison, 61, 76, 112

Vonnegut, Kurt, 353

Vorse, Mary Heaton, 67

Wakefield, Dan, 204

Walker, Alice, 460

Weizmann, Chaim, 56

Williams, William Carlos, 489

Wright, James, 505

Yeats, W.B., 477

Index

"Abbie" (Krassner), 452–54
Abortion, 454–59
  Blacks and, 459–63
Acheson, Dean, 193
Acion, Fecundo, 262
ACT UP (AIDS Coalition to Unleash Power), 444
Adams, Brooks, 360–64
Adams, Henry, 361–62, 365
Adams, John Quincy, 21, 362, 364
Addictions, 353–56
After Long Silence (Straight), 339
"After the Ball" (Jones), 494
Age of Reason, The (Sartre), 176
Agee, James, 178–82, 211
Agnew, Spiro T., 275
AIDS, 436–46
Alcoa, 153–58
Alcoholics Anonymous, 353–56
Algren, Nelson, 187–89
Alinsky, Saul, 290
Alsace-Lorraine, 28
Aluminum Company of America, 153–54
Aluminum Ltd., 153
American Birth Control League, 100–01
"American Christmas, 1952" (Algren), 187–89
American Civil Liberties Union (ACLU), 23, 33
American Eductional Association, 135
American Empire, 358–66
American Jewish Committee, 310
"American Liberalism" (Hays), 23
American Mercury, The (Mencken), 53
American Tragedy, An (Dreiser), 224
"Americans and Their Myths" (Sartre), 176–78
Amiel, Frederick, 50
Anarchists, 15–19, 118–19
  Sacco and Vanzetti case, 83–89
  Anarcho-Syndicalists, 118
Anger, Kenneth, 271
Ann Veronica, 83
Anti-imperialist movement, 19–21
Anti-Saloon League, 55
Anti-semitism, 171–75
Arbiter, Petronius, 55
Arbuckle, Fatty, 54
"Are We Training Cuban Guerillas?", 241–42
Arendt, Hannah, 171–75
Armstrong, Hamilton Fish, 141–42
Armstrong, Louis, 232
"Arrival, The" (Cardenal), 503–04
"Art" (Danto), 446–52

Artiguenave, Sudre d', 40
"As We See It," 274–77
Asch, Sholom, 124
Ash, Timothy Garton, 333
Atwood, Margaret, 501–02
Auden, W.H., 178, 182, 479
Auntie Mame, 219
Austen, Jane, 209, 213
Austria-Hungary, 29

Babbit (Lewis), 47
Bacon, Reginald, 390
Baer, Barbara L., 288–99
Baker, Wallace, 25, 158, 263, 266, 268
Bakunin, Mikhail Alexandrovich, 116
Balabonov, Angelica, 120
Baldwin, James, 261–69
Baldwin, Stanley, 142
Balfour Declaration, 56
Balzac, Honoré de, 159, 184, 213, 390
Banque Nationale d'Haiti, 39
"Bare Almond Trees" (Lawrence), 471
Barnes, Ben, 372
Barnet, Richard, 463–66
Barr, Alfred Hamilton Jr., 276
Batt, William L., 154
Beals, Carleton, 96–100
"Bear, The" (Frost), 472
"Beat the Devil" (Cockburn), 397–401
Beck, James M., 24
Beckwith, Byron de la, 273
Beethoven, Ludwig van, 54
Begin, Menachem, 308, 316–17
Bel Geddes, Barbara, 219
Belgium, 28
Bell, Daniel, 347
Ben-Elissar, Elie, 316
Benchley, Robert C., 24–26
Bennett, Bruce, 180
Bergen, Sol, 151–53
Berger, Victor, 26
Berman, Marshall, 389
Between The Lines (Wakefield), 204
Bickel, Mary, 129
Bidault, M., 192
Big News, The, 227
"Big Parade–1936 Model" (Dos Passos), 133–36
"Bill of Rights Day," 189–92
"Blacklist = Black Market" (Trumbo), 221–30
Blackmun, Harry, 285

Blacks,
and abortion, 459–63
in Georgia, 62–66
Jesse Jackson's campaign, 403–09
Negro artists, 72–76
see also Civil rights
Blaine, James G., 113
Blanko, Marko, 371
Blondell, Joan, 152
Blum, Léon, 142
Blunt, Anthony, 339
Bly, Robert, 497–98
Bogan, Louise, 476
Bogart, Humphrey, 179, 181
Bolshevists, 23, 26, 32, 54, 91
Bond, Julian, 276
Bonfire of the Vanities, The (Wolfe), 388–97
Boniecki, Adam, 419–20
Book of Daniel, The (Doctorow), 352
Book reviews,
Corporate Crimes and Violence (Mokhiber), 422–32
Thomas Wolfe's Letters to His Mother (Terry, ed.), 158–60
T.S. Eliot's poetry, 70–71
Ulysses (Joyce), 41–46
Borges, Jorge Luis, 367
Bourke-White, Margaret, 121–23
Boxing, 129–33
Boyle, Sarah Patton, 214–19
Bradley, Mamie, 206
Brandley, Mandy, 207
Brando, Marlon, 246
Brave One, The (Rich), 225, 227
Bread and Roses Too (Newfield), 270
Breland, J.J., 206
Breshkovsky, Katherine, 120
Brezhnev, Leonid, 329
Brickner, Balfour, 315
British Labor Party, 23
Broder, David, 274
Broffault, Robert, 124
Broun, Heywood, 102–05
Brown, John, 67, 85, 89
Brown, Rap, 303
"Brueghal Nativity, A" (Williams), 489–91
Bryan, W.J., 93
Bryant, Anita, 305
Bryant, Roy, 205, 207–08
Brzezinski, Zbigniew, 312–13, 343–44
Buckley, Bill, 390
Bulgaria, 28–29
Bumpers, Eleanor, 390
Bunker, Arthur H., 153
Bunyan, John, 224
Burger, W., 285
Bush, George, 463
"Bush's Splendid Little War" (Barnet), 463–66

Butterfield, Fox, 338

Cabell, Branch, 127
Cabrera, Guillermo, 367
Caldwell, Erskine, 121
Calvert, Greg, 302, 305
Camus, Albert, 172–75, 273
Cape Haitien (Haiti), 37–38
Capital punishment, 386–88
Anarchists' execution, 15–19
Capote, Truman, 389
Cardenal, Ernesto, 503–04
Carlino, Resto del, 150
Carlton, C. Sidney, 207
Carnegie Foundation, 35
Carter, James Earl (Jimmy), 308, 310, 312, 317–18, 344
"Casting Out the 'People's Church' " (Lernoux), 416–22
Castro, Fidel, 241, 340
Cather, Willa, 49–52
Cervantes, Miguel de, 224
Chamber Music (Joyce), 41
Chamberlain, John, 124–25
Chambers, Robert, 390
Chambers, Whittaker, 189, 191
Chaney, James, 303
Chaplin, Charlie, 179
Chapman, John Jay, 191
Charles II, 138
Chase, Stuart, 127
Chatham, Gerald, 205
Chavez, Cesar, 288–89, 292, 296, 298
Chavez, Helen, 296–97
Chekhov, Anton, 211
Chestnutt, Charles, 74
Chile, 366–68
China, 28
Church, in Latin America, 416–22
Church, Frank, 344
Circus clowns, 15
Civil League, 24
Civil liberties,
blacklisting, 221–30
loyalty oaths, 334–36
Pro-German List, 25
Rosenberg case, 351–52
surrogate motherhood, 372–83
Civil Rights Act, 272
Clark, William, 276
"Class Justice in Germany" (Hitler), 66–67
Clements, Bill (Governor), 371
Clowns, 15
Clurman, Harold, 219–21
Coburn, Judith, 301
Cockburn, Alexander, 339, 389–401
Coe, David Allan, 371
Cohen, Leonard, 271

Cohen, John S., 63
Cohen, Stephen F., 383–85
Cold war, 325–32, 343–44
"Cold War II" (Grossman), 342
Cole, Lester, 223
Collier, Peter, 333, 337
Columbia, Church's influence in, 416–22
Commager, Henry Steele, 286
Communism,
  in El Salvador, 319–25
  loyalty oaths, 334–36
  U.S. liberalism and, 332–51
Community Service Organization, 290
Condon, Richard, 242–45
Confucius, 365
Connally, John, 372
Connelly, Mike, 229
"Conquest of Haiti, The" (Seligmann), 36–40
Conyers, John, 276
Cooke, Cardinal, 283
Coolidge, Calvin, 96
Copernicus, 137–38
"Corporate Crime and Violence" (Mokhiber), 422–32
Coughlin, Charles Edward, 191
Coward-McCann, 129
Cowley, Malcolm, 127
Cozzens, James Gould, 348
Craig, Willie, 263
Crane, Stephen, 213, 367
Criticism, literary, 53–56
Cromwell, Richard, 138
Cronkite, Walter, 306
Cros, Charles, 231
Crotty, Ron, 231–32
Crow, Jim, 63, 66
Crowder, A. Don, 370–71
Cummings, E. E., 367
Czardom, in Russia, 31

Da Vinci, Leonardo, 176
Dahlberg, Edward, 109
Dai, Bao, 193
Daifullah, Nagi, 290
Daley, Richard, 276
"Danger of the Hour, The" (Godkin), 2
Daniels, Josephus, 134
Dante, 224
Davis, Bette, 151
Dayan, Moshe, 315
De la Cruz, Juan, 290, 295–96
De la Cruz, Maximina, 295
De Maupassant, Guy, 24
"Deadly Costs of an Obsession, The" (Rist), 436–46
Death Comes for the Archbishop (Cather), 49
"Death of the Sheriff, The" (Lowell), 483–84
Death penalty, 386–88

Debs, Eugene, 32–33, 95
Debs, Theodore, 33
Declaration of Independence, 192
Dedalus, Stephen, 41, 44–46
"Delirious New York" (Leonard), 388–97
Democratic National Committee, 154
Dempsey, Jack, 130
Denby, David, 333, 339
Denton, Jeremiah, 336
Descartes, René, 139, 176
Dewey, George, 362
Diary of a Scoundrel, 219
Dickens, Charles, 184, 187, 189
Dickinson, Emily, 473–74
Dickey, Christopher, 368
"Dilemma of American Jewry, The" (Samuelson), 308–18
Dillinger, John, 249
Dillman, Bradford, 221
"Disarmament Conference, The 1932" (Einstein), 110–11
Disney, Walt, 114–16
Divine Comedy, (The) 45
Doctorow, E.L., 352
Donovan, Ray, 390
Doren, Mark Van, 70–71
Dos Passos, John, 10, 67–70, 133–36
Dostoevski, Fyodor, 187, 189, 211
Douglas, Aaron, 76
Douglas, William O., 191
Douglass, Frederick, 263
"Dream, The" (Bogan), 476
Dreiser, Theodore, 189, 213
Dreyfus Case, 85
Du Bois, W.E.B., 62–66
Duberman, Martin Bauml, 442–46
Dublin, 43
Dubliners (Joyce), 41
Dulles, John Foster, 195–97, 309, 332, 356, 359
Dunbar, Paul Laurence, 74
Duncan, Robert, 495–96
Durr, Cliff, 154
"Dust Changes America" (Bourke-White), 121–23
Dylan, Bob, 271–72, 274

East Prussia, 28
"East, West—Is There a Third Way?" (Thompson), 325–32
Eastman, Crystal, 76–80
Editorials,
  "As We See It," 274–77
  "Bill of Rights Day," 189–92
  "For Jesse Jackson and His Campaign," 403–10
  "It's Only Nikita, After All," 239–40
  "Justice Underfoot" (Villard), 83–89

"Long Shadow, The" (Navasky), 351–52
"One World or None" (Kirchwey), 168–71
"Revenge of Ahab, The" (Kopkind), 268–70
Edwards, Douglas, 227
Egypt, 28
  Sadat's peace initiatives, 308–18
Eichenberg, Fritz, 467
Eichmann in Jerusalem (Arendt), 171
Eighty Days Around the World, 225
Einstein, Albert, 110–11, 138, 151–53, 359
"Einstein in Hollywood" (Kaufman), 151–53
Eisenhower, Dwight, 284, 309
Eisenstein, Sergei Mikhailovich, 89–91
El Salvador, State Department's white paper
  on, 319–25
Eldridge, Florence, 221
Eliot, T.S., 70–71, 114
Ellington, Duke, 232
Ellis Island, 34
Emunim, Gush, 315
En-Lai, Chou, 197
End of Ideology, The (Bell), 347
Endore, Guy, 185–87, 228
Ericson, Eric, 51
Erskine, Dr., 53
Ervine, St. John, 47
Espionage Act, The, 23, 32–33
Esposito, Frank, 232
Evers, Charles, 276
Evers, Medgar, 243
Ewing, Oscar, 154
"Execution of the Anarchists, The" (Godkin),
  15–19
Exiles (Joyce), 41

Façade (Walton), 231
Fadiman, Clifton, 129
Fagans, Myron, 187
Falange, 148
"Fall of Joe Louis, The" (Farrell), 129–33
Fallow, Peter, 390
Farr, Fred S. (Senator), 249, 253
Farrell, James T., 129–33
Farrow, John, 225
Faulkner, William, 183, 188, 213, 367
Fear and Loathing on the Campaign Trail '72
  (Thompson), 245
Featherstone, Ralph, 303
Federal Bureau of Investigation (FBI), 199
Fein, Leonard, 318
Feland, General, 98
Felder, Ronald, 263
Ferguson, Allyn, 232, 234
Ferlinghetti, Lawrence, 488
Fielding, Henry, 83
Film, of Eisenstein, 89–91
Fine Clothes to the Jew (Hughes), 72
Fire Next Time, The (Baldwin), 261

"First Glance" (Van Doren), 70–71
Fischer, Louis, 66–67, 147–50
Fisher, Rudolph, 76
Fitzgerald, Ella, 232
Five Fingers (Wilson), 225
Flacks, Charles Wright, 304
Flacks, Mickey, 304
Flacks, Mark A.J., 304
Flaherty, Robert, 226
Flaubert, Gustav, 41, 177, 209
"For Jesse Jackson and His Campaign,"
  403–10
"For the Jews – Life or Death?" (Stone),
  160–62
Foreman, Carl, 227
Forrestal, James, 189
Fox, Paula, 389
France, 28
  racism in, 410–15
France, Anatole, 125
Franco, Francisco, 141, 146–50, 162
Francois-Poncet, 283
"French Existentialism" (Arendt), 171–75
Freud, Sigmund, 90, 136, 151, 246, 347
Friedan, Betty, 349
Friedheim, Jerry, 286–87
Friendly Persuasion (West), 225
Froine, John, 306
Frost, Robert, 472
Fuentes, Carlos, 366–68
Fuller (Governor), of Massachusetts, 84–86
Fulton, Hugh, 155–57
Funston (General), 20

Gallo Brothers, 298
Gamblers Anonymous, 353–56
"Game at Salzburg, A" (Jarrell), 485–86
Gandhi, 350
Gang of Six. See SDS (Students for a
  Democratic Society)
Gannett, Lewis, 124–28
Garrison, Wendell Phillips, 19–21
Gay issues, AIDS, 436–46
Geismar, Maxwell, 263
Generalnaya Linya, 91
"Georgia: Invisible Empire State" (Du Bois),
  62–66
Germany,
  class justice in, 66–67
  Imperial Government, 27
Gershwin, George, 177
Ghorbal, Ashraf, 314
Gide, André, 109
Gilpin, Charles, 74
Ginsberg, Allen, 271
Gitlin, Todd, 299–307
Glasgow, Ellen, 127
Gleason, Ralph, 244

Go Tell It On The Mountain (Baldwin), 261
Godkin, E.L., 2–5, 12–19
Goebbels, Joseph, 286–87
Goering, Hermann, 287
Goetz, Bernie, 390
Gold, Mike, 104
Goldman, Emma, 25–26, 116–20
  political exiles, 116–20
Goldmann, Dr. Nahum, 313
Goldwater, Barry, 270, 275
Gompers, Samuel, 55
Goodman, Paul, 303
Gorbachev, Mikhail, 383–85
Gorman (Senator), of Maryland, 112
Gotti, John, 390
Gottlieb, Bob, 301
Grafton, Samuel, 160
Graham, Billy, 271, 283
Grant, Ulysses S., 364
Gray, Jimmy Lee, 386
Great Powers, 29, 35
*Great Schism: Stalinism and the American
  Intellectuals, The* (O'Neill), 349
Great Shark Hunt, The (Thompson), 245
Green, William, 135
Greenbaum Village, Bolsheviki of, 54
Grenada, invasion of, 463–66
Grieg, Edvard, 51
Gritz, John, 81
Grossman, Robert, 342
Gruening, Ernest, 277–82
Guatemala, 366–68
Gustafson, Gus, 232

Haber, Alan, 303
Haig, Alexander, 340
Haiti,
  Banque Nationale d', 39
  Conquest of,
  Cape Haitien, 37
  Lieutenant Muth, 37
  Monroe Doctrine, 37
  Panama Canal, 37
  Port au Prince, 37
  President Vilbrun Guillaume Sam, 37
  United States and, 36–40, 366–68
Hamilton, Alexander, 364
Hamlet (Shakespeare), 83, 136
Hamm, Daniel, 263, 266–68
Hamsun, Knut, 50
Hanoi, 286–88
Hansen, Harry, 125
Harpers (Ash), 333
Hawkins-Humphrey bill, 306
Hawthorne, Nathaniel, 209
Hay, John, 362
Hayden, Tom, 304
Hayes, Helen, 219

Hays, Arthur Garfield, 23
Hays, Will H., 151
Hearst, William Randolph, 23, 135
Hegel, Georg W., 345
Hell's Angels (Thompson), 245–51
Hemingway, Ernest, 183, 213, 367
Henry, Aaron, 276
Herbst, Josephine, 208–14
Herford, Oliver, 46
Herod, 64
Herrick, Margaret, 226
Herriot (Prime Minister), of France, 85
Herter (Secretary of State), 240
Herz, Alice, 304
Herzen, 116
Herzog, Chaim, 313
Hesse, Herman, 271
Hidden Persuaders, The (Packard), 348
Hill, Joe, 249
Hilton, Ronald, 241–42
Hippies, 270–74
"Hippopotamus, The" (Eliot), 71
Hiss, Alger, 351–52
Hitchens, Christopher, 386–88
Hitler, Adolf, 66–67, 118, 133, 142, 150,
  162, 169–70, 194, 244, 282, 284–88
"H.L. Mencken" (Mencken), 53–56
Hoffman, Abbie, 452–54
Holt, Tim, 179–80
Homer, 114
Homosexuals, AIDS and, 436–46
Honneger, Arthur, 231
Hoover, Herbert, 112–14
Hope, Thomas, 390
Horowitz, David, 333, 337
Howe, Irving, 311, 333, 337, 389
Hoyt, Eunice, 83
"Hubris of a President" (Shirer), 282–88
Huerta, Dolores, 288–94, 296–98
Hughes, Charles E., 104
Hughes, Langston, 72–76, 231
Hugo, Victor, 224
Humphrey, Hubert, 275–77, 279, 306
Huston, John, 179–82
Huston, Walter, 179–81
Huxtable, Ada Louise, 389

"I Stand with the Spanish People" (Mann),
  144–46
I.F. Stone (Levine), 156
Illustrations,
  "*Cold War II*" (Grossman), 342
  I.F. Stone (Levine), 156
  "*It's Only a Theory*" (Sorel), 402
  Sacco and Vanzetti (Shahn), 88
  Woodcuts (Eichenberg), 467
Ilschenko, Annelise, 371
Imperial Government, German, 27, 37

Imperialism, anti-imperialist movement, 19–21
In Search of New York, 388–97
"In the Heart of Le Pen Country" (Singer), 410–16
"Injustice" (Neruda), 509–10
International Red Cross, 161
International Workingmen's Association, 119
"Is Literature Possible?" (Trilling), 106–09
Israel,
    Palestine and, 432–36
"It Seems to Heywood Broun" (Broun), 102–05
"*It's Only a Theory*" (Sorel), 402
"It's Only Nikita, After All," 239–40
Ivins, Molly, 369–72

Jackson, Henry, 343
Jackson, Jesse, 274, 403–10
Jacobsen, Josephine, 511–12
James, Henry, 5–12, 41, 43, 182–83, 209–10, 213–14
    "Saratoga," 5–12
    The Noble School of Fiction, 5
Jarrell, Randall, 485–86
Jarrico, Paul, 227
"Jazz Poetry" (Rexroth), 231–34
Jefferson, Thomas, 166, 284, 364
Jenkins, Al, 151–53
Jenner (Senator), 191
Jews,
    American, 308–18
    in New Left movement, 301
    Palestine's political agenda and, 432–36
Johnson, Edward Earl, 386–87
Johnson, Lyndon, 2–3, 275–76, 278–81, 283, 338, 410
"Johnson's Cabinet Watched by Ants" (Bly), 497–98
Jolson, Al, 177
Jones, Jesse, 154–57
Jones, Le Roi, 494
Jonson, Ben, 224
Jordan, Barbara, 410
Josephson, Matthew, 127
Joyce, James, 41–47, 108–09, 114–15, 183
    Freeman's Journal, 43
Judea, 311
Julius Caesar, 115
Jungle, The (Sinclair), 80
"Justice in Summer" (Wakefield), 204–08
"Justice Underfoot" (Villard), 83–89

Kafka, Franz, 173, 209, 211
Katz, Fred, 68, 231, 233
Katz, Shmuel, 317
Kaufman, George S., 151–53
Kellum, J. W., 207
Kennedy, John F., 241–44, 272, 306, 314

Kent, Duchess of, 134
Kent, Duke of, 134
Keyserling, Leon, 343
Khan, Genghis, 54
Khrushchev, Nikita, 240, 384–85
King Brothers, 226
King, Martin Luther, Jr., 139, 254–61, 275, 303
    civil rights, 254–61
Kipling, Rudyard, 359
Kirchwey, Freda, 76, 100–02, 116, 139–44, 168–71
    world government, 168–71
Kirkpatrick, Jeane, 340
Kissinger, Henry, 287, 384
Klutznick, Phillip, 313
Kopkind, Andrew, 332–51, 368–69
Kosinski, Jerzy, 333
Kramer, Lawrence, 390
Krassner, Paul, 452–54
Kronenberger, Louis, 129
Kropotkin, Peter, 116
Krupskaya, Nadezhda, 89
Krutch, Joseph Wood, 129
Ku Klux Klan, 65, 101, 123
La Follette, Bob, 113
La Follette, Philip, 113
Labor issues, Passaic strike, 67–70
LaGuardia, Fiorello, 135
Laird (Defense Secretary), 279
Lamorisse, Albert, 226
"Land of Jekyll and Hyde" (Fuentes), 366–68
LaPorte, Roger, 303
Lardner, Ring, 213
Lardner, Ring Jr., 223
Lasky, Jesse Jr., 226
"Last Steep Ascent, The" (King), 254–61
Latin America,
    Church in, 416–22
    El Salvador and U.S., 319–25
    Haiti, 36–40, 366–68
    U.S. and, 366–68
Lattimore, Owen, 193
Law,
    abortion, 454–59
    capital punishment, 386–88
    corporate crime, 422–32
    surrogate motherhood, 372–83
Lawrence, D. H., 55, 108–09, 212, 471
Lawson, Jack, 223
Le Pen, Jean Marie, 410–11
League of Nations, 28–29, 141–42
Leary, Timothy, 271, 273
Lee, Herbert, 303
Legion of Valor, 134
Lehman Corporation, 153
Lehman (Governor), 135, 191
LeMay, Curtis, 274

Lenin, Vladimir, 32–33, 116, 300, 319
Lennon, John, 271
Leonard, John, 388–97
Lernoux, Penny, 416–22
Les Mouches (Sartre), 175
Let There Be Light (Huston), 182
Levertov, Denise, 499–500
Levine, David, 156
Lewis, Flora, 333
Lewis, Sinclair, 47–49, 128, 189
Liberalism, 55, 332–51
  cold war and, 343–44
  in U.S., 23
  Vietnam war attitudes, 336–38
Liberia, 28
Library of Congress, 192
"Life on the Blacklist" (Endore), 185–87
Lincoln, Abraham, 21, 105, 165, 180, 191, 275, 284, 364
Lindbergh, Charles, 96
Lingeman, Richard, 356
Lippmann, Walter, 274–75
Lipset, Seymour Martin, 317
Lipton, Lawrence, 231, 233–34
Literature,
  Old-World novels, 8
  Lionel Trilling, 106–10
  Criticism, 53–56
Little Review, 209
Locke, Bobby, 369
Lodge, Henry Cabot, 26, 55, 113, 361
Loeffler, Tom, 369–70
Loew's Inc., 228
London, Jack, 182
Lonely Crowd, The (Packard), 348
Long Day's Journey Into Night (O'Neill), 219–21
"Long-Legged Fly" (Yeats), 477
"Long Shadow, The" (Navasky), 351–52
Lorca, Federico Garcia, 475
Lords of Discipline, The, 350
Louis, Joe, 129–33
"Love Song of J. Alfred Prufrock, The" (Eliot), 71
Lovett, Robert Morss, 129
Lowell, Robert, 483–84
Loyalists, 148
Loyalty oaths, 334–36
Lynch, Thomas C., 248, 250, 253

McAllister (Judge), 17
Macbeth (Shakespeare), 219
McCall, Mary, 187
McCarran, 189
McCarthy, Joe, 191–92, 276–77
McCarthy, Mary, 124–29, 189
McCarthy period, 333, 337
McCarthyism, 189, 343, 349

McCord, Ted, 180
McCoy, Sherman, 390, 392
MacDonald, William, 27–32
MacDowell, Gerty, 44
McEldowney, Carol, 303
McGovern, George, 298, 343–44
McKinley, William, 362
Mclean, Donald, 339
MacLeish, Archibald, 163–68
McWilliams, Carey, 234, 245, 269–70, 288
Maddox, Lester, 272
"Madness at Versailles, The" (MacDonald), 27–32
Main Street (Lewis), 47
Maistre, Joseph de, 391
"Making Defense Safe for Alcoa" (Stone), 153–58
"Making of a Red, The" (Benchley), 24–26
Malatesta, Enrico, 116, 120
Maltz, Albert, 227
Man With the Golden Arm, The (Algren), 187
" 'Manchurian Candidate' in Dallas" (Condon), 242–45
Mann, Thomas, 108, 144–46
Mannix, Eddie, 222
Mao Tse-tung, 304
March, Fredric, 221
"March to a Crossroads on Abortion" (Tax), 454–59
Marcus, Yoel, 310, 318
"Marsh, Hawk" (Atwood), 501–02
Margin of Hope, An Intellectual Autobiography, The (Howe), 333
Márquez, Gabriel García, 367
Marseilles (France), racism in, 410–15
Marshall, Margaret, 124–29, 178–82
Marx, Karl, 116, 136, 300, 319–22, 340, 347, 349
Maslow, Alfred, 194
"Mass Movies" (Eisenstein), 89–91
"Matthew Arnold" (Auden), 479
Matthews, Glenna, 288–99
Maxim Gorky as Artist (Baldwin), 261
May, Andy, 223
Meany, George, 276
Meese, Edwin, 388
Meiklejohn, Alexander, 191
Meir, Golda, 313, 316
Meller, Raquel, 74
Melville, Herman, 209
"Memory" (Sandburg), 480
Mencken, H. L., 53–56, 127, 189
Menelaus, 115
Menuhin, Yehudi, 95
Messinger, Ruth, 388
Mexico, U.S. and, 366–68
Mühsam, Erich, 119
Michel, Louise, 116

Milam, J. W., 205, 207–08
Milhaud, Darius, 231
Military spending, 22
Miller, Arthur, 197–204
Miller, Henry, 158–60
Mills, Dick, 232, 234
Milton, John, 137, 224
"Mind Is an Enchanting Thing, The" (Moore), 481–82
Mingus, Charles, 231
Minh, Ho Chi, 192–97
"Minnesota: The Norse State" (Lewis), 47–49
Minority Report, 386–88
Mittelman, 194
Mitterrand, Francois, 333
"Modest Proposal, A" (Miller), 197–204
Mokhiber, Russell, 422–32
Molotov, 197
Monroe Doctrine, 37
Moore, Brew, 232
Moore, Marianne, 481–82
"Moral of Tweed's Career, The" (Godkin), 12–14
Morgan, J. P., 55
"Morning at the Window" (Eliot), 71
Morocco, 28
Morris, Wayne, 152
Morrison, Norman, 303
Morrissey, John, 6
Morton, Thruston, 242, 244
Moses, Robert, 389
"Mother-Worship" (Eastman), 76–80
Motion Picture Association of America, 228
"Motorcycle Gangs, The" (Thompson), 245–53
Moynihan, Daniel, 343
Murphy, Ray, 135
Murrow, Edward R., 170
Muskie, Edmund S., 275–76
Mussolini, Benito, 118, 120, 150, 154, 194
Muste, A. J. , 303
Muth (Lieutenant), 37
My Antonia (Cather), 49

Nader, Ralph, 234–39
Napolean, 150, 288, 361
Nasser (President), 313
National Association for the Advancement of Colored People (NAACP), 62, 215
National Jewish Community Relations Advisory Council, 315
National Labor Relations Act, 289
Navasky, Victor S., 351–52, 356–57
"Nebraska: The End of the First Cycle" (Cather), 49–52
"Negro Artist and the Racial Mountain, The" (Hughes), 72–76
Nelson (Senator), 48

Nelson, Truman, 263
Neruda, Pablo, 367, 509–10
"Net Spread in Vain, A" (Shaw, Villard), 61
New Left, 299–307
  Abbie Hoffman and, 452–54
New York, 386–97
  Boss Tweed's career, 12–14
Newfield, Jack, 270–74
Newman, 129
Newton, Isaac, 138
Nhu, Madame, 250
Niagara Movement, 62
Nicaragua, U.S. and, 96–99, 366–68
Nietzsche, Friedrich, 54
"Nightfall" (Paz), 508
Nitze, Paul, 343
Nixon, Richard, 240, 274–79, 282, 284–88, 338, 343
No Exit (Sartre), 176
"Noble School of Fiction, The" (James), 5
Nobody Knows My Name (Baldwin), 261
Notes of a Native Son (Baldwin), 261
Noyes, Alfred, 22

Oberon, Merle, 151
O'Brien, Willis, 226
Obstructionists, 25
O'Casey, Sean, 209
October (Eisenstein), 91
" 'Odyssey' of Disney, The" (Thurber), 114–16
Oedipus, 174
Oglesby, Carl, 302
Oglesby (Governor), 16–17
O'Leary, Jeremiah, 25
Oliver, King, 232
"On an Old Horn" (Stevens), 478
"On Being Modern-Minded" (Russell), 136–39
"On Vietnam" (Gruening), 277–82
"One Cheer for the Hippies" (Newfield), 270–74
"One World or None" (Kirchwey) 168–71
O'Neill, Eugene, 219–21
O'Neill, William L., 349
Organization Man, The (Packard), 348
Original Prosepectus for The Nation (Richards), 1
Origins of Totalitarianism, The (Arendt), 171
Ortega, Daniel, 389
Ortiz, Lupe, 293
Orwell, George, 351
Ostreovsky, George Alexander, 219
Oswald, Lee Harvey, 243–44
"Our Critics, Right or Wrong" (McCarthy, Marshall), 124–29
"Out of Bondage" (Kirchwey), 100–02

"Pacifist's Dilemma, The" (Thomas), 139–44
Packard, Vance, 348

Paine, Tom, 143, 263
Paitch, Marty, 233
Palestine, political agenda, 432–36
Panama Canal, 37
Papen, Fritz von, 25
"Paradise Reagan-ed" (McWilliams), 269–70
Parsons, Louella, 151
Passaic strike, 67–70
"Passport Nuisance, The" (Pound), 92–95
Patchen, Kenneth, 231–32, 234
Pavlov, Ivan, 90
Paz, Octavio, 367, 508
Peace Conference, 27–32
Peale, Norman Vincent, 283
Pena, Ralph, 233
"People Are Indivisible, The" (MacLeish),
    163–68
Peralte, Charlemagne, 39
Perelman, S. J., 225
Perkins, Max, 158
Perkoff, Stuart, 234
Persephone (Stravinsky), 231
"Pesky Imperialist, The" (Garrison), 19–21
Peters, Horace W., 24–26
Petras, James, 319–25
Phillippe, Louis, 213
Phillips, Channing, 276
Phillips, Wendell, 89
Place in the Sun, A (Wilson), 224
"Plain Sense of Things, The" (Stevens), 487
Plath, Sylvia, 492
Podhoretz, Norman, 317, 343
Poe, Edgar Allan, 367
Poe, James, 225
Poetry, 471–512, *see also* individual poems by
    name.
Poetry Magazine, 209
Politics,
    Boss Tweed's career, 12–14
    exiles of, 116–20
    Jesse Jackson's campaign, 403–09
    liberalism in U.S., 332–51
    New Left, 299–307
    Palestine's political agenda, 432–36
    Students for a Democratic Society (SDS),
        299–307
    in Texas, 369–72
    Versailles treaty, 27–32, 142
Pollitt, Katha, 372–83
Polyphemus, 115
"Poor Me and Pure Boston" (Sinclair), 80–83
Populist Party, 64
Port au Prince (Haiti), 37–38
Port Huron Statement, 299
Portrait of the Artist as a Young Man, A
    (Joyce), 41
"Pot and the Kettle, The" (Villard), 112–14
Potemkin (Eisenstein), 89–91

Pound, Ezra, 92–95, 367
    Little Review, 209
    Poetry Magazine, 209
Powell, Lewis, 285
"Preludes" (Eliot), 71
Preminger, Otto, 221
Presley, Elvis, 304, 307
Prokosch, Frederic, 124
Prophetic Minority (Newfield), 270
Proteus, 115
Proust, Marcel, 109, 183
Prussianism, 25
Public Ledger, The, 32
Pucelik, Anton, 51

Quakers, 161
Quintero, Jos, 219

Rabin, Yitzhak, 316
Racism,
    in France, 410–15
    New Left and, 302–05
Rader, Paul, 226
Radosh, Ronald, 333
Rand, Ayn, 348
Rangel, Maria-Luisa, 294–95
Rathbone, Basil, 151
Ratzinger, Cardinal Joseph, 420–21
Reagan, Ronald, 269–70, 272, 296, 323, 336,
    340, 343, 350, 358, 368
Reconstruction, plan of, 2
"Red China at Geneva" (Snow), 192–97
Red Balloon, The (Lamorisse), 226
Red Scare, 24–26
Redgrave, Michael, 219
Reds, 350
Reed, Willie, 207
Rehnquist, 285
Reiss, Winold, 75
"Report from Occupied Territory" (Baldwin),
    261–69
"Requiem for the American Empire" (Vidal),
    358–66
"Return of Cold War Liberalism, The" (Kop-
    kind), 332–51
"Revenge of Ahab, The" (Kopkind), 368–69
Revere, Ann, 228
Revolt in the South, Dan Wakefield, 204
Rexroth, Kenneth, 231
"Rhapsody on a Windy Night" (Eliot), 71
Rice, Robert, 263
Rich, Robert, 225–26
Richards, Joseph, 2
Riesman, David, 348
"Right to Life, The" (Walker), 460–63
Rilke, Rainer Maria, 214
Rist, Darrell Yates, 436–42
Robards, Jason, 221

Robeson, Paul, 74, 76
Rockefeller, Nelson, 277
Rodó, Jos Enriqué, 367
Roewer, George, 83
Rogdayeve, Nicholai, 119–20
Rogers, Shorty, 232–33
Rojas, Clemente Marroquin, 241
Rolling Stone, 333
Romanovs, 119
Roosevelt, Theodore, 22, 55, 102, 105, 110, 112–13, 161–62, 191, 222, 284, 360–64
Rose, Aggie, 298
Rosenbergs, The, 351–52
Rosenfeld, Stephen, 335
Ross, Fred, 290–91
Rostow, Eugene, 343
Rousseau, Jean Jacques, 224
Rudd, Mark, 306
"Ruins of Memory, The" (Herbst), 208–14
Ruskin, John, 12
Russell, Rosalind, 219
Russell, Bertrand, 136
Russell, Colonel John, 39

Saar Basin (Germany), 28
Sabadado, Marie, 297
Sacco, Nicola, 83–89
Sacco-Vanzetti case, 83–89, 102
Sadat, Anwar, 308, 310, 312, 314, 317
Sade, Marquis de, 272–73
"Safe Car You Can't Buy, The" (Nader), 234–39
Safer, Morley, 334
Said, Edward, 432–36
Saint-Saens, Camille, 50
Saint-Simon, 389
Salinger, J. D., 348
Sam, Vilbrun Guillaume, 37
Samaria, 311
Samuelson, Arthur H., 308–18
San Francisco Symphony Orchestra, 95
San Peitro (Huston), 182
Sanders, Ed, 270
Sandburg, Carl, 480
Sandino, Augusto Csar, 96–100
Sanger, Margarey, 100
Santayana, George, 45, 136
"Saratoga" (James), 5–12
Sartre, Jean-Paul, 166, 172–78, 273
Sazulich, Vera, 116
Schary, Dore, 222
Schell, Jonathon, 341
Schindler, Alexander, 310–13, 318
Schlesinger, Arthur, Jr., 332, 335
Schleswig (Germany), 28
Schmeling, Max, 129
Schnitzler, Arthur, 47
Schwerner, Michael, 303

Scott, Adrian, 223
Scudder, Vida, 69
SDS (Students for a Democratic Society), 299–307
Seaton, George, 226–27, 229
Second Stage, The (Friedan), 349
Seldes, Gilbert, 41–46
Seligmann, Herbert T. J., 36–40
Sergius, Grand Duke, 26
Seven Lively Arts, The (Seldes), 41
Sexton, Anne, 493
Shahn, Ben, 88
Shakespeare, William, 22, 136–37
Sharkey-Slocum case, 2
Shaw, Bernard, 61
Shaw, Raymond, 243
Shaw, T. E., 114
Sherrill, Robert, 422–32
Shirer, William L., 282–88
Siam, 28
Siegfried, André, 100–01
Siegman, Henry, 314–15
Silesia, 28
Sinatra, Frank, 232
Sinclair, Upton, 80–83, 364
Singer, Daniel, 410–16
Sleeping Prince, The, 219
Smerdyakov, Dostoevski, 389
Smith, Al, 101
Smith, Bessie, 76
Smith, Clara, 74
Smith, Gerald L. K., 187
Smith, Hoke, 64–65
Smith, Holland M., 225
Smith, Robert B., 205
Smith, Susan, 127
Smollett, Tobias, 83
SNCC (Student Non-violent Coordinating Committee), 302–06
Snow, Edgar, 192–97
Social Action Commission of the Union of American Hebrew Congregations, 315
Socialists, 23
Socrates, 210
Sondergaard, Gale, 228
"Song of the Little Death" (Lorca), 475
Sontag, Susan, 339, 341
Sorel, Edward, 402
Sorkow, Harvey (Judge), 372–73, 376–77, 380
Soskin, William, 125–26
Souls of Black Folk, The (Du Bois), 62
Soviet Union, 118
    cold war, 325–32
    Latin America and, 319–25
    reforms in, 382–85
"Sovieticus" (Cohen), 383–85

"Sowing the Wind to Reap the Whirlwind" (Villard), 33–36
"Spain's Tragic Anniversary" (Fischer), 147–50
Spellman, Cardinal, 274
Spender, Stephen, 182–85
Spicer, Jack, 231
Spillane, Mickey, 250
Spinoza, Baruch, 137–38
Spiridonova, Maria, 120
"Spit in the Devil's Eye" (Boyle), 214–19
Stafford, Frank, 263, 266
Stalin, Josef, 349, 384
Stalinism, 340
"Starry Night, The" (Sexton), 493
Steffens, Lincoln, 189
Stein, Gertrude, 54
Steinbeck, John, 183
Steinbrenner, George, 388
Stendahl, 213
Stern, Elizabeth, 374–76
Stern, William, 374–77, 380, 383
Stevens, Wallace, 478, 487
Stevenson, Adlai, 187
Stewart, Michael, 390
Stimson (Secretary), 169
Stoddard, Lothrop, 101
Stolberg, Benjamin, 127
Stone, I. F., 153–58, 160–62
Stone, Lawrence, 378
Stout, William, 227
Strachey, Lytton, 126
Straight, Michael, 339
"Strange Case of Baby M, The" (Pollitt), 372–83
Stravinsky, Igor, 231
Strayhorn, Billy, 232
Stresemann, Gustav, 140
Strider, H.C., 206
Student Non-violent Coordinating Committee (SNCC), 302–06
Students for a Democratic Soicety (SDS), 299–307
Subversion-terorism equation, 339–40
Sugar, Margit, 267–68
Sun Also Rises, The (Hemingway), 246
Surrogate motherhood, 372–83
Swango, Curtis, 205
"Sweeney Poems, The" (Eliot), 71
Swenson, May, 507
Synagogue Council of America (SCA), 314

Talisman, The, 115
Tang, Truong Nhu, 338
Tarbell, Ida, 127
Tate, Alan, 276
Tawney (Congressman), 22
Tax, Meredith, 454–59

Taylor, Telford, 286
Tchaikovsky Concerto, 95
"Tears" (Jacobsen), 511
"Teeth" (Swenson), 507
Tenney, Jack, 187
Terrorism, liberalist views and, 339–40
Terry, John Skally, 158
Tess of the D'Urbervilles (Hardy), 83
Texas, politics in, 369–72
Thayer (Judge), 85–87
These United States, W.E.B. Du Bois, 62
Thieu, Nguyen Van, 287
Thomas, J. Parnell, 223
Thomas, Norman, 112–14, 139–44
Pacifist's dilemma, 139
Thomas, Walter, 263
Thompson, E. P., 325–32, 341
Thompson, Hunter S., 245–53
Thurber, James, 114–16
Till, Emmett Louis, 205, 208, 213
Tisch, Larry, 310
"To a Blossoming Pear Tree" (Wright), 505–06
Tolstoy, Leo, 209, 211
Toomer, Jean, 74, 76
The Torture of Mothers (Nelson), 263
"Tough as Bob War and Other Stuff" (Ivins), 369–72
Touring Club de France, 93
"Tragedy of the Political Exiles, The" (Goldman), 116–20
Traven, B., 179, 181
Treasure of the Sierra Madre, The (Huston), 178–82
Treaty of Versaille, 27–32, 94, 142
Trevor-Roper, Hugh, 284
Trillin, Calvin, 356–58
Trilling, Lionel, 106–09
Troilus and Cressida, 219
Tropic of Cancer (Miller), 158
Tropic of Capricorn (Miller), 158
Trotzky, Leon, 26, 32–33
Truman Harry S., 153–55, 168–70, 193, 284
Trumbo, Dalton, 221–30
Trump, Donald, 388
Tuchman, Barbara, 310
Tunney, Gene, 130
Turkey, 28–29
Tut-ankh-amen's tomb, 46
Twain, Mark, 21, 363
Tweed, William Marcy "Boss", 12–14
"Two Views of a Cadaver Room" (Plath), 492

Ulysses (Joyce), 41–46, 114–15
Un-American Activities Committee, 186
"Uncivil Liberties" (Trillin), 356–58
Union of American Hebrew Congregations, 315

Union of Socialist Soviet Republics. See Soviet Union
United States,
American Empire, 358–66
corporate crime in, 422–32
El Salvador and, 319–25
Grenada invasion, 463–66
Haiti and, 36–40, 366–68
Latin America and, 96–99, 366–68
liberalism, 23
military spending, 22
Soviet relations and cold war, 325–32
United States Marine Corps, 38–39
"Up Rising" (Duncan), 495–96

Valry, Paul, 126
Vance, Cyrus, 344
Vanzetti, Bartolomeo, 83–89
Versailles treaty, 27–32, 142
Alsace-Lorraine, 28
Czardom, 31
Great Powers, 30
Hungary, 31
Peace Conference, 30
Posen, 28
Russia, 31
Saar Basin, 28
Silesia, 28
Woodrow Wilson, 30–31
Vidal, Gore, 358–66
Vietcong, 250
Vietnam war, 397–401
liberal attitudes following, 336–38
Villard, Oswald Garrison, 33–36, 61, 83, 96, 103–05, 112–14
Vogel, Albert, 390
Voltaire, 224
Vonnegut, Kurt, 353–56
Vorse, Mary Heaton, 67–70
Voting Rights Act, 256

Wakefield, Dan, 204–08, 214
Wales, C. H., 230
Walker, Alice, 460–63
Walker, Mickey, 130
Wallace, Henry, 272–76, 345
Walter, Francis, 223
Walton, William, 231
Wanger, Walter, 222
"War in Passaic, The" (Vorse), 67–70
Warhol, Andy, 271
Warner, Jack L., 223
Warner Brothers, 151
Warnke, Paul, 344
Warren, Earl, 153, 387
Washington, Booker T., 62
"Waste Land, The" (Eliot), 71
Watson, Tom, 64

Waugh, Evelyn, 391
Weary Blues, The (Hughes), 72
Weathermen, 299, see also New Left
Week, The, 15
Week, The, Lenin and Trotzky, 32–33
Week, The, Tut-ankh-amen's tomb, 46
Weiseltier, Leon, 341
Weiss, Abe, 390
Weiss, Peter, 272
Weizman, Ezer, 316
Weizmann, Chaim, 56–61
Welles, Orson, 226
West, Jessamyn, 225
West, Rebecca, 126, 129
"What Happened the Day a Poet Was Appointed Postmaster" (Ferlinghetti), 488
"What Were They Like?" (Levertov), 499–500
Wheeler, William, 222, 229
White (Ambassador), 324
White, Horace, 113
White, Mark, 370
"White-Collar Thuggery" (Sherrill), 422–32
"White Paper on the White Paper" (Petras), 319–25
Whitehead, Mary Beth, 373–83
Whitman, Walt, 183, 367
Whitney, John Hay, 244
Whitten, John, 207–08
Whyte, William, 348
Wiesel, Elie, 310
Wild One, The, 246
Wild Palms, The (Faulkner), 367
Wilhelm II, 288
Will, George, 343
Willey, Clair, 232
Williams, Roger, 191
Williams, William Carlos, 489–91
Wilson, Michael, 224–28
Wilson, Charles E., 206
Wilson, Charlie, 371
Wilson, Edmund, 129
Wilson, Woodrow, 23, 27, 32, 55, 92–93, 113, 284
"With Sandino in Nicarugua" (Beals), 96–100
Wolfe, Julia Elizabeth, 158
Wolfe, Tom, 158, 389–90, 392–96
"Women of the Boycott, The" (Baer, Matthews), 288–99
Women's rights,
abortion and, 454–59
fertility planning, 100–102
surrogate motherhood, 372–83
Woodcuts (Eichenberg), 467
Woolf, Virginia, 126
World Jewish Congress, 313–14
World of Our Fathers (Howe), 311
World Zionist Organization, 56

"Worst Addiction of Them All, The" (Vonnegut), 353–56
Wotan, 133
Wright, Harold Bell, 127
Wright, James, 505–06
Wright, Moses, 205–06
"Writers in America" (Spender), 182–85
Wylie, Reggy, 44

X, Malcolm, 303

Ydigoras (President), of Guatemala, 241
Yeats, W.B., 45
You Have Seen Their Faces (Bourke-White), 121

You Never Even Called Me By My Name (Coe), 371
Young, Andrew, 344
Yurande, Ester, 293

Zablocki (Congressman), of Wisconsin, 240
Zamor, Haitian goverment, 39
Zedong, Mao, 350 (*see also* Mao Tse-tung)
Ziegler, Ronald, 286
"Zionism–Alive and Triumphant" (Weizmann), 57–61
Zionism, *see* Israel
Zionist Organization of America, 314
Zola, 224
Zoshchenko, Mikhail, 89